David Jobber
and Geoff Lancaster

7th Edition

Selling and Sales Management

 Prentice Hall
FINANCIAL TIMES

An imprint of **Pearson Education**
Harlow, England • London • New York • Boston • San Francisco • Toronto • Sydney • Singapore • Hong Kong
Tokyo • Seoul • Taipei • New Delhi • Cape Town • Madrid • Mexico City • Amsterdam • Munich • Paris • Milan

Pearson Education Limited
Edinburgh Gate
Harlow
Essex CM20 2JE
England

and Associated Companies throughout the world

Visit us on the World Wide Web at:
www.pearsoned.co.uk

First published as *Sales Technique and Management* by Macdonald & Evans Ltd in 1985
Second edition published by Pitman Publishing, a division of Longman Group UK Ltd in 1990
Third edition published by Pitman Publishing, a division of Longman Group UK Ltd in 1994
Fourth edition published by Pitman Publishing, a division of Pearson Professional Ltd in 1997
Fifth edition published by Financial Times Management, a division of Financial Times
Professional Limited in 2000
Sixth edition published 2003
Seventh edition published 2006

© Macdonald and Evans Ltd 1985
© David Jobber and Geoff Lancaster 1990
© Longman Group UK Ltd 1994
© Pearson Professional Ltd 1997
© Financial Times Professional Ltd 2000
© Pearson Education Limited 2003, 2006

ISBN 978-0-273-69579-0

British Library Cataloguing-in-Publication Data
A catalogue record for this book is available from the British Library

Library of Congress Cataloging-in-Publication Data
A catalog record for this book is available from the Libaray of Congress

10 9 8 7 6 5 4 3
11 10 09 08 07

Typeset in 9.25 on 12 in Stone Serif by Fakenham Photosetting Limited, Fakenham, Norfolk
Printed by Ashford Colour Press Ltd., Gosport

The publisher's policy is to use paper manufactured from sustainable forests.

Contents

Part Two Sales Environment   75

3   Consumer and Organisational Buyer Behaviour   77

4   Sales Settings   110

Supporting resources
Visit www.pearsoned.co.uk/jobber to find valuable online resources

For instructors
- An Instructor's Manual, including sample answers for selected material in the book
- Customisable PowerPoint slides, including key figures and tables from the main text

For more information please contact your local Pearson Education sales representative
or visit www.pearsoned.co.uk/jobber

About the Authors

David Jobber BA (Econ), MSc, PhD is an internationally recognised marketing academic and is Professor of Marketing at the University of Bradford School of Management. Before joining the faculty at the School of Management, he worked in sales and marketing for the TI Group and was Senior Lecturer in Marketing at Huddersfield University. He has wide experience of teaching sales and marketing at undergraduate, postgraduate and executive levels and has held visiting appointments at the universities of Aston, Lancaster, Loughborough and Warwick. Supporting his teaching is a record of achievement in academic research and scholarship. David has published four books and over 100 research papers in such internationally-rated journals as the *International Journal of Research in Marketing*, the *Journal of Personal Selling and Sales Management*, and the *Strategic Management Journal*. His eminence in research was recognised by his appointment as Special Adviser to the Research Assessment Exercise panel.

Geoff Lancaster MSc, PhD, FCIM, FLCC, MCMI, MCIPS is Professor of Marketing at Liverpool John Moores University. He is Chairman of a corporate communications company Durham Associates Group Ltd, Castle Eden, County Durham with offices in London, Hull, Bahrain, Kingdom of Saudi Arabia, Oman and the Republic of South Africa. The company is in receipt of the Queen's Award for Export Achievement. He was previously Senior Examiner and Senior Academic Adviser to the Chartered Institute of Marketing and Chief Examiner to the Institute of Sales and Marketing Management. He has also published marketing and research methods textbooks with McGraw-Hill, Macmillan, Butterworth-Heinemann and Kogan-Page.

List of Figures

List of Tables

Preface

Premise

This text covers what must still be the most important element of the marketing mix for most students and practitioners. With a move away from the selling function towards more esoteric areas of marketing over the past few years, this vital aspect of marketing has been somewhat neglected. However, in the end it has to be face-to-face contact that eventually wins the order, and this text therefore explains and documents the selling and sales management process from both the theoretical and practical viewpoints.

Book Structure

More precisely, the text is split into five logical parts: **Sales Perspective**, **Sales Environment**, **Sales Technique**, **Sales Management** and **Sales Control**.

Sales Perspective examines selling in its historical role and then views its place within marketing and a marketing organisation. Different types of buyers are also analysed in order to help us achieve an understanding of their thinking and organise our selling effort accordingly. **Sales Technique** is essentially practical and covers preparation for selling, the personal selling process and sales responsibility. **Sales Environment** looks at the institutions through which sales are made; this covers channels, including industrial, commercial and public authority selling followed by selling for resale. International selling is an increasingly important area in view of the ever increasing 'internationalisation' of business and this merits a separate chapter. **Sales Management** covers recruitment, selection, motivation and training, in addition to how we must organise and compensate salesmen from a managerial standpoint. Finally, **Sales Control** covers sales budgets and explains how this is the starting point for business planning. Sales forecasting is also covered in this final section, and a guide is given to the techniques of forecasting and why it is strictly a responsibility of sales management and not finance. Each chapter concludes with a mini-case study and practical exercises, together with formal practice questions typical of those the student will encounter in the examination room.

New to this Edition

This seventh edition provides an integration of recent cutting-edge selling and sales management research into chapters throughout the book. Also the 'Key Account Management' and 'Internet and IT Applications in Selling and Sales Management' chapters have been substantially rewritten and updated. The authors are grateful to John O'Connor, chief executive, Deep-Insight, for his work on the 'Internet and IT Applications' chapter. A fuller discussion of the role of selling as part of an integrated marketing communications programme and enhanced coverage of the role of the sales force as gatherers of market intelligence are also included. The section on negotiation is expanded to reflect its important role in today's business environment. This seventh edition features new and updated cases to support the effective teaching of selling and sales management. The chapter ordering has also changed to make the sequence more logical. Finally, we have increased the use of case histories to show how principles can be applied in practice. As always, this edition continues to place emphasis on international aspects of selling and sales management to reflect the importance of international markets in today's global economy.

Target Market

This text will be invaluable to those students studying for the examinations of the Chartered Institute of Marketing, the Communication, Advertising and Marketing Education Foundation, the London Chamber of Commerce and Industry higher stage selling and sales management subject, marketing specialisms on Higher National Certificate and Diploma in Business Studies, first degrees with a marketing input, and postgraduate courses like the Diploma in Management Studies and Master of Business Administration that have a marketing input. In addition, the text emphasises the practical as well as the theoretical, and it will be of invaluable assistance to salespersons in the field as well as to sales management.

Acknowledgements

We would like to thank Richard Cork, Belinda Dewsnap, Martin Evans, Jason Greenaway, Diana Luck, Paul Miller, Lynn Parkinson and Michael Starkey for providing excellent material on the applications of IT in sales. We also wish to thank all of the case contributors for supplying excellent case studies to enhance the practical aspects of the book. We also thank the reviewers who provided feedback for this edition. They include:

Russell Campbell, University of Paisley
Suzanne Cole, University of Wales, Newport (UWCN)
Laura Cuddihy, Dublin Institute of Technology
Belinda Dewsnap, Loughborough University
Raj Komaran, Singapore Management University/Smartberry Research International
Adrian Pritchard, Coventry University

Finally, we would like to thank our editorial team at Pearson Education led by Senior Acquisitions Editor Thomas Sigel, for helping make this new edition possible.

Acknowledgements

We are grateful to the following for permission to reproduce copyright material:

Figure 1.1: Characteristics of modern selling reprinted from Moncrief, W.C. and Marshall, G.W. (2005) The evolution of the seven steps of selling, *Industrial Marketing Management*, 34, pp. 13–22, Fig. 1. Copyright © 2005 with permission; Table 1.1: The top ten success factors in selling reprinted from Marshall, G.W., Goebel, D.J. and Moncrief, W.C. (2003) Hiring for success at the buyer-seller interface, *Journal of Business Research*, 56, pp. 247–255. Copyright © 2003 with permission from Elsevier; Table 1.2: Marketing strategy and sales management from Strakle, W. and Spiro, R.L. (1986) Linking market share strategies to salesforce objectives, activities and compensation policies, *Journal of Personal Selling and Sales Management*, August, pp. 11–18; Figure 3.1: The consumer decision-making process from Blackwell, R.D., Miniard, P.W. and Engel, J.F. (2000) *Consumer Behaviour*, 7th Edition, Orlando, Florida: Dryden. Reprinted with permission of South-Western, a division of Thomson Learning, www.thomsonrights.com. Fax: 800–730–2215. Copyright © 2000; Table 3.1: Social class categories adapted from National Readership Survey, July 2000–June 2001; Table 5.1: Top ten criteria used by sales agents to evaluate principals reprinted from Merritt, N.J. and Newell, S.J. (2001) 'The extent and formality of sales agency evaluations of principals', *Industrial Marketing Management*, 30, pp. 37–49. Copyright © 2001 with permission; Table 8.1: Types of question used in personal selling from R. DeCormier and D. Jobber (1993) The counsellor selling method: concepts, constructs and effectiveness, *Journal of Personal Sales and Management*, 13(4), pp. 39–60; Figure 9.1: Traditional (bow-tie) buyer-seller relationship adapted from Shipley, D. and Palmer R. (1997) 'Selling to and managing key accounts' in Jobber. D. (1997) *The CIM Handbook of Selling and Sales Strategy*, Butterworth-Heinemann, Oxford, p. 95 Copyright © 1997, reprinted with permission from Elsevier; Figure 9.2: Key account (diamond) based relationship adapted from Shipley, D. and Palmer R. (1997) 'Selling to and managing key accounts' in Jobber. D. (1997) *The CIM Handbook of Selling and Sales Strategy*, Butterworth-Heinemann, Oxford, p. 95 Copyright © 1997, reprinted with permission from Elsevier; Table 9.6: KAM key success factors from Abratt, R. and Kelly, P.M. (2002) Customer–supplier partnerships: perceptions of a successful key account management program, *Industrial Marketing Management*, 31, pp. 467–476. Copyright © 2002 with permission from Elsevier; Figure 11.1: Expenditure on direct marketing in Europe adapted from Direct Marketing Expenditure and Direct Marketing

Expenditure per capita, reprinted from *European Marketing Pocket Book 2005*. Copyright © 2005, reprinted by permission of the World Advertising Research Centre; Figure 12.2 From Foss B. and Stone M. (2001) *Successful Customer Relationship Marketing*, Kogan Page: London; Figure 13.1: Important qualities of salespeople from D. Jobber and S. Millar (1984) The use of psychological tests in the selection of salesmen: a UK survey, *Journal of Sales Management*, 4, p. 1; Table 13.2: Qualities required of trainee and senior sales executives from Mathews, B. and Redman, T. (2001) Recruiting the wrong salespeople: are the job ads to blame?, *Industrial Marketing Management*, 30, pp. 541–550. Copyright © 2001 with permission from Elsevier. Figure 13.2: How companies attract applicants from outside the company from D. Jobber and S. Millar (1984) The use of psychological tests in the selection of salesmen: a UK survey, *Journal of Sales Management*, 4, p. 1; Figure 14.6: Criteria used to evaluate training courses from Stamford-Bewley, C. and Jobber, D. (1989) *A Study of the Training of Sales People in the UK*, University of Bradford School of Management working paper; Table 14.7: Methods used to train sales managers and Table 14.8: Topics covered in sales training programmes from R.E. Anderson, R. Mehta and J. Strong (1997) An empirical investigation of sales management training programs for sales managers, *Journal of Personal Selling and Sales Management*, 17(3), pp. 53–66; Page 17: 'Meeting customer's needs in growth markets — online gaming' excerpt from case study found at http://www.thetimes100.co.uk/case_study; Page 18: 'Application of segmentation' excerpt from case study found at http://www.thetimes100.co.uk/case_study; Page 29: 'Travis Perkins' customers and the marketing mix' excerpt from case study found at http://www.thetimes100.co.uk/case_study; Page 40: Practical exercise: Telcontar. Courtesy of PR Artistry Limited, Cedar Court, 9-11 Fairmile, Henley on Thames, Oxon RG9 2JR. Reproduced with the permission from www.prartristry.com. Page 45: 'Application of PEST analysis to Corus' excerpt from case study found at http://www.thetimes100.co.uk/case_study; Page 129: 'Example of franchising' excerpt from case study found at http://www.thetimes100.co.uk/case_study; Page 132: 'Extended marketing mix' excerpt from case study found at http://www.thetimes100.co.uk/case_study; Page 150: Practical exercise: xstreammedia. Courtesy of PR Artistry Limited, Cedar Court, 9–11 Fairmile, Henley-on-Thames; Page 196: Practical exercise: Syplan. The publishers are grateful to NI Syndication Limited for an extract adapted from an article by Sarah Gracie on Syplan published in the *Sunday Times* 23rd June 2002 © Sarah Gracie/Times Newspapers Limited 2002; Page 215: 'British Gas and ethics' excerpt from case study found athttp://www.thetimes100.co.uk/case_study; Page 218: 'The importance of business ethics in Cadbury Schweppes excerpt from case study found at http://www.thetimes100.co.uk/case_study; Page 221: Practical exercise: 'Chevron Texaco cuts losses with Innovetra Fraud Alerter' excerpt from case study found at http://www.thetimes100.co.uk/case_study; Page 256: Excerpt from case study 'Acton Mobile Industries ...' courtesy of the Chapman Group, www.chapmanhq.com. Reprinted with permission; Page 307: Excerpt from case study 'GTSI, Chantilly, Virginia, USA' courtesy of the Chapman Group, www.chapmanhq.com. Reprinted with permission; Page 309: 'Total quality management' excerpt from case study found at http://www.thetimes100.co.uk/ case_study; Page 323: Practical exercise: Focus Wickes – 'Fusion' excerpt from case study found at http://www.thetimes100.co.uk/case_study; Page 475: 'Alternative types of budgeting' excerpt from case study found athttp://www.thetimes100.co.uk/case_study.

In some instances we have been unable to trace the owners of copyright material, and we would appreciate any information that would enable us to do so.

Part One

Sales Perspective

Part one of *Selling and Sales Management* consists of two introductory chapters that set the context for the remainder of the book.

The first chapter introduces the nature and role of selling and sales management before relating this to the marketing concept. The incontrovertibly interlinked relationship between selling and sales management is then explained and the notion of more sophisticated marketing thought is described as having its roots in sales. Philosophies, or orientations, of production, sales and marketing are explained as well as how the marketing concept is implemented in practice, namely through the marketing mix. Key concepts such as market segmentation and targeting and the 'four Ps' marketing mix variables of price, product, promotion and place are introduced. The chapter then concludes with a more detailed explanation of the relationship between marketing strategy and personal selling.

Sales strategies and how these relate to marketing planning form the basis of the second chapter. The traditional marketing planning process is explained with emphasis on issues like targeting, pricing, customer retention and the allocation and control of resources to assist implementation of the plan. The place of selling in the marketing plan is examined in detail, explaining how pivotal the sales function is in achieving success, along with a related discussion of how the notion of 'inside-out' planning is being replaced by 'outside-in' thinking. Selling is traditionally referred to as an element of the 'promotional mix', but the view is taken that this should more correctly be described as the 'communications mix'. An explanation is given of the place of selling alongside traditional elements in the communications mix, namely advertising, sales promotion and publicity/public relations. More contemporary elements of the communications mix, namely direct marketing and interactive/internet marketing are also examined in terms of how these interface with the sales process.

1

Development and Role of Selling in Marketiing

Objectives

After studying this chapter, you should be able to:

1 Understand the implications of production, sales, and marketing orientation
2 Appreciate why selling generally has a negative image
3 Know where selling fits into the marketing mix
4 Identify the responsibilities of sales management
5 Recognise the role of selling as a career

Key Concepts

- break-even analysis
- business to business (B2B)
- business to consumer (B2C)
- exclusive distribution
- intensive distribution
- market penetration
- market segmentation
- market skimming
- marketing concept
- marketing mix
- product life-cycle
- sales management
- selling
- target accounts
- targeting

1.1   Background

Perhaps no other area of business activity gives rise to as much discussion among and between those directly involved and those who are not involved as the activity known as selling. This is not surprising when one considers that so many people derive their livelihood, either directly or indirectly, from selling. Even those who have no direct involvement in selling come into contact with it in their roles as consumers. Perhaps, because of this familiarity, many people have strong, and often misplaced, views about selling and salespeople. Surprisingly, many of these misconceptions are held by people who have spent their working lives in selling, so it might well be a case of 'familiarity breeds contempt'.

It is important to recognise that **selling** and sales management, although closely related, are not the same and we shall start in this chapter by examining the nature and role of selling and sales management in the contemporary organisation and exploring some of the more common myths and misconceptions.

We shall also look at the developing role of selling because, like other business functions, it is required to adapt and change. Perhaps one of the most important and far reaching of these business changes has been the adoption of the concept and practice of marketing, due to changes in the business environment. Because of the importance of this development to the sales function, we shall examine the place of marketing within the firm and the place of selling within marketing.

1.2   The Nature and Role of Selling

The simplest way to think of the nature and role of selling (traditionally called salesmanship) is that its function is to make a sale. This seemingly obvious statement disguises what is often a very complex process, involving the use of a whole set of principles, techniques and substantial personal skills, and covering a wide range of different types of selling task. Later we will establish a more precise meaning for the term *selling*, but first we will examine the reasons for the intense interest in this area of business activity.

The literature of selling abounds with texts, ranging from the more conceptual approaches to the simplistic 'how it is done' approach. Companies spend large sums of money training their sales personnel in the art of selling. The reason for this attention to personal selling is simple: in most companies the sales personnel are the single most important link with the customer. The best designed and planned marketing efforts may fail because the salesforce is ineffective. This front-line role of the salesperson means that for many customers the salesperson *is* the company. Allied with the often substantial costs associated with recruiting, training and maintaining the salesforce, there are powerful reasons for stressing the importance of the selling task and for justifying attempts to improve effectiveness in this area. Part Three of this text addresses this important area of sales techniques.

The term *selling* encompasses a variety of sales situations and activities. For example, there are those sales positions where the sales representative is required primarily to deliver the product to the customer on a regular or periodic basis. The emphasis in this type of sales activity is very different to the sales position where the sales representative is dealing with sales of capital equipment to industrial purchasers. In addition, some sales representatives deal only in export markets whilst others sell direct to customers in their homes. One of the most striking aspects of selling is the wide diversity of selling roles.

Irrespective of this diversity, one trend common to all selling tasks is the increasing emphasis on professionalism in selling. This trend, together with its implications for the nature and role of selling, can best be explained if we examine some of the myths and realities that surround the image of selling.

1.3 Characteristics of Modern Selling

Today, a salesforce must have a wide range of skills to compete successfully. Gone are the days when salespeople required simple presentational and closing skills to be successful. Today selling requires a wide array of skills, which will be identified in the next section. In this section we discuss the characteristics of modern selling. Salespeople who don't understand these characteristics will be ill-equipped to tackle their jobs.

The characteristics of modern selling are given in Figure 1.1.

1 *Customer retention and deletion.* Many companies find that 80 per cent of their sales come from 20 per cent of their customers. This means that it is vital to devote considerable resources to retaining existing high volume, high potential and highly profitable customers. Key account management has become an

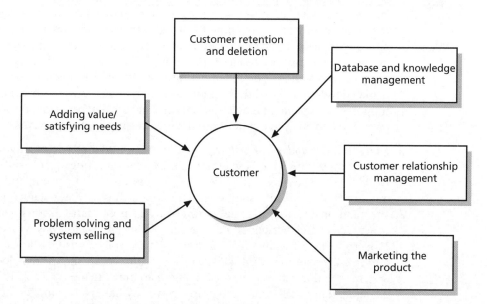

Figure 1.1 Characteristics of modern selling
Source: Adapted from Moncrief, W.C. and Marshall, G.W. (2005) 'The evolution of the seven steps of selling', *Industrial Marketing Management*, 34, pp. 13–22.

important form of sales organisation because it means that a salesperson or sales team can focus their efforts on one or a few major customers.

At the other end of the spectrum, companies are finding that some small customers actually cost the organisation money. This is because servicing and distribution of products to those customers may push costs beyond the revenue generated. Larger companies may have to change to telemarketing and/or the Internet as a means of servicing these small customers or drop them altogether.

2 *Database and knowledge management.* The modern salesforce needs to be trained in the use and creation of customer databases, and how to use the internet to aid the sales task (e.g. finding customer and competitor information). In the past salespeople recorded customer information on cards and sent in orders through the post to head office. Today, technological advances such as email, mobile phones and video conferencing have transformed the way knowledge is transferred. Laptops mean that salespeople can store customer and competitor information, make presentations and communicate with head office electronically. Furthermore, information supplied by the company, such as catalogues and price lists, can be held electronically.

3 *Customer relationship management.* Customer relationship management requires that the salesforce focuses on the long-term and not simply on closing the next sale.[1] The emphasis should be on creating win-win situations with customers so that both parties to the interaction gain and want to continue the relationship. For major customers, relationship management may involve setting up dedicated teams to service the account and maintain all aspects of the business relationship. This form of organisational structure, key account management, is discussed in Chapter 9, and Chapter 10 is devoted to relationship selling.

4 *Marketing the product.* The modern salesperson is involved in a much broader range of activities than simply planning and making a sales presentation. Indeed, face-to-face presentations can now sometimes be replaced by information presented on web pages and by email attachments that give the customer up-to-date information on many topics quicker, more comprehensively and in a more time-convenient manner than many face-to-face interactions.[2] The role of the salesperson is expanding to participation in marketing activities such as product development, market development and the segmentation of markets, as well as other tasks that support or complement marketing activities such as database management, provision and analysis of information, and assessing market segments.[3]

5 *Problem solving and system selling.* Much of modern selling, particularly in business-to-business situations, is based upon the salesperson acting as a consultant working with the customer to identify problems, determine needs, and propose and implement effective solutions.[4] This approach is fundamentally different from the traditional view of the salesperson being a smooth fast-talker who breezes in to see a customer, persuades the customer to buy and walks away with an order. Modern selling often involves multiple calls, the use of a team-selling approach and considerable analytical skills. Further, customers are increasingly looking for a systems solution rather than the buying of an individual product. This means, for example, that to sell door handles to a company like Ford a supplier must not only be able to sell a door system which includes door handles as well as locking and opening devices but also have a thorough knowledge of door technology, and the ability to suggest to Ford solutions to problems that may arise.

6 *Satisfying needs and adding value.* The modern salesperson must have the ability to identify and satisfy customer needs. Some customers do not recognise they have a need. It is the salesperson's job in such situations to stimulate need recognition. For example, customers may not realise that a machine in the production process has low productivity compared to newer, more technologically advanced machines. The salesperson's job is to make customers aware of the problem in order to convince them that they have a need to modernise the production process. In so doing, the salesperson will have added value to the customer's business by reducing costs and created a win-win situation for his or her company and the customer.

1.4 Success Factors for Professional Salespeople

A key issue for aspiring and current salespeople and sales managers is an understanding of the key success factors in selling. A study by Marshall, Goebel and Moncrief (2003) asked sales managers to identify the skills and knowledge required to be successful in selling.[5] Table 1.1 shows the top ten success factors.

This book addresses all of these issues. It is important to recognise these success factors since such knowledge has the potential to improve the overall efficiency and effectiveness of the salesperson–customer interaction in several ways. First, sales managers can use this knowledge of widely accepted sales success factors to improve their recruitment and training practices. Second, candidates for sales jobs can use this knowledge of success factors to ensure they work towards high levels of proficiency in those key areas they can control, and do as well as possible emphasising their own capabilities during the job interview. Third, sales educators at universities and colleges have information upon which to ensure their curricula best reflect the skills and knowledge most valued by practitioners.[6]

Table 1.1 The top ten success factors in selling

1 Listening skills
2 Follow-up skills
3 Ability to adapt sales style from situation to situation
4 Tenacity – sticking to the task
5 Organisational skills
6 Verbal communication skills
7 Proficiency in interacting with people at all levels within an organisation
8 Demonstrated ability to overcome objections
9 Closing skills
10 Personal planning and time management skills

Source: Reprinted from Marshall, G.W., Goebel, D.J. and Moncrief, W.C. (2003) 'Hiring for success at the buyer-seller interface', *Journal of Business Research,* 56, pp. 247–55. Copyright © 2003, with permission from Elsevier.

The diverse nature of the buying situation means that there are many types of sell-ing job: selling varies according to the nature of the selling task. Figure 1.2 shows that there is a fundamental distinction between order-takers, order-creators, and order-getters. Order-takers respond to already committed customers; order-creators do not directly receive orders since they talk to specifiers rather than buyers; whereas order-getters attempt to persuade customers to place an order directly.

There are three types of order-takers: inside order-takers, delivery salespeople and outside order-takers. Order-creators are termed missionary salespeople. Finally, order-getters are either front-line salespeople consisting of new business, organis-ational or consumer salespeople, or sales support salespeople who can be either technical support salespeople or merchandisers. Both types of order-getters operate in situations where a direct sale can be made. Each type of selling job will now be discussed in more detail.

Order-takers

Inside order-takers

Here the customer has full freedom to choose products without the presence of a salesperson. The sales assistant's task is purely transactional – receiving payment and passing over the goods. Another form of inside order-taker is the telemarketing sales team who support field sales by taking customers' orders over the telephone.

Delivery salespeople

The salesperson's task is primarily concerned with delivering the product. In the UK, milk, newspapers and magazines are delivered to the door. There is little attempt to

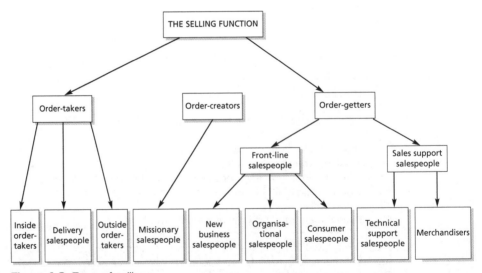

Figure 1.2 Types of selling

persuade the household to increase the milk order or number of newspapers taken: changes in order size are customer driven. Winning and losing orders will be dependent on reliability of delivery and the personality of the salesperson.

Outside order-takers

These salespeople visit customers, but their primary function is to respond to customer requests rather than actively seek to persuade. Outside order-takers do not deliver and to a certain extent they are being replaced by more cost efficient tele-marketing teams.

Order-creators

Missionary salespeople

In some industries, notably the pharmaceutical industry, the sales task is not to close the sale but to persuade the customer to specify the seller's products. For example, medical representatives calling on doctors cannot make a direct sale since the doctor does not buy drugs personally, but prescribes (specifies) them for patients. Similarly, in the building industry, architects act as specifiers rather than buyers, and so the objective of a sales call cannot be to close the sale. Instead, in these situations the selling task is to educate and build goodwill.

Order-getters

The final category, called order-getters, consists of those in selling jobs where a major objective is to persuade customers to make a direct purchase. These are the front-line salespeople.

New business salespeople

The task is to win new business by identifying and selling to prospects (people or organisations who have not previously bought from the salesperson's company).

Organisational salespeople

These salespeople have the job of maintaining close, long-term relationships with organisational customers (i.e. industrial buyers, buying for resale and institutional buyers – e.g. the latter of whom typically sell to educational establishments, the police service and local authorities). The selling job may involve team selling where mainstream salespeople are supported by product and financial specialists.

Consumer salespeople

These people sell physical products and services such as double glazing, security equipment, cars, insurance and personal pension plans to individuals. Much selling in this category tends to be 'one-off' and salespeople are generally rewarded through commission. Therefore, the impetus to attain an order is paramount and it is this category that has attracted much criticism in terms of 'high pressure' being put on customers to make a purchase.

Technical support salespeople

This group of order-getters provides sales support to front-line salespeople. Where a product is highly technical and negotiations are complex, a salesperson may be supported by product and financial specialists who can provide the detailed technical information required by customers. This may be ongoing as part of a key account team or on a temporary basis with the specialists being called into the selling situation as and when required.

Merchandisers

These people provide sales support in retail and wholesale selling situations. Orders may be negotiated nationally at head office, but sales to individual outlets are supported by merchandisers who give advice on display, implement sales promotions, check stock levels and maintain contact with store managers.

Selling as a career

The subdivisions of the sales roles just outlined give an idea of the range of sales positions that are available. Generally, there is much less personal pressure involved in being an order-taker than an order-maker and a prime attribute for an order-maker is a pleasant, non-combative personality. However, the opportunity for higher rewards belongs to order-takers as their remuneration normally rests on some kind of commission or bonus where payment is linked to the amount of orders they take. It is an acknowledged fact that in many business situations the opportunity to earn really high incomes at a relatively young age is present in this kind of situation.

With such a large range of selling situations and positions in sales, it is not possible to provide a specific prescription of the qualities required for a successful sales career. There is no definitive test or selection procedure that can be used to distinguish between successful and less successful salespeople and apart from 'trying it out' there is no way of knowing if a person is suited to a career in sales. However, there are a number of key qualities that are generally recognised as being important:

1 *Empathy and an interest in people.* Such a skill will help in more accurately identifying customers' real needs and problems in terms of thinking oneself into the other person's mind and understanding why the customer feels as he or she does.

2 *Ability to communicate.* This means an ability to get a message across to a customer and, more importantly, an ability to listen and understand. The skill of knowing when to stop talking and when to listen is essential.

3 *Determination.* Although the salesperson must be able to take no for an answer, this should not come easily to someone who wants to succeed in selling. It is a fact that customers might say no when they really mean maybe, which can ultimately lead to yes. Determined salespeople have a need and a will to succeed and success can mean closing a sale.

4 *Self-discipline and resilience.* Most salespeople spend much of their time unsupervised and, apart from seeing customers, they are alone. As part of their job they can expect setback, rejections and failures. A salesperson thus needs to be both self-disciplined and resilient to cope with these facets of the sales task.

1.6 Image of Selling

Mention of the word *selling* will prompt a variety of responses. It will evoke a high proportion of negative, even hostile, responses, including 'immoral', 'dishonest', 'unsavoury', 'degrading' and 'wasteful'. Is such an unfavourable view justified? We suggest not. In fact the underlying attitudes to selling derive from widely held misconceptions about selling, some of which are outlined below.

1 *Selling is not a worthwhile career.* This notion is held by many, the common attitude being that if one has talent then it will be wasted in sales. Unfortunately this attitude is often held by those in a position to advise and influence young people in their choice of careers. In some circles it is fashionable to denigrate careers in selling, and the consequence is that many of our brighter graduates are not attracted to a career in selling.

2 *Good products will sell themselves and thus the selling process adds unnecessarily to costs.* This view assumes that if you produce a superior product then there will always be buyers. This may be all right if a firm can produce a technologically superior product, but then it is likely that additional costs will accrue in terms of research and development, and there will be continued research and development costs involved in keeping ahead. In addition, as developed later in the text, the role of selling is not solely to sell; it can be used to feed back information from customers to the firm – particularly product performance information – and this is of direct use to research and development.

3 *There is something immoral about selling, and one should be suspicious about those who earn their living from this activity.* The origin and reason for this most pervasive and damaging of the misconceptions about selling stems from the 'foot in the door' image that has been perpetuated. Such attitudes can make life difficult for the salesperson who has first to overcome the barriers which such mistrust erects in the customer/salesperson relationship.

There are a number of elements in the sales task that act as demotivators:

1 Because of their perceived low status, salespeople are constantly exposed to the possibility of rejection and often have to suffer 'ego punishment' such as being kept waiting, appointments cancelled at short notice and 'put downs' from customers to which they cannot adequately respond as buyers have the power in such circumstances. Thus, in **business to business (B2B)** and **business to consumer (B2C)** selling in particular a certain amount of psychological risk is involved.

2 In B2B situations in particular, salespeople visit buyers in their offices, so they are effectively working in 'foreign' territory and might sometimes feel uneasy

when entering the premises. The customer might keep the salesperson waiting, thus heightening discomfort.

3 The salesperson tends to work alone, often staying away from home for periods. An attraction is independence, but it can be a lonely existence. Thus there is a certain amount of psychological risk attached to such situations.

Selling is therefore not an easy task, and those who are concerned to improve its image must be more vociferous, yet objective, in presenting its case and recognise that misconceptions invariably have some basis in fact. There are always unscrupulous individuals and companies ready to trade on the ignorance and gullibility of unsuspecting customers. These individuals are not salespeople: at best they are misguided traders and at worst criminals. At some times in our lives we inevitably feel that we have purchased something we did not really want or on terms we could not really afford because we were subjected to high-pressure selling.

Selling then is not entirely blameless, but salespeople are becoming more professional in their approach to customers. Some of the worst excesses in selling have been curbed – some through legal means, but increasingly voluntarily. To overcome some of these misconceptions, selling needs to sell itself and the following facts about selling should be more universally aired:

1 *There is nothing immoral or unscrupulous about selling* or about those involved in this activity. Selling provides a mechanism for exchange and through this process customers' needs and wants are satisfied. Furthermore, most people, at some stage, are involved in selling – even if only selling their skills and personalities in an attempt to obtain a job.

2 *Selling is a worthwhile career.* Many of those who have spent a lifetime in selling have found it to be a challenging, responsible and rewarding occupation. Inevitably a career in selling means meeting people and working with them, and a selling job often offers substantial discretion in being able to plan one's own work schedule.

3 *Good products do not sell themselves.* An excellent product may pass unnoticed unless its benefits and features are explained to customers. What appears to be a superior product may be totally unsuited to a particular customer. Selling is unique in that it deals with the special needs of each individual customer, and the salesperson, with specialist product knowledge, is in a position to assess these circumstances and advise each customer accordingly.

Why sales skills are the key to a firm's success

Successful entrepreneurs all have one thing in common – the ability to sell. Patrick Dunne, a director with 3i, the venture capitalist, says: 'It's not just selling products to new customers. You also need sales skills to get the first people to work for you. And the cleverest ones are very good at getting suppliers and others to give them credit.'

But entrepreneurs often stumble in their enthusiasm to get started warns Patrick Joiner, Chief Executive of the Institute of Sales & Marketing

Management: 'The most essential skill of selling,' he says, 'is to put yourself in your client's shoes. This is where entrepreneurs fall down. They are often people with a special knowledge about their industries or a technology that helped them to come up with their business ideas. But being totally fired up by their own products, they're locked into seeing it from their own perspectives. Entrepreneurs also tend to be very driven and enthusiastic, which means they can come across as overbearing.' He goes on to say: 'You should always be trying to build a relationship with your customer. You need more than just something different or low cost or even effectiveness in selling – the market changes quickly and you will keep these advantages for only so long. What you need most of all is a good relationship with your customers.'

Source: *Sunday Times*, 5 May 2002, p. 13.

1.7 The Nature and Role of Sales Management

In the same way that selling has become more professional, so too has the nature and role of **sales management**. The emphasis is on the word *management*. Increasingly, those involved in management are being called upon to exercise in a professional way the key duties of all managers, namely, planning, organising and controlling. The emphasis has changed from the idea that to be a good sales manager you had to have the right personality and that the main feature of the job was ensuring that the salesforce were out selling sufficient volume. Although such qualities may be admirable, the duties of the sales manager in the modern company have both broadened and changed in emphasis.

Nowadays the sales manager is expected to play a much more strategic role in the company and is required to make a key input into the formulation of company plans. This theme is developed in Chapters 2 and 15. There is thus a need to be familiar with the techniques associated with planning, including sales forecasting and budgeting (dealt with in Chapter 16). The sales manager also needs to be familiar with the concept of marketing to ensure that sales and marketing activities are integrated – a theme expanded in this chapter. In many companies the emphasis is less on sales volume and more on profits. The sales manager needs to be able to analyse and direct the activities of the salesforce towards more profitable business. In dealing with a salesforce, the sales manager must be aware of modern developments in human resource management.

Looked at in the manner just outlined, the role of the sales manager may seem formidable; that person must be an accountant, a planner, a personnel manager and a marketer. However, the prime responsibility is to ensure that the sales function makes the most effective contribution to the achievement of company objectives and goals. In order to fulfil this role, sales managers will undertake specific duties and responsibilities:

- the determination of salesforce objectives and goals

- forecasting and budgeting

- salesforce organisation, salesforce size, territory design and planning

- salesforce selection, recruitment and training
- motivating the salesforce
- salesforce evaluation and control

Because these areas encompass the key duties of the sales manager, they are discussed in detail in Parts Four and Five.

Perhaps one of the most significant developments affecting selling and sales management in recent years has been the evolution of the marketing concept. Because of its importance to selling, we will now turn our attention to the nature of this evolution and its effect upon sales activities.

1.8   The Marketing Concept

In tracing the development of the **marketing concept** it is customary to chart three successive stages in the evolution of modern business practice:

1 Production orientation.

2 Sales orientation.

3 Marketing orientation.

Production orientation

This era was characterised by focusing company efforts on producing goods or services. More specifically, management efforts were aimed at achieving high production efficiency, often through the large-scale production of standardised items. In such a situation other functions such as sales, finance and personnel were secondary to the main function of the business, which was to produce. More importantly, the underlying philosophy was that customers would purchase products, provided they were of a reasonable quality and available in sufficiently large quantities at a suitably low price.

Such a philosophy was initiated by Henry Ford when he mass produced the Model T Ford in Detroit in 1913. His idea was that if he could produce a standard model vehicle in large quantities using mass production techniques, then he could supply a potential demand for relatively cheap private transport. At the time Ford was correct; there was such a demand and his products proved successful. A production orientation to business was thus suited to an economic climate where potential demand outstripped supply, as was the case in the USA at that time. However, times change, and such a philosophy is not conducive to doing business in today's economic climate, where potential supply usually outstrips demand.

Sales orientation

With the large-scale introduction of mass production techniques in the 1920s and 1930s, particularly in the USA and Western Europe, and the rapid worldwide increase in competition which accompanied this, many firms adopted a sales orientation.

The sales-orientated company is one where the focus of company effort switches to the sales function. The main issue here is not how to produce but, having products, how to ensure that this production is sold. The underlying philosophy towards customers in a sales-orientated business is that, if left to their own devices, customers will be slow or reluctant to buy. In any case, even those customers who are seeking to purchase the type of product or service the company produces will have a wide range of potential suppliers. This situation is exacerbated when, in addition to sufficient capacity on the supply side, demand is depressed. Such was the case in many of the developed economies in the 1930s, and it was in this period that many 'hard sell' techniques developed. Many of these were dubious, even dishonest, and much of the tainted image accompanying selling derives from their use.

Many companies still adopt a sales-orientated approach to doing business, even though customers are better protected against its worst excesses, as discussed in Chapter 13.

Marketing orientation

It is unclear exactly when the idea of marketing or customer orientation began to emerge; indeed in some ways the central importance of the customer has perhaps always been recognised in the long history of trading. Not until the 1950s, however, did the ideas associated with the marketing concept begin to emerge and take shape. The marketing concept – initially an American phenomenon – arose partly as a result of a dissatisfaction with the production and sales orientations, partly as a result of a changing environment, and partly as a result of fundamental business sense.

The marketing concept holds that the key to successful and profitable business rests with identifying the needs and wants of customers and providing products and services to satisfy them. On the surface such a concept does not appear to be a far-reaching and fundamentally different philosophy of business, but in fact the marketing concept requires a revolution in how a company thinks about, and practises, its business activities as compared with production or sales orientation. Central to this revolution in business thinking is the emphasis given to the needs and wants of the customer. The contrast between this approach and, for example, that of a sales-orientated company is shown in Figure 1.3.

Increasingly, companies have come to recognise that this different approach to doing business is essential in today's environment. Consumers are now better educated and more sophisticated. Real incomes have increased steadily over the years and consumers now have considerable discretionary spending power to allocate between an increasingly diverse range of products and services. Too many companies have learned the hard way that having what they feel to be a superior product, efficient production and extensive promotion – laudable though these may be – are not sufficient to confer automatic success. To have any chance of success, customer needs must be placed at the very centre of business planning. In part, this stress on understanding the consumer explains the development of those concepts and techniques aimed at understanding buyer behaviour. In Chapter 3 we develop a framework within which consumer and organisational buying behaviour may be analysed.

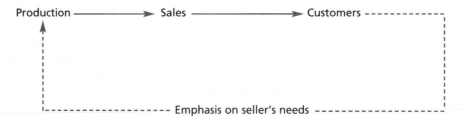

(a) Sales orientation

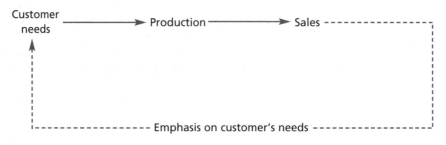

(b) Marketing orientation

Figure 1.3 Sales versus market orientation

Implementing the Marketing Concept

For a company to be marketing orientated requires that a number of organisational changes take place in practices and in attitudes. To become of value it requires that the discipline of marketing contributes what might be termed a technology of marketing. By this we mean that management requires the development of a set of tools (techniques and concepts) to implement the marketing concept. We have already mentioned that the behavioural sciences can lead to an understanding of buyer behaviour; another example is the development of quantitative and qualitative techniques of marketing research for analysing and appraising markets. Some of the more important and useful concepts in marketing are now discussed.

Market segmentation and targeting

Because marketing focuses on customer needs and wants, this requires that companies identify these needs and wants and then develop marketing programmes to satisfy them as a route to achieving company objectives. The diversity of customer needs and wants, and the multiplicity of ways in which these may be satisfied, means that few if any companies are in a position effectively to serve all customers in a market in a standardised manner. **Market segmentation** is the process of identifying those clusters of customers in a market which share similar needs and wants and will respond in a unique way to a given marketing effort. Having identified the various segments in a market, a company can then decide which of them are most attractive and to which segments it can market most effectively. Company marketing efforts can then be tailored specifically to the needs of these segments on which the company has decided to target its marketing.

Market segmentation and **targeting** are two of the most useful concepts in marketing, and a set of techniques has been developed to aid companies in their application. Some of the more important benefits of effective segmentation and targeting are as follows:

- a clearer identification of market opportunities and particularly the analysis of gaps (where there are no competitive products) in a market

- the design of product and market appeals that are more finely tuned to the needs of the market

- focusing of marketing and sales efforts on those segments with the greatest potential

There are a number of bases for segmenting markets, which may be used singly or in combination. For example, a manufacturer of toothpaste may decide that the market segments best on the basis of age, i.e. the seller discovers that the different age groups in the market for the product have different wants and needs and vary in what they require from the product. The seller will find that the various segments will respond more favourably, in terms of sales, if the products and marketing programmes are more closely tailored to the needs of each segment. Alternatively, the seller may find that the market for toothpaste segments on the basis of income – the different income groups in the market vary in their product requirements. Finally, the seller may find that the market segments on the basis of a combination of both income and age characteristics (see box).

Meeting customers' needs in growth markets – online gaming

It is important to recognise that an overall market usually consists of discrete segments made up of consumers with different needs. Two obvious segments for broadband are business and household. Both can be broken down into sub-components where relevant.

Household customers can be defined by age or income in addition to the type of use they make of the web:

- educational – research for homework
- communication – email, instant messaging
- sport – navigating pages about football
- music – downloading tracks
- online gaming

BT identified that customers with a gaming interest had a high propensity to adopt broadband technology. Two tiers of online gamers have been identified.

- Tier 1 consists mainly of males aged 16–35.
- Tier 2 consists of family users, i.e. parents whose children are potential online users. *(continued on following page)*

Research showed that customers are passionate about gaming and that they enjoy using new technology with the latest games and up-to-date consoles. Customer research showed that the social aspect of gaming is important – users enjoy playing against their friends.

Source: *http://www.thetimes100.co.uk/case_study* with permission

Among some of the more frequently used bases for segmentation are the following:

1 Consumer products/markets
   - age
   - sex
   - income
   - social class
   - geographical location
   - type of residence (A Classification of Residential Neighbourhoods – ACORN)
   - personality
   - benefits sought
   - usage rate, e.g. heavy users versus light users

2 Industrial products/markets
   - end-use market/type of industry/product application
   - benefits sought
   - company size
   - geographical location
   - usage rate

Whatever the base(s) chosen to segment a market, the application of the concepts of segmentation and targeting is a major step towards becoming marketing orientated.

Application of segmentation

When marketing a product category, firms need to identify different market segments. Segmentation involves identifying sets of characteristics that distinguish particular groups of customers from others. For example:

1 *Based on demographics, i.e. dividing up the population into groups based on age, gender etc.* BIC uses this approach, recognising that different retailers appeal to different types of consumer based on age profiles and income, and different groups of end consumers seek different products, e.g. male and female shaver requirements. Promotion, advertising and presentation of products are therefore tailored to these differences.

2 *Based on usage.* In addition to its world-leading range of pocket lighters, BIC introduced BIC Megalighter designed to light barbecues and candles in 2004.

3 *Based on the behaviour/needs of consumers.* BIC's research into its stationery product category showed that there were three distinct types of writing instrument shopper:

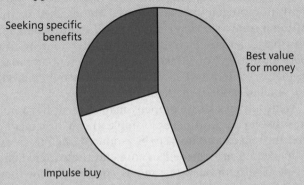

Best value for money

This type is typically bought by offices and households that have writing instruments in virtually every room. Everyone is allowed to use any available pen, so there is no great problem if one is misplaced. Households tend to seek lower priced pens and regularly make new purchases of assortments of writing instruments based on current needs.

Seeking specific benefits

Here consumers are looking for a more personalised item – something they regard as 'my pen'. It will be kept in a private place belonging to that individual, who may be reluctant to let anyone borrow it. Buying decisions will typically take longer and involve careful consideration over choice. Key features looked for will include the pen's being comfortable to hold and its capacity for producing smooth writing that reflects the individual, e.g. by colour or handwriting style. Marketing activity therefore needs to focus on these more sophisticated individual needs.

Impulse buy

Impulse buys are unplanned. Innovative designs will attract this segment, largely because the consumer is buying for pleasure. Purchasing in this segment is far more emotional, so the skilful marketer will seek to create 'objects of desire'. Attention grabbing Point of Sale displays are essential to stimulate impulse buys.

BIC aims to create a balanced product portfolio, including:

- reliable, value for money products for regular household purchasers;
- premium high quality products for the consumer that wants 'something special';
- novel, attractive products, sometimes with a fairly short life cycle.

Source: *http://www.thetimes100.co.uk/case_study* with permission

The marketing mix

In discussing the notion of market segmentation, we have frequently alluded to the company marketing programme. By far the most important decisions within this marketing programme, and indeed the essence of the marketing manager's task within a company, are decisions on the controllable marketing variables: decisions on what E. Jerome McCarthy[7] termed the 'four Ps' of *price*, *product*, *promotion* and *place* (or distribution). Taken together, these four variables, plus the chosen market segments, comprise what Neil Borden termed the **marketing mix** – a concept which is central to modern marketing practice.[8]

Generally speaking, company management has a number of variables or ingredients that it can control. For example, the management of a company has discretion over the range of products to be produced, their features, quality levels, etc. The task of marketing management is to blend these ingredients together into a successful recipe. The term *marketing mix* is appropriate, for there are many marketing mix ingredients and even more ways of combining them. Each element of the four Ps requires that decisions are taken:

1 *Price*: price levels, credit terms, price changes, discounts.

2 *Product*: features, packaging, quality, range.

3 *Promotion*: advertising, publicity, sales promotion, personal selling, sponsorship. More correctly, the combination of these five elements is termed the communications mix. Getting these five elements to work together in harmony is termed 'integrated marketing communications'. The emergence of the internet and the increased use of direct marketing techniques in particular have more recently led to a greater emphasis on this aspect of the marketing mix.

4 *Place*: inventory, channels of distribution, number of intermediaries.

It will be seen that personal selling is considered to be one component of the promotional decision area of the marketing mix. We shall return to the place of selling in the mix later in this chapter, whilst the notion of a promotional mix is considered in more detail in Chapter 2. At this stage we will consider in greater detail the other elements of the mix.

Product

Many believe that product decisions represent the most important ingredient of the marketing mix. Decisions in this area, they argue, have the most direct and long-lasting influence on the degree of success which a company enjoys. At first glance this may seem to constitute evidence of a production as opposed to marketing orientated stance. However, it does not. There is no doubt that product decisions are the most important of the marketing decisions which a company makes. It is true that unless there is a potential demand (a true market need) for a product, then no matter how good it is, it will not succeed. This is not to say that decisions about products should be made in isolation. It is also true that there are many examples of products which had considerable market potential, but failed because of poor promotional, pricing and distribution decisions. In effect, product decisions determine the upper limit to a company's sales potential. The effectiveness of decisions on other elements of the mix determines the extent to which this potential is realised.

The term *product* covers anything a company offers to customers to satisfy their needs. In addition to physical, tangible products offered for sale, there are also services and skills. Non-profit organisations also market their services to potential customers. Increasingly, charities, educational establishments, libraries, museums and political candidates make use of the techniques of marketing. There are a number of ways of classifying products, depending upon the basis chosen for classification. For example, a broad distinction can be made between consumer and industrial products, the basis for classification here being the end-user/buyer.

Regardless of the basis of classification, one important factor to bear in mind is that the customer is purchasing a package of benefits, not product features. This concept of a product is yet another example of a market-orientated approach to doing business. It looks at the product from the point of view of what the customer is actually purchasing, i.e. needs and wants. For example, when people purchase cosmetics they are purchasing attractiveness. Theodore Levitt[9] provides us with a graphic example of this concept of a product when he states: 'Purchasing agents do not buy quarter inch drills; they buy quarter inch holes.' Viewing the product in this way can provide insights that can be used in marketing a product. In the sales area it can be used to develop the sales presentation by emphasising ways in which the product or service provides a solution to the customer's problems.

The product life-cycle

One of the most useful concepts in marketing derives from the idea that most products tend to follow a particular pattern over time in terms of sales and profits. This pattern is shown in Figure 1.4 and is known as the product life-cycle curve.

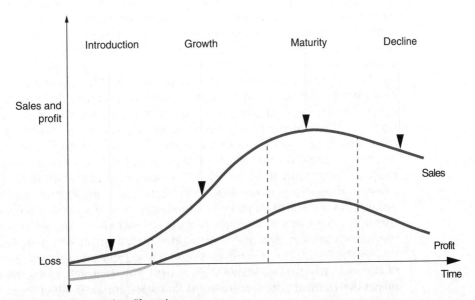

Figure 1.4 The product life-cycle curve

The **product life-cycle** is analogous to the life-cycle pattern of humans and has four distinct stages – introduction (birth), growth, maturity and eventually decline. Its shape can best be explained by outlining briefly the nature of each of the stages.

1 *Introduction.* In this stage, sales growth is relatively slow. Dealers must be persuaded to stock and promote the product. Consumers must be made aware of its existence, persuaded to be interested and convinced that it is a worthwhile purchase. They may have to be educated in how to use the product and their existing purchasing and lifestyle habits might change (e.g. microwave ovens and their associated convenience). There are few profits at this stage and heavy launch costs often mean a financial deficit.

2 *Growth.* After initial slow acceptance, sales begin to escalate at a relatively rapid pace. There is a snowball effect as word-of-mouth communication and advertising begin to take effect. Dealers may request to stock the product. Profits begin to be made, especially if a newly introduced product can command high initial prices (known as **market skimming**).

3 *Maturity.* The growth of sales begins to slow as the market becomes saturated. Few new buyers are attracted to the product and there is a high proportion of repeat sales. Attracted by the high profit and sales figures, competitors have now entered the market. Partly because of this increased competition, profits, having peaked, then begin to decline.

4 *Decline.* Sales begin to fall and already slim profit margins are depressed even further. Customers might have become bored with the product and are attracted by newer, improved products. Dealers begin to de-stock the product in anticipation of reduced sales.

Implications of the product life-cycle

Not all products exhibit such a typical cycle of sales and profits. Some products have hardly any life-cycle at all (many new products are unsuccessful in the marketplace). Similarly, sales may be reduced abruptly even in a period of rapid sales growth as a result of, perhaps, the introduction of a new and better competitive product. Products vary too in the length of time they take to pass through the life-cycle. Unlike the human lifespan, there is no average life expectation for products. Nevertheless, the fact that a great number of products do tend to follow the generalised life-cycle pattern has a number of implications for marketing and sales strategies. Some of these are considered in more detail in Chapter 2. Two of the more important implications of the product life-cycle concept are considered now.

The first obvious implication of the concept is that even the most successful products have a finite life. Further, there is some evidence which suggests that intensifying competition and rapid technological change are leading to a shortening of product life-cycles. This explains the importance and emphasis now attached to the continued development of new products. The salesforce has an important role to play in this process. Because of their often daily contact with customers, they are usually the first to detect signs that products are about to embark upon the period of decline. Such detailed knowledge of customers, competitors and market requirements makes them potentially a valuable source of new product ideas.

A second implication of the life-cycle concept is that different marketing and sales strategies may be appropriate to each stage. For example, in the introductory stage the emphasis may be on locating potential prospects. In the growth stage, the salesforce may find themselves having to deal with the delicate issue of rationing products to their customers as demand increases more rapidly than capacity. In the maturity and decline stages, the salesforce will increasingly have to rely on competitive pricing and special offers in order to combat increasing competition and falling sales. Again, this is covered in more detail in Chapter 2.

Product adoption and diffusion

This theory was first put forward by Everett Rogers in 1962[10] and is closely related to the product life-cycle. It describes innovative behaviour and holds that the characteristics of a new product can affect its rate of adoption. Figure 1.5 describes its characteristics.

Consumers are placed into one of five 'adopter' categories, each with different behavioural characteristics. These adopter categories contain percentages of first-time buyers (i.e. not repeat buyers) that fall into each category. What will attract first-time buyers to a product or service, and the length of time it will take for the diffusion process to be completed, will depend upon the nature of the product or service.

If we consider a new range of female fashions, then the time taken for the diffusion process to be completed might be less than one year. Here, the innovators (i.e. the first 2.5 per cent) are likely to be fashion-conscious rich people. However, if we consider a new type of computer software then innovators are more likely to be technically minded computer 'experts' and the time for diffusion will be over a longer period. Similarly, although microwave ovens were developed almost 30 years ago, they have not yet totally diffused through the marketplace as they are now in the 'laggard' stage. Having said this, many potential consumers will never adopt for

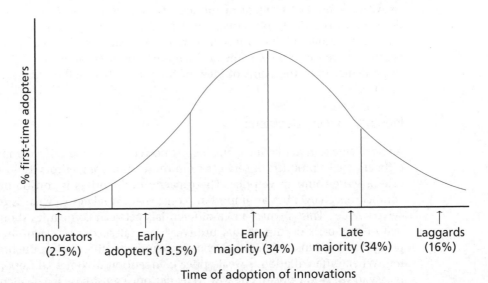

Figure 1.5 The adoption of innovations

a variety of reasons (e.g. some people refuse to have a television because it destroys the art of conversation). A number of factors can determine the rate at which the innovation is taken up:

- its *relative advantage* over other products or services in the marketplace

- the extent to which it is *compatible* with the potential needs of customers

- its *complexity* in terms of how it can be used and understood

- its *divisibility* in terms of how it can be tried beforehand on some kind of test basis before a commitment is made to purchase

- its *communicability*, which is the degree to which the innovation can be described or demonstrated prior to purchase (see box).

How to protect your dark clothes

Is it annoying when after just a few washes your favourite dark clothes fade to a dull grey colour and have to be consigned to the back of your wardrobe? Now you can keep your dark clothes from fading for longer with Dreft Dark. It is a specially formulated liquid detergent with ingredients that will enable your darks to stay dark for longer whilst removing stains effectively. It is gentle enough to be used on your whole family's clothes and is the leader in its field. It is suitable for both machine and hand washing and is now available from Sainsbury's and many other leading supermarkets.

Source: Adapted from promotional article in *Best*, 2 July 2002.

Pricing

As with the product element of the mix, pricing decisions encompass a variety of decision areas. Pricing objectives must be determined, price levels set, decisions made as to credit and discount policies and a procedure established for making price changes. Here we consider some of the more important inputs to pricing decisions, in particular from the point of view of how they affect selling and sales management.

Inputs to pricing decisions

A vital element in marketing is the buying power of customers. If a company cannot differentiate its products or services from those of its competitors it must be able to offer a more competitive price. The capacity to set prices is constrained by what competitors charge, but an important consideration relates to what is termed 'perceived value'. This is where price differentials between companies should be justified on the basis of 'differential utility'. Some salespeople concentrate on selling product features instead of taking the opportunity to differentiate the product offering. When differentiation is weak, price competition becomes all important and it is easy to sell at low prices. The way to reduce price sensitivity is a challenge to make the product more distinctive. It should, however, be recognised that customers will differ a great deal in terms of sensitivity. For some, price is the overriding criterion, but for others factors like delivery, service and image are more important.

Market based pricing as opposed to cost based pricing is where a firm acknowledges that price represents value and not just costs. Conventionally, companies add their direct and indirect costs and overheads plus profit to arrive at a selling price. Once the price is set, the salesperson's task is to convince clients that the product being offered is worth it. Depending on the volume demanded, price can then be lowered if demand is small or raised if demand is large. A cost based approach ignores customers and competition. Market based pricing commences by considering the worth or value customers see in owning a product and considering their opportunities for acquiring comparable products or brands. Value to customers is a function of the product, the services that supplement it, how the company relates to customer needs and the impression the customer has of the product.

Increased value inevitably means higher costs in terms of better products and levels of service. The secret is to attain a balance between what customers will offer and the costs related to this approach.

In the determination of price levels, a number of factors must be considered. The main factors include the following:

1 *Company objectives.* In making pricing decisions, a company must first
   determine what objectives it wishes its pricing to achieve within the context of
   overall company financial and marketing objectives. For example, company
   objectives may specify a target rate of return on capital employed. Pricing levels
   for individual products should reflect this objective. Alternatively, or
   additionally, a company may couch its financial objectives in terms of early
   cash recovery or a specified payback period for the investment.

2 *Marketing objectives.* These may shape the pricing decision. For example, a
   company may determine that the most appropriate marketing strategy for a
   new product which it has developed is to aim for a substantial market share as
   quickly as possible. Such a strategy is termed a **market penetration** strategy. It
   is based on stimulating and capturing demand backed by low prices and heavy
   promotion. At the other extreme, the company might determine that a market
   skimming strategy is appropriate. Here, high initial prices are set – again often
   backed by high levels of promotional spending – and the cream of the profits is
   taken before eventually lowering the price. When the price is lowered, an
   additional, more price-sensitive band of purchasers then enters the market.
   Whatever the financial and marketing objective set, these determine the
   framework within which pricing decisions are made. Such objectives should be
   communicated to sales management and to individual members of the sales
   team.

3 *Demand considerations.* In most markets the upper limit to the prices a company
   can charge is determined by demand. Put simply, one is able to charge only
   what the market will bear. This tends to oversimplify the complexities of
   demand analysis and its relationship to pricing decisions. These complexities
   should not, however, deter pricing decision-makers from considering demand
   in their deliberations. One of the most straightforward notions about the
   relationship between demand and price is the concept of a demand curve for a
   product, as shown in Figure 1.6. Although it is a simple concept, the demand

curve contains much useful information for the decision-maker. It shows that at lower prices, higher quantities are normally demanded. It is also possible to read off the curve the quantity demanded at any given price. Finally, it is possible to assess how sensitive demand is to changes in price. In other words, we can calculate the percentage change in quantity demanded for any given percentage price increase or decrease. Such information is useful for making pricing decisions, but obtaining information about the relationship between the price and demand is not easy. Factors other than price have an important effect on demand. Despite this, pricing decisions must reflect demand considerations and some estimate should be made of the likely relationship between demand levels and price. Here again, the salesforce can play a key role in the provision of such information and many companies make full use of this resource when pricing their products.

A final point to be considered is the slope of the demand curve. Figure 1.6 is a 'conventional' curve, in that it slopes downwards to the right, which means that at lower prices higher quantities are demanded. However, it is dangerous to assume that this is always the case. In some circumstances it is possible to charge too low a price for a product or service; far from increasing demand, such low prices actually reduce it. This can be the case for products that are bought because they *are* highly priced, i.e. where there is some prestige attached to having purchased what everyone knows is an expensive product. Similarly, low prices may cause the customer to suspect the quality of a product.

4 *Cost considerations.* If demand determines the upper threshold for price, then costs determine the lower one. In a profit-making organisation, in the long run, prices charged need to cover the total costs of production and marketing, with some satisfactory residue for profit. In fact companies often begin the process of making decisions on price by considering their costs. Some techniques of pricing go further with prices being determined solely on the basis of costs; for example, total costs per unit are calculated, a percentage added for profit and a final price computed. Such cost-plus approaches to pricing, although

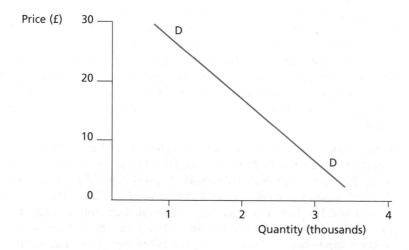

Figure 1.6 The demand curve

straightforward, have a tendency to neglect some of the more subtle and important aspects of the cost input. As with demand, cost considerations can be quite complex. One of the important distinctions that a cost-plus approach often neglects is the distinction between the fixed and variable costs of producing a product. Fixed costs are those which do not vary – up to the limit of plant capacity – regardless of the level of output, e.g. rent and rates. Variable costs do differ with the level of output – as it increases, so too do total variable costs, and vice versa as production is decreased, e.g. direct labour costs, raw materials, etc. This apparently simple distinction is very useful for making pricing decisions and gives rise to the technique of **break-even analysis**.

Figure 1.7 illustrates this concept. Fixed, variable and total costs are plotted on the chart, together with a sales revenue curve. Where the revenue curve cuts the total cost curve is the break-even point. At this point the company is making neither profit nor loss. From the break-even chart it is possible to calculate the effect on the break-even point of charging different prices and, when this is combined with information on demand, break-even analysis is quite a powerful aid to decision-making. Sales managers should understand the different costing concepts and procedures and, whilst they do not need detailed accounting knowledge, they should be familiar with the procedures that go into the costing of products they are responsible for selling.

5 *Competitor considerations*. Few companies are in the position of being able to make pricing decisions without considering the possible actions of competitors. Pricing decisions, particularly short-term tactical price changes, are often made as a direct response to the actions of competitors. Care should be taken in using this tactic, particularly when the movement of price is downwards. Once lowered, price can be very difficult to raise and, where possible, a company should consider responses other than price reduction to combat competition.

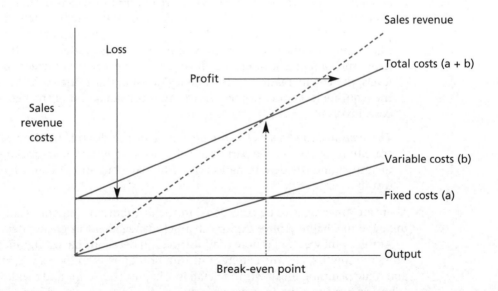

Figure 1.7 A simple break-even chart

Distribution

The distribution (or place) element of the marketing mix, particularly the management of physical distribution, has long been felt to be one of the areas in business where substantial improvements and cost savings can be made. Representing, as it often does, a substantial portion of total costs in a company, the distribution area has in recent years attracted considerable attention in terms of new concepts and techniques designed better to manage this important function. The management of distribution is now recognised as a key part of the strategic management of a company and in larger organisations is often the responsibility of a specialist. Because of this we can do no more here than give a non-specialist overview of some of the more important aspects of this element of the mix.

In its broadest sense distribution is concerned with all those activities required to move goods and materials into the factory, through the factory and to the final consumer. Examples of the decision areas encompassed in the distribution element of the marketing mix are as follows:

1 *The selection of distribution channels*. This involves determining in what manner, and through which distribution outlets, goods and services are to be made available to the final consumer. Marketing channels may be very short, e.g. where goods and services are sold direct to the customer such as via mail order. Alternatively, the channel may include a whole set of intermediaries, including brokers, wholesalers and retailers. In addition to selecting the route through which products will reach consumers, decisions must also be made as to the extent of distribution coverage. For example, some companies have a policy of **exclusive distribution** where only a small number of selected intermediaries are used to distribute company products. In other cases, a company may decide that it requires as wide a distribution cover as possible (**intensive distribution**), and will seek a large number of distribution outlets.

2 *Determining the level of customer service*. In addition to selecting channels of distribution, decisions must also be made as to factors such as delivery periods and methods of transportation. Reduced delivery times can provide a significant advantage to a company in marketing its products. On the other hand, such a policy is often accompanied by a necessity to increase inventory levels, thereby increasing costs. A policy decision must, therefore, be made as to the requisite level of customer service, after consideration of the benefits and costs involved.

3 *The terms and conditions of distribution*. Included under this heading would be conditions of sale on the part of distributors, minimum order/stocking quantities and the determination of credit, payment and discount terms for distributors.

There are other areas to be considered in the distribution element of the marketing mix, and in Chapter 10 we explore channel management in greater detail.

At this point we should note that distribution decisions have a significant impact on sales activities, e.g. the extent of distribution directly influences territory design and route planning (dealt with in detail in Chapter 16). Terms and conditions of distribution influence the framework within which sales are negotiated. The management of physical distribution influences the all-important delivery terms which the salesforce are able to offer their customers. Probably no other area of the marketing mix has such a far-ranging influence on the sales process.

Communications

This final element of the marketing mix has the most direct influence on sales because personal selling itself is considered as one element of the total promotional mix of a company. Other elements of this communications sub-mix (sometimes called a promotional sub-mix) include advertising, sales promotion, publicity and sponsorship.

The notion of the integrated **communications mix** was first put forward by Shultz, Tannenbaum and Lauterborn in 1992.[11] The view was taken that the various sub-elements of communications have traditionally been considered as separate entities. They advocated linking all of these together to convey a cohesive message to target markets, one in which each aspect supports other parts of the communications programme. The American Association of Advertising Agencies defines integrated marketing communications as:

> A concept of marketing communications planning that recognises the added value of a comprehensive plan that evaluates the strategic roles of a variety of communications disciplines and combines them to provide clarity, consistency and maximum communications impact through the seamless integration of discrete messages.

The implication of the integrated communications mix for selling is that the salesforce must be kept fully informed of any new sales promotions, direct marketing and advertising campaigns. Sometimes promotional campaigns have been counterproductive because sales staff have not been informed. It is clearly unsatisfactory when customers are the first to tell sales staff about a special offer that has been made through an advertising campaign of which they are not fully aware.

All of these sub-elements are covered throughout the text in a variety of contexts and their relationships with selling are fully examined.

Travis Perkins' customers and the marketing mix

- The internal customer – all employees and associates of the business are important; they are the point of contact with the external customer.
- The external customer – they buy goods from the business and they are also customers the business hopes to attract in the future.

Travis Perkins must strive to continuously improve performance and be better than the competition in keeping existing, and attracting new, customers. In order to pursue competitive advantage Travis Perkins is constantly reviewing and adjusting its marketing mix, paying attention to the little things that make a difference.

(continued on following page)

Price

Travis Perkins does not aim to be the cheapest. Its aim is to provide value for money and a service that customers can rely upon. Customers may have tight deadlines. A reliable supply to finish the job is essential.

Some customers are more price sensitive than others. Account customers are given preferential rates depending on their product requirements and purchasing habits. Volume and overall spend are two key drivers to create the correct price levels for a specific customer. Goods can also be delivered from the yard or direct from manufacturers to produce the most competitive rate.

Product

Travis Perkins needs to be aware of lifestyle and fashion changes when it decides which products are offered for sale. Many products are standard building materials but adding value to the product is important.

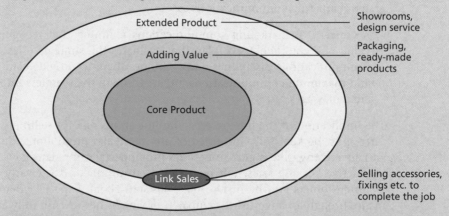

Place

Accessibility for customer and supplier is vital to the success of any business. It must also consider how to display goods within its premises, for instance, placing similar or complementary products close to each other and labelling products clearly.

Promotion

All businesses need to tell the customer what they have to offer. It is important that Travis Perkins considers carefully the most effective methods of promotion to maximise sales. Strategies might include special offers, online ordering, point of sale offers, trade shows and exhibitions.

The marketing mix for Travis Perkins:

Price

- standard prices for one-off customers
- differentiated discounts for account holders/frequent purchasers

- discounts on many products
- value for money and an excellent service.

Place

- branches need to be accessible by road
- adequate car and van parking
- space for loading/unloading
- complementary products need to be near each other
- impulse buys at point of sale
- associated services such as hire, kitchen planning where appropriate
- safe and friendly environment.

Product

- needs to reflect lifestyle changes
- needs to reflect legislation and technology advances
- needs added value, such as pre-packed bags of sand and cement for easy transportation
- ready-made wooden constructions such as trellis, fence panels, doors and windows
- link selling to ensure the customers buy associated products such as fixings and finishing materials.

Promotion

- website *www.travisperkins.co.uk*
- online ordering
- online tool hire
- exhibitions
- customer surveys
- special offers and value lines – Spotlight and Red Hot Offers feature the very best deals each month
- catalogues/direct mail
- sports sponsorship.

Source: *http://www.thetimes100.co.uk/case_study* with permission

1.10   The Relationship between Sales and Marketing

Throughout this chapter we have examined the nature and roles of selling and sales management and have discussed a general move towards marketing orientation. In addition, we have seen that sales efforts influence and are influenced by decisions taken on the ingredients of a company's marketing mix, which in turn affect its overall marketing efforts. It is essential, therefore, that sales and marketing be fully integrated. The adoption of the marketing concept has in many companies been accompanied by changes in organisational structure, together with changes in the view of what constitutes the nature of selling.

Examples of the possible organisational implications of adopting the marketing concept are shown in Figure 1.8 which shows the organisation charts of a sales orientated and a marketing orientated company.

Perhaps the most notable difference between the pre- and post-marketing orientated company is the fact that sales are later seen to be a part of the activity of the marketing function. In the marketing orientated company, the marketing function takes on a much wider controlling and co-ordinating role across the range of company activities. This facet of marketing orientation is often misunderstood by those in sales, and a great deal of resentment is often engendered between sales and marketing. Such resentment is often due to insensitive and undiplomatic management when making the changes necessary to reorientate a company. Selling is only a part of the total marketing programme of a company and this total effort should be co-ordinated by the marketing function. The marketing concept, however, does not imply that sales activities are any less important, nor that marketing executives should hold the most senior positions in a company.

In addition to changes in organisational structure, the influence of the marketing function and the increased professional approach taken to sales has meant that the nature and role of this activity has changed. Selling and sales management are now concerned with the analysis of customers' needs and wants and, through the company's total marketing efforts, with the provision of benefits to satisfy these

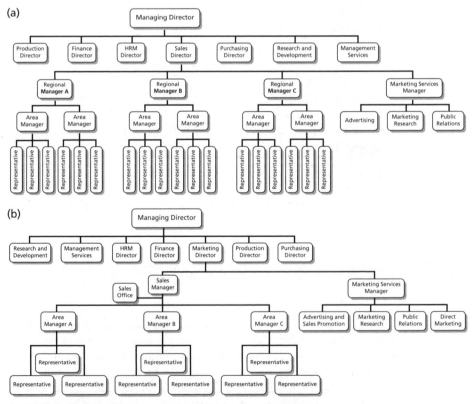

Figure 1.8 Organisational implications of adopting the marketing concept:
(a) company organisation chart, sales orientated company;
(b) company organisation chart, marketing orientated company

needs and wants. Figure 1.9 gives an overview of the relationship between marketing and personal selling and outlines the key areas of sales management.

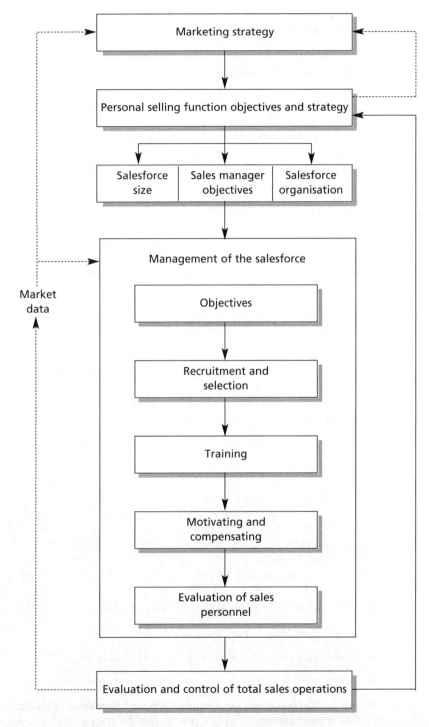

Figure 1.9 Marketing strategy and management of personal selling

As with all parts of the marketing mix, the personal selling function is not a stand-alone element, but one that must be considered in the light of overall marketing strategy. At the product level, two major marketing considerations are the choice of target market and the creation of a differential advantage. Both of these decisions impact on personal selling.

Target market choice

The definition of a target market has clear implications for sales management because of its relationship with target accounts. Once the target market has been defined (e.g. organisations in a particular industry over a certain size), sales management can translate that specification into individual accounts to target. Salesforce resources can then be deployed to maximum effect.

Differential advantage

The creation of a differential advantage is the starting point of successful marketing strategy, but this needs to be communicated to the salesforce and embedded in a sales plan that ensures they can articulate it convincingly to customers. There are two common dangers:

1 The salesforce undermine differential advantage by repeatedly giving in to customer demands for price concessions.

2 The features that underlie the differential advantage are communicated, but customer benefits are neglected. Customer benefits need to be communicated in terms that are meaningful to customers. This means, for example, that advantages such as higher productivity may require translation into cash savings or higher revenue for financially minded customers.

The second way in which marketing strategy affects the personal selling function is through strategic objectives. Each objective – build, hold, harvest and divest – has implications for sales objectives and strategy, outlined in Table 1.2. Linking business or product area strategic objectives with functional area strategies is essential for the efficient allocation of resources and effective implementation in the marketplace.

As we have seen, selling objectives and strategies are derived from marketing strategy decisions and should be consistent with other elements of the marketing mix. Indeed, marketing strategy will determine if there is a need for a salesforce at all, or whether the selling role can be better accomplished using some other medium such as direct mail. Objectives define what the selling function is expected to achieve. Objectives are typically defined in terms of the following:

- sales volume (e.g. 5 per cent growth in sales volume)

- market share (e.g. 1 per cent increase in market share)

- profitability (e.g. maintenance of gross profit margin)

- service levels (e.g. 20 per cent increase in number of customers regarding salesperson assistance as 'good or better' in annual customer survey)

Table 1.2 Marketing strategy and sales management

Strategic marketing objective	Sales objective	Sales strategy
Build	Build sales volume	High call rates on existing accounts
	Increase distribution	High focus during call
	Provide high service levels	Call on new accounts (prospecting)
Hold	Maintain sales volume	Continue present call rates on current accounts
	Maintain distribution	Medium focus during call
	Maintain service levels	Call on new outlets when they appear
Harvest	Reduce selling costs	Call only on profitable accounts
	Target profitable accounts	Consider telemarketing or dropping the rest
	Reduce service costs and inventories	No prospecting
Divest	Clear inventory quickly	Quantity discounts to targeted accounts

Source: Strakle, W. and Spiro, R.L. (1986) 'Linking market share strategies to salesforce objectives, activities and compensation policies', *Journal of Personal Selling and Sales Management*, August, pp. 11–18.

- salesforce costs (e.g. 5 per cent reduction in expenses)

Salesforce strategy defines how those objectives will be achieved and the following may be considered:

(a) call rates

(b) percentage of calls on existing versus potential accounts

(c) discount policy (the extent to which reductions from list prices is allowed)

(d) percentage of resources

- targeted at new versus existing products
- targeted at selling versus providing after-sales service
- targeted at field selling versus telemarketing
- targeted at different types of customer (e.g. high versus low potential)

(e) improving customer and market feedback from the salesforce

(f) improving customer relationships

Given this link between sales and marketing, it is important that personnel in these functions work effectively together. In particular, sales personnel who manage the external relationship with customers must collaborate internally with their colleagues in marketing to agree joint commercial objectives and to develop marketing programmes (for example, new products and promotions) that meet the needs of trade customers and that receive ready adoption by them. Any lack of collaboration between sales and marketing has the potential to jeopardize the supplier's successful marketing to the trade customer, and, consequently, the firm's overall success in the marketplace.[12]

Unfortunately, the sales–marketing relationship, while strongly interdependent, is reported as being neither particularly collaborative nor harmonious. The relationship appears to be characterised by a lack of cohesion, poor co-ordination, conflict, non-cooperation, distrust, and dissatisfaction.[13] Research by Dewsnap and Jobber (2004) found that improved working relations can result when senior management actively supports the close collaboration between the two functions, and when sales and marketing personnel are placed in physical proximity to one another in the company.[14]

1.11   Conclusions

The nature and role of selling and sales management have been outlined and discussed and some of the more widely held misconceptions about these activities explored. It was suggested that selling and sales management are becoming more professional, and those individuals involved in these activities must now be trained and skilled in a range of managerial techniques.

One of the most significant developments in modern business thinking and practice has been the development of the marketing concept. Companies have moved from being production orientated, through being sales orientated to being market orientated.

Some of the key concepts in marketing were outlined, including market segmentation and targeting, the product life-cycle and the marketing mix. The implications of marketing orientation for sales activities and the role of selling in the marketing programme have been demonstrated.

Because of the emphasis given in marketing to the needs and wants of the customer, Chapter 3 is concerned with exploring further the nature of consumer and organisational buying behaviour.

References

1 Beverage, M. (2001) 'Contextual influences and the adoption and practice of relationship selling in a business-to-business setting: an exploratory study', *Journal of Personal Selling and Sales Management*, 21, pp. 207–15.

2 Moncrief, W.C. and Marshall, G.W. (2005) 'The evolution of the seven stages of selling', *Industrial Marketing Management*, 34, pp. 13–22.

3 Leigh, T.H. and Marshall, G.W. (2001) 'Research priorities in sales strategy and performance', *Journal of Personal Selling and Sales Management*, 21, pp. 83–93.

4 Rackham, N. and DeVincentis, J. (1999) *Rethinking the sales force: redefining selling to create and capture customer value*, McGraw-Hill, New York.

5 Marshall, G.W., Goebel, D.J. and Moncrief, W. (2003) 'Hiring for success at the buyer-seller interface', *Journal of Business Research*, 56, pp. 247–55.

6 Marshall, G.W., Goebel and Moncrief (2003) op. cit.

7 McCarthy, E.J. (1960) *Basic Marketing: A Managerial Approach*, Irwin, Homewood, IL.

8 Borden, N.E. (1964) 'The Concept of the Marketing Mix', *Journal of Advertising Research*, (4), June, pp. 2–7.

9 Levitt, T. (1962) *The Marketing Mode*, McGraw-Hill, New York.

10 Rogers, E.M. (1962) *Diffusion of Innovations*, The Free Press, New York.

11 Schultz, D.E., Tannenbaum, S.I. and Lauterborn, R.F. (1992) *Integrated Marketing Communications*, McGraw-Hill, New York, NY.

12 Corstjens, J. and Corstjens, M. (1995) '*Store wars – the battle for mindspace and shelfspace*', Wiley, Chichester.

13 Anderson, R.E. (1996) 'Personal selling and sales management in the new millennium', *Journal of Personal Selling and Sales Management*, 16, pp. 1–16; Corstjens and Corstjens (1995) op. cit; Strahle, W.M., Spiro, R.O. and Acito, F. (1996) 'Marketing and sales: strategic alignment and functional implementation', *Journal of Personal Selling and Sales Management*, 16, pp. 1–20; Wood, V.R. and Tandon, S. (1994) 'Key components in product management success (and failure): a model of product managers' job performance and job satisfaction in the turbulent 1990s and beyond', *Journal of Product and Brand Management*, 3 (1), pp. 19–38.

14 Dewsnap, B. and Jobber, D. (2000) 'The sales-marketing interface in consumer packaged-goods companies: a conceptual framework', *Journal of Personal Selling and Sales Management*, 20, pp. 109–119; Dewsnap, B. and Jobber, D. (2002) 'A social psychological model of relations between marketing and sales', *European Journal of Marketing*, 36, pp. 874–94; Dewsnap, B. and Jobber, D. (2004) 'The antecedents of sales-marketing collaboration: an empirical investigation', *Proceedings of the European Marketing Academy*, Murcia, Spain.

Practical Exercise

Mephisto Products Ltd

'Yet another poor year,' reflected the senior executive of Mephisto Products. 'Profits down by 15 per cent, sales and turnover static in a market that was reckoned to be growing at a rate of some 20 per cent per annum. It cannot go on.' These were the thoughts of Jim Bullins, and he contended that the company would be out of business if the next year turned out to be as bad.

Jim Bullins had been senior executive at Mephisto for the past three years. In each of these years he had witnessed a decline in sales and profits. The company produced a range of technically sophisticated electromechanical control devices for industry. The major customers of Mephisto were in the chemical processing industry. The products were fitted to the customer's processing plant in order to provide safety and cut-out mechanisms, should anything untoward happen in the manufacturing process.

The products were sold through a UK salesforce of some 12 people. Each represented a different area of the country and all were technically qualified mechanical or electrical engineers. Although some 95 per cent of Mephisto's sales were to the chemical industry, there were many more applications for electromechanical control devices in a wide variety of industries.

The reason that sales were concentrated in just the one industry was historical, in that the firm's founder, James Watkinson, had some 30 years earlier married the daughter of the owner of a major detergent manufacturer. As an engineer, Watkinson had seen the potential for such devices in this type of manufacture and, with the aid of a small loan from his father-in-law, had commenced manufacture of such devices, initially for his father-in-law's company and later for wider application in the chemical industry. Watkinson had long since resigned from active participation in Mephisto Products, although he still held a financial interest. However, the philosophy that Watkinson had brought to the company was one which still pervaded business thinking at Mephisto.

The essence of this philosophy was centred on product and production excellence, backed by strong technical sales support. Watkinson believed that if the product was right, i.e. well designed and manufactured to the highest level of quality, there would be a market. Needless to say, such a product then needed selling (because customers were not necessarily aware that they had a need for such safety mechanisms) and salespeople were encouraged to use what may be described as high-pressure salesmanship, pointing out the consequences of not having such mechanisms in a manufacturing plant. They therefore tended to emphasise the negative aspects (of not having such devices) rather than the positive aspects (of how good they were, time saving in the case of plant breakdown, etc.). Needless to say, in Watkinson's day such products then needed selling and, even though sales were to industrial purchasers, it was felt that such selling techniques were justified. This philosophy still pertained and new salespeople were urged to remember that, unless they were pressed, most customers would not consider updating their control equipment.

Little advertising and sales promotion were carried out, although from time to time, when there was some spare cash, the company did purchase advertising space in *The Chemical Processors' Quarterly*. Pricing was done on a cost-plus basis, with total costs being calculated and a fixed percentage added to account for profits. Prices were thus fixed by the accounts department and sales had no say in how they were established. This led to much dissent among the salespeople, who constantly argued that prices were not competitive and if they were cut, sales could be increased substantially.

Delivery times were slow compared with the average in the industry and there were few discounts for large order quantities, with the salesperson first having to clear such discounts with accounts before agreeing to such an arrangement. Again, Watkinson's old philosophy still prevailed: 'If they want the product badly enough, they will wait for it' and 'Why offer discounts for large quantities – if they did not want that many they would not order them.'

During the previous five years, from being a relatively successful company, market share for Mephisto Products dropped substantially. The market became much more competitive with many new entrants, particularly from EU countries, coming into the UK market that had traditionally been supplied by UK manufacturers. Many of these market entrants had introduced new and updated products, drawing upon recent advances in electronics. These new products were seen by the market as being technically innovative, but the view taken by Mephisto management was that they were faddish and, once the novelty had worn off, customers would come back to their superior products.

Unlike many of his colleagues, Jim Bullins was worried by developments over the past five years and felt there was a need for many changes. He was aware that the more successful new entrants to the industry had introduced a marketing philosophy into their operations. Compared with ten years ago in this type of business, it was now common practice for companies to appoint marketing managers. Furthermore, he knew from talking to other people in the industry that such companies considered sales to be an integral part of marketing. At a recent meeting with his senior staff, he mentioned to the sales manager the possibility of appointing a marketing director. The sales manager, who was shortly expecting to be made sales director, was scathing about the idea. His view was that marketing was suitable for a baked beans manufacturer but not for a company engaged in the manufacture and sale of sophisticated control devices for the chemicals industry. He argued that Mephisto's customers would not be swayed by superficial advertising and marketing ploys.

Although Jim Bullins always took heed of advice from his senior managers, recent sales figures had convinced him that the time had now come to make some changes. He would start, he decided, by appointing a marketing manager in the first instance. This person would have marketing experience and come most probably from the chemical industry. The person appointed would have equal status to the sales manager, and ultimately either the new appointee or the existing sales manager would be promoted to the board of directors.

Discussion Questions

1 Criticise Mephisto Products' approach to sales and marketing.

2 Comment upon the following as they exist now at Mephisto Products:

   (a) marketing orientation

   (b) the marketing mix

   (c) the product life-cycle

3 What problems can you anticipate if Jim Bullins goes ahead and appoints a marketing manager?

4 What general advice can you give to the company to make it more marketing orientated?

Practical Exercise

Telcontar

Telcontar, a leading supplier of software and services for real-time, location-based solutions, has announced the appointment in May 2004 of Graham Page as Managing Director Europe. Based in London, Page will be responsible for all European operations planned for the UK, Germany and other major countries. He will also be a member of the corporate executive management team, located in California, USA.

Telcontar provides software and integration services to providers of location-based applications, including vehicle telematics systems, wired internet solutions, wireless internet and cell phone applications. The location-based services supplied range from driving directions, real-time traffic data and maps. Telcontar's map management software and multidimensional spatial data access products allow location-based service providers to integrate digital maps with traditional database content drawn from multiple services. This provides fast accurate access to comprehensive map and data services.

Page has a strong background of general management, including sales, marketing, implementation and support of application software throughout Europe. Previous roles include Vice President Europe at both Sherpa Corporation and ASK Computer Systems and Managing Director at Numetrix. In each case Page was responsible for restructuring and building successful, profitable operations.

'The demand for location-based information is immense, and increasing all the time, particularly in the wireless and telematics sectors. Telcontar has the leading technology platform for providing these services,' Page commented. 'I am looking forward to setting up the European operation for Telcontar's products and services in what is going to be a fast-moving and dynamic market. We already have several significant deals with high profile organisations in the pipeline, so watch this space!'

Telcontar is the provider of the premier software platform for location-based services. Telcontar's clients use its Drill Down Server (to offer their own customers such services as driving directions, real-time traffic information, and maps. Telcontar's services are also used by vehicular or personal emergency response call centres as well as for fleet tracking and dispatch. The company specialises in integrating digital maps with traditional database content drawn from multiple sources.

In March 2003, Telcontar secured $US23.5m of second round funding from a consortium of companies led by Ford Motor Company.

Telcontar is privately owned and headquartered in San Jose, California, with field offices in Los Angeles, Dallas and the United Kingdom. Telcontar® and Drill Down Server® are trademarks of Telcontar.

Source: PR Artistry Limited, Cedar Court, 9–11 Fairmile, Henley on Thames, Oxon RG9 2JR. Reproduced with permission from *www.prartistry.com*

Discussion Questions

1 Do you feel that Page's background in sales and marketing is the right kind of experience for this type of new venture? Might not a more technical background be more appropriate?

2 Page's immediate task is to recruit members of the sales team. Advise Page as to the type of salespeople he should be looking for.

Examination Questions

1 Discuss the place of selling in the marketing mix.

2 How does the role of selling tend to differ between

(a) industrial products and

(b) consumer products?

3 Differentiate between production, sales and marketing orientation.

4 Give reasons as to why the shape of the curve of the product life-cycle is similar to that of the adoption of innovations curve.

2 Sales Strategies

Objectives

After studying this chapter, you should be able to:

1   Understand and appreciate the differences between sales and marketing strategies
2   Appreciate where the key marketing concepts fit into the planning process
3   Identify component parts of the communications mix
4   Differentiate between objectives, strategies and tactics

Key Concepts

- branding
- budget
- external audit
- internal audit
- promotional mix
- push and pull strategies

- PEST/PESTLE/STEEPLE analysis
- sales forecast
- sales planning process
- SWOT analysis
- TOWS matrix

2.1 Sales and Marketing Planning

To be effective, sales activities need to take place within the context of an overall strategic marketing plan. Only then can we ensure that our sales efforts complement, rather than compete with, other marketing activities. Accordingly, sales strategies and management are afforded a more holistic perspective and tend to cover the whole organisation. Hence, the current general consensus is that sales strategies and tactics may only be arrived at, implemented and assessed against a framework of company-wide objectives and strategic planning processes. Before discussing sales strategies and tactics, the nature and purpose of strategic market plans and the place of selling in these plans is outlined and discussed.

2.2　The Planning Process

The nature of the **sales planning process** is outlined in Figure 2.1. This process can be likened to that of operating a domestic central heating system. We first determine the temperature required, timing, etc. (setting objectives) and procedures which must be followed to make sure that this is achieved (determining operations). Next we have to implement appropriate procedures, including ensuring that the necessary resources are available (organisation). At this stage we can commence operation of the system (implementation). Finally, we need to check how the system is operating, in particular the temperature level that has been reached (measuring results). Any deviations in required temperature are then reported and corrected through the thermostatic system (re-evaluation and control).

This planning process can be described through the acronym MOST which describes the process from the general to the specific: mission, objective, strategy, tactics.

2.3　Establishing Marketing Plans

There is no universal way of establishing an ideal marketing plan; neither is the process simple in practice because every planning situation is unique. Conceptually, however, the process is straightforward, consisting a series of logical steps. The marketing plan (Figure 2.2) can be portrayed as a hierarchy consisting of three levels:

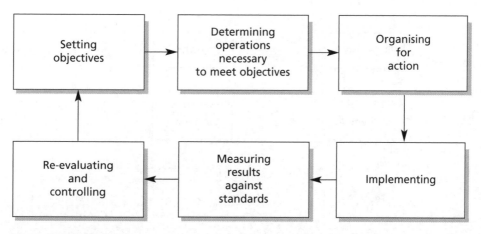

Figure 2.1 The planning process

- Objectives: Where do we intend to go? (*goals*)

- Strategies: How do we intend to get there? (*broadly descriptive*)

- Tactics: The precise route to be taken (*detailed*)

Business definition (corporate mission or goal)

As a prerequisite to the determination of marketing plans, careful consideration should be given to defining (or redefining) the overall role or mission of the business. This issue is best addressed by senior management's asking and answering the question: 'What business are we in?' The definition of the role of a business should be in terms of what customer needs are being served by a business rather than in terms of what products or services are being produced. For example, the manufacturer of microcomputers might define the company as being in the business of rapid problem-solving. In the automobile industry, companies might define their business as being the provision of transport, conferring status, etc., rather than manufacturing cars.

This process of business definition is important. Not only does it ensure that a company thinks in terms of its customers' wants and needs, but also in terms of the planning process, it forms a focusing mechanism for more detailed aspects that follow.

Situation analysis/marketing audit

The precise content of this step in preparing the marketing plan will vary from company to company, but will normally consist of a marketing analysis and an analysis of strengths/weaknesses, opportunities and threats (SWOT).

Market analysis (or marketing audit)

Examples of data and analysis required under the **internal audit** include:

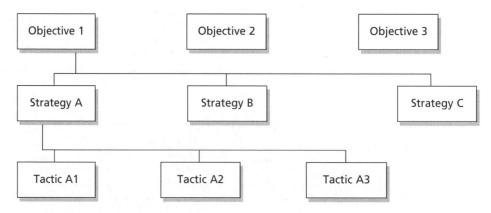

Figure 2.2 Hierarchy of the marketing plan

1 Current and recent size and growth of market. In the multi-product company this analysis needs to be made in total, by product/market and by geographical segment.

2 Analysis of customer needs, attitudes and trends in purchasing behaviour.

3 Current marketing mix.

4 Competitor analysis, including an appraisal of:

   • current strategy

   • current performance, including market share analysis

   • their strengths and weaknesses

   • expectations as to their future actions.

As well as analysing existing competition, potential new entrants should be appraised.

The **external audit** consists of an analysis of broad macro-environment trends – Political, Economic, Socio-cultural and Technological (**PEST**) – that might influence the future of the company's products. This original description was first extended to SLEPT with the introduction of Legal factors, and then to **PESTLE** with the introduction of Environmental factors and now to **STEEPLE** with the introduction of Ecological factors.

Application of PEST analysis to Corus

Corus examined its construction strategy in light of the external environment to identify future market needs. By linking Corus competencies and technical knowledge to future market needs, Corus aims to develop products that give the company a competitive advantage in construction. PEST analysis is a powerful tool that can be used to help analyse the external construction environment. This analysis involves examining the current situation with regard to the following factors:

Political
UK government policy and EU directives, for example, planning and environmental issues, including sustainability, affect the construction industry.

Economic
The health of the economy and interest rates affect demand for commercial and residential property. The UK government is using taxation as a means to encourage improving environmental performance, e.g. The Climate Change Levy, Aggregates and Landfill taxes. The construction industry is increasingly interested in whole life costs of buildings, which include initial capital costs, operating and maintenance costs – understanding how better design can improve all these costs.

Social
Changes in the birth/divorce rates and the average number of people living in a household affect the demand for housing. Increasing crime, ageing population,

(continued on following page)

and people's well-being are part of the social dimension. Research shows that the highest number of disagreements amongst neighbours is due to car parking.

Technology
New construction technologies affect working practices, for example in the building industry, constructing more component systems in factories rather than on building sites.

PEST analysis can be extended to SLEPT through the addition of Legal factors including legislation that regulates industry. A PESTLE analysis is extended further and includes two additional factors.

Legislation
UK and European governments believe the construction industry is highly fragmented and the only way to improve the performance of the industry in terms of safety and environmental performance is to increase legislation.

Environmental
Two of the main issues here are meeting the Kyoto Agreement in reduction of carbon dioxide from the burning of fossil fuels and waste going to land fill.

Note: When using PESTLE as a tool for analysis it is possible to get overlap between a specific issue which can be put into two sections. What is important is to identify the changes and to understand the impact those changes will have on the construction industry.

The factors identified in the analysis are concerned with the current situation. However, it is essential to plan for the future through forecasting events over the next 20 years using factors from the PESTLE analysis. This is partly due to the need to have accreditation for products. This is a testing regime carried out by an independent body against relevant UK/International standards and building regulations. On successful outcomes of the tests, a performance certification is issued for the specific product in the specific application – generally stating structural, fire, acoustic, thermal and durability performance of the product. This is important as the construction industry is generally conservative and hence, to introduce a new product, it is essential to have third party validation that the product will perform as the manufacturer states. Achieving this accreditation can take up to two years and it then takes a substantial amount of time to develop the product for today's construction industry.

The process of forecasting future events is known as Road Mapping. It allows Corus to understand changes in PESTLE factors over time and identify how these affect the construction industry and link product developments to these changes. It also allows Corus to identify market opportunities, develop products to meet these and identify which existing technologies can manufacture them.

Source: *http://www.thetimes100.co.uk/case_study* with permission

Both internal and external audits are deliberate and detailed coverage of the internal and external elements that have been described. It can be carried out by people within marketing or from other departments and, most importantly, they must have the backing of top management as they are central to both the marketing planning and corporate planning horizons of the company.

Analysis of strengths/weaknesses, opportunities and threats

Here management must make a realistic and objective appraisal of *internal* company strengths and weaknesses in the context of potential *external* opportunities and threats (**SWOT analysis**). Opportunities for the future of a business and threats to it stem primarily from factors outside the direct control of a company and in particular from trends and changes in those factors which were referred to earlier as the macro-environment – namely political, economic, socio-cultural and technological factors. It is important to recognise that the determination of what constitutes an opportunity/threat, and indeed the appraisal of strengths and weaknesses, must be carried out concurrently. An 'apparent' strength, for example, a reputation for quality, becomes a real strength only when it can be capitalised on in the marketplace.

A SWOT analysis is not a lengthy set of statements; it is simply a number of bullet points under each heading. It should be short and uncomplicated as it is from the SWOT that marketing strategies are generated.

Statement of objectives

On the basis of the preceding steps, the company can now determine specific objectives and goals that it wishes to achieve. These objectives, in turn, form the basis for the selection of marketing strategies and tactics.

A company may have several objectives. Although marketing objectives usually tend to support business objectives, business and marketing objectives may also be one and the same. It should be pointed out that there are several types of objectives, such as financial and corporate objectives. Additionally, objectives may be departmental or divisional. However, regardless of the type or format, each objective requires its own strategy.

Objectives are needed in a number of areas – production objectives, financial objectives, etc. In a market driven company, marketing objectives are the most important as they reflect customer needs and how the company can satisfy these. In a market driven company, marketing plans come first in the overall corporate planning process. The objectives of other areas must then be consistent with marketing objectives. In addition to this element of consistency, objectives should be expressed unambiguously, preferably quantitatively, and with an indication of the time span within which the objectives are planned to be achieved. The acronym SMART describes the requirement for such objectives: Specific, Measurable, Achievable, Realistic and Time related.

This time span of planned activities often gives rise to some confusion in planning literature. Marketing plans are often categorised as being short range, intermediate range and long range. The confusion arises from the fact that there is no accepted definition of what constitutes the appropriate time horizon for each of these categories. What is felt to comprise long-term planning in one company (say five to ten years) may be considered intermediate in another. It is suggested that the different planning categories are identical in concept, although clearly different in detail. Furthermore, the different planning categories are ultimately related to each other – achieving long-term objectives requires first that intermediate and short-term objectives be met. The following criteria are necessary for setting objectives:

1 *Ensure objectives focus on results*

- Because the effects of marketing activity are essentially measurable, sales and marketing strategies should enable the quantification of marketing achievement.

2 *Establish measures against objectives*

- Return on investment.

3 *Where possible have a single theme for each objective*

- Imprecise objectives such as 'reduce customer defections by 20 per cent through best-in-class service' are not acceptable. There are at least two objectives here and each should be quantified.

4 *Ensure resources are realistic*

- Best practice: attempt to answer common marketing problems through the use of test and roll-out plans.

- Because testing enables roll-out costs to be estimated reasonably accurately, this should ensure that campaign running costs are realistic. (Of course, overheads or labour cost may not be.)

5 *Ensure marketing objectives are integral to corporate objectives*

- This is indisputable, because there will be a serious mismatch if corporate objectives differ from marketing objectives, e.g. general corporate objectives suggest expansion into new member countries of the European Union, and specific marketing objectives only include current members of the EU.

Example of establishing an objective

Saga Holidays – Meeting the needs of empty nesters

Saga Holidays was set up to provide holidays for people with a high proportion of leisure time, people defined as either 'retired' or 'empty nesters'. The holidays would be outside school holidays and other peak periods.

Original objective: Sell long-stay holidays and cruises

Success: Negotiating strength

But what were their options for business expansion?

Either   1 Sell holidays to other market sectors.

Or   2 Sell other products and services to established customers.

So what did Saga do?

Instead of expanding out of a profitable market segment into less profitable segments, Saga met other needs of the retired/empty nester market by selling insurance, savings and other suitable products. The business is thus now defined as a *retired market service provider* rather than merely a *specialist holiday organisation*.

Saga followed what Michael Porter would term a Focus Business Strategy as opposed to a differentiation strategy or cost leadership strategy.

In today's competitive market, it is not uncommon for companies to diversify their product offering to an established customer base. With customer acquisition, customer service and database management costs already met, this may indeed be the most profitable expansion option.

Saga offers a practical example of 'WHAT WOULD OUR CUSTOMERS WANT TO BUY FROM US NEXT?'

A most important document in a company is the annual marketing plan, which the sales manager plays a key part in preparing. The remainder of this chapter discusses planning in the context of the preparation of this annual document.

Determine sales and market potential and forecast sales

A critical stage in the development of marketing plans is the assessment of market and sales potential followed by the preparation of a detailed **sales forecast.** Market potential is the maximum possible sales available for an entire industry during a stated period of time. Sales potential is the maximum possible portion of that market which a company could reasonably hope to achieve under the most favourable conditions. Finally, the sales forecast is the portion of the sales potential that the company estimates it will achieve. The sales forecast is an important step in the preparation of company plans. Not only are the marketing and sales functions directly affected in their planning considerations by this forecast, but other departments, including production, purchasing and human resource management, will use the sales forecast in their planning activities. Sales forecasting, therefore, is a prerequisite to successful planning and is considered in detail in Chapter 16.

Generating and selecting strategies

Once marketing objectives have been defined and market potential has been assessed, consideration should be given to the generation and selection of strategies. Broadly, strategies encompass the set of approaches that the company will use to achieve its objectives.

This step in the process is complicated by the fact that there are often many alternative ways in which each objective can be achieved. Although several strategies may be evaluated, only one strategy can be employed, hence giving rise to the formula: one strategy per objective. For example, an increase in sales revenue of

10 per cent can be achieved by increasing prices, increasing sales volume at the company level (increasing market share) or increasing industry sales. At this stage it is advisable, if time consuming, to generate as many alternative strategies as possible. In turn, each of these strategies can be further evaluated in terms of their detailed implications for resources and in the light of the market opportunities identified earlier. Finally, each strategy should be examined against the possibility of counter-strategies on the part of competitors.

The vignette that follows was provided by PR Artistry and concerns one of their clients, MCRL. It provides an illustration of how the planning process is implemented through the application of what the company has termed GOSPA.

GOSPA for MCRL

GOSPA is a corporate performance management process that implements and produces measurable results. It stands for *Goals, Objectives, Strategies, Plans and Actions*.

Using this process improves communication, control, morale, measurement and performance through a set of easy to implement steps. It gives management a structure for business planning, change, restructuring, measurement and consistent communication after an initial short training period. It is appropriate for organisations both large and small.

Goals in relation to press relations for MCRL in Europe

G1   To build a strong brand and market for MCRL by raising awareness in the press and amongst potential customers within the retail sector in the UK, France, Italy and Germany

G2   For MCRL to be an immediate shortlist choice as a supplier to the 'Enterprise Service Bus' in terms of content integration and digital media/store-innovation projects within retailers in the UK, France, Italy and Germany

Objectives

O1   Implement a regular press release service, issuing a target of one release per month per country to a specific target press list concentrating on quality rather than volume starting January 2007

O2   Produce articles and opinion pieces for the target press using James Pemberton, Michael Jaszczyk and Mike Camerling to position MCRL as the company that provides the technology for retailers to adopt what is next in retail starting January 2007

O3   Produce additional case studies of customers to illustrate how MCRL applications can benefit customers, in-store staff, operations and IT departments starting January 2007

O4   Monitor forward feature opportunities in target publications, contributing relevant and authoritative material whenever possible beginning December 2006

O5   Provide a coordinated approach to the press in the UK, France, Italy and Germany

Strategies

S1   To target three distinct audiences within retailers – marketing, operations and IT. To agree key messages for each of these audiences e.g. for IT to give advice and guidance as to how to provide the 'Enterprise Service Bus' concept

S2   For Mary Phillips of PR Artistry to work with James Pemberton of MCRL to produce an opinion piece per quarter for proactive placement with the retail press

S3   To build a selected list of target publications in each country and a target list of freelance writers in the retail sector. Possibly three sub-lists dealing with the three target audiences mentioned in S1

S4   Proactively identify and target forward features in the target press on a continuous basis, making submissions wherever possible

Plans for January, February, March
P1   Produce Media lists for each country

P2   Prioritise the first six press releases for each country:
  • Metro – shopping list management

  • HIT – PSA in use since July at Dohle Retail Group

  • Wincor Nixdorf partner release regarding Retail Management System (RMS)

  • PSA uses Flash MX for the first time

  • Retail Framework to integrate with Portable Shopping Systems (PSS) to by-pass Point of Sale (POS)

  • MCRL and RMS certified SIF (Store Integration Framework) by IBM

P3   Write and issue the first three press releases

P4   Agree and prioritise the first two opinion pieces – possible topics:
  • MCRL provide the infrastructure necessary for retailers to benefit from the next wave of in-store systems, including in-store digital media, kiosks, PSA, PDA and intelligent scales

  • Digital Signage – MCRL shows the right approach to get meaningful ROI metrics and a sustainable and manageable solution. 'There's more to it than just hanging a few screens with TV commercials'

  • Flash comes of age to make the shopping experience easier and more fun

P5   Write and get the first two articles placed

Actions
A1   Meeting in Paris on 9 December – MCRL, PRA and MN

A2   PRA to write the first press release and then PRA and MN to introduce MCRL to the target press

A3   Agree topic for the first opinion piece

Source: *http://www.gospaplanning.com* with permission

Examples of strategies

We begin by supposing that the objective is to maximise profit from dealings with established customers.

Strategy 1: Targeting

To the marketer, targeting is equivalent to segmentation. A segmentation/targeting strategy may be based on any or all of the following:

- value (high or low consumption, value of goods purchased)

- customer preference (telephone/email ordering service, type of products/services purchased)

- lifestage (status of relationship between supplier and customer: active/lapsed/dormant customer/months since last purchase)

At this point it is important to emphasise that:

- segments must be potentially profitable

- segments are not mutually exclusive

- segments are not stable

Hence, a consumer may fall into more than one segment or different segments at different times. If the segment requires a special effort to reach or appeal to it, then it must have sufficient potential purchasing power to justify the effort.

Strategy 2: Pricing

In line with the classic marketer's approach, the following pricing strategies may be adopted:

- make short-term tactical reductions

- establish price premiums

- elevate perceived quality

Thus, the classic principle of elevating the perceived quality of a brand so that it can command a higher selling margin may be adopted. Additionally, a discount has more value if the worth of what is being discounted is understood.

Discounting is of course prevalent in all marketing. In Fast Moving Consumer Goods (FMCG) markets it tends to be driven by competitive or retailer pressures. Often, tactical cuts are seen as defensive.

Strategy 3: Customer retention

Because advanced technology enables suppliers to track the progress of an enquirer or customer, focus is increasingly shifting from mere product profitability to the profitability of customer relationships. However, customer profitability will be determined by:

- the cost of acquisition

- the losses of customers or would-be customers at various key stages in the relationship

Key stages in the customer relationship could be revised as:

- enquiry

- conversion to customer

- repeat purchase

- up-trade

- threatened dormancy

- recovery

The probability of loss usually declines with the length of the relationship. In consumer markets (but not in business markets) most often the duration of a relationship outweighs rate of spending in determining the lifetime value of the relationship. Here, a customer database will not only facilitate measurement of this relationship, but more importantly enable corrective action to be undertaken more easily. Thus, an offer may be triggered to prevent the customer 'going dormant'. Consequently, if the customer fails to respond and does go dormant, further offers may be made to recover the customer and re-start the relationship/recovery.

Additionally, there could be a customer development and retention strategy, which could provide the means to retain customers. There may be a retention strategy based on customer care and a development strategy based on sales promotion.

From this list of alternative strategies a choice must be made with regard to the broad marketing approach which the company considers will be the most effective in achieving objectives. This must then be translated into a strategy statement which must be communicated to and agreed with all those managers who will influence its likely degree of success or failure. Once again, the specific contents of such a strategy statement will vary between companies, but as an example a strategy statement might encompass the following areas:

1 A clear statement of marketing objectives.

2 A description of the choice of strategies for achieving these objectives.

3 An outline of the broad implications of the selected strategies with respect to the following key areas in marketing:

- target market

- positioning

- marketing mix

- marketing research.

At this stage the strategy statement should give a clear and concise indication of where the major marketing efforts of the company will be focused. Once this has been discussed and agreed we can progress to the next step of preparing a detailed plan of action.

There are many tools available for generating strategic options, the most popular of which are the Boston Matrix and the GE/McKinsey Matrix. A description and application of such tools is more appropriate to corporate strategy and strategic marketing planning texts and not within the sphere of this text. However, analysis using the product life-cycle concept and diffusion of innovations is appropriate in this context and these have been discussed in Chapter 1. SWOT analysis is a useful method of generating strategies. A number of stages are necessary:

1 Evaluate the influence of environmental factors (STEEPLE/PEST) on the company.

2 Make a diagnosis about the future.

3 Consider company strengths and weaknesses in relation to all key areas of the company.

4 Develop strategic options.

For example, in Figure 2.3 let us consider the case of a specialist, low-volume UK sports car producer.

Strategic possibilities using SWOT analysis

As an illustration, here are two strategic possibilities for the sports car producer mentioned in Figure 2.3: use existing strong, well-established brand to raise production levels through automation to market to other European countries (S1, S2, W1, W2, O2, T2). Raise the basic price (S4, W3, O1, T1, T2).

This is an application of the use of SWOT matrix which in essence takes elements of SWOT and brings them together to form marketing strategies. It was first proposed by Weihrich in 1982.[1]

Preparing the marketing programme

The strategy statement prepared in the previous section provides the input for the determination of the detailed programme required to implement these strategies. The first step in the preparation of this programme is the determination of the mar-

Strengths	Weaknesses
1 Well-established brand name	1 Production only semi-automated
2 In business since 1920	2 Maximum production 30 units per week
3 Cult following	
4 Low price	3 Long waiting list
5 Consistently good press reviews	4 Only sold in UK, USA, Germany, Holland, Belgium and Scandinavia
Opportunities	**Threats**
1 USA market can take twice their allocation	1 Some purchasers not prepared to wait
2 Other European countries would like to purchase	2 Other volume manufacturers now producing niche models like this

Figure 2.3 SWOT matrix for a sports car producer

keting mix. Detailed decisions must be made with respect to product policy, pricing, promotion and distribution. Care should be exercised to ensure that the various elements of the marketing mix are integrated, i.e. that they work together to achieve company objectives in the most effective manner.

At this stage of the planning process what has previously been an outline plan for guiding decision-making becomes a detailed operational plan and this section is inevitably the lengthiest part of the planning document. It is on the basis of this part of the plan that day-to-day marketing activities and tactics of the company will be organised, implemented and assessed.

Allocating resources – budgeting

Having made detailed decisions with respect to the elements of the marketing mix, the next step is to assemble a **budget** for each of these elements. In most companies limited resources ensure that managers from the different functional areas have to compete for these scarce resources. It is likely that much discussion will take place between those responsible for each element of the marketing mix. In addition it may be found that initial marketing objectives, strategies and detailed plans for the marketing programme to achieve the forecast level of sales may, in the light of financial and other resource constraints, be unrealistic. In this event modifications to the original plan may have to be made.

It should be noted that at this stage an estimate can be made of both costs and revenues and a forecast profit and loss statement prepared.

Implementation

The procedure so far should have resulted in the preparation of a detailed document setting out what is to be done, when it will be done, who is responsible and estimated costs and revenues, as well as agreed time frames for the various activities in the plan. Once approved, details of the marketing plan should be communicated to everyone involved. This communication is an essential and sometimes neglected aspect of marketing planning. Many companies have elaborate marketing plans that are not implemented because key people have not been informed or have not agreed the proposed plan.

Control

Finally, the plan should contain an outline of the control mechanisms that will be applied. This should include details of major objectives and key parameters in the measurement of the degree of success in achieving the objectives, enabling corrections and modifications to be made as the plan unfolds. This control part of the marketing plan should specify what is to be measured, how it is to be measured and what data are required for measurement. It may also include details of what action is to be taken in the light of deviations from the plan. This contingency planning is a key feature of any planning process, recognising as it does that plans need to be flexible in order to accommodate possible unforeseen or unpredictable changes in the market. The overall marketing planning process is summarised in Figure 2.4.

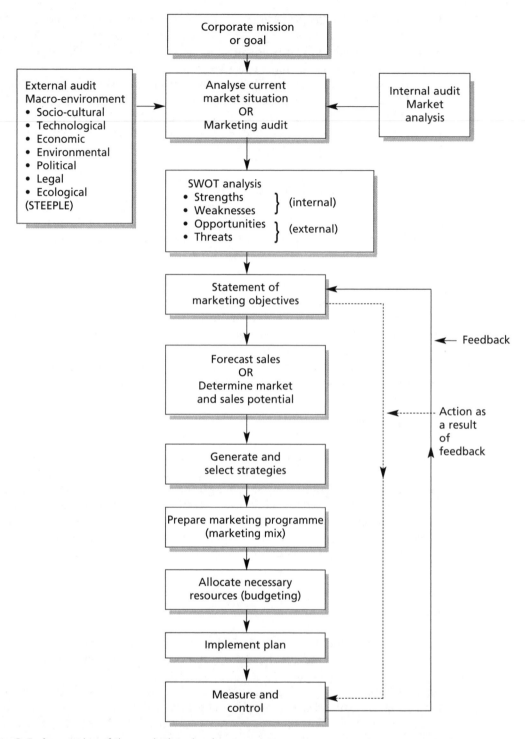

Figure 2.4 An overview of the marketing planning process

2.4   The Place of Selling in the Marketing Plan

We have examined how marketing plans are prepared. The sales function has an important role to play in this process and we now look at the nature of this role and, in particular, the contribution that the sales function makes to the preparation of the marketing plan and how the sales function itself is influenced by the marketing plan.

Contribution of the sales function

Throughout the planning process alternative courses of action need to be identified and decisions taken as to which of these alternatives is the most appropriate. Contingency planning measures like these involve identifying alternatives and choosing between them, which requires accurate and timely information. A key role of the sales function in the planning process is the provision of such information. This becomes clearer if we examine some of the stages in the planning process where the sales function can make a valuable contribution:

(a) analysis of current market situation (marketing audit)

(b) determining sales potential/sales forecasting

(c) generating and selecting strategies

(d) budgeting, implementation and control

Toyota

By constantly finding out what its customers will want to buy next, Toyota has achieved profitable line extension and replacement. In fact, by being able to make additional low-cost sales to its established customers, Toyota has not only achieved sustainable competitive advantage through customer retention, but is also in a stronger position to invest in expansion.

Analysis of current market situation (marketing audit)

The proximity of the sales function to the marketplace places it in a unique position to contribute to the analysis of the current market situation facing the company. In particular, sales is often well placed to contribute to the analysis of customer needs and trends in purchasing behaviour. The sales manager can also make a valuable contribution with respect to knowledge about competitors and their standing in the marketplace. This informational role of sales managers should not be ignored because, through the salesforce, they are ideally equipped to provide up-to-date, accurate information based on feedback from customers.

Determining sales potential/sales forecasting

As we later see in Chapter 16, an important responsibility of the sales manager is the preparation of sales forecasts for use as the starting point for business planning. Short-, medium- and long-term forecasts by the sales manager form the basis for allocating company resources in order to achieve anticipated sales.

Generating and selecting strategies

Although decisions about appropriate marketing strategies to adopt rest with marketing management, the sales manager must be consulted and should make an input to this decision. Again, the sales function is ideally placed to comment on the appropriateness of any suggested strategies.

The sales manager should actively encourage sales staff to comment upon the appropriateness of company marketing strategies. The field salesforce are at the forefront of tactical marketing and can more realistically assess how existing target markets will respond to company marketing initiatives. Indeed, the fact that there are front-line people who benefit from the most contact with customers should not be overlooked.

Budgeting, implementation and control

Preparation of the sales forecast is a necessary precursor to detailed marketing plans. The sales forecast is also used in the preparation of the sales budget.

On the basis of the sales forecast, the sales manager must determine what level of expenditure will be required to achieve the forecasted level of sales. The important thing to remember about this budget is that it is the cornerstone of the whole budgeting procedure in a company. Not only the activities of the sales department, but also production, human resource management, finance and research and development will be affected by this budget. Because of this importance, sales budgets are considered in detail in Chapter 16. At this stage it is sufficient to note that in preparing the sales budget the sales manager must prepare an outline of the essential sales activities required to meet the sales forecast, together with an estimate of their costs. The precise contents of the annual sales budget will vary between companies, but normally include details of salaries, direct selling expenses, administrative costs and commissions and bonuses.

Having agreed the sales budget for the department, the sales manager must assume responsibility for its implementation and control. In preparing future plans, an important input is information on past performance against budget and, in particular, any differences between actual and budgeted results. Such 'budget variances', both favourable and unfavourable, should be analysed and interpreted by the sales manager as an input to the planning process. The reasons for budget variances should be reported, together with details of any remedial actions that were taken and their effects.

Influence of marketing plan on sales activities: strategies and tactics

Any planning process is effective only to the extent that it influences action. An effective marketing planning system influences activities, both strategic and tactical, throughout the company. The classical marketing approach favours the inside-out planning model proposed by Schultz, Tannenbaum and Lauterborn[2] (Figure 2.5).

However, the reverse outside-in planning model is becoming more and more popular. Figure 2.6 shows an outside-in planning sequence, starting with a calculation of the cost per sale to current customers, then to lapsed customers and prospects on the database, and finally to new customers. The cost-per-sale calculations determine the sales target in each case.

This process is followed by a strategy for each discrete segment. A product may not, for example, be offered to each segment at the same price. Similarly, types of communication will be different for each segment.

Both the segment strategy and the content of communications will, ideally, be tested against reasonable alternatives. The most successful alternatives on testing will then be rolled out to the remaining population in each segment.

Although the inside-out model is financially driven, it is much less safe than the customer-oriented planning model. Perhaps this influence is most clearly seen through decisions relating to the marketing programme or marketing mix. Sales strategies are most directly influenced by planning decisions on the promotional element of the marketing mix. Here we will consider briefly the notion of a 'mix' of promotional tools, outlining the considerations in the choice of an appropriate mix and the implications for sales strategies. In particular, the important and often misunderstood relationship between advertising and selling is explained and discussed. We conclude this section by examining briefly the nature of sales tactics.

The promotional mix

Earlier in this chapter we suggested that an important facet of marketing planning is the preparation of a marketing programme, the most important step in this preparation being the determination of the marketing mix – product, price, distribution

Monetary objective
⇓
Costs
⇓
Contribution margin
⇓
Marketing funds
⇓
Allocations against prospects
⇓
Communication choices
⇓
Implementation

Figure 2.5 Inside-out planning model

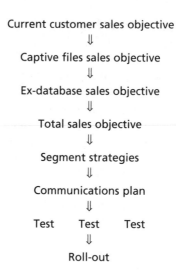

Current customer sales objective

⇓

Captive files sales objective

⇓

Ex-database sales objective

⇓

Total sales objective

⇓

Segment strategies

⇓

Communications plan

⇓

Test   Test   Test

⇓

Roll-out

Figure 2.6 Outside-in planning model

and promotion. As selling is only one element in the promotion part of this mix, it is customary to refer to the **promotional mix** (or more correctly the communications mix) of a company. This traditional promotional mix is made up of four major elements:

1 Advertising.

2 Sales promotion.

3 Publicity/public relations.

4 Personal selling.

To these traditional elements can now be added:

5 Direct marketing.

6 Interactive/internet marketing.

In most companies all four traditional elements can contribute to company sales, but a decision has to be made as to where to place the emphasis. This decision is made at the planning stage. In addition, it is important that the elements of the promotional mix work together to achieve company objectives. An important planning task of management is the co-ordination of promotional activities.

Several factors influence the planning decision as to where to place emphasis within the promotional mix. In some firms the emphasis is placed on the salesforce with nearly all promotional budget being devoted to this element of the mix. In others, advertising or sales promotion is seen as being much more efficient and productive than personal selling. Perhaps the most striking aspect of the various promotional tools is the extent to which they can be substituted for each other. Companies within the same industry differ markedly in where they place the promotional emphasis. This makes it difficult to be specific about developing the promotional mix within a particular company. As a guide, some of the more important factors influencing this decision are now outlined.

1 *Type of market.* In general, advertising and sales promotion play a more important role in the marketing of consumer products, whereas personal selling plays the major role in industrial marketing. The reasons for this stem from differences between industrial and consumer marketing, which are outlined in Chapter 3. An obvious contrast is the marketing of fast-moving consumer goods (FMCG) with the marketing of often highly technical, expensive capital goods to industry. Despite this, it is a mistake to conclude that advertising does not have a role to play in the marketing of industrial products. Indeed, the contribution of advertising is often undervalued by sales personnel and discounted as a waste of company resources. The relationship between advertising and sales is considered later in this chapter.

The 'new' promotional mix increasingly involves e-commerce possibilities and this is highlighted through developments in this field and numbers of companies using this facility. In addition, the use of freephone facilities is also making communication easier and cost-free to the potential customer. These more contemporary issues are highlighted in the two vignettes that follow.

E-commerce is made e-asy with new site

PSICommerce is a new e-commerce package designed by PSINet to open up the world of global trading to small and medium businesses. It claims to make merchandising on the web a simple and cost-effective process.

The PSICommerce basic package costs from £125 for SMEs to register and get the package components to be connected to the internet. An ongoing connection charge starts at £100 a month.

A Government Competitiveness White Paper says UK e-commerce transactions are currently worth around $US4.5 billion. Growth over the next three years could reach $US47 billion, with 70–80 per cent of e-commerce revenues expected to involve small and medium sized enterprises, either in business-to-business or business-to-consumer roles.

Valerie Holt, Managing Director of PSINet UK and Vice President of Europe, said SMEs' appetite for e-commerce was rapidly developing. But adoption of it was being throttled because of fear of costs related to the technical complexities of developing and building an internet 'shop' and integrating to the credit card payment systems.

'The benefits of the package will allow any small business to instantly trade globally on the internet. They may have only 2 or 30 clients worldwide but the internet enables them, by negating location, to overcome the physical barrier to trade,' said Holt.

Source: *www.psi.commerce.com*

Benefits to business of marketing numbers

Many companies do not realise that telephone numbers can be an effective marketing tool in terms of generating revenue and increasing customer bases. Research shows that marketing numbers can increase calls by up to 300 per cent. Patrick Naughton of Telecom One has suggested a number of benefits when using marketing numbers and has given a number of questions to be asked when weighing up the pros and cons:

- Are you trying to increase awareness of the company, products and services?
- Are you trying to improve the quality of your customer service?
- Are you trying to broaden the reach of your business?
- Do you already have a solid customer base and want to generate a new revenue stream?

The facilities that are available include:

Freephone (0800/0808) – customers can reach you free of charge; you pay 8p per minute.

Local rate or Lo-call (0845/0844) – customers pay 8p per minute weekdays, 4p evenings, and 2p at weekends, regardless of where in the country they call from.

National rate (0870/0871) – a single, location independent number. Calls are the same cost as local rate calls. Customers pay national rate charges and your business benefits by revenue generated from every call you receive.

Gold numbers – a memorable number that will stick in a customer's memory. It is likely to be used more frequently than others and thus generate more business.

Alphanumeric numbers – dialling a word in place of a number, e.g. 0800 BUSINESS (can only be used in countries that have this facility).

Websites *www.theidm.com* (Institute of Direct Marketing) *www.telecom1.com* and *www.oftel.com*.

Source: *www.whattobuyforbusiness.co.uk* Edition 252, March 2002

2 *Stage in the buying process.* In Chapter 3 it is suggested that for both industrial and consumer products it is useful to consider the stages through which the prospective purchaser passes en route to making a purchase decision. Although there are a number of ways in which this process may be conceptualised, essentially it consists of the potential purchaser moving from a position of being unaware of a company and/or its products, to being convinced that its products or services are the most appropriate to the buyer's needs. The sequential nature of this process is shown in Figure 2.7.

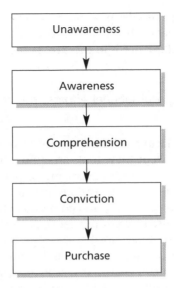

Figure 2.7 Stages in the buying process

For a given outlay, advertising and publicity are more effective in the earlier stages of moving potential purchasers through from unawareness to comprehension. Personal selling is more cost effective than other forms of promotional activity at the conviction and purchase stages. This is not to suggest that 'cold calling' is not an important area of sales activity but, as we see later, such cold calling is rendered much more effective if the customer is already aware of the company's products.

3 *Push versus pull strategies.* One of the most important determinants in the choice of promotional mix is the extent to which a company decides to concentrate its efforts in terms of its channels of distribution. This can perhaps be best illustrated if we contrast a push strategy with that of a pull strategy:

A **push strategy** is one in which the focus of marketing effort is aimed at pushing the product through the channel of distribution. The emphasis is to ensure that wholesalers and retailers stock the product in question. The idea is that if channel members can be induced to stock a product they in turn will be active in ensuring that your product is brought to the attention of the final customer. In general a push strategy entails a much greater emphasis on personal selling and trade promotion in the promotional mix.

A **pull strategy** relies much more heavily on advertising to promote the product to the final consumer. The essence of this approach is based on the notion that if sufficient consumer demand can be generated for a product this will result in final consumers asking retailers for the product. Retailers will then ask wholesalers for the product, who will contact the producer. In this way the product is 'pulled' through the channel by creating consumer demand via assertive advertising. (Channel management is considered in detail in Chapter 10 and in particular the diminishing role of wholesalers is examined.)

4 *Stage in the product life-cycle.* Chapter 1 introduced the concept of the product life-cycle. There is evidence to suggest that different promotional tools vary in their relative effectiveness over the various stages of this cycle. In general,

advertising and sales promotion are most effective in the introduction and growth stages of the life-cycle, whereas it is suggested that the emphasis on personal selling needs to increase as the market matures and eventually declines.

Co-ordinating promotional efforts: the relationship between advertising and selling

In discussing factors affecting choice of promotional tools, it may have appeared that to some extent these tools are mutually exclusive – for example, one chooses to concentrate either on advertising or personal selling. This is not the case. The relationship between the various promotional tools, including personal selling, should be complementary and co-ordinated. Perhaps this obvious point would not need to be stressed were it not for the fact that often this complementary relationship is misunderstood. Nowhere is this misunderstanding more evident than in the relationship between advertising and selling.

It is unfortunate that many sales managers and their salesforces believe that expenditure on advertising is a waste of company resources. Very rarely, they argue, does a customer purchase simply because a product is advertised, particularly where that customer is an industrial purchaser. Because of this, the argument continues, the money 'wasted' on advertising would be better spent where it will have a direct and immediate effect – on the salesforce. Increasingly, evidence suggests the notion that advertising money is wasted in industrial markets is misplaced. Among the functions that advertising can perform in such markets are the following:

1 Corporate advertising can help to build the reputation of a company and its products.

2 Advertising is particularly effective in creating awareness among prospective clients. The sales representative facing a prospect who is unaware of the company or product faces a much more difficult selling task than the representative who can build on an initial awareness.

3 Advertising can aid the sales representative in marketing new products by shouldering some of the burden of explaining new product features and building comprehension.

4 Advertising using return coupons may be used to open up new leads for the salesforce.

Overall, by far the greatest benefit of advertising in industrial markets is seen, not through a direct effect on sales revenue, but in the reduction of overall selling costs. Evidence suggests that, given adequate frequency, this reduction in selling costs to customers exposed to advertising may be as high as 30 per cent. Conversely, non-advertisers may find themselves at a disadvantage. The cost of selling to customers exposed to competitors' advertising may be increased by as much as 40 per cent.

In marketing consumer goods, **branding** and brand image are very important and advertising is generally thought to be the most effective promotional tool. However, personal selling and a well-trained salesforce can contribute significantly to increased market penetration by influencing stockists to allocate more shelf space to company products and persuading new dealers to stock them.

At all times, sales and advertising should be co-ordinated to achieve company objectives. It is important for sales personnel to be informed about company advertising campaigns. This advertising should be utilised in selling, the advertising theme being reinforced in the sales presentation.

From sales strategies to tactics

We have seen that a number of factors influence the setting for sales strategies. It was suggested that this influence is most direct in determining the relative emphasis to be given to sales activities in overall company and promotional strategy. Sales strategies are of course also influenced by the marketing and sales objectives specified in the marketing plan. As an illustration, a marketing objective of increased market share may mean that the sales manager has to ensure that sales in the forthcoming year increase by 10 per cent. Furthermore, the planning document should specify the route or strategy by which this objective will be accomplished, e.g. 'Additional sales effort is to be targeted on the opening of new accounts'. Sales objectives and strategies, therefore, also stem directly from the planning process, after consulation and agreement with relevant personnel.

However, not all researchers support the merits of relationship marketing, and opposing this outlook, Shaw[3] argues: 'Marketers must stop their obsession with loving customers since it has become a distraction from the basics of selling and tracking the origins of sale success.' Having agreed these strategic guidelines, a more detailed set of activities must be built into the planning process. The sales manager must determine the specific actions required to achieve sales goals, i.e. tactics.

Tactics encompass the day-to-day activities of the sales function in the achievement of marketing and sales objectives. Tactics also include actions which need to be taken in response to unexpected short-term events in the marketplace, for example, a special promotional effort by a competitor. The relationship between objectives, strategies and tactics is shown in Figure 2.8.

Tactical decisions represent the 'fine tuning' of sales activities and encompass many decision areas covered in greater detail elsewhere; for example, the deployment of sales personnel – territory design and planning (Chapter 15) – can be considered a tactical aspect of sales. Similarly, the design of incentive systems (Chapter 15) should form part of a tactical plan, designed to accomplish sales goals within the framework of sales strategies.

The importance of tactics should not be underestimated; even the best-formed strategies fail for want of proper tactics. As an example of the use and importance

Figure 2.8 The relationship between objectives, strategies and tactics

of tactics in selling, we consider briefly an aspect of purchasing which is of vital interest to many companies, namely brand/supplier loyalty.

Brand/supplier loyalty

If we examine the purchase of products and services over time, we find that often the purchasing sequence of individuals indicates that they repeatedly buy the same brand of a product or, if the product is an industrial one, they consistently buy from a particular supplier. For such individuals, if we imagine that the brand or supplier in question is called X, the purchasing sequence would be as shown below:

Purchase occasion	1	2	3	4	5	6
Brand purchased/supplier	X	X	X	X	X	X

There is no doubt that brand/supplier loyalty does exist. Moreover, the cultivation of such loyalty among customers often accounts for a significant part of tactical marketing and sales effort, representing, as it does, a substantial market asset to a company.

By favouring a longer term perspective, such a cultivation of customer loyalty complements traditional brand-building techniques. Indeed, as Martin[4] insists, customer relationships with brands help insulate brands from competitors, 'the customer-brand linkage can be viewed as an important subset of relationship marketing'.

Additionally, while Reichheld and Schefter[5] also support this theory when they claim 'a large group of customers are influenced primarily by brand' and that these customers 'are looking for stable long-term relationships', Curtis[6] succinctly summarises that 'customers need to feel that they are part of a brand's crusade'.

Before considering the part that sales tactics can play in this process of cultivating brand loyalty, it is important to explain precisely what is meant by brand loyalty. This apparently simple notion gives rise to some misunderstanding.

Let us return to the purchasing sequence just shown. Although we have suggested that such a sequence is associated with a brand-loyal customer, the existence of such an array of purchases for a customer does not, of itself, constitute evidence that this customer *is* brand loyal. There are a number of possible explanations for this purchasing behaviour. One such explanation might be that this customer concentrates much of his or her purchasing in one particular retail outlet and it so happens that this particular retail outlet only stocks brand X of this product, i.e. the customer exhibits loyalty, but to the store, rather than the brand. Another possible explanation is that this customer pays little regard to the particular brand or supplier; s/he is not consciously brand loyal at all, but rather has simply slipped into the habit of purchasing this brand and cannot be bothered to switch. In this second example it is true to say that the customer must be reasonably satisfied with the brand being purchased consistently. If this were not the case, or the customer became dissatisfied, s/he would then make the decision to switch. Nevertheless, the fact is that this is not true brand loyalty.

True brand or supplier loyalty exists when customers make a conscious decision to concentrate their purchases on a particular brand because they consider that supplier or brand superior to others. There may be a number of reasons/bases for such perceived superiority, e.g. superior quality, better delivery and after-sales services, the availability of credit, or some combination of these or other factors. In discussing possible reasons for brand/supplier loyalty, we enter the realms of motives, perceptions, attitudes, etc, and more complex behavioural areas discussed in Chapter 3.

The concept of brand/supplier loyalty is a difficult one and care should be taken in interpreting the often conflicting evidence for its causes. Nevertheless, there are some indications that the salesperson can play a key role in helping to establish brand/supplier loyalty amongst a company's customers. One of the reasons for this is that learning theory suggests we have a tendency to repeat experiences that give us pleasure and to avoid those that do not. Among the most powerful and lasting impressions that serve as a source of pleasure or displeasure in purchasing activities are experiences in the face-to-face encounters with sales staff. Favourable attitudes and behaviour of sales personnel in dealing with their customers can contribute significantly to the creation of brand/supplier loyalty.

2.5 Conclusions

A framework for sales strategies and tactics has been established. We have seen that these are developed and operated within the framework of marketing planning. The sales function makes a valuable contribution to the establishment of marketing plans, providing, as it does, key data on customers, markets, competitors, sales forecasts and budgets. In turn, selling activities are directly influenced by decisions taken at the marketing planning stage. In the meantime, the increasingly essential role of databases should not be ignored.

We have looked at planning decisions for the marketing programme or marketing mix and, specifically, at the communications mix in a company. Factors such as type-of-product market, steps in the buying process, push versus pull strategies and stage in the product life-cycle have all been shown to influence promotional and consequently sales strategies.

Finally, we examined sales tactics, the relationship between advertising and selling, and the important area of brand/supplier loyalty. It was shown that advertising plays a key role in aiding the sales effort, reducing selling costs and easing the sales task. Brand/supplier-loyal customers are a valuable asset to any company and the salesforce is central to the establishment and maintenance of such customer loyalty.

References

1 Weihrich, H. (1982) 'The TOWS matrix – a tool for situational analysis', *Long Range Planning*, 15(2), pp. 54–66.

2 Schultz, D.E., Tannenbaum, S.I. and Lauterborn, R.F. (1993) *Integrated Marketing Communications*, NTC Business Books, Lincolnwood, IL.

3   Shaw, R. (1999) 'Customers are about sales, not false friendships', *Marketing*, January, p. 20.

4   Martin, C.L. (1998) 'Relationship marketing: a high-involvement product attribute approach', *Journal of Product & Brand Management*, 7(1), pp. 6–26.

5   Reichheld, F. and Schefter, P. (2000) 'E-Loyalty', *Harvard Business Review*, July/August, pp. 105–13.

6   Curtis, J. (2000) 'Get some decent exposure', *Revolution*, 12 July, pp. 32–6.

Practical Exercise

Welsh Lamb & Beef Promotions Ltd

Welsh Lamb & Beef Promotions Ltd (WLBP) was established by a group of like-minded Welsh livestock farmers who believe that Welsh lamb and beef have a reputation for excellence that needs to be promoted to a wide consumer audience.

The company is now one of the UK's largest farmer co-operatives with over 7,500 farmer members, and is dedicated to the promotion and marketing of branded, farm-assured Welsh lamb and beef in target markets worldwide. WLBP believes that livestock farming is of significant commercial importance to rural Wales, with the preservation of the family farm critical to the maintenance of Welsh culture and the scenic beauty of the Welsh countryside.

Wales is a land famous for its mountains, lakes, valleys, history, legends and song. For centuries it has been home to native Welsh sheep breeds. They have thrived on natural grassland available all year round. Welsh lamb is considered to have a good colour and a sweet, succulent flavour. The unique reputation and qualities enjoyed by the product worldwide come from traditional husbandry methods and feeding the animals on abundant grazing. The character of Welsh lamb arises from the influence of the traditional hardy Welsh breeds from the mountains, providing good quality breeding stock that forms the basis of lowland flocks.

Welsh lamb provides the consumer with a natural, versatile, tender, succulent meat with the distinct flavour of Wales. Welsh lamb (Cig Oen Cymru) together with the Welsh lamb dragon logo, is a guarantee of consistent high quality.

Welsh beef, however, is the hidden treasure of Wales and has now established its own identity (Cig Eidion Cymru). The foundation of this brand is the high quality of Welsh stock. With over 86 per cent of the land down to grass, Welsh beef farmers are renowned for their ability to convert quality grassland into top quality beef. The alluvial soils of the Welsh valleys are rich in minerals that are perfect for producing the finest quality beef. Cattle thrive in this unspoilt environment, producing beef that is succulent and of the highest standard. Its unique character arises from the influence of traditional beef breeds that dominate Welsh herds and from the topography of the country, coupled with the expertise of livestock farmers that has been handed down over generations.

Welsh producers were hit hard by the ban imposed during the foot-and-mouth crisis, but WLBP are confident that old markets are being reclaimed and new ones created. 'The export market has always been very important,' says Linda Jones, spokeswoman for WLBP. 'Before foot-and-mouth we were exporting £100 million of Welsh branded lamb, mainly to Spain and Southern Europe, and added to this was £10 million worth of beef, mainly to the Netherlands.'

Despite the heavy blow of the export ban, consumers and buyers on the continent have retained their enthusiasm for Welsh meat, if events since the ban was lifted towards the end of 2001 are anything to go by. 'We've been out of the market for a year, but within a week after the ban had been lifted they wanted Welsh lamb,' says Linda Jones. 'In December 2001 we met the Eroski group of Spanish buyers and they want Welsh beef as well as lamb.' The recovery of Welsh beef into export markets will take longer than Welsh lamb as a result of the 'Date Based Export Scheme'.

An application has been lodged with the EU to give Welsh lamb and beef the status of 'Protected Geographical Indication' – similar to that given to champagne.

Meanwhile, representatives of the group have been meeting with buyers across Europe to promote Welsh meat. Don Thomas, managing director of WLBP, said, 'The effort placed on the recovery of our valuable export markets must not be underestimated. It is vital for the long term commercial security of rural Wales that we re-establish the export of Welsh meat in key European countries as soon as possible. The reputation of Welsh meat in these target European markets needs to be reaffirmed.' He went on to say, 'A branded product will prevail in the export market, not a commodity. It is now important that the industry works together to exploit these opportunities with vigour. We can now positively implement our commercial strategies with existing and new customers to recover these vital export markets.'

In a UK context, Safeway's latest promotion for Welsh lamb backs up suggestions that supermarkets are taking home-produced meat more seriously following the foot-and-mouth crisis. A ten-week campaign, launched on 6 June 2002, specifically promotes Welsh lamb in-store. Dennis Hobbs, Sales Director of Safeway's dedicated lamb supplier, H M Bennett, says, 'We hope this major initiative will give Safeway customers the opportunity to support farmers by buying more lamb and the rural economy by visiting the countryside.'

Four years after Safeway's launch of Welsh mountain lamb, the first of the regional meat marketing campaigns by the multiples, it is clear that consumer demand has been more enthusiastic than anticipated. The campaign was more than just an in-store promotion. It required the creation of a new supply chain as the Welsh industry's infrastructure for procurement, killing and distribution of hill lambs to major retailers was inadequate and unstable. But according to Safeway category manager, Kelly Hathway, 'Our lamb initiatives have gone from strength to strength since we launched Welsh mountain lamb.'

Source: Adapted from articles by Paul Carey and Thomos Livingstone in *The Western Mail*, 17/5/02, pp. 3, 5; a news item in *The Grocer*, 15/6/02, p. 23; *www.welshlambandbeef.co.uk*

Discussion Questions

Acting as an external marketing consultant to WLBP, prepare a report for management that:

1 Provides strategic guidelines for promoting WLBP products both in the UK and internationally following the foot-and-mouth crisis. Justify reasons for including the various elements of the communications mix that you have suggested.

2 Suggest how other multiples like Safeway, which is now actively promoting WLBP products, can now be persuaded to promote WLBP products.

Practical Exercise

Auckland Engineering plc

Jim Withey, Sales Manager for Auckland Engineering plc, a well-established engineering company in the Midlands, received the following memo from D C Duncan, his recently appointed Marketing Director.

> **Memo**
> *To*: J Withey, Sales Manager
> *From*: D C Duncan, Marketing Director
> *Date*: 16 January 2006
> *Subject*: Preparation of annual marketing plan

You will recall that at our series of preliminary meetings to discuss future marketing plans for the company I suggested that I was unhappy with the seemingly haphazard approach to planning. Accordingly, you will recall it was agreed between departmental heads that each would undertake to prepare a formal input to next month's planning meeting.

At this stage I am not seeking detailed plans for each product market, rather I am concerned that you give thought to how your department can contribute to the planning process. Being new to the company and its product/markets, I am not fully up to date on what has been happening to the market for our products, although as we all know our market share at 35 per cent is down on last year. I would particularly like to know what information your department could contribute to the analysis of the situation.

To help in your analysis I have summarised below what came out of our first planning meetings.

1 **Business definition.** It was agreed that the business needs redefining in customer terms. An appropriate definition for our company would be: 'Solutions to engine component design and manufacturing problems'.

2 **SWOT analysis**

Our main *strengths* are:

- Excellent customer awareness and an image of reliability and quality.

- Salesforce is technically well qualified.

- Manufacturing flexibility second to none – we respond quickly and effectively to individual customer needs.

Our main *weaknesses* are:

- Prices approximately 10 per cent above industry average.

- Spending higher proportion of turnover on advertising than most main competitors.

- Salesforce not skilled in generating new leads.

Our major *opportunities* are:

- Some major competitors having difficulty keeping customers because of quality and delivery problems.

- Recent legislation means research and development programme on new TDIX component, emphasising lower exhaust emission levels, should prove advantageous.

- Recent and forecast trends in the exchange rate should help export marketing efforts.

- Buyers in the industry seem prone to switching suppliers.

Our major *threats* are:

- Our largest customer threatening to switch owing to our higher average prices.

- Apart from TDIX programme, we have not been keeping pace with rapid technological change in the industry.

- Some major export markets are threatened by possibility of import restrictions.

3 **Objectives**

Financial

- To increase return on capital employed by 5 per cent.

- Net profit in the forthcoming year to be £4 million.

Marketing

- Sales revenue to be increased to £35 million in the forthcoming year.

4 **Marketing strategy**

Target markets

- Major manufacturers of diesel engines worldwide.

Positioning

- Highest engineering quality and after-sales service in supply of specialist low-volume diesel engine components.

I would welcome your comments on my analysis, together with any views on the appropriateness of the objectives I have set.

For the next meeting I suggest that as sales manager you give some thought as to where the relative emphasis should be placed in our promotional effort. As I have mentioned, we seem to be spending an excessive amount on advertising compared with our competitors. Perhaps you could give me your thoughts on this, as I understand you were in favour of raising our advertising budget from 1 per cent to 2 per cent of turnover last year. As you are aware, from a limited budget, we must decide where to place the relative emphasis in our communications mix. Perhaps you can indicate what you feel are the major considerations in this decision.

Discussion Questions

1 Give a brief outline of ways the sales manager can contribute to the marketing planning process at Auckland Engineering.

2 Looking at Duncan's analysis of the previous meeting, what issues/problems do you see that are of relevance to the activities of the salesforce?

3 How would you respond to Duncan's comments on the promotional mix and in particular to his comments about the level of advertising expenditure?

4 What is the logic in conducting a SWOT analysis in this context?

Practical Exercise

Flying high

Graham Keddie, appointed Managing Director late 2004, believes the magnetic effect of attracting two low-cost airlines has now succeeded in putting East Midlands Airport (EMA) firmly on the map. It has been a long-held view that EMA suffered from an identity problem; situated on the fringes of three major cities – Birmingham, Nottingham and Leicester. However, the announcement that 210,545 people flew from the airport in April 2005 – an incredible increase of 47.4 per cent on the previous year – shows that a point has clearly been proved.

Many passengers came from outside the region and one of the attractions has been the cheap flights with Go and bmibaby. Graham Keddie has started to fulfill the seemingly unlimited potential of EMA. Those living in the huge catchment area can now fly from their local airport to the destination of their choice. There is more than enough room for Go and bmibaby to thrive at EMA. There has been no need for a winner in the battle for supremacy and both airlines report that sales have exceeded expectations.

It has been a challenge for the airport because the dramatic increase in passengers came virtually overnight, but the workforce has put in a tremendous amount of work to make things go smoothly. In the long term a new terminal will need to be built, and plans are being worked upon but will take years to complete the entire project.

Keddie has said that the breakthrough has been made and proved what people have been claiming for many years. However, he feels there is still a lot more potential to be fulfilled. Suddenly people want to do business with the airport and that is good news for the many people who want to travel from EMA.

The international scheduled market showed an increase of 135.3 per cent in April 2005 compared to 12 months ago, with Malaga as the most popular destination. Domestic scheduled flights also experienced a large upturn with passengers increasing 30.6 per cent year on year – due entirely to the launch of the Go service between EMA and Edinburgh.

Source: Adapted from article originally in *Flightscene News Magazine of East Midlands Airport*, 50, Summer 2002.

Discussion Questions

1 Suggest a general outline marketing planning strategy for 12 months ahead for Graham Keddie.

2 What part should the sales function play when drawing up a detailed 12 months operational marketing plan for EMA?

3 Discuss the pros and cons of providing a long-term marketing plan, given the relative volatility of the market.

Examination Questions

1 Explain the differences between marketing strategies and sales strategies.

2 What is the relationship between objectives, strategies and tactics?

3 Discuss the component parts of the communications mix.

4 What is the relationship between SWOT analysis and the SWOT matrix?

5 What is meant by contingency planning and when is it required in the marketing planning process?

Part Two

Sales Environment

Chapter 3 provides a detailed examination of consumer and organisational buyer behaviour. In particular, their differences are considered in terms of how each purchasing situation calls for an entirely different sales approach. Consumer buying behaviour is then considered in more detail. The important marketing to buying organisations is then examined in terms of important factors that affect this process, including buy class and product type. Developments in purchasing practice, especially centralised purchasing and 'just-in-time' or lean manufacturing, and how these have affected the seller/purchaser relationship are then examined. The notions of 'reverse marketing' and 'relationship marketing' have sprung out of these developments and these are then described in terms of their influence on the practice of selling.

Sales settings are examined from a macro point-of-view in Chapter 4 and environmental and managerial forces acting upon sales are discussed, including issues such as rising consumer and organisational buyer expectations and the expanding negotiation power of major buyers. Technological forces linked to IT are discussed as are new managerial techniques that have developed largely as a result of these developments. The bulk of the remainder of this chapter is concerned with sales channels and their selection, appraisal and characteristics. It analyses categories of industrial, commercial and public authority selling and how these differ from selling to consumers, along with issues like concentration of markets, the complexity of purchasing decisions, long-term relationships and reciprocal trading. Selling for resale including a separate discussion on franchising is discussed, and this is followed by the selling of services. Sales promotions to consumers and to trade customers are then analysed. The respective effectiveness of exhibitions and public relations in supporting sales activities is discussed.

International selling issues are examined in Chapter 5, and consideration is given to economic issues like the balance of payments, UK share of international trade and the European Union. A micro view is then taken in terms of how international selling operates at the company level. Cultural factors are an important element of international business and Chapter 5 addresses issues like aesthetics, religion, social organisation and cultural change. How international selling is organised is also an important business issue and to this extent a distinction is made between multinational marketing, international marketing and exporting. Agents, distributors, licensing and joint ventures are methods of overseas trading arrangements and these are discssed with special consideration being given to international pricing issues.

Chapter 6 concerns law and ethical issues. Law is considered in terms of contract issues including terms and conditions. This is followed by terms of trade and general business practices. The chapter concludes with a discussion of ethical issues, covering matters like bribery, deception and reciprocal trading.

3 Consumer and Organisational Buyer Behaviour

Objectives

After studying this chapter, you should be able to:

1 Understand the different motivations of consumer and organisational buyers

2 Formulate strategies for approaching consumer and organisational buyers

3 Recognise the importance of relationship management

Key Concepts

- ACORN
- brand personality
- buy class
- buy phase
- buying centre
- centralised purchasing
- choice criteria
- consumer decision-making process
- creeping commitment
- decision-making unit (DMU)
- financial lease
- interaction approach
- just-in-time (JIT) delivery/purchasing
- life-cycle costs
- lockout criteria
- operating lease
- organisational buying behaviour
- reference group
- relationship management
- reverse marketing
- strategic partners
- total quality management
- value analysis

Differences Between Consumer and Organisational Buying

There are a number of important differences in emphasis between consumer and organisational buying which have important implications for the marketing of goods and services in general and the personal selling function in particular.

Fewer organisational buyers

Generally, a company marketing industrial products will have fewer potential buyers than one marketing in consumer markets. Often 80 per cent of output, in the former case, will be sold to perhaps 10–15 organisations. This means that the importance of one customer to the business-to-business marketer is far in excess of that to the consumer marketing company. However, this situation is complicated in some consumer markets where the importance of trade intermediaries, for example, supermarkets, is so great that, although the products have an ultimate market of many millions of people, the companies' immediate customers rank alongside those of important organisational buyers.

Close, long-term relationships between organisational buyers and sellers

Because of the importance of large customers, it makes sense for suppliers to invest in long-term relationships with them. This is reflected in the growth of key account selling where dedicated sales and marketing teams are employed to service major customers. Customers too see the advantages of establishing close relationships with suppliers. Ford, for example, has reduced its number of suppliers from 30,000 to 3,000 and many now have single-supplier status. The nature of relationships in many consumer markets is different: customers and manufacturers rarely meet and for many supermarket products, brand switching is common.

Organisational buyers are more rational

Although organisational buyers, like all people, are affected by emotional factors, for example, like or dislike of a salesperson, the colour of office equipment, etc., it is probably true that on the whole organisational buying is more rational. Often decisions will be made on economic criteria. This is because organisational buyers have to justify their decisions to other members of their organisation. Caterpillar tractor salespeople based their sales presentation on the fact that, although the initial purchase price of their tractors was higher than the competition, over the life of the tractor costs were significantly lower. This rational economic appeal proved very successful for many years. Customers are increasingly using life-cycle cost and value-in-use analysis to evaluate products. Rail companies, for example, calculate the life-cycle costs including purchase price, running and maintenance costs when ordering a new locomotive.

Organisational buying may be to specific requirements

It is not uncommon in business-to-business marketing for buyers to determine product specifications and for sellers to tailor their product offerings to meet them.

This is feasible because of the large potential revenue of such products, for example, railway engines. This is much less a feature of consumer marketing, where a product offering may be developed to meet the need of a market segment but, beyond that, meeting individual needs would prove uneconomic.

Reciprocal buying may be important in organisational buying

Because an organisational buyer may be in a powerful negotiating position with a seller, it may be possible to demand concessions in return for placing the order. In some situations the buyer may demand that the seller buys some of the buyer's products in return for securing the order. A buyer of tyres for a car manufacturer may demand that, in return for the contract, the tyre producer buys its company cars from the car manufacturer.

Organisational selling/buying may be more risky

Business-to-business markets are sometimes characterised by a contract being agreed before the product is made. Further, the product itself may be highly technical and the seller may be faced with unforeseen problems once work has started. For example, Scott-Lithgow won an order to build an oil rig for British Petroleum, but the price proved uneconomic given the nature of the problems associated with its construction. GEC won the contract to develop the Nimrod surveillance system for the Ministry of Defence but technical problems caused the project to be terminated with much adverse publicity. Another example was British Rail which encountered technical problems with the commissioning of the Class 60 diesel locomotive built by Brush Traction, although these were eventually resolved.

Organisational buying is more complex

Many organisational purchases, notably those which involve large sums of money and are new to the company, involve many people at different levels of the organisation. The managing director, product engineers, production managers, purchasing manager and operatives may influence the decision of which expensive machine to purchase. The sales task may be to influence as many of these people as possible and may involve multi-level selling by means of a sales team, rather than an individual salesperson.[1]

Negotiation is often important in organisational buying

Negotiation is often important in organisational buying because of the presence of professional buyers and sellers and the size and complexity of organisational buying. The supplier's list price may be regarded as the starting point for negotiation, but the price actually paid will depend on the negotiation skills and power bases of buyers and sellers.

Consumers are individuals who buy products and services for personal consumption. Sometimes it is difficult to classify a product as either a consumer or an organisational good. Cars, for example, sell to consumers for personal consumption and to organisations for use in carrying out their activities (e.g. to provide transport for a sales executive). For both types of buyer, an understanding of customers can only be obtained by answering the following five questions:

1 *Who* is important in the buying decision?

2 *How* do they buy?

3 *What* are their choice criteria?

4 *Where* do they buy?

5 *When* do they buy?

This chapter addresses the first three of these questions since they are often the most difficult to answer.

Who buys?

Many consumer purchases are individual. When purchasing a Mars bar a person may make an impulse purchase upon seeing an array of confectionery at a newsagent's counter. However, decision-making can also be made by a buying centre, such as a household. In this situation a number of individuals may interact to influence the purchase decision. Each person may assume a role in the decision-making process. Blackwell, Miniard and Engel[2] describe five roles. Each may be taken by husband, wife, children or other members of the household:

1 *Initiator* – the person who begins the process of considering a purchase. Information may be gathered by this person to help the decision.

2 *Influencer* – the person who attempts to persuade others in the group concerning the outcome of the decision. Influencers typically gather information and attempt to impose their choice criteria on the decision.

3 *Decider* – the individual with the power and/or financial authority to make the ultimate choice regarding which product to buy.

4 *Buyer* – the person who conducts the transaction: who calls the supplier, visits the store, makes the payment and effects delivery.

5 *User* – the actual consumer/user of the product.

One person may assume multiple roles in the buying centre. In a toy purchase, for example, a child may be the *initiator* and attempt to *influence* his/her parents who are the *deciders*. The child may be *influenced* by a sibling to buy a different brand. The *buyer* may be one of the parents, who visits the store to purchase the toy and brings it back to the home. Finally both children may be *users* of the toy. Although the purchase was for one person, marketers have four opportunities – two children and two parents – to affect the outcome of the purchase decision.

The marketing implications of understanding who buys lie within the areas of marketing communications and segmentation. Identifying the roles played within the buying centre is a prerequisite for targeting persuasive communications. As the previous discussion has demonstrated, the person who actually uses or consumes the product may not be the most influential member of the buying centre, nor may they be the decision-maker. Even when they do play the predominant role, communication to other members of the buying centre can make sense when their knowledge and opinions may act as persuasive forces during the decision-making process. The second implication is that the changing role and influences within the family buying centre are providing new opportunities to creatively segment hitherto stable markets (e.g. cars).

The consumer decision-making process – how they buy

Behavioural scientists regard the **consumer decision-making process** as a problem-solving or need-satisfaction process. Thus, an electronic calculator may be bought in order to solve a problem – inaccuracy or slowness in arithmetic – which itself defines the need – fast and accurate calculations. In order to define which calculator to buy, a consumer may pass through a series of steps,[3] as illustrated in Figure 3.1.

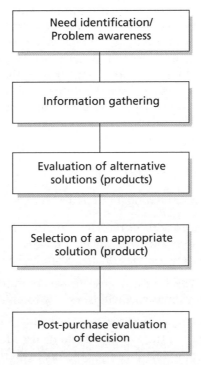

Figure 3.1 The consumer decision-making process
Source: From *Consumer Behavior* 9th edition by Blackwell. © 2001. Reprinted with permission of South-Western, a division of Thomson Learning: www.thomsonrights.com. Fax: 800–730–2215.

Needs

In the case of the calculator, the needs (stimulated by problem identification) are essentially *functional*. In this situation the salesperson would be advised, after identifying the buyer's needs, to demonstrate the speed and accuracy of the calculators s/he is selling. Successful selling may involve identifying needs in more detail; for example, are special features required or does the buyer only have to perform a standard, basic set of calculations, implying a less elaborate and cheaper calculator? For other products need satisfaction may be *emotional* or *psychological*. For example, a Sheaffer pen is bought largely for its status rather than any marginal functional superiority over other pens. An accurate assessment of the kinds of needs which a product is satisfying will enable a salesperson to plan the sales presentation correctly, presenting the product as a means of satisfying the buyer's needs or solving the buyer's problems.

How do needs arise? They may occur as a natural process of life; for example, the birth of children in a family may mean that a larger car is required. They may also arise because of stimulation. An advertisement for video-recorders or a salesperson's talk may create the need for extra in-house entertainment and, at the same time, provide a means of satisfying that need.

Information gathering

Many needs can only be satisfied after a period of information search. Thus a prospective car purchaser who requires a small, economical car may carry out a considerable search before deciding on the model which best satisfies these needs. This search may involve visiting car showrooms, watching car programmes on television, reading car magazines and *Which?* reports and talking to friends. Clearly, many sources of information are sought besides that provided by the salesperson in the showroom. Indeed, in some situations the search may omit the salesperson until the end of this process. The buyer may reduce the number of alternatives to a manageable few and contact the salesperson only to determine the kind of deal offered on the competing models.

Evaluation of alternatives and selection of the best solution

Evaluation may be thought of as a system, as depicted in Figure 3.2.

1 *Evaluative (choice) criteria*. These are the dimensions used by consumers to compare or evaluate products or brands. In the car example, the relevant evaluative criteria may be fuel economy, purchase price and reliability.

2 *Beliefs*. These are the degrees to which, in the consumer's mind, a product possesses various characteristics, e.g. roominess.

3 *Attitudes*. These are the degrees of liking or disliking a product and are in turn dependent on the evaluative criteria used to judge the products and the beliefs about the product measured by those criteria. Thus beliefs imply knowledge, e.g. model X does 36 miles per gallon at a steady 56 miles per hour, whereas attitudes imply liking or disliking, e.g. model X is poor with regard to fuel economy.

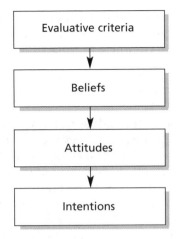

Figure 3.2 The evaluation system

4 *Intentions*. These measure the probability that attitudes will be acted upon. The assumption is that favourable attitudes will increase purchase intentions, i.e. the probability that the consumer will buy.

Given this system, it makes sense for a salesperson to find out from a prospect the evaluative criteria being used to judge alternative products. For example, a stereo system salesperson will attempt to find out whether a potential buyer is evaluating alternative stereo units primarily in terms of external design or sound quality. Further, it can be effective to try to change evaluative criteria. For example, if the stereo system salesperson believes that the competitive advantage of the product range lies in its sound quality, but the buyer's criterion is primarily external design, the salesperson can emphasise the sound quality of the product and minimise the importance of external design. Alternatively, if the primary consideration of the buyer is sound quality but a competitor's system is preferred, the sales task is to change attitudes in favour of their own system. Tools at their disposal include the use of performance comparisons from hi-fi magazines and in-shop demonstrations.

Post-purchase evaluation of decision

The art of effective marketing is to create customer satisfaction. Most businesses rely on repeat purchasing, which implies that customers must gain satisfaction from their purchases (otherwise this will not occur). Festinger[4] introduced the notion of 'cognitive dissonance' partly to explain the anxiety felt by many buyers of expensive items shortly after purchase. The classic case of this is the car buyer who assiduously reads car advertisements after having bought the car in an effort to dispel the anxiety caused by not being sure that s/he has made the correct purchase.

Salespeople often try to reassure buyers, after the order has been placed, that they have made the right decision, but the outcome of the post-purchase evaluation is dependent on many factors besides the salesperson's reassurance. The quality of the product and the level of after-sales service play an obvious part in creating customer goodwill, and it is the salesperson who can help buyers in ensuring that the product they buy best matches their needs in the first place. This implies that it may not be in the salesperson's long-term interest to pressure buyers into buying higher priced items which possess features not really wanted – although this may increase short-term profit margins (and commission), it may lead to a long-term fall in sales as consumers go elsewhere to replace the item.

Choice criteria

Choice criteria are the various features (and benefits) a customer uses when evaluating products and services. They provide the grounds for deciding to purchase one brand or another. Different members of the buying centre may use different choice criteria. For example, a child may use the criterion of self-image when choosing shoes whereas a parent may use price. The same criterion may be used differently. For example, a child may want the most expensive video-game while the parent may want a less expensive alternative. Choice criteria can change over time due to changes in income through the family life-cycle. As disposable income rises, price may no longer be a key choice criterion but may be replaced by considerations of status or social belonging.

Choice criteria can be economic, social or personal. *Economic criteria* include performance, reliability and price. *Social criteria* include status and the need for social belonging. For example, Nike, Reebok and Adidas trainers need 'street cred' to be acceptable to large numbers of the youth market. Social norms such as convention and fashion can also be important choice criteria, with some brands being rejected as too unconventional (e.g. fluorescent spectacles) or out of fashion (Mackeson stout).

Personal criteria concern how the product or service relates to the individual psychologically. An important issue here is self-image, which is the personal view we hold of ourselves. For example, one person might view herself as a young, upwardly mobile, successful executive and wish to buy products that reflect that image. Audi tried to appeal to such a person when they ran an advertising campaign that suggested Audi drivers 'arrived' more quickly than other drivers. Many purchase decisions are 'experimental' in that they evoke feelings of fun, pride, pleasure, boredom or sadness. Such feelings need to be taken into account when marketing products or services. For example, in retail marketing, stores such as Next and Principles recognise the importance of creating the right atmosphere through the correct choice of in-store colour and design.

Salespeople and marketing managers need to understand the choice criteria being used by consumers when they evaluate their products or services. Such knowledge allows the salesperson to tailor the correct appeal to each customer s/he talks to and provides marketing managers with the basis for product or service design and the correct messages to use in advertising.

3.3   Factors Affecting the Consumer Decision-making Process

There are a number of factors which affect the consumer decision-making process and its outcome. These can be classified under three headings:

1   the buying situation

2   personal influences

3   social influences

The buying situation

Howard and Sheth[5] identified three types of buying situation:

(a) extensive problem-solving

(b) limited problem-solving

(c) automatic response

When a problem or need is new, the means of solving that problem is expensive and uncertainty is high, a consumer is likely to conduct extensive problem-solving. This involves a high degree of information search and close examination of alternative solutions. Faced with this kind of buyer, the salesperson can create immense good-will by providing information and assessing alternatives from the product range in terms of how well their benefits conform to the buyer's needs. The goodwill gener-ated with this type of buyer in such a situation may be rewarded by a repeat pur-chase when the buying situation changes to one of limited problem-solving. Thus successful car salespeople often find themselves with a group of highly loyal buyers who purchase from them, even if the dealership changes, because of the trust built up during this stage.

Limited problem-solving occurs when the consumer has some experience with the product in question and may be inclined to stay loyal to the brand previously purchased. However, a certain amount of information search and evaluation of a few alternatives occurs as a rudimentary check that the right decision is being made. This process provides a limited opportunity for salespeople of competing products to persuade consumers that they should switch model or brand by providing rel-evant comparative information and, perhaps, by providing risk-reducing guaran-tees, for example, free replacement of any defective parts.

Companies who have built up a large brand franchise will wish to move their cus-tomers to the state of automatic response. Advertising may be effective in keeping the brand in the forefront of the consumer's mind and in reinforcing already favourable attitudes towards the brand. In this situation, personal selling to the ulti-mate consumer may be superfluous. Companies selling consumer durables may offer generous trade-in terms for their old models. Black and Decker have used this technique whereby an old, unusable lawnmower could be traded in as part payment on a new model.

A key influence on whether a consumer conducts extensive or limited problem-solving or automatic response is his or her level of involvement with the purchase. High involvement is associated with important purchases that are of high personal relevance. When a purchase affects one's self-image, has a high degree of perceived risk, has social (e.g. status) implications, and the capacity to give a lot of pleasure, it is likely to be high involvement. When the opposite is the case, the consumer is likely to experience low involvement with the purchase. Figure 3.3 shows the relationship between involvement and the buying situation.

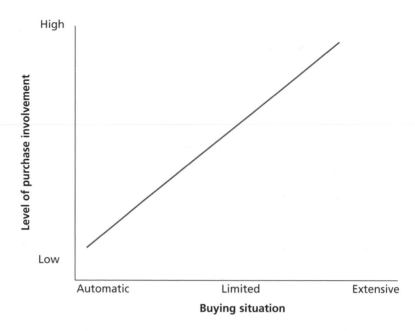

Figure 3.3 Level of purchase involvement and the buying situation

In high involvement situations (e.g. car or house purchase), the customer is looking for lots of information upon which to make a decision. A salesperson must be able to provide that information and answer in-depth queries. In low involvement situations, the customer is not likely to be an active searcher for information. Repetitive advertising is often used for these kinds of purchases.

Personal influences

A second group of factors that influences the consumer decision-making process concerns the psychology of the individuals concerned. Relevant concepts include personality, motivation, perception and learning.

Although personality may explain differences in consumer purchasing, it is extremely difficult for salespeople to judge accurately how extrovert or introvert, conventional or unconventional, a customer is. Indeed, reliable personality measurement has proved difficult, even for qualified psychologists. Brand personality is the characterisation of brands as perceived by consumers. Brands may be characterised as 'for young people' (Levis), 'brash' (Castlemaine XXXX) or 'intelligent' (Guinness). This is a dimension over and above the physical (e.g. colour) or functional (e.g. task) attributes of a brand. By creating a brand personality, a marketer may create appeal to people who value that characterisation. Research by Ackoff and Emsott[6] into brand personalities of beers showed that most consumers preferred the brand of beer that matched their own personality.

Sellers need to be aware of different buyer personality types. Buzzotta, Lefton and Sherberg[7] proposed a two-dimensional approach to understanding buyer psychology. They suggest that everyone tends to be warm or hostile, dominant or submissive. Although there are degrees of each of these behaviours, they believe it is meaningful to place individuals in one cell of a two-by-two matrix. Each behaviour is defined as follows:

1 *Dominant.* In face-to-face situations, dominance is the drive to take control of others. It implies a need to lead in personal encounters, to have control of situations and to have a strong desire to be independent.

2 *Submissive.* Submission is the disposition to let others take the lead. It implies a willingness to be controlled, a need to comply with the wishes of others and an avoidance of confrontation.

3 *Warm.* Warmth is having a regard for others. A warm person is described as one who is outgoing, good humoured, optimistic and willing to place trust in others.

4 *Hostile.* Hostility is having a lack of regard for others. It suggests a person who is cold, distrustful and disdainful of others. Hostile people like to be in a position to say 'I told you so'.

Figure 3.4 shows this dimensional model of buyer behaviour.

Buzzotta, Lefton and Sherberg[8] claim that, although there are as many distinctions as people, in general each person primarily falls into one of the four groups. To help identify each type, the salesperson must look for their hallmarks:

Q1: Dominant-hostile

These people are loud, talkative, demanding and forceful in their actions. They are hard-nosed, aggressive and assertive. They are usually difficult to get along with and can be offensive. They tend to distrust salespeople.

Q2: Submissive-hostile

These people are cold, aloof and uncommunicative. They tend to be loners and work in jobs that demand concentration rather than socialisation, for example, research, accountancy and computer programming. When responding to questions, they tend to be short and terse: 'maybe', 'all right', 'possibly'. Q2s prefer to avoid sales interviews, but if they cannot avoid them they take on a passive, almost detached role.

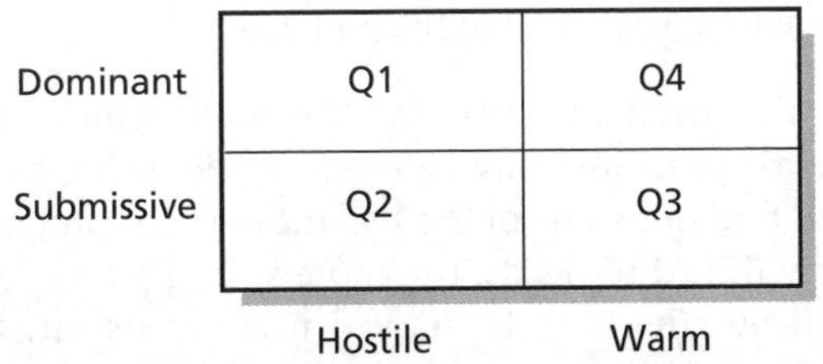

	Hostile	Warm
Dominant	Q1	Q4
Submissive	Q2	Q3

Figure 3.4 Dimensional model of buyer behaviour

Q3: Submissive-warm

These people are extrovert, friendly, understanding, talkative and positive-minded people who are not natural leaders. They prefer to buy from someone they like and view a sales interview as a social occasion. Generally they accept most of what the salesperson tells them, but if they feel any doubt they will postpone the decision to buy – possibly to seek advice from friends.

Q4: Dominant-warm

These people are adaptable and open minded but not afraid to express their ideas and opinions. They tend to want proof of sales arguments and become impatient of woolly answers. They are not hesitant to buy from anyone who can prove to their satisfaction that there is a benefit to be gained. They like to negotiate in a business-like manner and can be demanding and challenging in a sales interview.

Implications for selling

What are the implications for selling? Decormier and Jobber[9] argue that salespeople should modify their behaviour accordingly.

Q1 To win the respect of *dominant-hostile* people, the appropriate salesperson behaviour is to adjust their dominance level upward to meet that of the buyer. This would involve sitting upright, maintaining eye contact, listening respectfully (but passively) and answering directly. Once Q1 buyers realise that the salesperson is their psychological equal, a meaningful discussion can take place.

Q2 When first meeting with a *submissive-hostile* Q2 buyer, a salesperson should not attempt to dominate, but gradually try to gain his or her trust. The salesperson should match the buyer's dominance level and ask open-ended questions in a slow, soft manner. The salesperson should lower his or her stature, keeping eyes and head at the same level as the buyer.

Q3 *Submissive-warm* people like and trust people. The salesperson should satisfy their social needs by being warm and friendly. S/he should not attempt to dominate, but should instead share the social experience. Once liking and trust have been established, the salesperson should guide the interview towards the goal of decision-making.

Q4 *Dominant-warm* people consider respect more important than being liked. To gain respect, the salesperson should match the Q4's dominance level while maintaining a warm (empathetic) manner. Sales arguments need to be backed up whenever possible by evidence.

Sellers also need to probe for the motivations of the buyer. The true reason or motive for purchase may be obscure. However, by careful probing a salesperson is likely to find out some of the real motives for purchase some of the time. Motivation is clearly linked to needs; the more strongly a need is perceived by a consumer, the more likely s/he is to be moved towards its satisfaction. Thus, a salesperson can increase buyer motivation by stimulating need recognition, by showing the ways in which needs can be fulfilled and by attempting to understand the various motives which may be at work in the decision-making process. These may be functional, for example, time saved by a convenience food, or psychological, e.g. the status imparted by the ownership of a Jaguar or BMW car.

Not everyone with the same motivations will buy the same products, however. One of the reasons for this is that how someone decides to act depends upon his or her *perception* of the situation. One buyer may perceive a salesperson as being honest and truthful while another may not. Three selective processes may be at work on consumers.

1 *Selective exposure*. Only certain information sources may be sought and read.

2 *Selective perception*. Only certain ideas, messages and information from those sources may be perceived.

3 *Selective retention*. Only some of them may be remembered.

In general, people tend to forget more quickly and to distort or avoid messages that are substantially at variance with existing attitudes.

Learning is also important in consumer decision-making. Learning refers to the changes in a person's behaviour as a result of his or her experiences. A consumer will learn which brand names imply quality and which salespeople to trust.

Lifestyle

Lifestyle patterns have attracted much attention from marketing research practitioners. *Lifestyle* refers to the patterns of living as expressed in a person's activities, interests and opinions. Lifestyle analysis, or *psychographics*, groups the consumers according to their beliefs, activities, values and demographic characteristics such as education and income. For example, Research Bureau Ltd, a UK marketing research agency, investigated lifestyle patterns among housewives and found eight distinct groups:

1 *Young sophisticates:* extravagant, experimental, non-traditional; young, ABC1 social class, well educated, affluent, owner-occupiers, full-time employed; interested in new products; sociable with cultural interests.

2 *Home centred:* conservative, less quality conscious, demographically average, middle class, average income and education; lowest interest in new products; very home centred; little entertaining.

3 *Traditional working class:* traditional, quality conscious, unexperimental in food, enjoy cooking; middle aged, DE social group, less education, lower income, council house tenants; sociable; husband and wife share activities, like betting.

4 *Middle-aged sophisticates:* experimental, not traditional; middle aged, ABC1 social class, well educated, affluent, owner-occupiers, full-time housewives, interested in new products; sociable with cultural interests.

5 *Coronation Street housewives:* quality conscious, conservative, traditional; DE social class, tend to live in Lancashire and Yorkshire TV areas, less educated, lower incomes, part-time employment; low level of interest in new products; not sociable.

6 *Self-confident:* self-confident, quality conscious, not extravagant; young, well educated, owner-occupier, average income.

7 *Homely:* bargain seekers, not self-confident, houseproud, C1C2 social class, tend to live in Tyne Tees and Scottish TV areas; left school at an early age; part-time employed; average level of entertaining.

8 *Penny-pinchers:* self-confident, houseproud, traditional, not quality conscious; 25 to 34 years, C2DE social class, part-time employment, less education, average income; enjoy betting, enjoy saving, husband and wife share activities, sociable.

Lifestyle analysis has implications for marketing since lifestyles hae been found to correlate with purchasing behaviour. A company may choose to target a particular lifestyle group (e.g. the middle-aged sophisticates) with a product offering, and use advertising which is in line with the values and beliefs of this group. As information on readership/viewing habits of lifestyle groups becomes more widely known, so media selection may be influenced by lifestyle research.

Social influences

Major social influences on consumer decision-making include social class, reference groups, culture and the family. The first of these factors, social class, has been regarded as an important determinant of consumer behaviour for many years. Social class in marketing is based upon the occupation of the head of the household or main income earner. The practical importance of social class is reflected in the fact that respondents in market research surveys are usually classified by their social class, and most advertising media give readership figures broken down by social class groupings. These are shown in Table 3.1. However, the use of this variable to explain differences in purchasing has been criticised. It is often the case that people within the same social class may have different consumption patterns. Within the C2 group, i.e. skilled manual workers, it has been found that some people spend a high proportion of their income on buying their own houses, furniture, carpets and in-home entertainment, while others prefer to spend their money on more transitory pleasures such as drinking, smoking and playing bingo.

Such findings have led to a new classificatory system, A Classification of Residential Neighbourhoods (ACORN), which classifies people according to the type of area they live in. This has proved to be a powerful discriminator between different lifestyles, purchasing patterns and media exposure.[10]

The term *reference group* is used to indicate a group of people that influences a person's attitude or behaviour. Where a product is conspicuous, for example, clothing or cars, the brand or model chosen may have been strongly influenced by what the buyer perceives as acceptable to his or her reference group (e.g. a group of friends, the family, or work colleagues). Reference group acceptability should not be confused with popularity. The salesperson who attempts to sell a car using the theme that 'it's very popular' may conflict with the buyer's desire to aspire to an 'exclusive' reference group, for which a less popular, more individual model may be appropriate.

Culture refers to the traditions, taboos, values and basic attitudes of the whole society within which an individual lives. It is of particular relevance to international

Table 3.1 Social class categories

	Social grade	All adults 15+ (%)
	A	3.0
	B	20.8
	C1	27.3
	C2	21.2
	D	17.4
	E	10.3

KEY:

Social grade	Social status	Occupation
A	Upper middle class	Higher managerial, administrative or professional
B	Middle class	Intermediate managerial, administrative or professional
C1	Lower middle class	Supervisory or clerical and junior managerial, administrative or professional
C2	Skilled working class	Skilled manual workers
D	Working class	Semi and unskilled manual workers
E	Those at the lowest level of subsistence	State pensioners or widows (no other earner), casual or lowest grade workers

Source: Adapted from *National Readership Survey*, July 2000–June 2001.

marketing since different countries have different cultures, affecting the conduct of business and how products are used. In Arab countries, for example, salespeople may find themselves conducting a sales presentation in the presence of a competitor's salesperson. In France chocolate is sometimes eaten between slices of bread.

The family is sometimes called a primary reference group and may play a significant part in consumer buyer behaviour. The decision as to which product or brand to purchase may be a group decision, with each family member playing a distinct part. Thus, in the purchase of motor cars, traditionally the husband decided upon the model, while his wife chose the colour.[11] The purchase of cereals may be strongly influenced by children. The cleaning properties of a carpet fibre may be relatively unimportant to the principal breadwinner but of greater significance to the partner who performs the housework tasks. When a purchase is a group decision, a salesperson will be wise to view the benefits of his or her products in terms of each of the decision-makers or influencers.

3.4 Organisational Buyer Behaviour

Organisational buyer behaviour has usefully been broken down into three elements by Fisher.[12]

1 *Structure.* The 'who' factor – who participates in the decision-making process and their particular roles.

2 *Process.* The 'how' factor – the pattern of information getting, analysis, evaluation and decision-making which takes place as the purchasing organisation moves towards a decision.

3 *Content.* The 'what' factor – the choice criteria used at different stages of the process and by different members of the decision-making unit.

Structure

An essential point to understand in organisational buying is that the buyer or purchasing officer is often not the only person who influences the decision, or who actually has the authority to make the ultimate decision. Rather, the decision is in the hands of a **decision-making unit (DMU),** or buying centre as it is sometimes called. This is not necessarily a fixed entity. The people in the DMU may change as the decision-making process continues. Thus a managing director may be involved in the decision that new equipment should be purchased, but not in the decision as to which manufacturer to buy it from. Bonoma[13] and Webster[14] have identified six roles in the structure of the DMU:

1 *Initiators.* Those who begin the purchase process.

2 *Users.* Those who actually use the product.

3 *Deciders.* Those who have the authority to select the supplier/model.

4 *Influencers.* Those who provide information and add decision criteria throughout the process.

5 *Buyers.* Those who have authority to execute the contractual arrangements.

6 *Gatekeepers.* Those who control the flow of information, e.g. secretaries who may allow or prevent access to a DMU member, or a buyer whose agreement must be sought before a supplier can contact other members of the DMU.

The factors which influence the nature of the DMU will be examined later. Obviously, for different types of purchase the exact formation will vary. For very important decisions the structure of the DMU will be complex, involving numerous people within the buying organisation. The salesperson's task is to identify and reach the key members in order to convince them of the product's worth. Often, talking only to the purchasing officer will be insufficient, since this may be only a minor influence on which supplier is chosen. Salespeople need to avoid two deadly sins:

1 Working within their 'comfort zone'. This is where they spend too much time with people they like and feel comfortable with, but who are unimportant with regard to which product to buy or which supplier to use.

2 Spending too much time with 'nay sayers'. These are people who can say 'no' (the power of veto) but who do not have the authority to say 'yes'. It is the latter group, i.e. the decision-makers, to whom most communicational effort should be channelled.

When the problem to be solved is highly technical, suppliers may work with engineers in the buying organisation in order to solve problems and secure the order. An example where this approach was highly successful involved a small US company that secured a large order from a major car company owing to its ability to work with the company in solving the technical problems associated with the development of an exhaust gas recirculation valve.[15] In this case, its policy was to work with company engineers and to keep the purchasing department out of the decision until the last possible moment, by which time it was the only company qualified to supply the part.

Where DMU members are inaccessible to salespeople, advertising may be used as an alternative. Also, where users are an important influence and the product is relatively inexpensive and consumable, free samples given by the salespeople may be effective in generating preference.

Process

Figure 3.5 describes the decision-making process for an industrial product.[16] The exact nature of the process will depend on the buying situation. In certain situations

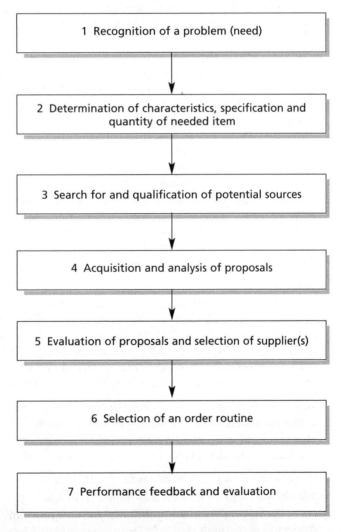

Figure 3.5 The organisational decision-making process (buy phases)

some stages will be omitted; for example, in a routine re-buy situation the purchasing officer is unlikely to pass through stages 3, 4 and 5 (search for suppliers and an analysis and evaluation of their proposals). These stages will be bypassed, as the buyer, recognising a need – perhaps shortage of stationery – routinely reorders from the existing supplier.

In general, the more complex the decision and the more expensive the item, the more likely it is that each stage will be passed through and that the process will take more time.

1 *Need or problem of recognition*. Needs and problems may be recognised through either internal or external factors. An example of an internal factor would be the realisation of undercapacity leading to the decision to purchase plant or equipment. Thus, internal recognition leads to active behaviour (*internal/active*). Some problems which are recognised internally may not be acted upon. This condition may be termed *internal/passive*. A production manager may realise that there is a problem with a machine but, given more pressing problems, decides to live with it. Other potential problems may not be recognised internally and only become problems because of *external cues*. A production manager may be quite satisfied with the production process until being made aware of another more efficient method. Clearly these different problems have important implications for the salesperson. The internal/passive condition implies that there is an opportunity for the salesperson, having identified the condition, to highlight the problem by careful analysis of cost inefficiencies and other symptoms, so that the problem is perceived to be more pressing and in need of solution (internal/active). The internal/active situation requires salespeople to demonstrate a differential advantage of one of their products over the competition. In this situation, problem stimulation is unnecessary, but where internal recognition is absent, the salesperson can provide the necessary external cues. A forklift truck sales representative might stimulate problem recognition by showing how their trucks can save the customer money, due to lower maintenance costs, and lead to more efficient use of warehouse space through higher lifting capabilities.

2 *Determination of characteristics, specification and quantity of needed item*. At this stage of the decision-making process the DMU will draw up a description of what is required. For example, it might decide that five lathes are required to meet certain specifications. The ability of a salesperson to influence the specifications can give their company an advantage at later stages of the process. By persuading the buying company to specify features that only their product possesses (*lockout criteria*), the salesperson may virtually have closed the sale at this stage.

3 *Search for and qualification of potential sources*. A great deal of variation in the degree of search takes place in organisational buying. Generally speaking, the cheaper, less important the item and the more information the buyer possesses, the less search takes place.

4 *Acquisition and analysis of proposals*. Having found a number of companies which, perhaps through their technical expertise and general reputation, are considered to be qualified to supply the product, proposals will be called for and analysis of them undertaken.

5 *Evaluation of proposals and selection of suppliers*. Each proposal will be evaluated in the light of the criteria deemed to be important to each DMU member. It is important to realise that various members may use different criteria when judging proposals. Although this may cause problems, the outcome of this procedure is the selection of a supplier or suppliers.

6 *Selection of an order routine*. Next the details of payment and delivery are drawn up. Usually this is conducted by the purchasing officer. In some buying decisions this stage is merged into stages 4 and 5 when delivery is an important consideration in selecting a supplier.

7 *Performance feedback and evaluation*. This may be formal, where a purchasing department draws up an evaluation form for user departments to complete, or informal through everyday conversation.

The implications of all this are that a salesperson can affect a sale through influencing need recognition, through the design of product specifications and by clearly presenting the advantages of the product over competition in terms which are relevant to DMU members. By early involvement, a salesperson can benefit through the process of **creeping commitment**, whereby the buying organisation becomes increasingly committed to one supplier through its involvement in the process and the technical assistance it provides.

Content

This aspect of organisational buyer behaviour refers to the **choice criteria** used by members of the DMU to evaluate supplier proposals. These criteria are likely to be determined by the performance criteria used to evaluate the members themselves. Thus a purchasing manager who is judged by the extent to which s/he reduces purchase expenditure is likely to be more cost conscious than a production engineer who is evaluated in terms of the technical efficiency of the production processes s/he designs.

As with consumers, organisational buying is characterised by both functional (economic) and psychological (emotive) criteria (see Table 3.2). Key functional considerations for plant and equipment may be return on investment, while for

Table 3.2 Choice criteria

Economic	Emotional
Price	Prestige
Delivery	Personal risk reduction
Productivity – cost versus revenues	Office politics
Life-cycle costs	Quiet life
Reliability	Pleasure
Durability	Reciprocity
Upgradability	Confidence
Technical assistance	Convenience
Commercial assistance	
Safety	

materials and component parts they might be cost savings, together with delivery reliability, quality and technical assistance. Because of the high costs associated with production down-time, a key concern of many purchasing departments is the long-run development of the organisation's supply system. Psychological factors may also be important, particularly when suppliers' product offerings are essentially similar. In this situation the final decision may rest upon the relative liking for the suppliers' salesperson. A number of important criteria are examined below.

Quality

The emergence of **total quality management** (TQM) as a key aspect of organisational life reflects the importance of quality in evaluating a supplier's products and services. Many buying organisations are unwilling to trade quality for price. In particular, buyers are looking for consistency of product or service quality so that end products (e.g. motor cars) are reliable, inspection costs reduced and production processes run smoothly. They are installing **just-in-time** (JIT) delivery systems which rely upon incoming supplies being quality guaranteed. Jaguar cars under Sir John Egan moved from a price-orientated purchasing system to one where quality was central and purchasing departments were instructed to pay more, provided the price could be justified in terms of improved quality of components.

Price and life-cycle costs

For materials and components of similar specification and quality, price becomes a key consideration. For standard items, such as ball-bearings, price may be critical to making a sale given that a number of suppliers can meet delivery and specification requirements. However, it should not be forgotten that price is only one component of cost for many buying organisations. Increasingly buyers take into account **life-cycle costs**, which may include productivity savings, maintenance costs and residual values, as well as initial purchase price, when evaluating products. Marketers can use life-cycle costs analysis to break into an account. By calculating life-cycle costs with a buyer, new perceptions of value may be achieved.

Continuity of supply

One of the major costs to a company is a disruption of a production run. Delays of this kind can mean costly machine down-time and even lost sales. Continuity of supply is therefore a prime consideration in many purchase situations. Companies which perform badly on this criterion lose out, even if the price is competitive, because a small percentage price edge does not compare with the costs of unreliable delivery. Supplier companies who can guarantee deliveries and realise their promises can achieve a significant differential advantage in the marketplace. Organisational customers are demanding close relationships with 'accredited suppliers' who can guarantee reliable supply, perhaps on a just-in-time basis.

Perceived risk

Perceived risk can come in two forms: functional risk, such as the uncertainty with respect to product or supplier performance, and psychological risk, such as criticism from work colleagues. This latter risk – fear of upsetting the boss, losing status, being ridiculed by others in the department, or indeed losing one's job – can play a determining role in purchase decisions. Buyers often reduce uncertainty by gathering information about competing suppliers, checking the opinions of important others in the buying company, only buying from familiar and/or reputable suppliers and by spreading risk through multiple sourcing.

Office politics

Political factions within the buying company may also influence the outcome of a purchase decision. Interdepartmental conflict may manifest itself in the formation of competing 'camps' over the purchase of a product or service. Because department X favours supplier A, department Y automatically favours supplier B. The outcome not only has purchasing implications but also political implications for the departments and individuals concerned.

Personal liking/disliking

A buyer may personally like one salesperson more than another and this may influence supplier choice, particularly when competing products are very similar. Even when supplier selection is on the basis of competitive bidding, it is known for purchasers to help salespeople they like to 'be competitive'. Obviously, perception is important in all organisational purchases, as how someone behaves depends upon the perception of the situation. One buyer may perceive a salesperson as being honest, truthful and likeable while another may not. As with consumer behaviour, three selective processes may be at work on buyers:

- *selective exposure*: only certain information sources may be sought

- *selective perception*: only certain information may be perceived

- *selective retention*: only some information may be remembered

The implications of understanding the content of the decision are that, first, a salesperson may need to change the sales presentation when talking to different DMU members. Discussion with a production engineer may centre on the technical superiority of the product offering, while much more emphasis on cost factors may prove beneficial when talking to the purchasing officer. Second, the choice criteria used by buying organisations change over time as circumstances change. Price may be relatively unimportant to a company when trying to solve a highly visible technical problem, and the order will be placed with the supplier who provides the necessary technical assistance. Later, after the problem has been solved and other suppliers become qualified, price may be of crucial significance.

3.5   Factors Affecting Organisational Buyer Behaviour

Cardozo[17] identified three factors which influence the composition of the DMU, the nature of the decision-making process and the criteria used to evaluate product offerings:

- the buy class
- the product type
- the importance of the purchase to the buying organisation

These three factors are illustrated in Figure 3.6.

The buy class

Industrial purchasing decisions were studied by Robinson, Faris and Wind,[18] who concluded that buyer behaviour was influenced by the nature of the **buy class**. They distinguished between a new task, a modified re-buy and a straight re-buy.

Figure 3.6 Influences on organisational purchasing behaviour

A *new task* occurs when the need for the product has not arisen previously so that there is little or no relevant experience in the company, and a great deal of information is required. A *straight re-buy*, on the other hand, occurs where an organisation buys previously purchased items from suppliers already judged acceptable. Routine purchasing procedures are set up to facilitate straight re-buys. The *modified re-buy* lies between the two extremes. A regular requirement for the type of product exists and the buying alternatives are known, but sufficient change has occurred to require some alteration of the normal supply procedure.

The buy classes affect organisational buying in the following ways. First, the structure of the DMU changes. For a straight re-buy, possibly only the purchasing officer is involved, whereas for a new buy, senior management, engineers, production managers and purchasing officers are likely to be involved. Modified re-buys often involve engineers, production managers and purchasing officers, but senior management, except when the purchase is critical to the company, is unlikely to be involved. Second, the decision-making process is likely to be much longer as the buy class changes from a straight re-buy to a modified re-buy and then, a new task. Third, in terms of influencing DMU members, they are likely to be much more receptive for new task and modified re-buy situations than straight re-buys. In the latter case the purchasing manager has already solved the purchasing problems and has other problems to deal with. So why make it a problem again?

The first implication of this buy class analysis is that there are big gains to be made if the salesperson can enter the new task at the start of the decision-making process. By providing information and helping with any technical problems which can arise, the salesperson may be able to create goodwill and creeping commitment, which secures the order when the final decision is made. The second implication is that since the decision process is likely to be long and many people are involved in the new task, supplier companies need to invest heavily in sales human resources for a considerable period of time. Some firms employ missionary sales teams comprising their best salespeople to help secure big new-task orders.

Salespeople in straight re-buy situations must ensure that no change occurs when they are in the position of the supplier. Regular contact to ensure that the customer has no complaints may be necessary, and the buyer may be encouraged to use automatic recording systems. For the non-supplier, the salesperson has a difficult task unless poor service or some other factor has caused the buyer to become dissatisfied with the present supplier. The obvious objective of the salesperson in this situation is to change the buy class from a straight re-buy to a modified re-buy. Price alone may not be enough since changing supplier represents a large personal risk to the purchasing officer. The new supplier's products might be less reliable and delivery might be unpredictable. In order to reduce this risk, the salesperson may offer delivery guarantees with penalty clauses and be very willing to accept a small (perhaps uneconomic) order at first in order to gain a foothold. Supplier acquisition of a total quality management standard such as BS5750 may also have the effect of reducing perceived buyer risk, or it may be necessary to agree to undertake a buyer's supplier quality assurance programme. Many straight re-buys are organised on a contract basis and buyers may be more receptive to listening to non-supplier salespeople prior to contract renewal.

Value analysis and life-cycle cost calculations are other methods of moving purchases from a straight re-buy to a modified re-buy situation. **Value analysis**, which can be conducted by either supplier or buyer, is a method of cost reduction in which components are examined to see if they can be made more cheaply. The items are studied to identify unnecessary costs that do not add to the reliability or functionality of the product. By redesigning, standardising or manufacturing by less expensive means, a supplier may be able to offer a product of comparable quality at lower cost. Simple redesigns like changing a curved edge to a straight one may have dramatic cost implications.

Life-cycle cost analysis seeks to move the cost focus from the initial purchase price to the total cost of owning and using a product. There are three types of life-cycle costs:

- purchase price

- start-up costs

- post-purchase costs

Start-up costs include installation, lost production and training costs. Post-purchase costs include operating (e.g. fuel, operator wages), maintenance, repair and inventory costs. Against these costs would be placed residual values (e.g. trade-in values of cars). Life-cycle cost appeals can be powerful motivators. For example, if the out-supplier can convince the customer organisation that its product has significantly lower post-purchase costs than the in-supplier, despite a slightly higher purchase price, it may win the order. This is because it will be delivering a *higher economic value* to the customer. This can be a powerful competitive advantage and at the same time justify the premium price.

The product type

Products can be classified according to four types:

1 *Materials* to be used in the production process, e.g. steel

2 *Components* to be incorporated in the finished product, e.g. alternator

    Product constituents

3 *Plant and equipment*

4 Products and services for *maintenance, repair and operation (MROs)*, e.g. spanners, welding equipment and lubricants

    Production facilities

This classification is based upon a customer's perspective – how the product is used – and may be applied to identify differences in organisational buyer behaviour. First, the people who take part in the decision-making process tend to differ according to product type. For example, it has been found that senior management tend to get involved in the purchase of plant and equipment or, occasionally, when new materials are purchased, if the change is of fundamental importance to company operations; for example, if a move from aluminium to plastic is being contemplated. Rarely do they involve themselves in component or MRO supply. Similarly, design engineers tend to be involved in buying components and materials but not normally MRO and plant and equipment. Second, the decision-making process tends to be slower and more complex as product type moves from:

MRO → Components → Materials → Plant and equipment

For MRO items, 'blanket contracts' rather than periodic purchase orders are increasingly being used. The supplier agrees to resupply the buyer on agreed price terms over a period of time. Stock is held by the seller and orders are automatically printed out by the buyer's computer when stock falls below a minimum level. This has the advantage to the supplying company of effectively blocking the efforts of the competitors' salesforces for long periods of time.

Classification of suppliers' offerings by product type gives the salesforce clues as to who is likely to be influential in the purchase decision. The sales task is then to confirm this in particular situations and attempt to reach those people involved. A salesperson selling MROs is likely to be wasting effort attempting to talk to design engineers, whereas attempts to reach operating management are likely to prove fruitful.

Importance of purchase to buying organisation

A purchase is likely to be perceived as important to the buying organisation when it involves large sums of money, when the cost of making the wrong decision, for example in lost production, is high and when there is considerable uncertainty about the outcome of alternative offerings. In such situations, many people at different organisational levels are likely to be involved in the decision and the process is likely to be long, with extensive search and analysis of information. Thus extensive marketing effort is likely to be required, but great opportunities present themselves to sales teams who work with buying organisations to convince them that their offering has the best payoff; this may involve acceptance trials (e.g. private diesel manufacturers supplying rail companies with prototypes for testing, engineering support and testimonials from other users). Additionally, guarantees of delivery dates and after-sales service may be necessary when buyer uncertainty regarding these factors is high.

3.6 Developments in Purchasing Practice

A number of trends have taken place within the purchasing function which have marketing implications for supplier firms. The advent of just-in-time purchasing and the increased tendency towards central purchasing, reverse marketing and leasing have all changed the nature of purchasing and altered the way in which suppliers compete.

Just-in-time purchasing

The **just-in-time (JIT)** purchasing concept aims to minimise stocks by organising a supply system which provides materials and components as they are required. As such, stockholding costs are significantly reduced or eliminated and thus profits are increased. Furthermore, since the holding of stocks is a hedge against machine breakdowns, faulty parts and human error, they may be seen as a cushion which acts as a disincentive to management to eliminate such inefficiencies.

A number of JIT practices are also associated with improved quality. Suppliers are evaluated on their ability to provide high-quality products. The effect of this is that suppliers may place more emphasis on product quality. Buyers are encouraged to specify only essential product characteristics, which means that suppliers have more discretion in product design and manufacturing methods. Also the supplier is expected to certify quality, which means that quality inspection at the buyer company is reduced and overall costs are minimised since quality control at source is more effective than further down the supply chain.

The total effects of JIT can be enormous. Purchasing inventory and inspection costs can be reduced, product design can be improved, delivery streamlined, production down-time reduced and the quality of the finished item enhanced.

However, the implementation of JIT requires integration into both purchasing and production operations. Since the system requires the delivery of the exact amount of materials or components to the production line as they are required, delivery schedules must be very reliable and suppliers must be prepared to make deliveries on a regular basis – perhaps even daily. Lead times for ordering must be short and the number of defects very low. An attraction for suppliers is that it is usual for long-term purchasing agreements to be drawn up. The marketing implications of the JIT concept are that to be competitive in many industrial markets (e.g. motor cars), suppliers must be able to meet the requirements of this fast-growing system.

An example of a company that employs JIT is the Nissan car assembly plant at Sunderland in the UK. The importance of JIT to its operations has meant that the number of component suppliers in the north-east of England has increased from 3 when Nissan arrived in 1986 to 27 in 1992. Nissan has adopted what they term 'synchronous supply' – parts are delivered only minutes before they are needed. For example, carpets are delivered by Sommer Allibert, a French supplier, from its nearby facility to the Nissan assembly line in sequence for fitting to the correct model. Only 42 minutes elapse between the carpet being ordered and fitted to the car. The stockholding of carpets for the Nissan Micra is now only ten minutes. Just-in-time practices do carry risks, however, if labour stability cannot be guaranteed. Renault discovered this to their cost when a strike at its engine and gearbox plant caused its entire French and Belgian car production lines to close in only ten days.

Centralised purchasing

Where several operating units within a company have common requirements and there is an opportunity to strengthen a negotiating position by bulk buying, **centralised purchasing** is an attractive option. Centralisation encourages purchasing specialists to concentrate their energies on a small group of products, thus enabling them to develop an extensive knowledge of cost factors and the operation of suppliers. The move from local to centralised buying has important marketing implications. Localised buying tends to focus on short-term cost and profit considerations whereas centralised purchasing places more emphasis on long-term supply relationships. Outside influences, for example, engineers, play a greater role in supplier choice in local purchasing organisations since less specialised buyers often lack the expertise and status to question the recommendations of technical people. The type of purchasing organisation can therefore give clues to suppliers regarding the important people in the decision-making unit and their respective power positions.

Reverse marketing

The traditional view of marketing is that supplier firms will actively seek the requirements of customers and attempt to meet those needs better than the competition. This model places the initiative with the supplier. Purchasers could assume a passive dimension, relying on their suppliers' sensitivity to their needs and technological capabilities to provide them with solutions to their problems. However, this trusting relationship is at odds with a new corporate purchasing situation that developed during the 1980s and is gaining momentum. Purchasing is taking on a more proactive, aggressive stance in acquiring the products and services needed to compete. This process whereby the buyer attempts to persuade the supplier to provide exactly what the organisation wants is called **reverse marketing**.[19] Figure 3.7 shows the difference between the traditional model and this new concept.

The essence of reverse marketing is that the purchaser takes the initiative in approaching new or existing suppliers and persuading them to meet their supply requirements. The implications of reverse marketing are that it may pose serious threats to uncooperative in-suppliers but major opportunities to responsive in-suppliers and out-suppliers. The growth of reverse marketing presents two key benefits to suppliers who are willing to listen to the buyer's proposition and carefully consider its merits. First, it provides the opportunity to develop a stronger and longer lasting relationship with the customer. Second, it could be a source of new product opportunities that may be developed to a broader customer base later on.

Figure 3.7 Reverse marketing

Leasing

A *lease* is a contract by which the owner of an asset (e.g. a car) grants the right to use the asset for a period of time to another party in exchange for payment of rent. The benefits to the customer are that a leasing arrangement avoids the need to pay the cash purchase price of the product or service, is a hedge against fast product obsolescence, may have tax advantages, avoids the problem of equipment disposal, and with certain types of leasing contracts avoids some maintenance costs. These benefits need to be weighed against the costs of leasing, which may be higher than outright buying.

There are two main types of lease: financial (or full payment) leases and operating leases (sometimes called rental agreements). A **financial lease** is a longer term arrangement that is fully amortised over the term of the contract. Lease payments, in total, usually exceed the purchase price of the item. The terms and conditions of the lease vary according to convention and competitive conditions. Sometimes the supplier will agree to pay maintenance costs over the leasing period. This is common when leasing photocopiers, for example. The lessee may also be given the option of buying the equipment at the end of the period. An **operating lease** is for a shorter period of time, is cancellable and not completely amortised. Operating lease rates are usually higher than financial lease rates since they are shorter term. When equipment is required intermittently this form of acquisition can be attractive since it avoids the need to let plant lie idle. Many types of equipment such as diggers, bulldozers and skips may be available on short-term hire as may storage facilities.

Leasing may be advantageous to suppliers because it provides customer benefits that may differentiate product and service offerings. As such it may attract customers who otherwise may find the product unaffordable or uneconomic. The importance of leasing in such industries as cars, photocopying and data processing has led an increasing number of companies to employ leasing consultants to work with customers on leasing arrangements and benefits. A crucial marketing decision is the setting of leasing rates, which should be set with the following in mind:

(a) the desired relative attractiveness of leasing versus buying (the supplier may wish to promote/discourage buying compared with leasing)

(b) the net present value of lease payments versus outright purchase

(c) the tax advantages of leasing versus buying to the customer

(d) the rates being charged by competition

(e) the perceived advantages of spreading payments to customers

(f) any other perceived customer benefits, e.g. maintenance and insurance costs being assumed by the supplier

3.7   Relationship Management

The discussion of reverse marketing gave examples of buyers adopting a proactive stance in their dealings with suppliers and introduced the importance of buyer–seller relationships in marketing between organisations. The Industrial Marketing and Purchasing Group[20] developed the **interaction approach** to explain the complexity of relationship management. This approach views these relationships as taking place between two active parties. Thus reverse marketing is one manifestation of the interaction perspective. Both parties may be involved in adaptations to their own process or product technologies to accommodate each other, and changes in the activities of one party are unlikely without consideration of, or consulation with, the other party. In such circumstances a key objective of industrial markets will be to manage customer relationships. Not only should formal organisational arrangements such as the use of distributors, salespeople and sales subsidiaries be considered, but also the informal network consisting of the personal contacts and relationships between supplier and customer staff. Marks & Spencer's senior directors meet the boards of each of its major suppliers twice a year for frank discussions. When Marks & Spencer personnel visit a supplier, it is referred to as a 'royal visit'. Factories may be repainted, new uniforms issued and machinery cleaned. This reflects the exacting standards that the company demands from its suppliers and the power it wields in its relationship with them.

The reality of organisational marketing is that many suppliers and buying organisations have been conducting business between themselves for many years. For example, Marks & Spencer has trading relationships with suppliers that stretch back almost 100 years. Such long-term relationships can have significant advantages to both buyer and seller. Risk is reduced for buyers since they get to know people in the supplier organisation and know who to contact when problems arise. Communication is thus improved and joint problem-solving and design management can take place. Sellers gain through closer knowledge of buyer requirements, and by gaining the trust of the buyer an effective barrier to entry for competing firms may be established. New product development can benefit from such close relationships. The development of machine-washable lambswool fabrics and easy-to-iron cotton shirts came about because of Marks & Spencer's close relationships with UK manufacturers. Sellers can also gain through information which buyers provide. Buyers often gather and pass on information about market developments that is relevant to the seller's business.[21]

Close relationships in organisational markets are inevitable as changing technology, shorter product life-cycles and increased foreign competition place marketing and purchasing departments in key strategic roles. Buyers are increasingly treating trusted suppliers as **strategic partners**, sharing information and drawing on their expertise when developing cost-efficient, quality-based new products. Such partnerships can form a strong barrier to entry for competitors wishing to do business with a buying organisation. For example, when an outside supplier's offer involves lower costs, higher quality, or even more advanced technology, buying organisations such as Honda, Toyota and Daimler Chrysler will work with their present strategic partners, giving them the opportunity to match or exceed the offer within a given time frame, which can be as long as 18–24 months.[22] The marketing implication is that successful organisational marketing is more than the traditional manipulation of the four Ps – product, place, promotion and price. Its foundation rests upon the skilful handling of customer relationships. This had led some companies to appoint customer relationship managers to oversee the partnership and act in a communicational and co-ordinated role to ensure customer satisfaction. Still more companies have reorganised their salesforces to reflect the importance of managing key customer relationships effectively. This process is called 'key' or major account management. It should be noted, however, that strategic partnerships and key account management may not be suitable for all companies. For example, small companies may not be able to afford the resources needed to make such processes work. [23]

3.8 Conclusions

Understanding buyer behaviour has important implications for salespeople and sales management. Recognition that buyers purchase products in order to overcome problems and satisfy needs implies that an effective sales approach will involve the discovery of these needs on the part of the salesperson. Only then can s/he sell the offering from the range of products marketed by the company which best meets these needs.

When the decision-making unit is complex, as in many organisational buying situations, the salesperson must attempt to identify and reach key members of the DMU in order to persuade them of the product's benefits. S/he must also realise that different members may use different criteria to evaluate the product and thus may need to modify his or her sales presentation accordingly.

The next chapter is concerned with the development of sales strategies which reflect the buyer behaviour patterns of the marketplace.

References

1 Corey, E.R. (1991) *Industrial Marketing: Cases and Concepts*, 4th edn, Prentice-Hall, Englewood Cliffs, NJ.

2 Blackwell, R.D., Miniard, P.W. and Engel, J.F. (2003) *Consumer Behaviour*, Orlando FL: Dryden.

3 Blackwell, R.D., Miniard, P.W. and Engel, J.F. (2003) *Consumer Behaviour*, Orlando FL: Dryden.

4 Festinger, L. (1957) *A Theory of Cognitive Dissonance*, Row & Peterson, New York.

5 Howard, J.A. and Sheth, J.N. (1969) *The Theory of Buyer Behaviour*, Wiley, New York.

6 Ackoff, R.L. and Emsott, J.R. (1975) 'Advertising at Anheuser-Busch, Inc.', *Sloan Management Review*, Spring, pp. 1–15.

7 Buzzotta, V.R., Lefton, R.E. and Sherberg, M. (1982) *Effective Selling Through Psychology: Dimensional Sales and Sales Management*, Wiley, New York.

8 Buzzotta, V.R., Lefton, R.E. and Sherberg, M. (1982) *Effective Selling Through Psychology: Dimensional Sales and Sales Management*, Wiley, New York.

9 Decormier, R. and Jobber, D. (1993) 'The counsellor selling method: concepts, constructs and effectiveness', *Journal of Personal Selling and Sales Management*, 13(4), pp. 39–60.

10 Baker, K., Germingham, J. and MacDonald, C. (1979) 'The utility to market research of the classification of residential neighbourhoods', *Market Research Society Conference*, Brighton: March, pp. 206–17.

11 Doyle, P. and Hutchinson, J. (1973) 'Individual differences in family decision-making', *Journal of the Market Research Society*, 15, p. 4.

12 Fisher, L. (1976) *Industrial Marketing*, 2nd edn, Business Books, London.

13 Bonoma, T.V. (1982) 'Major sales: who really does the buying', *Harvard Business Review*, May–June, pp. 111–19.

14 Webster, F.E. (1995) *Industrial Marketing Strategy*, Roland, New York.

15 Cline, C.E. and Shapiro, B.P. (1978) *Cumberland Metal Industries (A)*, case study, Harvard Business School.

16 Robinson, P.J., Faris, C.W. and Wind, Y. (1967) *Industrial Buying and Creative Marketing*, Allyn & Bacon and the Marketing Science Institute, New York.

17 Cardozo, R.N. (1980) 'Situational segmentation of industrial markets', *European Journal of Marketing*, 14, pp. 5–6.

18 Robinson, P.J., Faris, C.W. and Wind, Y. (1967) *Industrial Buying and Creative Marketing*, Allyn & Bacon and the Marketing Science Institute, New York.

19 Blenkhorn, D. and Banting, P.M. (1991) 'How reverse marketing changes buyer-seller relationships', *Industrial Marketing Management*, 20, pp. 185–91.

20 Turnbull, P. and Cunningham, M. (1981) *International Marketing and Purchasing*, Macmillan, London.

21 Walter, A., Ritter, T. and Gemünden, H.G. (2001) 'Value creation in buyer–seller relationships', *Industrial Marketing Management*, 30, pp. 365–77.

22 Henke, Jr, J.W. (2000) 'Strategic selling in the age of modules and systems', *Industrial Marketing Management*, 29, pp. 271–84.

23 Sharland, A. (2001) 'The negotiation process as a predictor of relationship outcomes in international buyer-seller arrangements', *Industrial Marketing Management*, 30, pp. 551–9.

Practical Exercise

The lost computer sale

Jim Appleton, managing director of Industrial Cleaning Services, had decided that a personal computer could help solve his cash flow problems. What he wanted was a machine which would store his receipts and outgoings so that at a touch of a button he could see the cash flow at any point in time. A year ago he got into serious cash flow difficulties simply because he didn't realise that, for various reasons, his short-term outflow greatly exceeded his receipts.

He decided to visit a newly opened personal computer outlet in town on Saturday afternoon. His wife, Mary, was with him. They approached a salesperson seated behind a desk.

Jim:	Good afternoon. I'm interested in buying a personal computer for my business. Can you help me?
Salesperson:	Yes, indeed, sir. This is the fastest growing network of personal computer centres in the country. I have to see a colleague for a moment but I shall be back in a few minutes. Would you like to have a look at this brochure and at the models we have in the showroom? [*Salesperson gives them the brochures, and leaves them in the showroom.*]
Mary:	I don't understand computers. Why are some bigger than others?
Jim:	I don't know. What baffles me are all these buttons you have to press. I wonder if you have to do a typing course to use one? [*Jim and Mary look round the showroom asking each other questions and getting a little confused. The salesperson arrives after five minutes.*]
Salesperson:	Sorry to take so long but at least it's given you a chance to see what we have in stock. You tell me you want a computer for work. I think I have just the one for you. [*Salesperson takes Jim and Mary to a model.*] This could be just up your street. Not only will this model act as a word processor, it will do your accounts, financial plans and stock control as well. It has full graphic facilities so that you can see trend lines on the screen at the touch of the button. You can also send emails and access the Internet.
Mary:	It looks very expensive. How much will it cost?
Salesperson:	A lot less than you think. This one costs £1,000, which is quite cheap.
Mary:	I've seen advertisements in newspapers for computers which are a lot less expensive.
Salesperson:	Yes, but do they have an Intel 1.8 MHz Pentium IV processor with 256 megabytes of SDRAM and a 20 Gb hard drive? And do they contain ATI's best selling Radeon graphics card and the latest CD/DVD drive?
Mary:	I don't know, but they looked quite good to me.
Jim:	It looks very complicated to use.
Salesperson:	No more complicated than any of the other models. The computer comes with a full set of instructions. My 12-year-old son could operate it.
Jim:	What's this button for?
Salesperson:	That moves the cursor. It allows you to delete or amend any character you wish.

Jim: I see.

Salesperson: I've left the best till last. Included in the price are three software pro-
                grams which allow the machine to be used for spreadsheet analysis,
                stock control and word processing. I'm sure your business will benefit
                from this computer.

Jim: My business is very small. I only employ five people. I'm not sure it's
                ready for a computer yet. Still, thank you for your time.

Discussion Questions

1 What choice criteria did Jim and Mary use when deciding whether to buy a
   computer and which model to buy?

2 Did the salesperson understand the motives behind the purchase? If not, why
   not? Did s/he make any other mistakes?

3 Imagine that you were the salesperson. How would you have conducted the
   sales interview?

Examination Questions

1 Compare and contrast the ways in which consumers and organisations buy
   products and services.

2 Of what practical importance is the study of organisational buyer behaviour to
   the personal selling function?

4 Sales Settings

Objectives

After studying this chapter, you should be able to:

1 Understand the forces impacting selling and sales management
2 Appreciate why channels are structured in different ways
3 Evaluate push and pull promotional strategies and tactics
4 Understand the unique problems and forces that surround organisational and service sales settings
5 Evaluate the usefulness and application of exhibitions as a promotional medium
6 Understand the nature and role of public relations as a selling tool

Key Concepts

- channels of distribution
- environmental and managerial forces
- exhibitions
- franchising/vertical marketing system (VMS)
- physical distribution management (PDM)
- public relations
- 'pull' techniques

- 'push' techniques
- sales channels
- sales promotions
- services
- strategic customer management
- supply chain integration (SCI)
- trade marketing
- unique sales proposition (USP)

In this chapter we analyse the major forces that affect selling and sales management. We then consider specific sales settings such as sales channels, industrial/commercial/public authority, retail and services selling. Related activities that support selling activities, namely sales promotions, exhibitions and public relations, are also examined.

Environmental and Managerial Forces Impacting Sales

A number of major environmental (behavioural and technological) and managerial forces impact on how selling and sales management are and will be carried out.[1,2] These are outlined in Table 4.1.

Behavioural forces

As customers adjust to a changing environment, so sales has to adapt to a variety of influences:

(a) rising consumer and organisational buyer expectations

Table 4.1 Forces affecting selling and sales management

Behavioural forces
Rising customer expectations and being concerned with fulfilling more than basic needs More professionally minded organisational buyers Customer avoidance of buyer–seller negotiations Expanding power of major buyers Globalisation of markets Fragmentation of markets

Technological forces
Sales force automation • laptop computers and more sophisticated software • electronic data interchange • desktop videoconferencing • extranet Virtual sales offices Widespread adoption of credit cards as charging platforms and use of such facilities as opportunities for creation of databases Electronic sales channels • internet • television home shopping

Managerial forces
Direct marketing • direct mail • telemarketing Blending of sales and marketing • intranet Qualifications for salespeople and sales managers

Source: Adapted and updated from Anderson, R.E. (1996) 'Personal selling and sales management in the new millennium', *Journal of Personal Selling and Sales Management*, 16(4), pp. 17–52.

(b) customer avoidance of buyer–seller negotiations

(c) expanding power of major buyers

(d) globalisation of markets

(e) fragmentation of markets

Rising consumer/organisational buyer expectations and fulfilment of higher order needs

As consumers experience higher standards of product quality and service, so their expectations are fuelled to expect even higher levels in the future. This process may be hastened by experiences abroad, and new entrants to industries (possibly from abroad) that set new standards of excellence. The chief executive of customer satisfaction research firm J.D. Power explained: 'What makes customer satisfaction so difficult to achieve is that you constantly raise the bar and extend the finish line. You never stop. As your customers get better treatment, they demand better treatment.' The implication for salespeople is that they must accept that both consumer and organisational buyer expectations for product quality, customer service and value will continue to rise. They must respond to this challenge by advocating and implementing continuous improvements in quality standards. The same is of course true in respect of organisational buyers, especially in view of trends highlighted in Chapter 7.

Customer avoidance of buyer–seller negotiations

Studies have shown that the purchase of a car is the most anxiety-provoking and least satisfying experience in retail buying.[3] Some car salespeople are trained in the art of negotiation supported by high pressure sales tactics. Consequently, customers have taken to viewing the purchase as an ordeal to be tolerated rather than a pleasurable occasion to be savoured. In response, some car companies have moved to a fixed price, no pressure and full book value for the trade-in approach. This was used for the successful launch of the Saturn by General Motors in the USA and is the philosophy of Daewoo cars in the UK.

Expanding power of major buyers

The growing dominance of major players in many sectors (notably retailing) is having a profound influence on selling and sales management. Their enormous purchasing power means that they are able to demand and get special services, including special customer status (key account management), just-in-time inventory control, category management and joint funding of promotions. Future success for salespeople will be dependent on their capabilities to respond to increasing demands of major customers.

Globalisation of markets

As domestic markets saturate, companies are expanding abroad to achieve sales and profit growth. Large companies such as Coca-Cola, Colgate-Palmolive and Avon

Products now earn the largest proportion of their revenues in foreign markets. The global challenge includes a correct balance between expatriate and host country sales personnel, adapting to different cultures, lifestyles and languages, competing against world-class brands and building global relationships with customers based in many countries. For example, 3M has a variety of global strategic accounts from industrial high-tech (e.g. Motorola, Hewlett-Packard, IBM, Texas Instruments) to original equipment manufacturers in electronics, appliances, automotive, electrical, aerospace, furniture, consumer products and health care.[4] A major challenge for such transnational corporations is the co-ordination of global sales teams that sell to companies like Nortel, Samsung, Siemens or P&G, where the customer may be located in over 20 countries and require special terms of sale, technical support, pricing and customisation of products. This complexity means that strategic account managers require both enhanced teamwork and co-ordination skills to ensure that customers receive top quality service.

Fragmentation of markets

Driven by differences in income levels, lifestyles, personalities, experiences and race, markets are fragmenting to form market segments. This means that markets are likely to become smaller with an increasing range of brands marketed to cater for diverse needs (both functional and psychological) of customers. Marketing and sales managers need to be adept at identifying changes in consumer tastes and developing strategies that satisfy an increasingly varied and multicultural society.

Technological forces

The importance of technological forces on selling and sales management is reflected in the attention given to this topic in Chapter 12. Three major forces are at play:

* salesforce automation

* virtual sales offices

* electronic sales channels

Salesforce automation includes laptop and palmtop computers, mobile telephones, fax, email and more advanced sales software which aid such tasks as journey and account planning, and recruitment, selection and evaluation of sales personnel. In addition, electronic data interchange (EDI) provides computer links between manufacturers and resellers (retailers, wholesalers and distributors), allowing direct exchange of information. For example, purchase orders, invoices, price quotations, delivery dates, reports and promotional information can be exchanged. Technological innovations have made possible desktop videoconferencing, enabling sales meetings, training and customer interaction to take place without the need for people to leave their offices.

Improved technology has encouraged the creation of virtual offices, allowing sales personnel to keep in contact with head office, customers and co-workers. The virtual office can be home or even a car. This means cost and time savings and enhanced job satisfaction for salespeople who are spared time waiting in traffic that is a feature of the job.

The fastest growing electronic sales channel is undoubtedly the internet, which will be discussed in Chapter 12. Its impact is not simply to reduce the size of salesforces but to change the focus of the sales team. For example, the Dell salesforce are encouraged to convert customers to buy using the internet. The objective is to free expensive salesperson time from transactional selling (which Dell's website does better, faster and cheaper) so that more time can be devoted to closing big new orders.[5]

However, another emerging channel is worthy of mention as it will reduce the need for field salesforces. This is television home shopping, which is popular in the USA. Viewers watch cable television presenters promote anything from jewellery to consumer electronics and order by telephone. In effect, the presenter is the salesperson.

Managerial forces

Managers can respond to the changes in the environment by developing new strategies and tactics to enhance sales effectiveness, including:

(a) employing direct marketing techniques

(b) improving co-operation between sales and marketing

(c) encouraging salespeople to attend training programmes and gain professional qualifications

The increased role of direct marketing, including direct mail and telemarketing, will be discussed in Chapter 12. However, an emerging change is the use of computer stations, especially in US retail outlets, to replace traditional salespeople. In Europe the serious use of computer stations began in car showrooms with Daewoo's employment of kiosks where customers gather product and price information. The process has moved further in the USA where several Ford dealerships have installed computer stations that fully replace salespeople. Customers can compare features of competitive models, calculate running costs, compute monthly payments, and use the computer to write up the order and transmit this to the factory, without the intervention of a salesperson.

The development of effective relationships between sales and marketing is recognised, but in practice, blending the two functions into an effective whole is sometimes hampered by poor communication. The establishment of intranets that link employees, suppliers and customers through their PCs can improve links and improve information exchange. Intranets are used for such functions as email, team projects and desktop publishing. Their adoption can enhance the effectiveness of the field salesforce that requires fast access to rapidly changing information such as product specifications, competitor news and price updates, and allows the sharing of information between sales and marketing.

The result of these forces is to change the role and operation of the traditional sales organisation from a focus on order-taking and order-making to **strategic customer management**.[6] The challenge is to reposition sales as a core element of a firm's competitiveness, where the sales organisation is closely integrated into marketing strategy and planning.[7] This process places the customer at the centre of the company's focus with the sales organisation charged with taking a strategic view of designing and implementing superior customer relationships.[8] This requires sales management to work towards the total integration of how customer relationships are designed, established, managed and sustained. For example, companies like Cisco have developed sales strategies that use personal selling when the purchase is important, complicated and the decision uncertain – usually the first sale to a customer or a new application – leaving subsequent purchases to be made via the internet.[9]

Strategic customer management requires three activities to be performed:[10]

- Intelligence: enhancing customer knowledge to add value to customer relationships.

    A key finding in an investigation into corporate purchasers' views of world class sales organisations is that their salespeople show a deep understanding of the customer's business, so that they can identify needs and opportunities ahead of the customer.[11] The idea is that sellers can gain competitive advantage by identifying new opportunities in the end-user markets of their customers. This requires the seller to move from a simple knowledge of the customer's organisation to understanding the customer's markets. For example, when Johnson Controls in the USA won the business for the seats and electronic controls in Ford's F-series trucks, it was not by discussing seats and switches with Ford. Johnson's competitive advantage was a better understanding of truck driver's seating and control preferences than Ford.

- Interfaces: refocusing salesforce efforts into the management and exploitation of critical interfaces that affect customer value (for example, with customer relationship management and key account management).

    Strategic customer management requires that the traditional salesperson and sales management processes integrate with the new challenges of doing business that have emerged through developments in technology. For example, the US firm Western and Southern Financial Group has added to its field salesforce of 2,200 representatives, call centre and online sales operations. The challenges include developing a new collaborative sales representative role, working with and through the new channels, relying on building salesperson trust to encourage information sharing and a seamless customer relationship across all the channels.[12] The aim is to produce an effective customer relationship management system that allows customer choice of channel while creating an efficient system of delivering customer value.

- Integration: the process of welding all the company's activities and processes that affect customer value into a single, integrated and sustained point of value delivery to customers.

    Similar to the previous activity but broader in scope is the need for cross-functional and cross-border integration to deliver superior customer value. The lack of such co-ordination has proven harmful to customer relations. For example, the lack of integration between sales and supply chain management caused problems for one company when the sales director realised that a major customer was ordering irregularly as and when stock control indicated the need for more supplies. He recognised that his stock cover could be reduced if the customer could be persuaded to adopt continuous replenishment. Two days after the customer agreed to move to the new system, the sales director received a telephone call from the distraught customer complaining that he was almost out of stock and on the point of taking his business elsewhere. The sales director ran to the distribution depot to identify the problem. The answer was simple: the distribution system placed highest priority on large orders. Unfortunately the change to continuous replenishment meant that the customer was placing many small orders which received lowest priority and were often not fulfilled by the end of the day.

Another example shows the dramatic consequences of a lack of integration between sales and operations.[13] In a major clothing company, the sales manager was instructed to increase sales targets irrespective of production capacity. Encouraged by his sales manager, a salesperson secured a major order from a national retailer. The result was that production could not deliver, the customer was furious, the salesperson was demotivated, and the sales manager was acutely embarrassed.

Having examined the major forces impacting the sales function, we will now consider the specific settings where selling takes place, and some of the activities, such as sales promotions and exhibitions, that support selling activities.

4.2   Sales Channels

Distribution channels involve two separate, yet closely connected, activities: logistics, or **physical distribution management (PDM)**, and **channels of distribution**. Historically, distribution was simple, with producers selling to their immediate neighbours, who often collected goods themselves. Modern-day manufacturing, more cosmopolitan consumers, better transportation and communications, and business specialisation has meant that channel decisions are now quite complex. Distribution costs have risen relative to production. However, as a result of automation and computerisation, production costs as a percentage of total cost are now considerably lower than they were only a few years ago. Each of the two elements of distribution is now considered.

Logistics or physical distribution management (PDM)

The terms *logistics* and *PDM* are interchangeable, although some writers infer that logistics is more concerned with strategic issues whereas PDM relates to tactics. Basically, logistics means the effective and economic planning, implementing and controlling the physical flow of materials in their unprocessed state through to finished goods from the point of origin to delivery to the end consumer. Logistics conventionally starts with customers and works back towards the original source of supply. The term '**supply chain ingegration**' **(SCI)** is sometimes used to describe its effective co-ordination, and this is discussed in detail in Chapter 10, 'Relationship selling'.

The logistics mix describes the functional elements involved in this process and each of these is now considered:

1 *Order processing*. This first stage calls for close liaison with the customer and a well-designed system should have simple administrative procedures and be speedy and effective.

2 *Materials handling.* This is usually a function of the product in terms of physical chacteristics like weight, bulk related to value and perishability and this will determine how it is stored and transported. Here, a balance between levels of service that the company provides (e.g. ex-stock delivery as opposed to, say, one month) and costs is a decisive factor.

3 *Warehousing.* The location of depots and warehouses relative to end customers is very important in some industries (e.g. agricultural machinery where spare parts must be immediately available during the harvesting period). Warehouses can carry buffer stock and help to even out peaks and troughs in production. Again, this process requires a balance between service levels and costs.

4 *Inventory control.* With the widespread adoption of just-in-time, or lean, manufacturing, this has become a critical issue. It is now customary to think of stockholding in terms of hours rather than days or weeks. An accounting rule of thumb suggests that the physical act of stockholding can add 25 per cent to the costs of inventory without adding to its value, so the advantages of lean manufacturing are understandable.

5 *Transportation.* This involves the physical delivery of goods to customers, and the organisation of materials from suppliers to be used in the production process. It is, of course, a critical factor in companies that operate a lean manufacturing system and this usually means that it is more costly because of smaller batch and load sizes, often resulting in partial loads.

6 *Packaging.* Packaging design for the container that is displayed on the shelf of a supermarket is normally a marketing communications issue, but in terms of outer containers and appropriate packaging for shipping via various modes of transport, this falls under the logistics mix classification

There are two philosophical standpoints in relation to logistics. One considers it as a 'systems concept' whereby management regards logistics as a system of interrelated components. The other views it as a total cost approach where management attempts to minimise the cost of using the components taken as a whole.

Channels of distribution

Management should constantly reappraise channels of distribution to make cost savings. Marketing channels are determined by company policy and this determines how the salesforce should be organised.

A **sales channel** is the route that goods take through the selling process from supplier to customer. Sometimes the channel is direct, especially where goods sold are incorporated into a manufacturing process. Final goods might then be sold through a different channel. A product example is fuel injection systems that are sold to automobile manufacturers; automobiles are then sold to car distributors and the car distributors sell to end consumers. When we consider a product from the raw material stage to the end product, many different sales channels can be involved at different stages of manufacturing. A sales channel can also be indirect, whereby a manufacturer sells to a wholesaler or agent, who sells in smaller lots to other customers. This is known as 'breaking bulk'.

Research has shown that channel management is a key role of the sales manager.[14] This is a major responsibility since for most manufacturers success or failure is partially determined by how efficiently and effectively their products are sold through their marketing channel members (e.g. agents, wholesalers, distributors and retailers). The implication is that sales managers require training in how to deal with issues related to channel management.[15]

Reedform of Wokingham

Good supply chain management is seen as both a key driver of business and one of the toughest problems for UK managers. Procurement is an often neglected part of business. A survey of chief executives and finance directors by the Chartered Institute of Purchasing & Supply found that 48 per cent could not recall their annual expenditure on goods and services, yet had no problem listing turnover, sales, profits and salary costs. This was odd, considering that most companies spend more on goods and services than on wages.

The starting point for managers should be in understanding how goods flow through the firm. This means mapping out the connections from suppliers to the company and on to customers, then charting the flow of information: orders, schedules, shipping notes, invoices, and so on. With a clearer picture of the supply chain, a company can work out a strategy that fits an overall scheme for the enterprise.

Reedform realised that its traditional business of printing forms was dying so it realigned its strategy and became a print 'broker'. It now commissions orders – everything from brochures to golf umbrellas – from printers. It then stores finished products for clients (who are short of space and glad to outsource their storage and stock management) and despatches them to their clients' customers as required. This new strategy meant building relationships with print suppliers and finding ways to add value for their clients by knowing what they needed and offering flexible arrangements. This involved investment in IT, but improvements were possible only because managers had formed a clear picture of what they wanted for the business.

Source: Adapted from 'Going with the flow', *Management Today* Supplement, May 2002.

Selecting/reappraising sales channels

When selecting or reappraising channels, the company must take into consideration:

- the market
- channel costs
- the product
- profit potential

- channel structure

- product life-cycle

- non-marketing factors

The market

This must be analysed to ensure that as many potential consumers as possible will have an opportunity to purchase the product or service. Channel compatibility with similar products in the marketplace is important. Consumers tend to be conservative and any move from the accepted norm can be viewed with suspicion. Unless there are sound reasons for so doing, it does not make sense to go outside the established channel. For instance, a canned food producer would not normally consider selling through mail order unless the company was providing a very specialist type of food or perhaps providing it as part of a hamper pack. Instead, the company would use traditional distribution outlets like food multiples and cash and carry.

Channel costs

Generally, short channels are the costliest. A company selling direct may achieve large market coverage, but in addition to increased investment in the salesforce, the firm also incurs greater transportation and warehousing costs. This is balanced against the fact that there will be a greater profit margin, by virtue of the fact that distributive intermediaries are obviated and their margins will not have to be met. In addition to such financial criteria, short channels have an advantage of being nearer to end-users, which means the company is in a better position to anticipate and meet their needs.

There has been a trend in recent years for manufacturers to shorten their channels to control more effectively distribution of their products, particularly where advertising has been used to pre-sell the goods to consumers.

The product

Normally, low-cost, low-technology items are more suited to longer channels. More complex items, often requiring much after-sales service, tend to be sold through short channels. This is why most industrial products are sold direct from the producer to user. The width of the product line is important, in that a wide product line may make it worthwhile for the manufacturer to market direct because the salesperson has a larger product portfolio with which to interest the customer that makes for more profit-earning potential.

A narrow product line is more suited to a longer channel because along the distribution chain it can be combined with complementary products of other manufacturers, resulting in a wider range of items with which to interest the customer. In this case, distributive intermediaries and not manufacturers are performing the final selling function. An example here is a manufacturer of bathroom fittings who sells through builders' merchants. Builders' merchants then sell these fittings to builders alongside other materials they require.

Profit potential

There comes a point when the costs of obtaining more sales through a channel outweigh revenue and profits to be gained from increased sales. For instance, a manufacturer of an exclusive perfume would not distribute through supermarkets or
advertise during peak-time television viewing. If the company did, then sales would
no doubt increase, but costs of achieving those sales would make it unprofitable. It
is an accounting problem and a balance must be struck between channel expense,
profit and gross margins.

A manufacturer using short channels is more likely to have high gross margins,
but equally higher channel expenses. A manufacturer using longer channels will
have relatively lower gross margins, coupled with lower channel expenses.

Channel structure

To some extent a manufacturer's choice of distributive intermediaries is governed by
the members in that channel. If members of the channel are strong (by virtue of,
say, their size), then it will be difficult for a manufacturer to go outside the established channel.

In some cases it may be difficult to gain entry to the channel unless the product
is differentiated by way of uniqueness or lower price than those products already
established in the channel. An example is the potential difficulty that a new detergent manufacturer would have in attempting to sell products through larger supermarkets. The manufacturer would have to convince members of the channel that
the detergent was in some way better than those already on the market, or offer
advantageous prices and terms. In addition, detergent is mainly marketed using a
'**pull**' strategy that relies on consumer advertising to create brand loyalty and pre-
sell the product to end customers. A new manufacturer would have to spend a lot
on mass advertising to create brand loyalty for the product, or attempt to '**push**' the
product through the channel by providing trade incentives, with probably a lower
end price than competitive products coupled with larger profit margins for retailers.
It can be seen that it would be a daunting task for a new detergent manufacturer to
enter the market in a big way without large cash resources at its disposal.

Product life-cycle

Consideration must be given to how far the product is along the product life-cycle.
A new concept or product just entering the life-cycle might need intensive distribution to start with to launch it on the market. As it becomes established it may be
that after-sales service criteria become important, leading to a move to selective distribution, with only those dealers that are able to offer the necessary standard of
after-sales service being allowed to sell the product. Conversely, sales are low
initially in keeping with diffusion theory discussed in Chapter 1. It would then be
the case that only a select few distributors are needed in the early stages of the life-
cycle.

In the case of televisions the wheel has turned full circle, from intensive distribution to selective distribution (for reasons just mentioned) and back to intensive
distribution. This is because servicing of televisions is now relatively simple, in that
televisions are constructed similarly and standard units are replaced when repairs

are needed. A television repairer no longer needs to be a specialist in one particular model. Television manufacturers realise that with comparative parity between models, consumers are less likely to be drawn towards a particular brand because of its supposed technical superiority or standard of after-sales service. The most crucial factor now is ensuring the customer is able to see the brand and compare it with competitors' brands. Thus, maximum exposure at point of sale is a manufacturer's distribution objective.

Non-marketing factors

Non-marketing factors relate to the amount of finance available. In the case of an innovative product, it could be that the firm is unable to exploit this to its fullest advantage because of financial constraints. The firm may have to distribute through a middleman because it cannot afford to employ a field salesforce. Conversely, the firm may use a non-conventional channel such as mail order, which requires minimal investment in salespeople, although the physical characteristics of the product might not make it suitable for mail order.

Non-marketing factors often apply when selling internationally, as many companies view export orders as a supplement to home trade and are prepared to offer an agency to anybody who is likely to obtain orders, irrespective of their commercial standing. A fuller discussion of international aspects is in Chapter 5, but it should be noted that there are cases of companies that entered into export agency agreements when they were small and exporting was relatively unimportant. As the companies grew they came to regard exporting as essential, but it proved difficult and expensive to unwind hastily-entered-into agency agreements. Such companies in many cases had to persevere with the original arrangements, often against long-term best interests.

Characteristics of sales channels

Marketing channels are one of the more stable elements in the marketing mix. A channel is costly and complex to change, unlike price, which is relatively easy to manipulate. For instance, a switch from selective to intensive distribution is a policy decision that will have a direct effect upon salesforce numbers, and even upon the type of selling methods to be used.

The main problem that companies have to face is in choosing the most appropriate channel. From the viewpoint of sales management this includes the type of sales outlet that must be serviced. Basically, a manufacturer has the choice of one of four types of distribution:

1 *Direct*. The manufacturer does not use a middleman and sells and delivers direct to the end customer.

2 *Selective*. The manufacturer sells through a limited number of middlemen who are chosen because of special abilities or facilities to enable the product to be better marketed.

3 *Intensive*. Maximum exposure at the point of sale is needed and the manufacturer sells through as many outlets as possible. Servicing and after-sales

aspects are less important. Examples are cigarettes, breakfast cereals and detergents.

4 *Exclusive.* The manufacturer sells to a restricted number of dealers. An example is the car industry where distributors must provide levels of stockholding, after-sales service, etc., deemed appropriate by manufacturers as their reputations depend ultimately upon service back-up given by distributors.

4.3   Industrial/Commercial/Public Authority Selling

These categories are grouped together as the sales approach is similar and behavioural patterns exhibited by each conform to organisational behaviour (discussed in Chapter 3). A number of characteristics in these types of market distinguish them from consumer markets.

Fewer customers

Institutions and businesses purchase goods either for use in their own organisations or for use in the manufacture of other goods. There are few potential purchasers, each making high-value purchases.

Concentrated markets

Industrial markets are often highly concentrated, an example being the UK textile industry which is centred in Lancashire and Yorkshire. An industrial salesperson who sells into one industry may deal with only a few customers in a restricted geographical area.

Complex purchasing decisions

Buying decisions often involve a large number of people, particularly in the case of a public authority where a purchasing committee may be involved in a major purchase.

Many industrial buying decisions involve more than the buyer; in some cases the technical specifier, production personnel and finance personnel are involved and this is where the decision-making unit (as discussed in Chapter 3) can be seen in practice. This can lengthen negotiation and decision-making processes. Salespeople have to work and communicate with people in a variety of positions and tailor their selling approaches to satisfy individual needs. For example, specifiers need to be convinced of the technical merits of the product, production people want to be assured of guaranteed delivery and buyers will be looking for value for money.

For technically complicated products, selling is sometimes performed by a sales team, with each member working with their opposite number in the buying team, e.g. a sales engineer works with engineers in the buying company.

Long-term relationships

A life insurance policy salesperson might make a sale and never meet the customer again. The nature of selling in industrial, commercial and public authority settings is that long-term relationships are established and both parties become dependent upon each other, one for reliable supplies and the other for regular custom.

There is a tendency to build up strong personal relationships over a long time and high-pressure sales techniques could be counter-productive. A more considered approach involving salespeople identifying needs of individual customers and selling the benefits of the product to satisfy those needs is more likely to be successful. The ability of salespeople to deal with complaints and provide a reliable after-sales service is important. It is suggested that the effective salesperson must understand how to develop and sustain relationships with key customer groups, along the lines of relationship selling (Chapter 10).

Reciprocal trading

This is an arrangement whereby company A purchases certain commodities manufactured by company B and vice versa. Such arrangements tend to be made at senior management level and are often entered into when there is a financial link between the companies, such as those within the same group (referred to as intergroup trading) or between companies whose directors simply want to formalise an arrangement to purchase as much of each other's products as possible.

Such arrangements can be frustrating for salespeople and buyers alike, as they deter free competition. Buyers do not like to be told where they must purchase from, just as salespeople do not like having a large part of a potential market permanently excluded because of a reciprocal trading arrangement.

Types of production

This relates mainly to industrial sales. The type of production operated by the firm to whom the salesperson is selling can determine the type of selling approach to be used. There are a number of different types of production:

1 *Job (or unit or project) production.* An item is produced or constructed to individual customer requirements. It is difficult to forecast demand in such circumstances. Examples are ships, tailormade suits and hospital construction.

2 *Batch production.* A number of products or components are made at the same time, but not on a continuous basis. As with job production, batches are normally made to individual customer requirements, but sometimes batches are produced in anticipation of orders. Product examples are books, furniture and clothes.

3 *Flow (or mass or line) production.* This is continuous production of identical or similar products that are made in anticipation of sales. Examples are motor cars, video recorders and washing machines.

4 *Process (or continuous) production.* The production unit has raw materials coming into the manufacturing process and a finished product emerging at the end. Examples are chemicals, brewing and plastic processes.

Salespeople selling in a combination of such settings have to adopt a different approach for each. With flow production the salesperson has to anticipate model changes to ensure the firm is invited to quote at the outset, and follow up the quotation in the expectation of securing an order which will be fulfilled over the life of the product. If the salesperson is unsuccessful at this stage, then he or she may not have the opportunity of selling to the firm again until the next model change, when it will be difficult dislodging an established supplier.

Just-in-time manufacturing is normally operated in flow production situations. As will be discussed in Chapter 10, reliability of quality and delivery are of prime importance as manufacturers work on minimal stockholding of components and raw materials. Long-term relationships with suppliers are prevalent. 'Zero defects' is the goal suppliers must strive to achieve in terms of quality.

With job production, losing an order is not normally as critical, because as long as the firm has been professionally represented, it should be invited to quote for the next order and perhaps be successful then. Losing a potential order is serious, but with job production it might mean waiting a short period before being asked to quote again for a different job, whereas with flow production it might be years before the model is changed and an opportunity provided to quote again (by which time the buyer might have forgotten the existence of the salesperson).

4.4   Selling for Resale

This includes selling to retailers, most of whom are multiples like Tesco, Sainsbury's and Asda which effectively perform their own wholesaling functions. Independents purchase from wholesalers or cash and carry operators like Makro. Some retailers belong to voluntary chains like SPAR. Much buying is centralised and in many cases the buyer visits the seller (unlike industrial selling when the seller normally visits the buyer). A look at changing patterns of retailing since the end of World War II illustrates how retailing has been revolutionised.

Before examining these changing patterns of retailing, we first categorise seven different types of selling outlet:

1 *Multiples.* Classed as belonging to a retail organisation with ten or more branches, each selling a similar range of merchandise. This has been one of the fastest growing areas of retailing and in the UK multiples now dominate fast-moving consumer goods (FMCG) retail trading.

2 *Variety chains.* Similar to multiples except that the qualifying number of branches is five and they sell a wider range of merchandise.

3 *Co-operative societies.* Owned and controlled by the people who shop there, each society is governed by a board of directors elected from its own members.

Anybody can be a member by purchasing one share. The movement can be traced back to 1844 when it started in Rochdale. Its principles are:

- open membership

- democratic control (one person, one vote)

- payment of limited interest on capital

- surplus arising out of the operation to be distributed to members in proportion to their purchases – originally distributed through dividends, but later paid through trading stamps; this has been generally abandoned in favour of lower prices

- provision of education

- co-operation amongst societies, both nationally and internationally

4 *Department stores*. Stores with five or more departments under one roof and at least 25 employees, selling a wide range of commodities, including significant amounts of household goods and clothing.

5 *Independents*. Traders who own their own retail outlets. There are variations, the first being where the independent belongs to a retail buying association. This is an informal grouping whereby retailers (usually within a specific geographical area) group together to make bulk purchases. A higher profile arrangement is when a wholesaler or group of wholesalers invites retailers to affiliate to them and agree to take the bulk of their purchases from them. Such arrangements are termed voluntary groups (individual wholesaler sponsored) or voluntary chains (group wholesaler sponsored). Participating independent retailers have an identifying symbol (and for this reason they are termed 'symbol shops' – like SPAR) in addition to their customary title. Retailers voluntarily agree to abide by the rules of the group or chain, including matters of accounting procedures, shop facilities and group marketing/promotional schemes.

6 *Mail order*. This activity has expanded significantly in recent years. The most popular type of arrangement is the mail order warehouse that carries a large range of goods. Business is conducted through the medium of glossy catalogues held by appointed commission agents who sell to families and friends. Mail order is also carried out by commodity specialists dealing in items like gardening produce, government surplus and hi-fi. They advertise in appropriate specialist press and through direct mail. This type of business has expanded largely as a result of the expansion of Sunday colour supplements. Many companies deal in more general ranges of goods and use such colour supplements to advertise. Some department stores offer postal services and sometimes provide catalogues.

7 *Direct selling*. Party plan companies have sold direct to customers in their homes for a number of years. Tupperware produces a range of high-quality kitchenware and other merchandise for food and drink storage. A direct salesperson demonstrates products to a group of guests, invited by the host in whose home the demonstration takes place. The host's compensation is a percentage commission on orders taken. A long-established company in the

field of direct selling is Avon Cosmetics whose part-time agents sell to people in a specific locality through the medium of a catalogue. This company is the subject of a case study at the end of this chapter. Buying from a 'travelling shop' was popular after World War II, but as people became more mobile its popularity waned. However, there is now a new trend to sell bespoke items through this medium.

Fashion on wheels

The Polyanna boutique zooms about Britain bringing rails of designer labels to its clients. The company was formed 35 years ago as Barnsley's first fashion boutique and has now expanded to include lifestyle menswear and accessories departments, and an in-house café – Le Croque. Mark, son of the founder, now zooms around the country in a van packed with high-fashion labels, visiting clients as far afield as Glasgow and London. His clients largely find out about the company from the website **www.pollyanna.com**

Source: *The Times*, 3 May 2002, pp. 16–17.

The success of the multiples has meant that manufacturers have had to reappraise their sales channels, with the concentration of purchasing power in fewer hands. In the FMCG field, manufacturers have become increasingly involved in controlling distribution of their products and in merchandising activities to support their 'pull' marketing strategies. This has meant heavy advertising expenditures, and concurrent merchandising activity at point of sale has been necessary to ensure that goods are promoted in-store to back up national advertising. As a result, large manufacturers operating a 'pull' strategy have been able to exercise control over their distributive intermediaries; such intermediaries could only dismiss demand created through advertising and branding at the risk of losing custom. This control has meant lower margins for retailers, with manufacturers being able to dictate the in-store location of their particular products. The weight of advertising put behind major brands has given these manufacturers influence over their distributive outlets.

Although there was initially some resistance on the part of manufacturers to the development of the multiples, they eventually found it to their advantage to deal with them directly. This was because multiples purchased in bulk, often for delivery to a central depot, and placed large orders well in advance of the delivery date, thus enabling the manufacturer to organise production more efficiently.

The implications for selling as a result of these developments have been that salespeople of FMCGs are no longer compelled to sell the products in the old-fashioned 'sales representational' sense as advertising has already pre-sold goods for them. Selling to multiples is more a matter of negotiation at higher levels whereby the buyer and the sales manager negotiate price and delivery and salespeople merely provide an after-sales service at individual outlets. Sometimes salespeople carry out merchandising activities such as building up shelf displays, providing window stickers and in-store advertising, although such duties may also be carried out by separate merchandiser teams, particularly when some form of demonstration or product promotion is required.

The growing importance of retailers is reflected in the formation of **trade marketing** teams to service their needs. A combination of key account management on the part of the salesforce and brand management's lack of appreciation of what retailers actually want has promoted many European consumer goods companies to set up a trade marketing organisation. A key role is to bridge the gap between key account management and the salesforce. Trade marketers focus on retailer needs:

- the kinds of products they want

- in which sizes

- with which packaging

- at what prices

- with what kind of promotion

Information on trade requirements is fed back to brand management who develop new products, and to the salesforce who can then better communicate with retailers. An important role for trade marketers is to develop tailored promotions for supermarkets.

Tailored promotion

A supermarket chain that owned a group of hotels demanded from a drinks supplier that the next competition promotion offer holiday breaks in its hotels as prizes (paid for by the supplier).

Wholesalers have suffered since and many have gone out of business because their traditional outlet post-World War II (independents) have also suffered. This is why wholesalers established voluntary groups or chains, in order to meet the challenge of multiples and offer a similar type of image to the public. However, this has largely failed because of inferior purchasing power and because wholesalers must try to make their independent retailing members behave like multiples, using voluntary means. The wholesaler's only sanction against non-cooperating members is to expel them from the group, whereas in the case of multiples a store manager can be quickly removed.

Since the late 1960s we have witnessed the growth of large-scale retailing, including growth in the size of retail establishments, first to supermarkets, then to superstores, then hypermarkets and finally to megastores. Because of the large size of site required for such outlets, but also for customer convenience, the trend has been towards out-of-town sites where easy parking is facilitated. Patterns of shopping have changed, with shoppers for most goods prepared to dispense with the personal service of the shopkeeper, and self-service and self-selection readily accepted in the interests of lower overheads and more competitive prices. There has been a growth in mass marketing because improved standards of living have meant that products that were once luxury goods are now utility goods and required by the mass of the population, e.g. cars, foreign holidays, televisions, telephones and mobile phones. Because supply normally exceeds demand for consumer goods, there has been a large increase in advertising and other forms of promotion in an attempt to induce brand loyalty, with FMCGs being pre-sold to consumers by means of 'pull' promotional strategies. At the same time retailers have encouraged shoppers to become 'store loyal' through the introduction of loyalty card schemes. Thus, retailing has been one of dynamic change which has affected ways in which salespeople operate.

Franchising

A more recent trend in European retailing has been contractual systems of **franchising**. It is a corporate **vertical marketing system (VMS)** as its power is based at a point in the channel that is one or more stages removed from the end customer. The franchisor initiates the franchise and provides the link to the ultimate franchisee in specific stages of the manufacturing/distribution process. Franchising was originally a British development under the 'tied public house' system. Landlords who owned their own premises were tied to a brewery under an agreement to purchase only that brewery's products. However, modern franchising is a US phenomenon that was introduced to the UK in the 1950s. Since then it has grown enormously and now has a code of conduct that is administered through a voluntary body called the British Franchising Association. Franchising comes in a number of forms:

1 *From manufacturers to retailers*: e.g. a car manufacturer (the franchisor) licenses car distributors (franchisees) to sell its products.

2 *From manufacturers to wholesalers*: popular in the soft drinks industry, here manufacturers sometimes supply concentrate (i.e. the 'secret recipe') which wholesalers then mix with water and bottle for distribution to local retail outlets (e.g. Pepsi Cola, Coca-Cola). Manufacturers are the driving force behind the brand image of the product and stringent consistency and control of quality is of paramount importance.

3 *From wholesalers to retailers*: in decline for a number of years as a result of the rise of the multiples mentioned. The most successful example is the voluntary group 'SPAR', which does not manufacture, but its large wholesale buying power means it can pass on cost savings to independent retailers who join the group and display the SPAR logo. They must abide by rules of the group in relation to matters like price promotions, standards of store layout and opening hours that the group uses as part of advertising: 'SPAR – your eight till late shop'.

4 *Service firm sponsored franchises to retailers*: this area has achieved the largest growth over recent years. Examples are found in the fast food business (e.g. Burger King, McDonald's, Little Chef, KFC, Spud-U-Like, Pizza Hut); car rentals (e.g. Avis, Budget, Hertz); office services (e.g. Prontaprint); hotels and resorts (e.g. some Sheraton and Holiday Inn hotels are owned by individuals or groups who operate on a franchise basis).

Franchising arrangements have a common set of procedures:

1 The franchisor offers expert advice on such matters as location, finance, operational matters and marketing.

2 The franchisor promotes the image nationally or internationally and this provides a well-recognised name for the franchisee.

3 Many franchise arrangements have a central purchasing system where franchisees buy at favourable rates or where a successful 'formula' is central to the operation of the franchise (e.g. KFC).

4 The franchise agreement provides a binding contract to both sides. This contract governs such matters as hours of opening, hygiene and how the business is operated in terms of its dealings with customers. Indeed, on this latter point, organisations like Little Chef employ 'mystery shoppers' who call unannounced and order a meal anonymously. They check up on the operation of franchisees to ensure they are following the franchise rules of operation. The mystery shopper investigates matters such as how the customer is greeted, whether or not they were kept waiting, whether or not certain extra items of food were offered, cleanliness of restroom facilities and if such facilities were checked in the last two hours from a chart that is displayed on the wall.

5 The franchisor often provides initial start-up and then continuous training to the franchisee.

6 A franchise arrangement normally requires the franchisee to pay a royalty or franchise fee to the franchisor. However, the franchisee owns the business and is not employed by the franchisor.

This system of marketing has become popular over recent years. It provides an advantage to both large-scale business (the franchisor) and the small-scale business (the franchisee). In the case of the latter, the opportunity to become self-employed and in control of their own destiny is a strong motivating factor to work hard and make a success of the business. The fact that the name is internationally recognised means that business is assured straight away.

Example of franchising

McDonald's is an example of brand franchising. McDonald's, the franchisor, grants the right to sell McDonald's branded goods to someone wishing to set up their own business, the franchisee. The licence agreement allows McDonald's to insist on manufacturing or operating methods and the quality of the product. This is an arrangement that can suit both parties.

Under this franchise, McDonald's owns or leases the site and the restaurant building. The franchisee buys the fittings, the equipment and the right to operate the franchise for twenty years. To ensure uniformity throughout the world, all franchisees must use standardised McDonald's branding, menus, design layouts and administration systems.

Source: *http://www.thetimes100.co.uk/case_study* with permission

4.5　Selling Services

Just like tangible products, a service must satisfy needs of buyers. However, benefits are less tangible than physical products in that they cannot be stored or displayed and satisfaction is achieved through activities (e.g. transportation from one place to another rather than, say, a seat on a train). **Services** come in many forms and examples include:

- transportation – air, sea, rail and road
- power – electricity, gas and coal
- hotels and accommodation
- restaurants
- communications – telephone, fax, email, text messages
- television and radio services
- banking
- insurance
- clubs – social, keep fit, sporting, special interests
- repair and maintenance
- travel agencies
- accounting services
- business consultancy – advertising, marketing research, strategic planning
- architectural
- cleaning
- library
- public (local) authority services and undertakings – disposal of refuse and road repairs
- computing services
- stockbroking services

There are more and they can be applied to both consumer and industrial users. The selling approach to each category differs, depending upon customer needs, just as selling approaches differ when considering physical products.

In the UK the service sector has grown tremendously over recent years, so much so that it is now primarily a service rather than a manufacturing economy. There are many reasons for this. For example, more women work full time and the division of responsibilities between men and women is breaking down more equitably. This has put pressure on the service sector to provide services that can perform tasks which have hitherto been seen as the province of being provided in the home (e.g. more eating out in restaurants and more holidays – often two per year – because of increased disposable income).

Better technology has assisted the development and provision of a more comprehensive range of services (e.g. banks offer internet banking, credit cards, instant statements, quicker decisions on loans and longer term services like house loans). Building societies now provide a broader range of services and have moved into areas traditionally viewed as the province of the banks and the major ones have now become banks. This has been a result of the 'liberalisation' of their activities through the Financial Services Act (1986).

In addition to expansion of existing services in the financial sector, more services are now available (e.g. professional drain clearing through the 'Dyno-rod' franchise). Public services have become more marketing orientated and have to be seen to be more accountable to the publics (e.g. the police service is now more public relations conscious than in the past). Local authorities spend money that is raised through council tax and the public now questions more closely how money they have contributed is being spent. Thus, these organisations have to be seen to be spending money wisely as they are publicly accountable. They have to communicate with their public and explain how services they provide are of value. Special characteristics of services include:

(a) Intangibility.

(b) The difficulty of separating production from consumption as many services are consumed as they are produced.

(c) Services are not as 'standard' as products and are more difficult to assess (in terms of value).

(d) It is not possible to 'stock' services (e.g. unsold hotel rooms) unlike products.

Table 4.2 illustrates these characteristics more graphically.

The final criterion, ownership, shows that, unlike a product, the consumer does not secure ownership of the service, but pays to secure access to the use of the service (e.g. a recreational facility like exercise in a gymnasium).

The four Ps have been extended to include an extra three Ps; thus we have the 'seven Ps' of service marketing. The three extra Ps are People, Process and Physical evidence.

- *People* are an important element in carrying out a service, especially those who are directly involved with customers. Employees must be well trained and have a friendly demeanour when handling customers.

- *Process* relates to how the service is provided and it deals with customers at the point of contact in the supply of the service. Consistency and quality of service must be well planned and managed.

Table 4.2 Characteristics of services and products

Products		Services
Low	Intangibility	High
Low	Inseparability	High
Low	Variability (i.e. non-standard)	High
Low	Perishability (i.e. inability to stock)	High
Yes	Ownership	No

- *Physical evidence* is included because of the intangibility of services. Marketing should highlight the nature of the service being offered. This should be communicated to customers by emphasising such matters as levels of quality, types of equipment and physical facilities.

With this background in mind, the task of selling services is perhaps more difficult than selling products because of its more abstract nature. A distinguishing feature is that those who provide the service are often the ones who sell that service. Thus, providers of services must be more highly trained in sales technique, and sales negotiation forms an important part of such interaction. It is important too that close attention is paid to image building (e.g. banks and insurance companies must be seen to be stable, reliable institutions, but with a friendly, non-intimidating attitude – an image on which banks in particular have spent a lot of money). Above all, as McDonald[16] has pointed out, unlike a physical product it is never possible to know precisely what will be received until the service is rendered, so an element of trust is essential in selling services.

Extended marketing mix

People: Argos places great emphasis on training staff and ensuring they provide good customer service. If staff are friendly, know what they are talking about and are eager to serve customers this can provide an important competitive advantage in retailing.

Process (i.e. the buying process): In 2002 Argos introduced 'Text and Take Home' which allows potential buyers to text at any time to discover if a product is available in their local store, and, if they wish, reserve it to pick up later. The company expects 700,000 users per year for this service. Over 40 million text messages are sent in the UK every day so the potential is huge and Argos is tapping into this growth area. Alongside the Argos website and telephone service, 'Text and Take Home' is designed to make buying more convenient.

Argos has also improved the in-store buying experience by introducing 'Quick Pay' – a system that enables customers in-store to check availability, order and pay for goods themselves by credit or debit card, thereby avoiding the tills.

This service makes shopping easier for customers and reduces queues in-store during busy periods; it currently accounts for 6% of all Argos sales. Given the growth of Internet shopping, where customers can buy direct at any time of the day or night, Argos has responded by being technologically innovative to ensure the process of buying is as easy as possible. The success of these developments has been recognised with many top awards.

Physical environment: In retailing, the look and layout of stores can be an important factor when attracting customers. Argos has recently invested heavily in store improvements to ensure customers are attracted.

Source: *http://www.thetimes100.co.uk/case_study* with permission

4.6   Sales Promotions

Sales promotions include techniques that organisations can use as part of their marketing effort. Objectives that can be achieved through sales promotional activities include:

- encouragement of repeat purchases
- building of long-term customer loyalty
- encouragement of consumers to visit a particular sales outlet
- building up of retail stock levels
- widening or increasing the distribution of a product or brand

Sales promotions include:

- price reductions
- vouchers or coupons
- gifts
- competitions
- lotteries
- cash bonuses

Techniques cover:

- consumer promotions
- trade promotions
- salesforce promotions

The importance of sales promotions has increased since the 1960s, as has the sophistication of methods used. It is sometimes implied that sales promotion is a peripheral marketing activity, but companies increasingly realise the importance of a well-planned and co-ordinated programme of sales promotion.

Within the UK, sales promotional activities have matured since the 1970s. At that time few attempts were made to measure their effectiveness. Advertising agencies branched out into sales promotions with the aim of offering an all-inclusive package to clients in an attempt to combat competition from emerging sales promotion agencies. The mid-1980s brought increased economic pressure to bear on business activities that had the effect of making advertising agencies become more concerned about reductions in company advertising budgets. They began to pay more attention to the effectiveness of sales promotions and adopted a more integrated approach to advertising. There was a move towards fee-based sales promotional agencies, which implied a longer term relationship between agency and client, rather than the existing ad hoc commission structure.

As a result of increased competition from sales promotional agencies, advertising agencies have tended since the mid-1980s to take sales promotion seriously and now offer sales promotion alongside advertising as an integrated communications package. Since the late 1970s there has been a gradual erosion of the line between sales promotion and advertising. Sales promotions can be divided into three main areas of activity:

- consumer promotions
- trade promotions
- personnel motivation

Consumer promotions

These are often referred to as **pull techniques**, since they are designed to stimulate final demand and move products through the sales channel, with consumers providing the impetus. The most widely used consumer promotion is the price reduction or price promotion:

1 The item is marked '*x* pence off'. This can be manufacturer or retailer originated. This technique has to be used with caution by UK manufacturers, as recent legislation now makes it illegal to state this unless the previous price has been applied for a substantial period of time.

2 An additional quantity is offered for the normal price, e.g. 'buy one get one free (BOGOF)' or '10 per cent bigger – same price as usual'.

3 Price-off coupons, either in- or on-pack, may be redeemed against future purchases.

4 Introductory discount price offers on new products.

A view held by many organisers of such promotions is that the consumer, in economically difficult times, is more likely to be attracted by the opportunity to save money than by incidental free offers or competitions. Price promotions are predominantly used by FMCG producers, especially in the grocery trade.

Premium offers

Premium offers are techniques that give extra value to goods or services in the short term as part of a promotional package:

1 *Self-liquidating premiums*. An offer of merchandise is communicated to the customer on or off the pack. The price charged to the customer covers the cost of the item to the promoter. The promoter is able to purchase such merchandise in bulk and pass savings on to customers, who feel that they are getting something of additional value. These promotions are usually linked with the necessity to collect labels or cut out tokens from a number of purchases of the same, or same range of, products. The premium need not be connected with the product that carried the premium. The idea is to stimulate purchases of the product and selling the premium is of secondary importance.

2 *On-pack gifts*. Here the premium is usually attached to the product. The premium may be product related, e.g. a toothbrush attached to toothpaste, or

not product related, e.g. an item of merchandise such as a CD taped to a magazine.

3 *Continuities*. These are sets of merchandise that can be collected through a series of purchases, e.g. picture cards, chinaware, glassware, etc. The premium is either with the product or the purchaser has to send off for the premium.

4 *Coupon plans*. Coupons, contained within the pack, may be collected over time and exchanged for a variety of products in a catalogue. Coupon techniques may be used by one producer or supplier as a promotion for its goods or services, or the plan may include a number of different producers' products under one name. These schemes have in the main replaced trading stamps, which were used in a similar way. However, trading stamps and purchase vouchers that can be redeemed for cash or goods are making a comeback in specialist retailing situations (e.g. petrol purchases).

5 *Free samples*. These are sample packs of products offered with brand-related products, attached to magazines, given away separately in retail outlets, delivered door-to-door, etc.

Merchandise as a premium does not have the appeal of money, but it may have a more pointed appeal than cash or a price reduction. The premium chosen, and the way it is offered, may preselect a specific type of customer, but the offer can at least be targeted at the right market segment. Providing the additional response generated more than covers the cost of the premium and administration/distribution costs, the promotion should be cost effective.

The choice of premium and sales promotional technique is crucial. The problem is to find a premium that is 'different' or unusual, has broad customer appeal and is available in sufficient quantity to meet demand.

Competitions are popular in the UK and Germany. The advantage of running a competition is that it should be cost effective if the cost of the prizes is spread over a large enough number of entrants. Competitions for consumer goods are usually promoted on the pack concurrent with in-store promotion, with an entry form located on or near the product. It is usually required that each entry is accompanied by proof of purchase. More recently, free draws have become popular whereby a purchase is not necessary and the shopper merely fills in his or her name on an entry form and 'posts' it in an entry box in the retail outlet.

There is scope for individuality and creativity in this method of promotion. It needs much pre-planning and administration, which is probably the reason why competitions tend to be aimed at the national level and involve high value prizes such as holidays and cars, so that consumer response is great enough to cover the costs of the promotion. Lotteries and sweepstakes are also used as promotional techniques, particularly by retail outlets, which use them to attract custom into the store.

Joint promotions are not specific to consumer goods and are used increasingly as companies attempt to find new promotional techniques. They can involve two or more companies, which tend to be related not by product type but rather by similar customer profiles (e.g. the gin and tonic campaign that links two manufacturers – Gordons and Schweppes). There are a number of such arrangements:

(a) Between retailers and producers, where a branded good may carry a voucher redeemable at a particular retail outlet.

(b) Between two or more producers, where one manufacturer's product carries a promotion for the other, and vice versa. Here the relation is by customer profile and not by product.

(c) Between a service organisation and a producer, e.g. between a travel company and a breakfast cereal manufacturer, or a dry cleaner and a clothes manufacturer.

Trade promotions

The aim is usually to **push** products through the channel towards the customer. Similar to consumer promotions, incentives are offered through extra rewards like discounts, increased margins on sales, dealer competitions, exhibitions, provision of demonstrators and free holidays (often in the guise of a conference or product launch). The objectives of retailer–distributor promotions are:

- to achieve widespread distribution of a new brand

- to move excess stocks onto retailers' shelves

- to achieve required display levels of a product

- to encourage greater overall stockholding of a product

- to encourage salespeople at distributor levels to recommend the brand – particularly in the case of non-consumer products

- to encourage support for overall promotional strategy

There are problems associated with trade promotions. Too frequent use can mean that a salesperson directs attention to the product involved and neglects other products in the line. The objectives of the promoter may conflict with those of the retailer or distributor; some sales employees are not permitted to accept incentives or participate in trade contests because their management wishes to maintain control over their selling activities. There is also a danger that a trade promotion may be used to push another brand or inferior product. Consequently, long-term measures to promote sales are not feasible and manufacturers would be better advised to look to product improvement as part of long-term strategy. The British Code of Sales Promotion Practice states:

> No promotion directed towards employees should be such as to cause conflict with their loyalty to their employer. In case of doubt, the prior permission of the employer, or the responsible manager, should be obtained.

Although business gifts are not strictly sales promotions, they are relevant here. The business gift sector is characterised by seasonal demand and it is estimated that 80 per cent of this business is conducted in the last two months of every year. Apart from the obvious connotation that it puts the recipient under some moral obligation to purchase, it also serves as an advertising medium if the company logo is incorporated in the gift. From as early as 1981 the Chartered Institute of Purchasing and Supply took a serious and critical interest in the use of business gifts, especially where the 'giving' was tied to the placing of orders. They argued that such gifts could influence the buyer's objectivity and should be restricted to nominal items like calendars, diaries, pens, etc. Recently, the giving of business gifts has declined as employers have placed restrictions upon what their employees may receive. The Chartered Institute of Purchasing and Supply has published a 'blacklist' of companies operating what they consider to be gift schemes over and above items of nominal value.

Personnel motivation

These are promotions to the salesforce, but some apply to distributors and retailers. The most widely used salesforce promotion is the sales incentives scheme. Rewards are offered to participants on an equal basis which are over and above normal sales compensation. They can be prizes in a competition to individuals or groups who perform best against specific objectives. The problem is that average or below-average performers may not feel sufficiently motivated to put in any extra effort if they consider that only top performers are likely to win. Thus, competitions tend to be used for group or area salesforce motivation.

When establishing a salesforce incentive scheme one must consider objectives, timing, scoring methods and prizes/rewards. Typical objectives of such schemes include:

- introduction of a new product line
- movement of slow-selling items
- obtain wider territory coverage
- develop new prospects
- overcome seasonal sales slumps
- obtain display
- develop new sales skills

The timing of the scheme may depend on the size of the salesforce, the immediacy of action required and the nature of the objectives to be achieved. An incentive programme runs on average for between two and six months.

Scoring or measuring performance may be based upon value or unit sales. In order to overcome territorial differences, quotas may be established for individual regions, areas or salespeople. Points, stamps, vouchers, etc., may be awarded on the achievement of a pre-stated percentage of quotas or level of sales, and continue to be awarded as higher levels are achieved. Such tokens may then be exchanged for merchandise, cash, etc., by the recipient. Sometimes catalogues are supplied giving a range of merchandise for the salesperson or family to choose from. Vouchers for redemption or exchange in retail stores can be used as prizes or rewards.

During a scheme, additional bonus points may be awarded for the attainment of more specific short-term objectives such as increased sales of a particular product, increased numbers of new customers or training and display objectives. In this way a long-running scheme can be kept active and exciting for participants. Another form of motivation is the award of recognition in the form of a trophy or 'salesperson of the year' award.

4.7 Exhibitions

Exhibitions are tangentially related to sales settings as the objective is not to sell from display stands, although in some circumstances (e.g. glassware and decorative ware sales from importers and manufacturers to the trade) exhibitions and trade fairs are where most business takes place. Generally speaking, their function is to build up goodwill and prepare the way for future sales. Exhibitions were once regarded as a luxury item in a company's marketing budget and exhibition stand personnel often looked upon staffing an exhibition stand as an easy option to their normal duties. They were regarded as being a tool of public relations. Companies are now more aware of their value as part of overall marketing and sales efforts.

The term *exhibitions* covers a wider spectrum than that described. At a simple level *event management* concerns activities that promote the organisation, but it is often an excuse to provide hospitality to customers. *Corporate hospitality* is an honest definition, but for reasons of not wishing to draw attention to marketing expenditure that might be regarded as trivial, this term is rarely used. This can take the form of the provision of seats or a box for invited guests at an event like Royal Ascot, the Grand Prix at Silverstone or a Test match. At a more sophisticated level, *conferences* can be sponsored that reflect the interests of the sponsoring company, but provide a more serious forum for participants.

A study was undertaken by one of the authors to investigate how trade exhibitions could be better used as part of a communications programme. These results (Lancaster and Baron, 1977) are now presented together with updating information.[17]

Characteristics of a good exhibition include:

- a wide range of products

- a large number of competitors

- a good amount of information on the products on show made available beforehand (emphasising the importance of pre-exhibition mailing)

- a large number of new products

- nearness to the buyer's home base

- good exhibition hall facilities

- a simple stand that is always neat (no personal effects on display) and not cluttered with unsuitable display material

Characteristics of a good exhibitor include:

- exhibiting a full range of products, particularly large items that cannot be demonstrated by a travelling representative

- stand always staffed by personnel who do not spend time conversing with colleagues

- well-informed and approachable stand staff

- informative literature available

- seating area or an office provided on the stand

- refreshments for visitors (and stand staff only using refreshment facility when with customers)

- staff not using mobile telephones in public when on duty

- staff spending time with potential and known customers, making future appointments and filtering away time wasters and freeloaders

- actively following up sales leads and debriefing the stand team afterwards

Use of trade exhibitions is on the increase and companies increasingly need to establish a more scientific method of managing this function as it requires an understanding of how an exhibition stand communicates itself to the public. Setting exhibition objectives and measuring results are important, as is the identification and comprehension of elements in the exhibition event. Management should plan, coordinate and control the exhibition mix. Figure 4.1 explains how the exhibition communication process works.

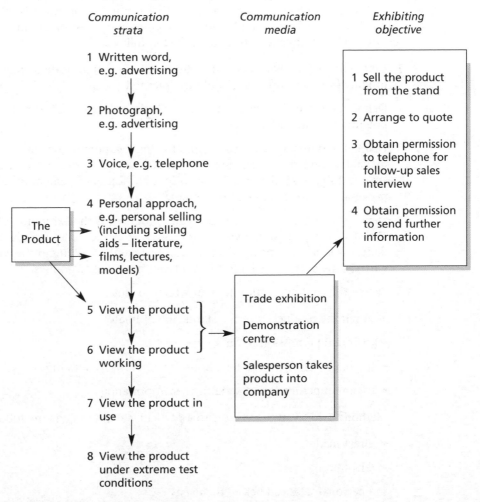

Figure 4.1 A model of the exhibition communication process

Different communication problems exist for different types of product, including materials, services and small or large, simple or complex machinery. With materials the selling feature or **unique sales proposition (USP)** may be communicated quite simply or through a low communication medium, e.g. the written word. The USP of a large piece of complex machinery might only be communicated by the potential customer viewing the machinery working. The different methods of communicating the USP of different types of product are termed *communication strata*. A product with a simple USP can be communicated through a low communication stratum, whereas a product with a complex USP can best be communicated through a high communication stratum.

Having selected the stratum needed to put across the USP, the other methods of communication used must be organised to complement it. For example, if trade exhibitions are selected as the ultimate communication medium, all other marketing inputs, e.g. salesforce and media advertising, must be co-ordinated with the programmed trade exhibition. If strata 5 or 6 (see Figure 4.1) are needed, there are three communication media that can be used, such as trade exhibitions, demonstration centres or the salesperson taking the product into the firm.

In the management of any function, the setting of objectives is vital; without this, there is no basis for planning, co-ordination, control or measurement of results. Such objectives can be enumerated as follows:

1 Define the market with which it is intended to communicate by region, by product or by any other segmentation method.

2 Define the value of potential purchases. Is the exhibition effort to be aimed at potentially small or large users?

3 Define the status of contact at whom to aim, e.g. purchasing manager, managing director, etc. High-status contacts cannot normally be attracted to small exhibitions – they may wish to speak to top management or require a personal invitation plus entertainment.

4 Define the preference towards company products. Is the exhibition effort to be aimed at present customers? Is it principally to launch a new product? The danger is that stand personnel time can be taken up talking to the converted, whereas the objective should be to interest potential customers.

5 Define the communication level at which to aim:

- to sell the product from the stand (the ultimate)

- to obtain permission to quote

- to obtain permission to telephone for a follow-up sales interview

- to obtain permission to send further information

Methods used to attract visitors to a particular stand include the following:

- direct mail

- telephoning

- a personal sales call before the event

- an advertisement in the technical or trade press

Once there, attractions can include the following:

- a buffet

- give-aways

- advertising material

- films and seminars at the exhibition

- attention-gaining exhibits on the stand

The exhibition stand itself should have a number of elements:

1 Products on show will depend upon the target market. The more products, the higher the number of prospects that will be interested, although a balance has to be struck so as not to provide so wide a range as to make it confusing.

2 Literature should not be on a self-service display. When a prospect comes to the stand looking for literature, this should be an ideal opportunity for the salesperson to establish contact and obtain details of the prospect.

3 Graphics should include at least a display board featuring the product literature. Such aids make the stand look more attractive. Models of the item being marketed are useful when the product being sold is too large or bulky to be physically displayed.

4 An office or interview room can take up a lot of expensive display space. An alternative is to demonstrate the product and then ask the visitor to a nearby seating area to conduct the interview.

5 Refreshment facilities on the stand are good attractors and from the results of the study were a major drawing force.

6 An area should be designated for storage of coats, briefcases, literature, materials, etc., to avoid clutter and distractions from the main aim of the exhibition.

7 An expensive, eye-catching stand can be a double-edged weapon. It might attract visitors, but the study indicated that visitors' attitudes towards such ostentation were that it might be reflected in the price of products.

The stand should be planned as early as possible by drawing up a checklist of everything required, checking limitations on stand design, drawing up a checklist of stand services required and a progress chart for the preparation of all products and exhibits, including their manufacture, transportation to the exhibition, assembly and dismantling.

Exhibition stand personnel must be able to communicate the USP of the products and have a sound commercial and technical knowledge. They may come from a variety of backgrounds such as sales, marketing and technical, and should be briefed upon a number of areas beforehand:

1 Objectives of the exhibition and set procedures to be used in achieving these objectives.

2 Features of the stand, who else is on the stand and the geography of the stand in the exhibition complex. Who is the exhibition stand manager?

3 How to approach stand visitors, how to interview them and how to deal with irrelevant visitors.

4 Tips on physical appearance before staffing the exhibition stand.

With professional pre-planning and management, exhibitions can be a powerful sales tool and not the expensive luxury that many companies at one time regarded them to be.

4.8   Public Relations

Nature and role of public relations

Public relations covers a broader spectrum than selling or indeed marketing. Its application is wider and encompasses the entire organisation and its various external and internal 'publics'. Its role, however, is increasingly important as an ancillary to selling, both in the receiving and giving senses. Selling needs public relations to assist it in its everyday operation and selling is often called upon to disseminate a public relations message. Since the first edition of this book was published, there has been a general recognition of the strategic role of public relations; no longer is it viewed as a means of 'covering up' when something has gone wrong. It has a positive role to play in an organisation and that role is now emphasised.

The public relations practitioner has to conduct activities that concern every public with which the organisation has contact. The specific nature of such groups will vary according to circumstances. Jefkins identifies seven basic publics:[18]

- the community
- employees
- government
- the financial community
- distributors
- consumers
- opinion leaders

Definition

The task of defining the exact nature of PR is difficult. A number of definitions exist, each emphasising a slightly different approach and each attempting to arrive at a simple, yet brief and accurate, description. The difficulty in developing a single acceptable definition reflects the complexity and diversity of the subject. We look at three definitions:

PR practice is the deliberate, planned and sustained effort to establish and maintain mutual understanding between an organisation and its public.
(Institute of Public Relations, IPR)

The essential features of this definition are first that PR practice should be *deliberate*, *planned* and *sustained* – not haphazard (e.g. when responding to the accidental pollution of a river). Second, *mutual understanding* is necessary in order to ensure that the communication between the organisation and its publics is clear (i.e. the receiver perceives the same meaning as the sender intended).

An alternative definition is given by the late Frank Jefkins who widely authored on this subject:[19]

PR consists of all forms of planned communication, outwards and inwards, between an organisation and its publics for the purpose of achieving specific objectives concerning mutual understanding.

This modified version of the IPR definition adds two dimensions:

(a) *Public* becomes *publics*, since PR addresses a number of audiences.

(b) The inclusion of *specific objectives* makes PR a tangible activity.

If we accept Jefkins's definition, then we accept its further implication – that PR exists whether an organisation likes it or not. Simply by carrying out its day-to-day operations, an organisation necessarily communicates certain messages to those with whom it interacts. Opinions are formed about the organisation and its activities. It is thus necessary that PR orchestrates these messages in order to help develop a *corporate identity* or *personality*.

A more precise and comprehensive description of PR is provided by the Public Relations Society of America:

1 Anticipating, analyzing and interpreting public opinion, attitudes and issues which might impact, for good or ill, on the operations and plans of the organization.

2 Counseling management at all levels with regard to policy decisions, courses of action and communication.

3 Researching, conducting and evaluating, on a continuing basis, programs of action and communication to achieve informed public understanding necessary for the success of the organization's aims.

4 Planning and implementing the organisation's efforts to influence or change public policy.

5 Managing the resources needed to perform the functions of public relations.

(Public Relations Society of America)

Communication is central to PR. The purpose of PR is to establish a two-way communication process to resolve conflicts by seeking common ground or areas of mutual interest. This is, of course, best achieved by word of mouth and is why the role of selling as the communication medium is so potentially important for PR to be successful.

Corporate identity

The concept of corporate identity, or personality, is inextricably linked to PR. All PR activities must be carried out within the framework of an agreed and understood corporate personality. This personality must develop to reflect the style of the top management, since they control the organisation's policy and activities.

A corporate personality can become a tangible asset if it is managed properly and consistently. However, it cannot be assumed that all managers will consider the role of personality when they make decisions. A PR executive thus needs to be placed so that s/he is aware of all issues, policies, attitudes and opinions that exist in the organisation which have a bearing upon how it is perceived by the organisation's publics.

The use of the word *personality* rather than *image* is deliberate. An image is a reflection or an impression which may be a little too polished or perfect. True PR is deeper than this. To use a common denigrating quote of a 'PR job' implies that somehow the truth is being hidden behind a glossy or false facade. Properly conducted, PR emphasises the need for *truth* and full information. The public relations executive, as a manager of the corporate personality, can only sustain in the long term an identity that is based upon reality.

What public relations *is not*

Misunderstanding as to the nature of PR has led to confusion about its role. Certain distinctions are clarified:

1 *PR is **not** free advertising.* Advertising complements selling. PR is informative, educational and creates understanding through knowledge. PR is not free. It is time consuming and costs money in terms of management expertise. Editorial space and broadcasting time have more credibility than advertisements. Every organisation, consciously or unconsciously, has PR. PR involves communications with many groups and audiences, not just potential customers.

2 *PR is **not** propaganda.* Propaganda is designed to indoctrinate to attract followers. It does not necessarily call for an ethical content, so facts can be distorted or falsified for self-interest. PR, on the other hand, seeks to persuade by securing the willing acceptance of attitudes and ideas.

3 *PR is **not** publicity.* Publicity is a result of information being made known. The result may be uncontrollable and either good or bad. PR is concerned with the behaviour of an organisation, product or individual that leads to publicity. It will clearly seek to control behaviour in such a way as to attempt to ensure that the publicity is good.

Objectives of public relations

PR is used in order to create a better environment for the organisation and its activities. The objectives may include the following:

• attract sales inquiries

- reinforce customer loyalty

- attract investors

- attract merger partners or smooth the way for acquisition

- attract better employees

- dissolve or block union problems

- minimise competitor advantage while you catch up

- open a new market

- launch a new product

- reward key people with recognition

- bring about favourable legislation

In order to achieve such objectives, PR is viewed as part of a total marketing communications strategy, the principal part of which is the selling function. At any point in a marketing programme there can be PR activity, for the reason that PR is concerned with human relations and is a two-way process. There is a PR element in every facet of marketing (e.g. a salesperson who exaggerates, cheats or lets down customers is a PR liability).

Manufacturers have to get closer to people. In order to reach different groups, each with separate interests, they must employ the techniques of press relations, house journals, seminars, works visits, private demonstrations, exhibitions, videos, professionally designed websites, and other aids. Moreover, they have to consider those who influence opinion, sales channels and all communication media that express ideas and news.

Corporate public relations

This is concerned with group image and based on a long-term, carefully planned programme designed to achieve maximum recognition and understanding of the organisation's objectives and performance which is in keeping with realistic expectations.

The main medium for corporate PR is prestige advertising (e.g. ICI's 'pathfinders', which present to the public a progressive image of the huge conglomerate). Another medium is house style (e.g. a specific logo like the woolmark sign devised by the International Wool Secretariat and displayed on hats and uniforms worn by people they sponsor). Sponsorship is important for such sporting activities as golf, football, cricket and motor racing. It can include partial funding for, and the resultant publicity of, such events as concerts and community projects.

Sponsorship is defined by Meenaghan[20] as 'an investment in cash or in kind, in an activity, in return for access to the exploitable commercial potential associated with that activity'.

Effective public relations

Effective PR depends upon the following:

- Setting specific objectives that are capable of evaluation.
- Fully integrating the PR function into the organisation.
- Selecting the right personnel to carry out the PR function.

We now examine each in more detail.

Objective setting

This is an essential requirement of PR practice. Bowman and Ellis state:[21]

> If a PR programme is to be effective, then it is vital that its objectives be defined; that means of achieving them shall then be determined ... and that progress, success and failure be reviewed.

Although it is sometimes difficult to decide how an objective can be measured, an obvious objective can be cited in terms of increased sales, although it is sometimes difficult to determine whether such an increase in sales was due to PR activity or to some other marketing activity.

Crisis PR tends to dictate its own objectives. If information is to be prevented from reaching the press, then the yardstick that determines success or failure is whether that information reaches the press or not. If the objective is to maintain the company's reputation, then some attempt must be made to define 'reputation' in useful terms such that it can be measured and evaluated.

A traditional method of measuring PR activity is in terms of column centimetres gained from press coverage. This method does not, however, account for the quality of such coverage. Furthermore, the value of editorial cannot be quantified against equivalent advertising cost because of the greater credibility of editorial.

As PR matures, the call for more objectivity is likely to become greater. As Worcester and English state:[22]

> Just as it is now difficult to conceive of marketing without measurement, a PR agency seeking to change the perception of its clients ... will begin by quantifying the scale of the problem ... and the effect of its activities over time.

Integration

The integration of the PR function into the organisation is important. It should be decided whether PR should act in a 'technician' or 'policy-making' role, the implication being that a technician simply carries out top management orders whereas the policy-maker inputs into corporate strategic plans. Modern thinking favours the latter role because every decision has PR implications. If PR is not involved in policy formation, then top management is implicitly assuming the PR mantle.

The role that is suggested for PR is far reaching, involving communication with large numbers of people. This requires co-operation with other organisational functions. PR must then be a reasonably autonomous unit so that it can serve all departments equally. A staff function should be positioned so that it can funnel its services to the organisational levels that may be the public face of the organisation to outside groups. The importance of PR at lower hierarchical levels cannot be overstated (e.g. from the way the secretary answers the telephone to the attitude of the company's delivery person).

The extent of PR responsibility has to be established initially by senior management and this can be achieved by objective setting and well-defined job analyses. PR as a staff function exists to serve and facilitate line functions. Such lack of PR authority is desirable since it minimises conflict and ensures that the emphasis is upon co-operation and consultation between line and staff. It also recognises that day-to-day business and executive authority are vested in line management. It does, however, mean that it is essential that PR has direct access to the board in order that PR programmes can be sanctioned and executed with full backing from top management.

Selection

The selection of the 'right' personnel is especially important for potential PR practitioners. The practice of PR covers such a wide diversity of tasks that flexibility is very important. The Institute of Public Relations (IPR) recognises: 'There is no single set of ideal qualifications and no formal path into the profession.'

The IPR even states that formal qualifications are not necessary for PR personnel. However, such a view sugggests that you 'learn by your mistakes' which can be costly. There are clearly some PR principles that can be formally taught and it may be that PR as a profession has now 'come of age' because Stirling University introduced the first Master's degree in Public Relations back in 1988 and Bournemouth University introduced the first Bachelor's degree in 1989.

Practitioners have identified a number of skills and attributes necessary to be successful:

- sound judgement
- personal integrity
- communications skills
- organisational ability
- strong personality
- team player

The traditional importance of media relations has resulted in a strong journalist contingent in the PR profession. However, some find it hard to adapt as the required writing style is different, as are planning horizons and work routines. As the wide range of necessary qualities and skills illustrates, relevant experience can be obtained from almost any background. Personality is really of far more importance, together with a sense of empathy and the ability to be adaptable. It goes without saying that an ability to write and speak fluently is vital.

The use of public relations consultancies

In some situations, it is more cost effective to use a PR consultancy, especially in areas where the organisation is inexperienced (e.g. the City or Parliament). Quite often larger companies find that a better interaction comes from an in-house PR department and an external specialist. Consultancies are an integral part of the PR industry and possess certain advantages of experience, independence and specialist skills that may not be evident internally. External PR activities can be grouped as follows:

1   Freelance writers/consultants, who are generally technical authors able to produce PR feature articles.

2   PR departments of advertising agencies, which can vary from a small press office handling product publicity to augment an advertising campaign, to a large comprehensive PR department not unlike the agency set-up itself.

3   PR subsidiary of an advertising agency, where there is a desire to permit a fuller development of PR activity on the part of the advertising agency and indeed whose clients will provide a useful source of potential business. Its association with an advertising agency can have benefits through shared services such as art studios and production.

4   Independent PR consultants, who usually specialise in a particular class of business, which clients can take advantage of for ad hoc or short-term assignments. Such consultants specialise in charities and appeals, theatre, finance, agriculture, building, shipping, travel, fashion, etc.

5   PR counsellors, who advise but do not carry out the PR work.

4.9   Conclusions

This has been a lengthy chapter of necessity as it has placed sales settings in their respective contexts. It has been shown that different selling approaches must be adopted, depending upon the situation in which one is selling.

Environmental and managerial forces have been discussed and their importance illustrated. Various sales settings including sales channels, industrial/commercial/ public authority, reseller and services selling have been examined.

Sales promotions relate to all types of sales setting and their growth and importance have been shown in respect of consumer markets, trade markets and as an aid to sales personnel motivation. The role of exhibitions has also been examined.

Public relations has been discussed in some detail, as this area has expanded most over recent years and its relationship to the selling function is very direct as the salesforce is increasingly being called upon to carry out PR activity.

The next chapter is concerned with international selling, which is a further example of a sales setting. It is, however, treated separately because of its diversity and ever-increasing importance, especially in view of European Union legislation and changes that impact on the selling function.

References

1 Anderson, R.E. (1996) 'Personal selling and sales management in the new millennium', *Journal of Personal Selling and Sales Management*, 16(4), pp. 17–52.

2 Magrath, A.J. (1997) 'A comment on "personal selling and sales management in the new millennium",' *Journal of Personal Selling and Sales Management*, 17(1), pp. 45–7.

3 *Business Week* (1996) 'Revolution in the showroom', *Business Week*, 19 February, pp. 70–6.

4 Magrath, A.J. (1997) 'A comment on "personal selling and sales management in the new millennium",' *Journal of Personal Selling and Sales Management*, 17(1), pp. 45–7.

5 Piercy, N.F. and Lane, N. (2003) 'Transformation of the traditional salesforce: imperatives for intelligence, interface and integration', *Journal of Marketing Management*, 19, pp. 563–82.

6 Lane, N. and Piercy, N. (2004) 'Strategic customer management: designing a profitable future for your sales organisation', *European Management Journal*, 22 (6), pp. 659–68.

7 Stephens, H. (2003) 'CEO' *American Marketing Association Summer Educators' Conference*, The H.R. Challey Group, August, Chicago.

8 Lane and Piercy (2004) op. cit.

9 Royal, W. (1999) *'Death of salesmen'*, 17 May, pp. 59–60. Available from: <www.industryweek.com>

10 Lane and Piercy (2004) op. cit.

11 H.R. Challey Report (1997) *'The customer selected world class sales executive report'*, The H.R. Challey Group, Cincinnati, OH.

12 Dixon, D. (2003) 'New challenges for the salesforce', *American Marketing Association Summer Educators' Conference*, Western and Southern Financial Group, August, Chicago.

13 Lane and Piercy (2004) op. cit.

14 Metha, R., Rosenbloom, B. and Anderson, R. (2000) 'The role of the sales manager in channel management: impact of organisational variables', *Journal of Personal Selling and Sales Management*, 20, Spring, pp. 81–8.

15 Anderson, R.E., Mehta, R. and Strong, J. (1997) 'An empirical investigation of sales management training programs for sales managers', *Journal of Personal Selling and Sales Management*, 17, Summer, pp. 53–66; Mehta, R., Dubinsky, A. J. and Anderson, R.E. (2002) 'Marketing channel management and the sales manager', *Industrial Marketing Management*, 31, pp. 429–39.

16 McDonald, M. (1988) *How to Sell a Service*, Heinemann, London.

17 Lancaster, G. and Baron, H. (1997) 'Exhibiting for Profit', *Industrial Management*, November, pp. 8–14.

18 Jefkins, F. (1989) *Jefkins School of Public Relations – A Broadsheet*.

19 Jefkins, F. (1989) *Jefkins School of Public Relations – A Broadsheet.*

20 Meenaghan, T. (1989) 'The role of sponsorship in the marketing communications mix', *International Journal of Advertising*, 10.

21 Bowman, P. and Ellis, E. (1982) *Manual of Public Relations*, Heinemann, Oxford.

22 Worcester, R.M. and English, P. (1985) 'Time for PR to mature?' *PR Week*, 1 November.

Practical Exercise

xstreammedia

Gain market share by implementing effective eCRM. In other words make eCRM work for your company, fast and with ease, even if you don't have deep pockets! eCRM can benefit any company or business that has customers, and contrary to popular belief, is not just for call centres or large companies.

For most companies simply offering better products than their competitors is not enough. You need to provide a better quality of service to customers to ensure they do not take their business elsewhere. A company of any size can implement a successful eCRM system without breaking the bank to do so. These are the claims of xstreammedia who go on to answer a number of questions.

Why do we need CRM?

The internet is here to stay. It is pervading business in every way, and we are seeing this in the development of e-business. E-business has already gone through two waves of development and is now entering a third. In the first wave we saw websites that were really just glorified brochures – content. The second wave concentrated on transactions – placing orders. The third wave is the most difficult, but also the most lucrative if you get it right, and this is relationships.

CRM

Customer Relationship Management means different things to different people. Most suppliers of CRM software will choose the description that most closely reflects the strengths of the system they have to offer. It can be extended to include almost any front office system.

Companies should decide upon their own definition for CRM. In the process of finding this definition, focus will be on aspects of relationships with customers that are most important to the business. This process will naturally give a good indication as to what type of system is being sought.

xstreammedia believes that Customer Relationship Management is about better communication with customers. Making sure that the right hand knows what the left hand is doing. To achieve this you need a database that links details of all customer contact whatever the medium, i.e. telephone, email, fax, web, post or face-to-face meetings. Whenever the customer contacts you, whoever responds will know exactly what has been happening with that customer and respond in the most appropriate manner.

eCRM

e-Customer Relationship Management can mean using the internet technology to achieve CRM objectives to share knowledge company wide, or extending CRM to include customer interactions taking place over the internet. xstreammedia believes it is both. Additionally, eCRM should allow you to take a proactive role so you can help customers before they know they need help. For instance, if someone is filling in a form on your website but they get stuck, there should be a mechanism that allows them to ask for live interactive help.

What are the benefits of eCRM

Market and customer intelligence eCRM will integrate all sources of information about customers into one easily accessible place. This enables businesses to see an accurate picture of their customer base, giving a solid foundation from which to take strategic decisions about market segmentation and sales channels.

Projections from Datamonitor show that the way we communicate with customers is undergoing huge change. Systems used to track customers need to reflect new methods of communication like web chat, collaborative browsing and voice over IP telephony.

Turns browsers into buyers

Figures issued recently by the government show that UK SMEs (Small and Medium-sized Enterprises) are leading Europe in the use of e-commerce. If your organisation is using the internet to contact your customers or you are planning to do so, turning browsers into buyers is going to be one of your biggest challenges. Research indicates that only 2 per cent of browsers ever get around to buying. If you could increase that figure by just 1 per cent you would double your sales.

More repeat business at a lower cost

By giving your customers high-quality after-sales service you build customer loyalty and perceived added value for your brand. This leads to increased repeat business and prevents customers moving to competitors. This in turn means that each customer becomes more profitable, particularly when compared to the high cost of finding new customers.

Streamline your e-commerce operation

Thirty-one per cent of people find websites confusing. If you add to this the fact that most sites do not respond to e-mail within 24 hours, it is no surprise that people do not complete their online purchases in the majority of cases. Gaining a market share in the online shopping world is going to be very lucrative.

Companies invest time and money developing a website that reflects their individuality and this in itself can lead to confusion as every website is different. People surfing at home often have only one phone line. This means that if they want to ask a question they have to drop the connection in order to make a telephone call. In practice they probably just won't bother. eCRM will enable you to 'chat' to visitors to your site whilst they are online either by means of a virtual agent, text-based web chat, or utilising voice over IP to speak directly via their PC. This means you can offer real time help to your browsers and help reduce the abandoned shopping cart syndrome.

So why do we hear so much about failed CRM projects?

Fifty per cent of technology-enabled CRM projects fail. The reasons for this high failure rate are:

Timing. This is critical. If it takes 18 months to implement a system, then it will be no good by the time you come to use it because the market has moved on. Because CRM can be such an all-encompassing concept, projects typically become very complicated as more and more issues are uncovered as it goes along. Time constraints add to the pressure, sometimes meaning that parts of the project are left out or glossed over.

It is vital to know what you want to achieve in advance and allow enough time. Then you need to find the simplest, scaleable solution that will allow you to meet those objectives within your timescales.

Integration. One of the main attractions of implementing a CRM system is so staff can have access to all customer data from within one system. This usually means integrating to all the legacy systems that your business is already using. The biggest challenge here is to integrate the CRM system with the website and software that supports other channels of communication. Customers should be able to use each channel interchangeably and at the same time, without having to explain who they are and what they want each time.

Finding a CRM package that can easily export and import data from and to other systems will overcome this problem. Instead of trying to replace all systems with one huge one, it is better to find a system that will glue them all together and can be implemented in bite-sized chunks.

Only one department buys in. One department in isolation will not be able to implement a true CRM system. CRM is not just a marketing tool! It covers all staff that are customer facing, including sales, marketing and customer support as well as IT.

To ensure a project is successful you need representatives from all of these areas, as well as board level commitment.

What's the answer?

Solutions for Small and Medium-sized Enterprises. You don't have to be a large corporate to want to get more profitable business from existing customers. You may have all the same challenges in terms of sharing customer knowledge across the organisation, but the solution can be a lot simpler and a lot more cost effective.

How can XeRM help?

XeRM is the latest eCRM solution from xstreammedia, designed specifically for Small and Medium-sized Enterprises (SMEs). XeRM is a modular product which means that you can choose the combination of functionality that exactly fits your requirements – you don't have to buy the whole system. XeRM consists of the following modules:

- call management
- CTI to desktop
- E-mail management
- electronic facsimile processing
- web chat
- web collaboration
- customer profiling
- remote data access
- database integration

Frequently asked questions

What if I don't even have a customer database?

In many ways this is good news, because it means that you can start from scratch. The tools supplied with XeRM can build databases very simply and quickly.

What if I don't have a website?

You can still benefit from the CRM aspects of XeRM and if/when you are ready to deploy your website, the system you have will be ready to incorporate the new channels of communication from your customers and partners from day one.

How much should I budget for?

The main server software will cost around £10,000 to £15,000. After that you need to allow around £1,000 per concurrent user. Concurrent user licences are based on the number of people that are logged in using the system at any one time. Most CRM packages are licensed by number of seats. This is the absolute number of people that will have access to the system and will obviously be a much higher number – one of the reasons that traditional CRM systems can be so expensive.

Source: PR Artistry Limited, Cedar Court, 9-11 Fairmile, Henley on Thames, Oxon RG9 2JR. Reproduced with permission.

Discussion Questions

1 Currently xstreammedia's promotion is through the electronic media. They know that they are 'ahead of the game' in developments in this field. They are considering using some form of sales representation to boost sales and have asked you to provide guidelines in the form of a report as to how such a salesforce should be recruited, trained and incentivised.

2 They are also considering other kinds of promotional campaigns and have sought your advice as to whether this should be based on a 'push' or a 'pull' strategy. Advise the company and give justification for this advice.

Practical Exercise

Yee Wo Plastic Piping Components Ltd

Johnny Tan is the sales manager for Yee Wo Plastic Piping Components Ltd, which is a subsidiary of a Taiwanese multinational that manufactures a large range of diverse products. Their markets are mainly in the civil and chemical engineering industries.

Yee Wo Plastic Piping Components is solely involved in the manufacture and sale of plastic pumps, valves, fittings, pipes and gauges. Such products have applications in, for example, chemical plants, dyehouses and swimming baths. Their growth in the marketplace is virtually assured because they are largely replacing steel and malleable cast iron products at less cost and with greater efficiency.

In the ASEAN region, five manufacturers market similar products. The two largest are Yee Wo Plastic Piping Components and Shun Tak Fittings, each with about 40 per cent of the ASEAN market, with the remaining 20 per cent being shared amongst the other three. Each of the five manufacturers charges around the same price for their products, but the smaller companies are more prone to negotiation downwards on the factory price.

Distribution is almost wholly through stockists and the sales representatives' tasks are twofold:

1 To persuade stockists to hold a full range of the company's products to ensure a complete service to the end-user.

2 To persuade end-users to specify the company's products when purchasing from distributors.

Only Yee Wo Plastic Piping Components and Shun Tak Fittings provide a complete product range and this probably accounts for their success. However, a disturbing trend has emerged amongst the smaller distributors, and this has been to stock only the fastest moving lines from marginally cheaper sources from smaller manufacturers. Yee Wo's representatives are increasingly being called upon to supply less popular lines at very short notice.

Several of Yee Wo's representatives have become disturbed by this trend and two have recently resigned because of the adverse effects upon their sales commission. Replacing these with the right calibre people will be difficult and Johnny Tan realises that there are three courses of action to help solve this problem.

- restrict supplies to licensed distributors only

- persuade representatives to concentrate more upon the productive market sectors (e.g. large chemical plants)

- sell direct and cut out distributors

Discussion Questions

1 What can Johnny Tan do to revitalise his demoralised salesforce?

2 What are the implications of pursuing each of the three courses of action suggested by Johnny Tan?

Practical Exercise

Gardnov Ltd

Richard Booth is worried. It is the end of his first month as the newly appointed sales manager of Gardnov Ltd and things have not gone as well as expected. He joined the company with considerable enthusiasm and optimism, feeling that his experience and logical, positive approach would stand him in good stead in his new post, even though he had not previously worked for a company dealing with similar types of merchandise. His selling background was based in the more aggressive product fields of double glazing and home security products.

Gardnov Ltd was established ten years ago to supply garden products to the retail trade. Essentially a wholesaler, Gardnov stocks a very comprehensive range of garden products including garden tools, pumps and pond products, barbecues and garden furniture. It carries a Gardnov branded line of garden ornaments and these are made by manufacturers to Gardnov designs and specifications – the most popular being a range of garden gnomes featuring the likenesses of famous political figures. Most leading UK branded products are carried, together with some of the major overseas suppliers' brands. All these products are included in the company's annual catalogue which is mailed out to garden centres and retail outlets throughout the UK, regardless of whether or not they are existing customers.

Although retail customers may order direct from the catalogue (and a number do), some 90 per cent of all sales are obtained through the company salesforce of six salespeople, all male, organised to cover the UK on a regional basis. The salesforce are each paid a straight salary which in 2006 averaged £21,600 each, within a range of £16,900 to £29,300. The position of a salesperson within this range depends upon his age and length of time he has been with the company. A mid-range company car is provided, together with an expense account that covers fuel costs and a modest entertainment allowance.

Richard Booth has worked in sales for some 20 years and had previously been regional sales manager for a leading manufacturer of double glazing and home security products. On commencing his appointment at Gardnov Ltd (the previous sales manager having retired), Booth decided that he would spend his first four weeks simply observing how the salesforce operated by accompanying them on sales visits and talking to customers. He felt this would give him a sound basis on which to assess the current situation and he could then put together a strategic sales plan for the future.

What he found out during those four weeks now forms the basis of his present worries. Essentially, what he has seen and heard suggests that the company salesforce is generally lethargic and lacking in motivation. Although sales have increased by some 5 per cent on average over each of the past ten years, the total market, as Booth established from secondary marketing research data, has been growing at an annual rate of over 10 per cent.

Some of the more worrying elements that Booth established in his first four weeks are as follows. Each salesperson is assigned a region to cover. In each region the previous sales manager had divided accounts into three categories – A, B, C – according to their sales potential. A accounts are major customers to be visited weekly. B accounts are visited once every two weeks and C accounts once a month. Booth also established that each salesperson had been allocated a non-incentivised target for opening new accounts in his region.

What Booth has discovered is that over the past two years virtually all of the salesforce had only called regularly on A category customers, while B category customers were being visited about once in six weeks and C category customers were hardly ever visited. In addition, only one new account had been opened during the past four months, against five that had been lost.

Even worse, Booth visited a sample of customers in each region and was dismayed to hear that even regular customers felt that they did not relate closely to Gardnov's salesforce. A number of customers commented that recently the salesforce had been more like order-takers rather than order-makers. In addition, a high proportion of the customers suggested that Gardnov's salesmen were unable to answer questions about some of the products in the catalogue. They felt that the salesmen showed little interest in their customers and had little enthusiasm for the products they were selling. Their main aim seemed to be to minimise the time spent with the customer, even when a visit *was* made.

Booth knew that all six of the salesforce were experienced salesmen and had been with the company for an average of five years, falling within a range of two to twelve years, in an industry where the average length of stay for sales representatives was only three years. He was not sure what the problem was but knew that he would have to take immediate steps to improve sales performance.

His problem is that he does not want to start his career with Gardnov by antagonising the salesforce, but he is determined to increase motivation and ultimately sales. First, he needs to gain their co-operation and confidence. Then he hopes to be able to remedy the present situation.

Discussion Questions

1 What steps should Richard Booth take to investigate further the problems highlighted by his initial research, while at the same time gaining the co-operation of the salesforce? In your answer indicate what information Booth will require.

2 What are the disadvantages of the present salary-only compensation plan? What advice would you give to Booth about devising and implementing a new system of compensation for the salesforce?

Practical Exercise

Allwarm Knitting Ltd

Allwarm Knitting Ltd has been producing and selling yarns from their base in Huddersfield for 98 years. The soft water of the surrounding Pennine hills makes it a perfect place for production because of the scouring and cleansing processes that wool goes through before the final yarn is ready. In order to obtain a sliver that can be satisfactorily spun into a woollen thread, the following operations are necessary: willowing, oiling and blending, teasing, carding, condensing and roving. The Pennines are also suitable for the rearing of different breeds of sheep that produce different wool types and ultimately yarns for warmth, softness and breathability.

Many of these wools are still produced to the same formula today, and this fact is emphasised in the company's promotion that emphasises tradition and skill. It is still a private company and the directors have never seen the need to go to the market to raise additional capital. The company has always sold through specialist shops and some department stores under the brand name 'Yorkshire wool'. Ten years ago they were approached by a large department store group to produce a range of knitting yarns under the group's brand name. Management rejected the idea as they saw it as the first step towards giving up control of a brand that had been built up over 100 years.

The company's product range has always been extensive and currently includes a wide range of colours and yarn types. It has always been their policy to be a full-range producer, which has entailed the holding stocks of a large variety of qualities and colours at the factory for immediate dispatch to customers. A recent problem has been that financing such a large stock of finished yarns has severely drained working capital, such that the first ever overdraft facility has now been arranged with the bank.

The company's hand-knitting yarns are produced using pure new wool or blends of wool and more exclusive natural fibres such as mohair, angora and cashmere. The company has taken consistent pride in the quality of its products and believes that its brand name is well known and respected throughout the world by customers and the trade alike. For this reason, the company has always withstood moves to produce knitting yarns containing artificial fibres, despite price advantages and wear-resistance qualities.

In the 1960s knitting was popular and its main purpose then was to provide cheap garments such as sweaters for utility rather than aesthetic appeal. After a lull in the late 1970s to the mid-1980s when hand-knitting became less popular, the years since then have witnessed a return to knitting at home. One reason for this has been that it has become fashionable to wear hand-knitted garments. Younger women in particular like the idea of being able to knit an individual garment using top quality material at a fraction of the cost of a similar shop-bought item. Major fashion houses now make knitwear a prominent feature of their collections. Another reason for the return to home knitting has been the development of knitting machines that are simple to use and have come down in price dramatically since the 1980s.

Changes in fashion are reflected in the consumption statistics for hand-knitting yarns (see Table 1). Shown alongside these statistics is the percentage share of the total market held by Allwarm Knitting Ltd as well as the volume taken up by artificial fibres.

Despite a steady market, Allwarm's market share has tended to diminish over recent years and management decided that some action should be taken to arrest this decline in sales. A market research study was commissioned to establish facts and data in relation to consumption patterns. This study was completed at the end of 2002.

The research found that although total hand-knitting yarn consumption was steady between 1992 and 2006, of the total amount sold, yarns incorporating artificial fibres had increased at the expense of natural fibre yarns. The principal reason for this was found to be the price advantage of artificial yarns over natural yarns (approximately 30 per cent cheaper). The study also found that there had been a shift by distributors (especially department stores) from stocking branded yarns to unbranded yarns as they were cheaper. It was also discovered that many of the cheaper hand-knitting yarns were being sold through market outlets as manufacturers' seconds. Such yarns would not pass stringent quality tests carried out by

Table 1 Consumption statistics for hand-knitting yarns

Year	UK sales (kg millions)	% share which is purely artificial fibres	Allwarm % share of UK sales
1983	10.0	not available	7.2
1984	9.8	not available	7.3
1985	9.6	0.9	7.3
1986	10.4	1.4	7.2
1987	11.1	2.0	7.0
1988	12.0	3.1	6.8
1989	14.1	4.2	6.5
1990	14.8	4.8	6.1
1991	15.1	5.3	6.0
1992	15.4	5.9	5.8
1993	15.6	6.2	5.6
1994	15.4	6.4	5.5
1995	15.3	7.0	5.2
1996	15.2	7.4	5.2
1997	15.4	8.1	5.1
1998	15.2	8.3	5.0
1999	15.2	8.5	4.9
2000	15.5	8.6	4.8
2001	15.2	8.6	4.9
2002	15.4	8.7	5.0
2003	15.6	8.8	4.7
2004	15.5	8.5	4.6
2005	16.0	8.2	4.8
2006	15.9	8.0	4.8

Note: Per cent share of mixed fibres in relation to total sales is not known.

Allwarm and other quality manufacturers. There is no legal requirement to subject yarns to quality testing and although many such yarns were classed as seconds, many were not really seconds in the true sense of the word. They were actually manufactured to less rigorous standards and market traders were using the 'seconds' ploy as a selling technique to allow buyers to think they were getting a bargain.

The survey also pointed out the fact that although quantities of imported hand-knitting yarns were negligible at the moment, there was a strong likelihood that this would increase considerably. Yarns from the former East Germany had made inroads into the UK market, especially those incorporating artificial mixed fibres.

Allwarm does not own any distribution outlets. It does have a mill shop on the factory site for the sale of yarn that is of 'second' quality on a relatively minor basis of colour imperfection or the yarn blend not being quite up to specification. All substandard yarn in terms of its strength and the likelihood of breakage is always disposed of or reprocessed and never sold to the general public.

A UK salesforce of ten sells direct to specialist knitting yarn shops (accounting for 85 per cent of sales) with department stores accounting for the remainder. This concentration is historic because Allwarm feel that the specialist shop is the most appropriate way to sell their high-quality 'Yorkshire wool' branded yarns. Many customers seek advice from retailers when they purchase hand-knitting yarns and the company has always believed that its reputation in the trade is such that specialist retailers are likely to recommend their product to customers in preference to cheaper unbranded or mixed yarn products.

The salesforce is remunerated on a fixed salary, reviewed annually on the basis of sales. All employees share an annual bonus payable before Christmas. This is based on a percentage of the employee's annual salary. The bonus was typically around 10 per cent until 1996 and then around 5 per cent until 2001, but since then nobody has received a bonus.

Another market research study has been commissioned using discussions with groups of ten housewives in categories C1 and C2 who knit at home. As yet the research has to be formally reported, but initial findings suggest that brand name seems to be relatively unimportant when choosing a brand of knitting yarn. In a C1 focus group only three out of ten were able to recall 'Yorkshire wool' spontaneously although they all said they had heard of the brand when prompted. A C2 focus group was worse in that not a single respondent was able to spontaneously recall the 'Yorkshire wool' brand and only half had ever heard of it after prompting. In total, six focus groups will be completed together with a report within four weeks.

Discussion Questions

1 Allwarm Knitting has decided to attempt, through its distributors, to obtain a database of its end customers in order to be able to target them directly with promotional material from the company in order to build up the strength of the brand. How do you envisage that such a system should work? Explain the difficulties and the potential expense of setting up and servicing such a system.

2 Do you feel that some kind of direct marketing facility might be appropriate to help the company to arrest its declining share of the market? How might such a facility work in terms of targeting both distribution outlets and end customers?

3 The company has an email facility for business-to-business purposes. It is now contemplating setting up a website for end customers to encourage a knitting club. Advise them upon the type of information that should be incorporated in this website.

4 Allwarm Knitting's centenary is only two years away. Suggest ways in which they might celebrate this event and use it as a means of boosting their marketing effort.

Quality Chilled Foods Ltd

The company manufactures a range of up-market chilled foods in a market that covers the counties of Norfolk, Suffolk, Essex, parts of Cambridgeshire and parts of North East London. The region consists of more than 10 million people. The company's customers are quality delicatessens and some of the smaller non-chain supermarkets.

The following report has been published in the *East Anglian Times*, a newspaper covering the area in which the company's products are sold. This paper is an evening paper and has a very high readership.

> Listeria bacteria have been found in a high percentage of chilled foods through-out East Anglia. This information comes from a report published by Essex County Council and it is confirmed by Norfolk and Cambridgeshire County Councils.
>
> The report says that the virulent bacteria – which is particularly dangerous to children, elderly people and pregnant women – has been found in food such as cooked chickens, cooked meats and pâtés in supermarkets and stores. The report is to be studied in more detail later in the month by Essex authority's environmental health sub-committee.
>
> It has been drawn up following a widespread survey in the towns of Chelmsford, Southend and Colchester. At the same time similar surveys have been conducted in Ipswich and Cambridge, and although these results are not fully confirmed, their respective county councils state that their findings are likely to be similar to the findings from Essex.

It concludes: 'The relatively high percentage of commercial chilled foods which were positive gives cause for concern – not least because the large majority of these foods were ready to eat without further cooking or reheating.'

The Chief Environmental Health Officer for Essex said: 'The report is hardly a shock – it confirms a similar government finding of last year.'

Discussion Question

1 Quality Chilled Foods have asked you, a public relations consultant, to advise them what to do in relation to their retail customers in particular and the public in general. The company has absolute proof that none of their products contain listeria bacteria because their chilling process is unique and has in-built safety checks to ensure against this kind of eventuality.

   Prepare your advice in the form of a report, with special reference to the role which could be played by the salesforce.

Examination Questions

1 In the context of sales channels why is it important to engage in segmentation and targeting?

2 How can sales promotion techniques be used to help the sales effort?

3 Using appropriate illustrations, explain how PR assists the sales function.

4 Explain the meaning of 'push' and 'pull' promotional techniques. How can each help the salesperson to plan sales more effectively?

5 What is meant by the USP? How is it of use to the salesperson?

6 How can new methods of promotion through the internet assist the sales process?

5 International Selling

Objectives

After studying this chapter, you should be able to:

1 Understand key economic terms relating to international trade

2 Appreciate the nature of different types of overseas representational arrangements

3 Have a working knowledge of many of the world's trading blocs

4 Evaluate the role of culture in international selling

5 Know how to organise for international selling

6 Appreciate the effects of worldwide sourcing and buying alliances

Key Concepts

- agent
- balance of payments
- culture
- distributor
- exporting
- export houses
- invisible trade
- indirect and direct (selling)

- international marketing
- joint venture
- licensing
- multinational marketing
- subsidiary
- theory of comparative costs
- trade surplus and deficit

5.1 Introduction

In this chapter we explore aspects of international selling and examine issues and problems that stem from these. Companies contemplating entering overseas markets will need to develop specialist knowledge and expertise in these areas.

Some sales managers feel that selling abroad is impossibly difficult, but most who try it see that, although it is 'different', it is no more demanding than selling in the home market. Success depends largely on the attitude and approach of the firm and the personal qualities of the salespeople – not every salesperson is suited to such a task from the point of view of understanding and empathy with the foreign market concerned. Whilst it is hoped that this text will contribute to the development of the personal qualities necessary for successful salesmanship, the chapter concentrates specifically on those aspects of international selling with which a firm either exporting or contemplating it should be familiar.

Each year companies that have never been involved in selling abroad join the important, and often highly profitable, league of exporters or licensors and some establish joint ventures or subsidiary companies in overseas countries. One of the problems for the UK economy is that, despite government exhortations for companies to become involved in selling overseas, many executives remain apprehensive because of the mystique which often surrounds the subject. We now attempt to dispel some of this mystique by examining the more important economic aspects of international selling.

5.2 Economic Aspects

Many goods we purchase are imported, and everywhere we read that companies are striving to increase exports. Successive governments have exhorted, threatened and promised to persuade the business community to become involved in foreign markets and export more. Exporting is necessary for economic survival.

The UK is not self-supporting. Much of our raw materials and food must be purchased in world markets and imported. In turn, to pay for these commodities, we must export. The ledger for these transactions is represented by the balance of trade accounts which shows the difference between our overseas earnings and overseas expenditure. The difference between our export earnings and import expenditure (including 'invisibles' dealt with later) is termed the **balance of payments**. We now take a more detailed look at what this means.

The balance of payments

Goods passing from one country to another have to be paid for; trading between countries thus involves the creation of debts between countries. Over a period of, say, one year a country will add up how much it has paid or still owes for goods imported from foreign countries. In the same way, the country will add up how much has been paid or is still owed from overseas countries for goods exported to them. When the amount exported exceeds the amount imported the country is said to have a favourable balance of trade or a **trade surplus**. If the import of goods exceeds exports, then the country is said to have an adverse balance of trade or a **trade deficit**.

Payments for physical goods are not the only items involved in international trade. Debts also arise between countries because of services performed by one country for another. Because one cannot actually see such services they are referred to as **invisible** exports or imports. For example, the UK supplies insurance services for other countries and premiums payments due from those countries are received in the UK. Payment for shipping services, income from tourism, banking services and interest payments from international loans are other examples of invisibles.

To find how a country stands in respect of international trade – its balance of payments – we must compare the country's total exports (visible and invisible) with its total imports (visible and invisible). In the long term, a country's payments for imports and receipts for exports should balance. If a country finds itself in deficit, it can do one of two things to put matters right:

1 Reduce expenditure on imported foreign goods, reduce expenditure overseas on such items as defence and foreign aid and attempt to discourage its citizens from travelling overseas to stop money being spent abroad.

2 Sell more goods and services overseas to increase foreign revenue. It can encourage foreign tourists in the country to spend money or it can encourage foreign investment that will provide income.

Whilst the first alternative can be effective to some extent, there is a limit to which expenditure of this kind can be reduced. It is therefore to the second alternative that countries should look – selling goods and services overseas – if they are to maintain and improve their living standards and avoid a balance of payments crisis. We look briefly at the issues involved to fully understand these points.

A country that has a balance of payments surplus may receive payment from the debtor's foreign exchange reserves, receive the balance in gold, leave the money in the debtor country and use it to purchase goods and services in the future, or lend the debtor country the money to pay off the debt and receive interest on the loan in the meantime. In the same way, a country that has a deficit on its balance of payments will either have to run down its foreign exchange reserves; pay over gold; borrow the money to pay off the debt from other countries; or hold money, in terms of credit, that the creditor country can use to purchase goods and services in the future.

In essence, the balance of payments is an accounting record, with information from various sources being entered on the basis of double entry bookkeeping. If there is a deficit on the current account, i.e. if we import more goods and services than we export, this deficit must be matched by a surplus on the capital account to make the account balance. The capital account records purchases and sales of assets such as stocks, bonds, land, etc. There is a capital account surplus, or a net capital inflow, if our receipts from the sale of stocks, bonds, land, bank deposits and other assets exceed our payments for our own purchase of foreign assets.

If the government is to achieve a balance in the accounts in a current account deficit, it means either borrowing from abroad or reducing the government's stocks of gold and/or foreign exchange reserves. These borrowings and/or reductions are entered in the capital accounts as a positive figure and hence counteract the negative entry represented by a current account deficit, so the books balance.

As you will appreciate, a country can fund a continuing current account deficit only if it has limitless reserves of gold and foreign exchange or unlimited foreign borrowing power. In the long run, persistent current account deficits are difficult and costly to sustain and damaging to an economy. Total exports must pay for total imports, so if a country's exports fall then imports should also fall, unless the deficiency in exports can be made good in the ways specified. We now appreciate the importance to a country of keeping up its volume of exports.

UK share of international trade

The UK's share of exports by the main manufacturing nations has declined dramatically since the end of World War II. At the same time, some major competitors like Japan and Germany have increased their share. The problems to which this has given rise are compounded when one examines our import record. On the import side there has been a trend comprising two related factors:

- the tendency for real imports per unit of real gross domestic product to increase

- the rising share of manufactured goods accounted for by imports

The effect of such trends on British manufacturing industry has been serious. In the late 1980s to the present day the UK has experienced an imbalance in the balance of payments. In fact, the cost of physical imports has exceeded the value of exported products for over a century. This has been undesirable, but not of critical importance because our income from invisible exports has made good the difference. However, for a variety of reasons, income from invisible exports has failed to keep pace with expenditure on physical imports, resulting in an overall deficit throughout this period.

Whatever the reasons for the current situation, selling overseas has been and will remain one of the keystones of our national prosperity. Not only is it in the national interest, but in the interest of every industry, company, employer and employee.

Further economic factors

It is appropriate to consider some of the more important developments in world trade over the past 20 years. It is difficult to comment on the general effect of these developments as different industries and individual companies have been affected in different ways. Some companies feel that they have had a beneficial effect on their trading situation, while others feel that their competitive position has been seriously undermined.

European Union (EU)

The EU was at first called the Common Market, and indeed reference is still made to this title. The Common Market was legally established on 25 March 1957 by the signing of the Treaty of Rome between the governments of France, West Germany, Italy, the Netherlands, Belgium and Luxembourg. Since then, the ranks of Europeans have been swelled by the accession of Ireland, Denmark, Greece, Spain, Portugal and the UK, to be joined later by the former East Germany, following the reunification of Germany. More recently, Austria, Sweden and Finland were admitted, and in 2005 Poland, Hungary, Latvia, Estonia, Slovakia, Slovenia, Lithuania, Malta, Cyprus and the Czech Republic were admitted. Turkey, Romania, Croatia and Bulgaria are now seeking membership. The Common Market was also known as the European Economic Community (EEC), and subsequently the European Community (EC). The EC title is still used, but now stands for European Commission. These name changes resulted from the fact that, as the organisation expanded and matured, it began to see its role as being more of a political union than merely a trading bloc. More recently, its title has been changed to the European Union (EU), which is a reflection of its current influential political role.

The initial objective of the treaty was to remove all restrictions on the free movement of goods and services and individuals within 12 years (i.e. by 1969), by removing taxation differentials, frontier controls and other forms of restriction. Since those early days, the movement towards this goal has been slow for economic and political reasons. In fact, it was this political aspect that kept the UK out of the EU for many years. The UK was not seen to be truly European – a contention that many say holds true today, epitomised by a national reluctance to adopt the euro – and its tendency to view the EU as an economic, rather than as a political union.

By 1982 (the EU's twenty-fifth birthday) the momentum for a Single European Market had come to a virtual standstill. Many non-tariff barriers remained. The free movement of goods was hindered by varying taxation systems, public procurement restrictions (to include tenders only from domestic providers) and different technical and consumer protection standards. For example, rates of value added tax still differ beween individual countries.

A turning point came in 1984 when Jacques Delors (former French finance minister) assumed the presidency of what was then the EC. He developed the concept of an open market within the community to create the largest single market in the Western world. Although this was essentially nothing new, his statement came at the end of the economic recession of the late 1970s and early 1980s, during which member states had turned economically inwards, defending their national markets against European competition. A programme for removing the remaining obstacles to trade by 31 December 1992 was drawn up by Lord Cockfield, EC Commissioner in charge of the internal market portfolio. The programme was presented to heads of government at a summit meeting in Milan in June 1985, and eventually the Single European Act (SEA) came into force in July 1987. The Act lists 300 measures which were to be completed if the single market philosophy was to proceed to schedule. In order to hasten the decision-making process, power of veto was removed and these resolutions could be passed by a 'qualified majority'. These 300 initial proposals were subsequently reduced to 279 by the withdrawal of certain proposals and the grouping of others into single proposals. The main features of the Single European Act are:

(a) establishment of a Single European Market

(b) products approved in any one EU country can be freely marketed throughout the EU

(c) progressive opening up of government and public body contracts to all EU contractors on an equal basis

(d) more competitive and efficient Europe-wide services in telecommunications and IT

(e) removal of red tape on road haulage and shipping services between member countries to be provided on equal terms, and more competition on air routes with lower overall fares

(f) banks should be free to provide banking and investment services anywhere within the EU; insurers should have greater freedom to cover risks in member countries

(g) restrictions on the movement of capital to be abolished

(h) harmonisation of national laws on patents and trademarks

(i) professional qualifications gained in one country to be acceptable throughout the EU

There are, of course, other features, but these are the most significant ones.

A pamphlet produced by the Department of Trade and Industry perhaps best summed up how companies could take advantage of the single market in terms of protecting their existing markets and developing new ones.[1] This is ironic because other members of the EU have more of a European mentality. They tend to regard each other's markets as their own 'home' markets, whereas UK companies still tend to regard selling to EU countries as exporting. This is highlighted by the fact that since the UK joined the EU with its current population of almost half a billion people, it has always operated with a net deficit on its balance of trade with its European partners. The DTI pamphlet recommended that companies should ask a number of key questions in relation to their businesses:

1 How has the market changed our business?

2 Should we become a European business, looking upon Europe as our primary market rather than just the UK?

3 Would becoming a European business alter the scale of the targets in our plans?

4 In what ways will we be vulnerable to more competition in our present markets?

5 Should we form links, merge or acquire business to strengthen our market presence, broaden our range of products and services, and spread our financial risk?

6 Is our management and structure appropriate to exploit new opportunities or defend our position?

7 What training in languages and other skills do we need to be ready for this single market?

8 Who in our firm is going to be responsible for deciding how to make the most of the single market?

The pamphlet might have stated the obvious, but it did at least focus thinking in a formal manner to the issues of 1992. More specifically, it recommended that in the field of *selling* the company should ask five key questions. The solutions to each of these questions were volunteered through a list of suggestions:

1 How do you reach the customers?

   • Investigate the trade structure such as wholesalers and retailers.

   • Identify buying points.

   • Find out about buying procedures, terms and practices, such as the preferred currency of invoicing (now, with exceptions, standardised as the euro).

   • Consider how far you need to know the local language.

   • Examine different selling approaches, including brokers and agents.

   • Find out how your competitors are using advertising, promotion and trade discounts.

2 How can you sell into this market?

   • Consider regional test marketing.

   • Establish your sales targets.

   • Decide on your total sales and promotion budget.

   • Decide on your selling organisation.

3 What sales literature is necessary?

   • Assess suitability of existing material for European markets.

   • Consider the need to redesign to appeal to new customers.

   • Arrange translation where necessary.

4 How should you advertise?

   • Examine your existing advertising.

   • Assess differences in national media availability and costs.

   • Decide on your advertising budget.

5 How will you provide after-sales service?

   • Consider relative merits and costs of direct provision or subcontracting.

The prospect of a single market is no longer a future scenario but a reality. Companies that have failed to plan for the changes which the single market has brought, and will continue to bring, find themselves faced with increased competition for which they are ill-prepared. Successful companies will increasingly be those who prepared for the single market some years ago. A Confederation of British Industry survey of 200 companies, undertaken in 1990, found that three-quarters had undertaken strategic reviews in response to 1992. It is important to remember that in many ways 1992 represented just one more step, albeit a major one, in a 40-year journey towards genuine free trade within the EU.

At a more general level, by the terms of the Treaty of Rome that first initiated the EU in 1957, member countries are independent of their national governments and not able to accept instructions from them. Their proposals are subject to the official sanctions of the (European) Council of Ministers and the democratically elected members of the European Parliament. This means that many of the decisions which ultimately affect UK industry are outside the direct control of the UK government, and in many areas of trade negotiations are carried out on our behalf by the EU as a whole. This process of Europeanisation was taken further by the terms of the Maastricht Treaty, which was controversial in the domestic political arena of the UK. There is still deep division within political parties as to the relative merits of the proposals in the treaty. The point being made is that although it is ultimately envisaged that the EU will be similar to the USA, with each member country being akin to a state (it is even termed the United States of Europe), can this ever be a reality when one considers differences in attitude, culture, language and even religion? It is difficult to envisage a homogeneous pan-European marketing programme not unlike that of the USA. A continuing trend towards political and economic unity will pose many opportunities (and threats) to companies within the EU, but things will not change overnight. This will be more of a slow transitionary period and could well take decades before an integration similar to that in the USA today. We have seen the first steps towards this goal, with the introduction of a common monetary unit – the euro – that has been accepted by an overwhelming majority of member countries.

An interesting proposition is that postulated by Charles Betz of the European consultancy organisation Carré Orban and Paul Ray International that each European country will adopt a particular expertise:

- **Germany** will specialise in high technology engineering.

- **The Netherlands** will concentrate on service industries (e.g. storage and distribution of petrochemicals).

- **Belgium** will form the hub of the community through Brussels, adopting a bureaucratic role.

- **France** will become more technical.

- **Switzerland** will remain outside the EU, acting as the financial centre and neutral protector of money.

- **Austria** could play a major role as the bridge between the EU and other Eastern European countries.

- **Turkey** (which is currently seeking membership) will become a cheap manufacturing base producing goods for the Middle East and North Africa.

- **Italy**, **Spain** and **Greece** will be the 'winners' as they have reasonable levels of readily available, cost-effective labour.

- **Portugal** has low labour costs and is basically an agrarian economy, making it a natural country from which to sell winter grown vegetables to the more affluent northern countries.

- **Denmark** has traded its Scandinavian independence for an ability to trade within the EU and should do well with innovative designs.

- **Ireland** will hopefully solve its political problems with the North and its low labour costs will put it in a good position to compete in manufacturing and assembly.

- **United Kingdom** will show leadership in financing the consolidation of industries across national boundaries.

- **Sweden and Finland** will develop their established expertise in precision machinery and telecommunications equipment.

This is merely one expert's conjecture, but inevitably there will be movement towards specialisation by individual member countries of the EU.

World Trade Organisation (WTO)

Perhaps one of the most important developments of the last few years has been a steady but widespread trend towards protectionism. The greater part of world trade is subject to the General Agreement on Tariffs and Trade (GATT). Basically this is a complex agreement, but its most important features can be summarised in four fundamental principles:

1 *Non-discrimination*. Each member country agrees that any tariff concession or trade advantage granted to one country, whether or not a member of GATT, shall be granted to all member countries.

2 *Consultation*. Member countries are required to meet under GATT auspices to discuss any trade problems that may arise.

3 *Tariff negotiation*. That tariffs should be open to negotiation is the idea that originally inspired GATT. The hope was that these negotiations would be aimed at reducing and eventually removing customs duties.

4 *Trade liberalisation*. The overriding aim of the WTO, and from which the principles described derive, is a continuing liberalisation of world trade. With this aim in mind, import quotas and licensing requirements, restrictions that nations have traditionally used to limit volume and types of imports, are prohibited. The idea is that temporary protection shall be afforded to each nation's domestic industry exclusively through the customs tariff.

The effect of GATT over post-war years has been to remove some of the protection afforded to national markets. As a result, GATT agreements have been responsible – in part – for considerable growth in world trade referred to earlier. This liberalisation of trade has since been slowed by a series of actions. There has been widespread adoption of restrictive trade measures falling outside formal GATT rules, e.g. voluntary export restraints and anti-dumping legislation.

The WTO has suggested that, excluding agricultural products, the volume of international trade so affected now represents more than 5 per cent of the total volume of world trade and is expanding steadily. However, the WTO principles resulted in the average tariff on manufactured goods falling from 40 per cent in 1947 to only 4.7 per cent in 1979, and it has continued to fall marginally ever since.

Such tariff reductions are negotiated in GATT rounds of meetings – the eighth round began in Uruguay in 1986 and was originally set for completion in December 1990. The fact that this only finished in 1995 reflects the lengthy and difficult negotiations involved. The Uruguay round made slow progress on new rules and tariff reductions, including a new general agreement on trade in services. However, a major stumbling block to reaching agreement was the dispute between the USA and the EU members regarding the Common Agricultural Policy. The USA insisted that reform of subsidies allocated to EU farmers was essential to a GATT agreement and called for the abolition of all farming subsidies over a period of ten years. Initially, it seemed that the USA and the EU would not be able to agree on the farm subsidies issue and that the Uruguay round would degenerate into a stalemate with a return to protectionist policies, especially on the part of the USA. However, after intensive talks and diplomacy and following the recent Doha round of negotiations, issues were largely resolved and the WTO was able to move forward, albeit somewhat haltingly.

Eastern Europe

A significant development in recent years has been the collapse of communism and the changes in Eastern Europe this has precipitated. The nature and significance of these changes are lengthy topics, but suffice it to say that many of the previously 'closed' Eastern European countries are now open to trade with their neighbours and countries worldwide. In attempting to develop their economies, many of these previously centrally planned economies are now eager and willing trade partners for those companies able to organise themselves to do business with them.

The continuing need to export

Undoubtedly the world economy is experiencing basic changes in the composition and direction of international trade, terms of trade and in size, direction and character of capital movements. The UK has moved from being heavily reliant on oil imports to self-sufficiency. Related to this, our balance of payments accounts showed a surplus until the 1980s when they fell back into deficit again. Despite this, the imperative need to export remains as strong as ever. While these changes pose a challenge to exporters, it can only be hoped that the response they evoke will be conducive to the well-being and prosperity of all.

Although increased exports of goods and services is in the national interest, individual firms have more selfish objectives and the most positive inducement to them to sell overseas is the existence of profitable opportunities. However, there are other factors that must be considered and these are now discussed.

5.3 International Selling at Company Level

The fact that national economic prosperity depends on selling overseas is not without relevance to individual companies. There are a number of more pressing reasons why companies benefit from selling overseas:

1 *Trade due to non-availability of a particular product.* Such trade is clearly beneficial when a country is able to import a commodity it could not possibly produce itself. For example, the UK imports rubber because it cannot be grown here. It may be that a product or process is protected by a patent and can only be produced if a firm purchases the patent right or enters a licensing agreement.

2 *Trade due to international differences in competitive costs.* The basis for international trade between countries can be explained in terms of the economist David Ricardo's **theory of comparative costs**. The theory states that countries will gain if each exports products in which costs of production are comparatively lower and imports products in which costs of production are comparatively higher. Although this principle is applied mainly in connection with international trade, one can see it in operation in all forms of production. It is a similar concept to the benefit of division of labour, in that benefits are to be gained not by persons doing what they can do best, but by persons doing what they can do relatively better than other people. The more productive country would still benefit from specialisation in those goods it produces best, and should then import those goods it is comparatively less good at producing.

3 *Trade due to product differentiation.* In many industries each firm's product has some point of difference that distinguishes it in some way from products manufactured by other firms. Differentiation may be in terms of quality, design or even an intangible difference such as customers' perceived image of the product. This latter factor is in evidence in relation to cars, which explains why the UK both imports cars from and exports cars to other countries.

It is important to note that the decision to export and import in a free market economy is not made by the country as a collective unit. It is made by individual firms who hope to benefit through foreign trade. We have looked at three broad reasons why individual firms become involved in selling overseas, but there are other more situation specific reasons:

(a) To become less vulnerable to the effects of economic recession, particularly in the home market, and to counter market fluctuations.

(b) Loss of domestic market share due to increased competition.

(c) To take advantage of faster rates of growth in demand in other markets.

(d) To dispose of surplus or to take up excess capacity in production.

(e) Loss of domestic market share due to product obsolescence. Products that become technically obsolete in more developed economies may still be appropriate in less advanced economies. For example, flypaper has been replaced by aerosol fly killers, but this product is relatively inexpensive and still in demand in developing countries.

(f) To achieve the benefits of long production runs and to gain economies of scale: if the firm can expand its production it will lead to a reduction in average cost and hence a reduction in price, not only in overseas markets but also in the home market, which may lead to further domestic market expansion.

(g) The firm has special expertise or knowledge of producing a product that is not available in a foreign market.

(h) Simply the existence of potential demand backed by purchasing power which is probably the strongest incentive of all.

So far we have looked at some of the main economic factors concerned with selling overseas. This coverage is not exhaustive as entire texts have been written on the economics of international trade.

At the beginning we stated that selling overseas was different to selling in the home market. Whilst economic factors are important, only non-economic factors can explain the different patterns of consumption of two different countries with similar per capita incomes. Selling overseas is a cultural as well as an economic phenomenon and it is to the area of cultural influences in overseas markets that we now turn.

5.4   Cultural Factors in International Selling

In essence, **culture** is the distinctive way of life of a people that is not biologically transmitted. Such learned behaviour is passed on from one generation to the next, evolving and changing over time. A society organises itself in such a way that people adhering to cultural norms are rewarded while those who deviate are 'punished' to a greater or lesser degree depending on the culture. As a society's needs change and evolve, so cultural norms will change and 'old' patterns of behaviour will no longer be rewarded, whereas new patterns will. In this way, society sustains itself and produces the types of behaviour and responses it needs to survive.

This reward and punishment principle of culture is important when selling overseas. The culture in which a person lives affects their consumption patterns and perceptions of specific products and meanings attached to them. Because of this, only certain products and selling practices that the individual perceives as normal and acceptable to their particular culture will be acceptable. It follows that overseas salespeople need to understand how culture functions in individual overseas markets so that sales approaches can be tailored accordingly. In order to be able to offer value to the market, a salesperson must understand the value system of the foreign market and this means a knowledge of the influence of cultural factors.

Culture includes both abstract and material elements. Abstract elements include values, attitudes, ideas and religion. These are learned patterns of behaviour that are transmitted from one generation to another. Material elements of the culture are levels and type of technology and consumption patterns within that society.

The Prahalad and Doz Integration and Responsiveness Model (Figure 5.1) has proven to be a valuable model in portraying the approach that firms may adopt in their international operations.[2]

According to this model, a firm may opt to maintain its standardised products/services across its international markets (i.e. Coca-Cola) or choose to adapt its product offerings according to the cultural needs of the respective country (e.g. Levi jeans). However, according to this model, sustained competitiveness would

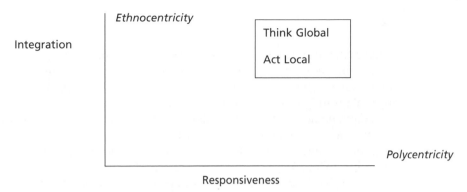

Figure 5.1 Prahalad and Doz Integration and Responsiveness Model
Source: Prahalad, C.K. and Doz, Y.L. (1991) 'Managing DMNCS: A Search for a New Paradigm',
Strategic Management Journal, 12, pp. 145–64.

ideally be achieved if companies strive to achieve the balance of *Think Global Act Local*. Subsequently, not only would the firm and its employees be able to integrate fully within the culture, but they would also be able to respond appropriately to the cultural demands and needs of the specific market – hence achieving a win-win situation.

An understanding of the way a society organises its economic activities and the type of technology used is important for selling overseas. It stands to reason that a firm would find difficulty selling advanced microelectronic machinery to a culture with a primitive, agriculturally based economy. In such a case 'appropriate' technology will have a greater chance of acceptance.

Salespeople should develop cultural skills. These provide them with an ability to relate to different cultures even when they do not know the elements of the culture in detail. Cateora, Graham and Ghauri[3] suggest that people with cultural skills can:

- convey respect and communicate verbally and non-verbally a positive attitude and interest in people and their culture

- cope with ambiguity and the frustrations that sometimes occur when faced with an unfamiliar culture

- show empathy by understanding other people's needs and viewpoints

- avoid judging other people by their own value systems

- control the use of self-reference criteria whereby assumptions are made based upon one's own culture and values

- use humour to prevent frustration levels rising when things do not work out as planned

We now explore some of these elements within cultures in the knowledge that in some countries factors such as religion have inhibited the acceptance of Western materialism and industrialisation.

Aesthetics

A non-material cultural factor which may have an influence on the development of overseas markets is aesthetics. This refers to a culture's ideas concerning beauty and good taste, together with an appreciation of colour and form. The exporter must be aware of positive and negative aspects of its designs, packaging, advertising, etc. The company should be sensitive to local preferences and tastes and items such as company logos should incorporate local preferences.

Colour is important, the most quoted example being that black represents mourning in the West, whereas in Eastern countries the colour of mourning is white. This has implications for pack design. Music is important, particularly when used in advertising and promotion. Many non-Western cultures use a type of music not applied in the West, which has symbolic meaning to the members of the culture. An attempt should be made to understand this symbolism and turn it to positive selling advantage.

Religion

Material culture and aesthetics are outward manifestations of a culture and give an indication of how consumers in a particular culture behave. The firm selling overseas needs an understanding of why consumers behave in that way. The religion practised by a culture can give insights into its members' behaviour. For illustrative purposes, two of the largest religions – Hinduism and Islam – are now discussed.

Hinduism is followed by 85 per cent of India's population and is as much a way of life as a religion. An understanding of the tenets of Hinduism is necessary for an understanding of the Indian culture. Important doctrines of Hinduism include the caste system, the joint family, the veneration of the cow and the restriction of women. Any product or selling activity that offends the tenets of Hinduism would have small chance of success because such views are deep-rooted in Indian culture.

Islam takes the Koran as its ultimate guide; anything not mentioned in the Koran is likely to be rejected by the faithful. An important element in Islamic belief is that everything which happens proceeds from the divine will. This belief restricts any attempt to bring about change because to attempt to change may be contrary to what Allah has ordained. Firms entering overseas markets must bear this in mind when introducing new products or services.

A company must therefore be aware of religious differences in its foreign markets and be prepared to make adaptations both in selling operations and the products themselves.

Education

Analysing educational information for relevant markets gives the firm an insight into the nature and sophistication of consumers in different countries. In some countries many people are not formally educated in the three Rs, although they may be educated in ways of culture.

In marketing a new product in a foreign country, the firm is itself trying to educate consumers in uses and benefits of the product. The success of this sales communication will be constrained by the general level of education within the culture. If consumers are largely illiterate, then company advertising, packaging and labelling will need to be adapted. Complex products that need written instructions may need to be modified into diagrams to meet the educational level and skills of the particular culture.

Language

The language of a culture is important. For example, a literal translation by someone not familiar with its deeper cultural meaning may result in serious mistakes. If the brand name is standardised worldwide in English it may be found to have an unfavourable meaning in some countries, or not be pronounceable in languages that lack certain letters of the alphabet. A famed example of the former (and now denied by Rolls-Royce) is that the Rolls-Royce Silver Shadow was nearly called Silver Mist which would have been most unfortunate when selling to the German market. A good example of the latter is Signal toothpaste which was called Shield toothpaste.

Understanding language in international selling

A key ingredient in international selling is a command of foreign languages. As the former German Chancellor, Willy Brandt, once said, 'If I am selling to you I will speak English, but if you are selling to me dann mussen Sie Deutsch sprechen!'

Salespeople also need to understand both the nuances of the foreign language and the silent language. A salesperson needs to know that Japanese 'yes' often means 'no', but that a Chinese 'no' often means 'yes'! Silent languages are also important as the following example illustrates.

A European salesperson visits a Saudi businessperson to sell him machinery. The Saudi offers the salesperson coffee which is politely refused (he had been drinking coffee earlier). He sits down and crosses his legs exposing the sole of his shoe. He passes sales literature to the Saudi with his left hand, asks about the Saudi's wife and stresses the need to make a quick decision.

Unwittingly, the European has offended the Saudi five times. He turned down his host's hospitality, showed disrespect, used an 'unclean' hand, was over-familiar and showed impatience with his host. Although the Saudi may realise that the actions were unintentional, the salesperson is left in a weakened position.

Sources: Based on Cateora, P.R. (1998) '*International Marketing*', Irwin, Boston; Egan, C. and McKiernan, P. (1994) '*Inside Fortress Europe: Strategies for the Single Market*', Addison Wesley, Wokingham.

Social organisation

Social organisation differs between cultures. The primary kind of social organisation is based on kinship and in many less-developed nations this takes the form of a large extended family. A company operating in such a society must realise that the extended family means that decisions on consumption are taken by a larger unit and in different ways. A firm selling overseas may find difficulty determining the relevant consuming unit (e.g. is it the family, the household or an individual?).

In many Asian and African countries, social organisation is in tribal groupings which may be a clue to effective market segmentation. Social class is more important and more rigid in many foreign countries, e.g. the Indian caste system. The selling firm must be aware of the cultural variations in social organisation when targeting sales efforts to a particular social segment of the population.

Political factors

Culture includes all activities that characterise the behaviour of particular communities such as legal, political and economic factors. Nationalism and dealings with governments are often considered to be a major problem facing firms selling overseas. Most governments play either participating or regulatory roles in their economies. In India, for example, certain sectors of the economy are reserved exclusively for government enterprise.

Government legislation and economic policy may affect a firm's pricing and credit policy and there may be regulations concerning products and promotions. Factors like nationalism, international relations, political stability and the level of capitalism and democracy in the foreign country will all have an impact on overseas sales strategy.

General cultural attitudes and values

In some cultures selling and trade in general have low social approval. A company selling overseas may thus have difficulty in recruiting appropriate sales personnel and selling products through the channel of distribution. Many Eastern cultures put spiritual values before material values.

Different cultures also have different 'time values'. A much quoted example is in Latin American cultures, where sales representatives are often kept waiting a long time for a business appointment. In our culture this would be unorthodox and at best would be seen as being ill mannered. A delay in answering correspondence in the UK usually indicates that the matter has low priority. A similar delay in Spain could mean something different because there close family relatives take absolute priority. No matter how important other business is, all non-relatives are kept waiting. In the West we are used to business deadlines, but in many Middle Eastern cultures a deadline is taken as an insult and such behaviour may well lose business for the overseas salesperson.

The concept of space has a different meaning to different cultures. In the West the size of an executive's office is often an indication of his or her status. In the Arab world this is not so. The managing director may use the same office as the general

The Chinese culture and sales negotiations

Cultural differences mean that salespeople need to understand and respect the values of overseas customers and alter their expectations and behaviour accordingly. Visiting salespeople may be required to attend long banquets when engaging in negotiations with Chinese people. The banquets may begin in either the late morning or early evening. Frequent toasts are usual and some Chinese hosts regard the visitor as having a good time if s/he becomes a little intoxicated.

In China, negotiations often take much longer than in many Western countries and arriving late for a business appointment is deemed acceptable behaviour. To do so in Hong Kong, however, would result in the visitor 'losing face', a serious issue in Chinese culture. When conducting sales negotiations, visiting salespeople should avoid creating a position where a Chinese person might 'lose face' by finding themselves in an embarrassing situation (e.g. by displaying lack of knowledge or understanding). Chinese people tend to elicit as much information as possible before disclosing their hand to avoid losing face or displaying ignorance. Business relations should be built on the basis of harmony and friendship. Contracts are accepted as much as a basis for business relationships as a legal document.

Many salespeople fall into the trap of using 'self-reference' criteria when selling abroad. They assume that what is acceptable and highly valued in their own country is equally valued in all cultures. To avoid this fallacy, salespeople need training in the special skills of selling to people from different cultures.

Sources: Based on Bradley, F. (1998) *International Marketing Strategy*, Prentice Hall, London; Jeannet, J.P. and Hennessey, H.D. (1995) *Global Marketing Strategies*, Houghton Mifflin, Boston.

clerks, so the salesperson must be careful how s/he speaks to people. In the West, business agreements are carried out at a distance, say two metres or more. In Middle Eastern and Latin American countries, business discussions are carried out in very close proximity, involving physical contact, which many Western salespeople find uncomfortable.

In the West, business is discussed over lunch or dinner in the businessperson's home. In India, to discuss business at home or at any social occasion is a violation of hospitality rules. In the West we rely on the law of contract for all business agreements, but in the Muslim culture a man's word is just as binding. In fact, a written contract often violates a Muslim's sensitivities because it challenges his honour.

Subcultural influences must not be overlooked, because these are sometimes the dominant force in the country. Examples include the following:

- nationality groups, e.g. French- and English-speaking Canadians

- religious groups, e.g. Protestant and Catholic groupings in Northern Ireland

- geographical areas, e.g. the North and South of England may be thought of as separate markets for many products

- racial groups, e.g. within South Africa the divide still remains between races

- social stratification, e.g. the caste system in India

Cultural change

A company following the marketing concept overseas – trying to satisfy needs and wants of target markets at a profit – must keep abreast of changes in the cultural environment that affect people's attitudes and values and hence, indirectly, their needs and wants of products and services. In our own society the cultural values towards debt have changed. Debt has lost its stigma and is part of everyday life with the universal acceptance of credit cards. Our society's moral values have changed and we are more liberal and tolerant of matters like entertainment. Products and services demanded have reflected this change in cultural values. A firm must therefore be aware that its products may face obsolescence in overseas markets, not because of technical advance but because of cultural change.

Not only are a firm's existing products vulnerable to cultural change, but the company may also miss new opportunities by not being informed of changes in culture. The impact of culture is especially important if the company is dealing with a foreign culture seeking rapid industrialisation. It is necessary for a company operating in this type of environment to monitor trends and adapt as necessary. Not only must the firm selling overseas be versed in the economics, law and politics of a foreign country, but it will also have to understand the more subtle, less tangible meanings, values and languages of the culture itself.

| 5.5 | Organisation for International Selling |

Organisation to implement international sales operations can be complex. Decisions must be made on arranging the interface between manufacturing and sales and in delegating responsibility for international operations. Each problem can have alternative solutions and an optimal decision must be tailored for each firm.

Some companies are so deeply involved in international trade that it forms the majority of sales turnover, whilst others are simply content to supply export orders. A distinction is made between **multinational marketing, international marketing** and **exporting** and each is now considered:

1 *Multinational marketing* relates to companies whose business interests, manufacturing plants and offices are spread throughout the world. Although their strategic headquarters might be in an original country, multinationals operate independently at national levels. Multinationals produce and market goods within the countries they have chosen to develop. Examples of multinationals are Shell, Ford, Coca-Cola, Microsoft and McDonald's. To be successful multinationals need to understand their competences and weaknesses. The Microsoft case history examines this company's bright and dark side.

2 *International marketing* covers companies that have made a strategic decision to enter foreign markets, have made appropriate organisational changes and marketing mix adaptations.

3 *Exporting* is at the simple end of the scale and the term is applied to companies that regard exporting as a peripheral activity, whose turnover from exporting is less than 20 per cent.

Microsoft's soul

Steve Ballmer has drawn up a map of multinational Microsoft's soul. There is a 'bright side' and a 'dark side' to the software company says Ballmer in a slide presentation he has shown to staff at the Seattle headquarters.

The bright side

- The company is 'totally about intelligence'. It is stocked with some of the brightest people.
- Microsoft 'loves, loves, loves' technology.
- It is super-competitive.
- Internally the company is honest and self-critical.
- The individual rules the roost. 'One great guy. One great idea.'

The dark side

- Internal competition is too fierce. Departments see each other as enemies.
- The company is sometimes focussed on the wrong things.
- It is too reliant on 'brilliant leaders'.
- It is 'opinionated but not decisive'.
- There is a lack of team work.

Source: Adapted from an article by Dominic Rushe, *The Sunday Times*, 23 June 2002.

Whatever the form of organisation for overseas selling, it is important that there should be a senior manager charged with responsibility for exporting who is able to advise and influence colleagues.

In choosing how to organise for international selling there is a division into **indirect** and **direct** methods. Some of the more common forms of overseas sales organisation are now described. The choice of organisation depends on a number of factors: the proportion of total turnover accounted for by overseas business; the nature of the product; relative advantages and disadvantages of each form of organisation. There is no single uniform approach to the task. The keynote is flexibility and adaptability. We first consider indirect approaches to international selling.

Types of intermediary and their selection

It is estimated that agents and distributors alone, acting on behalf of overseas companies, handle over half the world's overseas trade. The term *intermediary* is used to describe all persons and organisations providing the service of representation between sellers and buyers.

Few manufacturers are able to cover a market adequately without the service of some form of intermediary. The decision faced by firms as to which intermediary to use and the policies to be adopted is critical to the firm's future in the market.

Agents

An **agent** is a firm or individual acting on behalf of another. This is one of the main forms of overseas representation. The most common form of agency is where agents, acting as independent operators, obtain orders on behalf of an exporter on a commission basis and the exporter acts as principal. Agents also work on behalf of purchasers and some specialise in certain tasks, for example, transport and distribution, advertising and market research.

Care should be exercised in appointing the right agent, and a company entering overseas markets should satisfy itself as to the agent's reputation and financial position. The agent may have other interests and the firm should ensure that these do not conflict with its own. Agents are often key figures in a firm's overseas operations and success overseas will depend on the ability and commitment of the agent. Care therefore needs to be exercised in the choice of agent and organisations like banks will advise and assist in their selection. In assessing the suitability of an agent, the principal needs clear answers to the following questions:

1 When was the agency founded?

2 What other interests does the agency have, i.e. what other agencies are held?

3 Does the agent provide the required coverage for your market?

4 What is the agent's standing in the business community of the market in terms of professional integrity and reputation, reliability, etc.?

5 Is the agent the type of person or company that will fit in with the way your company carries out its business?

6 Will you be able to work with the agency?

7 Does the agent possess the resources necessary to carry out the task adequately, i.e. financial resources, transport, offices, warehouses and human resources?

8 Is the agent able to provide technical support or after-sales service arrangements if these are necessary?

This list is not exhaustive and more specific details may be necessary depending on the market, industry and type of product. Once a suitable agent has been found, progress should be monitored. Agents are usually appointed for a trial period, with extensions to the contract after that.

Training agents is important to indirect selling in overseas markets, particularly if products are technically complex. Without proper knowledge and technical appreciation of the product range, the agent will be ill equipped to conduct negotiations with professional buyers who may be experts in their field. Training may have to take place at the principal's manufacturing plant and should form a compulsory part of any agreement. Training may need to be continuous, with periodic updating sessions, especially if the firm is involved in new product development or if technology is changing rapidly.

Sales meetings and conferences in the principal's own country can be used for training purposes and as a forum for tackling specific problems and discussing future promotional strategies. Such meetings will also have a social function, bringing agents together for a few days to exchange ideas, discuss common problems and be made to feel part of the company.

Once a suitable agent has been found, the right kind of working relationship must be nurtured. Many companies feel that the appointment of a good overseas agent is an alternative to involvement in the market themselves. This is *not* so as the principal has to be actively involved; if the relationship is to be successful then it must be based on partnership and co-operation. The principal should visit the agent in the market to create a sense of value, importance, belonging and encouragement. Such visits also keep the agent informed of developments in the principal's country and of the principal's products. The principal will gain valuable market information on competitive actions, the overseas business environment and feedback on promotions and new products. All of this will lead to a better understanding of the dynamics of the overseas market and improvement in sales strategy.

The principal can also give assistance to the agent by helping in commercial negotiations between the agent and important customers, assisting with special discounts or credit arrangements in order to secure business. Frequency of visiting abroad by the principal will depend on the importance of the market, the competence of the agent and distance from home base. Important markets should be visited more frequently, particularly if technical assistance or after-sales service are required.

In some cases, agents feel insecure as companies often regard them as a temporary method of servicing overseas markets. Once the market expands and matures, many companies dismiss their agents and enter direct selling or open a subsidiary company. Therefore, the very success of an agent can sometimes mean downfall. In anticipation of this eventuality, agents sometimes collect a large number of agencies, resulting in a diffusion of effort and possible conflict of interests. This problem can be overcome by negotiating a long-term arrangement once the agent has been proved, or by inserting a gradual run-down clause into the agency agreement. In the latter case, the agent can often make a valuable contribution to, say, the setting up of a new overseas subsidiary company, or even manage the subsidiary. Thus, fair treatment of agents and ex-agents cultivates a reputation as a good and fair employer, and this in turn will probably be reflected in future dealings in that country.

An insight into the factors in which principals should excel in order to attract top performing agents is given in a research study by Merritt and Newell (2001)[4] which identified the criteria sales agents use to evaluate principals. The top ten criteria are listed in Table 5.1

Distributors

Distributors act in a different capacity to agents as they actually buy and sell the goods, whereas agents work principally on commission. Like an agent, a distributor will usually be a local firm or individual and a specialist in the requirements of the local market. They should be familiar with local business practices/customs, structure

Table 5.1 Top ten criteria used by sales agents to evaluate principals

---

  1 Loyalty of principal to agency
  2 Product quality
  3 Trustworthiness of the principal
  4 Exclusiveness of territories
  5 Timeliness of orders received
  6 Potential sales growth
  7 Principal–agency teamwork
  8 Principal action on complaints
  9 Commission or reward structure
10 Attitudes of principal personnel

Source: Merritt, N.J. and Newell, S.J. (2001) 'The extent and formality of sales agency evaluations of principals', *Industrial Marketing Management*, 30, pp. 37–49.

of the market and various socio-cultural factors. Distributors differ from agents as follows:

(a) They will be able to finance their own stockholding of goods.

(b) They will usually be able to purchase in larger quantities, thus saving on delivery costs.

(c) Acting as principal, they will be commercially and legally responsible for all business transactions in the market.

(d) They are entrepreneurs and accept risks involved in the purchase and reselling of goods, such as local falls in demand and currency fluctuations.

(e) In some cases they may provide an after-sales service.

A frequent complaint from companies using distributors is that, because they are independent businesses acting independently, they can decide the final selling price to the customer. If price is thought to be a significant factor in the product's success, then the manufacturer should only deal with distributors who are willing to agree a mark-up and selling price with the manufacturer.

As with agents, it is important for the manufacturer to develop good working relationships with overseas distributors as commitment to the commercial relationship is needed from both sides. Although distributors purchase goods from the manufacturer to resell on their own account, they are more than just another customer. The manufacturer relies on the distributor to achieve their own objectives, but the manufacturer must consider that distributors have objectives and interests of their own. It is in the firm's interests to give distributors as much technical and sales assistance as possible. As with agents, distributors can be used in an information-gathering capacity to report on trends and developments in the marketplace.

A decision will also have to be made whether to use a number of smaller local distributors or a small number of large national distributors. Using a number of small distributors has the advantage of good coverage and is advantageous where there are regional differences in culture or business practices. However, large national distributors give economies of scale as goods can be shipped in bulk.

In some cases it may be desirable to have an exclusive agreement with the distributors, otherwise they might offer competitors' products to customers if they offer a higher margin.

Licensing

Licensing is another alternative open to a firm contemplating an indirect venture into overseas markets. It assumes that the company has some unique product or process (preferably protected by patent) that an overseas company will want to manufacture. This is a good way of entering and remaining in more distant markets, or in a market where it is difficult or impossible to export finished goods. In such markets, direct selling or selling via agents and distributors might be impractical, or it might be the case that import duties and other non-tariff barriers might present obstacles to exporters.

The costs of setting up a manufacturing subsidiary might be prohibitive or the foreign country might be politically unstable. Licensing avoids the danger of the firm's overseas assets being expropriated and, in some situations, repatriation of profits is sometimes difficult for a manufacturing subsidiary. Where the product is bulky and expensive to transport relative to its value, licensing might be the only way to produce that product at a competitive price. If a firm has a good product idea but is short of capital to expand and exploit the commercial opportunity itself, licensing allows the earning of at least some profit or, more precisely, royalty, without having to commit scarce financial resources.

The main problem is that if a licensing arrangement exists with a company in a politically sensitive area then, for many reasons, royalties due might not be paid. This a danger of licensing and clearly the licensee has to be chosen with care. There are two suggestions to try to overcome this situation. One is to ensure that the licensing arrangement means the acceptance of certain component parts from the licensor and if there are problems in payment then components can be withheld. The other suggestion is that where the product under licence is technically advanced it is likely that it will be continually improved through innovation; the sanction here is that if there are royalty payment problems then the latest innovation can be withheld. However, such suggestions indicate a negative aspect of licensing and the majority of such arrangements are successful. The answer is to choose a licensee of integrity in a politically stable country (the problem being that in such a situation there are probably more lucrative export arrangements than licensing).

Assuming that a licensing arrangement is agreed, then regular checks should be made as to the quality of the licensee's finished products and defined quality standards should be part of the licensing agreement.

Export houses

The use of **export houses** is an alternative to the manufacturer having their own export department. Export houses are usually home-based organisations that carry out some or all the overseas activities in place of the manufacturer, often using their own agents, distributors or other intermediary. They are a useful alternative for small companies whose overseas operations are limited, not warranting the expense of direct involvement. They are also used by larger firms that are only marginally involved in smaller markets, or they use export houses until a market has expanded sufficiently to warrant their own overseas operation.

Manufacturers can delegate some or all of their overseas operations to an export house or they may delegate parts of the actual selling task to the export house. Thus, export houses offer flexibility and a range of services:

1 Export factoring – handling finance and credit arrangements on behalf of manufacturers.

2 Factory representation – a sales supervisor supervising sales activities of distributors or dealers on behalf of the manufacturer.

3 Market intelligence gathering in overseas markets.

4 Handling export procedures and documentation.

5 Help in selecting agents, distributors and dealers.

6 Confirming orders – paying the manufacturer on confirmation of an order from an overseas buyer and receiving commission, although here the export house is not actually paying the manufacturer, but merely confirming liability for payment.

Having looked at services that export houses can offer, we now look at the reasons why a manufacturer might want to use one:

1 Lack of resources to carry out overseas operations by the manufacturer.

2 When overseas selling operations are only small scale and it would not make economic sense to carry out such operations oneself.

3 Where the export house has particular expertise in a country or an industry.

4 Where the manufacturing company is predominantly production orientated and lacks marketing expertise.

There are a number of disadvantages, the main one being lack of direct contact with the market. The manufacturer may also experience difficulty in monitoring developments and changes in the overseas market and adapting to these changes in good time.

Having examined indirect approaches to selling, we now look at more direct methods.

Direct methods of overseas selling

Subsidiary companies

The **subsidiary** may be a selling or manufacturing organisation or both. A selling subsidiary usually replaces agents and distributors with the company's own permanent staff. In certain cases it is possible for a firm to start its own sales organisation with little investment. The usual way, however, is for a company to start by using an agent; then to open its own sales office with a limited number of staff. Once profits start to show, the unit can become self-sufficient and ultimately expand into manufacturing.

The above scenario is a generalisation and sales subsidiaries may require a larger investment than many companies can afford, especially where after-sales service has to be offered and stocking a large volume of spare parts is necessary. Manufacturing subsidiaries range from simple assembly plants to complete production units.

A simple assembly plant subsidiary is useful where the product is bulky and freight costs are high. By using local assembly, the final cost of transport may be reduced as it is often more economical to ship containers of parts for assembly than to ship finished bulky manufactured products. In addition, local employment is created that promotes goodwill towards the company, which in itself assists in developing markets further.

Reasons for establishing overseas manufacturing subsidiaries differ from company to company, but the following are important:

1 *Production capacity.* Where overseas markets are expanding, a firm may find problems in serving the market from the home base.

2 *Non-tariff restrictions.* Where such restrictions exist, the setting up of a subsidiary may be the only way round them. Many foreign governments give grants and incentives to firms to set up manufacturing bases in their countries and their purchasing strategies favour goods made at home. In some cases restrictions placed against imports might take the form of complex (and unnecessarily prohibitive) safety or packaging regulations.

3 *Costs.* Labour and manufacturing facilities are often more economical in overseas countries and setting up a manufacturing base saves transportation costs.

4 *Explicit import restrictions.* Where these exist, the setting up of a manufacturing subsidiary may be the only way to enter or stay in the market.

When establishing a subsidiary, local legal and taxation regulations must make it possible to set up a profitable subsidiary and allow the parent company to extract profits from the country. It may be prudent for a firm to gain experience in the market through agents and distributors before venturing directly into setting up a manufacturing subsidiary. Many firms employ the staff of a previous agent or distributor to form the nucleus of the new company.

Although it may seem that the establishment of a foreign subsidiary exposes a firm to many of the risks that licensing minimises, a venture of this kind can offer the greatest potential. Not only may local employment and production be beneficial for reasons mentioned, but the parent company can offer the subsidiary the wealth of its business experience and resources. Other advantages are that employees working direct for a company are often better motivated than those of an intermediary and it is easier to control a subsidiary because it is under the parent company's direct control. The disadvantage is that economic or political instability within the country may cause problems outside the control of the parent company.

Joint ventures

A **joint venture** is where usually two but sometimes more firms manufacture and sell products on a joint basis. As such it can be an indirect as well as direct method of exporting, depending upon the arrangement. This is common in the transport, construction and high technology sectors of business. Such agreements have financial benefits as the cost of development is shared, but friction and disagreement sometimes arise between members to the agreement.

Direct selling

Despite the strengths of using intermediaries, some companies find that selling direct from the home country to overseas markets offers more advantages. Direct selling requires a firm to take responsibility for establishing contact with potential customers.

Direct selling provides a degree of control that is impossible to achieve through intermediaries over matters such as price, credit, after-sales service, etc. The chief disadvantage is that more frequent travel is involved and a lack of a permanent presence in the market can cause problems. The firm may find difficulty keeping abreast of developments in the market and will have to rely on customers to provide market information. Customers may also view this lack of permanent presence as a lack of definite commitment to the market. Firms supplying technically complex products that require technical service and advice often place a sales engineer in the market on a semi-permanent basis, which tends to obviate the lack of commitment criticism. The following guidelines show where direct selling is most appropriate:

1 *Buyer-specified work*. Where individual orders are large and custom-made it may be necessary for the manufacturer and purchaser to get together to discuss each job as a unique contract.

2 *Continuous supply*. Once set in motion this requires only a periodic visit to negotiate such matters as price changes. Such contracts are normally able to run smoothly without a permanent overseas presence.

3 *Products are technically complex with a clearly defined market*. Here problems can be discussed directly between the supplier and user.

4 *Geographical proximity*. For example, countries in Western Europe can sometimes be serviced direct from the UK because of good communication facilities.

5 *Few customers but large or high-value orders*. In such situations time and expense involved travelling abroad are sometimes small compared with size and value of orders.

In selling direct to a customer overseas, there is an opportunity to build up close relationships with individual customers based on trust, commitment and understanding. A close interactive commercial relationship is beneficial, particularly if the exporting company is unfamiliar with the market. Speaking the language of the country is more important in direct selling than if the firm deals through an intermediary. If the salesperson is to build up a close personal relationship with customers, s/he must understand the cultural, religious and business practices of the country. There may be many mental barriers to a foreign buyer placing an order with an overseas salesperson and patience will be required to break down these barriers. Thus, emphasis must be placed upon gradual acceptance rather than the expectation of instant success. This involves careful planning in building up contacts and nurturing them and not taking the first 'no' for an answer.

Freight considerations

Pricing as an element of the marketing mix has been covered in Chapter 1. In considering pricing decisions for international markets the same rationale applies. There are, however, a number of additional factors that must be considered, the most significant of which is the potentially greater logistical problem of getting the goods to their destination. This normally involves extra packaging to withstand lengthy sea journeys, although with containerisation it is possible to rent a full or partial container, so this is less of a problem for goods where containerisation is appropriate. Air freight is a quick medium of transport, especially for goods that are perishable, or where weight is low and value high in relation to volume.

Transport adds to costs and this must be considered in relation to the price at which goods will be charged when they reach their ultimate market. For this reason many manufacturers tend to accept lower margins for export orders so they will still be competitively priced. Quotations for export orders are sometimes a simple ex-works price that does not include freight charges to the end customer. At the other extreme, the price can include delivery to the customers' works. These various price quotations form part of the legal document of contract and are considered in the next chapter.

Import considerations

A factor when calculating price is that of tariffs that might be levied on goods entering the customer's country. This will have to be considered in the light of an additional cost before the goods reach the marketplace. Import considerations might also include a quota restriction on particular goods, which means that a numerical restriction is placed upon the amount that can be imported during a particular period. In such cases the importing country sometimes raises extra revenue by selling off these quotas to the highest bidder. An import licence is sometimes required, which apart from costing money sometimes entails a lengthy process in terms of negotiating with authorities in the country concerned. This process is detailed and complicated and only companies with large international trading departments could handle such detail internally. For smaller companies, the services of shipping and handling agents would be necessary, all of which add to the landed cost of goods.

Purchasing alliances

Larger companies have an inbuilt advantage as they are able to form worldwide purchasing alliances between each other and, in a multi-country manufacturing organisation, between its own subsidiaries (the implications of the latter being discussed in the next section). Such an alliance might be in the form of reciprocal trading (see Chapter 10). On the other hand, a number of companies, particularly in the automobile industry, purchase component parts from each other; for example, one company might use another's engines for use in their vehicles. The implication for international selling is that such arrangements might impede free competition as certain markets might simply not be available because of such arrangements. The selling company should be aware of such alliances so as not to waste time exploring fruitless avenues. However, the parallel argument is that such alliances do not necessarily last for ever, so selling companies should be aware of the possibility of an alliance being broken up in good time by using market intelligence, of which the salesforce can be a good contributor.

Transfer pricing

This is perhaps one of the most intriguing aspects of pricing and can be controversial in that it often involves detailed investigation by customs and excise and taxation authorities if they feel companies are abusing positions of relative privilege. It is of particular benefit to large international companies with manufacturing and assembly bases situated in different countries around the world.

Transfer pricing works when component parts and finished products are moved between manufacturing or assembly plants in different countries as part of the manufacturing or marketing process. Different countries have different rates of corporation tax and import duties also vary between countries. There is, therefore, an incentive to an international company to make as much profit as possible in a country with a low rate of corporation tax. In fact, some countries offer 'tax-free holidays' for a specific period to companies willing to set up manufacturing bases.

What happens is that component parts from one country can be transferred to a high duty country in which the company also has a manufacturing base at a low transfer price to minimise import duty. Components can also be transferred into countries with higher rates of corporation tax at high transfer prices in order to minimise profits. In addition, parts or finished products can be transferred at high prices into a country from which transfer of profits is difficult owing to currency restrictions or perhaps where there is an unstable currency, and so depress the profits of the manufacturing or assembly plant in that country.

In view of possible abuses of the transfer pricing system it can be seen why customs and excise and tax authorities tend to view such arrangements with a certain amount of suspicion.

5.7 Japan – A Study in International Selling

The objective of this chapter has not been to provide a comprehensive guide to international selling and exporting. Rather, the general case for exporting for the good of the economy and for the good of individual companies has been covered, together with an overview of organisational and cultural issues. The specific type of information that is of direct use to a potential exporter is that which follows in respect of exporting to Japan. This information has been taken from an article in the *Journal of Sales Management* for which the second author was then editor.[5]

Successful selling to Japan requires patience and sensitivity to customs and business practices not altogether appreciated by Westerners. Business in Japan is still conducted in a traditional Confucian manner where civility, politeness and the search for constructive relationships are of essence, and successful business follows the establishment of such relationships.

In many ways the Japanese do not respond in the same way as Westerners. For the most part, the Japanese keep their emotions under control and culture demands that a person of virtue will not show a negative emotion when shocked or upset by sudden bad news. This ideal of an expressionless face in situations of great anxiety was strongly emphasised in *bushido* (the way of the warrior) which was the guideline for samurai and the ideal for many others. Furthermore, not only are negative emotions suppressed, but the control of an outward show of pleasant emotions in public is also rarely relaxed in Japan. Women tend to cover their mouths while laughing and males show true merriment (and true anger) mainly after hours when their culture allows them greater freedom of behaviour while drinking alcohol. Thus the poker-faced ideal is very common in public settings in Japan. The moral of these observations is that one must develop a sensitivity to the reactions of the Japanese because of the difficulty in telling how they are reacting.

Another noteworthy aspect is that shame is intolerable in Japan. This means that one should never put one's Japanese counterpart in a position that will force him or her to accept blame for a project going wrong, being delayed, etc. This characteristic has important implications for two elements of the sales process: handling objections and the close. The Japanese may avoid explicit objections because politeness demands that the seller does not lose face. Similarly, an attempted close may put the Japanese in a position where they are concerned for the seller's loss of face if the answer is to be negative. The deft footwork associated with the persuasion approach to selling clashes with the Japanese character and is completely opposed to the spirit of Japanese negotiations.

In some countries it is considered socially acceptable to compliment someone directly on his or her business accomplishments or the accomplishment of the company, but in Japan anything in the way of a compliment is made indirectly. Instead, say, of complimenting someone directly on his or her taste and sophistication, the Japanese practice is often to approach this particular problem indirectly and pick out some aspect of the room which reflects the other person's taste and sophistication and comment on that.

With regard to business correspondence, Japanese companies may fail to answer written enquiries concerning possible business relationships. This does not necessarily mean a lack of interest. There can be a number of reasons for a slow response. Decision-making tends to be much slower and this is often the reason. Japanese companies are accustomed to being able to talk face-to-face with suppliers as this is the usual way of conducting business in Japan.

Personal introductions are commonly executed by a third party rather than through, say, the medium of a telephone call requesting a meeting. The person making the introduction will explain to the person one wishes to meet approximately what subjects are to be discussed, what company one comes from and one's position within that company. Because there will usually be a common understanding between the two Japanese, the Japanese businessperson whom one wishes to meet will generally be more favourably disposed to hearing one's opinion than if one walks in without an introduction.

The key to a successful business relationship in Japan is a successful personal relationship and nowhere in the world are business and personal relationships so intertwined. However, such friendship only opens the door. Thereafter the hard reality of the benefits to be gained and the risks to be run will take over. Friendships in Japan take more time to form, are deeper and last longer than those in the West and often these obligations extend to business relationships. For example, during a recession a large firm will commit itself to its suppliers and subcontractors for continued orders to tide them over. The lesson of these observations is that one must be prepared to operate within this two-tier business structure; establish friendship first and then move to the second stage of actual business negotiations.

To Westerners, Japanese business seems formal and ritualistic. To a degree this is true, but business relationships do no more than reflect the formality of relationships generally. As in all societies, ritual is particularly important when meeting someone for the first time. It is used to establish and signal that one has identified initial relationships. The first meeting is also a time when transgressions are most likely to cause lasting damage.

One of the most powerful forms of non-verbal communication is dress. The usual dress for Japanese businesspeople is a dark suit for men and sober dress for women. However, most Japanese businesspeople acquainted with foreigners have come to expect a certain variety within reasonable limits in the dress of foreign businesspeople. It is not, therefore, expected that one should imitate the Japanese mode of dress. However, one should avoid extremes in dress which may cause uneasiness. For example, loud clothing will create the disturbing feeling among the Japanese businesspeople that the foreigner has perhaps failed to take them as seriously as s/he might have, by failing to observe that the common practice in dress in Japan is some degree of formality.

At the beginning and end of every meeting, the Japanese businessperson will bow very formally to the members of the other side in the negotiations. This is generally observed at the first meeting and to a somewhat lesser extent at subsequent meetings. Most Japanese with experience in dealing with Westerners will be expecting to use a handshake rather than a bow. The appropriate strategy is perhaps to wait to determine whether the Japanese businessperson is prepared to offer his hand for a handshake or whether he is going to bow. The question of whether the non-Japanese should imitate the bow of the Japanese is controversial within Japan itself. Generally, a nod of the head or a slight bow is considered acceptable for the non-Japanese party. One should be aware that reciprocal bowing behaviour is dependent on the status relationship of participants; the inferior must begin the bow, and his bow is deeper, while the superior determines when the bow is complete. When participants are of equal status, they must both bow the same way and begin and end the bow at the same time.

One of the most obvious differences between Japanese and Western business practices is the use of business calling cards, or *meishi*. These are exchanged on every occasion where one businessperson meets another. The prime purpose is to enable the recipients of the cards to know the other's status so that not only do they bow correctly, but also use the proper form of language. Japan is a hierarchical society and the Japanese are very status conscious in that they use different forms of language and bow in different manners according to the status relationship with another individual. Business cards also serve the function of not having to memorise instantaneously the names and positions of one's business counterparts and they provide a record for future reference.

Such cards are a standard pattern and size, so that they will fit in the Japanese filing systems. They must have square corners for males and round corners for females. The typical business card that the non-Japanese businessperson should have will show the Japanese translation of the individual's name on one side, along with his/her company, its address and the person's title. The other side will have the same information in English (which is the most common foreign language used in Japanese business).

The exchange of business cards is a very important part of the process of introduction in Japan. For this reason, cards should be exchanged one at a time and with some care. The courteous method is to present it, Japanese side up, with the printing facing the receiver.

One of the peculiarities of these business cards is that there is no single standard set of English translations for the ranks and positions in Japanese companies. As mentioned earlier, Japan is a very hierarchical and status conscious society, so an understanding of the ranks in business is very important. Table 5.2 translates some of the more common Japanese business titles.

The basic titles in a Japanese firm are usually very clear and the level of the position within a company, as indicated by the title, is usually closely related to the age of the individual. This system of ranking and responsibility, corresponding closely with age and years of service in the company, is one unique characteristic of Japanese organisations.

While the details of negotiations may be left to a representative in Japan, the managing director of the foreign firm (or some other high official in the company) should establish an initial contact with his or her equal in the Japanese firm. This is termed the *aisatsu*, or the greeting. The purpose of this is to establish a presence.

The Japanese term *hai* is literally translated as 'yes', although it can also mean 'I see' or 'I understand' and does not necessarily mean agreement. Furthermore, the Japanese are very reluctant to give a direct 'no' answer because Japanese culture emphasises harmony rather than confrontation. Instead of the answer 'no', one is more likely to hear something non-committal such as 'Let me think.' One must therefore learn to read the negative response signs such as hesitancy or an unwillingness to be more specific.

Postponements of negotiations are common in Japan, largely because decision-making follows a prescribed process called the *ringi* system. This means that a

Table 5.2 Translations of common Japanese business titles

Japanese title	Description and/or usual translation
No title	New graduate, aged 23–33
Kakaricho	Manager, aged 34–43
Kacho	Section Chief, aged 44–47
Bucho	Bureau Chief, aged 48+, Senior Manager
Torishimariyaku	Director
Fuku Shacho	Vice-President (more senior director)
Shacho or Daihyo Torishimariyaku	President (Managing Director)
Kaicho	Chairman

Source: Japanese External Trade Organisation (1976) 'Selling to Japan: know the business customs', *International Trade Forum*, 12.

proposal must be circulated among various sections and departments which will be affected by the proposal, with much discussion and correction ensuing. The *ringisho* (request for a decision) goes back and forth and eventually a consensus is achieved among the interested parties, with the president giving final approval.

During negotiations long periods of total silence are common. This is because the Japanese like time to think over what has been said and what alternatives are open to them when they next speak. Silence is also part of the Japanese communication procedure and they tend to rely heavily upon non-verbal communication. Westerners often find such silences embarrassing and feel obliged to say something unnecessary to relieve the supposed tension. The best way to handle such silences is to exercise restraint and outwait the silence.

Japanese businesspeople have little confidence in detailed contracts which attempt to provide for all possible contingencies. Their preference is for broad agreements and mutual understanding. Contracts are drawn up with an eye to flexibility and a contract is often considered an agreement to enter into a general course of conduct rather than something fixing precise terms. The Japanese like to negotiate each issue as it arises and there is an assumption that each party is prepared to make substantial accommodations to the other. This should not be interpreted as an attempt to violate the contract, but rather the desire of the Japanese to allow both sides the ability to adjust to unforeseen circumstances. One should not expect to obtain a detailed contract, but once a commitment is made it is for the long term. Japanese firms prefer long-term, reliable and exclusive business relationships and tend to turn to established channels to develop new business initiatives.

Because of the consciousness of using the correct level of language in a conversation or discussion, any interpreter one engages may unconsciously modify statements going from English to Japanese and back to English again, according to the rank of the people involved. For example, if a senior official of a Western company is speaking with a high-level Japanese manager, the interpreter will feel in an inferior position to both of them. The statement that the senior official intends to have translated verbatim for a Japanese counterpart may end up as being something quite different.

Entertainment in Japan plays a major role in establishing personal and business relationships. Unlike the West, business luncheons are a rarity and evening entertainment almost never takes place in the home. The typical pattern is for the Japanese businessperson to eat at a restaurant in the evening and thereafter go to a bar or cabaret. Such evenings are for cementing business relationships rather than for discussing specific aspects of business.

The personal skills necessary to conclude negotiations successfully in Japan do not come naturally to the Westerner. What is perhaps even more disturbing is the inappropriateness of much sales training to the Japanese situation. Many skills such as reading body language are culture bound. The persuasion approach to selling seems diametrically opposed to the Japanese character and perception of the role of negotiations. Eight recommendations put forward by Bruderev[6] for selling to people in Japanese organisations are as follows:

1 *Describe your organisation in detail.* Japanese businesspeople welcome pamphlets and brochures that describe your organisation, its location, its products and your objectives for being in Japan. Ideally these should be in Japanese; if not, the main points should be summarised in Japanese.

2 *Manage meetings Japanese style.* Get a mutual acquaintance to introduce you. Don't be late or change appointments. Leave plenty of time for travel between meetings and bring a small gift (e.g. a modest novelty item made in your country, but not something made by your firm as this would be viewed as a paltry give-away).

3 *Recognise that decisions are often made by middle management.* On your first call you may meet the president, but this is a formality. The important person is probably the head of a department or division.

4 *Do not push for a close.* Even with the most attractive product and effective sales propositions, Japanese businesspeople will not make a decision at that meeting. They will want time to assess your proposal, your company and you personally. They will be thinking about establishing a long-term relationship, and so will demand time to consider all aspects of the sale. If they do not like your proposal, courtesy rules out their saying 'no' to your face.

5 *Use Japanese whenever possible.* Write sales and promotional material in Japanese using a native-born translator. If you have to write in English this will damage your image. Many Japanese businesspeople have a limited knowledge of English, so if you have to speak in English, speak slowly, using simple words. Learn some common Japanese expressions; the effort you have made will be appreciated.

6 *Make sales presentations low key.* Use a moderate, low-key, deliberate style to reflect their preferred manner of doing business.

7 *Establish a strong relationship.* Japanese people follow formal rules when beginning a relationship (e.g. the introduction, exchange of business cards, the gradual beginning of business talks) and expect you to cultivate relationships through sales calls, courtesy visits and the occasional lunch and other social events.

8 *Dress conservatively.* Japanese prefer plain, undemonstrative business dress. The objective should be to blend in quietly.

5.8 Conclusions

Broad economic aspects of international trade have been considered and their significance to the sales function has been established. This has included balance of payments and the UK's share of international trade. UK entry into the EU was examined, together with the effects of the General Agreement on Tariffs and Trade (GATT).

The advantages to companies entering international selling have been discussed, particularly in the context of how the sales approach should be adapted for different cultures, especially in relation to issues such as aesthetics, religion, education, language, social organisation and political factors.

Different types of organisation for international selling have been explained, including agents, distributors, licensing and export houses under indirect methods as well as direct methods like the use of subsidiary companies, joint ventures and direct selling. The chapter was concluded with a specific description of the problems involved in selling to Japan. The next chapter considers further broader issues of selling and relates to legal and social aspects.

References

1   Department of Trade and Industry (1989) *The Single Market – An Action Checklist for Business*, HMSO, London.

2   Prahalad, C.K. and Doz, Y.L. (1991) 'Managing DMNCS: A Search for a New Paradigm', *Strategic Management Journal*, 12, pp. 145–64.

3   Cateora, P.R., Graham, J.L. and Ghauri, P.J. (2000) *International Marketing*, Irwin/McGraw-Hill, Maidenhead.

4   Merritt, N.J. and Newell, S.J. (2001) 'The extent and formality of sales agency evaluations of principals', *Industrial Marketing Management*, 30, pp. 37–49.

5   Saunders, J.A. and Hon-Chung, T. (1984) 'Selling to Japan', *Journal of Sales Management*, 1, p. 1.

6   Bruderev, W. (1993) 'Bridging the divide', *Financial Times*, 3 June.

Practical Exercise

Syplan

For some weeks Russell Anderson had worried about work that was reaching him from Calcutta across his virtual private network in the Buckinghamshire headquarters of Syplan, the company he launched with colleague David O'Mahony in 2003. Syplan was betting its future on new software called Clear Thought, designed to help FTSE 100 companies analyse business performance. It had outsourced software development to a team in Calcutta. The team was committed to deliver the system by 1 January 2006, but this deadline had slipped and Anderson felt remote from the action.

'However carefully you specify a task, you cannot calculate time needed for effective human communication,' says Anderson. 'If I were dealing with a development team in this country, half the time would be spent hammering out specifications. The rest would be spent on informal discussion; the kind that motivates people and gets them talking so you naturally hear if anything is going wrong.'

The company started out providing consultancy to the likes of Nortel Networks, BUPA and British Airways, but in 2005 they decided on a change of direction. They felt that consultancy was changing as big companies sought to reduce reliance on armies of external consultants in favour of developing greater in-house capability.

They decided to develop software that would help companies to act as their own strategic analysts.

The Clear Thought product would enable companies to analyse performance of projects across many sites and areas of operation. Ideally, it would enable each person in an organisation, whether in finance, sales or logistics, to key in business improvement ideas and study the impact on other parts of the business. The idea was to design a system that would encourage creative commercial thinking at all levels.

The move was risky. As a consultancy, the company had low overheads and had built up sales of £375,000 for financial year ending March 2005, on which it made pre-tax profits of £240,000. But the software would cost more than £500,000 to develop and in the meantime Syplan's income would almost dry up because Anderson believed software development was not something that could be done in a half-hearted way.

'Many people questioned our timing,' says Anderson, 'but I believe it is a great time. Given the recent technology slump, it has never been cheaper to develop innovative software.'

Anderson spent January 2006 in Calcutta getting Clear Thought back on track. He learned some important lessons, particularly how communications can drive up productivity. A small example illustrates this. Before leaving Britain he had sent out a specification for a function in the software. When he arrived in India he found engineers busily writing their own code for it. But a brief bit of research showed that he could acquire a piece of software for £130 that would perform the function perfectly well. He was able to put the engineers to work on something for which there was no existing solution.

'This is the kind of thing that happens when you are not working in the same place,' says Anderson. 'I would now recommend using an outsourced team only for simple development tasks. Once we are bigger we will have our own team.'

Clear Thought is now due to be launched in August 2006, but this is just the start of the obstacle race. Syplan now faces its second hurdle, convincing FTSE 100 companies to use the system, which might cost anything from £100,000 to £1 million, depending on whether it is deployed within a single business area or across an entire company with operations in many countries. This is no easy task. The founders have credibility as consultants, but none as software developers. They are also selling new products in a climate of depressed business spending and slashed IT budgets.

Source: Adapted from an article originally written by Sarah Gracie, *The Sunday Times*, 23rd June 2002. © Sarah Gracie/Times Newspapers Limited 2002.

Discussion Questions

Syplan sees its challenges in three areas. Advise the company as to how it might resolve them:

1 Managing software development in Calcutta.

2 Persuading a blue-chip company to use the software and prove to others that it works.

3 Finding partners that can sell the software to their clients.

Practical Exercise

Wardley Investment Services (Hong Kong)

Private banking has been one of the main growth areas of the banking industry in the Association of South East Asian Nations (ASEAN) region over the past few years, but private bankers have found that newly rich ASEAN clientele can be quite a different market from the traditional customer in Europe and North America.

Mr Robert Bunker and Mr John Cheung, directors of Wardley Investment Services (Hong Kong) said both Wardley and its corporate parent, the Hongkong & Shanghai Bank Group, have adopted what has been described as the American interpretation of private banking in their approach to the ASEAN marketplace.

Mr Bunker explained, 'We provide a one-stop shop for financial services to high net worth individuals, drawing on the wide range of services available in the group. There are many smaller banks which have seen private banking as a profitable growth area, but it is difficult for them to provide the breadth of services with just a small representative office in the region. As a result, they struggle to develop the mass of business necessary to make a living.'

The demands of ASEAN customers do tend to differ from those of their counterparts in Europe and North America. Mr Cheung said that in Asia as a whole private banking is not as tax driven as it is in much of the West.

'There are other differences. For example, the division of corporate and private wealth in Asia is often blurred, and some Asian clients are very aggressive in the way they like to invest. Again, such tendencies can mean a different attitude on the part of the private bank,' he said.

Mr Bunker added, 'I think that you will notice in the marketing strategy of the group that we are trying to shrug off our traditional image and create a more adventurous and aggressive picture.' He said the infrastructure of the group provides a great boon. In the ASEAN region, the bank has a presence in one form or another in Singapore, Thailand and Indonesia.

European banks entering the ASEAN market find it a lot more difficult to rely on name or reputation to build their market share, particularly when many potential customers are not familiar with their names. A bank such as Banca della Svizzera Italiana (BSI), for example, despite its size and reputation in Europe, has to fight hard to get noticed in an already crowded marketplace.

But Mr Anton Jecker, BSI's chief representative in Hong Kong, believes his bank can offer a competitive service for its clients. He said, 'We see private banking as just that, knowing the individual needs and requirements of a customer and servicing those needs. We provide individually serviced accounts with an emphasis on the personal nature of banking. We provide safety and confidentiality as a Swiss bank, and investors do not put their money with us for us to speculate. So we do not target the entrepreneur so much and tend to go for personal assets on the whole. We make it clear where we can help from the beginning, and we do not do everything in the wide spectrum of banking services.'

Although BSI has a different emphasis to the Hongkong Bank Group, Mr Jecker still feels that there is a great future for private banking in the region. 'But it is difficult for European banks to enter such markets, especially given the dominance of US banks in the last 30 to 40 years. The same can be said for the Philippines which, despite its economic and political problems, still has a lot of potential for private banking.'

Discussion Questions

1 Give advice to a United Kingdom bank that has not previously been engaged in the ASEAN region as to what problems it might face when setting up in the area.

2 What segmentation possibilities might exist for a smaller bank in the region?

3 What research would you advise a small bank to undertake before setting up in the region for the first time?

4 Assume that a small bank you are advising has decided to set up in the region. What strategic guidelines would you give to the bank insofar as organising its selling activities is concerned?

Practical Exercise

Sapporo (Hong Kong) Ltd

Sapporo is part of a major Japanese conglomerate. They manufacture in Hong Kong, but mainly buy in from their own factory in China a range of consumable cleaning items, including household brushes, mops and cleaning cloths as well as similar products designed for industrial markets.

The raw material used is principally high-density woven material that has a relatively long lifespan. The company is regarded as being at the 'quality' end of the market for such products. Their goods are packaged and branded so as to make them stand out from the more traditional generic unbranded products.

Both industrial and consumer products are distributed through intermediaries and not direct. The salesforce sells to distributors for industrial products and to wholesalers for consumer products. Advertising plays a key role in the company's marketing efforts and products are brand managed in order to create an element of internal marketing competition.

Hong Kong sales for the past three years have been increasing steadily from HK$17.4 million in 2000–1, to HK$21.2 million in 2001–2 to HK$26.9 million in

2002–3. Press and television advertising (above the line) and sales promotional spending (below the line) as well as the maintenance of a company website have been about 5 per cent of sales during this period with 60 per cent being spent on television campaigns. The remainder has been spent on leaflets, in-store campaigns, trade magazines and the press.

The parent company had made a decision to expand more into the ASEAN market and has encouraged Sapporo to open up satellite manufacturing and distribution plants in the region. They are concerned that Sapporo chooses the right advertising agency for this planned expansion. The parent company uses two agencies in the ASEAN region and at one point they attempted to impose one of these agencies on Sapporo's Hong Kong operations. Sapporo (Hong Kong) Ltd resisted, saying that another country's agency would not understand the Hong Kong market. Now the Japanese parent company is using this same argument against Sapporo taking its Hong Kong advertising campaign (and Hong Kong advertising agency) into the ASEAN region.

Discussion Questions

1 Consider sales turnover figures and comment on whether or not the company is justified in engaging in so much above-the-line promotion, especially in view of its expansion into other ASEAN countries. Would it not be better to engage in more direct selling or use a direct marketing facility?

2 In view of planned ASEAN expansion Sapporo has decided to move its promotional mix from above-the-line promotion and go more towards selling/direct marketing, so the equation becomes half to each category. Comment on potential problems in relation to the choice of advertising agency to handle this and the possibility of incorporating a pan-ASEAN theme into its promotion.

Practical Exercise

Quality Kraft Carpets Ltd

This company was founded in 1991 by William Jackson and John Turner in Kidderminster, a UK town with a tradition of carpet-making going back hundreds of years. Carpet manufacture and related activities had been the major provider of employment in the area up until the late 1960s. However, since that date the carpet industry, like many other areas of British textiles, faced problems and decline.

Paradoxically, it was this decline that brought Quality Kraft Carpets into existence. William Jackson had been production manager with one of the largest carpet manufacturing firms in the area, with a worldwide reputation for quality carpets. John Turner had been a loom tuner (a maintenance engineer) responsible for maintaining over 100 carpet looms for another large company. Jackson had been made redundant as a result of a drastic decline in orders and Turner's company had gone into liquidation. They were good friends and since their unemployment had come at the same time they decided to start their own small company, specialising in the product they knew best – traditional, woven, good quality Axminster carpets.

Because so many firms in the area were either closing down or cutting back production, there was a steady supply of textile machinery being sold very cheaply by local auctioneers. By pooling their respective resources, plus help from the bank, they were able to acquire a 15-year lease on a small factory and purchase enough equipment to enable them to commence production.

Their policy was to weave best quality carpets made of 80 per cent wool and 20 per cent nylon. The market was good quality carpet shops and the contract market, especially hotels, restaurants, offices and large stores. They made a conscious decision not to deal with carpet superstores, largely because profit margins would be low, as bulk purchasing power enabled them to demand low margins. In addition, carpet superstores predominantly sold cheaper carpets, mainly tufted synthetic carpets purchased from North America. It was contended that purchasers looking for a good quality carpet would go to a conventional carpet shop and not a carpet superstore that they considered was more applicable to the lower end of the market.

At the time of setting up (1991) the main problems facing UK carpet manufacturers were a depressed economy and the fact that imports of carpets were taking an increasing share of a diminishing market. Thus, the recession made carpet purchasing a lower priority issue for those who already had carpets and the attitude was to make them last longer.

Imports now account for over 35 per cent of the UK carpet market and this percentage is increasing. The main imports are synthetic tufted carpets, mainly from North America but increasingly from EU countries – Belgium, followed by Germany and Holland. Nylon carpet is basically oil based, which gave the Americans a significant advantage until the late 1980s because of the cheapness of their oil. However, since then their oil prices have increased and the strength of the US dollar has made exports to the UK less competitive.

Despite the apparently depressing picture for UK manufacturers, the UK carpet industry is still amongst the largest in the world, particularly the high quality woven carpet sector. The UK has always been a net exporter of carpets and its reputation for quality has worldwide acclaim.

Since Quality Kraft Carpets commenced, its total sales have been as follows:

Quality Kraft Carpets Ltd sales (£000)

1991	1992	1993	1994	1995	1996	1997	1998	1999	2000	2001	2002	2003	2004	2005	2006
500	640	820	1,280	1,760	2,300	2,900	2,100	2,000	1,970	1,950	1,960	1,990	2,010	1,950	2,100

These sales are to two distinct markets:

• direct to quality retailers

• the contract market

The percentage of sales accounted for by each of these market segments is shown below.

Percentage of sales to each segment

	1991	1992	1993	1994	1995	1996	1997	1998	1999	2000	2001	2002	2003	2004	2005	2006
Retail	78	76	70	66	63	60	60	58	56	52	52	50	50	48	47	50
Contract	22	24	30	34	37	40	40	42	44	48	48	50	50	52	53	50

At the 1997 level of demand the company was operating at full capacity, but today it has an excess of manufacturing capacity. The company has not laid off any employees, but overtime has been cut out and some work that was given to outside contractors, e.g. final 'shearing' up of carpets, is now done in the company. An interesting facet of contract sales is that much of it is for customised carpet, often incorporating the customer's company logo in the design.

The company now feels that the industry is likely to remain depressed and foreign competition in the UK market likely to increase further. The company has not attempted to sell its products abroad, but feels that if it is ever to expand again, then overseas markets are the only feasible method. William Jackson and John Turner had a long discussion about exporting as they were both inexperienced in such matters. They listed the strengths and weaknesses of Quality Kraft Carpets in order to arrive at a decision as to which would be the most appropriate overseas market to enter and their conclusions were as follows:

1 Weaknesses

- Small and relatively new without the reputation of a long-established firm.

- Management has no knowledge of selling overseas, and although educated by experience, has little knowledge of finance, economics, languages, etc., which are of help when selling overseas.

- The more popular types of tufted carpets are not manufactured.

- The company cannot compete on price in the volume markets because of outdated equipment and small purchasing power.

- Although products are first class, they are expensive.

- The company does not directly employ such specialists as designers, but operates on a freelance/contractual basis.

2 Strengths

- Expertise in the manufacture of good quality, conventionally woven Axminster carpets.

- The company is small and flexible and can easily cope with new trends in designs.

- Proficiency is increasing in contract work and staff have specialist knowledge of such one-off tasks. Much repeat business is coming from satisfied contract customers.

- There is a loyal workforce who have flexible working arrangements in that the workers can each carry out a number of different jobs without demarcation disputes.

- The company is reasonably profitable and it has very little long-term debt.

- The retail part of the business contains loyal customers with much repeat business.

After discussions with the bank and advice from the British Overseas Trade Board, it was decided that the USA offered the best potential for the immediate future. The Middle East and Japan showed promise in the medium term. It was also decided that they should concentrate on the contract market. These decisions were based upon the following criteria:

1 The USA is now an established market for best quality Axminster carpet.

2 Although the USA does manufacture some conventionally woven Wilton carpet, it does not manufacture much good quality Axminster carpet.

3 In the contract market, quality seems to be more important than price and it would seem to be good for the company to concentrate on contract carpet sales.

4 Import tariffs into the USA from the UK are 9.5 per cent ad valorem (on top of the imported cost) for Axminster and 19.5 per cent for Wilton (higher to protect USA producers). This gives an undoubted advantage for the export of Axminster carpets.

5 A market research survey conducted in the USA had indicated that their interior designers liked Axminster because of the fact that any pattern or logo could be woven into the design. Most contract carpet in the USA is tufted and printed which only makes mass production runs feasible. This printing process, although much cheaper, is inferior to the design being actually woven into the carpet as is the case with Axminster.

6 The pound is quite good value against the US dollar, although it has strengthened in recent years, yet this makes the product good value in the USA.

7 Advice from the British Overseas Trade Board has indicated that the UK has a high reputation in the USA for quality carpets. They appreciate personal service and reliable delivery and British carpets might be seen as a status symbol.

Quality Kraft Carpets Ltd decided that they would immediately enter the North American market, but did not want to commit too much money to the venture in case it failed. On the other hand, if it was successful, they were prepared to commit more resources.

Discussion Questions

1 Draw up a short-, medium- and long-term sales strategy upon how Quality Kraft Carpets can enter, develop and remain in the US market.

2 What form of representation would you recommend for this new market – or would you consider setting up a manufacturing subsidiary? Give reasons for your decision.

3 How might your various strategies change and what further considerations would need to be made if, after initial success in the US market, the Middle East and Japan offered good export opportunities?

4 What would be your marketing communications and sales promotional strategies for the company in the USA? More specifically, outline your sales 'message' and the type of media you would use to communicate this message.

5 What, if any, further research needs to be undertaken before attempting to export to the USA?

Examination Questions

1 Discuss the contention that there is no such thing as 'overseas selling'; it is merely an extension of selling to the home market.

2 How does the role of an export agent differ from the role of an export salesperson?

3 Discuss the contribution that the WTO has made to a freeing up of international sales negotiations.

4 What are the differences that should be considered when international sales managers draw up their export plans?

5 How is the worldwide trend towards urbanisation and greater overseas travel affecting opportunities for international selling?

Law and Ethical Issues

After studying this chapter, you should be able to:

1 Understand the importance of consumer protection in the context of selling

2 Apply appropriate terms and conditions to a contract of sale

3 Appreciate how legal controls affect sales activities

4 Make voluntary and legal restraints work to the advantage of both the buyer and the seller

5 Appreciate ethical issues in sales

Key Concepts

- collusion
- consumer credit
- consumer protection
- contract
- ethical issues
- exclusion clauses
- false trade descriptions
- faulty goods
- inertia selling
- regulated agreements
- terms and conditions
- terms of trade
- unit pricing

Consumer protection by the law is very much a twentieth-century phenomenon. Before that the prevailing attitude can be described by the phrase caveat emptor – let the buyer beware. Much of the legislation has been drawn up since 1970 when there was a recognition that sellers may have an unfair advantage compared with consumers when entering into a contract of sale. The major laws controlling selling activity in Britain include the following:

- Weights and Measures Acts 1878, 1963, 1979

- Sale of Goods Acts 1893, 1979

- Resale Prices Acts 1964, 1976

- Restrictive Trade Practices Acts 1956, 1968, 1976

- Misrepresentation Act 1967

- Trade Descriptions Acts 1968, 1972

- Unsolicited Goods and Services Acts 1971, 1975

- Supply of Goods (Implied Terms) Acts 1973, 1982

- Fair Trading Act 1973

- Hire Purchase Act 1973

- Consumer Credit Act 1974

- Unfair Contract Terms Act 1977

- Consumer Safety Act 1978

- Consumer Protection Act 1987

In addition to these Acts, consumers are protected by a range of codes of practice covering such activities as advertising, market research and direct selling. Trade associations such as the Association of British Travel Agents, Society of Motor Manufacturers and Traders, and Radio, Electrical and Television Retailers' Association have also drawn up codes of practice which have been approved by the Office of Fair Trading.

The consumers' interest is also protected by the Consumers' Association, which campaigns for consumers and provides information about products, often on a comparative basis, allowing consumers to make a more informed, rational choice between products and brands. This information is published in their magazine *Which?* The National Consumer Council was established in 1975 to represent the consumer interest at national level and to issue reports on various topics of consumer concern, e.g. consumer credit.

6.1   The Contract

All this activity is centred upon the **contract** entered into when a seller agrees to part with a good or provide a service in exchange for monetary payment.

A contract is made when a deal is agreed. This can be accomplished verbally or in writing. Once an offer has been accepted a contract is formed and is legally binding. Thus if a builder offers to build a garage for £1,000 and this offer is accepted, the builder is obliged to carry out the work and the householder is under an obligation to pay the agreed sum upon completion. Although contracts do not have to be in writing – except, for example, house purchase – to place an offer and acceptance in writing can minimise the likelihood of misunderstanding over the nature of the agreement which has been struck and provide tangible evidence in the event of legal action. Important in written contracts are the terms and conditions which apply. This aspect of the contract will now be considered, before an examination of some business practices and the way in which they are controlled by law is undertaken.

In a binding contract, one party should have made a firm offer and the offer should have received an unequivocal acceptance. An offer should be distinguished from 'an invitation to treat'. An invitation to treat (negotiate) is not an offer. For example, the display of goods at a certain price in a shop is not an offer by the shopkeeper to sell. Rather it is an invitation to shoppers to make an offer to buy. Thus if a product is accidentally priced too low, the customer cannot demand to buy at that price.

6.2 Terms and Conditions

As the name suggests, **terms and conditions** state the circumstances under which the buyer is prepared to purchase and the seller is prepared to sell. They define the limit of responsibility for both buyer and seller. Thus both buyer and seller are at liberty to state their terms and conditions. Usually the buyer will state them on the back of the order form and the seller will do so on the reverse of the quotation form. Often a note is typed on the front of the form in red ink: 'Your attention is drawn to our standard terms and conditions on the reverse of this order.' Typical clauses incorporated into the conditions of a purchase order include the following:

1 Only orders issued on the company's printed order form and signed on behalf of the company will be respected.

2 Alterations to orders must be confirmed by official amendment and signed.

3 Delivery must be within the specified time period. The right to cancel is reserved for late delivery.

4 Faulty goods will be returned and expenses charged to the supplier.

5 All insurance of goods in transit shall be paid for by the supplier.

6 This order is subject to a cash discount of 2.5 per cent, unless otherwise arranged, for payment within 28 days of receipt. Any payment made is without prejudice to our rights if the goods supplied prove to be unsatisfactory or not in accordance with our agreed specification or sample.

7 Tools supplied by us for the execution of this order must not be used in the service of any other firm without permission.

Careful drawing up of terms and conditions is essential in business since they provide protection against claims made by the other party should problems arise in fulfilment of the contract. An example of a conditions of sale document for a seller is given in Figure 6.1.

CONDITIONS OF SALE

These Conditions apply except so far as they are inconsistent with any express agreement entered into between the Seller and the Buyer before the delivery.

1 Where the Seller delivers in bulk it is the Buyer's responsibility
   (a) to provide a safe and suitable bulk storage which complies in all respects with all relevant regulations made by H.M. Government or other competent authority.
   (b) to ensure that the storage into which delivery is to be made will accommodate the full quantity ordered and in the case of Petroleum Spirit to procure certification to this effect and also to the effect that the connecting hose is properly and securely connected to the filling point. In this regard the Buyer is referred to the regulations currently in force relating to the storage and use of petroleum spirit.
   (c) in the case of highly inflammable products and where otherwise applicable, strictly to observe any regulations laid down by H.M. Government or other competent authority in respect of the avoidance of smoking, naked lights, fires, stoves or heating appliances of any description in the vicinity of the storage and the fill, dip and vent pipes connected thereto.
   The Buyer will indemnify the Supplier against any damages, claims, expenses or costs which may arise as a result of the Buyer's non-observance of these conditions.

2 It is a condition of every bulk sale that the quantity shown by any measuring devices employed by the Seller shall for the purpose of accounts be accepted by the Buyer as the quantity delivered but the Buyer may be represented at the taking of these measurements in order to verify them if he so desires. The Seller cannot accept any responsibility whatever for discrepancies in the Buyer's tanks, dip rods or other measuring devices.

3 Prices include any Government Tax (other than Value Added Tax) in force at the time of supply. Any variation in the rate of existing tax, or any additional taxation, is for Buyer's account.

4 All products supplied are chargeable at the price ruling on the day of despatch irrespective of the date of the order or the amount of cash sent with order.

5 In the event of missing consignments, short delivery or damage the Seller can only investigate the circumstances if
   (a) In the case of damage the Buyer notifies the Railway or other Carrier and the Seller of the damage immediately upon receipt of the damaged goods, such notices to be in writing and quoting the invoice number;
   (b) In the case of non-receipt or short delivery the Buyer notifies the Seller in writing of non-receipt or short delivery. Such notice, quoting the invoice number, should be sent within 21 days of date of despatch.

6 Acceptance of goods will be treated as acceptance of the Seller's conditions.

Figure 6.1 Example of conditions of sale document

6.3 Terms of Trade

In addition to the tactical and strategic aspects of international selling discussed in Chapter 5, sellers and buyers need to be aware of the **terms of trade** which apply when trading overseas. Differences in the terms of trade can have serious profit consequences for the unwary. Terms of trade are used to define the following:

(a) who is responsible for control over the transfer of goods between importer and exporter

(b) who is responsible for each part of the cost incurred in moving the goods between importer and exporter

A number of terms are used to cover these aspects of delivery and cost. Variations in definitions led to the International Chamber of Commerce drawing up formal definitions in 1936. These were published under the title of INCOTERMS and have since been subject to update. For example, in 1980 a new edition of INCOTERMS covered two new terms which were required because of the increasing importance of container transportation.

Terms of trade are useful in that they cover a range of situations extending from the case where exporters merely make their goods available for collection by importers or their agents at their factory (ex works) to the case where the exporter agrees to deliver the goods to the importer's factory, thereby taking responsibility for the costs and administration of that delivery (free delivered). The following sections list the more commonly used terms.

Bills of lading

A bill of lading is a receipt for goods received on board a ship which is signed by the shipper (or agent) and states the terms on which the goods were delivered to and received by the ship. The Bills of Lading Act 1855 laid down the following principles:

1 It maintained the right of the shipper to 'stoppage in transit'. Thus an unpaid exporter could reclaim the goods during shipping.

2 It set up the principle of transferability which allowed the transfer of the bill of lading from the holder to a third person who then assumed ownership of the goods as well as any rights and liabilities stated in the bill.

3 It stated that the bill of lading was prima facie evidence that the goods had been shipped.

The bill of lading thus acts as evidence that the goods have been received by the shipper. It can also act as part of the contract between the shipper and person or organisation paying for the shipping. For example, if the goods are damaged upon arrival at the port of departure, a shipper can 'clause' the bill of lading to that effect. A bill of lading will usually cover the following details:

- name of the shipper

- ship's name

- description of the cargo

- payment details, e.g. whether freight has been paid or is payable at destination

- name of consignee

- terms of the carriage contract

- date when the goods were loaded in the ship

- who is to be notified on arrival of the shipment at its destination

- ports of departure and final destination.

In summary, the bill of lading is a receipt for the goods shipped, a transferable document of title to the goods allowing the holder to claim his or her goods, and evidence of the terms of the contract of shipping.

Ex works

An exporter may quote a price to an importer 'ex works'. This places the exporter's liability for loss or damage to the goods at a minimum and also means that the exporter's duties in delivering the goods are minimal. Ownership of the goods passes to the buyer once they leave the factory and the buyer pays all costs of exporting and accepts the risks once the goods pass through the factory gates. Quoting ex works may make sense if the goods are to be combined with those of another organisation to form a joint export cargo, or when the buyer has well-developed transportation facilities, e.g. buyers of commodity items such as tea and coffee beans. However, for other customers, quoting an ex works price may not meet their needs, since they cannot easily compare the actual cost of such goods against buying in their own country where prices are quoted with delivery.

Free on board (FOB)

This extends the responsibility, liability and costs of delivery for the exporter until the goods have been loaded on to the ship ('passed the ship's rail'). From this point, the importer pays the costs of insurance and freight. However, the exporter still has the right of 'stoppage in transit' should the importer fail to pay for those goods. Variations for land transport are 'free on rail' (FOR) and 'free on wagon' (FOW) which mean that the seller has the responsibility and cost of delivering goods on board a railway transporter or wagon.

Free alongside ship (FAS)

This term means that the exporter is responsible for and must pay all the costs of transport up to the point of placing the goods alongside the ship. A provision should be made covering who is responsible for any loss or damage before the goods are actually loaded on to the ship. The importer thus pays for the loading of the cargo and the cost of insurance and freight to its destination.

Cost, insurance and freight (CIF)

If a cost, insurance and freight agreement is reached, the exporter is responsible for the delivery of the goods on to the ship and pays the insurance on the part of the buyer against loss or damage while on ship. Should any loss or damage occur after the shipping company has received the goods and given the shipment a clean bill of lading, the buyer can take action against the ship owner or underwriter. Thus responsibility has passed from the exporter once the cargo is aboard ship, although it is the exporter who pays for the shipping to the importer's port.

The term *cost and freight* (C&F) is similar to CIF except, as its name suggests, the exporter is not responsible for insurance during shipping. Instead the importer incurs the cost of this insurance.

Free delivered

This places maximum responsibility and cost on the exporter, who undertakes to deliver the goods to the importer with all costs paid and all of the administrative duties (e.g. obtaining an import licence) carried out by the exporter. From a marketing perspective, quoting a delivered price has the advantage that it minimises customer uncertainty and workload since the costs of transport, obtaining documentation, arranging shipping, etc., are borne by the seller. Furthermore, it allows the customer to compare actual prices from a foreign source with local prices where delivery costs are included or are of minimal amount. However, customers who have an efficient importing system may prefer to pay 'ex works' or 'free on board' and organise carriage themselves, rather than pay the higher 'free delivered' price.

6.4 Business Practices and Legal Controls

False descriptions

Unscrupulous salespeople may be tempted to mislead potential buyers through inaccurate statements about the product or service they are selling. In the UK a consumer is protected from such practice by the Trade Descriptions Act 1968. The Act covers descriptions of products, prices and services and includes both oral and written descriptions.

Businesses are prohibited from applying a **false trade description** to products and from supplying falsely described products. The false description must be false to a material degree, and the Act also covers 'misleading' statements. Not only would salespeople be contravening the Act if they described a car as achieving 50 miles per gallon when in fact it only achieved 30 miles per gallon, they would also be guilty of putting a false trade description if they described a car as 'beautiful' if it proved to be unroadworthy.

The Trade Descriptions (Place of Production) (Marking) Order 1988 requires that where products are marked in such a way as to suggest they were made elsewhere than is the case, a clear statement of the actual place of manufacture must be made.

Misleading price indications are covered by the Consumer Protection Act 1987. This Act states that it is an offence to give a misleading indication of the price at which goods, services, accommodation or facilities are available. Agents, publishers and advertisers are covered by the Act as well as the person or organisation offering the goods or services. Prices can be misleading when:

- it is suggested that a price is less than it actually is
- it is suggested that other charges are included in the price when in fact they are not

- it is suggested that prices will increase, decrease or stay the same

- it is suggested that the price depends on certain circumstances or particular facts

- consumers are encouraged to depend on the truth of the price indication by circumstances which do not apply

The Act covers both products and services.

Confusion over value for money due to differing pack sizes can be reduced by **unit pricing** whereby packs are marked with a price per litre or kilogram, etc. An EU Directive which came fully into force in 1994 requires that many supermarket products, for example, must be marked with a unit price unless packed in EU-approved pack sizes.

Faulty goods

The principal protection for the buyer against the sale of **faulty goods** is to be found within the Sale of Goods Act 1979. This Act states that a product must correspond to its description and must be of merchantable quality, i.e. 'fit for the purpose for which goods of that kind are commonly bought as it is reasonable to expect'. An example is a second-hand car which is found to be unroadworthy after purchase; it is clearly not of merchantable quality, unless bought for scrap. Finally a product must be fit for a particular purpose which may be specified by the buyer and agreed by the seller. If, for example, a buyer bought a car in this country with the expressed desire to use it in Africa, a retailer may be committing an offence if s/he agrees that the car is fit to be used when in fact, because of the higher temperatures, it is not.

The condition that products must correspond to their description covers both private and business sales, whereas the merchantability and fitness for purpose conditions apply to sales in the course of a business only. The latter two conditions apply not only at the time of purchase but for a reasonable time afterwards. What exactly constitutes 'reasonable' is open to interpretation and will depend upon the nature of the product.

In order to protect the consumer against faulty goods, some companies give guarantees in which they agree to replace or repair those goods should the fault become apparent within a specified period. Unfortunately, before the passing of the Supply of Goods (Implied Terms) Act 1973, these so-called guarantees often removed more rights than they gave. However, since the passing of that Act it has been unlawful for a seller to contract out of the conditions that goods should be merchantable and fit for their purpose. Buyers can now be confident that signing a guarantee will not result in their signing away their rights under the Sale of Goods Act 1979.

The Consumer Protection Act 1987 came into operation in response to an EU Directive. This protects buyers if they suffer damage (e.g. death, personal injury or damage to goods for private use). They must be able to prove that the good was defective and that the damage was caused by the defect in the product. Usually liability falls on the manufacturer or importer of the finished product or of the defective component or raw material. A product is considered to be defective when it does not provide the safety which a person is entitled to expect (including instruction for use). A major defence against claims is the 'development defence' where the manufacturer proves that the state of technical knowledge when the product was launched did not enable the existence of the defect to be discovered.

Further consumer protection is provided by the Consumer Safety Act 1978 which prohibits the sale of dangerous products, and by various EU regulations. For example, the EU mark can only be used on aerosol containers if they conform to EU regulations regarding dimensions, strength, etc.

Inertia selling

Inertia selling involves the sending of unsolicited goods or the provision of unsolicited services to people who, having received them, may feel an obligation to buy. For example, a book might be sent to people who would be told that they had been specially chosen to receive it. They would be asked to send money in payment or return the book within a given period, after which they would become liable for payment. Non-payment and failure to return the good would result in letters demanding payment, sometimes in quite threatening terms.

The growing use of this technique during the 1960s led to a campaign organised by the Consumers' Association demanding that legislation be enacted curbing the use of the technique. As a result the Unsolicited Goods and Services Act 1971 was passed, followed by the Unsolicited Goods and Services (Amendment) Act 1975.

These Acts have not prohibited the use of the technique but have created certain rights for consumers which make the use of the method ineffective. Unsolicited goods can be treated as a free gift after a period of six months from receipt if the sender has not reclaimed them. Further, if the recipient notifies the sender that they are unsolicited, the sender must collect them within 30 days or they become the property of the recipient. The 30-day rule was felt to be a fair compromise between the rights of the recipient and the rights of the sender who may be the subject of a false order placed by a third party.

The practice of sending threatening letters demanding payment has been outlawed, as have the threats of legal proceedings or placing of names on a published list of defaulters.

Unsolicited services have also been controlled by law. For example, the practice of placing unsolicited entries of names of firms in business directories and then demanding payment has been controlled.

The law therefore gives sufficient rights to consumers effectively to deter the practice of inertia selling. Fortunately for the consumer, the trouble and costs involved in using this technique nowadays outweigh the benefits to be gained.

Exclusion clauses

Another practice which some sellers have employed in order to limit their liability is the use of an **exclusion clause**. For example, a restaurant or discotheque might display a sign stating that coats are left at the owner's risk, or a dry cleaners might display a sign excluding themselves from blame should clothes be damaged. This practice is now controlled by the Unfair Contract Terms Act 1977. A seller is not permitted to limit liability or contract out of his or her liability for death or injury arising from negligence or breach of contract or duty.

For other situations, where loss does not include death or injury, an exclusion clause is only valid if it satisfies the requirement of 'reasonableness'. This means that it is fair taking into account the circumstances prevailing when the sale was made. Relevant factors which are taken into account when making a judgement about 'reasonableness' include the following:

- the strength of the bargaining positions of the relevant parties

- whether the customer received an inducement to agree to the exclusion clause

- whether the customer knew or ought to have known of the existence of the exclusion clause

- whether the goods were produced to the special order of the customer

- for an exclusion clause which applies when some condition is not complied with, whether it was practicable for the condition to be met

Buying by credit

Before 1974 obtaining **consumer credit** through a hire-purchase agreement was treated differently, under the law, to consumer credit by means of a bank loan. However, from the consumer's point of view there is very little difference between paying for a good by instalments (hire purchase) or paying in cash through a bank loan which is itself repayable by instalments. The Consumer Credit Act 1974 effectively abolished this distinction. Almost all consumer credit agreements up to £15,000 are termed **regulated agreements**. A notable exception is a building society mortgage. Regulations concerned with 'truth in lending' provisions of the Act came into operation in 1985. The Act now replaces all former statutes concerning credit (e.g. hire purchase).

An important consumer protection measure which resulted from the Act was that a lender should disclose the true interest rate in advertisements and sales literature. This true rate now appears in advertisements as the annual percentage rate (APR) and enables consumers to compare rates of interest charged on a common basis. Prior to this Act, cleverly worded advertisements and sales literature could give the impression that the scale of charges was much lower than was the true case.

Control of credit trading was achieved by a system of licensing which is placed in the hands of the Director-General of Fair Trading. This system was designed to ensure that only people with a sound trading record are able to deal in credit. Not only finance companies but also retailers who arrange credit in order to sell their products must have a licence. Exempt from the Act, however, is weekly or monthly credit. Thus, many credit card agreements are exempt since total repayment is often required at the end of each month.

People entering credit agreements are entitled to receive at least one copy of the agreement so that they are informed of their rights and obligations. A 'cooling off' period is provided for in the Act when the agreement is preceded by 'oral representations' (sales talk) and the agreement was not signed on business premises. This provision was designed to control doorstep selling through credit arrangements. A consumer who wishes to cancel must serve notice of cancellation within five days of the date of receiving the copy of the signed agreement.

The Consumer Credit (Advertisements) Regulations 1989 laid down the minimum and maximum information which may be given in credit or hire advertisements. Advertisements are categorised as being simple, intermediate or full advertisements and the information content is regulated accordingly.

Collusion between sellers

In certain circumstances it may be in the sellers' interests to **collude** with one another in order to restrict supply, agree upon prices (price fixing) or share out the market in some mutually beneficial way. The Restrictive Trade Practices Act 1979 requires that any such trade agreement must be registered with the Director-General of Fair Trading, a post established under the Fair Trading Act 1973. If the Director-General of Fair Trading considers that the registered agreement is contrary to the public interest, s/he is empowered to refer it to the Restrictive Practices Court. If the Court agrees, the agreement may be declared void. The EU Commission also has powers over collusion and has had notable successes in breaking down price cartels, for example, in plastics.

6.5 Ethical Issues

Research into relationship marketing and personal selling highlights the importance of gaining customer trust in the establishment and development of mutually beneficial buyer–seller relationships.[1] Salespeople can partially create and keep trust by showing competence, reliability and customer focus. Of equal importance is the willingness to be honest, exercise fairness and refrain from unethical behaviours.[2] Salespeople face many **ethical issues** including bribery, deception, the hard sell and reciprocal buying. Most companies operate within a predetermined set of ethical guidelines (see box).

British Gas and ethics

Ethical decisions are integral in making investment decisions. BG Group's Statement of Business Principles sets out the fundamental values and ethical principles within which the company operates. BG Group will only enter countries where the company can operate in accordance with its business principles.

Important statistical and financial procedures are involved in making an investment decision, but it is important to emphasise the weight given to non-financial factors involved in such decisions. Gas is the cleanest fossil fuel, but any form of energy production involves some form of environmental cost, e.g. the sight of windfarms located in fields, or harmful release of greenhouse gases when burning fossil fuels.

(continued on following page)

BG Group will only bid to explore if it can operate within its ethical guidelines. This can sometimes be difficult since natural gas resources can be located in difficult areas, including sensitive environments, conflict zones and territories with indigenous peoples where land rights are contested or inadequately protected.

Source: *http://www.thetimes100.co.uk/case_study* with permission

Bribery

This is the act of giving payments, gifts or other inducements to secure a sale. Such actions are thought to be unethical because they violate the principle of fairness in commercial negotiations. A problem is that in some countries bribes are necessary simply to compete for business. Organisations need to decide if they are to market in such countries. Taking an ethical stance may cause difficulties in the short term but over a longer period the positive publicity (or lack of exposure to the risk of bad publicity) that can follow may be of greater benefit.

Deception

A problem which many salespeople face is the temptation to mislead the customer in order to secure an order. The deception may take the form of exaggeration, lying or withholding important information that would significantly lessen the appeal of the product. Such behaviour should be discouraged by training, sales management promoting ethical actions by their own words and behaviour and by establishing codes of conduct for their salespeople. Nevertheless, occasionally reports of malpractice in selling reach the media. For example, in the UK it was alleged that some financial services salespeople missold pensions products by exaggerating their expected returns. The scandal resulted in millions of pounds of compensation being paid by the companies to their clients. In the USA, the Prudential Insurance Company of America had to take a $2.6 billion charge against earnings to pay policy holders damages after the company allowed their salespeople to use deceptive sales practices.[3]

Secrets and lies of beauty industry laid bare by advertising watchdog

They are promoted as products that will rejuvenate, regenerate, tighten and tone, bringing instant smoothness to your skin and bounce to your hair.

The multibillion-pound industry of beauty creams, lotions, gels and ointments suffered a rebuke yesterday as two leading brands were found not to defy the ageing process or rigours of daily life, but medical science.

In a warning shot to an industry reliant on increasingly extreme claims, the Advertising Standards Authority upheld complaints about the promotion of an 'anti-cellulite' cream and an 'amino-acid replenishing' shampoo. Claims

attached to the two products were found to be misleading and unsubstanti-
ated, the watchdog ruled.

Source: Adapted from an article by Sam Lister in *The Times* 11 May 2005, News
Supplement p. 3

The hard sell

A criticism that is sometimes made of personal selling behaviour is the use of high-
pressure (hard sell) sales tactics to secure a sale. Some car dealerships have been
accused of such tactics to pressure customers into making hasty decisions on a complicated purchase that may involve expensive credit facilities. Such actions encouraged Daewoo to sell cars using non-commission customer advisors whose job it is to
help customers choose the car which best meets their needs rather than pressure
them into an ill-considered purchase.

15,000 a month hit by phone scam

Rogue salespeople are switching phone users to new suppliers without permission. People receive letters saying their landline accounts have been taken
over by firms they may never have heard of. They are victims of 'phone slam-
ming' which takes advantage of a legal loophole. Salespeople only need their
name, postcode and phone number. They do not have to obtain a signature or
evidence of consent, provided the customer is sent a letter giving them a 10-
day 'cooling off' period to cancel the switch. There are six steps:

1 Salesperson for phone company rings customer of rival firm and tries to get
their business with promises of lower bills.

2 Customer declines to be signed up, but agrees to be sent information by
post. Salesperson asks customer for their full address, including postcode.

3 Unbeknown to the householder, the salesperson – armed with their name,
address and phone number – registers them as a new customer and sends an
order to BT, to change the supplier to the new firm.

4 Once the order to switch has been made, the existing supplier, usually BT,
sends a letter telling the customer their account will end on a given date.

5 The new supplier sends a letter telling the customer the date the new service will begin and giving them ten days to cancel.

6 If the customer does not take the opportunity to cancel, their phone service is automatically switched. Bills are either sent in the post or cash taken
from the customer's bank via direct debit if these details have been given.

Providing the 'slammer' has given the householder the opportunity to cancel,
the whole process is within the law.

Source: Adapted from headline article in *Daily Mail* 25 April 2005.

Reciprocal buying

Reciprocal buying occurs when a customer agrees to buy from a supplier only if that supplier agrees to purchase something from the customer. This may be considered unethical if the action is unfair to other competing suppliers who may not agree to such an arrangement or not be in a position to buy from the customer. Proponents of reciprocal buying claim that it is reasonable for a customer to extract the best terms of agreement from a supplier, even if this means reaching agreement to sell to the supplier. Indeed, they argue, counter-trade where goods may be included as part payment for supplies has been a feature of international selling for many years and can benefit poorer countries and companies that can not afford to pay in cash.

The importance of business ethics in Cadbury Schweppes

Ethics concern an individual's moral judgments about right and wrong. Decisions taken within an organisation may be made by individuals or groups, but whoever makes them will be influenced by the culture of the company. The decision to behave ethically is a moral one; employees must decide what they think is the right course of action. This may involve rejecting a route that would lead to a bigger short-term gain.

Ethical behaviour and corporate social responsibility can bring significant benefits to a business. For example, they may:

- attract customers to the firm's products, thereby boosting sales and profits
- make employees want to stay with the business, reduce labour turnover and increase productivity
- attract more employees wanting to work for the business, reduce recruitment costs and enable the company to obtain the most talented employees
- attract investors and keep the company's share price high, possibly protecting the business from takeover.

Unethical behaviour and lack of corporate social responsibility may damage a firm's reputation and make it less appealing to stakeholders. Profits could fall as a result.

Along with good corporate governance, ethical behaviour is an integral part of everything that Cadbury Schweppes does. Treating stakeholders fairly is seen as an essential part of the company's success: *"A creative and well managed corporate and social responsibility programme is in the best interests of all our stakeholders – not just our consumers – but also our shareowners, employees, customers, suppliers and other business partners who work together with us."**

Ensuring that employees understand the company's corporate values is achieved by the statement of 'Our Business Principles' which makes clear the behaviour it seeks from employees.

Cadbury Schweppes' good practice was recognised when it was voted one of the 'most admired companies for community and environmental responsibility' by *Management Today* magazine in 2003. It was also ranked second in the Food and Drink sector in the Business in the Community 'Per Cent Club' index of corporate giving for 2003, with an investment in the community of around 3 per cent of its UK pre-tax profits.

*Cadbury Schweppes Corporate and Social Responsibility Report 2002

Source: *http://www.thetimes100.co.uk/case_study* with permission

6.6 Conclusions

This chapter has examined some of the laws and organisations which have been established to protect consumer interests. Unfortunately the unscrupulous few have made it necessary to enact laws which provide consumer protection.

Central to the study of the sale is an understanding of a contract and its associated terms and conditions. Next, a number of business practices and their related legal controls were described. Finally, ethical issues in sales were examined.

Part Three examines the techniques of selling.

References

1 Lewin, J.E. and Johnston, W.J. (1997) 'International salesforce management: a relationship perspective', *Journal of Business and Industrial Marketing*, 12, pp. 232–47; Hawes, J.M., Mast, K.E. and Swann, J.E. (1989) 'Trust earning perceptions of sellers and buyers', *Journal of Personal Selling and Sales Management*, 9, pp. 1–8.

2 Ferrell, O.C., Ingram, T.N. and LaForge, R.W. (2000) 'Initiating structure of legal and ethical decisions in a global sales organization', *Industrial Marketing Management*, 22, pp. 555–64.

3 O'Brien, B. (1999) 'Prudential fined $20 million by NASD over its sales of variable life insurance', *Wall Street Journal*, 9 (July), pp. 1–11.

Practical Exercise

Kwiksell Cars Ltd

John Perry spent £1,500 on a second-hand car bought from Roy Clarke, salesperson at Kwiksell Cars. He is rueing his decision. Perry had never bought a car before but believed that he was smart enough to tell a good car from a bad one. After several weekends of trying to buy a car from private sellers, he decided that going to a dealer was the only sensible option left to him if he wanted to buy one quickly.

A four-year-old Austin Astrada 1100 in the forecourt of Kwiksell Cars had caught his eye as he travelled to work by bus. It was advertised at £1,800 and looked in good condition.

When Perry and his girlfriend visited Kwiksell Cars the following Saturday he was greeted by Roy Clarke, who asked him which car he was interested in and took him to see the Astrada. Clarke described the car as 'in lovely condition', the mechanics having been overhauled recently and the engine tuned. Perry was concerned about petrol consumption and was told that he could expect around 40 mpg around town, increasing to nearly 55 mpg on long runs. Perry was very impressed but he was a little worried about the car's capacity to pull his father's caravan. 'There's no problem there,' said Clarke. 'The Astrada might have a small engine but the carburettor has been souped up and it will cope with a caravan. No problem!'

Clarke asked Perry if he and his young lady would like a test drive. Perry agreed and found the car quite good on acceleration, although the engine was a bit noisier than his father's car. 'That's the souped up engine,' said Clarke. 'It makes it sound a bit racey, doesn't it?'

To Perry, the car looked like the solution to his long search but he knew that, as a cash purchaser, he might be able to negotiate a lower price.

'The car seems to suit my purposes but the price is a little higher than I would be prepared to pay.'

'Yes, but it's not often a car in this condition comes on to the market, sir,' retorted Clarke.

'What would you be prepared to knock off the price for a cash deal?' asked Perry.

'Usually, the maximum I am allowed to go is £200, but if you are prepared to pay a deposit now, with the remainder on, say, Tuesday when you collect the car, I'm willing to reduce the price to £1,500.'

Perry felt pleased with himself, and in front of his girlfriend too! He agreed. He wrote a cheque for £500 and agreed to bring the balance in cash on the following Tuesday. Clarke asked him to sign a contract of sale and promised that the car and all the necessary documents would be ready by Tuesday.

Perry was pleased with his new purchase at first, but the following weekend on a long run, he noticed a knocking noise coming from the engine. The car also appeared to be using much more petrol than he expected. He decided to buy a car guide from WH Smith and check the petrol consumption figures. The guide stated that the Austin Astrada would achieve 30 mpg on the urban cycle and 40 mpg at a steady 56 mph. Perry was livid!

The knocking noise was still to be heard, so he took the car to his father's garage. The mechanic told Perry that the car's big ends were badly worn. It would cost £300 to be repaired. 'The engine's not souped up,' he said, 'it's kaput!'

'But I need the car next weekend. I'm going on holiday in my father's caravan,' said Perry.

'Well, I hope you're thinking of using your father's car,' said the mechanic. 'You'd blow the engine for sure with a car like the Astrada. It's only got an 1100 engine.'

Perry stormed into Clarke's office.

'I'm sorry you've had these problems but engine troubles are common with Astradas,' explained Clarke. 'I'd like to help but I did take you for a test drive.'

'You conned me!' shouted Perry.

'Not at all. You will see that the contract you signed clearly states that the responsibility to check for defects was the buyer's. That means that any faults which appear after sale are your responsibility to put right. You told me you knew a bit about cars. If you didn't you should have brought a mechanic with you. I knocked £300 off the price. That was to cover for any problems like this.'

Discussion Question

Did Clarke break the law regarding the sale of the car? Which laws are relevant to this case?

Practical Exercise

ChevronTexaco cuts losses with Innovetra Fraud Alerter

ChevronTexaco is an oil giant, active in over 180 countries and competitive in energy sectors. A key part of the UK operation is a network of Texaco-branded fuel stations with forecourt convenience stores across England and Wales. This part of the business operates in a competitive marketplace with historically low margins, putting a keen emphasis on efficiency and profitability.

Fraudulent transactions – a needle in a haystack

Like many retailers, Texaco recognises that shrinkage has a direct negative impact on the bottom line, and that internal theft is a major contributor to 'shrinkage of stock'. The company-operated network of sites has a team of ten auditors responsible for audit, loss prevention and compliance, and a key part of their brief is to detect and investigate cases of internal theft. With a large network of sites, many trading 24 hours a day, detecting fraud and non-compliance amongst millions of transactions is almost impossible, and much depends on random examinations noticing something unusual.

Reducing till-based fraud

Texaco wanted to reduce the level of shrinkage, and recognised that the most effective means of achieving this would be to improve the detection and prevention of till-based fraud.

Mike Noyce, European Security and Audit Manager for Texaco explains: 'We looked at various alternatives, and found that Managed Loss Prevention, suggested by Innovetra, provides a comprehensive approach to combating fraud.'

The implementation was managed under Innovetra's project planning process. Noyce comments: 'The system was up and running in eight weeks, the project went smoothly, and came in on budget.'

Direct to the field

Fraud Alerter automatically analyses and mines the transactions from all sites every night. The findings of the system are accessed directly by Loss Prevention Auditors in the field, with no need for help from specialised analysts. Each auditor spends a regular amount of time each week checking what has been found, and is then able to conduct a detailed investigation from their desktop, or to hit the road if a site visit seems necessary.

Early results

Texaco saw the benefit of the new system immediately. Noyce explains: 'We soon found a number of instances of internal fraud and thefts that would not have been detected without the new system. It helps root out fraud quickly, so we are able to nip it in the bud before it becomes a big problem.'

The speed with which the Loss Prevention Auditors are able to respond means that they can visit a site within days of a questionable event, making investigations more effective. 'Being able to confront people with the evidence so quickly after the event gives us a significant tool in the fight against this type of loss,' says Noyce.

Loss Prevention Auditors also find they can forward details of questionable events to the regional management team quickly and easily, bringing another resource to the fight against internal theft.

The deterrent effect has been significant. Site staff quickly became aware that frequent calls are being made to sites asking for an explanation of unusual events. This has had a measurable effect at many sites.

Training and compliance

Texaco is finding that Fraud Alerter helps identify and manage till-based training requirements and compliance issues. Noyce comments: 'Another benefit is that we have been able to identify areas where we need more staff training because Fraud Alerter shows where correct procedures are not being followed.'

A more effective team

The Loss Prevention team has become more productive and effective, and they are better able to prioritise their work. This has led directly to increased detection and resolution of fraud. The Loss Prevention Auditors are able to investigate suspicious events and access detailed till roll displays while working from home or their head office, allowing much of the investigative work to be done without the need to actually visit the retail site. This allows the investigators to be much more selective in deciding which sites to visit, resulting in fewer wasted, unproductive visits.

Managed Loss Prevention

Noyce says: 'MLP has enabled Texaco to fully benefit from the advanced technology now available. My team now have an additional, highly effective tool that complements our way of working and enables us to utilise our time more productively.' MLP and Fraud Alerter have provided Texaco with positive results. Having measured shrinkage both before and after the implementation, Texaco is able to accurately quantify the reduction which has occurred. 'Fraud Alerter has made a significant contribution to the reduction of losses since its implementation. The system has paid for itself in four months.'

About Innovetra

Founded in 1991 and based in North London, Innovetra specialises in business intelligence systems for the retail sector. Their range of products enables retailers to analyse information from their electronic point of sale (EPOS) and other systems to gain an understanding of their customers, increase sales and reduce loss making activities.

- Innovetra Performance Analysis enables fast analysis of all corporate data.

- Innovetra Basket Analysis is a powerful tool for analysing the basket mix, showing patterns within customer buying behaviour.

- Innovetra Retail Newswire is a browser based system for delivering timely alerts to field staff.

- Innovetra Fraud Alerter uses advanced searching and analysis technologies to identify potential fraudulent activity by retail staff. It highlights the areas of the business that need investigation and can dramatically cut loss from staff fraud.

High profile customers include BP Retail, Peacocks, Total UK, and Jacksons Convenience Stores.

Source: *www.thetimes100.co.uk/case_study* with permission

Discussion Question

How might the introduction of Innovetra in a group of retail establishments affect:

- The staff who work there including implications for training and recruitment?

- Managers of such retail establishments?

Examination Questions

1   What is a contract? Of what significance are contracts in buyer–seller relationships?

2   How well protected are customers from false trade descriptions and faulty goods?

3   How does the external legal environment affect the role of sales management?

Part Three Sales Technique

Part Three deals with the basics of selling. It begins with an overview of sales responsibilities including prospecting, customer records and information feedback, self-management, dealing with complaints, the provision of service and the implementation of sales strategies. Sales preparation issues such as product knowledge, knowledge of competitors' products and planning sales presentations are considered along with preparation for sales negotiations. In addition, negotiation techniques, including assessment of power, determination of negotiating objectives, concession analysis and proposal analysis are examined.

Chapter 8 explains personal selling skills and covers the 'sales routine' through the individual phases and associated tactics related to opening, need and problem identification, presentation and demonstration, handling objections, negotiation, closing the sale and follow up.

Chapter 9 is devoted to the important issue of key account management and how this is applied in practice. The KAM relational development model gives a strategic overview to this process and this leads to an explanation of the operation of the key account information and planning system.

Relationship selling is then discussed in Chapter 10 from a historical perspective, beginning with its roots in total quality management to customer care. 'Just-in-time' or 'lean' manufacturing has been the medium through which relationship marketing has developed and the notion of 'reverse marketing' introduced earlier in the text is expanded. The concept of supply chain integration is discussed along with the fact that powerful buyers wield increasing power in this relationship. Tactical issues in relationship selling are examined along with the task of the field salesforce becoming increasingly occupied in the process of gathering marketing information as an input to the company's marketing information system. Finally, the important role of the field salesforce in the task of servicing is considered.

Direct marketing is an element of modern marketing communications and this is looked at in Chapter 11 from the point of view of how this affects the selling process. The management of a direct marketing campaign is examined as is the practical application of database marketing, including such techniques as direct mail, telemarketing, catalogue marketing and direct response advertising.

How the internet complements selling activity concludes Part Three. It is explained in terms of how this has impacted on the roles of selling and sales management. An overview of IT techniques and their application to selling activities is provided. CRM is explained in terms of IT capabilities being used by firms to manage customer relationships. A separate discussion is provided in relation to how IT has affected retail selling including issues like EPOS, space management systems, category management, electronic data interchange, intranets and extranets.

7 Sales Responsibilities and Preparation

Objectives

After studying this chapter, you should be able to:

1 Itemise sales responsibilities
2 Evaluate sources of sales prospects
3 Take a systematic approach to keeping customer records
4 Understand the importance of self-management in selling
5 Assess what preparation is needed prior to selling
6 Understand the art of negotiation
7 Plan individual sales interviews

Key Concepts

- complaint handling
- diversion
- preparation
- presentation planning

- prospecting
- pure selling
- sales cycle
- sales negotiation

7.1 Sales Responsibilities

The *primary* responsibility of a salesperson is to conclude a sale successfully. This task will involve the identification of customer needs, presentation and demonstration, negotiation, handling objections and closing the sale. These skills are discussed in detail in Chapter 8. In order to generate sales successfully, a number of *secondary* functions are also carried out by most salespeople. Although termed secondary, they are vital to long-term sales success. These are:

- prospecting
- database and knowledge management
- self-management
- handling complaints
- providing service

Salespeople are also responsible for implementing sales and marketing strategies. This issue will be considered later in this chapter.

Prospecting

Prospecting is the searching for and calling upon customers who, hitherto, have not purchased from the company. This activity is not of uniform importance across all branches of selling. It is obviously far more important in industrial selling than retail selling; for example, a salesperson of office equipment may call upon many new potential customers, whereas a furniture salesperson is unlikely to search out new prospects – they come to him or her as a result of advertising and, perhaps, high street location.

A problem sometimes associated with salespeople who have worked for the same company for many years is that they rely on established customers to provide repeat orders rather than actively seeking new business. Certainly, it is usually more comfortable for the salesperson to call upon old contacts, but the nature of much industrial selling is that, because product life is long, sustained sales growth depends upon searching out and selling to new customers.

Sources of prospects

1   *Existing customers*. This is a highly effective method of generating prospects and yet tends to be under-used by many. A wealth of new prospects can be obtained simply by asking satisfied customers if they know of anyone who may have a need for the kinds of products or services being sold. This technique has been used successfully in life insurance and industrial selling but also has applications in many other areas.

    Having obtained the names of potential customers, the salesperson, if appropriate, can ask the customer if s/he may use the customer's name as a reference. The use of reference selling in industrial marketing can be highly successful since it reduces the perceived risk for a potential buyer.

2   *Trade directories*. A reliable trade directory such as *Kompass* or *Dunn and Bradstreet* can prove useful in identifying potential industrial buyers. The *Kompass* directory, for example, is organised by industry and location and provides such potentially useful information as:
    - name, address and telephone number of companies
    - names of board members

- size of firm, by turnover and number of employees
- type of products manufactured or distributed

For trade selling, the *Retail Directory* provides information regarding potential customers, organised by various types of retail outlet. Thus a salesperson selling a product suitable for confectioners and newsagents could use the listing of such retailers under the CTN heading (confectioners, tobacconists and newsagents) to obtain relevant names, addresses, telephone numbers and, also, an indication of size through the information given regarding number of branches.

3 *Enquiries.* Enquiries may arise as a natural consequence of conducting business. Satisfied customers may by word of mouth create enquiries from 'warm' prospects. Many companies stimulate enquiries, however, by advertising (many industrial advertisements use coupon return to stimulate leads), direct mail and exhibitions. This source of prospects is an important one and the salesperson should respond promptly. The enquirer may have an urgent need seeking a solution and may turn to the competition if faced with a delay. Even if the customer's problem is not so urgent, slow response may foster unfavourable attitudes towards the salesperson and his or her company's products.

　The next priority is to screen out those enquiries which are unlikely to result in a sale. A telephone call has the advantage of giving a personalised response and yet is relatively inexpensive and not time consuming. It can be used to check how serious the enquiry is and to arrange a personal visit should the enquiry prove to have potential. This process of checking leads to establish their potential is known as *qualifying.*

4 *The press and the Internet.* Perhaps under-used as a source of prospects, the press is nevertheless important. Advertisements and articles can give clues to potential new sources of business. Articles may reveal diversification plans which may mean a company suddenly becomes a potential customer. Advertisements for personnel may reveal plans for expansion, again suggesting potential new business. The Internet is also a vast resource for identifying new potential customers.

5 *Cold canvassing.* This method involves calling on every prospect who might have a need for the salesperson's product. A brush salesperson, for example, may attempt to call upon every house in a village. A variant of this method is the 'cool canvass', where only certain groups of people are canvassed such as those more likely to buy since they possess some qualifying feature; for example, only companies over a certain size may be judged viable prospects. Calling cold on big company buyers is unlikely to be successful, however. A more effective approach is to send a letter in advance explaining the business the company is in, followed by a call to make an appointment.[1]

Database and knowledge management

A systematic approach to customer record-keeping is to be recommended to all repeat-call salespeople. An industrial salesperson should record the following information:

1 Name and address of company

2 Name and position of contact(s)

3   Nature of business

4   Date and time of interview

5   Assessment of potential

6   Buyer needs, problems and buying habits

7   Past sales with dates

8   Problems/opportunities encountered

9   Future actions on the part of salesperson (and buyer).

The use of laptops enables salespeople to record key information which is then stored for future use.

Salespeople should also be encouraged to send back to head office information which is relevant to the marketing of company products. Test market activity by competition, news of imminent product launches, rumours of policy changes on the part of trade and industrial customers and competitors, and feedback on company achievement regarding product performance, delivery and after-sales service are just some of the kinds of information that may be useful to management.

Self-management

This aspect of the sales job is of particular importance since a salesperson is often working alone with the minimum of personal supervision. A salesperson may have to organise his or her own call plan. This involves dividing territory into sections to be covered day by day and deciding the best route to follow between calls. Often it makes sense to divide a territory into segments radiating outwards, from the salesperson's home at the centre. Each segment is designed to be small enough to be covered by the salesperson during one day's work.

Many salespeople believe that the most efficient routing plan involves driving out to the furthest customer and then zig-zagging back to home base. However, it can be shown that adopting a round-trip approach will usually result in lower mileage. Such considerations are important with respect to efficiency, as an alarming amount of time can be spent on the road as opposed to face-to-face with buyers. A survey conducted on behalf of the Institute of Marketing[2] into UK selling practice found that, on average, only 20–30 per cent of a salesperson's normal working day is spent face-to-face with customers. Although this study was conducted over 20 years ago, matters have not improved since then. In fact, this figure is now nearer 20 rather than 30 per cent because salespeople are increasingly called upon to carry out ancillary work such as customer surveys, service work and merchandising. Some companies take this responsibility out of the salesperson's hands and produce daily worksheets showing who is to be called on and in what order.

Another factor which may be the responsibility of the salesperson is deciding on call frequency. It is sensible to grade customers according to potential. For example, consumer durable salespeople may categorise the retail outlets they are selling to into A, B and C grades. The grade A outlets may be visited every fortnight, grade B every month and grade C once every three months. The principle applies to all kinds of selling, however, and may be left to the salesperson's discretion or organised centrally as part of the sales management function. The danger of delegating responsibility to salespeople is that the criteria used to decide frequency of visit are 'friendliness with the buyer' or 'ease of sale' rather than sales potential. On the other hand, it can be argued that a responsible salesperson is in the best position to decide how much time needs to be spent with each customer.

Handling complaints

Handling complaints may seem at first to be a time-consuming activity which diverts a salesperson from the primary task of generating sales. A marketing orientation for a salesforce, however, dictates that the goal of an organisation is to create customer satisfaction in order to generate profit. When dissatisfaction identifies itself in the form of a complaint, this necessary condition for long-term survival is clearly not being met.

Complaints vary in their degree of seriousness and in the authority which the salesperson holds in order to deal with them. No matter how trivial the complaint may seem, the complainant should be treated with respect and the matter dealt with seriously. In a sense, dealing with complaints is one of the after-sale services provided by suppliers. It is therefore part of the mix of benefits a company offers its customers, although it differs in essence since the initial objective is to minimise its necessity. Nevertheless, the ability of the salesperson to empathise with the customer and his or her problem and to react sympathetically can create considerable goodwill and help foster long-term relationships.

With this in mind, many companies give the customer the benefit of the doubt when this does not involve high cost, even though they suspect that the fault may be caused by inappropriate use of the product on the part of the customer; for example, garden fork manufacturers may replace prematurely broken forks, even though the break may have been caused by work for which the fork was not designed.

When the salesperson does not have the authority to deal with the complaint immediately, his or her job is to submit the relevant information in written form to head office so that the matter can be taken further.

Providing service

Salespeople are in an excellent position to provide a 'consultancy' service to their customers. Since they meet many customers each year, they become familiar with solutions to common problems. Thus an industrial salesperson may be able to advise customers on improving productivity or cutting costs. Indeed, the service element of industrial selling is often incorporated into the selling process itself, e.g. computer salespeople may offer to conduct an analysis of customer requirements and produce a written report in order to complete a sale. The salesperson who learns solutions to common problems and provides useful advice to his or her customers builds an effective barrier to competitive attacks and strengthens buyer–seller relationships.

Another area where salespeople provide service is in trade selling. They may be called upon to set up in-store displays and other promotions for wholesalers and retailers. Some companies employ people to do this on a full-time basis. These people are called merchandisers and their activities provide support to traditional salespeople, who can thus spend more time selling.

Retail salespeople also provide customer service. Selling audio equipment, for example, is an opportunity to help the customer to make the correct choice for a given budget. Richer Sounds is a UK-based chain of audio stores that prides itself on exceptional customer service (see box).

Customer service in retailing

At Richer Sounds, the UK-based audio chain, customer service begins when potential customers enter the door. Salespeople are trained to acknowledge customers by asking casually, 'Are you OK there?' or 'Are you happy browsing, sir/madam?' The purpose is not to sell them anything but to let customers know that the salesperson is aware of their presence and that they can contact him or her when they are ready. A sign over the door says 'Browsers Welcome' and they mean it – without the fear of being hassled by salespeople.

Customers should not be pre-judged. The same quality of service must be provided to customers who are shabbily dressed, pompous, flashy, aggressive, rude or boring. The whole selling operation should be transparent. There should be no pressure, no trying to disguise a poor product and no catches. Salespeople should be honest and if they do not have the right information should reply, 'I'm sorry I don't know but I shall try to find out.'

Sometimes it is not possible to make a sale because the product in question is not stocked. The salesperson should still provide a service by advising the customer where they might get it. Argos and Tandy catalogues are held for this purpose. Quite often customers will stop and think before they walk out to see if they can buy something as a mark of appreciation.

Richer Sounds advocates the policy of 'under-promise, over-deliver'. Over-promising can ruin long-term relationships so their salespeople never promise customers 'the moon' just to make a sale.

Even though Richer Sounds tries hard to give 100 per cent customer service, complaints are bound to happen. They even encourage them. They recognise that every disgruntled customer on average tells 20 people about it. By receiving complaints they have the chance to put things right and learn from their mistakes. A short, tear-off questionnaire is included with receipts. The questionnaire covers eight points including the customer's assessment of the quality of the service they have received, and there is space for comments. An after-sales service questionnaire which asks only four questions is also used to monitor service and invite complaints.

Salespeople should not change their customer focus once the sale is made. The service should be followed through until the customer is out of the shop. Salespeople should thank them for their custom, give them their name to contact if there are any problems, and perhaps help them to the car. If the customer is uncertain about their purchase, they will be told that the salesperson will call them after a few days to check that they are happy with the product.

Source: Based on Richer, J. (1995) *The Richer Way*, WMAP Business Communications.

Salespeople may also be called upon to provide after-sales service to customers. Sales engineers may be required to give advice on the operation of a newly acquired machine or provide assistance in the event of a breakdown. Sometimes they may be able to solve the problem themselves, while in other cases they will call in technical specialists to deal with the problem.

Implementing sales and marketing strategies

The salesforce is also charged with the responsibility of implementing sales and marketing strategies designed by management. Misunderstandings regarding strategy can have grave implications. For example, the credibility of a premium price and high-quality position in the marketplace can be seriously undermined by a salesforce too eager to give large price discounts. The solution might be to decide discount structure at managerial level (both sales and marketing management will have an input to this decision) based upon the price sensitivity of various market segments. The salesforce would then be told the degree to which price could be discounted for each class of customer. In this way the product's positioning strategy would remain intact while allowing the salesforce some discretion to discount when required.

Successful implementation can mean the difference between winning or losing new accounts. An effective method of gaining an account in the face of entrenched competition is the **diversion**. The aim is to distract a rival into concentrating its efforts on defending one account (and therefore neglecting another). The boxed case history provides a true account of how a salesperson for a computer company diverted a well-entrenched rival to defend an account (The Bank) in order to win another (The Insurance Company).

In this example, the stakes and costs were high. The management at A believed that the cost of loaning a £1 million computer system to The Bank was justified: (a) by a strategically important penetration of a major market; (b) by the potential profit to be gained by selling to The Insurance Company. This was a managerial decision and obviously dependent on judgement, but the example shows the principle of using 'diversion' as a method of winning major accounts.

The diversion

A computer company (A) was seeking its first high-profile installation in a major European city. A successful breakthrough sale was believed to be strategically important. It was considering two prospective customers: 'The Bank' and 'The Insurance Company'. *(continued on following page)*

At The Bank, a rival computer company (B) was entrenched. Using a network of contacts, A's salesperson did a thorough reconnaissance. He discovered that B's salesperson at The Bank was deeply entrenched through good service and effective relationship building. The conclusion was that the situation for A was hopeless. However, The Bank's information technology manager opined that if A offered them a free computer system (£1 million) The Bank would 'have to consider their offer'.

The Insurance Company was a customer of a third computer company (C) and company B. A's sales manager had senior contacts at The Insurance Company and found them dissatisfied with C, approaching a capacity shortage which would force the purchase of a large computer (likely to be over £10 million). The problem was that B was well respected by The Insurance Company. Also the same salesperson from B serviced both The Bank and The Insurance Company accounts. Fortunately, B's salesperson had not called upon The Insurance Company recently. The task: to perpetuate B's absence. To accomplish it, the 'diversion strategy' was used.

A called at The Bank and offered a computer 'free for a year' and made an occasional follow-up call, while selling diligently (but quietly) at The Insurance Company. The ensuing flap at The Bank was quite spectacular. The switching costs associated with A's complete replacement of B would have been significant, and so The Bank began to ask a lot of questions about switch-over plans and arrangements. (It was rumoured that B's salesperson was staying awake at night composing new questions that The Bank might ask of A!) In the face of these questions A's salesperson responded deliberately (after all, he was spending most of his time selling at The Insurance Company). The struggle at The Bank raged on with A's credibility relentlessly eroded by B's clever and determined defence.

In due course, B's sales team was successful in their defence of The Bank account. However, their gratification was dimmed by the news that A had won a larger order (£10 million) at The Insurance Company.

7.2 Preparation

The ability to think on one's feet is of great benefit to salespeople, since they will be required to modify their sales presentation to suit the particular needs and problems of their various customers and to respond quickly to unusual objections and awkward questions. However, there is much to be gained by careful **preparation** of the selling task. Some customers will have similar problems; some questions and objections will be raised repeatedly. A salesperson can therefore usefully spend time considering how best to respond to these recurring situations.

Within this section attention will be given to preparation not only for the selling task, in which there is little or no scope for the salesperson to bargain with the buyer, but also for where selling may involve a degree of negotiation between buyer and seller. In many selling situations, buyers and sellers may negotiate price, timing of delivery, product extras, payment and credit terms, and trade-in values. These will be termed **sales negotiations**. In others, the salesperson may have no scope for such discussions; in essence the product is offered on a take-it-or-leave-it basis. Thus, the salesperson of bicycles to dealers may have a set price list and delivery schedule with no authority to deviate from them. This will be termed **pure selling**.

Preparation for pure selling and sales negotiations

A number of factors can be examined in order to improve the chances of sales success in both sales negotiations and pure selling.

Product knowledge and benefits

Knowledge of product features is insufficient for sales success. Because people buy products for the benefits they confer, successful salespeople relate product features to consumer benefits; product features are the means by which benefits are derived. The way to do this is to look at products from the customer's point of view. Table 7.1 shows a few examples.

By analysing the products they are selling in this way, salespeople will communicate in terms which are meaningful to buyers and therefore be more convincing. In industrial selling, the salesperson may be called upon to be an adviser or consultant who is required to provide solutions to problems. In some cases this may involve a fairly deep understanding of the nature of the customer's business, in order to be able to appreciate the problems fully and to suggest the most appropriate solution. Thus the salesperson must not only know his or her products' benefits but the types of situation in which each would be appropriate. In computer selling, for example, successful selling requires an appreciation of which system is most appropriate given customer needs and resources. This may necessitate a careful examination of customer needs through a survey conducted by the seller. Sometimes the costs of the survey will be paid for by the prospective customer, later to be subtracted from the cost of the equipment should an order result.

Preparation of sales benefits should not result in an inflexible sales approach. Different customers have different needs which implies they seek different benefits from products they buy. One high-earning salesperson of office equipment attributed his success to the preparation he conducted before every sales visit. This involved knowing his product's capabilities, understanding his client's needs and matching these together by getting his wife to test him every evening and at the weekend.[3]

Table 7.1 Product features and customer benefits

Product feature	Customer benefit
Retractable nib on ballpoint pen	Reduces chances of damage
High rev. speed on spin dryer	Clothes are dried more thoroughly
High reach on forklift truck	Greater use of warehouse space
Streamfeeding (photocopiers)	Faster copying
Automatic washing machine	More time to spend on doing other less mundane activities

Knowledge of competitors' products and their benefits

Knowledge of competitive products offers several advantages:

1 It allows a salesperson to offset the strengths of competitors' products, which may be mentioned by potential buyers, against their weaknesses. For example, a buyer might say, 'Competitor X's product offers cheaper maintenance costs', to which a salesperson might reply, 'Yes, but these cost savings are small compared to the fuel savings you get with our machine.'

2 In industrial selling, sales engineers may work with a buying organisation in order to solve a technical problem. This may result in a product specification being drawn up in which the sales engineers have an influence. It is obviously to their benefit that the specification reflects the strengths and capabilities of their products rather than the competition. Thus knowledge of competitive strengths and weaknesses will be an advantage in this situation.

Competitive information can be gleaned from magazines such as *Which?*, sales catalogues and price lists, from talking to buyers and from direct observation (e.g. prices in supermarkets). It makes sense to keep such information on file for quick reference. Vauxhall gives its salespeople a brief with a résumé of the strengths and weaknesses of its car range, along with those of its competitors.

Sales presentation planning

Although versatility, flexibility and the ability to 'think on one's feet' are desirable attributes, there are considerable advantages to **presentation planning**:

1 The salesperson is less likely to forget important consumer benefits associated with each product within the range he or she is selling.

2 The use of visual aids and demonstrations can be planned into the presentation at the most appropriate time to reinforce the benefit the salesperson is communicating.

3 It builds confidence in the salesperson, particularly the newer, less experienced, that s/he is well equipped to do the job efficiently and professionally.

4 Possible objections and questions can be anticipated and persuasive counter-arguments prepared. Many salespeople who to an outsider seem naturally quick witted have developed this skill through careful preparation beforehand, imagining themselves as buyers and thinking of objections they might raise if they were in such a position. For example, many price objections can be countered by reference to higher product quality, greater durability, high productivity and lower offsetting life-cycle costs, for example, lower maintenance, fuel or human resources costs.

Setting sales objectives

The essential skill in setting call objectives is to phrase them in terms of what the salesperson wants the customer to do rather than what the salesperson will do. The type of objective set may depend upon the **sales cycle** of the product and the stage reached in that cycle with a prospective customer.

The sales cycle refers to the time that can reasonably be expected to pass before an order is concluded. With many retail sales this is short. Often, unless a sale is concluded during the first visit, the customer will buy elsewhere. In this situation it is reasonable to set a sales close objective. With capital goods such as aeroplanes, gas turbines and oil rigs, the sales cycle is very long, perhaps running into years. Clearly, to set a sales objective in terms of closing the sale is inappropriate. For producers with longer sales cycles, sensible objectives may be:

- for the customer to define clearly what his or her requirements are

- to have the customer visit the production site

- to have the customer try the product, e.g. fly on an aircraft

- to have the customer compare the product versus competitive products in terms of measurable performance criteria, e.g. for pile driving equipment this might be the number of metres driven per hour

The temptation, when setting objectives, is to determine them in terms of what the salesperson will do. An adhesive salesperson may decide that the objective of the visit to a buyer is to demonstrate the ease of application and adhesive properties of a new product. While this demonstration may be a valuable and necessary part of the sales presentation, it is not the ultimate goal of the visit. This may be to have the customer test the product over a four-week period, or to order a quantity for immediate use.

Understanding buyer behaviour

The point was made in Chapter 3 that many organisational buying decisions are complex, involving many people whose evaluative criteria may differ, and that the purchasing officer may play a minor role in deciding which supplier to choose, particularly with very expensive items.

The practical implication of these facts is that careful preparation may be necessary for industrial salespeople, either when selling to new companies or when selling to existing customers where the nature of the product is different. In both situations, time taken trying to establish who the key influencers and decision-makers are will be well rewarded. In different companies there may be different key people: for example, secretaries (office stationery); production engineers (lathes); design engineers (components); managing directors (computers). The salesperson needs to be aware of the real need to treat each organisation individually.

Other practical information which a salesperson can usefully collect includes the name and position of each key influencer and decision-maker, the times most suitable for interview, the types of competitive products previously purchased by the buying organisation, and any threats to a successful sale or special opportunities afforded by the situation. Examples in the last category would include personal prejudices held by key people against the salesperson, his or her company, or its products, while positive factors might include common interests which could form the basis of a rapport with the buyer, or favourable experiences with other types of products sold by the salesperson's company.

Preparation for sales negotiations

In addition to the factors outlined in the previous section, a sales negotiator will benefit by paying attention to the following additional factors during preparation.

Assessment of the balance of power

In the sales negotiation, seller and buyer will each be expecting to conclude a deal which is favourable to themselves. The extent to which each is successful will depend upon their negotiating skills and the balance of power between the parties. This balance will be determined by four key factors:

1 *The number of options available to each party.* If a buyer has only one option – to buy from the seller in question – then that seller is in a powerful position. If the seller, in turn, is not dependent on the buyer but has many attractive potential customers for the products, then again s/he is in a strong position. Conversely, when a buyer has many potential sources of supply and a seller has few potential customers, the buyer should be able to extract a good deal. Many buyers will deliberately contact a number of potential suppliers to strengthen their bargaining position.

2 *The quantity and quality of information held by each party.* ('Knowledge is power', Machiavelli.) If a buyer has access to a seller's cost structure then s/he is in a powerful position to negotiate a cheaper price, or at least to avoid paying too high a price. If a seller knows how much a buyer is willing to pay, then his or her power position is improved.

3 *Need recognition and satisfaction.* The greater the salesperson's understanding of the needs of the buyer and the more capable s/he is of satisfying those needs, the stronger will be the bargaining position. In some industrial marketing situations, suppliers work with buying organisations to solve technical problems in the knowledge that to do so will place them in a very strong negotiating position. The more the buyer believes that his or her needs can be satisfied by only one company, the weaker is the buyer's negotiating stance. In effect, the seller has reduced the buyer's number of options by uniquely satisfying these needs.

4 *The pressures on the parties.* Where a technical problem is of great importance to a buying organisation, its visibility high and solution difficult, any supplier who can solve it will gain immense bargaining power. If, on the other hand, there are pressures on the salesperson, perhaps because of low sales returns, then a buyer should be able to extract extremely favourable terms during negotiations in return for purchasing from him or her.

The implications of these determinants of the balance of power are that before negotiations (and indeed during them) salespeople will benefit by assessing the relative strength of their power base. This implies that they need information. If the seller knows the number of companies who are competing for the order, their likely stances, the criteria used by the buying organisation when deciding between them, the degree of pressure on key members of the decision-making unit, and any formula they might use for assessing price acceptability, an accurate assessment of the power balance should be possible.

This process should lessen the chances of pricing too low or of needlessly giving away other concessions like favourable payment terms. At this stage judicious negotiators will look to the future to assess likely changes in the balance of power. Perhaps power lies with the supplier now, but overpowering or 'negotiating too sweet a deal' might provoke retribution later when the buyer has more suppliers from which to choose.

Determination of negotiating objectives

It is prudent for negotiators to set objectives during the preparation stage. This reduces the likelihood of being swayed by the heat of the negotiating battle and of accepting a deal which, with hindsight, should have been rejected. This process is analogous to buyers at an auction paying more than they can afford because they allow themselves to be swept along by the bidding. Additionally, when negotiation is conducted by a team, discussion of objectives helps co-ordination and unity. It is useful to consider two types of objective:[4]

1 *'Must have' objectives*. The 'must have' objectives define a bargainer's minimum requirements; for example, the minimum price at which a seller is willing to trade. This determines the negotiating breakpoint.

2 *'Would like' objectives*. These are the maximum a negotiator can reasonably expect to get; for example, the highest price a seller feels s/he can realistically obtain. This determines the opening positions of buyers and sellers.

When considering 'must have' objectives it is useful to consider the Best Alternative to a Negotiated Agreement (BATNA).[5] This involves the identification of one's alternative if agreement cannot be reached. It sets a standard against which any offer can be assessed and guards against accepting unfavourable terms when pressured by a more powerful buyer. By having attractive BATNAs, higher 'must have' objectives can be set. For example, a person wishing to sell a house may set a 'must have' objective of £90,000. However, by considering his or her BATNA of renting the property, it may become clear that its rental value is equivalent to £100,000. This means that the 'must have' objective would rise by £10,000. Also during the negotiations themselves, its identification allows a comparison with each possible proposal that emerges with the BATNA to assess whether a negotiated agreement is better than the alternative.[6]

Finally, the notion of a BATNA encourages people without a strong alternative to create one. For example, before entering pay negotiations, the seller of services (employee) can strengthen his or her position by improving his or her BATNA by seeking and getting a favourable job offer elsewhere.

Figure 7.1 describes a negotiating scenario where a deal is possible since there is overlap between the highest price the buyer is willing to pay (buyer's 'must have' objective) and the lowest price the seller is willing to accept (seller's 'must have' objective). The price actually agreed will depend upon the balance of power between the two parties and their respective negotiating skills.

Concession analysis

Since negotiation implies movement in order to achieve agreement, it is likely that concessions will be made by at least one party during the bargaining process.

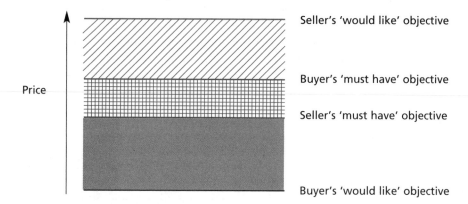

Figure 7.1 A negotiating scenario
Source: Adapted from Winkler, J. (1996) *Bargaining for Results*, Heinemann, Oxford.

Preparation can aid negotiators by analysing the kinds of concession which might be offered to the other side. The key to this concession analysis is to value concessions the seller might be prepared to make through the eyes of the buyer. By doing this it may be possible to identify concessions which cost the seller very little and yet are highly valued by the buyer. For example, to offer much quicker delivery than is usual may cost a seller very little because of spare capacity, but if this is highly valued by the buyer, the seller may be able to trade it in return for a prompt payment agreement. The kinds of issue that may be examined during concession analysis include the following:

- price
- timing of delivery
- the product – its specification, optional extras
- the price – ex works price, price at the buyer's factory gate, installation price, in-service price
- payment – on despatch, on receipt, in working order, credit terms
- Trade-in terms, e.g. cars

The aim of concession analysis is to ensure that nothing which has value to the buyer is given away freely during negotiations. A skilful negotiator will attempt to trade concession for concession so that ultimately an agreement which satisfies both parties is reached.

Proposal analysis

A further sensible activity during the preparation stage is to estimate the proposals and demands the buyer is likely to make during the course of negotiation, and the seller's reaction to them. This is analogous to the anticipation of objections in pure selling – it helps when quick decisions have to be made in the heat of the negotiation.

It is also linked to concession analysis, for when a buyer makes a proposal (e.g. favourable credit terms) s/he is really asking the seller to grant a concession. The skilful salesperson will ask for a concession in return – perhaps a less onerous delivery schedule. By anticipating the kinds of proposals the buyer is likely to make, the seller can plan the kinds of counter-proposals s/he wishes to make. In some situations, the appropriate response may be the 'concession close' (see Chapter 8).

7.3 Conclusions

This chapter has examined the responsibilities of salespeople to gain sales, to prospect for new customers, to maintain customer records and provide information feedback, to manage their work, to handle complaints and to provide service.

An important element in managing their work is preparation, which is examined in detail. A distinction is made between sales negotiations, where a certain amount of bargaining may take place, and pure selling, where the salesperson is given no freedom to bargain. The following elements are important during preparation:

(a) product knowledge and customer benefits

(b) knowledge of competitors' products and their benefits

(c) sales presentation planning

(d) setting sales and negotiation objectives

(e) understanding buyer behaviour

(f) assessing the power balance

(g) concession analysis

(h) proposal analysis

Chapter 8, on personal selling skills, considers how to use this preparation in the actual selling situation.

References

1 Lee, A. (1984) 'Sizing up the buyers', *Marketing*, 29 March.

2 PA Consultants (1979) *Sales Force Practice Today: A Basis for Improving Performance*, Institute of Marketing, London.

3 Kennedy, G., Benson, J. and Macmillan, J. (1980) *Managing Negotiations*, Business Books, London.

4 Kennedy, G., Benson, J. and Macmillan, J. (1980) *Managing Negotiations*, Business Books, London.

5 Fisher, R. and Ury, W. (1991) *Getting to Yes: Negotiating Agreement Without Giving In*, Business Books, London.

6 Pillutla, M. (2004) *'Negotiation: how to make deals and reach agreement in business'*, Format Publishing, Norwich.

Practical Exercise

The O'Brien Company

The O'Brien Company manufactures and markets a wide range of luggage, including suitcases, handbags and briefcases. The company is organised into two divisions – consumer and industrial. The consumer division sells mainly through retail outlets, whereas the industrial division markets direct to companies which buy luggage (especially briefcases) for use by their executives.

You have recently been appointed as a salesperson for the industrial division and asked to visit a new potential client with a view to selling him briefcases. The potential customer is Brian Forbes, the Managing Director (and owner) of a medium-sized engineering company in the Midlands with subsidiaries in Manchester, Leeds and Bristol. They employ a salesforce of 20 men selling copper piping. In addition, it is estimated that the company employs around 40 marketing, personnel, production and accountancy executives.

The O'Brien Company markets two ranges of executive briefcase. One is made from good quality plastic, with imitation hide lining. It is available in black only and priced at £25 for the lockable version and £22 for the non-lockable type. The other, a de-luxe range, is manufactured from leather and real hide and priced at £95. Colours available are black, brown, dark blue and claret. Additional features are a number-coded locking device, a variable depth feature which allows the briefcase to be expanded from its usual 87.5 mm to 137.5 mm, individual gilt initialling on each briefcase, an ink-resistant interior compartment for pens, and three pockets inside the lid to take different sized papers/documents. The plastic version has only the last of these features and is 75 mm in depth. Quantity discounts for both ranges are as shown below:

Quantity	Reduction %
10–19	2
20–39	3
40–79	4
80 or more	6

Very little is known about Brian Forbes or his company apart from the information already given. However, by chance, an acquaintance of yours who works as a salesperson for a machine tool company visited Mr Forbes earlier in the year.

1 What are your sales objectives? What extra information would be useful?

2 Prepare a sales presentation for the briefcases.

3 Prepare a list of possible objections and your responses to them.

Presenting New Standa Plus: the final word in hydraulic braking systems?

Standa is a hydraulic braking system that has been around for 15 years, used by most of the major truck and lorry manufacturers. It has been very reliable, but has perhaps lost its way and key customers are starting to specify other systems in their trucks. The reason for this is that there has been little in the way of product development. Until now!

New Standa Plus has been developed, which uses polytetrafluoroethylene (PTFE) to prolong the life of the system. PTFE is a very slippery coating that reduces friction wear dramatically (in the household it is used on non-stick pans). The use of this coating in hydraulic systems is revolutionary. The PTFE coating is a major advancement for the product type, as it will prolong the life of the system by up to 50 per cent (independent tests by Hydromatics Testers Ltd).

The reason the new PTFE coating is so special is that up until now it was impossible to get the PTFE to stick effectively to the piston metal. This was due to the fact that the hydraulic fluid would find any imperfections in the coating, and there were always some, and this would cause the PTFE to separate from the metal of the piston. The Standard Hydraulics R&D team have discovered a new process, using liquid nitrogen as the solvent for the PTFE, which delivers a blemish-free coating. The added bonus is that the coating can now be applied to both pistons and cylinders. Thus the system becomes virtually friction free and New Standa Plus is now guaranteed for a minimum of 15 years – longer than the lifetime of the average truck itself and certainly up to 50 per cent longer than the competition's products. The New Standa Plus PTFE coating technology is patented as 'SuperPTFE'. As such, it cannot be directly copied by any other hydraulic braking system manufacturer.

The advertising that will run for the product in the technical press is based upon the concept that New Standa Plus is built to last longer than the trucks.

In the role of sales representative for Standard Hydraulics you are required to put together a sales pitch to purchasing teams at potential new customers. You will need to convince the prospects to switch from their existing hydraulic system to New Standa Plus. You should assume that you will make a PowerPoint presentation to the buying group, which will consist of the manufacturing director, production manager, technical designer, financial director and managing director. You would be advised to include something for each of them to be impressed with. You should use the information given about the product to form the basis for your sales pitch. In your sales presentation you will need to communicate the following:

• The Standa hydraulic braking system has been radically improved by the addition of PTFE (polytetrafluoroethylene) coating to the hydraulic pistons and cylinders.

• The name of the new system is New Standa Plus.

• The effect of the product improvement is that it dramatically prolongs the working life of the bearings.

• The company is a leading edge manufacturer of hydraulics. You might consider using the corporate claim/slogan 'Standard Hydraulics, the new Standard in Hydraulics'.

Source: Written by Andrew Pressey, Lecturer in Marketing, University of East Anglia. Neville Hunt, Lecturer in Marketing, University of Luton.

Examination Questions

1 What considerations should be taken into account when deciding on the amount of prospecting a salesperson should do?

2 Discuss the contribution of preparation to the selling process.

8 Personal Selling Skills

Objectives

After studying this chapter, you should be able to:

1 Distinguish the various phases of the selling process
2 Apply different questions to different selling situations
3 Understand what is involved in the presentation and the demonstration
4 Know how to deal with buyers' objections
5 Understand and apply the art of negotiation
6 Close a sale

Key Concepts

- buying signals
- closing the sale
- demonstrations
- needs analysis
- negotiation

- objections
- personal selling skills
- reference selling
- sales presentation
- trial close

The basic philosophy underlying the approach to personal selling adopted in this book is that selling should be an extension of the marketing concept. This implies that for long-term survival it is in the best interests of the salesperson and his or her company to identify customer needs and aid customer decision-making by selecting from the product range those products which best fit the customer's requirements. This philosophy of selling is in line with Weitz[1] and the contingency framework, which suggests that the sales interview gives an unparalleled opportunity to match behaviour to the specific customer interaction that is encountered. This is called 'adaptive selling' since the salesperson adapts his or her approach according to the specific situation and it has been found to be a growing way of conducting sales interactions.[2] This is not to deny the importance of personal persuasion. In the real world, it is unlikely that a product has clear advantages over its competition on all points, and it is clearly part of the selling function for the salesperson to emphasise those superior features and benefits which the product possesses. However, the model for personal selling advocated here is that of a salesperson acting as a need identifier and problem-solver. The view of the salesperson as being a slick fast-talking confidence trickster is unrealistic in a world where most sellers depend upon repeat business and where a high proportion of selling is conducted with pro-fessional buyers.

Saxe and Weitz (1982) defined customer-orientated selling as 'the degree to which salespeople practice the marketing concept by trying to help their customers make purchase decisions that will satisfy customer needs'.[3] They characterised customer-orientated selling as:

1 The desire to help customers make satisfactory purchase decisions.

2 Helping customers assess their needs.

3 Offering products that will satisfy those needs.

4 Describing products accurately.

5 Avoiding deceptive or manipulative influence tactics.

6 Avoiding the use of high pressure sales techniques.

In order to foster customer-orientated selling, companies need to develop a corpor-ate culture that places understanding customers and creating value for them central to their philosophy and to use evaluation procedures that include measurement of the support given to customers, customer satisfaction with salesperson interactions, and the degree to which salespeople are perceived by customers to behave ethically. In addition, companies should include ethics in sales training courses, and employ sales managers who are willing to promote and enforce ethical codes and policies.[4]

Research studies[5] have shown that successful selling is associated with the following:

- asking questions
- providing product information, making comparisons and offering evidence to support claims
- acknowledging the customer's viewpoint
- agreeing with the customer's perceptions
- supporting the customer
- releasing tension
- having a richer, more detailed knowledge of customers
- increased effort
- self-confidence in one's own ability

These important findings should be borne in mind by salespeople when in a sales interview. They also suggest that sales training can improve sales performance, not

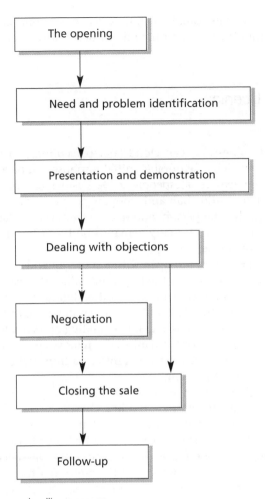

Figure 8.1 The personal selling process

only by improving skills, but by enhancing the self-confidence of the trainees in their perceived ability to perform well.[6]

As with the development of all skills, the theoretical approach described in this chapter needs to be supplemented by practical experience. Many companies use role playing as a method of providing new salespeople with the opportunity to develop their skills in a situation where sales trainees can observe and correct behaviour. An example of such an exercise, where students and salespeople can apply some of the techniques outlined in this chapter, is given at the end of Chapter 14.

In order to develop personal selling skills it is useful to distinguish seven phases of the selling process, shown in Figure 8.1. These phases need not occur in the order shown. Objections may be raised during presentation or during negotiation and a trial close may be attempted at any point during the presentation if buyer interest is high. Furthermore, negotiation may or may not take place or may occur during any of the stages. As Moncrief and Marshall (2005) report:[7]

'The evolved selling process assumes that the salesperson typically will perform the various steps of the process in some form, but the steps (phases) do not occur for each sales call. Rather, they occur over time, accomplished by multiple people within the selling firm, and not necessarily in any given sequence.'

8.1 | The Opening

Initial impressions can cloud later perceptions, so it is important to consider the ways in which a favourable initial response can be achieved.

Buyers expect salespeople to be businesslike in their personal appearance and behaviour. Untidy hair and a sloppy manner of dress can create a lack of confidence. Further, the salesperson who does not respect the fact that the buyer is likely to be a busy person, with many demands on his or her time, may cause irritation on the part of the buyer.

Salespeople should open with a smile, a handshake and, in situations where they are not well known to the buyer, introduce themselves and the company they represent. Common courtesies should be followed. For example, they should wait for the buyer to indicate that they can sit down or, at least, ask the buyer if they may sit down. Attention to detail, like holding one's briefcase in the left hand so that the right can be used for the handshake, removes the possibility of an awkward moment when a briefcase is clumsily transferred from right to left as the buyer extends his or her hand in greeting.

Opening remarks are important since they set the tone for the rest of the sales interview. Normally they should be business related since this is the purpose of the visit; they should show the buyer that the salesperson is not about to waste time. Where the buyer is well known and by his or her own remarks indicates a willingness to talk about a more social matter, the salesperson will obviously follow. This can generate close rapport with the buyer, but the salesperson must be aware of the reason for being there and not be excessively diverted from talking business. Opening remarks might be:

Trade salesperson:	Your window display looks attractive. Has it attracted more custom?
Industrial salesperson:	We have helped a number of companies in the same kind of business as you are in to achieve considerable savings by the use of our stock control procedures. What methods do you use at present to control stock?
Retail salesperson:	I can see that you appear to be interested in our stereo equipment. What kind of system do you have in mind?

The cardinal sin which many retail salespeople commit is to open with 'Can I help you?' which invites the response 'No thank you. I'm just looking.'

8.2 Need and Problem Identification

Most salespeople have a range of products to sell. A car salesperson has many models ranging from small economy cars to super luxury top-of-the-range models. The computer salesperson will have a number of systems to suit the needs and resources of different customers. A bicycle retailer will have models from many different manufacturers to offer customers. A pharmaceutical salesperson will be able to offer doctors a range of drugs to combat various illnesses. In each case, the seller's first objective will be to discover the problems and needs of the customer. Before a car salesperson can sell a car, s/he needs to understand the customer's circumstances. What size of car is required? Is the customer looking for high fuel economy or performance? Is a boot or a hatchback preferred? What kind of price range is being considered? Having obtained this information the salesperson is in a position to sell the model which best suits the needs of the buyer. A computer salesperson may carry out a survey of customer requirements prior to suggesting an appropriate computer system. A bicycle retailer should ask who the bicycle is for, what type is preferred (e.g. mountain or racing) and the colour preference, before making sensible suggestions as to which model is most suitable. A pharmaceutical salesperson will discuss with doctors the problems which have arisen with patient treatment; perhaps an ointment has been ineffective or a harmful side-effect has been discovered. This gives the salesperson the opportunity to offer a solution to such problems by means of one of his or her company's products.

This **needs analysis** approach suggests that early in the sales process the salesperson should adopt a question-and-listen posture. In order to encourage the buyer to discuss his or her problems and needs, salespeople tend to use 'open' rather than 'closed' questions. An open question is one which requires more than a one-word or one-phrase answer, for example:

- 'Why do you believe that a computer system is inappropriate for your business?'

- 'What were the main reasons for buying the XYZ photocopier?'

- 'In what ways did the ABC ointment fail to meet your expectations?'

A closed question, on the other hand, invites a one-word or one-phrase answer. These can be used to obtain purely factual information, but excessive use can hinder rapport and lead to an abrupt type of conversation which lacks flow:

- 'Would you tell me the name of the equipment you currently use?'

- 'Does your company manufacture 1000 cc marine engines?'

- 'What is the name of your chief mechanical engineer?'

In practice, a wide variety of questions may be used during a sales interview.[8] Thirteen types of questions and their objectives, together with examples, are given in Table 8.1.

Salespeople should avoid the temptation of making a **sales presentation** without finding out the needs of their customers. It is all too easy to start a sales presentation

Table 8.1 Types of question used in personal selling

Type of question	Objective	Example
Tie down question	Used for confirmation or to commit a prospect to a position.	You want the program to work, don't you?
Leading question	Direct or guide a prospect's thinking.	How does that coat feel on you?
Alternative question	Used to elicit an answer by forcing selection from two or more alternatives.	Would you prefer the red or blue model?
Statement/question	A statement is followed by a question which forces the prospect to reflect upon the statement.	This machine can spin at 5000 rpm and process three units per minute. What do you think of that productivity?
Sharp angle question	Used to commit a prospect to a position.	If we can get it in blue, is that the way you would want it?
Information-gathering questions	Used to gather facts.	How many people are you currently employing?
Opinion-gathering questions	Used to gather opinions or feelings.	What are your feelings concerning the high price of energy?
Confirmation questions	Used either to elicit agreement or disagreement about a particular topic.	Do my recommendations make sense?
Clarification questions	Reduce ambiguities, generalities and non-committal words to specifics.	When you say ... exactly what do you mean?
Inclusion questions	Present an issue for the prospect's consideration in a low-risk way.	I don't suppose you'd be interested in a convertible hard-top, would you?
Counterbiasing	To attain sensitive information by making a potentially embarrassing situation appear acceptable.	Research shows that most drivers exceed the speed limit. Do you ever do so?
Transitioning	Used to link the end of one phase to the next phase of the sales process.	In addition to that, is there anything else that you want to know? (No) What I'd like to do now is talk about ...
Reversing	Used to pass the responsibility of continuing the conversation back to the prospect by answering a question with a question.	When can I expect delivery? When do you want delivery?

Source: DeCormier, R. and Jobber, D. (1993) 'The counsellor selling method: concepts, constructs and effectiveness', *Journal of Personal Sales and Management*, 13(4), pp. 39–60.

in the same rigid way, perhaps by highlighting the current bargain of the week, without first questioning the customer as to his or her needs.

Questioning can also be useful in order to understand the customer's situation. Here is an account of how important this can be:

> 'We had a problem with a new customer and one of our young sales reps. We sent the CEO in to meet the customer. The customer was a new wine buyer for a large supermarket chain. This was when supermarkets had just started selling wine. The customer always seemed very defensive, and questioning revealed that he didn't know much about the wine trade. We invited him out for lunch at our premises and just talked to him. We found out that he liked Rugby League, so we talked to him about that. After that there was no problem; he relaxed and we understood that he was nervous about a new position. This enabled us to move from a $20,000 per year account to a $150,000 account.'[9]

At the end of this process, the salesperson may find it useful to summarise the points that have been raised to confirm an understanding with the buyer. For example:

> 'Fine, Mr and Mrs Jones. I think I have a good idea of the kind of property you are looking for. You would like a four-bedroom house within fifteen minutes' drive of Mr Jones's company. You are not bothered whether the house is detached or semi-detached, but you do not want to live on an estate. The price range you are considering is between £300,000 and £350,000. Does this sum up the kind of house you want, or have I missed something?'

8.3   The Presentation and Demonstration

Once the problems and needs of the buyer have been identified, the presentation follows as a natural consequence. The first question to be addressed is presentation of what? The preceding section has enabled the salesperson to choose the most appropriate product(s) from his or her range to meet customer requirements. Second, having fully discussed what the customer wants, the salesperson knows which product benefits to stress. A given product may have a range of potential features which confer benefits to customers, but different customers place different priorities on them. In short, having identified the needs and problems of the buyer, the presentation provides the opportunity for the salesperson to convince the buyer that they can supply the solution.

The key to this task is to recognise that buyers purchase benefits and are only interested in product features in as much as they provide the benefits that the customer is looking for. Examples of the relationship between certain product features and benefits are given in Chapter 7. Training programmes and personal preparation of salespeople should pay particular attention to deriving the customer benefits which their products bestow.

Benefits should be analysed at two levels: those benefits which can be obtained by purchase of a particular type of product, and those that can be obtained by purchasing that product from a particular supplier. For example, automatic washing machine salespeople need to consider the benefits of an automatic washing machine compared with a twin-tub, as well as the benefits that their company's automatic washing machines have over competitors' models. This proffers maximum flexibility for the salesperson in meeting various sales situations.

The danger of selling features rather than benefits is particularly acute in industrial selling because of the highly technical nature of many industrial products, and the tendency to employ sales engineers rather than salespeople. Perkins Diesels found this to be a problem with their sales team after commissioning market research to identify strengths and weaknesses of their sales and marketing operation,[10] but it is by no means confined to this sector. Hi-fi salespeople who confuse and infuriate customers with tedious descriptions of the electronic wizardry behind their products are no less guilty of this sin. A simple method of relating features and benefits in a sales presentation is to link them by using the following phrases:

- 'which means that'

- 'which results in'

- 'which enables you to'

For example, an estate agent might say, 'The house is situated four miles from the company where you work (product feature) which means that you can easily be at work within fifteen minutes of leaving home' (customer benefit). An office salesperson might say, 'The XYZ photocopier allows streamfeeding (product feature) which results in quicker photocopying' (customer benefit). Finally, a car salesperson may claim, 'This model is equipped with overdrive (product feature) which enables you to reduce petrol consumption on motorways' (customer benefit).

The term 'presentation' should not mislead the salesperson into believing that they alone should do all the talking. The importance of asking questions is not confined to the needs and problem identification stage. Asking questions as part of the presentation serves two functions. First, it checks that the salesperson has understood the kinds of benefits the buyer is looking for. After explaining a benefit it is sound practice to ask the buyer, 'Is this the kind of thing you are looking for?' Second, asking questions establishes whether the buyer has understood what the salesperson has said. A major obstacle to understanding is the use of technical jargon which is unintelligible to the buyer. Where a presentation is necessarily complicated and lengthy, the salesperson would be well advised to pause at various points and simply ask if there are any questions. This gives the buyer the opportunity to query anything that is not entirely clear. This questioning procedure allows the salesperson to tailor the speed and content of his or her presentation to the circumstances. Buyers have different backgrounds, technical expertise and intelligence levels. Questioning allows the salesperson to communicate more effectively because it provides the information necessary for the seller to know how to vary the presentation to different buyers.

Many sales situations involve risk to the buyer. No matter what benefits the salesperson discusses, the buyer may be reluctant to change from the present supplier or present model because to do so may give rise to unforeseen problems – delivery may be unpredictable or the new model may be unreliable. Assurances from the salesperson are, of themselves, unlikely to be totally convincing – after all, they would say that, wouldn't they! Risk is the hidden reason behind many failures to sell. The salesperson accurately identifies customer needs and relates product benefits to those needs. The buyer does not offer much resistance, but somehow does not buy; a likely reason is that the buyer plays safe, sticking to the present supplier or model in order to lessen the risk of aggravation should problems occur. How, then, can a salesperson reduce risk? There are four major ways:

(a) reference selling

(b) demonstrations

(c) guarantees

(d) trial orders

Reference selling

Reference selling involves the use of satisfied customers in order to convince the buyer of the effectiveness of the salesperson's product. During the preparation stage a list of satisfied customers, arranged by product type, should be drawn up. Letters from satisfied customers should also be kept and used in the sales presentation in order to build confidence. This technique can be highly effective in selling, moving a buyer from being merely interested in the product to being convinced that it is the solution to his or her problem.

Demonstrations

Chinese proverb: Tell me and I'll forget; show me and I may remember; involve me and I'll understand.

Demonstrations also reduce risk because they prove the benefits of the product. A major producer of sales training films organises regional demonstrations of a selection in order to prove their quality to training managers. Industrial goods manufacturers will arrange demonstrations to show their products' capabilities in use. Car salespeople will allow customers to test drive cars.

For all but the most simple of products it is advisable to divide the demonstration into two stages. The first stage involves a brief description of the features and benefits of the product and an explanation of how it works. The second stage entails the actual demonstration itself. This should be conducted by the salesperson. The reason behind this two-stage approach is that it is often very difficult for the viewers of the demonstration to understand the principles of how a product works while at the same time watching it work. This is because the viewers are receiving competing stimuli. The salesperson's voice may be competing for the buyers' attention with the flashing lights and noise of the equipment.

Once the equipment works, the buyers can be encouraged to use it themselves under the salesperson's supervision. If the correct equipment, to suit the buyers' needs, has been chosen for demonstration and it performs reliably, the demonstration can move the buyers very much closer to purchase.

There now follows more practical advice upon what must be regarded as an extremely important part of the personal selling process, for without a demonstration the salesperson is devoid of one of his or her principal selling tools.

Pre-demonstration

1 Make the process as brief as possible, but not so brief as not to be able to fulfil the sales objective of obtaining an order, or of opening the way for further negotiations. It is basically a question of balance, in that the salesperson must judge the individual circumstances and tailor the demonstration accordingly. Some potential buyers will require lengthier or more technical demonstrations than others.

2 Make the process as simple as possible, bearing in mind that some potential purchasers will be less technically minded than others. Never 'over-pitch' such technicality, because potential buyers will generally pretend that they understand and not want to admit that they do not because of loss of face. They will see the demonstration through and probably make some excuse at the end to delay the purchase decision. The likelihood is that they will not purchase (or at least not purchase from you). This point is deliberately emphasised because it is a fact that many potential sales are lost through demonstrations which are too technical.

3 Rehearse the approach to likely objections with colleagues (e.g. with one acting as an 'awkward' buyer). Work out how such objections can be addressed and overcome through the demonstration. The use of interactive video is useful here, as you can witness your mistakes and rehearse a better demonstration and presentation.

4 Know the product's *selling points* and be prepared to advance these during the course of the demonstration. Such selling points must, however, be presented in terms of benefits to the customer. Buyer behaviour must therefore be ascertained beforehand. By so doing, it will be possible to maximise what is euphemistically called the 'you' or 'u' benefits.

5 The demonstration should not go wrong if it has been adequately rehearsed beforehand. However, machines do break down and power supplies sometimes fail. Be prepared for such eventualities (e.g. rehearse an appropriate verbal 'routine' and have a back-up successful demonstration available on your laptop). The main point is not to be caught out unexpectedly and to be prepared to launch into a contingency routine as smoothly as possible.

Conducting the demonstration

1 Commence with a concise statement of what is to be done or proved.

2 Show how potential purchasers can participate in the demonstration process.

3 Make the demonstration as interesting and as satisfying as possible.

4 Show the potential purchaser how the product's features can fulfil his or her needs or solve his or her problems.

5 Attempt to translate such needs into a desire to purchase.

6 Do not leave the purchaser until s/he is completely satisfied with the demonstration. Such satisfaction will help to justify ultimate expenditure and

will also reduce the severity and incidence of any complaints that might arise after purchasing.

7 Summarise the main points by re-emphasising the purchasing benefits that have been put forward during the demonstration. Note that we state purchasing benefits and not sales benefits because purchasing benefits relate to individual buying behaviour.

8 The objectives of a demonstration should be: (a) to enable the salesperson to obtain a sale immediately (e.g. a car demonstration drive given to a member of the public); or (b) to pave the way for future negotiations (e.g. a car demonstration drive given to a car fleet buyer).

9 Depending upon the objective above, in the case of (a) ask for the order now, or in the case of (b) arrange for further communication in the form of a meeting, telephone call, letter, an additional demonstration to other members of the decision-making unit, etc.

Advantages of demonstrations

1 Demonstrations are a useful ancillary in the selling process. They add realism to the sales routine in that they utilise more human senses than mere verbal descriptions or visual presentation.

2 When a potential customer is participating in a demonstration, it is easier for the salesperson to ask questions in order to ascertain buying behaviour. This means that the salesperson will not need to emphasise inappropriate purchasing motives later in the selling process.

3 Such demonstrations enable the salesperson to maximise the 'u' benefits to potential purchasers. In other words, the salesperson can relate product benefits to match the potential buyer's buying behaviour and adopt a more creative approach, rather than concentrating upon a pre-prepared sales routine.

4 Customers' objections can be more easily overcome if they can be persuaded to take part in the demonstration process. In fact, many potential objections may never even be aired because the demonstration process will make them invalid. It is a fact that a sale is more likely to ensue if fewer objections can be advanced initially, even if such objections can be satisfactorily overcome.

5 There are advantages to customers in that it is easier for them to ask questions in a more realistic way in order to ascertain the product's utility more clearly and quickly.

6 Purchasing inhibitions are more quickly overcome and buyers declare their purchasing interest sooner than in face-to-face selling/buying situations. This makes the demonstration a very efficient sales tool.

7 Once a customer has participated in a demonstration there is less likelihood of 'customer remorse' (i.e. the doubt that value for money is not good value after all). By taking part in the demonstration and tacitly accepting its results, the purchaser has bought the product and not been sold it.

Guarantees

Guarantees of product reliability, after-sales service and delivery supported by penalty clauses can build confidence towards the salesperson's claims and lessen the costs to the buyer should something go wrong. Their establishment is a matter for company policy rather than the salesperson's discretion but, where offered, the salesperson should not underestimate their importance in the sales presentation.

Trial orders

The final strategy for risk reduction is for salespeople to encourage trial orders, even though they may be uneconomic in company terms and in terms of salespeoples' time in the short term, when faced with a straight re-buy (see Chapter 3). Buyers who habitually purchase supplies from one supplier may recognise that change involves unwarranted risk. It may be that the only way for a new supplier to break through this impasse is to secure a small order which, in effect, permits the demonstration of the company's capability to provide consistently high-quality products promptly. The confidence, thus built, may lead to a higher percentage of the customer's business in the longer term.

Acton Mobile Industries, Baltimore, Maryland, USA – Mobile office building supplier automates sales process for sales team

Focus

Acton Mobile Industries had historically managed their sales process with spreadsheets and other paper-based means. Under new management, the company made a business decision to automate their sales process using XSalerator.com™ in order to increase revenue and sales effectiveness through a shortened sales cycle, implementation of best practices, and the ability to provide senior management with accurate real-time forecasting data.

Client Overview

With headquarters in Baltimore, Maryland, and 15 offices in 12 states, Acton Mobile Industries has been servicing the mobile office and modular building industry since 1970. Through the ability to quickly deliver temporary space that makes job surveillance and project management both comfortable and convenient, the company has become the leader in providing mobile offices and modular buildings to suit customer specific needs. Acton Mobile Industries provides temporary space for construction sites, schools and industry in a variety of sizes and for varying lengths of time.

Situational Overview

Acton Mobile Industries made a business decision to automate their sales process with a web-based salesforce automation system in order to better manage the sales process from lead development to closed orders. The

Chapman Group was engaged to implement their proprietary salesforce automation solution (XSalerator.com™) through a 3-phase process consisting of an assessment, customisation, and implementation phase.

Efforts

The Chapman Group (TCG) worked with a client team consisting of senior members of Acton Mobile Industries in the corporate office and various members of the field salesforce in order to further develop the strategic objectives, goals and vision for the project. This provided an opportunity to gain valuable insight into Acton Mobile Industries' sales process in order to target key areas of improvement through the implementation of the new salesforce automation package. During this initial assessment phase, Chapman Group met with key stakeholders to create ownership of the proposed salesforce automation concept.

The next phase involved tailoring and customizing XSalerator.com™ to provide the sales team with a system that would enable them to meet their quotas more consistently and provide them with a reliable reinforcement of sales best practices. The user interface of the system was designed with key performance indicators from Acton Mobile Industries' market in mind, including a variety of charts, graphs and analysis. Each screen within XSalerator.com™ was reviewed during this process, culminating in a user-friendly, results-focused system.

Results

Since going live in February 2004, Acton Mobile Industries has experienced radical improvements in the areas of forecasting, prospect development, closed business and order fulfilment. Employees received an intensive one-day training session that introduced them to the system and provided them with a roadmap for future success. Results point to a more effective sales process and a renewed sense of strategy and direction of the sales division for all employees.

Source: *www.ChapmanHQ.com* with permission

8.4 Dealing with Objections

Objections are any concerns or questions raised by the buyer.[11] While some objections are an expression of confusion, doubt or disagreement with the statements or information presented by the salesperson, objections should not always be viewed with dismay by salespeople. Many objections are simply expressions of interest by the buyer. What the buyer is asking for is further information because s/he is interested in what the salesperson is saying. The problem is that the buyer is not as yet convinced. Objections highlight the issues which are important to the buyer. For example, when training salespeople, Ford makes the point that customers' objections are signposts to what is really on their minds.

An example will illustrate these points. Suppose an industrial salesperson working for an adhesives manufacturer is faced with the following objection: 'Why should I buy your new adhesive gun when my present method of applying adhesive – direct from the tube – is perfectly satisfactory?' This type of objection is clearly an expression of a desire for additional information. The salesperson's task is to provide it in a manner which does not antagonise the buyer and yet is convincing. It is a fact of human personality that the argument which is supported by the greater weight of evidence does not always win the day; people do not like to be proved wrong. The very act of changing a supplier may be resisted because it implies criticism of a past decision on the part of the buyer. For a salesperson to disregard the emotional aspects of dealing with objections is to court disaster. The situation to be avoided is where the buyers dig in their heels on principle because of the salesperson's attitude.

So, the effective approach for dealing with objections involves two areas: the preparation of convincing answers and the development of a range of techniques for answering objections in a manner which permits the acceptance of these answers without loss of face on the part of the buyer. The first area has been covered in the previous chapter. A number of techniques will now be reviewed to illustrate how the second objective may be accomplished. These are shown in Figure 8.2.

Listen and do not interrupt

Experienced salespeople know that the impression given to buyers by the salesperson who interrupts midstream is that the salesperson believes that:

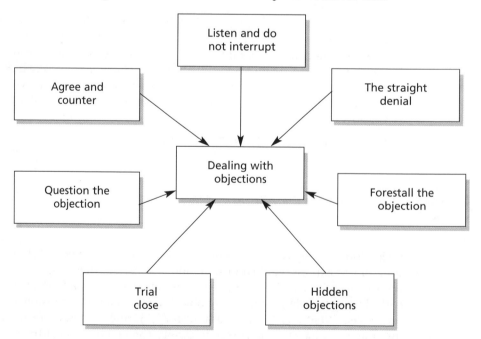

Figure 8.2 Dealing with objections

- the objection is obviously wrong

- it is trivial

- it is not worth the salesperson's time to let the buyer finish

Interruption denies the buyer the kind of respect s/he is entitled to receive and may lead to a misunderstanding of the real substance behind the objection. The correct approach is to listen carefully, attentively and respectfully. The buyer will appreciate the fact that the salesperson is taking the problem seriously and the salesperson will gain through having a clear and full understanding of what the problem really is.

Agree and counter

This approach maintains the respect that the salesperson shows to the buyer. The salesperson first agrees that what the buyer is saying is sensible and reasonable, before then putting forward an alternative point of view. It therefore takes the edge off the objection and creates a climate of agreement rather than conflict. For example:

Buyer: The problem with your tractor is that it costs more than your competition.

Salesperson: Yes, the initial cost of the tractor is a little higher than competitors' models, but I should like to show you how, over the lifetime of the machine, ours works out to be far more economical.

This example shows why the method is sometimes called the 'yes ... but' technique. The 'yes' precedes the agree statement, while the 'but' prefaces the counter-argument. There is no necessity to use these words, however. In fact, in some sales situations the buyer may be so accustomed to having salespeople use them that the technique loses some of its effectiveness. Fortunately there are other approaches which are less blatant:

- 'I can appreciate your concern that the machine is more expensive than the competition. However, I should like to show you ...'

- 'Customer XYZ made the same comment a year ago. I can assure you that he is highly delighted with his decision to purchase because the cost savings over the lifetime of the machine more than offset the initial cost difference.'

- 'That's absolutely right – the initial cost is a little higher. That's why I want to show you ...'

The use of the reference selling technique can be combined with the agree and counter method to provide a powerful counter to an objection. For example, salespeople of media space in newspapers that are given away free to the public often encounter the following objection:

Buyer [e.g. car dealer]: Your newspaper is given away free. Most of the people who receive it throw it away without even reading it.

Salesperson: I can understand your concern that a newspaper which is free may not be read. However, a great many people do read it to find out what second-hand cars are on the market. Mr Giles of Grimethorpe Motors has been advertising with us for two years and he is delighted with the results.

The straight denial

This method has to be handled with a great deal of care since the danger is that it will result in exactly the kind of antagonism which the salesperson is wishing to avoid. However, it can be used when the buyer is clearly seeking factual information. For example:

Buyer: I expect that this upholstery will be difficult to clean.

Salesperson: No, Mr Buyer, absolutely not. This material is made from a newly developed synthetic fibre which resists stains and allows marks to be removed simply by using soap, water and a clean cloth.

Question the objection

Sometimes an objection is raised which is so general as to be difficult to counter. For example, a customer might say s/he does not like the appearance of the product, or that the product is not good quality. In this situation the salesperson should question the nature of the objection in order to clarify the specific problem at hand. Sometimes this results in a major objection being reduced to one which can easily be dealt with.

Buyer: I'm sorry but I don't like the look of that car.

Salesperson: Could you tell me exactly what it is that you don't like the look of?

Buyer: I don't like the pattern on the seats.

Salesperson: Well in fact this model can be supplied in a number of different upholstery designs. Shall we have a look at the catalogue to see if there is a pattern to your liking?

Another benefit of questioning objections is that in trying to explain the exact nature of objections buyers may themselves realise these are really quite trivial.

Forestall the objection

With this method, the salesperson not only anticipates an objection and plans its counter, but actually raises the objection as part of his or her sales presentation.

There are two advantages of doing this. First, the timing of the objection is controlled by the salesperson. Consequently, it can be planned so that it is raised at the most appropriate time for it to be dealt with effectively. Second, since it is raised by the salesperson, the buyer is not placed in a position where, having raised a problem, s/he feels that it must be defended.

The danger with using this method, however, is that the salesperson may highlight a problem which the buyer had not thought of. It is most often used where a salesperson is faced with the same objection being raised time after time. Perhaps buyers are continually raising the problem that the salesperson is working for one of the smallest companies in the industry. The salesperson may pre-empt the objection in the following manner: 'My company is smaller than most in the industry which means that we respond quicker to our customers' needs and try that bit harder to make sure our customers are happy.'

Turn the objection into a trial close

A **trial close** is where a salesperson attempts to conclude the sale without prejudicing the chances of continuing the selling process with the buyer should they refuse to commit themselves.

The ability of a salesperson to turn the objection into a trial close is dependent upon perfect timing and considerable judgement. Usually it will be attempted after the selling process is well under way and the salesperson judges that only one objection remains. Under these conditions s/he might say the following: 'If I can satisfy you that the fuel consumption of this car is no greater than that of the Vauxhall Vectra, would you buy it?'

When dealing with objections, the salesperson should remember that heated arguments are unlikely to win sales – buyers buy from their friends, not their enemies.

Hidden objections

Not all prospects state their objections. They may prefer to say nothing because to raise an objection may cause offence or prolong the sales interaction. Such people may believe that staying on friendly terms with the salesperson and at the end of the interview stating that they will think over the proposal is the best tactic in a no-buy situation. The correct salesperson's response to hidden objections is to ask questions in an attempt to uncover their nature. If a salesperson believes that a buyer is unwilling to reveal their true objections, s/he should ask such questions as the following:

• 'Is there anything so far which you are unsure about?'

• 'Is there anything on your mind?'

• 'What would it take to convince you?'

Uncovering hidden objections is crucial to successful selling because to convince someone it is necessary to know what s/he needs to be convinced of. However, with uncommunicative buyers this may be difficult. As a last resort the salesperson may need to 'second guess' the reluctant buyer and suggest an issue which they believe is causing the problem and ask a question such as: 'I don't think you're totally convinced about the better performance of our product, are you?'

8.5 Negotiation

In some selling situations, the salesperson or sales team have a degree of discretion with regard to the terms of the sale. **Negotiation** may therefore enter into the sales process. Sellers may negotiate price, credit terms, delivery times, trade-in values and other aspects of the commercial transaction. The deal that is arrived at will be dependent upon the balance of power (see Chapter 7) and the negotiating skills of the respective parties.

The importance of preparation has already been mentioned in the previous chapter. The buyer's needs, the competition which the supplier faces and knowledge about the buyer's business and the pressures upon him or her should be estimated. However, there are a number of other guidelines to aid the salespeople actually engaged in the negotiation process.

Start high but be realistic

There are several good reasons for making the opening stance high. First, the buyer might agree to it. Second, it provides room for negotiation. A buyer may come to expect concessions from a seller in return for purchasing. This situation is prevalent in the car market. It is unusual for a car salesperson not to reduce the advertised price of a car to a cash purchaser. When considering how high to go, the limiting factor must be to keep within the buyer's realistic expectations; otherwise they may not be willing to talk to the seller in the first place.

Attempt to trade concession for concession

Sometimes it may be necessary to give a concession simply to secure the sale. A buyer might say that s/he is willing to buy if the seller drops the price by £100. If the seller has left some negotiating room, then this may be perfectly acceptable. However, in other circumstances, especially when the seller has a degree of power through being able to meet buyer requirements better than competition, the seller may be able to trade concessions from the buyer. A simple way of achieving this is by means of the 'if . . . then' technique.[12]

- 'If you are prepared to arrange collection of these goods at our premises, then I am prepared to knock £10 off the purchase price.'

- 'If you are prepared to make payment within 28 days, then I am willing to offer a 2.5 per cent discount.'

This is a valuable tool at the disposal of the negotiator since it promotes movement towards agreement and yet ensures that proposals to give the buyer something are matched by proposals for a concession in return.

It is sensible, at the preparation stage, to evaluate possible concessions in the light of their costs and values, not only to the seller but also to the buyer. In the example above, the costs of delivery to the seller might be much higher than the costs of collection to the buyer. The net effect of the proposal, therefore, is that the salesperson is offering a benefit to the buyer at very little cost to the seller.

Implement behavioural skills

Graham[13] reports on research carried out by the Huthwaite Research Group into negotiation effectiveness. By comparing skilled, effective negotiators with their average counterparts, the researchers identified a set of behavioural skills that are associated with negotiation success. These are:

- Ask lots of questions: questions seek information (knowledge is power) and identify the feelings of the buyer. They also give control (the person asking the questions directs the topic of conversation), provide thinking time while the buyer answers and are an alternative to outright disagreement.

- Use labelling behaviour: this announces the behaviour about to be used. Examples of labelling behaviour are 'Can I ask you a question?' 'I should like to make two further points' and 'May I summarise?'

- But do not label disagreement: a likely way of ensuring your argument does not get a fair hearing is to announce in advance to the other party that you are going to contradict their argument. Statements like 'I totally disagree with that point' or 'I cannot accept what you have just said' are bound to make the other party defensive.

- Maintain clarity by testing understanding and summarising: testing understanding is a behaviour which seeks to identify whether or not a previous contribution has been understood. Summarising is a behaviour which restates in a compact form the content of previous discussions. An example of this combined behaviour would be, 'Let me see if I've got this right. You are saying that if we could deliver next week, match the competition on price and provide a day's worth of free training, you would place an order with us today.'

- Give feelings: contrary to conventional wisdom, skilled negotiators are not poker faced. They express their feelings which makes them appear human, creates an atmosphere of trust and can be an alternative to giving hard facts.

- Avoid counterproposing: this is a proposal of any type which follows a proposal given by the other party without first demonstrating consideration of their proposal. Counterproposing is usually an instant turnoff. If the seller is not prepared to give due consideration to the buyer's proposal, why should the buyer listen to the seller's?

- Avoid the use of irritators: these are behaviours which are likely to annoy the other party through self-praise and/or condescension. Statements like 'Listen, young man, I think you're going to find this a very attractive and generous offer', are likely to be more irritating than persuasive. The response will be 'I'm best placed to judge your offer, and don't patronise me'.

- Do not dilute your arguments: common sense suggests that presenting as many arguments in favour of a proposal is the correct way to gain acceptance. The problem is that as more and more points are advanced they tend to become weaker. This allows the buyer to attack the weaker ones and the discussion becomes focused on them. The correct approach is to present only a few strong arguments rather than a complete list of both stronger and weaker points. This avoids the risk of the weak arguments diluting the power of the strong points.

In addition to these behavioural skills, Buskirk and Buskirk (1995) suggest a further one:[14]

- Avoid personalising the discussion: negotiations should never get personal. Negotiators should never say 'You're being ridiculous' or 'Your price is too low.' Calling someone's statement 'ridiculous' is an affront. Personal pronouns should be taken out of speech patterns. Instead say 'That price is too low.'

Buyers' negotiating techniques

Buyers also have a number of techniques which they use in negotiations. Sellers should be aware of their existence, for sometimes their effect can be devastating. Kennedy, Benson and Macmillan[15] describe a number of techniques designed to weaken the position of the unsuspecting sales negotiator.

First, the shotgun approach involves the buyer saying, 'Unless you agree immediately to a price reduction of 20 per cent we'll have to look elsewhere for a supplier.' In a sense, this is the 'if . . . then' technique played on the seller, but in this setting the consequences are more serious. The correct response depends upon the outcome of the assessment of the balance of power conducted during preparation. If the buyer does have a number of options, all of which offer the same kind of benefits as the seller's product, then the seller may have to concede. If the seller's product offers clear advantages over competition, then the salesperson may be able to resist the challenge.

A second ploy used by buyers is the 'sell cheap, the future looks bright' technique: 'We cannot pretend that our offer meets you on price, but the real payoff for you will come in terms of future sales.' This may be a genuine statement – in fact the seller's own objective may have been to gain a foothold in the buyer's business. At other times it is a gambit to extract the maximum price concession from the seller. If the seller's position is reasonably strong s/he should ask for specific details and firm commitments.

A final technique is known as 'Noah's Ark' – because it's been around that long! The buyer says, tapping a file with one finger, 'You'll have to do much better in terms of price. I have quotations from your competitors which are much lower.' The salesperson's response depends upon his or her level of confidence. The salesperson can call the buyer's bluff and ask to see the quotations; or take the initiative by stating that they assume the buyer is wishing for them to justify the price; or, if flushed with the confidence of past success, can say 'Then I advise you to accept one of them.'

8.6   Closing the Sale

The skills and techniques discussed so far are not in themselves sufficient for consistent sales success. A final ingredient is necessary to complete the mix – the ability to **close the sale**.

Some salespeople believe that an effective presentation should lead the buyer to ask for the product without the seller needing to close the sale. This sometimes hap-

Closing the Sale 265

pens, but more usually it will be necessary for the salesperson to take the initiative. This is because no matter how well the salesperson identifies buyer needs, matches product benefits to them and overcomes objections, there is likely to be some doubt still present in the mind of the buyer. This doubt may manifest itself in the wish to delay the decision. Would it not be better to think things over? Would it not be sensible to see what competitor XYZ has to offer? The plain truth, however, is that if the buyer does put off buying until another day it is as likely that s/he will buy from the competition. While the seller is there, the seller is at an advantage over the competition; thus part of the salesperson's job is to try to close the sale.

Why, then, are some salespeople reluctant to close a sale? The problem lies in the fact that most people fear rejection. Closing the sale asks the buyer to say yes or no. Sometimes it will be no and the salesperson will have been rejected. Avoiding closing the sale does not result in more sales, but rejection is less blatant. The most important point to grasp, then, is not to be afraid to close. Accept the fact that some buyers will inevitably respond negatively, but be confident that more will buy than if no close had been used.

A major consideration is timing. A general rule is to attempt to close the sale when the buyer displays heightened interest or a clear intention to purchase the product. Salespeople should therefore look out for such **buying signals** and respond accordingly. Purchase intentions are unlikely to grow continuously throughout the sales presentation. They are more likely to rise and fall as the presentation progresses (see Figure 8.3). The true situation is reflected by a series of peaks and troughs. An example will explain why this should be so. When a salesperson talks about a key benefit which exactly matches the buyer's needs, purchase intentions are likely to rise sharply. However, the buyer then perhaps raises a problem, which decreases the level, or doubts arise in the buyer's mind as to whether the claims made for the product are completely justified. This causes purchase intentions to fall, only to be followed by an increase as the salesperson overcomes the objection or substantiates the claim.

In theory the salesperson should attempt to close at a peak. In practice, judging when to close is difficult. The buyer may be feigning disinterest and throughout a sales interview several peaks may be expected to occur. Which peak should be

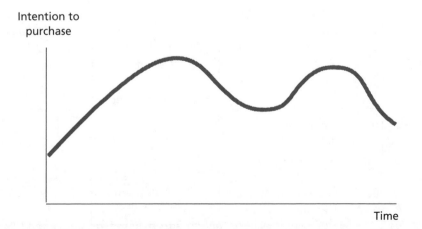

Figure 8.3 The level of buyer's purchase intentions throughout a sales presentation

chosen for the close? Part of the answer lies in experience. Experienced salespeople know intuitively if intentions are sufficiently favourable for a close to be worth-while. Also, if need and problem identification have been conducted properly, the salesperson knows that a rough guide as to when to close is after they match all product benefits to customer needs; theoretically, intentions should be at a peak then.

Not all buyers conform to this theoretical plan, however, and the salesperson should be prepared to close even if the planned sales presentation is incomplete. The method to use is the **trial close**. This technique involves asking for the order in such a way that if the timing is premature the presentation can continue with the minimum of interruption. Perhaps early in the presentation the customer might say, 'Yes, that's just what I'm looking for', to which the salesperson replies, 'Good, when do you think you would like delivery?' Even if the buyer says they have not made up their mind yet, the salesperson can continue with the presentation or ask the customer a question, depending on which is most appropriate to the situation.

A time will come during the sales interview when the salesperson has discussed all the product benefits and answered all the customer's questions. It is, clearly, decision time; the buyer is enthusiastic but is hesitating. There are a number of clos-ing techniques which the salesperson can use (see Figure 8.4).

Simply ask for the order

The simplest technique involves asking directly for the order:

- 'Shall I reserve you one?'

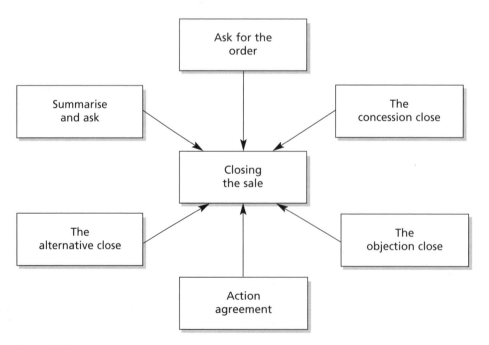

Figure 8.4 Closing the sale

- 'Would you like to buy it?'

- 'Do you want it?'

The key to using this technique is to keep silent after you have asked for the order. The salesperson has asked a closed question implying a yes or no answer. To break the silence effectively lets the buyer off the hook. The buyer will forget the first question and reply to the salesperson's later comment.

Summarise and then ask for the order

This technique allows the salesperson to remind the buyer of the main points in the sales argument in a manner which implies that the moment for decision has come and that buying is the natural extension of the proceedings.

'Well, Mr Smith, we have agreed that the ZDXL4 model meets your requirements of low noise, high productivity and driver comfort at a cost which you can afford. May I go ahead and place an order for this model?'

The concession close

This involves keeping one concession in reserve to use as the final push towards agreement: 'If you are willing to place an order now, I'm willing to offer an extra 2.5 per cent discount.'

The alternative close

This closing technique assumes that the buyer is willing to purchase but moves the decision to whether the colour should be red or blue, the delivery should be Tuesday or Friday, the payment in cash or credit, etc. In such circumstances the salesperson suggests two alternatives, the agreement to either thus closing the sale:

- 'Would you like the red one or the blue one?'

- 'Would you like it delivered on Tuesday or Friday?'

This technique has been used by salespeople for many years and consequently should be used with care, especially with professional buyers who are likely to have experienced its use many times and know exactly what the salesperson is doing.

The objection close

This closing technique has been mentioned briefly earlier in this chapter. It involves the use of an objection as a stimulus to buy. The salesperson who is convinced that the objection is the major stumbling block to the sale can gain commitment from the buyer by saying, 'If I can convince you that this model is the most economical in its class, will you buy it?' A positive response from the buyer and reference to an objective statistical comparison by the seller effectively seal the sale.

Action agreement

In some situations it is inappropriate to attempt to close the sale. For many industrial goods the sales cycle is long and a salesperson who attempts to close the sale at early meetings may cause annoyance. In selling pharmaceutical products, for example, salespeople do not try to close a sale but instead attempt to achieve 'action agreement' whereby either the salesperson or doctor agree to do something before their next meeting. This technique has the effect of helping the doctor–salesperson relationship to develop and continue.

A useful characteristic for salespeople is persistence. Making a decision to spend large quantities of money is not easy. In most sales situations, no one product is better than its competitors on all evaluative criteria. This means that the salespeople for all of these products stand some chance of success. The final decision may go to the one who is most persistent in his or her attempts to persuade the customer that the product meets the buyer's needs. Children learn very quickly that if they are initially refused what they want, asking a second or third time may be successful. The key is knowing where to draw the line before persistence leads to annoyance.

Once the sale is agreed, the salesperson should follow two rules. First, they should never display emotions. No matter how important the sale, and how delighted the salesperson feels, s/he should remain calm and professional. There will be plenty of opportunity later to be euphoric. Second, leave as quickly as is courteously possible. The longer s/he stays around, the greater the chance that the buyers will change their minds, and cancel the order.

8.7   Follow-up

This final stage in the sales process is necessary to ensure that the customer is satisfied with the purchase and no problems with factors such as delivery, installation, product use and training have arisen. Salespeople may put off the follow-up call because it does not result in an immediate order. However, for most companies repeat business is the hallmark of success and the follow-up call can play a major role by showing that the salesperson really cares about the customer rather than only being interested in making sales.

The follow-up call can also be used to provide reassurance that the purchase was the right one. As we have already seen, many customers suffer from cognitive dissonance, that is being anxious that they have made the right choice.

Advances in technology have changed the way the follow-up is made. Traditionally it was done with a telephone call, a letter thanking the customer for the sale and asking if the product was meeting expectations, or the salesperson 'dropping by' to see if any problems had arisen. Today, email is frequently used, particularly in business-to-business situations. Emails are quick and efficient at reaching customers, and allow them to respond quickly if difficulties arise.[16]

This chapter has stressed the importance of changing the sales approach according to the differing needs and circumstances of customers. The boxed case discussion continues this theme by showing how different British and German customers can be.

Selling in Germany

Salespeople have to be aware of the need to adapt their approach to differing customers and different ways of doing business. Major differences in the ways British and German companies do business were described by two German employees of British computer company Psion:

'With German firms there is much greater emphasis on bureaucracy and proper procedure. With British firms things are done in a much more off-the-cuff way which means that they can react more flexibly and it is possible to act on a client's requirements very rapidly. In Germany, particularly with big German companies, you have to go through a very long bureaucratic procedure.

'I think the Germans are very precise. Their attitude is "I want this thing by 10.15 am not at 10.16 am." If you order something in the UK, you ask "When will it arrive?" You will be told "You'll have it next month".'

The office hierarchy is very important in Germany. For example, office subordinates may not be willing to take even the smallest decision while their boss is away. Salespeople can waste a lot of valuable time under such circumstances by attempting to sell to persons not authorised to take the decision of whether to buy the product or not.

The Germans place great emphasis on personal contact and usually expect to meet business partners face-to-face. However, one-to-one meetings are rare, with senior executives normally bringing along at least one colleague. Sometimes they appear confident, almost arrogant. The correct response is to be polite and correct. Germans are not impressed by covering up uncertainty with humour, particularly not at first meetings.

German business people should be addressed by their title and surname: Herr Schmidt or Frau Strauss. Dress is sober. Lunch is an important element in German business negotiations, although it may well be in the company canteen since business guests are rarely invited out for lavish meals.

Often suppliers' salesforces are expected to negotiate with purchasing departments which may have considerable organisational power. Attempts to bypass the purchasing department may cause annoyance. Face-to-face contact at trade fairs and advertising campaigns are often used to communicate with engineers and other technical people.

Sources: Based on BBC2 Television (1993) 'Germany Means Business: The Frankfurt Contenders', January 5; Forden, J. (1988) 'Doing business with the Germans', *Director*, July, pp. 102–4; Welford, R. and Prescott, K. (1992) '*European Business*', London; Pitman Publishing, p. 208; and Wolfe, A. (1991) 'The Eurobuyer: how European businesses buy', *Marketing Intelligence and Planning*, 9(5), pp. 9–15.

8.8 ▷ Conclusions

The skills involved in personal selling have been explored in this chapter. The necessary skills have been examined under the following headings:

1 The opening.

2 Need and problem identification.

3 Presentation and demonstration.

4 Dealing with objections.

5 Negotiation.

6 Closing the sale.

7 The follow-up.

The emphasis in this chapter has been on identifying the needs and problems of the potential buyer and presenting a product or service as a means of fulfilling that need or solving that problem. Having identified the skills necessary for successful selling, in the next chapter we will examine the role of key account management in the selling process.

References

1 Weitz, B.A. (1981) 'Effectiveness in sales interactions: a contingency framework', *Journal of Marketing*, 45, pp. 85–3.

2 Marshal, G.W., Moncrief, W.C. and Lassk, F.G. (1999) 'The current state of sales force activities', *Industrial Marketing Management*, 28, pp. 87–98.

3 Saxe, R. and Weitz, B.A. (1982) 'The SOCO scale: a measure of the customer orientation of salespeople', *Journal of Marketing Research*, 19 (August), pp. 343–51.

4 Schwepker, Jr, C.H. (2003) 'Customer-orientated selling: a review, extension, and directions for future research', *Journal of Personal Selling and Sales Management*, 23 (2), pp. 151–71.

5 Schuster, C.P. and Danes, J.E. (1986) 'Asking questions: some characteristics of successful sales encounters', *Journal of Personal Selling and Sales Management*, May, pp. 17–27; Sujan, H., Sujan, M., and Bettman J. (1998) 'Knowledge structure differences between effective and less effective salespeople', *Journal of Marketing Research*, 25, pp. 81–6; Szymanski, D. (1988) 'Determinants of selling effectiveness: the importance of declarative knowledge to the personal selling concept', *Journal of Marketing*, 52, pp. 64–77; Weitz, B.A., Sujan, H. and Sujan, M. (1986) 'Knowledge, motivation and adaptive behaviour: a framework for improving selling effectiveness', *Journal of Marketing*, 50, pp. 174–91; Krishnan, B.C., Netemeyer, R.G. and Boles, J.S. (2002) 'Self-efficacy, competitiveness, and effort as antecedents of salesperson performance', *Journal of Personal Selling and Sales Management*, 20 (4), pp. 285–95.

6 Krishnan, B.C., Netemeyer, R.G. and Boles, J.S. (2002) op.cit.

7 Moncrief, W.C. and Marshall, G.W. (2005) 'The evolution of the seven steps of selling', *Industrial Marketing Management*, 34, pp. 13–22.

8 Decormier, R. and Jobber, D. (1993) 'The counsellor selling method: concepts, constructs and effectiveness', *Journal of Personal Selling and Sales Management*, 13(4), pp. 39–60.

9 Cross, J., Hartley, S.W., Rudelius, W. and Vassey, M.J. (2001) Sales force activities and marketing strategies in industrial firms: relationships and implications, '*Journal of Personal Selling and Sales Management*, 21 (3) pp. 199–206.

10 Reed, J. (1983) 'How Perkins changed gear', *Marketing*, 27 October.

11 Hunt, K.A. and Bashaw, R. (1999) 'A new classification of sales resistance', *Industrial Marketing Management*, 28, pp. 109–118.

12 Kennedy, G., Benson, J. and Macmillan, J. (1980) *Managing Negotiations*, Business Books, London.

13 Graham, R. (1997) 'Commercial negotiations', in Jobber, D. *The CIM Handbook of Selling and Sales Strategy*, Butterworth-Heinemann, Oxford, pp. 34–52.

14 Buskirk, R.H. and Buskirk, B.D. (1995) *Selling: principles and practice*, McGraw-Hill, New York.

15 Kennedy, G., Benson, J. and Macmillan, J. (1980) *Managing Negotiations*, Business Books, London.

16 Moncrief and Marshall (2005) op.cit.

Practical Exercise

Mordex Photocopier Company

You have an appointment to see George Kirby, sales office manager of Plastic Foods Ltd, with regard to the hire of a Mordex photocopier. You are bristling with anticipation as you know the present contract which Plastic Foods has with Clearprint, your closest competitor, is up for renewal. You have not met Mr Kirby before.

As you enter Mr Kirby's office you notice that he appears a little under pressure. After introducing yourself, you say, 'I'd like to talk with you about how we can improve the efficiency of your photocopying operation. I see that you use the Clearprint ZXR photocopier at the moment. What kinds of documents do you photocopy in the sales office?'

The discussion continues, with you attempting to assess his staff's requirements with regard to photocopying facilities and his attitude towards the Clearprint machine. One need is the ability of the photocopier to collate automatically, since some of the documents photocopied are quite lengthy. Another requirement is for the photocopy to be of the highest quality since it is usual for photocopies of standard letters to be sent to clients. The Clearprint photocopier does *not* have a collating facility and the quality, while passable, is not totally satisfactory. Further, there are sometimes delays in repairing the machine when it breaks down, although generally it is quite reliable.

At the end of the discussion you summarise the points that have been raised: staff time is being wasted collating lengthy documents; the quality of photostat is not totally satisfactory; repairs are not always carried out promptly. Mr Kirby agrees that this is a fair summary.

Discussion Questions

During the sales interview the following objections were raised. How would you deal with them?

1 'I'm sorry, I have an urgent meeting in ten minutes' time. Can we make it quick?'

2 'We haven't had any major problems with the Clearprint so far.'

3 'Doesn't your firm have a bad reputation?'

4 'Aren't your hiring charges much higher than Clearprint's?'

5 'How do I know your service will be any better than Clearprint's?'

6 'My staff have got used to using the Clearprint. I'll have to spend time showing them how to use your machine.'

7 'Let me think about it. The Clearprint rep is coming next week. I should like to discuss the points you've raised with him.'

Negotiation Exercise

Supermarket versus superbrand: co-operate to compete

Thomas Maggs is head buyer for cereals and cereal-related products at Morrisco Markets, one of the UK's top supermarket chains. Morrisco has a 14 per cent share of the UK grocery market with a mixture of in-town and out-of-town stores fairly evenly spread across the country. Like most retail grocery buyers, Maggs is tough on his suppliers. He has to be as competition among the big multiples is fierce and the ability to price low and retain a fair margin is the key to sustained financial success. The breakfast cereal market is highly competitive, fragmented and yet dominated by a number of 'power brands', such as Kellogg's Corn Flakes, Weetabix and Shreddies, all of which spend large budgets on advertising and promotions. Maggs favours deep price cutting promotional activity in this market as he knows that it shifts stock fast. The cereal manufacturers tend to resist this form of promotion as much as they can, preferring to 'add value' to their products rather than reduce price, which they feel tends to undermine premium brand imagery.

Sonya Farquahar is Key Accounts Manager at Morning Foods Ltd, a large manufacturer of breakfast cereals with one or two heavily supported 'power brands' in its portfolio, such as Powergrains, a protein-rich crunchy cereal enjoying 8 per cent of the cereal market and Slymbites, a tasty, low-fat cereal targeted at young women, ready sweetened with aspartame, a no calorie sugar substitute, enjoying 5 per cent of the market. With distinct product differentiators, these two brands hold premium price positions and the company favours added value 'themed' promotions. Each brand is heavily supported with TV advertising. Riding on the back of the success of the two brands, each of them has been recently brand extended to cereal bars, competing with Jordans and other brands. The brand team at Morning Foods want to run promotions on the two brands offering free cereal bars in-pack as a means of generating trial for each of the extensions. Given the importance of these brands, the company is trying to use this as a lever to gain separate distribution for the bars. It seems to be working with most of the supermarket chains, but Morrisco is proving difficult to persuade – they don't like to be dictated to and they don't want another as yet unproven cereal bar on their shelves. Maggs at Morrisco is insisting on some form of deep price oriented promotion.

Task

Students form three teams representing Morrisco Markets, Morning Foods Ltd and a team of observers. Each side has a set of objectives, ranked according to importance. Teams spend 20 minutes developing a negotiation strategy, identifying the objections that the other party is likely to make and preparing appropriate responses. Each team should nominate a representative or negotiating team. Each side is looking for a 'win-win' result. Each party has a fair idea what the other's negotiation objectives will be.

Objectives: Morning Foods Ltd

Must have:

- 'Added value' promotions agreed for both brands – Powergrains in sales period May/June; Slymbites in sales period September/October
- Trial of the cereal bar variants of each brand

Would like:

- Stocking of cereal bar brand variants adjacent to Jordans, etc.

Objectives: Morrisco Markets

Must have:

- Effective price-based promotions for each brand

- No agreement to stock cereal bars

Would like:

- Specially printed Morrisco promotional packs

- Special promotional TV support

Source: Written by Andrew Pressey, Lecturer in Marketing, University of East Anglia. Neville Hunt, Lecturer in Marketing, University of Luton

Practical Exercise

A controlled sales process?

Sales research undertaken at Loughborough University examined the duration and proportion of time that car dealership salespeople spend on selling and selling-related activities, and examined the role and effectiveness of controlled sales processes.

Controlled sales processes – in theory

A controlled sales process in a car dealership usually involves a customer information form to collect customers' contact details, details of their current car (and a valuation, if being considered as a part exchange), the car they are interested in, financing details, and information such as where they heard about the dealership.

For the process to be effective, a sales manager (or controller) issues and logs a customer information form to a salesperson for each customer that enters the showroom. The salesperson then gathers the details as part of the selling process with the customer, even if the customer is only browsing. The completed form is either retained by the salesperson or handed back to the controller. Each customer is discussed at sales meetings and action decided upon until the customer makes a purchase or the sale is lost. The process enables a sales manager to ensure that salespeople are managing prospects effectively.

This system, when used properly, does increase sales. It is especially important in car dealerships as many customers will be at the initial stage of information gathering and it may be months before they make a purchase. Therefore taking an interest in the customer, professionally collecting their details, undertaking courtesy follow-up calls and targeted promotional activity can help keep the dealership on the customer's shortlist.

Controlled sales processes in practice

In reality the research identified that although the dealers said they operated a controlled sales process, they did not. Most allowed the salespeople to hold on to and log their own customer information sheets, which reduces the effectiveness of the system. Salespeople are subject to social and personal prejudices like everyone else.

Consequently they interpret a situation and judge potential customers and determine whether or not they are a 'tyre kicker' (a time waster). Consequently many customers enter the showroom, are not interacted with professionally, are ignored and do not have their information collected or the information is collected but never followed up. How many times as a buyer in any sales situation have you felt that you weren't taken seriously?

Controlled sales systems do work and bring in business that would be lost. Another Loughborough University study found that in a dealership where a part-controlled system was in place, 50 per cent of customers were not followed up. Of those, 50 per cent had purchased elsewhere and 60 per cent of those purchased the same brand but at another dealership.

Sales are evidently lost when enquiries are not followed up. When enquiries are not even recorded, the potential loss of business is frightening.

Roadblocks to controlling a sales process?

One of the biggest roadblocks to implementing a controlled sales process is salespeople. They say: 'I haven't got time to follow up enquiries, I'm too busy with paperwork or dealing with "real" customers.' The research disagrees with this statement. The *average* proportion of time salespeople spent on their activities in a working week was as follows:

- In new car consultations with customers – 13 per cent

- In used car consultations with customers – 8 per cent

- Sales administration – 19.5 per cent

- Prospecting, following up enquiries – 10.5 per cent

- Other activities outside the sales process (e.g. having a break, chatting, reading a newspaper, collecting cars from other dealerships) – 49 per cent. In some dealerships this figure was as high as 70 per cent

It appears that there *is* time for operating and following up a full controlled sales process and consequently improving sales.

Source: Written by Jim Saker, Professor of Retail Management, Loughborough University Business School. Gary Reed, Lecturer, Loughborough University Business School. Vicky Story, Lecturer, Loughborough University Business School.

Discussion Questions

1 This case study is based on car dealerships. How representative is this of other industries?

2 Why do salespeople spend so much time unproductively? How can this be reduced?

3 What management tools and techniques could be used to ensure a controlled sales process is effective? Could information technology help?

4 What are the benefits of an effective controlled sales process for the customer, the salesperson, the sales manager and the company?

Examination Questions

1 If the product is right and the sales presentation is right, there is no need to close the sale. Discuss.

2 Discuss the ways in which a salesperson can attempt to identify buyer needs.

9 Key Account Management

Objectives

After studying this chapter, you should be able to:

1 Understand what a key account is and the advantages and disadvantages of key account management

2 Decide whether key account management is suitable in a given situation

3 Understand the criteria used to select key accounts

4 Appreciate the tasks and skills of key account management

5 Understand the special role and competences of global account management

6 Recognise the ways in which relationships with key accounts can be built

7 Identify the key components of a key account information and planning system

8 Appreciate the key success factors for key account management

Key Concepts

- global account management
- key account information and planning system
- key account management
- relationship building
- relational development model

Important changes are taking place in the personal selling function. Companies are reducing the size of their salesforces in response to increasing buyer concentration, the trend towards centralised buying, and in recognition of the high costs of maintaining a field salesforce. This latter factor has fuelled a move towards telemarketing. Perhaps the most significant change, however, has been the rise in importance of selling to, and managing key accounts resulting from, the growing concentration of buying power into fewer hands. These days companies often find over 70 per cent of sales coming from a few key customers. These key customers require special treatment since the loss of even one of them would significantly affect a supplier's sales and profits. In addition to the concentration of buying power, Weilbaker and Weeks (1997) have noted several business conditions that stimulated the movement to key account management.[1] These were that a small number of buying companies accounted for a large proportion of suppliers' sales, increased pressure by customers on suppliers to improve service and the wide geographic dispersion of buyers of the same company which encouraged some suppliers to adopt key account management as a way of presenting a co-ordinated front.

They also noted that there was increased pressure on buyers to reduce costs, greater pressure from customers to improve communications and a heightened desire to develop partnerships. Previously, the usual arrangement was for salespeople to be responsible for selling to companies only within their own geographic territory. As buyers demanded higher quality service and lower costs, some companies began assigning a single sales-person to manage and develop a few accounts. The improved service and responsiveness to the key account customer was valued by those customers who were looking to off-load some of the responsibilities normally handled by their own employees.[2] Furthermore, suppliers also appear to gain, as research by Homburg, Workman and Jensen (2000) shows that actively managing key accounts results in improved supplier performance.[3]

In this chapter we shall discuss what a key account is, the advantages and draw-backs to key account management, the factors which influence the move to key account management, the criteria used to select key accounts, the skills required and how to select, and sell to, key accounts. Since the objective of key account man-agement is to develop relationships over time, we shall also examine how to build account relationships. Next, we shall consider key account planning and evalu-ation. Finally, key success factors for key account management will be discussed.

9.1   What Is Key Account Management?

Key account management is a strategy used by suppliers to target and serve high poten-tial customers with complex needs by providing them with special treatment in the areas of marketing, administration and service. In order to receive key account status, a cus-tomer must have high sales potential. A second characteristic is that of complex buying behaviour; for example, large decision-making units with many choice criteria are often found in dispersed geographical locations. The decision-making unit may be located in different functional areas and varying operating units. Third, key account status is more likely to be given to customers willing to enter into a long-term alliance or partnership. Such relationships offer buyers many benefits including reliability of supply, risk reduc-tion, easier problem-solving, better communications and high levels of service. Key accounts that are geographically spread are often called national accounts.

Key account management has three features. First, key account management involves special treatment of major customers that is not offered to other accounts. This may involve preferential treatment in the areas of pricing, products, services, distribution and information sharing.[4] This may take the form of special pricing, customisation of products, provision of special services, customisation of services, joint co-ordination of distribution and workflow, information sharing and joint development of business processes and new products.[5] Second, it is associated with dedicated key account managers who typically serve several key accounts. They may be placed in the suppliers' headquarters, in the local sales organisation of the key account's country, or sometimes on the premises of the key account.[6] Third, key account management requires a multifunctional effort involving, in addition to sales, such groups as engineering, marketing, finance, information technology, research and development, and logistics.[7]

Key account handling requires a special kind of attention from the seller that may be beyond the capacity of the regular field salesforce. Some of the key responsibilities of key account managers are planning and developing relationships with a wide range of people in the customer firms, mobilising personnel and other resources in their own firms to assist the account, and co-ordinating and motivating the efforts and communications of their company's field salespeople in their calls on the various departments, divisions and geographical locations of the key account.[8]

According to Hise and Reid,[9] the six most critical conditions needed to ensure the success of key account management are as follows:

- integration of the key account programme into the company's overall sales effort

- senior management's understanding of, and support for, the key account unit's role

- clear and practical lines of communication between outlying sales and service units

- establishment of objectives and missions

- compatible working relationships between sales management and field salespeople

- clear definition and identification of customers to be designated for key account status

Some important distinctions between transactional selling and key account management are shown in Table 6.1.

Table 9.1 Distinctions between transactional selling and key account management

	Transactional selling	Key account management
Overall objective	Sales	Preferred supplier status
Sales skills	Asking questions, handling objections, closing	Building trust, providing excellent service
Nature of relationship	Short, intermittent	Long, more intense interaction
Salesperson goal	Closed sale	Relationship management
Nature of salesforce	One or two salespeople per customer	Many salespeople, often involving multifunctional teams

Advantages and Dangers of Key Account Management

A number of advantages to the supplier have been identified with key account management:

1 Close working relationships with the customer – the salesperson knows who makes what decisions and who influences the various players involved in the decision-making process. Technical specialists from the selling organisation can call on technical people (e.g. engineers) in the buying organisation, and salespeople can call upon administrators, buyers and financial people armed with the commercial arguments for buying.

2 Improved communication and co-ordination – the customer knows that a dedicated salesperson or sales team exists and they know who to contact when a problem arises.

3 Better follow-up on sales and service – the extra resources devoted to the key account means there is more time to follow up and provide service after a key sale has been concluded.

4 More in-depth penetration of the DMU – there is more time to cultivate relationships within the key account. Salespeople can 'pull' the buying decision through the organisation from the users, deciders and influencers to the buyer, rather than face the more difficult task of 'pushing' it through the buyer into the organisation, as is done with more traditional sales approaches.

5 Higher sales – most companies that have adopted key account selling techniques claim that sales have risen as a result.

6 The provision of an opportunity for advancement for career salespeople – a tiered salesforce system with key account selling at the top provides promotional opportunities for salespeople who wish to advance within the salesforce rather than to enter a traditional sales management position.

7 Lower costs through joint agreement of optimum production and delivery schedules, and demand forecasting.

8 Co-operation on research and development for new products and joint promotions (e.g. within the fast-moving consumer goods/retail sector).

However, Burnett[10] points out that key account management is not without its potential dangers. For example:

1 When resources are channelled towards a limited number of companies, the supplier runs the risk of increased dependence on, and vulnerability to, relatively few customers.

2 The risk of pressure on profit margins if a customer chooses to abuse its key account status.

3 The possible danger of a customer applying ever-increasing demands for higher levels of service and attention once they know that they have preferred customer status.

4 Focusing resources on a few key accounts may lead to neglect of smaller accounts, some of which may have high long-term potential.

5 The team approach required by key account management may be at odds with the career aspirations of certain high achievers who prefer a more individualistic approach and object to the dilution of praise which has to be shared with other people when a big order is won. Thus care is required when recruiting key account salespeople.

It should also be recognised that not all major customers may want to have close key account managed relationships. Some companies prefer to carry out their buying on a transactional selling model with their purchasing professionals trading off quality with price, and using their market power to extract the best deal. Some supermarkets are regarded by many of their suppliers as buying on such a basis.[11]

9.3 Deciding Whether to Use Key Account Management

An important question is the suitability of key account management to suppliers. Clearly it is only one form of salesforce organisation (others are discussed in Chapter 15 which covers organisation and compensation) and care is needed in deciding whether the extra resources and costs associated with its implementation can be justified. The greater the extent to which the following circumstances exist, the more likely a company is to move towards setting up key accounts:[12]

1 A small number of customers account for a high proportion of the supplier's sales.

2 There is potential for differentiation of the product and/or service provided by the supplier in a way that is highly valued by the customer.

3 Customers exhibit complex buying behaviour with large decision-making units applying varied choice criteria, often in multiple locations, meaning that a geographical organisational structure is inappropriate.

4 Multifunction contacts between supplier and customer are required.

5 Significant cost savings are possible through dealing selectively with a small number of large customers, and joint agreements of production and delivery schedules.

6 There is a danger of different salespeople from the supplier's salesforce calling upon the same customer to sell different products or offer conflicting solutions to problems.

7 The establishment of in-depth communications and strong relationships with customers may lead to the opportunity of tailoring products and services to specific customer needs.

8 Customers are centralising their operations.

9 Competition is improving its account handling by moving to key account management.

9.4 Criteria for Selecting Key Accounts

Traditionally the key criterion for designating particular customers as 'key accounts' was on the basis of the large quantity of output sold to a customer. On the basis that an organisation bought a considerable amount of product from a supplier, it deserved special treatment because of the high profit contribution it made. The supplier was motivated to provide the extra resources because the loss of that customer would significantly impact its own sales and profits.

As experience with key accounts has grown, the range of criteria used to select key accounts has grown based on the strategic or long-term importance of specific customers to a supplier.[13] These include:

- Accounts that have growth prospects through their ability to build sales and market share in their existing markets.

- Accounts with growth prospects through their position as major players in small or medium-sized but expanding markets.

- Customers that are willing to be partners in innovation by allowing joint new product development with a supplier and/or will allow a supplier to test new products in their production processes.

- Customers that are early adopters of new products and so aid the diffusion of such products in the marketplace.

- Highly prestigious accounts that improve the image and reputation of the supplier and can be used in reference selling by the salesforce.

- Accounts that are important to and currently served by competitors that the supplier has decided to attack.

9.5 The Tasks and Skills of Key Account Management

A study by the Bureau of Business Practice reported that choosing the best person to manage and co-ordinate key account programmes is second only in importance to obtaining support from top management.[14] Selecting the best person requires a full understanding of the tasks and skills required of the job. Simply choosing the company's top salesperson to handle the management of a key account is not recommended because the jobs are so different,[15] with the latter requiring a higher level of managerial ability (e.g. leadership, co-ordination, development of account strategies and communication). This is because powerful buyers in key accounts carry high expectations and are very demanding of suppliers. For example, they expect key account salespeople to act as partners in creating strategic solutions to their problems or to be experts who provide specialised category or product application knowledge.[16]

Wotruba and Castleberry[17] surveyed key account salespeople to identify the tasks performed and skills required of the job. The top ten of each are listed in Table 9.2.

This list can be used to choose criteria for the recruitment, selection and evaluation of key account managers. It is not surprising that relationship building skills are paramount, and this topic will be explored later in this chapter. Next, though, we consider the special selling skills required to sell to key accounts.

As can be seen in Table 9.2, an important responsibility of a key account manager is to establish and maintain a harmonious and mutually beneficial relationship between supplier and customer. Traditionally buyer–seller relationships were managed as illustrated in Figure 9.1 with interfirm contact being almost exclusively between the supplier's salesperson and the customer's purchasing manager.[18] This is called the 'bow-tie' relationship. Key account management requires a more sophisticated approach whereby the relationship is in the form of a diamond, as shown in Figure 9.2. The key account manager co-ordinates and encourages multifunctional levels of interaction involving various relevant functions of both organisations such as marketing, engineering, research and development and finance.

For this to occur, key account managers must have the skills and/or power to encourage functional specialists within their own company to interact with their counterparts in customer organisations. The problem for many key account managers is that their colleagues in other functions do not recognise the need or do not believe they have the time to meet customer personnel. They perceive this task to be the responsibility of sales and marketing and resist involvement with customers. Thus, key account managers require considerable persuasive skills, internal credibility and the authority that comes with top management support to convince colleagues outside the sales and marketing function that customer contact is an essential part of their job. Functional specialists themselves may require training to communicate effectively with specialist managers in customer organisations.

Table 9.2 Tasks performed and skills required by key account management

	Tasks	Skills
1	Develop long-term relationships	Relationship building
2	Engage in direct contact with key customers	Co-ordination
3	Maintain key account records and background information	Negotiation
4	Identify selling opportunities and sales potential of existing key accounts	Human relations
5	Monitor competitive developments affecting key accounts	Focus on specific objectives
6	Report results to upper management	Diagnosing customer problems
7	Monitor and/or control key account contracts	Presentation skills
8	Make high level presentations to key accounts	Generating visibility, reputation
9	Co-ordinate and expedite service to key accounts	Communication
10	Co-ordinate communications among company units servicing key accounts	Working in a team

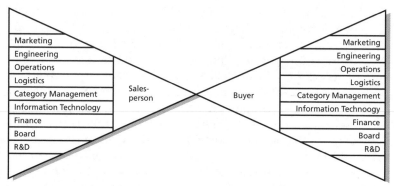

Figure 9.1 Traditional (bow-tie) buyer–seller relationship: communication is between salesperson and buyer
Source: Adapted from Shipley, D. and Palmer, R. (1997) 'Selling to and managing key accounts' in Jobber, D. (1997) *The CIM handbook of selling and sales strategy*, Butterworth-Heinemann, Oxford, p. 95. Copyright © 1997, reprinted with permission from Elsevier.

9.6   Key Account Management Relational Development Model

The development and management of a key account can be understood as a process between buyers and sellers. The key account management (KAM) **relational development model** plots the typical progression of a buyer–seller relationship based upon the nature of the customer relationship (transactional or collaborative) and the level of involvement with customers (simple or complex). It shows five of the

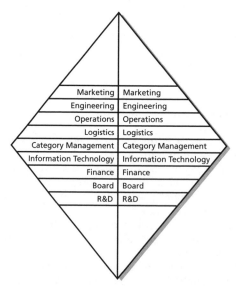

Figure 9.2 Key account (diamond) based relationship: key account manager co-ordinates communication which is direct between functions
Source: Adapted from Shipley, D. and Palmer, R. (1997) 'Selling to and managing key accounts' in Jobber, D. (1997) *The CIM handbook of selling and sales strategy*, Butterworth-Heinemann, Oxford, p. 95. Copyright © 1997, reprinted with permission from Elsevier.

six stages identified by Millman and Wilson:[19] pre-KAM, early-KAM, mid-KAM, partnership-KAM and synergistic-KAM (see Figure 9.3). A sixth stage (uncoupling-KAM) represents the breakdown of the relationship which can happen at any point during the process.

Pre-KAM

Pre-KAM describes preparation for KAM, or 'prospecting'. The task is to identify those accounts with the potential for moving towards key account status and to avoid wasting investment on those accounts that lack the potential. Pre-KAM selling strategies involve making products and services available while attempting to gather information about customers so that their key account potential can be assessed. Where an account is thought to have potential but breaking into the account is proving difficult, patience and persistence are required. A breakthrough may result from the 'in' supplier doing something wrong, e.g. refusing to quote for a low-profit order or failing to repair equipment promptly.

Early-KAM

Early-KAM involves the exploration of opportunities for closer collaboration by identifying the motives, culture and concerns of the customer. The selling company needs to convince the customer of the benefits of being a 'preferred customer'. It will seek to understand the customer's decision-making unit and processes, and the problems and opportunities that relate to the value adding processes. Product and service adaptations may be made to fit customer needs better. An objective of the

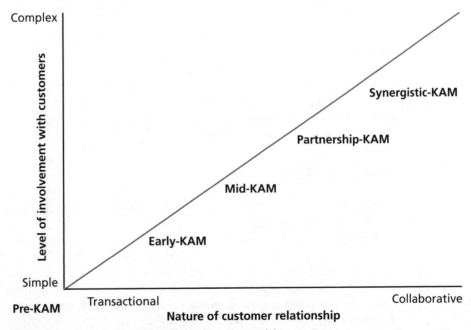

Figure 9.3 Key account relational development model

sales effort will be to build trust based on consistent performance and open com-munications.

Most communication is channelled through one salesperson (the key account manager) and a single contact at the buying organisation. This makes for a fragile relationship, particularly as it is likely that the seller is one of many supplying the account. The customer will be monitoring the supplier's performance to assess com-petence and to identify quickly any problems that might arise. The account man-ager will be seeking to create a more attractive offering, establish credibility and deepen personal relationships.

Mid-KAM

By now trust has been established and the supplier is one of a small number of pre-ferred sources of the product. The number and range of contacts increases. These may include social events which help to deepen relationships across the two organ-isations.

The account review process carried out at the selling organisation will tend to move upwards to involve senior management because of the importance of the cus-tomer and the level of resource allocation. Since the account is not yet exclusive the activities of competitors will require constant monitoring.

Partnership-KAM

This is the stage where the buying organisation regards the supplier as an important strategic resource. The level of trust will be sufficient for both parties to be willing to share sensitive information. The focus of activities moves to joint problem-solv-ing, collaborative product development and mutual training of the other firm's staff.

The buying company is now channelling nearly all of its business in the relevant product group(s) to the one supplier. The arrangement is formalised in a partnership agreement of at least three years' duration. Performance will be monitored and con-tacts between departments of the two organisations will be extensive. The buying organisation will expect guaranteed continuity of supply, excellent service and top quality products. A key task of the account manager is to reinforce the high levels of trust to exclude potential competitors.

Synergistic-KAM

Synergistic-KAM is the ultimate stage of the relational development model. Buyer and seller see one another not as two separate organisations, but as part of a larger entity. Top management commitment manifests itself in joint board meetings and joint business planning, research and development, and market research take place. Costing systems become transparent, unnecessary costs are removed and process improvements are mutually achieved. For example, a logistics company together with one of its retail key accounts has six cross-boundary teams working on process improvements at any one time.[20]

Uncoupling-KAM

This is where transactions and interactions cease. The causes of uncoupling need to be understood so that it can be avoided. Breakdowns are more often attributable to changes in key personnel and relationship problems than price conflicts. The danger of uncoupling is particularly acute in early-KAM when the single point of contact prevails. If, for example, the key account manager leaves to be replaced by someone who in the buyer's eyes is less skilled, or there is a personality clash, the relationship may end.

A second cause of uncoupling is a breach of trust. For example, the breaking of a promise over a delivery deadline, product improvement or equipment repair can weaken or kill a business relationship. The key to handling such problems is to reduce the impact of surprise. The supplier should let the buying organisation know immediately a problem becomes apparent. It should also show humility when discussing the problem with the customer.

Companies also uncouple through neglect. Long-term relationships can foster complacency and customers can perceive themselves as being taken for granted. Cultural mismatches can occur, for example, when the customer stresses price whereas the supplier focuses on life-cycle costs. Difficulties can also occur between bureaucratic and entrepreneurial styles of management.

Product or service quality problems can also provoke uncoupling. Any kind of performance problem, or perceptions that rivals now offer superior performance, can trigger a breakdown in relations. 'In' suppliers must build entry barriers by ensuring that product and service quality are constantly improved and that any problems are dealt with speedily and professionally.

Not all uncoupling is instigated by the buying company. A key account may be derated or terminated because of loss of market share or the onset of financial problems that impair the attractiveness of the account.

9.7   Global Account Management

Global account management (GAM) is the process of co-ordinating and developing mutually beneficial long-term relationships with a select group of strategically important customers (accounts) operating in globalising industries.[21] It has arisen as a way of managing global customers that are of strategic importance to suppliers. The growth in globalisation of business activities is making GAM an increasingly important issue for many multinational organisations.

Global key accounts are also usually multinational customers that have an expectation of being supplied and serviced worldwide in a consistent and co-ordinated way.[22] Multinational customers are increasingly buying on a centralised or co-ordinated basis and seek suppliers that are able to provide consistent and seamless service across countries.[23] Consequently, suppliers are developing and implementing GAM and are creating global account managers to manage the interface between seller and buyer on a global basis. At first sight GAM might be regarded as simply an extension of KAM, but there are some key differences that make the job fundamentally more complex:[24]

- cross-cultural issues (e.g. concerning people, systems and processes)
- management of globally dispersed and cross-cultural teams
- management of conflict that can stem from the issues of global versus local approaches to sales and marketing
- managing global logistics
- management of global communication
- location of global account managers

This complexity makes the job of the global account manager very demanding. Research has shown a range of roles and competences necessary to carry out the job.[25] These are displayed in Table 9.3. These competences are required because global account managers perform a boundary-spanning role across two important organisational areas. First they span the *internal* interface between global and national account management which is often part of a headquarters/subsidiary relationship. Second, they span the *external* interface between the supplier and the dispersed activities of its global accounts. In recognition of the need to navigate sensitive commercial and political issues while managing these interfaces, Wilson and Millman (2002) consider the global account manager to perform the role of political entrepreneur.[26]

Organisationally, a lead global account manager (sometimes called global client director, global relationship manager or global account team manager) normally manages a team of account managers. Although there is no one best way to organise for GAM, there are a number of principles that act as a guide when designing organisation structure and systems.[27]

Involvement of a senior corporate level manager as programme champion provides the political muscle to move the programme forward. The lead global account

Table 9.3 Roles and competences required of a global account manager

Roles	Competences
Global account strategist	Communication skills
Co-ordinator of the account's centralised and dispersed requirements	Global team leadership and management skills
Global account team manager/leader	Business and financial acumen
Information broker	Relationship management skills
Relationship facilitator/builder	Strategic vision and planning capabilities
Negotiator	Problem-solving capabilities
'Voice of the customer' (Customer's advocate)	Cultural empathy
Corporate 'culture carrier'	Selling skills (internal and external)
	Industry and market knowledge
	Product service knowledge

Sources: Based on Millman, T. (1999) 'From national account management to global account management in business-to-business markets', *Fachzeitschrift für Marketing THEXIS*, 16(4), pp. 2–9; Millman, T. and Wilson, K. (1999) 'Developing global account management competences', *Proceedings of the 15th Annual IMP Conference*, University College Dublin, September.

manager should be focused exclusively on managing the global relationship in order to avoid becoming embroiled in local politics with local country and national account managers assigned to local customer organisations.

The global account manager should have authority over the global team and the resources allocated to them and have sufficient status within the company hierarchy for this authority to be reinforced. Ideally, the global account manager should be located near the customer headquarters and supported by local account managers positioned near the customer's remote facilities. Further support should be provided by local dedicated staff and the expertise of corporate specialists.[28]

9.8 Building Relationships with Key Accounts

The importance of **relationship building** with customers is discussed in Chapter 10. However, there are certain ways in which suppliers can build relationships with key accounts. Five ways of building strong customer relationships will now be described.

1 Personal trust

The objective is to build confidence and reassurance.

Methods:

- ensure promises are kept
- reply swiftly to queries, problems and complaints
- establish high (but not intrusive) frequency of contact with key account
- arrange factory/site visits
- engage in social activities with customer
- give advance warning of problems

2 Technical support

The objective is to provide know-how and improve the productivity of the key account.

Methods:

- research and development co-operation
- before- and after-sales service
- provide training
- dual selling (supplier helps key account to sell)

3 Resource support

The objective is to reduce the key account's financial burden.

Methods:

- provide credit facilities
- create low interest loans
- engage in co-operative promotions to share costs
- engage in counter-trade (accept payment by means of goods or services rather than cash)

4 Service levels

The objective is to improve the quality of service provision.

Methods:

- reliable delivery
- fast/just-in-time delivery
- install computerised reorder systems
- give fast accurate quotes
- defect reduction (right first time)

5 Risk reduction

The objective is to lower uncertainty in the customer's mind regarding the supplier and the products/services provided.

Methods:

- free demonstrations
- free/low-cost trial period
- product guarantees
- delivery guarantees
- preventative maintenance contracts
- proactive follow-ups
- reference selling

Suppliers should consult the above checklist to evaluate the cost/benefit of using each of the methods of building strong relationships with each account. A judgement needs to be made regarding the value each key account places on each method and the cost (including executive and management time) of providing the item.

Managing relationships involves taking care in day-to-day meetings with customers. Table 9.4 gives a list of some key dos and don'ts of key account management.

9.9 Key Account Information and Planning System

The importance of key accounts means that suppliers need to consider the information which needs to be collected and stored for each account, and the objectives, strategies and control systems required to manage the accounts. This can be accomplished by a **key account information and planning system**. The benefits of planning systems include consistency, change monitoring, resource allocation and competitive advantage.

Consistency

The plan provides a focal point for decisions and action leading to better consistency and co-ordination between managers.

Table 9.4 Handling relationships with key accounts

Key account dos

Do work with the account to agree an actionable account plan.
Do understand key account decision-making:
- key choice criteria
- roles of decision-making unit
- how decisions are made
Do only ever agree to what can be delivered.
Do resolve issues quickly.
Do confirm agreements in writing.
Do communicate internally to identify unresolved problems (e.g. late delivery).
Do treat customers as 'experts' to encourage them to reveal information.
Do view issues from the customer's (as well as your own) perspective.
Do ask questions: knowledge is power.

Key account don'ts

Don't let a small issue spoil a relationship.
Don't expect to win everything, giving a concession may improve the relationship.
Don't divulge confidential information from other accounts.
Don't view negotiations as win-lose scenarios. Try to create win-win situations.
Don't be afraid to say 'No' when the circumstances demand it.
Don't deceive: if you do not know the answer, say so.

Monitoring of change

The planning process forces managers to review the impact of change on the account and to consider the actions required to meet the new challenges.

Resource allocation

The planning process asks fundamental questions about resource allocation. Some of the questions that require addressing are: Should the account receive more, the same or fewer resources? How should those resources be deployed? How should resources be allocated between accounts?

Competitive advantage

Planning promotes the search for better ways of servicing the account in order to keep out competing firms. The building block for the planning system is the account audit, which is based on the creation of an information system that collects, stores and disseminates essential account data. Table 9.5 shows the kind of data that may form such a system. Hard data record the facts and figures of the account such as the products sold and markets served and the sales volume (units), revenue and profits generated by the customer. Such general data provide the fundamental background information to the account.

Specific hard data cover issues that focus on the transactions between seller and customer such as the seller's sales and profits by product, supplier and competitor's price levels, competitor's products sold to the customer, their volume and revenue, details of discounts and contract expiry dates. Absolute levels, trends and variations from targets will be recorded.

Soft data complement hard data by providing qualitative (and sometimes more subjective) assessments of the account situation. A key requirement is the holding of buyer behaviour data such as the names, positions and roles of decision-making unit members, their choice criteria/perceptions/attitudes and buying processes. An assessment of the ongoing relationships should be made and any problems, threats and opportunities defined. The suppliers' and competitors' strengths and weaknesses should be analysed in both absolute and relative terms. Finally, external changes (such as declining markets, changes in technology and potential new competition) should be monitored as they may affect future business with the account.

The outcome of this account audit can be summarised in a strengths, weaknesses, opportunities and threats (SWOT) analysis (see Figure 9.4). The internal strengths and weaknesses of the supplier are summarised as they relate to the opportunities and threats relevant to the account. SWOT analysis provides a convenient framework for making decisions to improve the effectiveness of key account management and provides insights to develop the account plan. For example, action can be taken to exploit opportunities by building on strengths, and to minimise the impact of threats.

An account plan comprises objectives, strategies and control procedures.

Table 9.5 A key account information system

	Type of data	
	Hard	Soft
General	Addresses, telephone, fax and telex numbers, email addresses Customer products sold and markets served (size and growth rates) Sales volume and revenue Profits Capital employed Operating ratios (e.g. return on capital employed, profit margin)	Decision-making unit members Choice criteria Perceptions and attitudes Buying processes Assessment of relationships Problems and threats Opportunities Supplier's strengths and weaknesses Competitors' strengths and weaknesses Environmental changes affecting account now and in the future
Specific	Supplier's sales to account by product Supplier's price levels and profitability by product Details of discounts and allowances Competitors' products, price levels and sales Contract expiry dates	

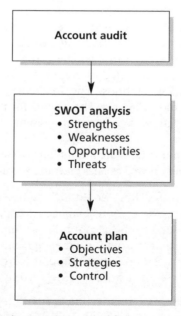

Figure 9.4 Key account planning system

Objectives

The account plan should set out clear objectives for the planning period. Typically objectives will be stated in terms of sales and profit-by-product for each account for the planning period. Pricing objectives will state target price changes for the period. Where more than one supplier services the account, share-of-business objectives may be set. For example, the SWOT analysis may identify an opportunity resulting from service problems associated with a competitor. This may encourage the development of an objective to raise the share of business from 40 to 55 per cent.

A long sales cycle is characteristic of many key account sales. It is, therefore, often sensible to couch objectives in terms of gaining customer commitment rather than of achieving a sales close, particularly if the account planning period is relatively short. Such objectives must be set in terms of customer responses, not seller actions. For example, suitable objectives may be to persuade the customer to visit the seller's site, agree to a product demonstration, or give the seller's new product an extended trial.

Strategies

Strategies are the means by which objectives are achieved. For example, the objective of persuading the customer to visit the seller's site would require a statement of who in the decision-making unit should be targeted, the identities of the people in the account management team responsible for reaching these people, what action they need to take to persuade the customer to make the visit, and activity completion deadlines. Obviously not every detail can be planned: scope should be provided for individual initiative and enterprise, but without a guiding framework, the activities may become uncoordinated or, worse still, the task neglected.

Control

An account planning control system checks progress on the achievement of objectives so that corrective action can be taken when needed. Computerised sales and profitability analysis can evaluate actual performance against objectives. Review meetings may be required to compare both quantitative and qualitative performance against expectations. The frequency, coverage and composition of review meetings should be agreed. The agenda for these meetings should be decided upon in time to gather, analyse and present information relevant to topics under discussion.

An important issue is the profitability of each key account. A check should be made on account costs as well as sales revenue. Account costs may be broken down as follows:

1 *Sales staff costs.* These would include the costs of all sales staff working on the account, e.g. the account manager, account executives and any field salesforce activity related to the account. For example, for a multiple retailer account, the account manager would reach an agreement with the field salesforce manager to provide a certain level of support (perhaps two visits per store per week). The costs of these visits would be included in the calculation of sales staff costs.

2 *Support staff costs.* In a technical environment such as telecommunications or information technology, this would comprise people such as systems engineers

who might undertake pre-bid analysis and planning, and also any dedicated maintenance people.

3 *Other sales and marketing costs.* These might include account-specific promotions, special packaging and special payment terms such as discounts. Special distribution arrangements, e.g. to individual stores rather than one central warehouse, would also fall into this category of account costs.

The above is an example of how a company may break down account costs, but organisations have the choice of how best to categorise account costs given their own circumstances and requirements. By itemising costs, results can be compared against budget and areas that require investigation will be revealed.

9.10 Key Success Factors for Key Account Management

A study by Abratt and Kelly (2002) investigated the perceptions of suppliers and key account customers regarding the success factors of key account relationships. They identified six critical issues that can assist management in the creation of enhanced and sustainable relationships (see Table 9.6).

Important issues relating to the suitability of the key account manager are his/her integrity, interpersonal skills, personality, general competence, and ability to relate to the culture of the key account. An in-depth knowledge and understanding of the key account customer's business was identified as the second key success factor. The primary reason for this was to anticipate their future needs. The third success factor was commitment to the key account programme. This involves giving sufficient time and resources to establish and build the relationship and to properly train key account managers. Suppliers should also have an effective system of evaluating the key account programme's core strengths and to apply them in ways that deliver the greatest value to their customers. In order to achieve this, the supplier requires an effective process for understanding the key account customer's needs. Cross-functional project teams can help by allowing both parties to develop a 'feel' for the value that each contributes to the relationship.

Trust is considered a key success factor, with suppliers regarding trust as the sharing of confidential information between the partners while key account

Table 9.6 KAM key success factors

---

1 Suitability of the key account manager
2 In-depth knowledge and understanding of the key account customer's business
3 Commitment to the partnership
4 Delivering value
5 Trust
6 Proper implementation and understanding of the KAM concept

Source: Reprinted from Abratt, R. and Kelly, P.M. (2002) 'Customer–supplier partnerships: perceptions of a successful key account management program', *Industrial Marketing Management*, 31, pp. 467–476. Copyright © 2002 with permission from Elsevier.

customers view trust as neither party breaching the contract. Finally, proper implementation and understanding of the KAM programme was seen to be a key success factor. Implementation requires an in-depth understanding, not only by key account managers but also by people in other functional areas. Such functions as operations, logistics, purchasing and marketing need to understand the reason for and the implications of the KAM programme. In addition, the key account customer needs to be informed and trained about the KAM programme. In particular, the customer should understand what the supplier is trying to achieve in establishing a KAM programme.

9.11 Conclusions

This chapter has examined the crucial task of selling to and managing key accounts. Selling skills tend to differ between low-cost and key sale situations. The additional skills and techniques necessary to sell to key customers have been examined.

An important ingredient in managing key accounts is the ability to manage relationships over a long period of time. We have discussed ways to build trust, provide technical and resource support, improve service levels and reduce risk for the customer. Additionally this chapter has examined ways of deciding whether a key account system is appropriate and, if it is, how to create a key account information and planning system.

References

1 Weilbaker, D.C. and Weeks, W.A. (1997) 'The evolution of national account management: a literature perspective', *Journal of Personal Selling and Sales Management*, 17(4), pp. 49–59.

2 See Weilbaker and Weeks (1997) op. cit.; Abratt, R. and Kelly, P.M. (2002) 'Customer–supplier partnerships: perceptions of a successful key account management program', *Industrial Marketing Management*, 31, pp. 467–476.

3 Homberg, C., Workman, Jr, J.P. and Jensen, O. (2002) 'A configuration perspective on key account management', *Journal of Marketing*, 66, April, pp. 38–60.

4 See Cardozo, R.N., Shipp, S.H. and Roering, K.J. (1992) 'Proactive strategic partnerships: a new business markets strategy', *Journal of Business and Industrial Marketing*, 7, pp. 51–63; Montgomery, D.B. and Yip, G.S. (2000) 'The challenge of global customer management', *Marketing Management*, 9, pp. 22–29.

5 Homberg, C., Workman, Jr, J.P. and Jensen, O. (2002) 'A configuration perspective on key account management', *Journal of Marketing*, 66, April, pp. 38–60.

6 See Dishman, P. and Nitse, P.S. (1998) 'National accounts revisited: new lessons from recent investigations', *Industrial Marketing Management*, 27, pp. 1–9; Wotruba, T.R.

and Castleberry, S.B. (1993) 'Job analysis and hiring practices for national account marketing positions', *Journal of Personal Selling and Sales Management*, 13(3), pp. 49–65.

7 Shapiro, B.P. and Moriarty, R.T. (1984) 'Support systems for national account management programs', *Marketing Science Institute Working Paper No. 84-102*, Cambridge, MA: Marketing Science Institute.

8 Worcester, R.M. and English, P. (1985) 'Time for PR to mature?' *PR Week*, 1 November.

9 Hise, R.T. and Reid, E.L. (1994) 'Improving the performance of the industrial sales force in the 1990s', *International Marketing Management*, 23, pp. 273–94.

10 Burnett, K. (1992) *Strategic Customer Alliances*, Financial Times/Pitman Publishing, London.

11 Piercy, N.F. and Lane, N. (2003) 'Transformation of the traditional salesforce: imperatives for intelligence, interface and integration', *Journal of Marketing Management*, 19, pp. 563–582.

12 Burnett, K. (1992) *Strategic Customer Alliances*, Financial Times/Pitman Publishing, London.

13 Shipley, D. and Palmer, R. (1997) 'Selling and managing key accounts' in Jobber, D. (1997) *The CIM Handbook of Selling and Sales Strategy*, Butterworth-Heinemann, Oxford, pp. 89–103.

14 Bureau of Business Practice (1986) 'National Accounts: Trends for the Eighties and Beyond', *Special Report*, 30 August, USA.

15 Maher, P. (1984) 'National account marketing: an essential strategy, or prima donna selling?' *Business Marketing*, December, pp. 34–45.

16 Delvecchio, S., Zamanek, J., McIntyre, R. and Claxton, R. (2004) 'Updating the adaptive' selling behaviours: tactics to keep and tactics to disregard', *Journal of Marketing Management*, 20, pp. 859–76.

17 Wotruba, T.R. and Castleberry, S.B. (1993) 'Job analysis and hiring practices for national account maketing positions', *Journal of Personal Selling and Sales Management*, 13(3), p. 49–65.

18 Shipley, D. and Palmer, R. (1997) op. cit.

19 Millman, T. and Wilson, K. (1995) 'From key account selling to key account management', *Journal of Marketing Practice*, 1(1), pp. 9–21.

20 McDonald, M. and Rogers, B. (1998) *Key Account Management*, Butterworth-Heinemann, London.

21 Wilson, K., Croom, S., Millman, T. and Weilbaker, D. (2000) 'The SRT-SAMA global account management study', *Journal of Selling and Major Account Management*, 2(3), pp. 63–84.

22 Millman, T. (1996) 'Global key account management and system selling', *International Business Review*, 5(6), pp. 631–45.

23 Montgomery, G. and Yip, P. (1999) 'Statistical evidence on global account management programs', *Fachzeitschrift Für Marketing THEXIS*, 16(4), pp. 10–13.

24 Holt, S. and McDonald, M. (2001) 'A boundary role theory perspective of the global account manager', *Journal of Selling and Major Account Management*, 3(4), pp. 11–31.

25 Millman, T. (1999) 'From national account management to global account management in business-to-business markets', *Fachzeitschrift Für Marketing THEXIS*, 16(4), pp. 2–9; and Millman, T. and Wilson, K. (1999) 'Developing global account management competences', *Proceedings of the 15th Annual IMP Conference*, University College Dublin, September.

26 Wilson, K. and Millman, T. (2003) 'The global account manager as political entrepreneur', *Industrial Marketing Management*, 32, pp. 151–158.

27 Millman, T. and Wilson, K. (2001) 'Structuring and positioning global account management programmes: a typology', *Journal of Selling and Major Account Management*, 4(1), pp. 11–38.

28 Millman, T. and Wilson, K. (2001) op. cit.

29 Abbratt, R. and Kelly, P.M. (2002) 'Customer supplier partnerships: perceptions of a successful key account management program', *Industrial Marketing Management*, 31, pp. 467–476.

Practical Exercise

Cloverleaf plc

Cloverleaf plc was a UK-based supplier of bottling machinery used in production lines to transport and fill bottles. Two years ago it opened an overseas sales office targeting Germany, France and the Benelux countries. It estimated that there were over 1,000 organisations in those countries with bottling facilities and that a key sales push in northern Europe was therefore warranted. Sales so far had been disappointing with only three units having been sold. Expectations had been much higher than this, given the advantages of their product over that produced by their competitors.

Technological breakthroughs at Cloverleaf meant that their bottling lines had a 10 per cent speed advantage over the nearest competition with equal filling accuracy. A key problem with competitor products was unreliability. Down-time due to a line breakdown was extremely costly to bottlers. Tests by Cloverleaf engineers at their research and development establishment in the UK had shown their system to be the most reliable on the market.

Cloverleaf's marketing strategy was based around high quality, high price competitive positioning. They believed that the superior performance of their product justified a 10 per cent price premium over their key competitors who were all priced at around £1 million for a standard production line. Salespeople were told to stress the higher speed and enhanced reliability when talking to customers. The sales organisation in northern Europe consisted of a sales manager with three salespeople assigned to Germany, France and the Benelux countries respectively. A technical specialist was also available when required. When a sales call required specialist technical assistance, a salesperson would contact the sales office to arrange for the technical specialist to visit the prospect, usually together with the salesperson.

Typically, four groups of people inside buying organisations were involved in the purchase of bottling equipment, namely the production manager, production engineer, purchasing officer and, where large sums of money were involved (over £0.5 million), the technical director. Production managers were mainly interested in smooth production flows and cost savings. Production engineers were charged with drawing up specifications for new equipment and in large firms they were usually asked to draw up state-of-the-art specifications. The purchasing officers, who were often quite powerful, were interested in the financial aspects of any purchase, and technical directors, while interested in technical issues, also appreciated the prestige associated with having state-of-the-art technology.

John Goodman was the sales executive covering France. While in the sales office in Paris, he received a call from Dr Leblanc, the technical director of Commercial SA, a large Marseille-based bottling company that bottled under licence a number of key soft drink brands. They had a reputation for technical excellence and innovation. Goodman made an appointment to see Dr Leblanc on 7 March. He was looking forward to making his first visit to this company. The following extracts are taken from his record of his sales calls.

March 7

Called on Dr Leblanc who told me that Commercial SA had decided to purchase a new bottling line as a result of expansion, and asked for details of what we could provide. I described our system and gave him our sales literature. He told me that three of our competitors had already discussed their systems with him. As I was leaving, he suggested that I might like to talk to M. Artois, their production engineer, to check specifications.

March 8

Visited M. Artois who showed me the specifications that he had drawn up. I was delighted to see that our specifications easily exceeded them but was concerned that his specifications seemed to match those of one of our competitors, Hofstead Gm, almost exactly. I showed M. Artois some of our technical manuals. He did not seem impressed.

March 11

Visited Dr Leblanc who appeared very pleased to see me. He asked me to give him three reasons why they should buy from us. I told him that our system was more technologically advanced than the competition, was more reliable and had a faster bottling speed. He asked me if I was sure it was the most technologically advanced. I said that there was no doubt about it. He suggested I contact M. Bernard, the purchasing manager. I made an appointment to see him in two days' time.

March 13

Called on M. Bernard. I discussed the technical features of the system with him. He asked me about price. I told him I would get back to him on that.

March 15

Visited Dr Leblanc who said a decision was being made within a month. I repeated our operational advantages and he asked me about price. I told him I would give him a quote as soon as possible.

March 20

Saw M. Bernard. I told him our price was £1.1 million. He replied that a key competitor had quoted less than £1 million. I replied that the greater reliability and bottling speed meant that our higher price was more than justified. He remained unimpressed.

March 21

Had a meeting with Mike Bull, my sales manager, to discuss tactics. I told him that there were problems. He suggested that all purchasing managers liked to believe they were saving their company money. He told me to reduce my price by £50,000 to satisfy M. Bernard's ego.

March 25

Told M. Bernard of our new quotation. He said he still did not understand why we could not match the competition on price. I repeated our technical advantages over the competition and told him that our 10 per cent faster speed and higher reliability had been proven by our research and development engineers.

March 30

Visited Dr Leblanc who said a meeting had been arranged for 13 April to make the final decision but that our price of £1.05 million was too high for the likes of M. Bernard.

April 4

Hastily arranged a meeting with Mike Bull to discuss the situation. Told him about Dr Leblanc's concern that M. Bernard thought our price was too high. He said that £1m was as low as we could go.

April 5

Took our final offer to M. Bernard. He said he would let me know as soon as a decision was made. He stressed that the decision was not his alone; several other people were involved.

April 16

Received a letter from M. Bernard stating that the order had been placed with Hofstead Gm. He thanked me for the work I had put into the bid made by Cloverleaf plc.

Analyse the reasons for the failure to secure the order and discuss the lessons to be learnt for key account management.

1 Discuss the differences between the characteristics of low and high value sales.

2 What are the key skills required of a key account manager?

3 What is global account management? What competences are required and do they differ from those required of the key account manager?

10 Relationship Selling

Objectives

After studying this chapter, you should be able to:

1. Relate to the ideas put forward by the early quality practitioners

2. See that quality now embraces the organisation as a whole rather than being the sole concern of manufacturing

3. Understand how freer world trade is driving companies towards accepting the need for quality in terms of their relationships with their customers and suppliers

4. Appreciate the role that is being played by just-in-time manufacturing in bringing about these changes

5. Understand the notion of reverse marketing and the change it is bringing about in the traditionally accepted roles of the field salesperson

6. Understand the notion of relationship selling as being the tactical marketing and sales key stemming from the adoption of reverse marketing

Key Concepts

- best practice benchmarking (BPB)
- business process re-engineering
- customer care
- marketing information system (MkIS)
- open accounting
- product or project champion
- relationship marketing
- relationship selling
- reverse marketing
- simultaneous engineering
- supply chain integration
- total quality management (TQM)

From Total Quality Management to Customer Care

When the buyer moves on does the relationship end?

Relationship marketing plays a significant role in modern sales management. Companies have for some time realised the benefits of practising a relational approach to selling rather than a transactional one. Nevertheless, many markets are volatile or else have long product life-cycles that make the practice of relationship selling challenging. This far-sighted quotation from 1954 came from Peter Drucker.[1]

> There is only one valid definition of business: to create customers. It is the customer who determines the nature of the business. Consequently, any business has two basic functions:
> * marketing (customer orientation)
> * innovation.

Much later, Zineldin[2] argued: 'The customer, individual or organisation alike, is at the centre of the organisation's activities and planning.' Reyes Pacios Lozano[3] agreed that 'the customer is at the centre of the organisation'. The importance of the customer remains clear. Several authors have stressed the implications of being 'customer orientated' as the most important component of relationship marketing and relationship selling.[4,5]

Supporting this line of thought, Gummesson[6] claims that 'customer focus' not only 'compels management to realise the firm's primary responsibility – to serve the customer', but also 'to recognise that customer knowledge is paramount to achieving market orientation'.

Another management thinker more often associated with engineering than management was W. Edwards Deming, who has been credited with guiding the Ford Motor Company (USA) towards a sharp focus on quality, not just in manufacturing but in all of its operations, including selling. Although Henry Ford is accredited with the production orientated notion of 'You can have any colour that you like as long as it is black', in the 1970s Deming formulated a mature theory of quality based upon his observations of Japanese manufacturing. His theory revolved around 14 points of philosophical thinking and he is widely regarded as being the modern quality guru. His thinking has changed the way that manufacturing companies operate, as was evidenced from earlier applications in the late 1970s and early 1980s through 'quality circles', or self-motivated works committees assigned to the improvement of quality.

This tactical thinking has now been replaced by the more mature and strategic view of **total quality management (TQM)** that dominates present-day thinking, not just in manufacturing, but in all areas of company activity. In line with the dynamics of TQM, in 1985, when General Motors announced the creation of the Saturn Corporation, calling it the 'the key to GM's long-term competitiveness, survival and success as a domestic provider', the new company's mission was not only to market compact vehicles 'developed and manufactured in the US', but perhaps more importantly to become a world leader in terms of quality, cost and customer satisfaction. Indeed, Saturn was an ambitious undertaking for GM. This positioning was further worsened by the established market share of imports, especially in the compact market. Additionally, the Saturn project was pursued at a time when the general feeling was that US manufacturers lacked the ability to make world-class compact cars,[7] and General Motors itself had already aborted several attempts to develop such cars. Yet after four years on the market, Saturn had succeeded in building from scratch one of the strongest brands from the USA. In fact, the brand was even compared to the Ford Mustang of the 1960s, the Ford Pinto of the 1970s and the Ford Taurus of the 1980s. According to Aaker,[8] the success of Saturn was not due to any key programme or specific policy, but rather to the total gestalt formed by a dozen Saturn decisions and practices revolving around creating a relationship between Saturn and the customer and the adoption of a team approach for the manufacturing of the product.

Taeger[9] contends that these early ideas of quality still tend to trigger mental pictures more related to manufacturing than to the business of selling. This is because its phraseology and concepts relate back to the origins of the quality philosophy of the manufacturing processes whence Deming took his inspiration. Taeger goes on to say that the difficulty in measuring the success of the quality process in sales is that, even when the initial phase has passed, there are rarely any positive pointers that can be identified as having been improved as a result of the introduction of TQM as part of the philosophy of selling. Indeed, as subsequently pointed out by Aaker,[10] even in the case of the Saturn success story it would have been unrealistic to measure quantitatively the role that any one element played in the ultimate performance of the company.

Despite some negative thinking that still exists in relation to the perception of quality, it is a fact that since the 1980s many bigger companies have recognised that the key to success is the need to evolve from a production- and cost-dominant stance towards one of serving a diverse range of customers through personal contact. A key factor in this transition relates to the process of forming relationships. As the strategic perspective of companies is changing from regional to global thinking, the selling model is changing from a 'transactions' to a 'relationships' focus.

This change of perspective in the commercial environment has been supported by academics from the 'Scandinavian School of Thought', namely Gronroos[11] and Gummesson.[12] In fact, by offering the Nordic perspective, these academics have led the argument that the marketing mix theory is inadequate in today's business environment. While Gronroos's main argument[13] that the traditional marketing mix approach is inadequate for operating in line with the marketing concept (i.e. satisfying customer needs and wants) appears to be based on the four Ps approach constituting a production-orientated definition of marketing and a reliance, at best, on mass marketing, Gummesson[14] argues that the marketing mix approach is supplier orientated as opposed to customer orientated. Hence, it excludes or treats marginally matters like complaints handling, invoicing, design and production. Additionally, Gummesson advocates that the 4Ps approach is narrowly limited to functions and is not an integral part of the total management process.

The general consensus about this change of focus lies mainly in the fact that, although customer focus prevails, relationship marketing aims to cover the whole organisation. Accordingly, Schill and McArthur[15] contend that this evolution is taking place now, with marketing adopting a more strategic dimension and with manufacturing, finance and human resource management being integrated and matched to support a coherent competitive strategy to assist marketing in such matters as cost leadership and product differentiation.

As the worldwide political and regulatory climate continues to be increasingly liberal towards the encouragement of free trade, it becomes more difficult to sustain market leadership based on short-term, sales-orientated transactions. Hence, in order to succeed in their search for new ways of gaining competitive advantage over rivals, sellers must engage in building and maintaining long-lasting relationships with their customers.

As competition intensifies, companies are seeking to differentiate their products not only via the *actual product* (the primary focus of the traditional marketing mix) by styling, packaging, brand image, quality and price benefits, but more holistically at the level of the *augmented product*. Accordingly, added benefits like sales support, guarantees and after-sales care that support purchase and consumption experiences are increasingly being provided.

Stalk, Evans and Schulman[16] cite the case of Honda's original success in motor-cycles resulting from the company's distinctive capability in dealer management, which departed from the traditional relationship between motorcycle manufac-turers and dealers. Honda provided operating procedures and policies of merchan-dising, selling, floor planning and service management. It trained all its dealers and their staff in these new management systems and supported them with a comput-erised dealer management information system.

Customer-focused quality is now essential because it involves a change from an operations-centred to a customer-targeted activity. As the move towards a global economy quickens, so customers demand quality in terms of their relationships with sellers, with increased emphasis being placed on reliability, durability, ease of use and after-sales service.

Supporting the argument that changes in the global environment are threaten-ing established value chains, Walters and Lancaster[17] offer an alternative view: tra-ditional value chains begin with the company's core competences, whereas evidence suggests that modern value chain analysis reverses this approach and uses customers as its starting point.

Building upon this contention, Zineldin[18] agrees: 'Effective marketers view making a first time sale not as an end of a process, but as a start of an organisation's relationship with a customer' and further argues 'to protect added value, a company needs to create and enhance long-term customer relationships'.

This leads to the modern notion of **customer care**. Customer care is a philosophy which ensures that products or services and the after-care associated with serving customers' needs at least meets, and in most cases exceeds, expectations. In support of this view, it is argued that customer loyalty can no longer be relied upon because there is greater product and service choice.

Modern studies repeatedly show how reduced marketing expenditures and life-time value based on commitment and trust make keeping of existing customers more cost effective than recruiting new ones. However, according to Sasaki[19] mar-keting must still react to this in a positive way by integrating new customers into a company in an attempt to develop a new relationship between them and the company. These new customers expect products or services to be in harmony with their lifestyles and values, and he contends that a winning product concept is gen-erated when designers and consumers share a contemporary atmosphere and inter-act with each other; in other words when customers feel more 'involved'. This is central to the notion of customer care. He further proposes that this atmosphere can be created as a result of technological advancements in mature cultures where style, tastes and demand can be better anticipated and suitable products can be developed.

Problems of integrating IT into building and maintaining customer relationships have not yet been solved in a comprehensive and satisfactory way. Zineldin[20] emphasises that IT tools should be used not only 'to provide relationship-building credibility and opportunities' but also to enable marketers to 'keep their finger on the customer's pulse and respond to changing needs'. Indeed, as companies look to possible customer needs for technological advancements, communication tools will 'provide great opportunities for creating long-term and close relationships'.

This view is evidenced by the approach of Nissan, the Japanese car manufacturer, when it saw that its market share was in decline. It changed its organisational structure and company philosophy to reflect, as its first priority, the concept of customer satisfaction. Development times were cut, leading to quicker lead times. Coupled with a greater awareness of what customers wanted, this had the effect of turning around the fortunes of the company and placing it in a more stable position in the marketplace. Further, more recent, evidence of the success that close attention to customer needs can create is provided by the Microsoft Corporation. Microsoft realised that the average person had little training or knowledge of computer software or programming. It replaced technical jargon with easily understandable icons and graphical representations of the tasks to be done. Microsoft is now the largest software company in the world and its founder, Bill Gates, one of the richest men in the world.

The idea of total product quality has been explored by Brooks and Wragg,[21] who contend that it is relevant to manufacturing companies adopting a market-driven approach to TQM. This infers that market-led quality can ensure that customers perceive quality is built into both the product and the service component of the total product offering, as illustrated in Figure 10.1.

Market-driven TQM and the development of a total product quality for manufacturing companies are concepts upon which companies should focus. As product parity is reached between different product offerings, so companies can gain a competitive advantage by increasing the total service component of their market offerings. This is more than simply offering an after-sales service – it is a programme of total customer care. This is illustrated in the example of GTSI, Chantilly, which put in a programme of sales coaching to replace the previous system of transactional purchasing.

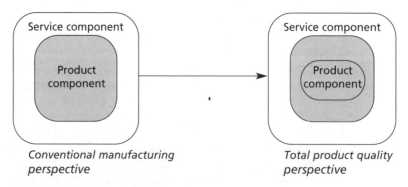

Conventional manufacturing perspective

Total product quality perspective

Figure 10.1 Internal to external focus of total quality perspective

GTSI, Chantilly, Virginia, USA

Situational overview

GTSI is a provider of technical solutions to the United States Federal Government. The company had identified that most sales were being conducted as 'transactional' purchases. Little value, beyond technology, was being communicated to the customer. GTSI had also identified that their sales representatives and account managers were not really networking within major agency accounts. These activities were positioning GTSI primarily as a 'commodity' resource with little perceived value and decreasing sales margins. In addition, turnover was increasing and competition was improving. It was GTSI's conclusion that due to minimal sales management input little, if any, coaching was taking place between management and sales representative.

Efforts

The Chapman Group was engaged to provide sales and management skills and process training to address these business issues. Initially, strategic sales training workshops that focused on enabling sales staff to communicate and demonstrate value to government agencies were developed. Sales management (coaching) processes and workshops were integrated into the sales organisation. Follow-up individualised training workshops were conducted, on an as-needed basis, including:
- Consultative value-added sales training programs
- Sales management and sales coaching curriculum
- Account management processes, plans, and communication systems

Results

- Sales grew from $400 million to $550 million in 12 months
- Per agency contracts grew by 20 per cent
- Sales margins increased approximately 2 per cent
- The company, as well as participants, captured all efforts on video for future re-use and review

Source: *http://www.chapmanHQ.com/our_clients/case_studies* with permission

10.2 From JIT to Relationship Marketing

Christopher, Payne and Ballantyne[22] absorbed the TQM ideas of bringing together quality, marketing and customer service, and labelled the resulting mixture **relationship marketing**. Although there is no consensus as to what relationship marketing constitutes (a study by Harker[23] revealed 26 definitions by a pantheon of authors), the general agreement is that relationship marketing means that organisations must be designed to enable them to pick up changes in the marketplace on a continuing basis. This is where the quality chain must be anchored.

This is the essence of what is termed **business process re-engineering**. For example, Toyota based its pioneering just-in-time (JIT) management system around the needs of customers. Work was reorganised to accommodate a variety of customer preferences in terms of the fastest possible response time and it is described as a system that delivers input to its production site at the rate and time it is needed. It thus reduces inventories within the firm and is a mechanism for regulating the flow of products between adjacent firms in the distribution system channel.

The notion of JIT has already been dealt with from a buyer behaviour point of view in Chapter 3. In this context it is argued that in a well-synchronised JIT manufacturing system, customer demands can be met and profits maintained or increased through a reduction in stockpiles and inventory levels which do not gain in value as they await the production process. In fact, they cost the organisation money in terms of financing an unproductive resource. In such a system the supplier and manufacturer relationship is critical and close associations must be developed. Typically this means a reduction in the number of suppliers and more long-term relationships. Rosenberg and Campbell[24] have said that salespeople spend less time selling and more time liaising between buyer, engineer and their own production management. This leads us to the notion of relationship selling which will be discussed later.

In contrast to the dynamics of the traditional marketing mix, which according to Peppers and Rogers[25] favours 'growth driven by mass marketing' and 'encourages businesses to chase short-term profits based on transaction volume', relationship marketing means that an organisation's marketing effort should be designed around a series of contacts with customers over time, rather than based on single transactions.

This means that more non-marketing people are involved in the process, and has led to the notion of what Gummesson[26] terms the *part-time marketer*, as these non-marketing people are increasingly brought into contact with customers at an operational level. He states that TQM has become an integrator between production orientation and marketing orientation, and the convergence of these two approaches towards the same goal aims to create customer-perceived quality and customer satisfaction.

This view is further supported by Clark and Fujimoto,[27] who contend that the traditionally held view of marketing is too assumption based and slow to respond to new customer demands. Traditional company and marketing structures are too hierarchical and rigid, and thus cannot respond to new segments or niches within a market. Clark and Fujimoto further state that in industries ranging from cars and computers to jet engines and industrial controls, new products are the focal point of competition. Developing high-quality products should be at the top of the competitive agenda for senior managers around the world.

Many companies now bring marketing into product development at a much earlier stage in the decision-making process. Temporary task forces are set up as project teams which involve personnel from different departments led by a team leader or project manager to oversee the introduction of new products. Such people are called **product champions** or **project champions**. In the automotive industry this normally starts at the design stage of a new vehicle when the product concept is being developed through initial brainstorming and lasts right through to the product's launch. As a result there is continuity of interest and impetus and it is not a matter of the project being 'handed over' to the next stage of the development through to launch process.

At a practical level the Department of Trade and Industry[28] have introduced what they term **best practice benchmarking (BPB)**. This involves an organisation forming a project team of people from multifunctional areas, such as marketing, production, quality and purchasing. The team's task is to obtain information about products or companies in their industry which have a higher level of performance or activity, and to identify areas in their own organisation that need improving. The team also needs to be given the facility for research on product development and quality. It is contended that the benefits of shared knowledge in such a multifunctional team mean that companies implementing BPB should find that this drives members of the team to meet new standards, or even to exceed them as discussed in Nissan's case (see box).

Total Quality Management

TQM is a key feature of Nissan's way of working. It involves making customer satisfaction top priority. Given this goal, everything the organisation and its people do is focused on creating high quality. To achieve this, Nissan has to:
- understand customer requirements
- consider the processes involved in providing quality, not just the end result
- prioritise and standardise tasks to deliver quality
- educate all employees to work in this way.

In practical terms TQM involves:
- identifying customers and their requirements
- establishing and using objectives (targets) for all areas of activity
- basing decisions on researched hard facts rather than on hunches
- identifying and eliminating the root causes of problems
- educating and training employees.

TQM is an ongoing process – a way of thinking and doing that requires an 'improvement culture' in which everyone looks for ways of doing better. Building this culture involves making everyone feel their contributions are valued and helping them to develop their capabilities.

A cycle of Plan, Do, Check, Action becomes part of every employee's thinking, because it represents Nissan's way of working.

Source: *http://www.thetimes100.co.uk/case_study* with permission

10.3 Reverse Marketing

At this juncture we reintroduce the concept of **reverse marketing**. The significance of this to the selling function is seen shortly. Reverse marketing has already been described in Chapter 3 (see Figure 3.7, p. 103). Although buyers have the purchasing power to initiate commercial transactions, it is traditionally the case within organisational buying situations that sellers tend to visit buyers, and this indeed forms the focus of this text. This is sometimes termed transactional marketing, where the emphasis is likely to be upon a single sale and the time horizon is usually short term. Quality is generally seen to be the concern of production and there tends to be an emphasis on product features and price.

To re-emphasise what was said earlier, the concept of reverse marketing occurs where buyers generally take the initiative and they source suppliers (sellers). This scenario is particularly applicable in retailing and in JIT manufacturing situations. JIT manufacturing has proved to be so economical and efficient that it will form an increasing trend in production line manufacturing situations where a relatively standardised product is being produced on a continuous basis. In this situation, buyers seek to source suppliers whom they will retain for a long period. The main criteria being sought from suppliers rest upon the quality of their goods and the reliability of their supplies as and when they are demanded. In JIT situations downtime on the production line resulting from faulty components or late delivery can prove very expensive. This view is supported by Deans and Rajagopal[29] who say that the cheapest component procured by driving hard bargains with multiple sources is not necessarily the least expensive in the long run. Once the cost of poor quality is factored in – down-time on the production line, rework, scrap, warranty work, legal fees, etc. – the cheapest may well prove to be the most costly.

Leenders and Blenhorn[30] state that many companies take a minimum of two years to achieve acceptable quality standards from suppliers in the situation just described. To discuss contracts for six months or one year is meaningless. Purchasing development costs must be recovered and this has to be done over longer periods of time. Suppliers and buyers form a long-term 'co-makership' agreement where both parties derive mutual benefits.

Kearney[31] conducted a wide-ranging study which concluded that the next wave of business improvement will not be obtained by looking at business in isolation, but by looking at the supply chain as a whole to find new opportunities to improve overall effectiveness. Additional areas of duplication and waste become evident and offer new sources of cost reduction. Service to the end customer can be driven to even higher standards by focusing the whole supply chain towards that goal, rather than diluting the efforts of individual companies through conflicting objectives. This broader vision is termed **supply chain integration (SCI)**.

Kearney concludes that closer relationships between suppliers and customers will become a competitive necessity. He does, however, caution that a naive belief in an ill-defined concept of partnership as a universal panacea will be counterproductive. A level of realism is required in SCI to take account of the practical difficulties of integration, the level of sophistication of the participants and the nature of competitive advantage and power within the supply chain. Each company has a different mix (or portfolio) of supply chain relationships operating at different levels and the key is to select the right one for the right supply chain.

The trend towards reverse marketing will gather momentum. Buyers as a group are becoming more professional and indeed such professionalism is needed in JIT purchasing situations. So how does a seller cope with buyer needs once the company is an 'in' supplier and a long-term relationship is anticipated? This brings us back to the notion of relationship marketing. Gronroos[32] argues that implementing the traditional view of marketing is unsatisfactory. He quotes the limitations of the four Ps and claims that other Ps, such as people and planning, have to be added in an attempt to cover new marketing perspectives. He agrees with the concept of a company basing its activities on customer needs and wants in target markets, but argues that this still smacks of production orientation since these ideas stem from the firm and not from the marketplace. His redefinition of marketing perhaps sums up the concept of reverse marketing and the resultant cognition of relationship marketing when he states: 'Marketing is to establish, maintain and enhance long-term customer relationships at a profit so that the objectives of the parties involved are met. This is done by a mutual exchange of promises.'

Building trade groups reject 'naive' partnership targets

Plans to step up the use of collaborative teams in construction projects ignore the need to integrate the wider supply chain, industry bodies have warned. There has been too much emphasis on forming integrated supply teams at the expense of understanding how to improve each organisation's individual supply chain.

This sentiment has been echoed by Brian Wilson, construction minister, who has called for the public sector to take a stronger lead in collaborative projects. 'We need teams and supply chains moving from one project to another, building up expertise that encourages innovation and a constant quest for better value,' he said.

Steven Ratcliffe, chief executive of the Construction Confederation has said: 'Each project will need to rely to some extent on local supply chains, which will be different from job to job.'

Source: Adapted from news item by Robin Parker, *Supply Management*, 18 July 2002, p. 10.

10.4   From Relationship Marketing to Relationship Selling

Cox, Hughes and Ralf[33] put forward a very interesting view from a procurement angle when they contend that substantial additional value could be secured in buyer–supplier relationships by placing a greater focus on the supply chain. From the purchasing point of view this involves an integrated approach to value acquisition from suppliers, value addition from manufacturing and value delivery to customers.

Added to this view is the fact that the most important feature of buyer–seller transactional relationships tends to revolve around price; indeed negotiation is one of the key issues in the sales presentation. However, a new view has emerged, based on the notion of **open accounting**. This kind of agreement is only possible when long-term relationships between buyers and sellers have been established in a typical JIT production situation. Here price negotiation does not feature in buyer–seller transactions because each side sees the other's price make-up. Buyers will have access to the seller's accounts in terms of the cost build-up for components or materials being supplied. These accounts will show the amount of material, labour and expenses plus overheads that have been incorporated into the cost of such products. As the term *open accounting* would suggest, complete open access is afforded. Equally, suppliers will have access to the manufacturer's accounts to conduct a similar analysis. A mutually acceptable margin for profit will then be agreed between the buyer and supplier so, in effect, the pricing element of the marketing mix has now become redundant, which perhaps gives additional credence to the earlier view relating to Gronroos's new definition of marketing.

All the above suggests that certain tactics are needed to implement relationship marketing. However, Slater and Narver[34] argue for a holistic concept of value: 'creating superior value for consumers requires a detailed understanding of the consumer's entire value chain (holistic needs), not only as it is today but also as it evolved over time (anticipated need).'

This type of marketing is about the strategic thinking that accompanies the new view of marketing brought about as a result of reverse marketing. It is contended that relationship selling concerns the tactical features of securing and building up the relationships implicit in relationship marketing. Thus, 'what establishes a firm's competitive advantages is their ability to serve customers' present and future needs (holistic needs)'.

Barnet *et al.*[35] observe striking differences between Western and Japanese approaches to the sharing of technological effort. In Europe, an average of 54 per cent of the approximate 6,800 engineering hours needed to produce a new model are contributed by subcontractors. In the USA only about 14 per cent of the 4,200 engineering hours needed are contributed by subcontractors. In Japan, the hours required to produce a new model are lower at 3,900 but about 72 per cent of those are supplied by subcontractors. The subcontractors' ability to participate in product design gives the Japanese customer the advantage of sharing the workload and reducing the time to market through what is called **simultaneous engineering**. In such a relationship it is common for the partners to provide access to shared technology.

Thus the role of marketing is changing. Selling is often viewed as a tactical arm of the marketing function and its role is also changing. In addition to the changes that have been identified so far, the marketing environment is changing in other ways. The penetration of the worldwide market by satellite and cable television means that 'blockbuster' promotional campaigns are becoming increasingly difficult to sustain owing to the fragmentation of viewers' patterns of watching television programmes. The increased abundance of channels had led to potential customers being dispersed into a wide variety of media audiences. Accordingly, the media are segmenting audiences more narrowly and, hence, it is more and more difficult to reach a wide audience through the same medium. Thus, in order to inform and persuade customers as well as to retain them, methods other than mass advertising ought to be given prominence.

Further, the massive increase in competition and increasing choice among customers in business and consumer markets coupled with increasing affluence in the last two decades has meant that customers have become, and continue to become, more sophisticated and demanding. Even when products offered are satisfactory, customers still seek and exercise their right to go from one supplier to another in order to purchase the products they need either at a better price, or merely to experience change and variety, as well as for many other reasons. Thus, brand loyalty has become more difficult to maintain.

Meanwhile, as the effectiveness of above-the-line media diminishes in general, so it will become a less attractive form of promotion for advertisers. Consequently, suppliers are considering different ways of keeping customers loyal to survive and prosper.

There will be a move towards below-the-line activity as more cost-effective campaigns can now be mounted through precisely targeted direct marketing approaches. This will lead to more effective ways of generating sales leads. 'Push' rather than 'pull' promotional techniques will become increasingly popular and, of course, a 'push' promotional strategy is very much the concern of the sales function. Whilst many suppliers, in particular retailers, have turned to such tactical devices as loyalty cards, other more visionary companies will be adopting a more strategic and philosophical approach to gaining customer loyalty through designing genuine relationship marketing programmes. This in turn implies a general increase in customer care programmes that can be viewed as an effective means of customer retention. Large companies, which might have viewed the unique selling proposition as being their 'winning card' when dealing with customers in the past, will be compelled to adopt more of a small business philosophy by staying adjacent to their customers in terms of understanding their needs and looking after them post-sale. Gronroos[36] contends that we are now experiencing, as a result of the growing awareness of the relationship marketing approach, a return to the natural systems-orientated way of managing customer relationships which existed before marketing became a 'clinical' decision-making discipline or an over-organised and isolated function.

Lancaster and Reynolds[37] suggest some of the activities that are increasingly becoming the responsibility of the sales function when they describe an expanded role for the modern salesperson. Some of the views of this enlarged role have been extended into what can now be regarded as a modern view of the tactics of relationship selling.

10.5   Tactics of Relationship Selling

Customer retention constitutes a prime objective of relationship selling. This can only be achieved in an organisational selling situation by having full regard to customers' needs and by working to form long and trustworthy relationships. In such situations it can be seen that the length of time individual salespersons stay in particular posts may well increase since buyers generally stay in their positions about twice as long as field salespeople. This new tendency has given rise to the associated concept of internal marketing, defined by Berry[38] as 'the means of applying the philosophy and practice of marketing to people who serve external customers so that (i) the best possible people can be employed and retained and (ii) they will do the best possible work.'

Just as in the case of external customers, there is a strong body of opinion that internal marketing should focus on long-term relationships and employee retention within company departments. Thus it is anticipated that under relationship selling circumstances the time individual salespeople spend in a particular post will move towards that of their purchasing counterparts. Why should this be the case? It can be postulated that buyers, because of the type of role they fulfil, have what may be termed a more 'sedate' occupational lifestyle than that of the traditional salesperson whose lifestyle 'on the road' can be quite hectic. Buyers are thus more 'settled' and stay in their posts longer. As buyers become more proactive in the marketplace under the system of reverse marketing, so their lifestyle will become more akin to that of the field salesperson. Although there is pressure to purchase effectively, this is different from the pressure to sell in terms of reaching sales targets and quotas in a given period.

At the same time, the role of the field salesperson will also experience a different kind of work pressure under reverse marketing. The pressure will focus on the longer-term goal of customer retention rather than sales targets and quotas. In fact, it is even contended that in such circumstances the traditional sales commission system might well disappear to be replaced by a higher basic salary plus bonuses shared by the expanded sales team whose ranks have been swelled by the concept of the part-time marketer. This might include production, quality and finance people, amongst others.

In their proposal of the 'virtuous circle', Reichheld and Schefter[39] advocate that the emphasis of this approach is placed on mechanisms which motivate employees to achieve as highly as possible. Hence, support mechanisms such as training programmes that enable employees to do their jobs to the best of their abilities are becoming of prime importance.

Different qualities will be required of field salespeople in relationship selling situations. There will be a move away from the qualities of salespeople that are quoted in Figure 13.1 (p. 385). The importance of features such as determination, self-motivation, resilience and tenacity, whilst still important when establishing long-term relationships, might well be overtaken by the greater relevance of features such as acceptability, attention to detail and a general ability to 'get along' with people on a long-term basis. To a certain extent the 'cut and thrust' that one traditionally associates with field selling positions will be supplanted by a calmer environment of working together as a team that includes members of both the salesperson's own company and the buyer's company.

Additionally, the attitudes of the buyer or customer towards the salesperson will also need to be taken into consideration. For instance, liking a specific salesperson will positively affect a buyer's attitude towards the products recommended by that person. However, caution must be exercised when interpreting selling relationships. Research by Kinniard[40] has shown that the sales role is attracting empathetic people who are not always successful because they mistake friendliness as meaning that a relationship has been established and naively anticipate that business will flow automatically.

Sales visits to individual customers are likely to be longer in duration and this will result in fewer individual sales calls being made. In fact, in some situations it can even be envisaged that there might well be somebody from the supplier's company permanently in place at the customer's company. This is already being practised by some high technology companies, for example those providing computer software and hardware to large retail organisations.

At a more practical level, the following two activities which currently tend to be regarded as ancillary to the task of selling will become more important: information gathering and servicing.

Information gathering

Information gathering in terms of collecting market information and intelligence is becoming an increasingly important part of the task of selling. Such information gathering feeds into the company's marketing information system as shown in Figure 10.2.

A company's **marketing information system (MkIS)** has three inputs: marketing research, market intelligence, and the company's own internal accounting system. These are inputs into the MkIS which captures the data on a database. Marketing research is provided by the marketing department from primary and secondary research and from commissioned survey data. The company's internal accounting system relates to sales analyses by customer purchases over periods of time by customer group, geographical area, size of order, and by any other combination that may be required. Market intelligence relates to information about competitors and the products and services they supply, plus information as to how they generally 'perform' with their customers. It also relates to the company's own customers.

Much of this intelligence comes from the company's own employees from executives, engineers, research personnel and more directly from field sales personnel who are extremely good collectors of market information and intelligence. The responsibility of salespeople as collectors of such information will expand and information technology skills will become increasingly important as individual salespeople interact in terms of input to and output from the MkIS as part of their routine activities. There is, of course, an output from the MkIS and this contributes to the strategic marketing planning system. Business in general is becoming more strategic and long term, and the MkIS is the principal data input into strategic marketing plans. The role of individual salespeople will become of more strategic value as their regular reports are incorporated into the MkIS, which in turn inputs into the organisation's longer term marketing plans. A formalised process for reporting this

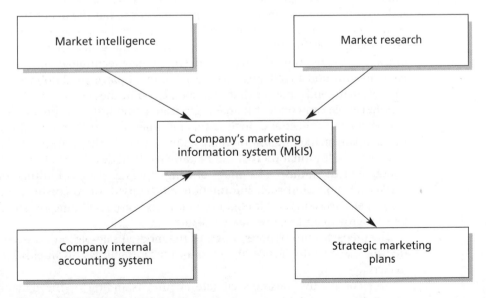

Figure 10.2 Marketing information system

information is an essential part of a contemporary marketing information system. It has already been mentioned that salespeople should be encouraged to send back information that is relevant to the marketing of the company's products to head office. In a lean manufacturing situation, the role of information gathering should be seen to be a prime part of the organisational salesperson's task.

It is widely acknowledged that the most effective form of marketing research is the personal interview and conducting research in this way provides the most accurate information as the interviewer is speaking directly with customers. It can, however, be an expensive form of interview because interviews take place at multiple times and locations. However, this expense is already covered when salespeople, as opposed to separate organisational marketing researchers, are encouraged to use the sales interview to gather marketing research data. It is also higher quality information as the salesperson has already established rapport with the customer, so responses will be more candid.

A number of advantages are associated with personal interviews in terms of being able to ask detailed questions, an ability to ask follow-up questions and the ability to use visual aids or samples. Respondents can be chosen who specifically comprise the target audience and they can also be called after the interview to verify or clarify what has been said in the research interview.

Concentrated markets are especially good for this kind of research as only a small number of competitors exist, and their activities can be easily investigated simply by asking buyers a few pertinent questions. Buyers will normally be willing to cooperate on the basis that divulging information, perhaps about competitors and how they perform against the salesperson's company, might mean that the salesperson's company will be able to offer the buyer an improved contract.

In fragmented markets that have many competitors it is often the case that Pareto's law exists whereby something like 80 per cent of total market revenues are accounted for by 20 per cent of the competition, so these are the 20 per cent that should be most closely investigated and the likelihood is that these are the customers whom salespeople visit on a more regular basis, e.g. in the computer industry there are hundreds of clone manufacturers, but the majority of the market is shared by manufacturers like HP/Compaq, IBM and Apple. It is, therefore, important to keep well informed about new and upcoming market players who might break into the big time through discovering a new technology or through aggressive marketing and advertising become a dominant player, and nobody is better able to spot such trends quicker than the salesperson in the field.

Salespeople can conduct marketing research amongst their organisational buyer customers and collect and analyse this information and then download this onto the company marketing information system for use in the strategic marketing planning process. Information that can be gathered includes information on the market structure of the industry, numbers of competitors as well as information on their market decisions and such information can be used for forecasting purposes and investment decisions and it might then lead to a more scientific assessment of competitive growth and relative market shares.

The preparation of reports is part of the modern salesperson's task, and presenting this market intelligence in a clear and meaningful way is important for policy makers.

In a competitive business climate an understanding of the dynamics of the market is an essential first step towards business success. A more precise assessment of product positioning based on an accurate market assessment is important along with a detailed understanding of consumer behaviour, motivation, needs and attitudes.

Such qualitative research on the part of salespeople means that the company can gain a greater insight into understanding how customers feel about their products alongside those of competitors, insights into buyer behaviour and feelings that might not come out in the course of a traditional sales interview and provide a vehicle through which the salesperson's company can benefit (i.e. through better market intelligence) and which will also benefit the customer (i.e. through the provision of a better designed and targeted service).

When monitored adequately, this process should be dynamic because interaction with customers is ongoing. The added benefits of such an integrated process include the following:

1 Reducing selling costs achieved through using information derived from the MkIS. New business response provides information to improve future targeting and, through experience of what works and what does not, improves the productivity of subsequent advertising and sales promotion.

2 More sales per customer, achieved through using customer case histories, leading to:
   • better identification and categorisation of customers
   • better segmentation and targeting
   • better presentation of relevant offers
   Identification of 'best customers' will determine future selling efforts; identify potential customers who warrant personal calls or special offers or even the type of representative who can best service each category of customer or enquirer.

3 Superior business forecasting achieved by:
   • analysing 'campaign' and customer case history data, using past performance as a guide to future performance
   • because the errors in past activities need not be repeated, efficiency should be subject to continuous improvement (control)

Servicing

Servicing is an area in which the role of the salesperson will become invaluable. This will include a certain amount of first-line servicing, so product application will be important as well as product knowledge, but what we refer to here is servicing in the broader sense of serving customers on a highly individualistic basis. The phenomenon of field sales personnel staying longer in such positions will provide them with more time to acquire such skills. Indeed, as highlighted by Reichheld, Mirkey and Hopton[41] employee retention is essential for profitability.

However, it is likely that such sales personnel will come from more technical backgrounds such as engineering or chemistry. Servicing will also include the provision of technical advice in relation to such matters as levels of quality, arranging after-sales service, establishing improved customer care programmes, and even offering consultancy services. More practical matters, such as agreeing delivery schedules, expediting individual orders and, occasionally, progressing payment for orders supplied, will also feature in this context. In JIT manufacturing situations the salesperson's company will form part of the supply chain, which stretches not only forwards to the end customer but also backwards towards the sources of prime manufacture, so buyers might need information from the salesperson's suppliers as part of the process of supply chain integration (SCI).

Swenson and Herche[42] used established scales as measures of salesperson performance and ascertained their ability or motivation to adapt their approach to meet customers' needs. The ability to become customer orientated as opposed to being sales orientated, and to determine whether or not the salesperson does actually use motivation to achieve the results that benefit both themselves and the customer, was ascertained. They concluded that the personal values of 'achievement', 'self-direction', 'self-respect' and 'self-accomplishment' were the key factors for successful salespeople. They further concluded that these social values could enhance the recruitment and selection of salespeople.

Does all of this suggest that the salesperson of the future will not need to be versed in any of the skills of selling? In a word, no. Prospecting skills will always be needed from leads that will be increasingly generated from direct marketing approaches rather than from cold calling. Skills of sales presentation will also be required in such circumstances. Negotiation skills too will still be needed. Communication skills have always been an important part of the field salesperson's armoury, but under traditional marketing such skills have been honed in such a way as to win orders through 'telling them what they want (or need) to know'. Under systems of reverse marketing, communications skills will still be essential, but the customer–salesperson dyad will be more in terms of equals than of an 'us and them' situation.

10.6   Conclusions

This chapter has examined current trends in the marketplace and looked at them in the context of likely future changes within the selling function.

It has traced the development of the movement towards relationship selling from its earliest roots based on quality issues through to the more mature notion of total quality management (TQM). In a more discerning marketplace customers desire and deserve the best in terms of quality. The selling implications of such expectations have been discussed.

Just-in-time (JIT) manufacturing is growing apace as a manufacturing technique, with the result that longer term selling relationships are becoming the norm. Traditional marketing is thus beginning to be replaced by reverse marketing, with buyers becoming more proactive in initiating commercial transactions, including long-term strategic relationships.

Relationship selling comprises the raft of sales tactics that actually delivers relationship marketing strategy to the company and to customers.

References

1 Drucker, P. (1973) *Management: Tasks, Responsibilities, Practices*, Harper & Row, New York, pp. 64–5.

2 Zineldin, M. (1999) 'Exploring the common ground of total relationship management (TRM) and total quality management (TQM)', *Management Decision*, 37(9), pp. 719–30.

3 Reyes Pacios Lozano, A. (2000) 'A customer orientation checklist: a model', *Library Review*, 49(4), pp. 173–8.

4 Kandampully, J. and Duddy, R. (1999) 'Relationship marketing: a concept beyond primary relationship', *Marketing Intelligence & Planning*, 17(7), pp. 315–23.

5 Rich, M.K. (2000) 'The direction of marketing relationships', *Journal of Business & Industrial Marketing*, 15(2/3), pp. 170–91.

6 Gummesson, E. (1991) 'Marketing orientation revisited: the crucial role of the part-time marketer', *European Journal of Marketing*, 25, pp. 60–75.

7 Aaker, D.A. (1996) *Building strong brands*, Free Press, New York.

8 Aaker, D.A. (1996) *Building strong brands*, Free Press, New York.

9 Taeger, D. (1992) '3Ms got it taped', *Total Quality Management*, December, pp. 353–5.

10 Aaker, D.A. (1996) *Building strong brands*, Free Press, New York.

11 Gronroos, C. (1994) 'Quo vadis marketing? Towards a relationship marketing paradigm', *Journal of Marketing Management*, 10, pp. 347–60.

12 Gummesson, E. (1999) *Total Relationship Marketing*, Butterworth-Heinemann, Oxford.

13 Gronroos, C. (1994) 'Quo vadis marketing? Towards a relationship marketing paradigm', *Journal of Marketing Management*, 10, pp. 347–60.

14 Gummesson, E. (1991) 'Marketing orientation revisited: the crucial role of the part-time marketer', *European Journal of Marketing*, 25, pp. 60–75.

15 Schill, R.L. and McArthur, D.N. (1992) 'Redefining the strategic competitive unit towards a new global marketing paradigm', *International Marketing Review*, 9(3), pp. 5–23.

16 Stalk, G., Evans, P. and Schulman, L.E. (1992) 'Competing capabilities: the new rules of corporate strategy', *Harvard Business Review*, March–April, pp. 57–69.

17 Walters, D. and Lancaster, G. (1999) 'Value and information – concepts and issues for management', *Management Decision*, 37(8), pp. 643–56.

18 Zineldin, M. (1999) 'Exploring the common ground of total relationship management (TRM) and total quality management (TQM)', *Management Decision*, 37(9), pp. 719–30.

19 Sasaki, T. (1991) 'How the Japanese accelerated new car development', *Long Range Planning*, 24, p. 17.

20 Zineldin, M. (2000) 'Beyond relationship marketing: technologicalship marketing', *Marketing Intelligence & Planning*, 18(1), pp. 9–23.

21 Brooks, R. and Wragg, T. (1992) 'Channelling customer loyalty', *Total Quality Management*, December, pp. 361–3.

22 Christopher, M., Payne, A. and Ballantyne, D. (1991) *Relationship Marketing*, Butterworth-Heinemann, Oxford.

23 Harker, M. J. (1999) 'Relationship marketing defined? An examination of current relationship marketing definitions', *Marketing Intelligence & Planning*, 17(1), pp. 13–20.

24 Rosenberg, L.J. and Campell, D.P. (1985) 'Just-in-time inventory control: a subset of channels', *Journal of the Academy of Marketing*, 13, pp. 124–33.

25 Peppers, D. and Rogers, M. (1999) 'Is your company ready for one-to-one marketing?' *Harvard Business Review*, 77(1), January/February, pp. 151–60.

26 Gummesson, E. (1991) 'Marketing orientation revisited: the crucial role of the part-time marketer', *European Journal of Marketing*, 25, pp. 60–75.

27 Clark, K.B. and Fujimoto, T. (1990) 'The power of product integrity', *Harvard Business Review*, November–December, p. 107.

28 Department of Trade and Industry (1993) *Best Practice Benchmarking*, DTI Publications, London.

29 Deans, K. and Rajagopal, S. (1991) 'Effective purchasing management', *Purchasing and Supply Management*, March, p. 15.

30 Leenders, M.R. and Blenhorn, D.L. (1998) *Reverse Marketing: the New Buyer–Seller Relationship*, Free Press, New York.

31 Kearney, A.T., Consultants (1994) *Partnership of Power Play*.

32 Gronroos, C. (1990) 'Marketing redesigned', *Management Decision*, 28(8), pp. 5–9.

33 Cox, A., Hughes, J. and Ralf, M. (1995) 'Influencing the strategic agenda: the challenge for purchasing leadership', *Purchasing and Supply Management*, pp. 36–41.

34 Slater, S.F. and Narver, J.C. (1994) 'Does competitive environment moderate the market orientation-performance relationship?' *Journal of Marketing*, 58, January, pp. 46–55.

35 Barnet, H., Hibbert, R., Curtiss, J. and Sculthorpe-Pike, M. (1995) 'The Japanese system of subcontracting', *Purchasing and Supply Management*, December, pp. 22–6.

36 Gronroos, C. (1994) 'Quo vadis marketing? Towards a relationship paradigm', *Journal of Marketing Management*, 10, pp. 347–60.

37 Lancaster, G.A. and Reynolds, P. (1998) *Marketing*, Butterworth-Heinemann, Oxford, pp. 229–30.

38 Berry, L.L. (1983) 'Relationship marketing', in Berry, L.L., Shostack, G.L. and Opah, G. (eds), *Emerging Perspectives on Services Marketing*, American Marketing Association, Chicago, IL.

39 Reichheld, F. and Schefter, P. (2000), 'E-loyalty', *Harvard Business Review*, July/August, pp. 105–13.

40 Kinniard, R.W. (1993) *How Europe Sells – Measuring the Effectiveness of the Field Sales Force*, R.W. Kinniard, Glasgow.

41 Reichheld, F., Mirkey Jr, R. and Hopton, C. (2000) 'The loyalty effect – the relationship between loyalty and profits', *European Business Journal*, 12(3), p. 134.

42 Swenson, J. and Herche, J. (1994) 'Social values and salesperson performance: an empirical examination', *Journal of the Academy of Marketing Science*, 22(3), pp. 283–9.

Practical Exercise

Microcom

When the buyer moves on does the relationship end?

Relationship marketing plays a significant role in modern sales management. Companies have for some time realised the benefits of practising a relational approach to selling rather than a transactional one. Nevertheless, many markets are volatile or else have long product life-cycles, which make the practice of relationship selling challenging.

James Vinewood is Managing Director of Microcom, a firm based in the UK that produces high-quality broadcasting equipment used by national networks such as the BBC, ITV and their equivalents abroad. The product is chiefly customised to customers' specific requirements and has a 10 to 15 year life. Mr Vinewood is troubled by the fact that at present the firm practises a largely transactional approach to selling. He is keen to adopt a relational selling approach, but is uncertain how he might achieve this. He suggests: 'A relationship is between people. The problem we have is when a company we have previously sold to requires new equipment and the original buyer has often left to go to another job, been promoted away from the buying function, retired, or in some circumstances may even have died.'

Although Mr Vinewood is keen to adopt a relational selling approach, his major reservation is that 'Relationship marketing cannot work because you can guarantee the places we sold to this year won't be in the market to buy again for 15–20 years.'

Typically Microcom will design and install the equipment (a process that can last anywhere between two months for small projects and up to three years for larger ones) and will then maintain contact with the customer for a time afterwards to ensure that the system is effective. These systems typically last for anywhere between 15 and 20 years before they must be replaced. There are generally a number of small orders that may crop up in the interim, but Microcom often does not bother with such minor orders as it typically needs a minimum of £20 million worth of business a year, which means that it usually only bids for the large orders. At present, however, Microcom has a poor retention record, with a rate of around 30 per cent, despite the fact that customers claim to be highly satisfied with the equipment and level of service provided by the firm.

Source: Written by Andrew Pressey, Lecturer in Marketing, University of East Anglia and Neville Hunt, Lecturer in Marketing, University of Luton.

Discussion Questions

1 Advise Mr Vinewood on the appropriateness of adopting a relational approach to selling.

2 Suggest and justify tactics that could be used.

Practical Exercise

Midlands Switchgear Limited

Midlands Switchgear Limited is a large manufacturing concern based in Wolverhampton. It was founded in 1904 and owed its initial growth to the expansion of tramway services in the early part of the twentieth century.

Today, the company relies largely upon sales to the regional electricity companies and to National Power and PowerGen, the national generators. Its products are widely used in the electricity distribution network, namely in electricity substations. It manufactures switchgear, but many of the component parts are bought in. Such bought-in components include current transformers, relays, switches and the cabinets in which they are housed. The company operates a sourcing policy of two preferred suppliers from a pool of five for each component that is purchased. This is to ensure continuity of supply in an industry that now demands 'instant' response. This is a trend that has become particularly prevalent since the privatisation of the electricity industry in the early 1990s.

The purchasing department is responsible for routine procurement, but inputs to the purchase decision such as to which suppliers to use come from the following personnel:

- Phil Stonehouse BSc (electrical engineering) who is the Commercial Director. He is responsible for sales and marketing, contracts and transportation.

- Martin Gilbert BSc (electrical engineering) and member of the Institute of Electrical Engineers, who is Director of Engineering. He is responsible for engineering and product design.

- Roy Young BSc (electrical engineering) and PhD (electronics) who is also a member of the Institute of Electrical Engineers. He is Technical Director, responsible for product development and acts as a 'troubleshooter' for customers' technical queries.

- Harold Charlesworth, a qualified member of the Chartered Institute of Management Accountants. He is in overall charge of the financial function, but his specialist input in this context is in the areas of budget setting and costing.

The domestic UK market for the company's products is not regarded as being particularly price sensitive. UK manufacturers have traditionally been sheltered from European and other competition by several non-tariff barriers. The principal one has been the ability of switchgear manufacturers to provide service backup at four hours' notice. The physical nature of power distribution in the UK differs from many other countries, including those in the European Union. Although there is no 'official' non-tariff barrier, the technicalities that must be understood and the infrastructure that must be developed before non-UK competitors can compete, can be quite daunting.

When purchasing components for switchgear, the following considerations are particularly important:

- customer specifications as to the manufacturer of instrumentation
- quality of products which usually means purchasing from 'approved' suppliers
- service and spares availability
- prompt delivery record
- price considerations

Discussion Questions

1 What are the drawbacks to the decision-making unit at Midlands Switchgear Limited from:

   (a) Midland Switchgear's viewpoint?

   (b) the viewpoint of a prospective company wishing to become an 'approved' supplier?

2 What do you feel are the main commercial threats facing Midlands Switchgear Limited? Having identified these threats, how do you feel the company should best reorganise to overcome these threats?

3 From the viewpoint of a company wishing to sell relays to Midlands Switchgear Limited, draw up an outline sales strategy of how you would approach the company.

Practical Exercise

Focus Wickes – 'Fusion': Winners, 2004 Retail Week Supply Chain Initiative Award

Mergers may bring long-term business benefits, but short-term there are problems with disparate IT systems and corporate culture. For Focus Wickes, with three major mergers in five years, streamlining supplier relations is a key priority – which is where the system termed Eqos that has been specifically produced for this task helps.

Giving them the tools

Focus Wickes has labelled its new supplier relationship initiative 'Fusion'. In the past five years the DIY chain has grown dramatically, acquiring Do It All in 1998 and both Great Mills and Wickes in 2000, to become the UK's second largest home improvements chain. Today there are more than 270 Focus outlets, including a dozen or so trading under the discount 'No Frills' fascia, and some 161 Wickes stores.

'Fusing' the inevitable disparate IT systems resulting from such expansion has been a major consideration in recent years. So, too, has been the need to build a coherent corporate culture that melds good supplier relations with a customer-centric strategy. 'We have seen something of a cultural revolution in the past few years,' says Justin Farrington-Smith, trading director for the Focus division. 'We're now giving much greater emphasis to understanding customer needs and also working more closely with suppliers.'

Wickes had been an early enthusiast for collaborative working, implementing the GXS TIE system back in 1998. 'We'd had several colleague changes since then,' explains Scott Holland, Supply Chain Development Controller, 'and the system had been poorly maintained so we felt it was time to take a fresh approach.' Around 98 per cent of Wickes' product assortment is own-label, so the company has always tended to work very closely with suppliers to develop new lines and share sales forecasts. What it wanted from the new tool was better communications to help cut lead times and improve 'on-shelf' availability, as well as something that could help suppliers become more involved in assortment planning and ranging, as the group moved towards a more structured category management model.

In recent months Wickes has aligned its business into three broad business units: 'Trade', 'DIY & Garden' and 'Showroom' – the sort of complete kitchens and bathrooms that tend to be delivered direct to customers. The aim was for the new integrated category teams, which make up the business units, to collaborate even more closely with suppliers. 'We needed something that would be simple for our suppliers to use, easy to link into their own IT systems and would also give us more flexibility in reporting,' recalls Fusion Project Manager Denis Antippa.

Why Eqos?

In August 2002 the company established a project group, bringing together a dozen suppliers, as well as representatives from both Focus and Wickes to define the requirements of the planned supplier relations platform. The resulting request for information was sent to twelve IT vendors of whom six were then invited to tender. 'In December 2002 we decided to go with Eqos' technology,' says Holland. 'It best matched our current and future requirements with good flexibility, rapid implementation and, importantly, the ability to work with a wide range of IT systems so it would be easy for both our suppliers and the different parts of the Focus Wickes group to integrate.'

Implementing an adaptable platform

Rather than putting in place a number of packaged solutions, Focus Wickes wanted an extensive, adaptable platform that would enable a series of collaborative SRM solutions, from performance monitoring through to new product development and vendor managed inventory.

The company signed a three-year agreement with Eqos to develop three operational modules with the flexibility to decide precisely which functions these would address as the system developed and users on both side of the trading partnership began to understand the options. This total platform has been called 'Fusion' with the first of the modules addressing product performance management (PPM). Work began in mid-March 2003, with the PPM component completed in 17 weeks and with 145 of Wickes' 150 suppliers live on the system by August.

'Fusion is one of the fastest business system deployments that we have undertaken in recent years. We did this through running a series of workshops and training sessions for suppliers,' says Denis Antippa. 'As the Eqos system is web-browser based it was very easy to use and most people didn't even need to read the manual.' The system is driven by daily downloads of store-level sales and stock data from both Focus and Wickes outlets. This is then consolidated centrally and input into Fusion, which is hosted by Eqos.

Consolidating data across the group can be especially helpful for those vendors selling to both divisions. Suppliers can access store and depot level information about their products to check sell-through rates, delivery performance and forecasts. Lines selling better than forecast are automatically highlighted with alerts e-mailed to relevant buyers and suppliers. This alerting system is a key aspect of Fusion usability.

Fusion is already initiating dialogue between suppliers and category managers to improve forecasts and streamline deliveries. As familiarity with the system increases, suppliers of items which go direct to stores, mostly heavy or bulky goods such as sacks of cement or garden sheds, are expected to play a greater part in helping store managers revise order quantities based on better supply chain visibility.

The benefits

Indications are that Fusion will help increase sales and margins in the first full year of operations by around 0.5 per cent, while stock-outs are on target to reduce by some 20 per cent. There are likely to be significant savings in logistics, as well as avoidance of overstocking. It all adds up to a likely annual saving of around £10 million across the group.

'Our suppliers are becoming much more proactive,' says Holland, 'and they've been able to use the information from Fusion to improve their own production schedules which they weren't able to do with the old TIE system. In future we might see a move to vendor managed inventory and greater use of collaborative planning, forecasting and replenishment techniques.'

At Focus, which began to roll-out the system to suppliers a month or so after Wickes, similar trends are starting to emerge. 'Suppliers can now see this information and suggest amendments based on greater visibility of supply chain and demand patterns,' says Jan Wilson, Focus Business Analyst. Like Wickes, Focus is moving to category management and has reorganised into business units 'Decorative', 'Home enhancement', 'Garden & Pets', and 'Core DIY' with some 26 category teams comprising planners, merchandisers, marketers and buyers.

Nearly 200 of the 220 Focus suppliers are live with Fusion. 'We've had very positive feedback,' says Farrington-Smith. 'This has really been a fundamental change in the way we work with our suppliers and it is very significant.' Currently suppliers only have access to their individual product performance data via Fusion, but in time greater involvement with overall category activity is likely.

Focus and Wickes are now conducting further workshops with their suppliers to decide on the next modules for Fusion. Among the possibilities are collaborative product development techniques and an 'open order book' system that would give all involved better visibility of the progress and status of purchase orders to help rid the supply chain of those all-too-familiar 'black holes'. 'We want our suppliers to drive much of the development,' says Holland, 'and they're already coming back to us with ideas for the next stage. The 'open order book' concept, for example, is something that they're suggesting.' At Focus, this new spirit of collaboration is already helping to realign the strategic business model. 'Traditionally Focus has sold largely branded merchandise,' says Farrington-Smith, 'but we'd like to move to around 30 per cent own-label in the near future and that means we must work more closely with suppliers.'

Source: *www.thetimes100.co.uk/case_study* with permission

Discussion Question

What would be the implications of Focus Wickes moving to 50 per cent own-label merchandise within the next year from the viewpoints of:
- end customers
- sales staff
- suppliers?

Examination Questions

1 Discuss the implications of the move towards relationship marketing in organisational buying/selling situations in the context of how this might change the role of selling.

2 Total quality management is a philosophy of management that should permeate every aspect of the organisation and not simply be the concern of production. What is meant by this statement in terms of how TQM can affect the selling function?

3 Describe the key elements of a customer care programme that would be appropriate in a manufacturing or service environment with which you are familiar.

4 What are the implications for salespeople of the adoption of supply chain integration by larger manufacturers?

11 Direct Marketing

Objectives

After studying this chapter you should be able to:

1. Understand the meaning of direct marketing
2. Appreciate the reasons for growth in direct marketing activity
3. Understand the nature of database marketing
4. Know how to manage a direct marketing campaign
5. Know the media used in direct marketing

Key Concepts

- business-to-business lists
- campaign management
- catalogue marketing
- consumer lifestyle lists
- consumer lists
- the creative brief
- database marketing

- direct mail
- direct marketing
- direct response advertising
- house list
- mailing houses
- mobile marketing
- telemarketing

A major change that is reshaping the face of selling is the growth of direct marketing. This chapter explores the major changes that are taking place, the key tools that can be used and how the direct marketing process can be effectively managed. It begins by explaining the meaning of direct marketing before discussing the use of database marketing. The management of direct marketing activities will then be explored, including setting objectives, targeting, achieving customer retention and creating action plans.

11.1 What is Direct Marketing?

Direct marketing attempts to acquire and retain customers by contacting them without the use of an intermediary. The objective is to achieve a direct response which may take one of the following forms:

- a purchase over the telephone or by post
- a request for a catalogue or sales literature
- an agreement to visit a location/event (e.g. an exhibition)
- participation in some form of action (e.g. joining a political party)
- a request for a demonstration of a product
- a request for a salesperson's visit

Direct marketing, then, is the distribution of products, information and promotional benefits to target consumers through interactive communication in a way which allows response to be measured. It covers a wide array of methods, including the following:

- direct mail
- telemarketing (both inbound and outbound)
- direct response advertising (coupon response or 'phone now')
- electronic media (internet, interactive cable TV)
- catalogue marketing
- inserts (leaflets in magazines)
- door-to-door leafleting
- text messaging (see box on p. 332)

Direct marketing has experienced growth in usage in Europe. Figure 11.1 illustrates its use in some European countries.

Smith outlines five factors that have fuelled the rise in direct marketing activity:[1]

1 *Market fragmentation.* The trend towards market fragmentation has limited the application of mass marketing techniques. As market segments develop, the capacity of direct marketing techniques to target distinct consumer groups is of increasing importance.

2 *Computer technology.* The rise in accessibility of computer technology and increasing sophistication of software, allowing the generation of personalised letters and messages, has eased the task of direct marketing.

3 *The list explosion.* The increased supply of lists and their diversity (e.g. 25,000 Rolls Royce owners, 20,000 women executives and 100,000 house improvers) has provided the raw data for direct marketing activities.

Millions of euros

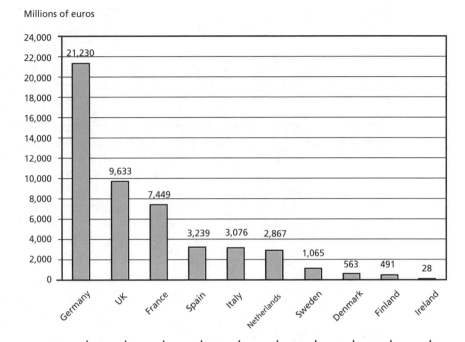

Direct marketing expenditure per capita (euro) 2002

Figure 11.1 Expenditure on direct marketing in Europe
Source: Adapted from Direct Marketing Expenditure and Direct Marketing Expenditure per capita, *European Marketing Pocket Book 2005*, World Advertising Research Centre, Henley-on-Thames. Reprinted with permission.

4 *Sophisticated analytical* techniques. By using geodemographic analysis, households can be classified into neighbourhood type (e.g. 'modern private housing, young families' or 'private flats, single people'). These in turn can be cross-referenced with product usage, media usage and lifestyle statements.

5 *Co-ordinated marketing systems.* The high costs of personal selling have led an increasing number of companies to take advantage of direct marketing techniques such as direct response advertising and telemarketing, to make the salesforce more cost effective. For example, a coupon response advertisement or direct mail may generate leads that can be screened by outbound telemarketing, or inbound telemarketing can provide the mechanism for accommodating enquiries stimulated by other direct marketing activities.

As with all marketing communications, direct marketing campaigns should be integrated both within themselves and with other communication tools such as advertising, publicity and personal selling. Uncoordinated communication leads to blurred brand images, low impact and customer confusion. The capability of direct marketing to transform markets is discussed in the boxed case history.

How direct marketing can change markets

The three classic cases of how direct marketing can transform markets are Dell Computers, First Direct's entry into banking and Direct Line's move into insurance.

Dell Computers was founded in 1984 by Michael Dell in the USA. His conception was to challenge existing players in the computers market by establishing a direct marketing operation that would allow customers to dial Dell to place an order for a computer. The computer, which was based upon customer specification, would be sent direct, eliminating the need for a distributor. Just-in-time production means that computers can be manufactured in four hours. Dell moved into internet marketing in 1996 and achieved over £14 million worth of web-enabled revenue per day in 1999.

First Direct moved into telephone banking in 1989. Its success was based on customer dissatisfaction with traditional branch banks that offered short opening hours, queues and bank charges. By centralising banking operations and offering direct access by telephone, First Direct was able to offer high levels of customer service at low cost. The new service offered 24-hour access and free banking. The operation has proved to be a huge success, with the number of customers far exceeding target and the highest level of customer satisfaction of any bank.

Direct Line saw a market opportunity in motor insurance. Traditional insurance companies used insurance brokers situated in towns and cities to provide the link to customers. Direct Line placed advertisements on television and in the print media to persuade prospects to phone their telemarketing operation with the inducement of a much cheaper quotation. The entire transaction is conducted over the telephone with the form being sent to the customer simply for signature. By eliminating the broker, Direct Line's cost structure enables it to reduce costs and pass on some of the savings to its customers. The success of its motor insurance has led the company to move into related areas such as home and contents insurance.

11.2   Database Marketing

Much direct marketing activity requires accurate information on customers so that they can be targeted through direct mail or telemarketing campaigns. This information is stored on a marketing database which comprises an electronic filing cabinet containing a list of names, addresses and transactional behaviour. Information such as types of purchase, frequency of purchase, purchase value and responsiveness to promotional offers may be held in the database. This allows future campaigns to be *targeted* at those people who are most likely to respond. For example, a special offer on garden tools from a mail order company can be targeted at those people who have purchased gardening products in the past. Another example would be a car dealer, which by holding a database of customer names and addresses and dates of car purchases could direct mail to promote service offers and new model launches.

A marketing database can also be used to strengthen relationships with customers. For example, Highland Distillers switched all of its promotional budget for its Macallan whisky brand from advertising to direct marketing. It built a database of 100,000 of its more frequent drinkers (those who consume at least five bottles a year), mailing them every few months with interesting facts about the brand, whisky memorabilia and offers.[2]

The UK supermarket Tesco has built a huge database through its successful loyalty card called Tesco Clubcard. The database is used to define market segments such as discount-driven 'price sensitives', 'foodies', 'heavy category users' and 'brand loyalists', testing response to promotions, and testing the effects of different prices. It is also used to target promotions, for example, targeting dog food offers to dog owners, sending direct mail to specific segments such as 'healthy living' types and tailoring email campaigns. Product assortments in stores can also be fine-tuned according to the buying habits of customers.[3]

A customer profile can be built up by including postcodes in the addresses of customers and employing the services of an agency that conducts geodemographic analysis, such as A Classification of Residential Neighbourhoods (ACORN). Direct mail can then be targeted at people with similar geodemographic profiles.

Database marketing is defined as an interactive approach which uses individually addressable marketing media and channels (such as mail, telephone and the salesforce) to:

(a) provide information to a target audience

(b) stimulate demand

(c) stay close to customers by recording and storing an electronic database memory of customers, prospects and all communication and transactional data.[4]

Typical information stored on a database includes the following:

1 *Information on actual and potential customers.* Basic data such as names, addresses and telephone numbers enable customers to be contacted. This may be supplemented by psychographic and behavioural data. In business-to-business markets, information on key decision-makers and their choice criteria may be held.

2 *Transactional information.* Such information as frequency of purchase, when the customer last bought and how much was bought for each product category may be stored. Cross-analysing this type of data with customer type can throw light on the customer profile most likely to buy a particular product and communications can be targeted accordingly.

3 *Promotional information.* Data covering what promotional campaigns have been run, customer response patterns and results in terms of contact, sales and profiles can be stored on a marketing database.

4 *Product information.* Information relating to which products have been promoted, how, when, where and associated responses can be held.

5 *Geodemographic information*. Information about the geographical areas of customers and prospects and the social, lifestyle or business categories to which they belong can be stored. By including postcodes in the addresses of customers and employing the services of an agency that conducts geodemographic analysis (such as ACORN) a customer profile can be built up. Direct mail can then be targeted at people with similar geodemographic profiles.

The importance of database marketing is reflected in its applications:

1 *Direct mail*. A database can be used to store customer information for mailings.

2 *Telemarketing*. A database can store telephone numbers of customers and prospects. Also when customers contact the supplier by telephone, relevant information can be held, including when the next contact should be made.

3 *Loyalty marketing*. Highly loyal customers can be drawn from the database for special treatment as a reward for their loyalty.

4 *Campaign planning*. The database can be used as a foundation for sending consistent and co-ordinated campaigns and messages to individuals and businesses.

5 *Target marketing*. Specific groups of individuals or businesses can be targeted as a result of analysing the database. For example, customer behaviour data stored by supermarkets can be used to target special promotions to consumers who are likely to be receptive to them, such as a promotion for wine aimed at wine purchasers exclusively.

6 *Distributor management systems*. A database can be the foundation upon which information is supplied to distributors and their performance monitored.

7 *Marketing evaluation*. By recording responses to marketing mix activities, for example, price promotions, special offers on products and direct mail messages, the effectiveness of different approaches to varying consumers and market segments can be evaluated.

QL Skincare 4U

Text messaging is set to become a tool in the marketing of cosmetics to its largest growing sector. Shiseido is set to use the favourite communication method of teens to sell them its revamped 'Pureness' range. Join the Puretext Club by texting the word Pure to 07887 926101, and beauty tips and special offers on Shiseido products will be sent directly to your mobile. Aimed at young women, 'Pureness' combats problems such as blemishes, enlarged pores and shine.

Source: *Sunday Times* 'Style Supplement', 1 September 2002, p. 41.

11.3   Managing a Direct Marketing Campaign

The starting point for **campaign management** is the marketing plan: direct marketing should be fully integrated with all marketing and promotional mix elements to provide a coherent marketing strategy. In particular direct marketers must understand how the product is being positioned in the marketplace in terms of its target market (where it is to compete) and differential advantage (how it is to compete). These issues will fundamentally affect who the campaign is targeted at and the persuasive messages used to convince the target consumer to buy. Figure 11.2 displays the stages in managing a direct marketing campaign.

Identifying and understanding the target audience

The target audience is the group of individuals at which the direct marketing campaign is aimed. For consumer markets the target audience may be described using market segmentation variables such as age, gender, social class and lifestyle. Of particular importance is the use of geodemographic bases for segmenting consumers. Population census data are used to classify households according to a wide range of variables such as household size, number of cars, occupation, family size and ethnic background. Using statistical techniques, small geodemographic areas (known as enumeration districts in the UK) are formed that share similar characteristics.

Figure 11.2 Managing a direct marketing campaign

ACORN, the best known system, describes different groups of households as Thriving, Expanding, Rising, Settling, Aspiring and Striving. Since each household in each group can be identified by its postcode (zip code), direct mail can be targeted at selected groups.

For business markets, the target audience will be described as the type of organisation that the direct marketer wishes to target and the type of individual within each organisation who should be reached. The first type of decision will be aided by segmentation based on such variables as organisational size, industry type, degree of purchasing centralisation, location and organisational innovativeness. Choosing the type of individual to select within the organisation will usually be based on an analysis of the decision-making unit (see Chapter 3). Often targeting will then be based on job title.

Once the target audience has been defined, a list is required which may be obtained from an in-house database or through an external broker. For example, in business markets, companies such as Kompass, and Dun and Bradstreet will provide adhesive labels with names and addresses drawn up to client specifications to facilitate direct mail campaigns. Direct marketers need to be aware of the possibility that mailing or telephone lists may be out of date or inaccurate.

Direct marketers also need to understand the buyer behaviour of the target audience. David Ogilvy, a famous advertising guru, once wrote 'never sell to a stranger'. What he meant by this was the importance of understanding the needs and purchasing behaviour of the target audience. In particular, understanding the needs and choice criteria of targeted individuals aids message development. For example, if we understand that price is an important choice criterion for our chosen target audience, we can stress the outstanding value for money of our direct marketing offer.

Setting campaign objectives

Campaign objectives can be set in different ways:

1 Financial objectives
   e.g. sales volume and value
        profit
        return on investment

2 Communication objectives
   e.g. awareness
        stimulate trial
        positioning of brand in consumers' minds
        remind and reinforce

3 Marketing objectives
   e.g. customer acquisition
        customer retention
        lead/enquiry generation
        number of orders
        response rate (proportion of contacts responding)

Despite this spread of possible objectives it is true to say that direct marketing usually is more concerned with making a sale – with immediate action – than with advertising. Linked to this objective is the acquisition and retention of customers. Acquiring new customers is usually much more costly than retaining existing ones.[5] Also maintaining customer loyalty has the additional advantage that loyal customers repeat purchase, advocate brands to their friends, pay less attention to competitive brands and often buy product line extensions.[6] Therefore, direct marketers should pay at least as much attention to retaining existing customers (and generating sales from them) as using tools such as direct mail and telemarketing to gain new customers.

When calculating the resources to be used to create new customers, the concept of lifetime value should be used. This is a measure of the profits of customers over their expected life with a company. Where lifetime value is high it can pay to invest heavily in customer acquisition, particularly if customers once attracted tend to stay loyal. This is why banks invest heavily in attracting students who in the short term do not have great value but over their lifetime are a very attractive proposition.

Equally, companies are paying considerable attention to retaining customers. This objective has spawned customer loyalty programmes such as frequent flyer schemes (airlines) and loyalty cards (supermarkets).

Creative decisions

Given that a usual objective of direct marketing is immediate sales generation, recipients of messages (particularly through direct mail and telemarketing) need to perceive a clear benefit in responding. As we saw in the boxed example, Direct Line grew its business by establishing a real customer benefit – substantial cost savings – communicated through direct response advertising and a highly efficient telemarketing scheme. In order to achieve their level of success, companies need to produce an effective **creative brief** which includes the following:

1 *Communication objectives*. This spells out what the campaign is hoping to achieve, such as sales volume and value, number of orders, customer retention and/or acquisition and lead generation.

2 *Target market analysis*. Target consumers will be identified, profiled and their needs and buyer behaviour analysed. This is essential so that the creative team adopts the Ogilvy philosophy of never selling to a stranger.

3 *Brand benefits (and weaknesses)*. The customer benefits that the brand's features create need to be identified. Features can be linked to benefits by the use of phrases like 'which results in' or 'which means that'. Any differential advantages need to be identified through an analysis of competitor brands' strengths and weaknesses.

4 *Development of the offer*. Potential offers should be pre-tested with the target audience to establish their attractiveness. This can take the form of small-scale individual tests or through the use of group discussions. Offers may be price related or take the form of free gifts (e.g. a free telephone/radio alarm to people taking out insurance).

5 *Message communication*. In direct mail the offer can be communicated by the envelope as well as the internal contents. Recipients must also be told clearly

how to respond. Including a freephone number as well as the usual freepost envelope can increase response by between 50 and 125 per cent.[7] In telemarketing, scripts are often used to communicate messages. When combined with powerful software and information technology, they can provide an efficient means of communicating with target consumers.

6 *Action plan.* An action plan focusing on when the campaign is to run, how often and recommendations regarding the most appropriate media to use needs to be drawn up. For telemarketing campaigns, practical details like how many operators are required and at what times need to be decided.

Media decisions

The direct marketer has a range of media that can be used to reach target audiences. Direct mail, telemarketing, direct response advertising and catalogue marketing will now be analysed. A fifth type of media – the internet – will be examined in Chapter 12.

Direct mail

Direct mail is material sent by post to a home or business address with the purpose of promoting a product and/or maintaining an ongoing relationship. An important factor in the effectiveness of a direct mail campaign is the quality of the mailing list. List houses supply lists on a rental or purchase basis. Since lists become out of date quickly it is usually preferable to rent. **Consumer lists** may be compiled from sub-scriptions to magazines, catalogues, membership of organisations, etc. Alternatively, **consumer lifestyle lists** are compiled from questionnaires. The electoral roll can also be useful when combined with geodemographic analysis. For example, if a company wished to target households living in modern private housing with young families, the electoral roll can be used to provide names and addresses of people living in such areas.

Business-to-business lists may be bought from directory producers such as the Kompass or Key British Enterprises directories, from trade magazine subscription lists (e.g. *Chemicals Monthly* or *Purchasing Managers' Gazette*), or from exhibition lists (e.g. *Which Computer Show*). Perhaps the most productive mailing list is that of a company's own customers which is known as the **house list**. This is because of the existing relationship that a company enjoys with its own customers. Also of use would be names of past buyers who have become inactive, names of enquirers and of those who have been 'referred' or recommended by present customers of the company. It is not uncommon for a house list to be far more productive than an externally compiled list. Customer behaviour such as the products purchased, most recent purchase, frequency of purchase and expenditure can also be stored in an in-house database. The management of direct mail involves asking five questions:

Who:	Who is the target market? Who are we trying to influence?
What:	What response is required? A sale, an enquiry?
Why:	Why should they buy or make an enquiry? Is it because our product is faster, cheaper, etc?
Where:	Where can they be reached? Can we obtain their home or working address?

When: When is the best time to reach them? Often this is at the weekend for consumers, and Tuesday, Wednesday or Thursday for business people (Monday can be dominated by planning meetings, and on Friday they may be busy clearing their desks for the weekend).

Other management issues include organisation for addressing and filling the envelopes. **Mailing houses** provide these services. For large mailings the postal service needs to be notified in advance so that the mailing can be scheduled.

Direct mail allows *specific targeting to named individuals*. For example, by hiring lists of subscribers to gardening catalogues, a manufacturer of gardening equipment could target a specific group of people who would be more likely to be interested in a promotional offer than the general public. Elaborate personalisation is possible and the results directly measurable. Since the objective of direct mail is immediate – usually a sale or an enquiry – success can easily be measured. Some organisations such as the *Reader's Digest* spend money researching alternative creative approaches before embarking on a large-scale mailing. Such factors as type of promotional offer, headlines, visuals and copy can be varied in a systematic manner and by using code numbers on reply coupons, responses can be tied to the associated creative approach.

The effectiveness of direct mail relies heavily on the quality of the mailing list. Poor lists raise costs and can contribute to the criticism of 'junk mail' since recipients are not interested in the contents of the mailing. Initial costs can be much higher than advertising in terms of cost per thousand people reached and the response can be low (an average response rate of 2 per cent is often quoted). Added to these costs is the expense of setting up a database. In these terms direct mail should be viewed as a medium- to long-term tool for generating repeat business from a carefully targeted customer group. An important concept is the *lifetime value* of a customer which is the profit made on a customer's purchase over his/her lifetime.

Telemarketing

Telemarketing is a marketing communications system where trained specialists use telecommunications and information technologies to conduct marketing and sales activities.

In North America, sales prospects have long been solicited through the medium of the telephone for relatively expensive products such as cars, freezers and home improvement. Telephonists work from prepared scripts designed to give different selling approaches according to the circumstances of the prospect, these circumstances being established before the sales talk. The idea is sometimes to 'smooth the way' for a salesperson's visit following the telephone call. Success rates may appear low, but it is a very cost-effective method and eliminates a lot of 'cold canvassing' by salespeople. However, telephone selling can be a very demanding task for the person soliciting over the telephone. This is reflected in the vernacular term applied to the location from which such solicitation takes place – 'the boiler room'.

Inbound telemarketing occurs when a prospect contacts the company by telephone, whereas outbound telemarketing involves the company calling the prospect. Developments in IT have affected both forms. For example, Quick Address is a package that enables telemarketing people handling inbound calls quickly to identify the address and account details of the caller with the minimum amount of typing time and also ensures it is accurate. The caller is asked for their name and postcode (either for the household or the company). From this the correct address will appear on the computer screen. If the caller wishes to purchase (e.g. using a credit card) over the telephone, the tedium of giving (and spelling) their address to allow posting is removed. This has gained penetration in such areas as selling football and theatre tickets. Even more sophisticated developments in telecommunications technology allow the caller to be identified even before the operator has answered the call. The caller's telephone number is relayed into the customer database and outlet details appear on the operator's screen before the call is picked up. This service, *integrated telephony*, has gained penetration in the customer service area.

Computerisation can also enhance productivity in outbound telemarketing. Large databases can store information that can easily be accessed by telephone marketing operators. Call lists can be automatically allocated to operators. Scripts can be created and stored on the computer so that operators have ready and convenient access to them on screen. Orders can be automatically processed and follow-up actions (such as call back in one month or send literature) can be recorded and stored. In addition, productivity can be raised by autodiallers.

An important technological advance is predictive dialling, which makes multiple outbound calls from a call centre. Calls are only delivered to agents when the customer answers, therefore cutting out wasted calls to answer machines, engaged signals, fax machines and unanswered calls. It is claimed to dramatically improve call centre efficiency by providing agents with a constant flow of calls. However, there is no time for call staff to psych themselves up for the call (they are alerted by a bleep and the relevant details appear on the screen). This means that call centre staff have to work extremely intensively.[8]

Telemarketing automation also allows simple keystroke retrieval of critical information such as customer history, product information or schedules. If the prospect or customer is busy, automated systems can reschedule a call-back and allow the operator to recall the contact on screen at a later date simply by pressing a single key.

Telemarketing is often conducted from *call centres* where trained operators accept and send thousands of calls a day. This process is described in the boxed case discussion.

Telemarketing: the development of call centres

The development in telemarketing activity has led to a rapid expansion in call centres. These are huge offices where perhaps over a hundred people operate telephones making and receiving calls. Their task is aided by automation, e.g. automatic dialling, computerised scripts and automatic order/ticket processing and addressing.

Staff are trained to communicate effectively over the telephone. First Direct's call handlers, for example, are given seven weeks' training before they come into contact with customers. Some companies such as Virgin Direct, the financial services firm, only contact customers who have called them first and agreed to further calls. This builds up trust and places the customer in control.

Call centres are also used to check on service levels. For example, Kwik Fit, the tyres, brakes and exhausts chain, employs a vast telemarketing team that contacts customers within 72 hours of their visit to an outlet to ensure the service was satisfactory. Its call centre staff also telephone 5,500 potential buyers of their motor insurance a night, their details drawn from a database of five million people who have used their repair centres. They claim a one in four success rate.

Technology is also helping the effectiveness of call centres. For example, a call-back button on a website allows a consumer to request a call back from a company's call centre at a time and date of their choosing. These days the responses from call centres are not necessarily by telephone. Intelligent email systems read and interpret incoming emails searching for key words and phrases before generating an automatic reply from a selection of responses.[9]

A useful set of guidelines for conducting a telemarketing call has been developed by the Bell Telephone System of America:

1 Identify yourself and your company.

2 Establish rapport: this should come naturally since you have already researched your potential clients and their business.

3 Make an interesting comment (e.g. to do with cost savings or a special offer).

4 Deliver your sales message: emphasise benefits over features (e.g. your production people will like it because it helps to overcome down-time through waiting for the material to set).

5 Overcome objections: be skilled at objection-handling techniques.

6 Close the sale: when appropriate do not be afraid to ask for the order (e.g. 'Would you like to place an order now?') or fulfil another objective (e.g. 'Can I send you a sample?').

7 Action agreement: arrange for a sales call or the next telephone call.

8 Express your thanks.

Mobile marketing

Mobile marketing (the sending of short text messages direct to mobile phones) is extremely successful. Every month in the UK over a billion chargeable text messages are sent. Marketers have been quick to spot the opportunities of this medium to communicate, particularly to a youth audience. Marketers now send out messages to potential customers via their mobile phones to promote such products as fast food, movies, banks, alcoholic drinks, magazines and books. A new acronym, SMS (short messaging service), has appeared to describe this new medium, which is available on all mobile phones that use the global system for mobile communications

(GMS), which dominates the second generation (2G) standard. The advantages of this approach for marketers are as follows.[10]

- *Cost effective*: the cost per message is between 15p and 25p compared with 50p to 75p per direct mail shot, including print production and postage.

- *Personalised*: like direct mail each message is sent to individuals, in contrast to traditional advertising.

- *Targeting*: given that SMS use among 15–25-year-olds is 86 per cent, and 87 per cent among 25–34-year-olds in the UK, mobile marketing has high potential as a youth targeting tool.[11]

- *Interactive*: the receiver can respond to the text message, setting up the opportunity for two-way dialogue.

- *Customer relationship building*: by establishing an ongoing dialogue with consumers it can aid the relationship-building process.

- *Time flexible*: unlike direct mail, mobile marketing can be sent at various times of the day, giving greater flexibility when trying to reach the recipient.

- *Immediate and measurable*: the results of the mobile campaign can be immediate (for example, the number of people taking up an offer) and the results measurable.

- *Database building*: creative use of mobile marketing allows marketers to gather consumer information, which can be stored on a database.

Mobile marketing does have certain limitations though.[12] These are as follows.

- *Short text messages*: the number of words in a text message is limited to 160 characters. Future technological advances may remove this limitation.

- *Visually unexciting*: 2G systems do not permit picture messaging. Although multimedia messaging services and 3G technology allow picture messaging, the extra cost may deter its widespread use.

- *Wear-off*: while mobile marketing is still novel, response rates are good, but sceptics argue that once the novelty has worn off and consumers receive more and more advertising/promotion-related messages, the effectiveness of the medium will wane.

- *Poor targeting*: as with poorly targeted direct mail, 'junk' text messages cause customer annoyance and lead to poor response rates.

At the moment, mobile marketing is not just acceptable, it is actually popular. Research by the Mobile Marketing Association showed that 68 per cent of consumers would be likely to recommend the service to their friends, and 43 per cent said they would respond to messages positively, perhaps by visiting a website or viewing an advertisement.[13]

Direct response advertising

Direct response advertising appears in the prime media such as television and the press but is different from standard advertising since it is designed to elicit a direct response such as a request for further information, an enquiry or an order. Usually a freefone telephone number is provided so that interested parties can contact the company. In this way, broadcast media are used to reach large numbers of consumers and direct marketing techniques are employed to allow a fast response by both consumers and the company.

Direct response television (DRTV) – or teleshopping as it is sometimes called – is slowly gaining in popularity and comes in many formats. The most basic is the standard advertisement with telephone number. Other variants are the 25-minute product demonstration (often called *infomercials*) and live home shopping programmes broadcast by companies like QVC.

In Europe a wide range of products is promoted (such as leisure products, household goods, books and beauty care products) through pan-European satellite channels such as Quantum International, Super Channel and NBC. Four factors tend to raise the probability of DRTV application and success:[14]

1 Products that require a demonstration or a service that needs to be explained.

2 Products that have mass appeal (although single interest channels provide a medium for specialist products).

3 An effective DRTV promotion must make good television to attract and maintain the interest of the target audience.

4 A successful DRTV promotion is usually supported by an efficient telemarketing operation to handle the response.

Catalogue marketing

Catalogue marketing is the promotion and sale of goods through catalogues distributed to agents and customers by mail or at outlets if the catalogue marketer is a store owner. Traditionally catalogue marketing was a form of mail order where agents passed the catalogue to relatives and friends who ordered through the agent. A key benefit to customers was the credit facility of weekly payment. More recently companies such as Next and Trois Suisse moved catalogue marketing more upmarket by targeting busy, affluent consumers who valued the convenience of choosing products at home.

A major UK success story has been Argos, which has built its business entirely on catalogue marketing. A wide range of products such as cameras, jewellery, toys, mobile phones, watches, household goods and gardening equipment is sold through their catalogues. A customer selects at home and then visits a town centre Argos store to purchase goods. Argos's success is built on this convenient form of shopping, plus low prices and an efficient service, and an inventory system that controls costs and ensures a low out-of-stock situation.

Catalogue marketing can provide a convenient method of shopping, a wide range of products, low prices and, sometimes, credit facilities. When the operation is centralised the expense of town centre locations is avoided. However, catalogues are expensive to print and require regular updating. The internet is a much cheaper way of displaying products to consumers. Like the internet, catalogues do not allow products to be tried (e.g. a hi-fi system) or tried on (e.g. clothing) before purchase. Furthermore there can be differences between the colour displayed in the catalogue and that of the product when it is delivered. This can be an important issue for products such as home furnishings.

Catalogues are also important in business-to-business markets, acting as a continual sales aid which allows customers to order at their convenience. More and more companies are moving to internet-based catalogues which are cheaper to produce and easier to update. Business-to-business catalogues often contain vast amounts of information including product specification and prices. Direct mail and telemarketing campaigns can be used to remind customers to buy from their catalogues. For many companies supplying other organisations such as component and office supply firms, the catalogue is an important marketing tool.

Campaign execution and evaluation

Once the creative and media decisions have been made, the action plan will be executed. This may be done in-house or through the use of a specialist direct marketing agency. The campaign should be evaluated against clearly defined objectives which include:

- sales volume and value
- response rate (the percentage of contacts responding)
- number of enquiries
- cost per order/enquiry/sale
- number of new customers
- number of existing customers re-buying
- conversion rate from enquiry to sale
- renewal rate
- repeat purchase rate

Most of these objectives measure the immediate (short-term) impact of a direct marketing campaign. Direct marketers should not ignore the longer term impact of a campaign which takes into account the lifetime value of a customer. A campaign in the short term may not appear cost effective, but when the impact through renewals and repeat purchase is taken into account its longer term value may be very positive.

11.4   Conclusions

This chapter has explored the growth of direct marketing as a means of selling products and services. Direct marketing activity has helped companies such as Direct Line, First Direct and Dell Computers to sell directly to customers without the need for traditional salespeople or distributors. The use of direct mail and telemarketing is reducing the need for a field salesforce, particularly for smaller customers.

Direct marketing activity needs to be carefully planned in order to produce integrated campaigns that make the best use of the tools available. Key media include direct mail, telemarketing, direct response advertising, catalogue marketing and internet marketing (discussed in the next chapter). They should be employed as part of a plan based on the identification and understanding of the target audience, the setting of campaign objectives, making creative and media decisions and the execution and evaluation of the campaign.

References

1 Smith, P.R. (1993) *Marketing Communications: An Integrated Approach*, Kogan Page, London, pp. 240–3.

2 Murphy, C. (2002) 'Catching up with its glitzier cousin', *Financial Times*, 24 July, p. 13.

3 Mitchell, A. (2002) 'Consumer power is on the cards in Tesco plan', *Marketing Week*, 2 May, pp. 30–1.

4 Stone, M., Davies, D. and Bond, A. (1995) *Direct Hit: Direct Marketing with a Winning Edge*, Pitman, London.

5 Rosenberg, L. and Czepeil, J.A. (1983) 'A marketing approach to customer retention', *Journal of Consumer Marketing*, 2, pp. 45–51.

6 Stone, Davies and Bond (1995) op. cit.

7 Roman, E. (1995) *The Cutting Edge Strategy for Synchronizing Advertising: Direct Mail, Telemarketing and Field Sales*, NTC Business Books, Lincolnwood, IL.

8 Miller, R. (1999) 'Phone apparatus', *Campaign*, 18 June, pp. 35–6.

9 Miles, L. (2001) 'Call centres exploit technology growth', *Marketing*, 18 October, pp. 35–6.

10 See Anonymous (2002) 'Can SMS Ever Replace Traditional Direct Mail?', *Marketing Week*, 26 September, 37; and McCartney (2003) op. cit.

11 Middleton, T. (2002) 'Sending out the Winning Message', *Marketing Week*, 16 May, pp. 43–5.

12 McCartney, N. (2003) 'Getting the Message Across', *Financial Times IT Review*, 15 January, p. 3.

13 Blythe, J. (2003) in Jobber, D. and Lancaster, G., *Selling and Sales Management*, Harlow, FT Pearson.

14 Carman, D. (1996) 'Audiences dial "S" for Shopping', *The European*, 4–10 April, p. 13.

Kettle Foods

Kettle Foods has discovered that its Chips brand does not need advertising support. Might this be a problem now supermarkets are promoting their in-house brands?

Kettle Chips were the first 'designer crisps' to come to Britain in the late 1980s in upmarket wine bars and delicatessens. Now they are everywhere. They are never advertised on television, the printed media or on poster sites, yet annual sales turnover of this type of snack in the UK is now almost £50 million.

In the UK, the snack market is worth around £3 billion a year, of which potato crisps forms one-third. This has remained steady for about ten years with the exception of the premium hand-cooked chips market (principally occupied by Kettle Chips) which is growing at 30 per cent per year. Kettle Chips are never advertised, so what is the secret of their success?

Cameron Healy had no working capital when he founded Kettle in Oregon in 1978. He contended that customers with sufficient discretionary income would be prepared to pay around £2 for a top quality packet of crisps. His idea turned out to be correct and he developed Kettle Chips. By 1982 they were the only hand-produced potato crisps in the USA. He came to Britain in 1987 to research 'natural foods' and set up crisp production with Tim Meyer in Norwich in 1988 and moved to larger premises in 1998. Since then year-on-year growth has been over 30 per cent and exports to Europe have grown at an even faster rate.

Josh Layish, joint Managing Director at Kettle, contends that company growth has been a direct result of not targeting a mass market. He says: 'Financial discipline is essential, but it cannot form the vision and direction for the company. We're not a volume driven business.' As Kettle is not a public company it has the managerial independence to make such decisions. Being a high-quality premium product encourages loyal consumers. 'Our customers are prepared to pay for premium products,' explains Layish. 'They're ABs – foodies and prosperous. Typically they haven't yet had kids, or they're older and their kids have left home and they want to be communicated with intelligently.'

The policy of not advertising was intuitive, based on the notion that in this way people could 'discover' the brand. 'We do a lot of communication with our customers,' says Layish. 'Any firm with a message like ours has to communicate it, but that's not the same as advertising in the 30-second commercial sense.'

Their communication strategy has the following components:

- Direct mail that extends to a database of 40,000 names obtained from customers who register at food fairs, county shows, English Heritage concerts, the BBC Good Food Show and such events as the National Wedding Show.

- A website that features a recipe book, plus a quarterly booklet for those who request it, as well as a free 0800 telephone facility.

- A PR strategy managed by Communications Plus which specialises in food and drink.

Kettle wants major sales through supermarkets, but it does not necessarily want this to be the first place where customers discover the brand. Originally it was marketed through delicatessens, but now it is offered in upmarket settings like Coffee Republic, All Bar One and Ha Ha's as the only hand-cooked crisp on offer.

When asked about competition from supermarket own brands, Layish responded: 'We are conscious of this, but we believe we can stay ahead on quality and innovation. Our seasonings are second to none.' Competition from own-label intrusion suggests a harder hitting marketing approach than Kettle has previously adopted. With 30 per cent growth from a firm that seems satisfied, what else can Kettle do?

Phil Teer, head of planning at St Luke's Communications Consultancy, argues that although Kettle Chips is perceived to be an innovative product with a modern pack design, we live in dynamic times and trends can quickly go out of fashion. With Kettle, they have successfully built an intense relationship between the brand and its customers, but he questions how strong that bond will be in two or three years. He suggests building a strong online community similar to the Friends Reunited website, as well as branding a TV programme. Teer contends that Kettle could create a strand of programming around its brand of crisps or its target market in the form of a deli-culture.

Teer says: 'I associate Kettle with the home . . . Kettle parties or events at high profile venues would enhance its out-of-home role and deepen the relationship in a contemporary way. You'd look to ensure that Kettle is a part of people's lives in a way that reflects how they're living it. People are smart. They look behind the brand and see that it's not some big corporation, but a small team who believe in what they do. That's a marketable quality.'

Layish is not persuaded with this view when he states: 'There is potential for a more targeted message, but we believe it is not a sufficiently rich message. We communicate a lot of information, but the more we have pulled back from volume-chasing promotional activity, the faster our acceleration in growth has been. We've seen real organic growth. If you have people who are passionate about natural products or the ethics of a company, it becomes a natural network.'

Source: Wynn, S. (2002) 'Crisp Growth Without Paying for the Ads', *Management Today*, May, pp. 70–72.

Discussion Questions

1 Which view is the more convincing – Teer's or Layish's? Give reasons to justify your answer.

2 Suggest ways in which Kettle Foods can surmount the threat from own-label brands, with particular reference to direct marketing.

3 How might Kettle sustain or even increase its 30 per cent year-on-year growth?

RU receiving me?

Text messaging (the sending of brief written messages directly to a cellular telephone) has been a phenomenon of the twenty-first century – it is an entirely new means of communication, suitable for an entirely new millennium. It was only really during 2001 that text messaging really took off. Cellular telephones became widely available to a young audience and, despite the belief in some quarters that text messaging would never catch on, the growth in the number of messages sent has been astronomical. During December 2001 alone, 1.3 billion chargeable text messages were sent across the four networks involved.

Marketers have never been slow to see the possibilities in a new communications medium, particularly one which has proved so popular with the younger end of the market. Marketers now send out text messages to potential customers via their mobile telephones; a way of reaching out directly to a potentially lucrative audience. A whole new acronym has appeared to encompass the new medium, and now SMS (short messaging service) is being used to promote movies, fast food, chocolate bars and even books.

Of course, if we were talking here about one-way advertising, public outcry would sink it without trace within weeks. It is reasonable to suppose that unsolicited text messages would prove as equally irritating as spamming on email. The lesson of spamming has not been lost on marketers, so the SMS system operates like any other direct marketing method, by being interactive with the recipients. SMS professionals are at some pains to ensure that spamming does not occur. They are prepared to police the system themselves in order to weed out any rogues who might damage customer trust. One useful factor which will help in this is that text messages are paid for by the sender, which makes indiscriminate texting an expensive operation.

In 2001, the EU ruled that SMS marketing in Europe should be an opt-in system, which means that marketers need to obtain people's permission to send them messages. First contact point is often an on-pack Instant Win device where the response mechanical is a text message. The telephone owner, by responding, gives permission for the SMS marketer to respond via text, so a 'mailing list' is built up in a more or less traditional way. Another way of developing a list is to run advertisements in magazines such as *Smash Hits* inviting readers to join the Pop Text Club. By joining the club, members will receive text messages about bands, gigs and latest releases from bands they are interested in.

From the recipient's viewpoint the advantages are obvious. The text messages themselves cost nothing (unless the recipient wants to respond) and the messages can be read at a convenient time. The brief nature of the message is an advantage too – compared with the average mailshot which may run to several thousand words of small print, a 160-character (maximum) message is positively refreshing. One industry leader, Flytxt, is so confident of the acceptability of the medium that it is planning to introduce a premium-rate group of text clubs which will charge the recipient for each message received. Obviously members of these clubs will know what they are getting into – but for traditional marketers, the idea that someone is prepared to pay to receive marketing messages must seem bizarre.

Research shows, however, that SMS is not only acceptable, it is actually popular. The research, carried out by the Mobile Marketing Association, showed that 68 per cent of respondents would be likely to recommend the service to their friends; 43 per cent said they would respond to messages positively, perhaps by visiting a website or viewing an ad.

Currently, the system is purely tactical, because of the limitations of the screen size and image quality. Technological advances embodied in the third-generation (3G) handsets mean that brand-building strategic campaigns became feasible during 2003 and 2004. In the meantime, SMS practitioners are content to use the system for tightly targeted direct marketing campaigns.

Source: Written by Jim Blythe, Reader in Marketing, University of Glamorgan.

Discussion Questions

1 Why might someone be prepared to pay to receive marketing messages?

2 What types of strategic messages might be delivered in future?

3 What factors might reduce the acceptability of SMS for customers?

4 What might account for the very positive response to SMS?

5 What type of company might benefit most from SMS?

Examination Questions

1 Compare the strengths and weaknesses of direct mail and telemarketing.

2 What is database marketing? Explain the types of information that are recorded on a database.

3 What are the stages of managing a direct marketing campaign? Why is the concept of lifetime value of a customer important when designing a campaign?

12 Internet and IT Applications in Selling and Sales Management

Objectives

After studying this chapter you should be able to:

1   Understand how a range of information technology developments have altered the selling and sales management functions

2   Understand how the internet impacts sales and marketing

3   Know how information technology can enable customer relationship management

4   Recognise the different generations of salesforce automation (SFA) software

5   Understand the specific information technology applications in retail selling and marketing

6   Discuss some of the newer technology trends relating to sales and sales management

Key Concepts

- customer relationship management
- customer relationship quality (CRQ)
- e-commerce
- extranets
- information technology
- intranets
- salesforce automation (SFA)

Developments in information technology are having profound effects on the way products are sold and the nature of selling and sales management activities. The chapter begins by providing a general overview of important developments in information technology (IT) and electronic commerce (e-commerce). The impact of the internet is then discussed before explaining the nature and effect of customer relationship management on selling and sales management. Salesforce effectiveness and salesforce automation (SFA) are then examined, followed by a brief look at specific developments and applications as well as some of the newer technology trends.

12.1   The Internet and e-Commerce Revolution

The changing nature of the salesforce

Information technology, the internet and electronic commerce (e-commerce) have each had a major impact on salesforce productivity and management. The extent to which such technology developments have affected salespeople's jobs can be gauged by the boxed account of a national account manager for a major company.

A sales practitioner's perspective

Over the last 15 years the role of information technology has rapidly explored nearly every possible avenue of our working and social lives from the emergence of ATMs to personal computers, domestic appliances and the wealth of information that is held about us as individuals whenever we make a transaction.

During my ten years' experience of field-based sales, many changes have occurred. I will now give a few examples of how communication methods have changed and how more efficient methods of operation have developed.

First, not so long ago most communication was by landline telephone and letter. This was followed by the fax and pagers. Then mobile phones and email arrived and communication between businesspeople became almost instantaneous.

Second, in the arena of a traditional salesperson, the raising of letters confirming arrangements, quotations, etc., passed in the post and several weeks were often needed to conclude simple transactional business deals. These have been replaced first by fax but now by email and web-based purchasing. In addition, the role of the secretary in this is becoming obsolete as the majority of salespeople generate their own letters from standard templates and quotation software.

In purely transactional purchases, customers can produce their own quotations by specifying certain criteria on a web-based purchasing system. The various fields are entered and the system automatically produces a quotation, which is legally binding on the company.

Within industrial sales many changes have occurred through technology. Historically, knowledge was power and the salesperson or sales engineer would know nearly everything about the customer-facing side of the relationship. Customer records were often randomly completed and 'deals or agreements' could often be verbal or have an unwritten verbal amendment. This was a potential cause for conflict, particularly if the personnel changed. On average people would change every three years in a typical industrial sales role.

With the introduction of IT, laptops and PDAs, much of this information can now be accessed not only by salespeople and their line managers but anyone

(continued on following page)

within the company who may have a requirement to be aware of what has been agreed previously with the customer (e.g. customer service, technical support, finance and logistics).

One of the major advantages of this is that any contact with the customer is entered into their file so everyone is fully aware of conversations, comments and offers made. These systems are becoming more commonplace, particularly in larger firms trying to manage their customer information more efficiently and with less reliability on memory or paper records.

Customer relationship management (CRM) is becoming commonplace in a wide range of sales related areas, including banks, industrial sales, catalogues and even taxi firms where a log of all previous transactions, enquiries, purchasing profiles and other communications is kept. In the most complex systems, details about a customer preference for hobbies, family anniversaries, pet likes or dislikes can be logged to assist in creating a more familiar relationship between individuals in the sales process.

The belief, where this is applied correctly, is that the customer can contact or be contacted by the company with an almost seamless approach. Questions about invoices, technical issues and quotations can be fielded by a whole range of employees within the organisation. However all this information needs to be gathered, entered and managed and the onus of this task often falls to the field salesperson in addition to getting the order.

These CRM systems offer great advantages in managing customers and identifying micro-segments within the overall customer base for highly focused marketing campaigns and promotions. These systems are now also capable of identifying and creating actual profit and loss statements on individual accounts, and the efficiency with which the salesperson and the company as a whole deals with each individual customer.

In effect a customer can be rated not only on the traditional basis of revenue generation but on actual net profit generated. This takes into account the level of service that is required to maintain the business from sales calls to technical services, discounts, and all the little extras that can often be given away in order to get the initial sale but then continue to cost the company for years afterwards.

The advantage of this mechanism is that expensive resources are not exhausted purely on the pet customer or the difficult customer but available to those who are in reality the lifeblood of the company. It also allows the salesperson to compile a service offering (or scale of offering) for individual clients which is in proportion to their current and potential worth to the organisation as a whole. This requires a great deal of trust from the parent company, as the salesperson needs to know the profitability of accounts and product lines. However, the potential advantage of the salesperson running their area as their own business and seeing business as more than just the sale on offer at a particular time has proven its worth within the added value sales arena.

The increased efficiency of sales resources utilising these types of IT systems I believe is proven in the field, but with them comes an additional level of responsibility and workload in managing them.

In summary, technology in all its facets has impacted greatly on today's working environment. In some cases it has replaced people; in others it has assisted not necessarily in reducing the overall workload but in increasing the time spent on profitable activities, reducing time on mundane tasks and increasing efficiencies.

There are only so many hours in a day and it is the responsibility of each company and their employees to find and utilise methods, devices and technologies to enable them to work smarter in today's environment.

Source: A perspective given by Mr Paul Miller, National Account Manager, BP Castrol Ltd. Part of BP Amoco Plc.

Paul Miller's account is typical of the changes that have taken place in sales and sales management over the last decade or more. The growth in the adoption of the internet in sales and marketing during this period has been phenomenal.

The rise of electronic commerce

One key capability of the internet is the ability to conduct and support electronic commerce (**e-commerce**), a term that is used mainly in connection with business-to-business (B2B) commerce, as opposed to its business-to-consumer (B2C) counterpart. Although the first wave of growth of internet usage was in the B2C domain, the B2B area is now between five and ten times larger.[1] E-commerce is any trading activity that is carried out over an electronic network such as the internet. As such it is not unique to the internet. For example, banks have been conducting business electronically for decades.

Electronic data interchange (EDI) has also allowed customers to place orders and suppliers to send invoices electronically for many years. However, the growth of internet use has seen an accompanying expansion of e-commerce through this medium. The boxed case study discusses how e-commerce has contributed to the success of Federal Express, Cisco, Dell and GE. This should not mislead anyone into believing that success on the internet is guaranteed. For every success story there are hundreds of expensive e-commerce failures. Poor website design, reluctance to conduct transactions through a new medium, problems with the adoption of common standards, difficulties with the integration of back-end systems and security fears are all barriers that hinder the faster adoption of e-commerce by consumers and businesses alike.

E-commerce in action

Internet-based e-commerce began in the mid-1990s when companies like Federal Express, Cisco, Dell and GE started to focus on online sales, customer service and

(continued on following page)

procurement. These companies recognised the advantages of the internet as a more flexible alternative to electronic data interchange (EDI). It allowed them to expand their electronic trading to smaller organisations and transactions now started to flow on the internet. The terminology changed also – people began to use terms like 'e-business', 'e-commerce' and 'business-to-business' (B2B) as the use of the internet increased as a networking mechanism. A good example is Siemens, the German giant with an annual procurement budget of around €35bn. The company buys all sorts of materials, from metals and plastics to pencils and desks, and spreads these over a dozen global divisions in sectors ranging from semiconductors and telecommunications to transportation and medicine. In 2002, 76 per cent of Siemens' procurement was offline and 24 per cent online. Of the online purchases, 90 per cent were conducted via EDI, the transfer of data between different companies using networks, and the remainder via the web. The reason for the high EDI usage is simply that this electronic service is still widespread in some industries, particularly vehicle manufacturing. The goal is to process 50 per cent of all purchases electronically by 2006, with at least half of these web-based.

Source: Based on O'Connor, J., Galvin, E. and Evans, M. (2004) *Electronic Marketing – Theory and Practice for the 21st Century*, Financial Times Prentice Hall, Harlow.

E-commerce can take place at four levels (see Figure 12.1).[2]

Publish

This is the provision of information to the customer electronically. It is one-way communication that may involve annual reports, press releases, information on products and services, recruitment opportunities and advertising. Sometimes

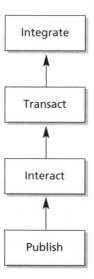

Figure 12.1 Four levels of e-commerce

referred to as 'brochureware', it is little more than the establishment of an online presence and has little to do with selling.

Interact

The next level refers to interactive engagement with the user on the internet. For example, Dell's website provides online technical support services including e-mail links to online technical support representatives. Again, this has little to do with sales but does provide an additional layer of functionality to the 'publish' level.

Transact

The third level of e-commerce allows goods and services to be bought and sold over the internet. Reaching this level can be costly in terms of initial investment, and although operating costs should be lower than more traditional ways of conducting business, usually costs need to be driven down in other areas of the business for cost savings overall to fall.

Integrate

The highest level of e-commerce is where integration of the computer system and processes of traders is achieved to create a strong, formalised relationship. This may involve the establishment of a business-to-business **extranet**, which is an electronic network linking companies to their trading partners. Extranets allow partners to exchange information such as that relating to ordering, delivery and invoicing in a secure environment. For example, Mobil's extranet allows the oil company to accept orders from 300 distributors globally.

The real impact of the internet on selling and sales management

To date, most of the commentary on the impact of the internet and information technology on sales and sales management has been anecdotal, offering exaggerated speculative forecasts of its future potential. Consequently, 'despite one view contending that the internet will become a major new retail format, replacing the traditional dominance of fixed location stores, little academic research exists to either disprove or support the claims of Internet penetration by retailers'.[3] Nonetheless, the internet channel continues to gain an increasing proportion of both B2C and B2B sales transactions.

With electronic commerce showing enormous potential to take over a significant share of sales, there has been an increasing need for companies to provide services that can reach individual users with different information profiles and levels of expertise.[4] Indeed, the internet has not only become a powerful tool, transforming the fundamental dynamics behind social and business interactions, but also more importantly, seems to be growing in both popularity and profitability.[5]

However, the application of the internet on selling and sales management remains a relatively new discipline with the potential to revolutionise the way companies build brands, sell products or services and develop relationships.

Although still in its infancy, this discipline represents a considerable ground for research with a fast pace of development. Nonetheless, as pointed out by some authors, few companies seem to have a focused strategy, let alone a clear understanding of this phenomenon.[6]

It should also be pointed out that while the initial objective of websites was to provide information, today increasing emphasis is being placed on the setting of lasting relationships between companies and customers.[7] As Martin suggests: 'The focus of marketing efforts are (and should be) shifting from marketing mix manipulation for the purpose of immediate exchange transactions to those that focus on longer-term exchange relationships.'[8] Accordingly, by developing a marketing strategy continuum focusing on steps to enable organisations to move from transaction cost marketing to relationship marketing, Grönroos not only complements Martin's argument, but further supports Scott's view that: 'Relationship marketing moves the dyadic exchange associated with personal selling from a short-term transaction orientation to a lifelong process where immediate closings must be postponed on the basis of more effectively meeting customer needs.'[9]

Not all researchers support the merits of this process and, opposing this outlook, Shaw argues: 'Marketers must stop their obsession with loving customers since it has become a distraction from the basics of selling and tracking the origins of sales success.'[10]

Nevertheless the internet has the potential to affect selling and sales management in many ways.

Building customer-centric selling arenas

The increasing use of the internet as a marketing and sales medium increases the power of the consumer by increasing the availability of comparative price information and the diversity of purchasing options. Customer focus not only compels management to realise the firm's primary responsibility of serving the customer, but also to recognise that customer knowledge is key to achieving market orientation.[11] As a result of this many organisations have successfully integrated strategies, tactics and web technologies to cement relationships with customers online.[12]

A major tool in creating customer-centric selling arenas is the emergence of extranets. These are secure sites accessible only to certain people and/or organisations. They allow transactions between buyer and seller to take place without the need for the involvement of expensive salespeople. Customers are able to log on to make routine purchases, allowing salespeople to focus on building customer relationships, developing customised solutions for customers and prospecting for new business. These business-to-business sites improve sales productivity and allow salespeople to build customer loyalty.[13]

Another internet-based selling arena is the open market catalogue site. These sites provide customers with product and price information and allow them to purchase from the site, rather like purchasing from a direct mail catalogue. The best known example is the online bookseller Amazon (www.amazon.com, www.amazon.co.uk, etc.).

Focusing on the right customer

Because the internet enables access to any online customer at any time and anywhere in the world, companies may be tempted to try to attract as many potential customers as possible. However, several authors warn against this lack of focus and advocate the necessity for companies to adhere to the principles of sales and marketing management such as targeting. For instance, Van Niekerk, Berthon and Davies stress that 'the temptation to be everything to everyone must be vigorously guarded against' and that 'a tighter focus on the specific target audience needs to be paramount'.[14]

When using the internet it is important that the organisation's website is designed to achieve a specific set of objectives and provides a focus, rather than just being a vehicle for promoting the company in general terms. These objectives can relate to servicing current customers when making purchases, cross-selling company products, encouraging new customers or building greater loyalty amongst existing customers. A method of encouraging response is to make a specific product or service offering or to ask for a website evaluation.

It is of course important that the website is simple to access, load and navigate with appropriate links. If it contains icons or banners to gain attention at the beginning, then these should not be used deeper in the site as they might prove to be distractions.

Data can be captured from those who respond to website offerings in terms of frequency of ordering, size of orders, types of purchase made, methods of payment, etc. This will provide a clearer picture of customers who can be profiled, segmented and targeted more easily along the lines suggested.

Creating quality in communications

The general consensus seems to be that the internet and its related technologies allow for swifter information exchange and more consistent communications.[15] However, researchers such as Reichheld and Schefter warn that 'with the freedom to do more comes the temptation to do too much'.[16]

Given the plethora of information now available, it is becoming increasingly important that evidence presented to the customer is kept to a manageable proportion.

Understanding buyer behaviour patterns

A study on consumer behaviour by Long and Schiffman clearly concludes: 'it pays to understand customers'.[17] Nonetheless, we still do not have a complete understanding of how users actually interact with the internet. Two factors seem critical to predicting consumer behaviour on the internet. The first factor questions whether the buyer builds a relationship with a selected vendor or searches for a different electronic vendor for each transaction. While the first pattern of behaviour will undoubtedly create an opportunity for the seller to tune regular offerings and promote loyalty, the second pattern precludes stable relationships. The other critical factor lies in the scope of the goods and services linking buyer and seller. Thus, the consumer is expected either to search for the provider of the best individual goods and services or favour a search for the best provider of a collection of goods and services.[18]

Based on these suggested patterns of behaviour, companies operating in varied industries will arguably find themselves in one or more of four competitive landscapes: Opportunity Spot, Opportunity Store, Loyal Link and Loyal Chains.

Opportunity spot occurs when purchasers exhibit no loyalty whatsoever. Each purchase is likely to be from a different supplier with no 'one-stop' shopping for a bundle of goods occurring. They may buy a ticket from British Airways one day and from United the next. When consumers show no loyalty or relationship continuity to brands or stores, but use intermediaries to put together bundles of goods, *opportunity store* markets occur. They may use Amazon.com one day and Buy.com another.

For *loyal links* to occur, consumers must show continuity when choosing vendors and services providers, although they may have no inclination to buy 'packages'. Consumers may be loyal to American Express for their credit card but see no reason to use that company for insurance. Consumers buying in categories that are described as *loyal chains* have preferred providers on whom they rely for a range of services and products. For example, Merrill Lynch might be used to help choose stocks, remind the consumers to write a will and arrange guardians for their children. Each type of consumer behaviour has marketing implications. For opportunity spot and opportunity store consumers, price is likely to be a key marketing mix variable. However, for loyal link markets the objective will be to retain the best customers through a careful blend of service and price. Dell Computers is an example of a company attempting to succeed in such a market. In practice, though, many companies have little information of the behaviour of their customers beyond sales figures and website hit rates.

Changing approaches to brand management

The internet is changing traditional approaches to brand management. While images and allusions are used to communicate branding messages in traditional marketing, on the internet product features and the provision of information are needed as a basis for branding as some consumers scan alternative product offerings and outlets for bargains. Furthermore, as consumers gain more experience of using the internet, they are more likely to search for alternative sources of information and to be less reliant on product branding.[19] Branding may become less dominant in consumer choice but still important.

Pricing

The internet makes the process of searching for the lowest price a simple task. Therefore, one prediction is that brands will have to become more price competitive to survive in the new electronic world. However, Reichheld and Schefter claim that 'contrary to common perception, the majority of on-line customers are not out to score the absolute lowest price ... Price does not rule the web; trust does'.[20] A contrary view is presented by Sinha who believes that 'cost transparency may weaken customer loyalty and create perceptions of price unfairness by encouraging dispassionate comparisons of price and features'.[21]

Creating interactive opportunities with consumers

The interactive opportunities afforded by the internet not only offer information about buyers' current tastes and preferences, but can also provide information about their potential needs and future market trends through marketing research.[22] It therefore represents a valuable source of new product ideas. The key is not only to design brands to be interactive, but also to equip customers with the ability and willingness to interact.[23]

Building customer relationships

Advances in information technology present new opportunities and challenges to establish, build and manage customer relationships. In fact, interactive communication is increasingly being hailed as the conductor to relationships, which cannot only drive brand value but more importantly provide up-to-date information on customers' needs and thoughts. For example, increasingly interactive databases have become the platform from which companies are tailoring the targeting of their messages to attract and retain customers. This is discussed in more detail in Chapter 11. Regarding the internet, the growth of email campaigns (as a replacement for direct mail) and extranets as forms of external communications and the growing complexity of intranet systems to facilitate internal communications show how information technology can aid (if done with care) buyer–seller relationships.

Performance measurement

Developments in information technology have increased the scope to collect, analyse and exploit customer information. The internet offers companies unprecedented opportunities for understanding their customers in depth and for customising offerings to meet their preferences. However, not only does the average website achieve less than 30 per cent of its full sales potential with each customer, but 'fewer than 20 per cent of companies even track customer retention rigorously let alone try to systematically learn from customer defection patterns'.[24] This lack of analysis means that strengths and weaknesses in past performance are not identified and opportunities to improve future performance are missed. Supporting this outlook, Kenny and Marshal argue that companies are so fixated on building web capacity and increasing their visitor counts, click-throughs and online sales that they overlook opportunities to cross-sell and upsell with a result that purchase value per customer is lower than it should be.[25] There is, therefore, considerable scope for improving the measurement of the effectiveness of websites and the information they provide.

12.2 Customer Relationship Management

Customer relationship management is a term for methodologies, technologies and e-commerce capabilities used by firms to manage customer relationships.[26] In particular, CRM software packages aid the interaction between customer and company, enabling the company to co-ordinate all the communication effort so that the customer is presented with a unified message and image. CRM companies offer a range of information technology-based services such as call centres, data analysis and website management. One basic principle behind CRM is that company personnel have a single-customer point of view of each client.[27] As customers are now using multiple channels more frequently, they may buy one product from a salesperson and another from a website. A website may provide product information which is used to buy the product from a distributor. Interactions between customer and company may take place through the salesforce, call centres, websites, email, fax services or distributors. Therefore it is crucial that no matter how customers contact a company, front-line staff have instant access to the same data about them such as their details and past purchases. This usually means consolidation of the many databases held by individual company departments into one centralised database that can be accessed by all relevant staff on a computer screen.

A model of customer management

Customer relationship management is much more than simply the technology. A good perspective of the CRM process is provided by the QCi Customer Management Model (see Figure 12.2). This model can be used by companies to understand how well they are managing their customers.[28] The model also shows the supporting role that IT plays in managing customers and sales relationships. Each of the elements of the QCi model will now be discussed.

Analysis and planning

Effective CRM begins by understanding the value, attitudes and behaviour of various customers and prospects. Once this has been achieved customers and prospects should be segmented so that planning activity can be as effective as possible. The planning will focus on such areas as the cost-effective retention and acquisition of customers. The boxed case history describes how a CRM system can be used to segment and target customers.

How CRM software can aid segmentation and targeting

A financial services company markets several financial service products and wants to identify new segments within its existing customer base for a cross-selling strategy. It wants to cross-sell Account Type A to those who have already purchased Account Type B. Through the application of CRM software, the company can easily identify those customers who have already purchased various of the company's products.

The company could target all those who have *not* bought A, but this would undervalue customer and transactional data as an asset. In addition, the company would also want the highest return on marketing investment. It is increasingly important to be accountable in terms of return on investment (ROI). So, instead the company could use this CRM software to interrogate existing customers who have both A and B accounts. Data mining can identify what makes these customers different from others and what makes them more or less likely to take both products. Transactional data can also be analysed for recency, frequency and monetary value (RFM) and long-term

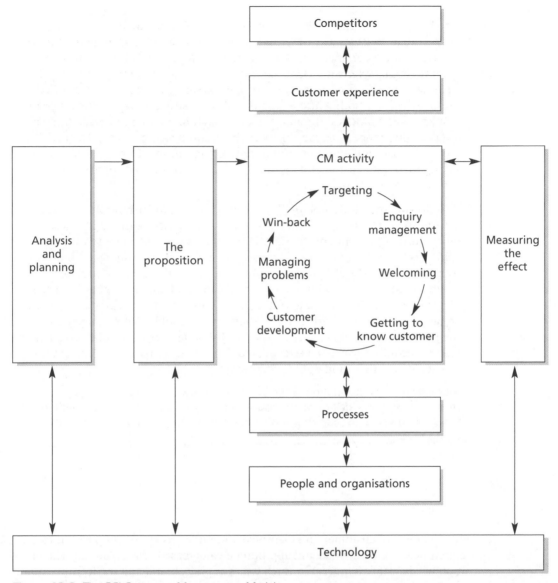

Figure 12.2 The QCi Customer Management Model
Source: From Foss, B. and Stone, M. (2001) *Successful Customer Relationship Marketing*, Kogan Page: London.

value (LTV) analyses. These are two important metrics in data-driven marketing and many software packages such as the one demonstrated here include algorithms for these further metrics. The results might show that the 'best' existing A and B account-holding customers come mainly from areas classified as blue-collar owners, high-income families, suburban semis, and low-rise council MOSAIC groups, income over £35,000, married, and aged in the 40 to 60 band.

However, the fullest benefit from existing customer data comes from looking at all the attributes together. The easiest way to achieve this is via CHAID,

(continued on following page)

which in this case is an integral component of the software being used and of most similar packages. CHAID (Chi-Squared Automatic Interaction Detection) is a form of cluster analysis which categorises individuals into groups based upon their characteristics. Here, various customer and transactional attributes have been investigated to see which best explain the characteristics of customers who have both A and B accounts. A 'tree' structure represents different 'hot and cold branches' through the data. Each branch represents a different level of importance in explaining who the A and B customers are. Each attribute is assessed and the most important or 'significant' forms the first split. Taking the entire customer base in this instance, 26 per cent of all customers have both A and B accounts.

By following the 'hottest branch', the company can understand the characteristics possessed by those customers who have purchased both A and B account types. Further branches of the CHAID tree might cascade down to even more segments based on whichever variables prove to be significant. Space prevents showing further stages here, but assume the analysis produced 60 target segments. Each of these would have significant and different characteristics. Targeting could be done on a 'test' basis in which a sample from each might be targeted and those with better response rates could then be targeted with the full 'roll-out' campaign. Also, each could be targeted with different treatments, according to whatever gender, age, marital status or geodemographic characteristic might underpin the 'creative' element.

Source: Based on a description of the Viper CRM software system owned by Smartfocus and provided by Martin Evans, Senior Teaching Fellow, Cardiff Business School. Thanks are given to Smartfocus for providing this example of their VIPER CRM software.

Proposition

Once segments of customers are identified and understood, the proposition to each segment needs to be defined and appropriate value-based offers planned. The proposition will be defined in terms of such issues as price, brand and service, and should drive the experience which the customer can expect when dealing with the organisation, its products and distributors. The proposition must then be communicated to both the customers and the people responsible for delivering it.

Information and technology

Information and technology provide the foundations for the whole model. Data needs to be collected, stored, analysed and used in a way that provides information which is consistent with the CRM strategy, the way people work and the way customers want to access the company. Technology enables an organisation to acquire, analyse and use vast amounts of data involved in managing customers. It needs to deliver the right information to the relevant people at the right time so that they can achieve their role in managing customers.

People and organisation

An organisation's front-line staff need to be recruited, trained, developed and motivated to deliver high standards of customer relations. Key elements are an organisational structure that supports effective customer management, role identification, training requirements and resources, and employee satisfaction.

Process management

In an environment where customer contact can take place at several different points, process can be difficult to implement and manage. Nevertheless, clear and consistent processes for managing customer relations need to be developed and reviewed in the light of changing customer requirements.

Customer management activity

This concerns the implementation of the plans and processes to deliver the proposition(s) to target segment(s) and involves the following:

1 *Targeting customer and prospect groups* with clear propositions (see earlier case history).

2 *Enquiry management*: this starts as soon as an individual expresses an interest and continues through qualification, lead handling and outcome reporting.

3 *Welcoming*: this covers new customers and those upgrading their relationship.It ranges from simple 'thank you' messages to sophisticated contact strategies.

4 *Getting to know*: customers need to be persuaded to give information about themselves. The information needs to be stored, updated and used. Useful information includes attitude and satisfaction information and relationship 'healthchecks'.

5 *Customer development*: decisions need to be made regarding which customers to develop through higher levels of relationship management activity and which to maintain or drop.

6 *Managing problems*: this involves early problem identification, complaint handling and 'root cause' analysis to spot general issues that have the potential to cause problems for many customers.

7 *Win-back*: activities include understanding reasons for loss, deciding which customers to try to win back, and developing win-back programmes that offer lost customers the chance to return and good reason to do so.

Customer experience

External measurement of customer experiences needs to take place and includes satisfaction tracking, loyalty analysis and mystery shopping.

Competitors

The strengths and weaknesses of competitors need to be monitored and the company's performance on the above issues evaluated in the light of the competition.

Measuring the effect

This final element occurs after the sale has been made and the service delivered. A core part of the CRM proposition is to ensure that customers' expectations are either met or exceeded, to the extent that those customers may become loyal and repeat purchasers in the future, and ambassadors or advocates to other potential customers. It sounds easy but, as mentioned earlier in this chapter, surprisingly few companies attempt to measure and manage customer retention in a systematic fashion. This is a subject we will pick up again in the next section.

CRM in selling and sales management

Customer retention and account management are sales activities that can be supported today by IT in a relatively sophisticated fashion. As the boxed example shows, the type of CRM technology available to today's sales managers can provide both a strategic overview of how well a company's portfolio of customers is being managed, and operational reports to guide individual sales managers to nurture their customers more effectively.

Getting a deep-insight into your customers

Most customer surveys miss the point. They don't account for the customer's feelings and trust. Furthermore, they are designed in a way that fail to capture the changing needs of customers. Let me start by clearing up a misunderstanding. I don't wish to play with semantics, but it is important to highlight the difference between Customer Loyalty and Customer Retention. Customer Loyalty is an elusive and intangible concept that cannot be measured and consequently *cannot* be *managed*. However, customer retention is a tangible concept that can be measured. If it can be measured, it *can* be *managed*! However, customer retention is a complex process.

Our research shows that the most important factor in customer retention is the measure of *Customer Relationship Quality (CRQ)*. This is an assessment of six factors, each of which can be measured:

- *the overall quality* of the firm's products or services,
- *customer satisfaction* (general assessment of what the firm does),
- *leading edge* (comparison with its competitors),
- *service performance* (reliability, responsiveness and customer care),
- *trust*, and
- *relationship commitment* (an intellectual and emotional link with a firm or a brand that reinforces one's self-identity).

We help customers measure and manage CRQ on an ongoing basis. We are also pragmatic enough to understand that sales directors need more operational measures to monitor the performance of their sales or account managers. At Deep-insight, we provide 'account manager packs' that provide an assessment of CRQ across different customer portfolios. That helps the sales director identify under-performing (and over-performing) sales managers, and helps the individual sales manager to identify the actions he or she needs to take on specific accounts to improve the quality of the relationship with (and future sales from!) that customer.

Online assessment tools like ours provide results within days, not weeks or months. More important, because the assessment takes only 12 minutes to complete, we get response rates of up to 75%. In other words, today's technology allows you to check the pulse of ALL your customers regularly, not just a small sample. Sales directors love that, because they can get regular and speedy feedback that allows them to take remedial action where necessary.

Source: A perspective from Dr Pierre Chenet, founder of the customer retention company Deep-insight (www.deep-insight.com).

Chenet's perspective is an example of true CRM in selling and sales management – attempting to gain a real understanding of, and insight into, the relationships that companies have with their customers. Armed with these insights, sales directors and account managers can focus on what they really need to do in order to make the next sale to these customers.

In the next section, we examine some of the more tactical uses of technology in the sales process. Note that much of what is described as salesforce automation (SFA) is an attempt at reducing the cost and improving the productivity of the salesperson. This is very important from a commercial perspective, but should not be confused with the true CRM activities described above, which are focused on the customer rather than the salesperson.

12.3   Improving Salesforce Effectiveness

Automating the salesforce

While sales representatives traditionally operated with limited technology support, in recent times, technology has been used to improve productivity. This technology, typically using laptop computers, is often referred to as salesforce automation (SFA).

Technology can increase the overall professionalism of salespeople as they work through the sales cycle with potential customers. Some of the benefits provided by this type of laptop software application include:

- Freeing salespeople from routine office administrative tasks, enabling them to spend more time with customers.

- Providing better customer service because the salesperson has immediate access to information such as stock levels or quotations.

- Capturing information that allows management to measure and monitor sales performance.

- Helping to create and manage sales opportunities so that a greater proportion is converted into sales.

The important caveat here is that salesforce productivity issues cannot be solved completely by technology. Selecting salespeople with the right skills, training them and motivating them with good incentives are also critical to salesforce productivity.

Three generations of salesforce automation (SFA) software

Salesforce automation software has developed through a series of different generations over the past decade.

Generation 1: Personal information and contact management

The first generation involved equipping the salesforce with laptops and other types of computing and data storage devices. At first, these machines contained the typical office productivity applications such as spreadsheets and word processors. Before long, salespeople clearly saw the value of Personal Information Managers (PIMs) and over time, these applications became tied into the other personal productivity applications on the PC. Products such as ACT!, Goldmine, and Maximizer were designed to help a salesperson manage contacts and time, and increase their selling effectiveness. Powerful time and contact management tools that had not existed previously were quickly developed and implemented.

Generation 2: The networked salesforce

As managers realised that this technology was helpful to their field sales representatives, they began to wonder how they might also harness this information for corporate purposes. The 'second generation' SFA tools were essentially networked versions of the first, connecting the contacts database and personal productivity tools of the salesforce to the corporate network. This was usually accomplished via data replication, by plugging the laptop into a phone-line, typically at night. While sales representatives retained their interest in time and contact management, these tools offered them little if any additional advantage over the first generation, although some were much smaller, more portable and lighter than their predecessors.

Generation 3: Technology-enabled selling

Technology-enabled selling is the name give to the latest generation of SFA tools. Technology-enabled sales systems incorporate a much richer variety of functions to help salespeople acquire and close more business, including some combination of the following:

- *Lead management.* The ability for sales to receive leads from marketing and other departments.

- *Opportunity management.* This organises all information around a sales opportunity to give a complete view of the sales cycle, co-ordinate schedules and resources, and bring the sales process to closure.

- *Account management.* The ability to track successfully closed opportunities. This can also track business contacts through companies, subsidiaries, branch offices, departments, etc. with multiple addresses and contacts.

- *Proposal management.* The ability of the salesforce to produce on-the-spot, customised, accurate product configurations and proposals. It is critically important for complex product and service sales opportunities.

- *Win/loss reporting.* The ability to evaluate wins, losses and return on investment objectively. It allows people and companies to learn and improve their sales and customer support processes.

There are literally hundreds of different software solutions aimed at the salesforce automation market. Some well-known US packages are shown in Table 12.1 below.

12.4 Other Applications of IT in Sales

Optimising sales territories

Another area of opportunity is the allocation of sales territories to particular sales-people. This can be an inefficient manual process that can be automated using statistical techniques to optimise the ratio of time spent with clients to time spent on the road. Zoltners and Lorimer (2000)[30] believe that many salesforces are losing millions of dollars each year because of sales territory imbalances. They cite a study of 4,800 sales territories from 18 companies in four different industries where more

Table 12.1 Well-known US salesforce automation (SFA) software packages

SFA solutions aimed at large enterprises	SFA solutions aimed at small–medium enterprises
Amdocs/Clarify (www.amdocs.com)	Pivotal (www.pivotal.com)
E.piphany (www.epiphany.com)	Onyx Software (www.onyx.com)
Firepond (www.firepond.com)	Interact Commerce (www.saleslogix.com)
J.D. Edwards (www.jdedwards.com)	
Oracle (www.oracle.com)	
PeopleSoft (www.peoplesoft.com)	
SAP (www.sap.com)	
Siebel Systems (www.siebel.com)	

Source: Gartner Research (2002).[29]

than half of the territories were imbalanced because they were either too large or too small. They also note that there are very real obstacles that prevent companies from optimising their sales territories:

- Salesforces resist change.

- Salesforce incentives and compensation plans can work against achieving the best alignment.

- Realignment is a cumbersome task.

- Data required for alignment is often not readily available.

These are the internal difficulties associated with any changes to existing sales territories. The realignment or optimisation of sales territories can also be problematic and confusing for customers. Zoltners and Lorimer believe that sales territory alignment is one of the most frequently overlooked areas of salesforce productivity and provide a methodology for overcoming the obstacles that includes obtaining buy-in from the salesforce and making territory decisions based on accurate data.

The boxed case shows an example of one implementation of territory management software.

IT applications in territory management

In the past, sales managers drew sales territory boundaries using a map, a thick felt pen, lots of pins and years of experience. The result was highly inefficient territories. At best this approach led to lots of unnecessary driving and at worst it meant lost sales as some areas were less well served than they should have been. Today software packages such as CACI Fieldforce Planning's *Insite Fieldforce* provide computerised territory planning. The package calculates the best possible balance of workloads and drive times to create efficient territories that allow the salesforce to spend less time driving and more time face-to-face with customers.

Territories are normally built around the locations of the salespeople – their home addresses or the local offices from which they travel – and the number of territories requested will be the number of salespeople in post. If more salespeople are to be recruited, extra 'floating locations' can be added and the package will work out the optimum location for each one. Alternatively, all territories can be based around floating locations to identify the best location for all salespeople. By default, territories of equal workload are produced. Account is taken of the greater time spent driving in more rural territories in Scotland, mid-Wales, East Anglia, Devon and Cornwall. Allowance is also taken of the distribution of calls around the sales base. For example, in one territory calls over an hour's drive time from the salesperson's home may be widely scattered while in another they may be concentrated in three towns where several calls can be made on the same day to reduce the total time spent driving. In this way efficient territories based on both drive time and workload can be designed.

A companion software package, *CallSmart*, allows sales calls to be placed in the best sequence to minimise drive time. It takes into account many factors such as call locations, call cycles, visit restrictions, fieldforce locations and driving times. It will deal with single and multiple frequency calls and plan tomorrow's visits or a set of call cycles for the next year. There are two versions of software, one allowing head office to plan calls and the other for use on the field salesperson's laptop.

The most efficient call sequence is achieved by using a matrix of drive times to and from any postcode. The package can then make the most efficient choice of when to plan each call. Call sequences can be viewed on a map to reassure users that the chosen plan is sensible, logical and efficient.

Source: Based on Shaw, M. and Williams, C. (1999) 'Putting territories on the map', *Journal of Targeting, Measurement and Analysis*, 8(2), pp. 135–52; www.caci.co.uk/ppf-insitefieldforce.htm; www.caci.co.uk/pff-callscheduling.htm

Geographic Information Systems (GIS) and Global Positioning Satellite (GPS) systems

One of the critical steps in realigning salesforce territories is the creation of an accurate territory database. Companies need to spend a significant amount of time creating, evaluating and verifying the geographic data that drive territory alignment decisions. In many Western countries, commercially-available geographic information systems (GIS) contain very good geographic data, based on detailed ZIP code or postal code information, to identify sales targets in metropolitan areas down to street level. CACI's *Insite Fieldforce* system (see box 'IT applications in territory management') is one example of a GIS that can be used for resource planning, territory planning and call scheduling.

In other countries where good geographic data are less easily available, the process is not so straightforward. Zoltners and Lorimer discuss the application of global positioning satellite (GPS) technology for creating the geographic account database. In one case in the Dominican Republic, a consumer products company equipped its salesforce with GPS readers. Salespeople stood at each account location and recorded account details (such as account name) while the GPS system captured the exact coordinates of the account location from satellite signals overhead. It took approximately one month to create an electronic database of the exact locations for over 20,000 accounts. Moreover, the salesforce also accepted the territory realignment process more readily because they were intimately involved in the data gathering activities.

Other sales support applications

Recruitment and selection

Recruitment and selection decisions can also be facilitated by IT applications. Specific software packages have been developed to assess the suitability of sales personnel. Packages assess candidates on the basis of key attributes for a salesperson, for example, intellect, motivation and sales ability. Some packages provide a suite of skill areas which can be selected according to the nature of the sales job and may include prospecting, lead qualification, handling objections, presentation skills, closing the sale, telephone technique and time management.

Such software packages can also be used in relation to the current sales team to diagnose underperformance and to identify training and motivational needs. For example, a sales manager can identify skills weaknesses and therefore focus on the area (e.g. presentation skills) in most need of attention. In relation to motivation, a manager can determine whether status is more important than money and adjust incentives accordingly.

Training

Implementation of *training* can also be assisted by IT. Computer-based training (CBT) packages can be used to deliver knowledge and develop skills in managing information. In particular, new product information can be delivered in this way. The software can be used to present information and challenge the salesperson to remember key points or to monitor knowledge levels. Some companies such as those in financial services (e.g. insurance) require their salespeople to achieve a minimum score before they are allowed to sell. A key advantage of computer-based training software is that it can be used at times and locations to suit the company and user. There has been growing interest in multimedia training packages. As more and more portable computers have CD-ROMs and training organisations install multimedia labs, this application has grown.

Sales forecasting

Computers have been used for *sales forecasting* purposes for many years. For example, the statistical software package SPSS can be used to forecast future sales using sophisticated techniques such as regression analysis. This takes account of variables such as advertising spend, disposable income and relative price levels to predict future sales. Without the power of the computer, the calculations would be time consuming, tiresome and prone to error.

Applications in retail sales and marketing

Some of the greatest changes in e-commerce have taken place within the field of retailing. This has major implications for the way in which business is conducted between suppliers and retailers, as described in the box below.

The changing relationship between supplier and retailer

The area of the relationship between a supplier and a retailer in the grocery industry has for a long time been a relationship built on personal contact. The personal contact between the salesforce of the supplier and representatives for the retailers (from store managers and 'upwards') has been the foundation of business relationships in the grocery sector. In recent years, the size of the salesforces have decreased, and more and more communication is done electronically between supplier and retailer. This is especially true in countries like the UK, where different forms of extranet, proprietary-nets based on internet technology, is increasingly the contact point between suppliers and retailers.

Source: Johansson, U. (2000) 'Consequences of information technology on supplier-retailer relationships in the grocery industry: a comparative study of Sweden and the UK', available at www.lri.lu.se/lifs/projects/it.htm

Johansson describes how suppliers access information on their sales and stocks, including promotions, with the retailers. He cites Safeway (now taken over by Morrisons), the fourth largest grocery retailer in the UK, which is linked to 500 of its suppliers, including all major ones, through the company's Supplier Information System (SIS). Tesco, the market leader in the UK, has its own system while Asda is argued to be even more advanced given that it is owned and operated by Wal-Mart, a retailer that builds its success largely on the use of state of the art information technology.

Suppliers need to be fully conversant with the technology employed by their trade customers and ensure their strategy and systems are consistent with their customer's approach. Suppliers need to be sensitive to the impact their own actions can have on a customer's technology and should take advantage of opportunities to assist the customer through the sharing of information and technological resources.

The pace of change in retailing continues to accelerate. Much of this change has been as a consequence on investment and focus on information technology by retailers of all sizes and made possible by falling infrastructure costs, such as the internet, which makes using data possible and cost effective.

We have already examined the role of electronic data interchange (EDI) applications in the retail industry. The following paragraphs give a brief insight into other applications used in the retail industry by both suppliers and retailers.

Supply chain management

Much of the drive for investment being made by retailers is to increase the efficacy of data relating to stock to allow efficiencies to be made in supply chain management. Supply chain management is the concept of the provision of products from suppliers' production lines to their sale at the retailers' tills. Supply chain management drives profitability as it ensures retailers and suppliers are focused on ensuring the right products are available in the right quantities at the right times to meet their individual customers' requirements. Accurate and real time data are the enablers for this.

Retailers are increasingly aware of the benefit of having collaborative relationships with their suppliers and are now making this data available to their suppliers, usually through web-based technology such as secure intranets and extranets. This allows the supplier to see the same data as their customers at the same time. Through the use of algorithm-based software packages both parties are able to use this data to manage the supply chain. Production and supply are harmonised to in-store demand, facilitating the concept of demand management. This can have the mutual benefits of sales being maximised, as stock-outs are reduced and lower levels of stock in the supply chain produce cost savings.

Retailers have taken the lead in this investment and thus now hold the balance of power in dealings with suppliers as they now possess more up-to-date and relevant real time data than their suppliers. This obviously gives a commercial advantage when negotiating with suppliers.

Electronic point of sale (EPOS) and electronic funds transfer at point of sale (EFTPOS)

Data is captured at the moment a product's unique bar code is scanned through at the till. Advances in technology have significantly aided the scope for data analysis. In addition to the original scanner-related data on sales rate, stock levels, stock turn, price and margin, retailers now have information about the demographics, socio-economic and lifestyle characteristics of consumers. They can also assess the impact of a whole host of variables, e.g. price, promotions, advertising, position in store, shelf position and number of facings. This information drives their choice of product mix, allocation of shelf space and promotional tactics. Some retailers also use customer loyalty cards as a means to capture data which can be analysed, allowing the retailer to engage in one-to-one marketing initiatives, e.g. information on new products and offers of discounts to retain customers.

EPOS has certainly changed the relationship between buyer and seller. Before the availability of scanner data, the trading relationship depended on information provided by manufacturers from retail audits, information that was at least several weeks old. More detailed, accurate and timely data from scanner systems gives the retailer significant bargaining power. Not surprisingly, therefore, information finds itself on the negotiating agenda. Manufacturers do buy EPOS data from their customers, but they can also trade the information and capabilities they have in exchange for it. Market knowledge is still the manufacturer's forte and this national market picture is of great use to the retailer. Additionally, armed with the retailer's EPOS data, the manufacturer could deliver well-targeted trade marketing programmes beneficial to both sides. In true trade marketing spirit, co-operation is the overall preferred approach.

EPOS depends on the inclusion of bar codes on all products to be scanned. This impacts directly on the manufacturer/supplier who should ensure that all packs carry a bar code and that the bar codes for any new line listings or promotional packs are entered into the customer's system before any goods are shipped.

Space management systems

Maximising the sales and profitability of selling space is critical. One of the reasons for retailers investing in supply chain management is to reduce the amount of storage space required in-store, allowing sales areas to be increased. To ensure the right amount of product is kept in-store and featured on the shelf, retailers use space management systems to construct virtual plannograms, which should maximise sales that can be achieved from each metre of selling space. To better understand the implications of these software packages on their products, suppliers have not only bought packages but also set up departments which specialise in space management. Opportunities exist for their proactive use by manufacturers, particularly in situations where the retailer is short of resources; importantly manufacturers can put themselves forward as produce category specialists. In the soft drinks sector, Coca-Cola Schweppes Beverages (CCSB) acts as the category specialist. A key function of the trade marketing role at CCSB is to advise the retail trade on the allocation of space to the soft drinks category in totality. An example of a software package that can accomplish this is *Nielsen's Spaceman*. Recently, however, retailers have become concerned that some suppliers may use this technology to favour their products at the expense of competitors at the key point of purchase.

Direct product profitability

Maximising the profitability of every product is critical in many areas of retailing where price figures highly in the marketing mix.

The output from direct product profitability (DPP) systems can affect retailer decisions on product stocking, store position, pricing and even trading terms demanded. It is vital therefore that the manufacturer understands DPP and the extent to and manner in which individual retailers use it.

DPP replaces gross margin as a much more accurate measure of a product's contribution to total company overhead and profit. It takes account of the fact that products differ with respect to the amount of resource they use, such as the amount of transport costs, warehouse and back-of-store space, staff handling time, share of shelf space, even head office costs. As a minimum, the manufacturer needs to be aware of how the retailer is using DPP and have sufficient expertise to question the results of the retailer's analysis. For example, a product with low DPP may still be essential to a retailer's success if it generates in-store customer flow, and if deleting it would lead to a loss of customers.

It can be used by manufacturers and retailers to examine the costs at their individual ends of the distribution chain, and by both to estimate the costs and profits in the other's field for use in negotiation. In some instances manufacturers have taken the lead in introducing DPP and in doing so have capitalised on the potential gains for both sides. Procter & Gamble (USA) claims it would modify its packaging, trading terms and other variables on the basis of DPP analysis. Proactive use of DPP by manufacturers works best with actual cost data from the retailer; without this only standard retail industry data can be used. In fact, to continue a theme already begun, manufacturer–retailer co-operation in the sharing of data is the preferred strategy in order to maximise gains for both parties.

Category management

Technology also enables category management. Scanning technology delivers information at a level of detail that allows customised merchandising strategies (tailored product assortments, space allocations, pricing, promotions) to be devised for categories or types of store. Furthermore, sophisticated computer modelling programs allow such marketing programmes to be pre-tested before they are implemented.

Retailers will best respond to those manufacturers who establish themselves as experts in the category and share their data on product sales, consumer behaviour and competitor activity with them. Manufacturers can add this data to their knowledge, analyse and identify significant consumer and category trends and use this to make strategic recommendations to the retailer on ranging, merchandising, products and promotions that will increase the overall profitability of the category. This, of course, presumes the adoption by the manufacturer of the relevant technology and applications, but the gains to the proactive manufacturer are substantial.

12.5 Other Trends

The wireless revolution

One significant trend in recent years is the move towards wireless technology, freeing the salesperson from his or her desk and allowing greater freedom to spend time with customers. Signorini (2001)[31] defines four areas into which the majority of these wireless data applications fall:

- *Field sales*. These include product inventory and pricing systems, access to customer account information, and real-time ordering.

- *Mobile office*. These include email, personal information management (PIM), access to corporate intranets and human resources systems.

- *Fleet management*. These solutions include despatch applications for courier companies, call scheduling systems for taxis and vans, location-tracking applications for managing the utilisation of large fleets of trucks, routing and mapping systems.

- *Field service*. These include the scheduling of work orders in the service and repair industry, access to customer records and information while on-site, financial services applications such as insurance claims handling and assessing, and access to national databases while 'on the road'.

Field sales constitute the single biggest use of wireless technology, accounting for more than a quarter of all applications in large organisations.[32] Wireless sales technology is typically used in one of two ways:

- The salesperson has a laptop computer that can be synchronised with head office by connecting a mobile phone to the laptop.

- The salesperson uses a personal digital assistant (PDA) that can transmit sales information to, and receive sales reports from, head office.

Although handheld devices are cheaper than laptops, it may well be the case that the overall cost per salesperson increases as a result of the introduction of mobile technology. If sales representatives retain their laptops, rather than replacing them with PDAs, then costs will certainly increase. There is also the potential for higher costs associated with the relative immaturity of some of the underlying technologies and standards.

Outsourcing of sales management applications

Another development worth noting is the trend towards outsourcing of sales management applications to specialist third parties. The business model can often be compelling, as many smaller companies do not have the resources to host their own salesforce applications. By using third parties, they avoid the need to develop and maintain their own software and sales systems. Their salespeople can gain access to the software using a standard internet browser and the data is then transferred to the company's database. One of the best examples of this is Salesforce.com (www.salesforce.com).

12.6   Conclusions

This chapter has explored the new developments in information technology that have impacted selling and sales management. Information technology is helping companies such as Wal-Mart, GE and Dell Computers to sell efficiently and effectively to customers. The internet is allowing customers to search for product and price information more easily than ever before, and to buy directly without the need for salespeople or distributors.

Developments in information technology such as email, fax and mobile phones are improving the communications links between salespeople, customers and head office. They are also bringing pressure on salespeople who are now expected to respond faster because of the speed at which these new technologies operate.

Customer relationship management software is allowing companies to understand the quality of their customer relationships better than they could historically. CRM software also provides company staff with access to the same data about the customer and so can respond in a unified way. This usually means the consolidation of the many databases held by individual departments into a centralised database that can be accessed by all relevant staff.

Sales management has also benefited from these developments. Salesforce automation (SFA) software has helped to increase the productivity of the salesperson, while IT is also employed to support territory management, journey planning, recruitment and selection, training, sales forecasting, salesforce size and evaluation systems.

Finally, an in-depth look at how IT has affected retail selling and marketing has identified applications in the areas of supply chain management, EPOS, space management systems, direct product profitability and category management.

References

1 Sharma, A. (2002) 'Trends in internet-based business-to-business marketing', *Industrial Marketing Management*, 31, pp. 77–84.

2 O'Connor, J. and Galvin, E. (1998) 'Creating value through e-commerce', *Financial Times Management*, FT Prentice Hall, London.

3 Hart, C. *et al.* (2000) 'Retailer adoption of the internet – implications for retail marketing', *European Journal of Marketing*, 34(8), pp. 954–74.

4 Aberg, J. and Shahmehri, N. (2000) 'The role of human web assistants in e-commerce: an analysis and a usability study', *Internet Research*, 10(2), pp. 114–25.

5 Birch, A., Gerbert, P., Schneider, D., OC&C and the McKenna Group (2000) *The Age of E-Tail*, Capstone Publishing, Tulsa, US; Chaffey, D., Mayer, R., Johnston, K. and Ellis-Chadwick, F. (2000) *Internet Marketing*, Pearson Education, Harlow; Evans, P. and Wurster, T.S. (2000) *Blown to Bits: How the New Economics of Information Transforms Strategy*, Harvard Business School Press, Boston; Simeon, R. (1999) 'Evaluating domestic and international web strategies', *Internet Research: Electronic Networking Applications and Policy*, 9(4), pp. 297–308.

6 See Cannon (2000) op. cit.; and Chaffey et al. (2000) op. cit.

7 Zineldin, M. (2000) 'Beyond relationship marketing: technologicalship marketing', *Marketing Intelligence and Planning*, 18(1), pp. 9–23.

8 Martin, C.L. (1998) 'Relationship marketing: a high-involvement product attribute approach', *Journal of Product and Brand Management*, 7(1), pp. 6–26.

9 Grönroos, C. (1994) 'Quo vadis, marketing? Toward a relationship marketing paradigm', *Journal of Marketing Management*, 10, pp. 347–60; Scott, M.P. (1995) 'Relationship selling', *Executive Excellence*, 12(1), p. 18.

10 Shaw, R. (1999) 'Customers are about sales, not false friendships', *Marketing*, January, p. 20.

11 Gummesson, E. (1996) 'Relationship marketing and imaginary organisations: a synthesis', *European Journal of Marketing*, 30(2), pp. 31–44.

12 Reichheld, F. and Schefter, P. (2000) 'E-loyalty', *Harvard Business Review*, July–August, pp. 105–13.

13 Shoemaker, M.E. (2001) 'A framework for examining IT-enabled market relationships', *Journal of Personal Selling and Sales Management*, 21(2), pp. 177–85.

14 Van Niekerk, D.N.R., Berthon, J.P. and Davies, T. (1999) 'Going with the flow', *Internet Research: Electronic Networking Applications and Policy*, 9(2), pp. 109–16.

15 Schwartz, D.G. (2000) 'Concurrent marketing analysis: a multiagent model for product, price, place, and promotion', *Marketing Intelligence and Planning*, 18(1), pp. 24–30.

16 Reichheld and Schefter (2000) op. cit.

17 Long, M.M. and Schiffman, L.G. (2000) 'Consumption values and relationships: segmenting the market for frequency program', *Journal of Consumer Marketing*, 17(3), pp. 214–32.

18 Clemons, E. and Row, M. (2000) 'Behaviour is key to web retailing strategy', *Financial Times*, p. 24.

19 Ward, M.R. and Lee, M.J. (2000) 'Internet shopping, consumer search and product branding', *Journal of Product and Brand Management*, 9(1), pp. 6–20.

20 Reichheld and Schefter (2000) op. cit.

21 Sinha, I. (2000) 'Cost transparency: the net's real threat to prices and brands', *Harvard Business Review*, March–April, pp. 43–55.

22 Li, T., Nicholls, J.A.F. and Roslow, S. (1999) 'The relationship between market-driven learning and new product success in export markets', *International Marketing Review*, 16(6), pp. 476–503.

23 Martin, C.L. (1998) 'Relationship marketing: a high-involvement product attribute approach', *Journal of Product and Brand Management*, 7(1), pp. 6–26.

24 Reichheld and Schefter (2000) op. cit.

25 Kenny, D. and Marshal, J.F. (2000) 'Contextual marketing: the real business of the internet', *Harvard Business Review*, November–December, pp. 119–25.

26 Foss, B. and Stone, M. (2001) *Successful Customer Relationship Marketing*, Kogan Page, London.

27 Dempsey, J. (2001) 'An elusive goal leads to confusion', *Financial Times Information Technology Supplement*, 17 October, p. 4.

28 See Foss and Stone (2001) op. cit.; and Woodcock, N., Starkey, J., Stone, J., Weston, P. and Ozimek, J. (2001) *State of the Nation II: 2002, An Ongoing Global Study of How Companies Manage Their Customer*, QCi Assessment Ltd, West Byfleet.

29 Close, W. and Eisenfeld, B. (2002). 'CRM sales suites: 1H02 magic quadrant,' *Gartner Research Note M-14-7938*, 1 March.

30 Zoltners, A. and Lorimer, S. (2000). 'Sales territory alignment: an overlooked productivity tool', *Journal of Personal Selling & Sales Management,* Summer.

31 Signorini, E. (2001) *The Enterprise Wireless Data Application Opportunity: A Segmentation Analysis*, The Yankee Group, December.

32 Yankee Group (2001) *Wireless Connectivity to the Enterprise: 2001 Survey Analysis*, The Yankee Group, March.

Practical Exercise

Computer assisted sales process (CASP)

Buying a car is a highly involved and lengthy process when compared to most other retail purchasing experiences. Today's car buyers are armed with far more information and can choose to buy vehicles online if they wish. However, the majority of customers still choose to buy a car through the traditional dealer network, despite the buying process remaining unchanged during the industry's 100-year history and surveys which suggest that customers view the process negatively. The motor manufacturers have started to address this issue by providing their dealership networks with more sophisticated tools aimed at improving customer handling and enhancing the consumer experience. One of these tools has been the computer assisted sales process (CASP). The CASP systems are usually designed with the following features:

A salesperson's diary assists in operating a controlled sales process, appointments for test drives, meeting with customers, vehicle handovers and follow-up calls to customers. The system encourages salespeople to collect prospect information such as name and contact details, what vehicle the customer currently has and what they like about it. The system automatically connects to the dealer management system and updates details of customers that are already held from previous car purchases or interactions with other departments in the dealership.

An electronic brochure guides the salesperson and customer through a structured presentation, allowing the customer to configure a car of their choice, which is then displayed on screen and includes vehicle model, engine size, colour and trim selection and factory options.

The CASP system also provides product reviews collected and added by the brand and marketing teams and also competitor vehicle comparisons – one of the weakest areas of salespeople's knowledge.

Following a test drive, the CASP can collect customer feedback on the driving experience. This aids constructive reflection for the customer, provides a 'closing' aid for the salesperson, and also provides an effective feedback mechanism for the manufacturer on the performance of their vehicles.

Should the customer have a vehicle to trade in, the system provides an on-screen part exchange price which adds an element of 'believability' for the customer and helps to provide a better trade-in price for the dealer.

The system also integrates into the manufacturer's national vehicle stock locator to source the customer's desired vehicle. Alternatively, if not available, it can place an order directly with the factory.

The finance presenter calculates and presents the various financing options and once chosen, it also credit checks the customer via a connection to the manufacturer's credit company. The system provides and prints either a comprehensive proposal with graphic images or an order confirmation document.

Finally, should the customer wish to make any amendments to a factory order, this can be done online from the salesperson's terminal.

In summary, the CASP should provide the customer with a coherent and clear process for buying a car, with the salesperson gaining the correct information to provide customers with the product or service they require.

Source: Written by Jim Saker, Professor of Retail Management, Loughborough University Business School. Gary Reed, Lecturer, Loughborough University Business School. Vicky Story, Lecturer, Loughborough University Business School.

Discussion Question

What do you see as the advantages and disadvantages from the point of view of the customer and also the salesperson?

Practical Exercise

Understanding customer value creation

The Customer Management Model (developed by QCi) described in this chapter may be used to analyse the contribution that customer management can make to the organisation. Adding value for stakeholders is an important aspect of a business proposition (e.g. improving share value, employability, etc.) but measuring this is usually not well performed and often results in poor understanding of critical success factors. Customer value is usually measured relative to what they have to pay either directly or indirectly (e.g. costs, taxation, etc.). In many cases, stakeholder and customer value are closely related. It is therefore important that organisations seek to enhance value to the customer which is only achievable through the 'value chain', that is, all parties involved in meeting the needs of customers. It is important to recognise and retain those customers that help the organisation shape its business proposition appropriately, to align its people, processes and infrastructure.

This exercise will get you thinking about how value is created and destroyed by organisations through the different activities they typically engage in to manage customers. Imagine you are a senior manager for a large organisation (pick a company with which you are familiar). For each of the following areas, list a couple of points under the headings: 'Value is created by' – 'Value is destroyed by'. For example:

Analysis and planning	Creating value through insight, knowledge and effective planning.
Value is created by	Understanding which customers you want to manage.
	Retaining those who are worth retaining.
Value is destroyed by	A lack of customer knowledge and insight.
	A mismatch of costs to revenues.
Proposition	Creating value through a proposition which helps you find, keep and develop those customers you want to manage.
People and organisation	Creating value through effective people and partners.
Processes	Creating value by being customer-centric.
Information and technology (including data)	Creating value through efficiency, service and intelligence.
Measurement	Creating value through understanding performance.

| **Customer experience** | Creating value through understanding the customer experience. |
| **Customer management activities** | Creating value through excellent acquisition, retention, development and recovery activities. |

This exercise will give you a list of factors that can be applied to the business in order to help you understand how effective and efficient they are at customer management.

Source: This exercise was prepared by Tracy Harwood, Senior Lecturer in Marketing, De Montfort University. Michael Starkey, Senior Lecturer in Marketing, De Montfort University.

Examination Questions

1 Choose five technological changes that have impacted selling and sales management. What effect have they had on selling and sales management practices?

2 What is e-commerce? E-commerce can take place at four levels. Discuss each of the four levels.

3 Discuss four ways that the internet has affected selling and sales management practices.

4 What is customer relationship management? Discuss how each of the elements of the QCi Customer Management Model can be used to understand how well customers are being managed.

Part Four Sales Management

Part Four considers issues related to the management of the salesforce. Chapter 13 examines the important elements of recruitment and selection. The job description acts as the blueprint for the personnel specification and this discussion is followed by the identification of sources of recruitment. Preparing a shortlist and the conduct of the interview are then examined along with the types of questioning techniques that are appropriate when considering the appointment of sales personnel.

Chapter 14 examines motivation and training of the field salesforce from the point of view of applying theories provided by Herzberg, Vroom, Adams and Likert along with the Churchill, Ford and Walker model of salesforce motivation. Sales management leadership is then considered, followed by sales training and the development of methods that improve selling skills.

Compensation is an important motivational element for salespeople. Chapter 15 looks at this and at how sales activities are organised. Such arrangements are geographical, product specialisation and customer-based structures, the latter of which breaks down into a number of sub-divisions. The establishment of sales territories is a determining factor when establishing the number of salespeople that might be required. Compensation plans are then considered around three main schemes: salary only, commission only and a mixture of salary and commission.

13 Recruitment and Selection

Objectives

After studying this chapter, you should be able to:

1   Appreciate that salesperson selection is a key to ultimate selling success

2   Apply interview and selection procedures in the context of recruiting salespeople

3   Understand the advantages and drawbacks of certain tests and procedures related to selection

Key Concepts

- empathy and ego drive
- interview
- job description
- personnel specification
- psychological tests

- recruitment
- role playing
- salesforce selection
- shortlisting

13.1   The Importance of Selection

In attempting to recruit and select a new sales representative, sales managers find themselves in an unaccustomed role. Instead of being a seller s/he for once takes on the role of buyer. It is crucial that this transition is carried out effectively because the future success of the salesforce depends upon the infusion of high-calibre personnel. There are a number of facts which emphasise the importance of effective **salesforce selection**:

1 There is wide variability in the effectiveness of salespeople. In the Institute of Marketing commissioned study[1] into salesforce practice, the following question was asked of sales managers: 'If you were to put your most successful salesperson into the territory of one of your average salespeople, and made no other changes, what increases in sales would you expect after, say, two years?'

   The most commonly expected increase was 16–20 per cent and one-fifth of all sales managers said they would expect an increase of 30 per cent or more. It must be emphasised that the comparison was between the top and average salesperson, not top and worst salesperson. Clearly, the quality of the sales representatives which sales managers recruit can have a substantial effect on sales turnover.

2 Salespeople are very costly. If a company decides to employ extra sales personnel, the cost will be much higher than just basic salary (and commission). Most companies provide a car if travel is required and travel expenses will also be paid. The special skills necessary to make a sale, rather than to receive an order, imply that training will be required. No company will want to incur all of these costs in order to employ a poor performer.

3 Other important determinants of success, such as training and motivation, are heavily dependent on the intrinsic qualities of the recruit. Although sales effectiveness can be improved by training, it is limited by innate ability. Like other activities where skill is required, such as cricket, football and athletics, ultimate achievement in selling is highly associated with personal characteristics. Similarly, motivational techniques may stimulate salespeople to achieve higher sales but they can do only so much. A lot will be dependent on the inborn motivation of the salesperson to complete a difficult sale or visit another prospect instead of returning home.

A study by Galbraith, Kiely and Watkins examined the features that attracted salespeople into selling and what they valued most about their work.[2] The results are given in Table 13.1.

Table 13.1 shows that working methods and independence are more important than earnings as the attraction for entering selling. This challenges the assumption

Table 13.1 Features of most interest and most value

Most interest	%	Most value	%
Working methods	60	Independence	40
Independence	13	Earnings	18
Earnings	12	Providing a service	14
Company status	5	Freedom	11
Good training	4	Dealing with people	8
Promotion chances	2	Job satisfaction	6
Professional status	2	Status	3
Exclusive territory	2	Promotion prospects	1

Source: Galbraith, A., Kiely, J. and Watkins, T. (1991) 'Sales force management – issues for the 1990s', *Proceedings of the Marketing Education Group Conference*, Cardiff Business School, July, pp. 425–45.

made by many companies that money is the main reason for embarking on a sales career. Independence is also highly valued when doing the selling job. The implication of these findings is that sales management should understand the reasons why people are attracted to selling in their industry to develop effective recruitment strategies. They certainly should not blindly assume that earnings are always paramount.

Sales managers are clearly faced with a difficult and yet vitally important task. However, many of them believe that the outcome of the selection process is far from satisfactory. In the Institute of Marketing survey,[3] nearly half of the sales managers reported that fewer than seven out of ten of the salespeople they had recruited were satisfactory.

Recruitment and selection is a particularly difficult task when operating in overseas markets. The boxed case discussion identifies some of the key issues.

Recruiting and selecting an international salesforce

A company wishing to recruit an international sales team has a range of options. Recruits could be expatriates, host-country nationals or third-country nationals. Expatriates (home-country salespeople) are well regarded by technical companies selling expensive products because they tend to possess a high level of product knowledge and the ability and willingness to provide follow-up service. Work overseas also provides companies with the opportunity to train managers and prepare junior executives for promotion. Furthermore, expatriates allow international companies to maintain a high degree of control over global marketing and sales activities. However, there are drawbacks. Expatriates are usually more expensive than local salespeople, they may not settle in the new country, and may fail to understand the cultural nuances required to sell successfully abroad.

The second option is to hire host-country nationals. The advantages are that they bring cultural and market knowledge, language skills and familiarity with local business tradition. This often means a shorter adjustment period for a company wanting to be active in a new overseas market. However, these benefits must be assessed in the light of several potential disadvantages. Often host-country nationals require extensive product training together with knowledge about the company, its history and philosophies. Second, in some countries such as Thailand, Malaysia and India salespeople are not held in high esteem. This restricts the supply of well-educated people into sales jobs and makes the task of recruiting local people more difficult. Finally, loyalty to a foreign company may be less than from expatriates.

The third option is to hire third-country nationals. When hired from similar countries in a particular region, they provide cultural sensitivity and language skills while allowing access to a more skilled and/or less costly salesforce than is available in the target country. Particularly for regionally focused companies, third-country nationals can be an effective compromise between expatriates and host-country nationals. However, the drawbacks are that the third-country national may have difficulty identifying with where and for

(continued on following page)

whom they work. They sometimes suffer from blocked promotions, lower salaries and difficulties in adapting to new environments.

Sources: Based on Boyacigiller, N. (1990) 'The role of expatriates in the management of interdependence, complexity and risk in multinational corporations', *Journal of International Business Studies*, 21(3), pp. 357–81; Honeycutt, Jr., E.D. and Ford, J.B. (1995) 'Guidelines for managing an international sales force', *Industrial Marketing Management*, 24, pp. 135–44; Zeira, Y. and Harari, E. (1977) 'Managing third country nationals in multinational corporations', *Business Horizons*, October, pp. 83–8.

There are a number of stages in the **recruitment** and selection process:

1 Preparation of the job description and personnel specification.

2 Identification of sources of recruitment and methods of communication.

3 Designing an effective application form and preparing a shortlist.

4 Interviewing.

5 Supplementary selection aids – psychological tests, role playing.

An understanding of each stage and the correct procedures to be followed will maximise the chances of selecting the right applicant.

13.2　Preparation of the Job Description and Specification

The production of an accurate **job description** should prove of little difficulty for the sales manager. S/he has intimate knowledge of what is required, having been a salesperson and out on the road with salespeople during training and evaluation exercises. Generally a job description will cover the following factors:

1 The title of the job.

2 Duties and responsibilities – the tasks which will be expected of new recruits, e.g. selling, after-sales service, information feedback, range of products/markets/type of customer with which they will be associated.

3 To whom they will report.

4 Technical requirements, e.g. the degree to which the technical aspects of the products they are selling need to be understood.

5 Location and geographical area to be covered.

6 Degree of autonomy – the degree to which salespeople will be able to control their own work programmes.

Once generated, the job description will act as the blueprint for the **personnel specification** which outlines the type of applicant the company is seeking. The technical requirements of the job, for example, and the nature of the customers which the salespeople will meet, will be factors which influence the level of education and possibly the age of the required recruit.

The construction of the personnel specification is more difficult than the job description for the sales manager. Some of the questions posed lead to highly subjective responses. Must the recruit have selling experience? Should such experience

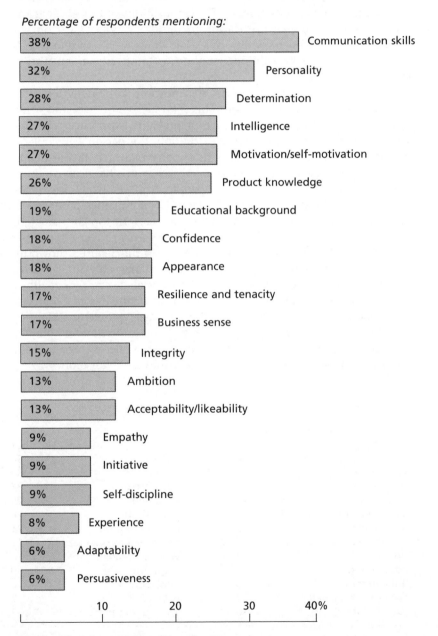

Percentage of respondents mentioning:

- 38% Communication skills
- 32% Personality
- 28% Determination
- 27% Intelligence
- 27% Motivation/self-motivation
- 26% Product knowledge
- 19% Educational background
- 18% Confidence
- 18% Appearance
- 17% Resilience and tenacity
- 17% Business sense
- 15% Integrity
- 13% Ambition
- 13% Acceptability/likeability
- 9% Empathy
- 9% Initiative
- 9% Self-discipline
- 8% Experience
- 6% Adaptability
- 6% Persuasiveness

10   20   30   40%

Figure 13.1 Important qualities of salespeople
Source: Jobber, D. and Millar, S. (1984) 'The use of psychological tests in the selection of salesmen: a UK survey', *Journal of Sales Management*, 1, p. 1.

be within the markets that the company serves? Should s/he be within a certain age range? Is it essential that the salesperson holds certain technical qualifications? If the answer to all of these question is yes, then the number of possible applicants who qualify is reduced.

The danger is that applicants of high potential in selling may be excluded. Graduates at universities often complain that jobs which they are confident they are capable of doing well are denied them because of the 'two years experience in selling' clause in the advertisements. The implications of this are that the job specification should be drawn up bearing in mind the type of person who would be *excluded* from applying if conditions are laid down with regard to such factors as previous experience. Is it really necessary or just more convenient since less training may then be required?

Another aspect of the personnel specification is the determination of qualities looked for in the new salesperson. This is a much more nebulous concept than the level of technical qualifications, age or previous experience. The qualities themselves may depend on the nature of the job, the personal prejudices of the sales manager (a good rule of thumb is that many managers favour people like themselves), or be based on more objective research which has been conducted into attributes associated with successful salespeople. A survey which investigated selection practice amongst sales managers in large UK companies produced a plethora of qualities deemed to be important. Figure 13.1 lists the top 20 characteristics and the percentage mentioning each.[4] A more recent survey of recruitment advertisements for trainee and senior sales executives identified the qualities shown in Table 13.2.[5]

Mayer and Greenberg produced a more manageable list.[6] Extensive research amongst over 1,000 companies in the USA revealed only two qualities essential to selling – empathy and ego drive. **Empathy** is defined as the ability to feel as the buyer does; to be able to understand the customers' problems and needs. This is distinct from sympathy. A salesperson can feel and understand without agreeing with that feeling. The other basic determinant of sales success, **ego drive**, is defined as the need to make a sale in a personal way, not merely for money.

Table 13.2 Qualities required of trainee and senior sales executives

	Trainee %		Executive %
Ambitious	27	Motivated	37
Motivated	26	Ambitious	25
Achievement-orientated	21	Enthusiastic	24
Enthusiastic	18	Communication	21
Communication	16	Achievement-orientated	11
Articulate	13	Work to deadlines	10
Committed	11	Committed	9
Intelligent	10	Intelligent	6
Work to deadlines	10	Articulate	7
Determined	10	Work under pressure	7

Source: Reprinted from Mathews, B. and Redman (2001) 'Recruiting the wrong salespeople: are the job ads to blame?' *Industrial Marketing Management*, 30, pp 541–50. Copyright © 2001, with permission from Elsevier.

Mayer and Greenberg claim that when an applicant has a large measure of both these qualities he or she will be successful at selling anything. Their research led them to believe that sales ability is fundamental, not the product being sold:

> Many sales executives feel that the type of selling in their industry (and even in their particular company) is somehow completely special and unique. This is true to an extent. There is no question that a data-processing equipment salesperson needs somewhat different training and background than does an automobile salesperson. Differences in requirements are obvious, and whether or not the applicant meets the special qualifications for a particular job can easily be seen in the applicant's biography or readily measured. What is not so easily seen, however, are the basic sales dynamics we have been discussing, which permit an individual to sell successfully, almost regardless of what he is selling.
>
> (Mayer and Greenberg 1964, p. 264)

Certainly, the evidence which they have provided, which groups salespeople into four categories (highly recommended, recommended, not recommended, virtually no chance of success) according to the degree to which they possess empathy and ego drive, correlated well with sales success in three industries – cars, mutual funds and insurance. Their measures of empathy and ego drive were derived from the use of a psychological test, the *multiple personal inventory* (discussed in section 13.6). In summary, a personnel specification may contain all or some of the following factors:

1 Physical requirements: e.g. speech, appearance.

2 Attainments: e.g. standard of education and qualifications, experience and successes.

3 Aptitudes and qualities: e.g. ability to communicate, self-motivation.

4 Disposition: e.g. maturity, sense of responsibility.

5 Interests: e.g. degree to which interests are social, active, inactive.

6 Personal circumstances: e.g. married, single, etc.

The factors chosen to define the personnel specification will be used as criteria of selection in the interview itself.

13.3 Identification of Sources of Recruitment and Methods of Communication

Sources

There are six main sources of recruitment:

- from inside – the company's own staff

- recruitment agencies

- educational establishments
- competitors
- other industries
- unemployed

Company's own staff

The advantage of this source is that the candidate will know the company and its products. The company will also know the candidate much more intimately than an outsider. A certain amount of risk is thereby reduced in that first-hand experience of the candidate's personal characteristics is available. However, there is no guarantee that s/he has selling ability.

Recruitment agencies

Recruitment agencies will provide lists of potential recruits for a fee. In order to be entered on such a list, reputable agencies screen applicants for suitability for sales positions. It is in the long-term interests of the agencies to provide only strong candidates. The question remains, however, as to the likelihood of top salespeople needing to use agencies to find a suitable job.

Educational establishments

It is possible to recruit straight from higher education personnel who have as part of their degree worked in industry and commerce. Most business degree students in the UK have to undergo one year's industrial training. Some of these students may have worked in selling, others may have worked in marketing. The advantage of recruiting from universities is that the candidate is likely to be intelligent and may possess the required technical qualifications. It should be borne in mind that the applicant may not see his or her long-term future in selling, however. Rather, they may see a sales representative's position as a preliminary step to marketing management.

Competitors

The advantage of this source is that the salesperson knows the market and its customers. The ability of the salesperson may be known to the recruiting company, thus reducing risk.

Other industries and unemployed

Both these categories may provide applicants with sales experience. Obviously careful screening will need to take place in order to assess sales ability.

Communication

Although some sales positions are filled as a result of personal contact, the bulk of recruitment uses advertisements as the major communication tool. Figure 13.2

shows how large companies attract applicants from outside the company. It is advisable to be aware of a number of principles which can improve the communication effectiveness of advertisements.

There is a wide selection of national and regional newspapers for the advertiser to consider when placing an advertisement. A major problem with such classified recruitment advertising is impact. One method of achieving impact is size. The trick here is to select the newspaper(s), check the normal size of advertisement which appears in it, then simply make your advertisement a little bigger than the largest. This should ensure a good position and its size will give the advertisement impact. Furthermore, the larger space will reduce the likelihood of the advertisement being poorly specified. This is an important consideration since research into sales job advertising in the printed media found the 'typical' ad to be ill specified, giving only a very rough sketch of the job and the organization concerned.[7] This method assumes, of course, adequate funds, although compared with selecting a lower quality salesperson, the extra cost to many companies is small.

The other component of impact is the content of the advertisement. The headline is the most important ingredient simply because if it does not attract and is not read, then it is very unlikely that *any* of the advertisement will be read. An inspection of any Friday night regional newspaper will highlight the lack of imagination employed in designing the average sales representative recruitment advertisement. There is plenty of scope, therefore, to attract attention by being different. As in the case of size, look at the newspaper which is to be used and ask the question: 'If I were contemplating changing jobs, what headline would attract my attention?'

Finally, if imagination is low and funds are high, it is worth considering employing a recruitment advertising specialist who will produce the advertisement and advise on media. Whether the advertisement is produced by the company itself or by a recruitment specialist, it is important to ensure that all of the major attractions

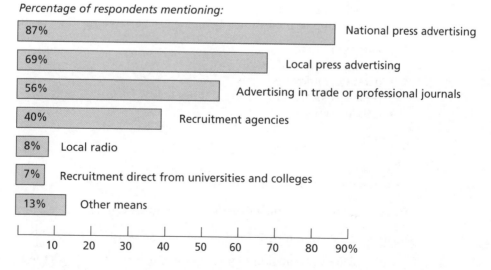

Figure 13.2 How companies attract applicants from outside the company
Source: Jobber, D. and Millar, S. (1984) 'The use of psychological tests in the selection of salesmen: a UK survey', *Journal of Sales Management*, 1, p. 1.

(not just features) of the job are included in the advertisement. This is necessary to attract applicants – the object of the exercise.

13.4   Designing an Effective Application Form and Preparing a Shortlist

The application form is a quick and inexpensive method of screening out applicants in order to produce a **shortlist** of candidates for interview. The questions on the form should enable the sales manager to check if the applicant is qualified vis-à-vis the personnel specification. Questions relating to age, education, previous work experience and leisure interests are often included. Besides giving such factual information, the application form also reveals defects such as an inability to spell, poor grammar or carelessness in following instructions.

The application form can reveal much about the person who is applying. Some applicants may be inveterate job-hoppers; others may have inadequate educational qualifications. Whatever the criteria, the application form will often be the initial screening device used to produce a shortlist. Its careful design should, therefore, be a high priority for those involved in selection. Four categories of information are usual on application forms:

1 *Personal*
   - name
   - address and telephone number
   - sex

2 *Education*
   - schools: primary/secondary
   - further and higher education: institutions, courses taken
   - qualifications
   - specialised training, e.g. apprenticeships, sales training
   - membership of professional bodies, e.g. Chartered Institute of Marketing

3 *Employment history*
   - companies worked for
   - dates of employment
   - positions, duties and responsibilities held
   - military service

4 *Other interests*
   - sports
   - hobbies
   - membership of societies/clubs

Such an application form will achieve a number of purposes:

(a) to give a common basis for drawing up a shortlist

(b) to provide a foundation of knowledge which can be used as the starting point for the interview

(c) to aid in the post-interview, decision-making stage

Having eliminated a number of applicants on the basis of the application form, an initial or final shortlist will be drawn up depending on whether the interviewing procedure involves two stages or only one stage. References may be sought for shortlisted candidates or simply for the successful candidate.

13.5 The Interview

The survey into the selection processes for salespeople of large UK companies[8] identified a number of facts pertinent to the **interview**:

1 Most companies (80 per cent) employ two-stage interviews.

2 In only one-fifth of cases does the sales manager alone hold the initial interview. In the majority of cases it is the human resources manager or human resources manager and the sales manager together who conduct the initial interview. This also tends to be the case at the final interview.

3 In 40 per cent of cases the HR manager and sales manager together make the final choice. In 37 per cent of cases the sales manager only makes the final decision. In other cases, marketing directors and other senior management may also be involved.

These facts highlight the importance of the sales manager in the selection process and indicate that selection normally follows two interviews – the screening interview and the selection interview. If the procedures described so far have been followed, the sales manager will have already produced a personnel specification including some or all of the factors outlined above and repeated here for convenience.

1 Physical requirements: e.g. speech, appearance, manner, fitness.

2 Attainments: e.g. standard of education, qualifications, sales experience and successes.

3 Aptitudes and qualities: e.g. ability to communicate, empathy, self-motivation.

4 Disposition: e.g. maturity, sense of responsibility.

5 Interests: e.g. identification of social interests, interests related to products that are being sold, active versus inactive interests.

The job specification will be used as a means of evaluating each of the shortlisted candidates. In reality other more personal considerations will also play a part in the decision. A candidate whom the sales manager believes would be difficult to work with or might be a troublemaker is unlikely to be employed. Thus, inevitably, the decision will be based upon a combination of formal criteria and other more personal factors which the sales manager is unable or unwilling to express at the personnel specification stage.

Having carried out the essential preparation necessary to form the basis of selection, what are the objectives and principles of interviewing? The overall objective is to enable the interviewers to form a clear and valid impression of the strengths and weaknesses of the candidates in terms of the selection criteria. In order to do this all applicants must be encouraged to talk freely and openly about themselves. However, at the same time the interviewer(s) must exercise a degree of control in order that the candidate does not talk at too great length on one or two issues, leaving insufficient time for other equally important factors (possibly where the candidate is weaker) to be adequately discussed.

The interview setting

The interview setting will have a direct bearing on the outcome of the interview. A number of examples will illustrate this point:

1 The room should be one where the sales manager is unlikely to be interrupted by colleagues or telephone calls. If this is not possible, visitors and telephone calls should be barred.

2 A very large room with just two or three people occupying it may not have the intimacy required to obtain a free, natural discussion.

3 A large desk situated between candidate and interviewer, particularly if littered with filing trays and desk calendars, can have the psychological effect of distancing the two parties involved, creating too formal an atmosphere and inhibiting rapport. A more relaxed, informal setting away from the manager's work desk is likely to enable the interviewee to relax more easily. The use of a low table which interviewers and interviewee can sit around (rather than sitting face-to-face) is a common method for achieving this effect.

Conducting the interview

Besides creating the right atmosphere by the judicious selection of the interview setting, the interviewers themselves can do much to help establish rapport.

What happens at the beginning of the interview is crucial to subsequent events. The objective at this stage is to set the candidate at ease. Most interviewees are naturally anxious before the interview and when they first enter the interview setting. They may feel embarrassed or be worried about exposing weaknesses. They may feel inadequate and lack confidence. Above all they may feel worried about rejection. These anxieties are compounded by the fact that the candidate may not have met his or her interviewers before and thus be uncertain about how aggressive they will be, the degree of pressure which will be applied and the types of question they are likely to ask. Some sales managers may argue that the salesperson is likely to meet this situation out in the field and therefore needs to be able to deal with it without the use of anxiety-reducing techniques on the part of the interviewers. A valid response to this viewpoint is that the objective of the interview is to get to know the candidate in terms of the criteria laid down in the personnel specification, or 'profile' as it is sometimes called. In order to do this candidates must be *encouraged* to talk about themselves. If sales ability under stress is to be tested, role playing can be used as part of the selection procedure. There are a number of guidelines which, if followed, should reduce anxiety and establish rapport:

1 One of the interviewers (preferably the sales manager) should bring the candidate into the room, rather than the candidate being sent for through a secretary or junior administrator. This reduces status differentials and hence encourages rapport.

2 Open the conversation with a few easy-to-answer questions which, although not directly pertinent to the job, allow the candidate to talk to the interviewers and gain confidence.

3 Continuing in this vein, questions early in the interview should be, if possible, open ended rather than closed. Open-ended questions allow the applicant scope for talking at some length on the topic, e.g. 'Can you tell me about your experiences selling pharmaceuticals?' Closed questions, on the other hand, invite a short answer, e.g. 'Can you tell me how long you worked for Beechams?' Some closed questions are inevitable, but a series of them makes it difficult for the candidate to relax and gain confidence. Indeed, such questions may give the impression that the applicant is uncommunicative, when really the problem lies with the interviewer.

4 Interviewers should appear relaxed and adopt a friendly, easy manner.

5 They should be courteous and appear interested in what the applicant says.

Having successfully established rapport and reduced anxiety, the interviewer will wish to encourage candidates to talk about themselves, their experiences, attitudes, behaviour and expectations. To do this the interviewer not only needs to develop the art of being a good listener but also needs to develop skills in making people talk. The skills required in the needs analysis stage of the selling process (discussed in Chapter 8) may be used in an interview to good effect. Specifically, the interviewer can use the following techniques:

1 the 'playback' technique

2 the use of rewards

3 the use of silence

4 the use of probes

5 summarising

6 the use of neutral questions

The 'playback' technique

The interviewer repeats the last few words of the candidate's sentence in order to elicit the reason for what has been said. For example, the candidate might say 'I worked for XYZ Company for two years, but I didn't like it very much.' The interviewer follows with 'You didn't like it very much?' Candidate: 'No, the sales manager was always on my back, checking to see that I was making my calls.'

The use of rewards

Obvious interest in the candidate's views, experiences and knowledge shown by the interviewer confers its own reward. This can be supplemented by what can only be described as encouraging noises such as 'Uh, uh' or 'Mmm, yes, I see'. The confidence which is instilled in the candidate will encourage further comment and perhaps revelations.

A further method of reward is through 'eye behaviour'. The subtle narrowing of the eyes, together with a slight nodding of the head can convey the message 'Yes, I see'. The correct use of such rewards comes only with experience, but their application is undoubtedly an aid in encouraging the candidate to talk freely.

The use of silence

Silence can be a very powerful ally of the interviewer. However, silence must be used with discretion, otherwise rapport may be lost and candidates may raise their barriers to open expression.

Its most common use is after the candidate has given a neutral, uninformative reply to an important question. A candidate, eager to impress, will feel uncomfortable and interpret silence as an indication that the interview is not going well. In such a situation s/he will normally attempt to fill the void, and it may be that the only way s/he can do this is by revealing attitudes or behaviour patterns which otherwise s/he would have been happy to have kept hidden. Alternatively, the pause may allow the candidate to formulate his or her thoughts and thus stimulate a more considered reply. Continuing with a follow-up question without a pause would have precluded this happening. Either way, extra, potentially revealing information can be collected by the discriminate use of silence.

The use of probes

The salesperson who is adept at needs analysis will be well acquainted with the use of probes. In an interview, comments will be made which require further explanation. For example, the applicant might say 'The time I spent on a sales training course was a waste of time,' to which the interviewer might say 'Why do you think that was?' or 'That's interesting, why do you say that?' or 'Can you explain a little more why you think that?' Such phrases are to be preferred to the blunt 'Why?' and are really alternatives to the 'playback' technique mentioned earlier.

A choice of phrases and techniques allows the interviewer to vary the approach to probing during the course of the interview. Although it may not always be possible to guarantee, probing of particularly embarrassing events such as the break-up of an applicant's marriage (if thought relevant to job performance) or failure in examinations should be left until the interview is well under way and certainly not be the subject of scrutiny at the start.

Summarising

During an interview, the interviewer will inevitably be attempting to draw together points which have been made by the applicant at various times in order to come to some opinion about the person under scrutiny. A useful device for checking if these impressions are valid in the subject's eyes is to summarise them and ask for his or her corroboration.

After a period of questioning and probing, the interviewer might say: 'So, as I understand it, your first period in sales was not a success because the firm you worked for produced poor quality products, inferior in terms of technical specifi-cations compared to competition and you felt inexperienced. But your second job, working with a larger, more well-known company, was more satisfactory, having received proper sales training and having the advantage of selling a recognised high-quality product line. Would you say that this was a fair summary?' Having obtained agreement, the interviewer can then move to another area of interest or continue to investigate the same area with the certainty that there has been no earlier misun-derstanding.

The use of neutral questions

A basic principle of good interviewing is to use neutral rather than leading ques-tions. The question 'Can you tell me about the sales training you received at your previous employer?' is likely to lead to rather different, less biased responses than 'I'm sure you learnt a lot from your sales training courses, didn't you?' Again, 'What do you feel about dealing with the type of customer we have?' is more neutral than 'I'm sure you wouldn't have any problems dealing with our customers, would you?'

Other considerations

There are other considerations which an interviewer is wise to bear in mind. First, he or she must not talk too much. The object is for most of the time spent inter-viewing to be used to evaluate the candidates. Second, part of the interview will be a selling task in order to ensure that the chosen applicant accepts. The balance between evaluation and selling is largely based upon judgement and no hard and fast rules apply, but obviously the competitive situation and the strength of the can-didate will be two factors which affect the decision.

Third, the interviewer must discreetly control the interview. A certain amount of time will be allocated to each candidate and it is the interviewer's responsibility to ensure that all salient dimensions of the candidate are covered, not only those about which the candidate wishes to talk. Some of the earlier techniques, used in reverse, may be necessary to discourage the candidate from rambling on. For example, the interviewer may look uninterested, or ask a few closed questions to discourage ver-bosity. Alternatively, the interviewer can simply interrupt with 'That's fine, I think we're quite clear on that point now' at an appropriate moment.

Finally, the interviewer will need to close the interview when sufficient infor-mation has been obtained. Usually, the candidate is forewarned of this by the inter-viewer saying 'OK, we've asked you about yourself. Are there any questions you would like to ask me (us)?' At the end of this session, the interviewer explains when the decision will be made and how it will be communicated to the candidate and then thanks him or her for attending the interview. They both stand, shake hands and the candidate is shown to the door.

13.6   Supplementary Selection Aids

Psychological tests

Although success at the interview is always an important determinant of selection, some firms employ supplementary techniques to provide a valid measure of potential. A number of large firms use **psychological tests** in this way. However, care has to be taken when using these tests and a trained psychologist is usually needed to administer and interpret the results. Further, there are a number of criticisms which have been levelled at the tests:

1   It is easy to cheat. The applicant, having an idea of the type of person who is likely to be successful at selling, does not respond truly but 'fakes' the test in order to give a 'correct' profile. For example, in response to a question such as 'Who is of more value to society – the practical man or the thinker?' they answer 'the practical man' no matter what their true convictions may be.

2   Many tests measure interest rather than sales ability. The sales manager knows the interests of successful salespeople and uses tests to discover if potential new recruits have similar interest patterns. The assumption here is that sales success can be predicted by the types of interests a person has. This is as unlikely as discovering a new George Best by measuring the interests of young footballers.

3   Tests have been used to identify individual personality traits which may not be associated with sales success. Factors such as how sociable, dominant, friendly and loyal a person is have been measured in order to predict sales success. While some of these factors may be useful attributes for a salesperson to possess, they have failed to distinguish between high- and low-performing sales personnel.

Earlier in the chapter, reference was made to the use of the multiple personal inventory in order to predict the degrees of empathy and ego drive which a person possesses. Mayer and Greenberg have shown that sales success can be reasonably accurately predicted once these characteristics are known.[9] The ideal is a person who possesses a high degree of both. A high degree of empathy (an ability to feel as the customer feels) and ego drive (the need to make a sale in a personal way) are usually associated with high sales performance. Plenty of empathy but little ego drive means that the salesperson is liked by the customers but sales are not made because of an inability to close the sale purposefully. A person with little empathy but much drive will tend to bulldoze his or her way through a sale without considering the individual needs of customers. Finally, the person with little empathy and ego drive will be a complete failure. Too many salespeople, say Mayer and Greenberg, fall into this last group.

The test itself – the multiple personal inventory – is based on the forced choice technique. Subjects pick those statements which are most like and least like themselves from a choice of four. Two of these statements may be termed favourable and the other two unfavourable. Mayer and Greenberg claim that the test is difficult to fake, since the two favourable statements are chosen to be equally favourable and the two unfavourable ones are equally unfavourable. The subject, then, is likely to be truthful. Since it is very difficult to produce statements which are *equally* favourable or unfavourable, the cautious conclusion is that the forced choice technique minimises cheating rather than completely eliminating it. The test also overcomes the criticism that psychological tests measure personality traits which may not be correlated with performance. Mayer and Greenberg describe empathy and ego drive as the 'central dynamics' of sales ability and produce evidence that scores on these characteristics correlate well with performance in the car, insurance and mutual funds fields.

If the multiple personal inventory, or any other psychological test, is to be used as a basis for selection of sales personnel, a sensible procedure would be to validate the test beforehand. Research has shown that other personality tests correlate with performance and that different types of people do well in different selling situations. Randall, for example, has shown that the type of person who was most successful selling tyres could be summarised as a 'grey man'.[10] His characteristics were those of a humble, shy, tender-minded person of below-average intelligence, quite unlike the stereotyped extrovert, happy-go-lucky, fast-talking salesperson. The explanation of why such a person was successful was to be found in the selling situation. Being in the position of selling a brand of tyre that was not widely advertised and had only a small market share, the salesperson had to hang around tyre depots hoping to make sales by solving some of the supply problems of the depot manager in meeting urgent orders. He was able to do this because his company provided a quicker service than many of its competitors. Thus, the personality of the man had to be such that he was prepared to wait around the depot merging into the background, rather than by using persuasive selling techniques.

This rather extreme example demonstrates how varied the sales situation can be. Contrast that situation with the skills and personality required to sell hi-fi equipment, and it becomes immediately apparent that successful selection should focus on matching particular types of people to particular types of selling occupations. Indeed Greenberg, since his earlier study, does seem to have moved position and recognised that successful selling depends on other personality dynamics 'which come into play depending on the specific sales situation'.[11] Consequently different psychological tests may be required for different situations.

Validation requires the identification of the psychological test or tests which best distinguish between a company's above-average and below-average existing salespeople. Further validation would test how the predictions made by the test results correlate with performance of new recruits. Recent research has cast doubt on the general applicability of the empathy/ego drive theory of sales success, but certainly the multiple personal inventory could be one psychological test used in this validation exercise, although it must be carried out under the supervision of a psychologist.

Finally, it must be stressed that the proper place of psychological tests is alongside the interview, as a basis for selection, rather than in place of it.

Role playing

Another aid in the selection of salespeople is the use of **role playing** in order to gauge the selling potential of candidates. This involves placing them individually in selling situations and assessing how well they perform.

The problem with this technique is that, at best, it measures sales ability at that moment. This may depend among other things on previous sales experience. Correct assessment of salespeople, however, should be measuring *potential*. Further, role playing cannot assess the candidate's ability to establish and handle long-term relationships with buyers and so is more applicable to those selling jobs where the salesperson–buyer relationship is likely to be short term and the sale a one-off. Role playing may, however, be valuable in identifying the 'hopeless cases', whose personal characteristics, e.g. an inability to communicate or to keep their temper under stress, may preclude them from successful selling.

13.7 Conclusions

The selection of salespeople, while of obvious importance to the long-term future of the business, is a task which does not always receive the attention it should from sales managers. All too often, the 'person profile' is ill-defined and the selection procedure designed for maximum convenience rather than optimal choice. The assumption is that the right candidate should emerge whatever procedure is used. Consequently the interview is poorly handled, the smooth talker gets the job and another mediocre salesperson emerges.

This chapter has outlined a number of techniques which, if applied, should minimise this result. Specifically, a sales manager should decide on the requirements of the job and the type of person who should be able to fulfil them. He or she should also be aware of the techniques of interviewing and the necessity of evaluating the candidates, in line with the criteria established during the personnel specification stage. Finally, the sales manager should consider the use of psychological tests (under the guidance of a psychologist) and role playing as further dimensions of the assessment procedure.

The next chapter examines two further key areas of sales management: motivation and training.

References

1 PA Consultants (1979) *Sales Force Practice Today: A Basis for Improving Performance*, Institute of Marketing, London.

2 Galbraith, A., Kiely, J. and Watkins, T. (1991) 'Sales force management – issues for the 1990s', *Proceedings of the Marketing Education Group Conference*, Cardiff Business School, July, pp. 425–45.

3 PA Consultants (1979) *Sales Force Practice Today: A Basis for Improving Performance*, Institute of Marketing, London.

4 Jobber, D. and Millar, S. (1984) 'The use of psychological tests in the selection of salesmen: a UK survey', *Journal of Sales Management*, 1, p. 1.

5 Mathews, B. and Redman (2001) 'Recruiting the wrong salespeople: are the job ads to blame?' *Industrial Marketing Management*, 30, pp. 541–50.

6 Mayer, M. and Greenberg, G. (1964) 'What makes a good salesman', *Harvard Business Review*, July/August, 42, pp. 255–68.

7 Mathews and Redman (2001), op cit.

8 Jobber, D. and Millar, S. (1984) 'The use of psychological tests in the selection of salesmen: a UK survey', *Journal of Sales Management*, 1, p. 1.

9 Mayer, M. and Greenberg, G. (1964) 'What makes a good salesman', *Harvard Business Review*, July/August, 42.

10 Randall, G. (1975) 'The use of tests and scored questionnaires in salesmen selection', in Millar, K.M. (ed.), *Psychological Testing in Personnel Assessment*, Gower, Aldershot.

11 Greenberg, G. and Greenberg, H.M. (1976) 'Predicting sales success – myths and reality', *Personnel Journal*, December, p. 61.

Practical Exercise

Plastic Products Ltd

Plastic Products Ltd is a company that produces and markets plastic cups, teaspoons, knives and forks for the catering industry. The company was established in 1974 in response to the changes taking place in the catering industry. The growth of the fast-food sector of the market was seen as an opportunity to provide disposable eating utensils which would save on human resources and allow the speedy provision of utensils for fast customer flow. In addition, Plastic Products has benefited from the growth in supermarkets and sells 'consumer packs' through four of the large supermarket groups.

The expansion of sales and outlets has led Jim Spencer, the sales manager, to recommend to Bill Preedy, the general manager, that the present salesforce of two regional representatives be increased to four.

Spencer believes that the new recruits should have experience of selling fast-moving consumer goods since essentially that is what his products are.

Preedy believes that the new recruits should be familiar with plastic products since that is what they are selling. He favours recruiting from within the plastics industry, since such people are familiar with the supply, production and properties of plastic and are likely to talk the same language as other people working at the firm.

Discussion Questions

1 What general factors should be taken into account when recruiting salespeople?

2 Do you agree with Spencer or Preedy or neither?

Examination Questions

1 Distinguish between the job description and the personnel specification. For an industry of your choice, write a suitable job description and personnel specification for a salesperson.

2 Discuss the role of psychological testing in the selection process for salespeople.

14 Motivation and Training

14.1   Motivation

Creating and maintaining a well-motivated salesforce is a challenging task. The confidence and motivation of salespeople are being constantly worn down by the inevitable rejections they suffer from buyers as part of everyday activities. In some fields, notably life insurance and double glazing, rejections may greatly outnumber successes; thus motivation may be a major problem. This is compounded by the fact that salesperson and supervisor are normally geographically separated, so the salesperson may feel isolated or even neglected unless management pays particular attention to motivational strategies which take account of his or her needs.

It is critical that sales managers appreciate that motivation is far more sophisticated than the view that all salespeople need is a 'kick up the pants'. Effective motivation requires a deep understanding of salespeople as individuals, their personalities and value systems. In a sense, sales managers do not motivate salespeople. What they do is provide the circumstances that will encourage salespeople to motivate themselves.

An understanding of motivation lies in the relationship between needs, drives and goals: 'The basic process involves needs (deprivations) which set drives in motion (deprivations with direction) to accomplish goals (anything which alleviates a need and reduces a drive)'.[1] Thus a need resulting from a lack of friends, sets up a drive for affiliation which is designed to obtain friends. In a work context, the need for more money may result in a drive to work harder in order to obtain increased pay.

Improving motivation is important to sales success as research has shown that high levels of motivation lead to:[2]

- increased creativity

- working smarter and a more adaptive selling approach

- working harder

- increased use of win-win negotiation tactics

- higher self-esteem

- a more relaxed attitude and a less negative emotional tone

- enhancement of relationships

In this chapter both applied theory and practice will be evaluated in order to identify the means of motivating a salesforce.

Motivational theories

Motivation has been researched by psychologists and others for many years. A number of theories have evolved which are pertinent to the motivation of salespeople.

Maslow's hierarchy of needs

Maslow's classic **hierarchy of needs** model proposed that there are five fundamental needs which are arranged in a 'hierarchy of prepotency'. Table 14.1 shows this hierarchy.

Maslow argued that needs form a hierarchy in the sense that, when no needs are fulfilled, a person concentrates upon his or her physiological needs. When these needs are fulfilled, safety needs become preponderant and important determinants of behaviour. When these are satisfied, belongingness becomes important – and so on up the hierarchy.

Table 14.1 Maslow's hierarchy of needs

Category	Type	Characteristics
Physical	1 Physiological	The fundamentals of survival, e.g. hunger, thirst.
	2 Safety	Protection from the unpredictable happenings in life, e.g. accidents, ill health.
Social	3 Belongingness and love	Striving to be accepted by those to whom we feel close (especially family) and to be an important person to them.
	4 Esteem and status	Striving to achieve a high standing relative to other people; a desire for prestige and a high reputation.
Self	5 Self-actualisation	The desire for self-fulfilment in achieving what one is capable of for one's own sake – 'Actualised in what he is potentially' (Maslow).

Although Maslow's belief that one set of needs only becomes important after lower order needs have been completely satisfied has been criticised, the theory does have relevance to salesforce motivation. First, it highlights the perhaps obvious point that a satisfied need is not a motivator of behaviour. Thus, a salesperson who already receives a more than adequate level of remuneration may not be motivated by additional payments. Second, the theory implies that what may act as a motivator for one salesperson may not be effective with another. This follows from the likelihood that different salespeople will have different combinations of needs.

Effective motivation results from an accurate assessment of the needs of the individual salespeople under the manager's supervision. The overriding need for one salesperson may be reassurance and the building of confidence; this may act to motivate him or her. For another, with a great need for esteem, the sales manager may motivate by highlighting outstanding performance at a sales meeting.

Herzberg

Herzberg's **dual factor theory** distinguished factors which can cause dissatisfaction but cannot motivate (hygiene factors) and factors which can cause positive motivation. Hygiene factors included physical working conditions, security, salary and interpersonal relationships. Directing managerial attention to these factors, postulated Herzberg, would bring motivation up to a 'theoretical zero' but would not result in positive motivation. If this were to be achieved, attention would have to be given to true motivators. These included the nature of the work itself which allows the person to make some concrete *achievement, recognition* of achievement, the *responsibility* exercised by the person, and the *interest value* of the work itself.

The inclusion of salary as a hygiene factor rather than as a motivator was subject to criticisms from sales managers whose experience led them to believe that commission paid to their salespeople was a powerful motivator in practice. Herzberg accommodated their view to some extent by arguing that increased salary through higher commission was a motivator through the automatic recognition it gave to sales achievement.

The salesperson is fortunate that achievement is directly observable in terms of higher sales (except in missionary selling, where orders are not taken, e.g. pharmaceuticals, beer and selling to specifiers). However, the degree of responsibility afforded to salespeople varies a great deal. Opportunities for giving a greater degree of responsibility to (and hence motivating) salespeople include giving authority to grant credit (up to a certain value), discretion to offer discounts, and handing over responsibility for calling frequencies. The results of an experiment with a group of British salespeople by Paul, Robertson and Herzberg showed that greater responsibility given to salespeople by such changes resulted in higher sales success.[3]

Herzberg's theory has been well received in general by practitioners, although academics have criticised it in terms of methodology and oversimplification.[4] The theory has undoubtedly made a substantial contribution to the understanding of motivation at work, particularly in extending Maslow's theory to the work situation and highlighting the importance of job content factors which had hitherto been badly neglected.

Vroom's expectancy theory

Basically **Vroom's expectancy theory** assumes that people's motivation to exert effort is dependent upon their expectations for success. Vroom[5] based his theory on three concepts – **expectancy**, **instrumentality** and **valence**.

1 *Expectancy*. This refers to a person's perceived relationship between effort and performance, i.e. to the extent to which a person believes that increased effort will lead to higher performance.

2 *Instrumentality*. This reflects the person's perception of the relationship between performance and reward; for example, it reflects the extent to which a person believes that higher performance will lead to promotion.

3 *Valence*. This represents the value placed upon a particular reward by a person. For some individuals promotion may be highly valued; for others it may have little value.

Thus, according to the theory, if a salesperson believes that by working harder s/he will achieve increased sales (high expectancy) and that higher sales will lead to greater commission (high instrumentality) and higher commission is very important (high valence), a high level of motivation should result. The nature of the relationships in the sales setting is depicted in Figure 14.1.

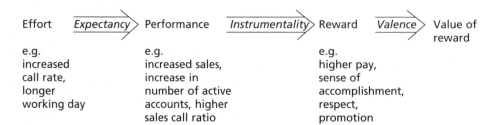

Figure 14.1 The Vroom expectancy theory of motivation

Clearly, different salespeople will have different valences (values) for the same reward. Some might value increased pay very highly, while for others higher pay may have less value. For some the sense of accomplishment and recognition may be very important, for others much less so. Also, different salespeople may view the relationship between performance and reward, and between effort and performance, in quite different ways. A task of sales management is to specify and communicate to the salesforce these performance criteria, which are important in helping to achieve company objectives, and to relate rewards to these criteria. Further, this theory supports the notion that for performance targets (e.g. sales quotas) to be effective motivators they should be regarded as attainable (high expectancy) by each salesperson; otherwise the first link in the expectancy model will be severed. Finally, this model provides a diagnostic framework for analysing motivational problems with individual salespeople and an explanation of why certain managerial activities can improve motivation. Training in sales skills, for example, can improve motivation by raising expectancy levels.

Adams's inequity theory

Feelings of inequity (unfairness) can arise when an individual's effort or performance on the job exceeds the reward which s/he receives. Salespeople who feel they contribute more than others to the organisation expect to receive proportionately greater rewards. This is the essence of Adams's **inequity theory**.[6] For a salesperson, inequity can be felt in the following areas:

- monetary rewards
- workload
- promotion
- degree of recognition
- supervisory behaviour
- targets
- tasks

The outcome of a salesperson perceiving significant inequities in any of these areas may be reduced motivation as a result of the feeling of unfairness. A study by Tyagi examined the effect of perceived inequities (rewards and favouritism) on motivation of life insurance salespeople.[7] The results showed that feelings of inequity in all areas investigated (monetary, promotion, recognition, supervisory behaviour and task inequities) had an adverse effect on motivation. Monetary reward inequity had a particularly strong effect on motivation. The implication is that sales managers must monitor their salesforce to detect any feelings of unfairness. This can be done informally during sales meetings or through the use of questionnaires. Some sales organisations survey their sales representatives periodically to measure their perceptions of inequity and the effectiveness of the company's motivational programme in general.

Motivation is often equated with incentives but Adams's work emphasises that the elimination of disincentives (e.g. injustices, unfair treatment) may be an equally powerful influence.

Likert's sales management theory

Unlike Herzberg, Maslow and Vroom, who developed 'general' theories of motivation, Likert based his **sales management theory** on research which looked specifically at the motivation of salespeople.[8] His research related differing characteristics and styles of supervision to performance. One of the hypotheses he tested was that the sales managers' own behaviours provide a set of standards which, in themselves, will affect the behaviour of their salespeople. He found that there was a link. High performing sales teams usually had sales managers who themselves had high performance goals.

His research also investigated the methods used by sales managers in the running of sales meetings. Two alternative styles were compared (see Figure 14.2). Sales managers who used the group method of leading sales meetings encouraged their team both to discuss sales problems which had arisen in the field and to learn from one another. Sales managers who monopolised the meeting discouraged interaction between salespeople and used it as an opportunity to lecture them rather than to stimulate discussion. There was a strong tendency for higher producing sales teams to use the group method.

Several reasons can be put forward to explain this. First, it is likely that a problem faced by one salesperson has been met previously by another who may have found a way of overcoming it; for example, a troublesome objection to one salesperson may have been successfully dealt with by another. The group method of leading a sales meeting encourages problem-solving and stimulates communication. Second, the more open style of meeting enables the sales manager to gain a greater understanding of the needs and problems of the salesforce. Finally, the group method promotes a feeling of group loyalty since it fosters a spirit of co-operation.

The research conducted by Likert, then, suggests that to produce a highly motivated salesforce, the sales manager should have high performance goals and encourage analysis and discussion of salespeople's performance and problems through the group method of conducting sales meetings.

The Churchill, Ford and Walker model of salesforce motivation

Churchill et al.[9] developed a model of salesforce motivation that integrated some of the ideas of Herzberg and Vroom (see Figure 14.3). This suggests that the higher the salesperson's motivation, the greater the effort, leading to higher performance. This

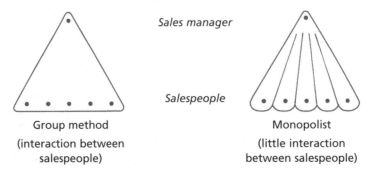

Sales manager

Salespeople

Group method
(interaction between
salespeople)

Monopolist
(little interaction
between salespeople)

Figure 14.2 Methods of conducting sales meetings

enhanced performance will lead to greater rewards which will bring about higher job satisfaction. The circle will be completed by the enhanced satisfaction causing still higher motivation.

The implications of this model for sales managers are as follows:

1 They should convince salespeople that they will sell more by working harder or by being trained to work 'smarter' (e.g. more efficient call planning, developing selling skills).

2 They should convince salespeople that the rewards for better performance are worth the extra effort. This implies that sales manager should give rewards that are valued and attempt to 'sell' their worth to the salesforce. For example, a sales manager might build up the worth of a holiday prize by stating what a good time s/he personally had when there.

They also found that the value of rewards differed according to salesperson type. Older salespeople who had large families valued financial rewards more. Younger, better educated salespeople who had no family or small families tended to value higher order rewards (recognition, liking and respect, sense of accomplishment).

Motivation in practice

A study into salesforce practice commissioned by the Chartered Institute of Marketing[10] asked sales managers to rank eight factors (excluding salary, bonus or commission) that could be effective in stimulating their salespeople to better their usual performance. The results of this research are given in Figure 14.4.

Figure 14.4 illustrates the importance of the manager/salesperson relationship in motivation. Individual meetings between manager and salesperson were thought to be the most effective of the eight factors investigated. Sales contests and competitions were ranked only sixth in importance, although a more detailed analysis of the answers revealed that this form of motivation was ranked first among the consumer goods companies replying to the questionnaire.

Surveys by Shipley and Kiely[11] and Coulaux and Jobber[12] investigated factors which motivated industrial and consumer goods salespeople. In both surveys self-satisfaction from doing a good job was ranked as the top motivator. Achieving targets and acknowledgement of effort were also highly ranked by both industrial and consumer salespeople. However, a major difference was the factor 'satisfy customer needs', with industrial salespeople ranking it second, while their consumer counterparts ranked it only sixth. The difference between industrial and consumer products and customers probably explains the discrepancy, with the former selling more technical products to customers with more complex needs (see Table 14.2).

Some of these factors, along with financial incentives, will now be evaluated in terms of their potential to motivate.

Figure 14.3 Salesforce motivation

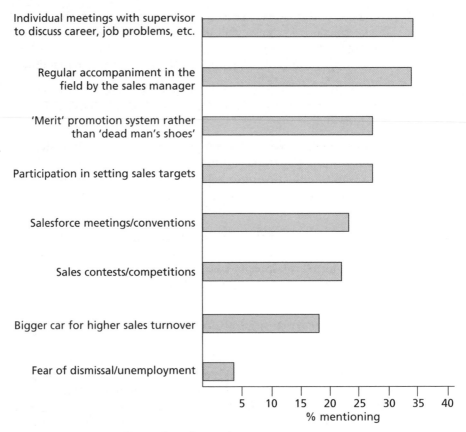

Figure 14.4 Motivating factors for salespeople

Financial incentives

Most companies, whether selling consumer or industrial goods, pay commission or bonus to their salespeople. The most usual form of payment is the salary plus commission system since this provides a level of security plus the incentive of higher earnings for higher sales. However, in some instances salespeople are paid on a straight commission basis so that earnings are entirely dependent upon achievement.

There are a number of variants of the commission system, each depending on the outcome of the following decisions:[13]

1 The commission base, e.g. sales revenue, or profits.

2 The commission rate, e.g. a set percentage of all sales or different for various products.

3 The starting point for commission, e.g. the first sale, or at some predetermined sales level.

A commission system may thus comprise a given percentage, e.g. 1.5 per cent of total sales revenue generated per salesperson; or a percentage, e.g. 5 per cent of sales revenue for all sales in excess of a sales quota. Some companies may construct more

Table 14.2 Motivational factors for salespeople in industrial and consumer goods markets

	Industrial Extremely strong	Moderately strong	Ranking*	Consumer Extremely strong	Moderately strong	Ranking*
Self-satisfaction from doing a good job	75	24	1	75	21	1
Satisfy customer needs	51	39	2	36	46	6
Achieve sales budgets	35	46	3	58	35	2
Acknowledgement of effort	36	43	3	50	37	4
Increase chance of promotion	89	29	5	58	31	3
Improve lifestyle	34	35	6	42	33	6
Meet family responsibilities	40	22	6	44	25	8
Make more money	38	22	8	46	33	5
Satisfy sales manager's expectations	24	32	9	29	35	9

*Note that the ranking is based on the sum of responses to extremely strong and moderately strong motivator with double weighting to the former category.
Sources: Industrial: Shipley, D. and Kiely, J. (1988) 'Motivation and dissatisfaction of industrial salespeople – how relevant is Herzberg's theory?' *European Journal of Marketing*, 22, 1. Consumer: Coulaux, C. and Jobber, D. (1989) *Motivation of Consumer Salespeople*, University of Bradford School of Management Working Paper.

complicated commission systems whereby different products have varying commission rates. Higher rates may be paid on higher profit items, lines regarded as being harder to sell or products with high inventory levels. Thus the commission system can be used not only to stimulate greater effort in general, but also to direct salespeople towards expending greater energy on those products the company particularly wants to sell.

Commission may work in motivating salespeople through providing a direct reward for extra effort (Vroom) and by giving recognition for achievement (Herzberg).

Setting sales targets or quotas

If a **sales target** or **sales quota** is to be effective in motivating a salesperson, it must be regarded as fair and attainable and yet offer a challenge to him or her. Because the salesperson should regard the quota as fair, it is usually sensible to allow him or her to participate in the setting of the quota. However, the establishment of the quotas is ultimately the sales manager's responsibility and s/he will inevitably be constrained by overall company objectives. If sales are planned to increase by 10 per cent, then salespeople's quotas must be consistent with this. Variations around this average figure will arise through the sales manager's knowledge of individual sales personnel and changes in commercial activity within each territory; for example, the liquidation of a key customer in a territory may be reflected in a reduced quota. The attainment of a sales target usually results in some form of extra payment to the salesperson.

Meetings between managers and salespeople

These were highly regarded by sales managers in the motivation of their sales teams. Managers have the opportunity to meet their salespeople in the field, at head office and at sales meetings/conventions. They provide a number of opportunities for improving motivation.

First, they allow the sales manager to understand the personality, needs and problems of each salesperson. The manager can then better understand the causes of motivation and demotivation in individual salespeople and respond in a manner that takes into account the needs, problems and personality of the salesperson. A study by Jobber and Lee showed the extent to which the perceptions of sales management and salespeople towards motivation and demotivation can differ.[14] They investigated the perceptions of what motivates and demotivates salespeople by asking a sample of life assurance salespeople and their sales directors. Figure 14.5 gives a summary of the results.

Sales management thought that competitions/prizes and incentives based on target setting motivated salespeople significantly more than the salespeople themselves did. Salespeople, on the other hand, valued fringe benefits higher than sales management. Perceptions of demotivating issues were also at variance. Sales management believed supervisory relations and personal problems demotivated salespeople significantly more than the salespeople did, whereas the salespeople believed that lack of advancement, lack of security and long hours of work were more a source of demotivation than the sales management believed. Such misunderstandings can lead to wasted managerial effort devising motivational schemes and compensation plans which are not valued by salespeople. The remedy is to meet regularly with the salesforce to understand their value systems, so that what is prescribed by management is effective in raising salesforce motivation.

Second, meetings in the field, which may form part of an evaluation and training programme, can also provide an opportunity to motivate. Sales technique can be improved and confidence boosted, both of which may motivate by restoring in the salesperson the belief that performance will improve through extra effort.

Third, according to Likert, **group meetings** can motivate when the sales manager encourages an 'open' style of meeting. Salespeople are encouraged to discuss their sales problems and opportunities so that the entire sales team benefits from each other's experiences. This leads to a greater sense of group loyalty and improved per-

	Motivators	Demotivators
Sales directors value these factors more highly	Competitions/prizes Incentives based on target setting	Supervisory relations Personal problems
Sales representatives value these factors more highly	Fringe benefits	Lack of advancement Lack of security Hours of work

Figure 14.5 Summary of differences between sales directors and sales representatives

formance. Finally, meetings between manager and salespeople provide the opportunity for performance feedback where weaknesses are identified and recognition for good work is given.

The study by Coulaux and Jobber found that almost half their sample of consumer salespeople wanted more meetings with their sales managers.[15] Table 14.3 shows the topics which they would most like to discuss. Three-quarters of the salespeople said that they would like more opportunity to analyse job problems and try to find a solution with their sales managers. Sales targets were second on the list of issues which they would like to discuss.

The work by Herzberg highlights the importance of **recognition** as a positive motivator and Maslow suggests that many people have a need to be accepted. Thus what sales managers say to their salespeople can have both motivational and demotivational effects, by giving and/or taking away recognition and acceptance. Giving recognition and acceptance (by a pat on the back or praise, for example) is called *positive strokes* and can act as a motivator. Withdrawing recognition and acceptance (for example, criticising or ignoring the person) is called *negative strokes* and can act as both a motivator or a demotivator depending on the circumstances. Such withdrawal can motivate when the salesperson is underperforming through lack of effort when that person has a strong desire for recognition and acceptance. However, many managers can demotivate almost unknowingly by what they say and do. Outside factors such as domestic problems may cause managers to give out negative strokes to people who do not deserve them. Under such circumstances they can have a demotivational effect. Table 14.4 gives a few examples.

A further example of the use of negative strokes was the sales manager of a financial services company who wanted to reduce his salesforce's expenses bill. The salespeople were provided with BMWs. To their astonishment the sales manager declared that from the following month the salesperson with the highest expenses would get to drive the company's new Skoda.

Promotion

Sales managers believe that a **merit-based promotion system** does act as a motivator. If the promotion is to a managerial position, there are grave dangers of promoting the company's best salesperson. The skills required of a sales manager are wider than those required of a salesperson. A sales manager must be able to analyse and control the performance of others, motivate and train them. These skills are not required to sell successfully.

Table 14.3 Topics salespeople would like to discuss more with their sales managers

Matters	%
Analyse job problems and try to find solutions together	75
Sales targets	70
Job problems	68
Promotion	45
Job career	45
Review performance together	30
Remuneration	22
Personal problems	22

Table 14.4 Positive and negative strokes

Strokes	Physical contact	Psychological
Positive	Handshake Pat on the back	Praise, smile, appreciative glance
Negative	Push Slap	Criticism, ridicule, ignore, sideways glance, frown

If promotion is to be tied to sales performance, it is sensible to consider the creation of a dual promotional route. The first path follows the normal managerial career sequence. The second is created to reward outstanding sales success. An example of such a merit-based promotional ladder is:

Salesperson → Senior Salesperson → National Account Executive

Sales contests

Sales contests are a popular form of incentive for consumer salesforces. The purpose of the sales contest varies widely. It may be to encourage a higher level of sales in general, to increase the sales of a slow-moving product or to reward the generation of new customers. The strength of a sales contest lies in its ability to appeal to the competitive spirit of salespeople and their need for achievement and recognition. As with other financial incentives, to be effective the contest must be seen to be fair and each salesperson must believe that s/he is capable of winning.

However, problems can occur. Contests can encourage cheating. In one company which used a sales contest to promote sales at a series of promotional events around the country with its dealers, salespeople 'stored up' orders achieved prior to the events in order to increase the apparent number of orders taken at the events. By pitching salesperson against salesperson, contests may militate against the spirit of mutual help and co-operation which can improve salesforce performance.

Sales managers need to be sensitive to the differences in cultural ideas and expectations of overseas salespeople when devising motivational programmes. Examples of how such differences can impact on salesforce motivation are given in the boxed case discussion.

Motivating international salespeople

The key to selecting appropriate salesperson motivation and compensation systems is to understand their values and expectations, and not to assume that what works at home will work in foreign markets. For example, in Europe money is often viewed as a key motivator whereas in the Middle East and Japan commission is little used, and non-financial factors such as increased responsibilities or higher job security are more effective. An understanding of local customs is required. For example, in Japan salary increases are usually based on seniority. Political factors can also determine the fixed salary/commission split and the level of fringe benefits provided for employees.

Perceptions of unfairness can arise when the overseas salesforce consists of a mixture of expatriates and local salespeople. Because a salary increase normally accompanies an expatriate's overseas move, they may be paid more than local recruits. If this becomes common knowledge, the motivation of locally recruited salespeople may suffer.

Sources: Based on Cundiff, E. and Hilger, M.T. (1988) *Marketing in the International Environment*, Prentice-Hall, Englewood Cliffs N.J.; and Hill, J.S., Still, R.R. and Boya, U.O. (1991) 'Managing the multinational sales force', *International Marketing Review*, 8(1), pp. 19–31.

14.2 Leadership

For motivation to be effective it must be channelled in the right direction, which is where leadership is crucial. Motivation provides the movement while leadership supplies the direction that allows both the company and the salesperson to achieve their objectives.[16] Leadership is the process of influencing the behaviour of people toward the accomplishment of objectives. In sales management, leadership usually focuses on the relationships between sales managers and their salespeople. However, it is also relevant for key, national or global account managers who manage account teams.

Leaders generate good performance from their sales teams by increasing their personal rewards from achieving objectives and by making the path to these rewards easier to follow through advice, training, reducing or removing obstacles and problems, and by increasing the opportunities for personal satisfaction.[17]

A key question is what is required to be a successful leader. An informal survey of sales managers' opinions on the characteristics of a successful leader produced the following comments:[18]

1 Leaders have a strong, defined sense of purpose. They know what needs to be done.

2 Leaders are effective communicators. They communicate their vision of the future. They provide an invitation to the sales team to link their prosperity to the success of the business. They communicate what is expected of people and how they are doing.

3 Leaders are persistent and hard working. They are prepared to invest whatever time and effort is required to achieve results.

4 Leaders are self-aware. They recognise their strengths, weaknesses, skills and abilities.

5 Leaders are learners. They welcome information, develop new skills and improve on existing ones.

6 Leaders love their work. They view work as an adventure and are constantly renewed and stimulated by it.

7 Leaders inspire others. They are able to unite people in a consolidated effort.

8   Leaders establish human relationships based on trust, respect and caring.

9   Leaders are risk takers. They are willing to explore and experiment.

10 Leaders are keen to help others attain their goals. They reduce or remove obstacles to the attainment of salespeople's goals and help them be successful in their jobs.

11 Leaders have the ability to motivate and inspire salespeople to grow and learn. Each of their salespeople feels they have control over their own destiny and feels important to their organisation.

An enormous amount of research has gone into exploring leadership.[19] While a review of all this work is beyond the scope of this book, one key study by Goleman will be reported as it links leadership styles to 'working atmosphere or climate' and performance.[20] The research is based on a study of almost 4,000 executives from around the world by the management consulting firm Hay McBer.

Six leadership styles were identified and are summarised in Table 14.5. The research indicated that effective leaders do not rely on one leadership style but use all or most of them, depending on the particular situation. Goleman drew a golfing

Table 14.5 Six leadership styles and key characteristics

Style	Operational characteristics	Style in a phrase	Underlying competences	When to use
Coercive	Demands compliance	'Do what I tell you'	Drive to achieve, self-control	In a crisis, with problem people
Authoritative	Mobilises people	'Come with me'	Self-confidence, change catalyst	When new vision and direction are needed
Affiliative	Creates harmony	'People come first'	Empathy, communication	To heal wounds, to motivate people under stress
Democratic	Forges consensus	'What do you think?'	Collaboration, team building	To build consensus, to get contributions
Pacesetting	Sets high standards	'Do as I do, now'	Initiative, drive to achieve	To get fast results from a motivated team
Coaching	Develops people	'Try this'	Empathy, self-awareness	To improve performance, to develop strengths

Source: Adapted from Goleman, D. (2000) 'Leadership that gets results', *Harvard Business Review*, March–April, pp. 78–90.

analogy: over the course of a game a golfer chooses clubs based on the demands of the shot. That is how highly effective leaders also operate.[21]

While coercion and pacesetting have their uses, the study showed that overall these styles can harm 'working atmosphere', reducing, for example, flexibility (how free employees feel to innovate unencumbered by red tape) and commitment to a common purpose. The other four leadership styles have a positive impact on 'working atmosphere' and financial performance. Goleman concludes that the best leaders are those who have mastered four or more styles, especially the positive ones (authoritative, affiliative, democratic, coaching) and have the ability to change styles as the situation demands. Effective leaders have the capability to match behaviour to the situation in an automatic, flexible, fluid and seamless way. Importantly, Goleman argues that the ability to use more than those leadership styles that come naturally can be taught (or coached). Therefore, sales managers who display, for example, only one or two of the necessary styles can be coached to expand their repertoire of styles and, therefore, become more effective leaders.

Consistent with these findings, Huczynski and Buchanan[22] conclude that leadership research suggests that effective leadership styles depend on context with no one style of leadership appearing universally better. However, they argue that a good deal of research suggests that a considerate, participative or democratic style of leadership is generally (if not always) more effective than an autocratic, coercive style. Two reasons are given:

1 It reflects the wider social and political trends towards increased personal freedom and the right to resist manipulation.

2 The need to tap the ideas of people with knowledge and experience and the need to get greater commitment through their involvement in decision-making.

Autocratic/coercive management stifles creativity, ignores available expertise and kills motivation and commitment. However, it can be necessary when time is short, the leader is the most knowledgeable person and where potential participants would never agree on a decision.[23]

14.3 Training

A study for the Learning International Organization[24] revealed seven sales challenges that organisations must meet if they are going to survive in the competitive marketplace:

1 *Distinguish between similar products and services.* Success in sales requires more than just having an exceptional product or service. The proliferation of 'me too' products is causing buyers to become confused. Excellent salespeople are needed to capitalise on product differences: that their offerings are better than the competitor's.

2 *Putting together groups of products to form a business solution.* As customers' requirements are continually becoming more complex, single product or service

selling is becoming obsolete. Their needs can only be met by a 'package' of products or services. The salesperson will have to be highly trained to put together a package to satisfy these needs.

3 *Handling the more educated buying population.* Today's customers are willing to work harder and take time to shop around for what they need. They are also more aware of the product features, benefits, options and prices. Today's professional salesperson must thus work harder to close the sale.

4 *Mastering the art of consultative selling.* The salesperson now needs to understand the specific business issues and problems faced by customers. His or her role is to lessen customers' responsibility to discover their own needs, and show how the product and service being offered will fill these needs.

5 *Managing a team selling approach.* In the future a team selling approach will have to be adopted to satisfy customer needs. The salesperson will have to draw on knowledge of technical staff, marketing staff and experts in other product areas.

6 *Knowing the customer's business.* Future sales will require in-depth knowledge of the customer's business, with salespeople well versed in the requirements of the market segment in which they sell. Relationship building with the customer is paramount and the customer's best interests are always placed at the forefront. Accurate marketing information is needed to provide each customer with the best possible service.

7 *Adding value through service.* When a product reaches a commodity status the salesperson's perceived value is diminished. They are reduced to 'order-takers'. Companies must continue to build up their relationship with customers by adding value through services such as business consultations and ongoing product support.

These challenges have assumed greater importance since the advent of the Single European Market. For the first time there is easy access to the European markets. Thus competition has increased and only the companies that are prepared to meet these challenges will survive.

Producing the best available product or service is not enough – it has to be sold. If companies are to survive they must attach the utmost importance to training their field salesforce, not just pay lip service to the concept. Top management must be totally committed to training and authorise sufficient investment for this to occur. They must also accept that the benefits derived from sales training may not be immediate; they take time to show through.

The potential benefits of sales training are immense ranging from enhanced skill levels, improved motivation (see the Vroom model)[25] and greater self-confidence in one's ability to perform well at selling, a factor that has been shown to be related to improved sales performance.[26]

On the whole, insufficient attention is paid to training. Presumably it is believed that salespeople will learn the necessary skills on the job. This approach ignores the benefits of a training programme that builds a reference frame within which learning can occur and provides the opportunity to practise skills with feedback which is necessary to identify the strengths and weaknesses of performance. For training to succeed the salesperson must accept that there is a problem with his or her performance, otherwise s/he is unlikely to try to rectify the problem.

Another approach to the training problem of new salespeople is to send them out with an experienced salesperson to observe how selling is done. This in itself is insufficient for successful sales training. Its virtues are that the trainee may gain insights not only into techniques which appear to be successful in selling, for example, certain closing techniques, but also into the kinds of objections raised by buyers. However, its value is greatly enhanced if supplemented by a formal sales training programme conducted by an experienced sales trainer who is skilled in lecturing, handling role-playing sessions and providing constructive feedback in such a way that it is accepted by the trainee.

Sales training provides particular challenges in the international environment. Differences in language and culture mean that care must be taken when training overseas sales teams. The boxed case discussion addresses some major points. Indeed, as individual nations become culturally diverse there is a growing need for cultural diversity training for companies that do not trade internationally.[27]

Training overseas salesforces

When training local salespeople cultural imperatives should be recognised. For example, when training Chinese and Japanese salespeople situations where 'loss of face' can occur should be avoided. Japanese salespeople receive on-the-job training in a ritualistic formal setting to ensure that constructive criticism does not result in 'loss of face' for the inexperienced salesperson. Also some selling approaches may not be applicable in certain cultures. For example, problem-solving techniques may not be suitable for Chinese or Japanese salespeople. Finally, care needs to be exercised when translating sales manuals into foreign languages.

For local recruits, training will include product knowledge and an appreciation of the company, its history and philosophies. For expatriates, language training may be required and familiarity with foreign business etiquette. Often initial on-the-job training is with an experienced expatriate. Training in the language, lifestyle and culture of the people of the new country should include the salesperson's spouse and children to reduce early burnout.

Sources: Based on Hill, J.S., Still, R.R. and Boya, U.O. (1991) 'Managing the multinational sales force', *International Marketing Review*, 8(1), pp. 19–31; Honeycutt, Jr, E.D. and Ford, J.B. (1995) 'Guidelines for managing an international sales force', *Industrial Marketing Management*, 24, pp. 135–44.

Skill development

There are four classic stages to learning a skill. These are shown in Table 14.6.

The first stage defines the situation before a trainee decides to enter a career in selling. S/he is unable to carry out the skills and has not even thought about them. By reading or being told about the skills involved, the trainee reaches the second stage of being consciously unable. S/he knows what to do but cannot successfully perform any of the skills.

At the third stage (consciously able) the trainee not only knows what to do but is reasonably proficient at putting the skills into practice individually. S/he is like a learner driver who can engage gear, release the clutch, look in the mirror, gently press the accelerator and release the handbrake as a series of separate operations, but not in a co-ordinated manner which successfully moves the car from a standing start. The trainee may be able to make a presentation successfully, handle objections and close a sale, but may be hopelessly adrift when s/he needs to handle objections, continue making the presentation and all the while look for signs to close the sale.

A successful training programme takes the trainee through this difficult barrier to the fourth stage (unconsciously able) when s/he can perform all the skills at once and has the ability to think a stage in advance so that s/he has control of the selling situation. A car driver reaches this stage when able to co-ordinate the skills necessary to start, move and stop a car without thinking; the timing of gear changes and braking, for example, become automatic, without conscious thought. Similarly, the salesperson can open the interview, move through the stages of need identification, presentation and handling objections in a natural manner, and can alter the approach as situations demand, before choosing the right moment and most appropriate technique to close the sale.

When salespeople become unconsciously able they are likely to be competent although, like a driver, football player or cricketer, there will always be room for further improvement and refinement of their skills.

Components of a training programme

A **training programme** will attempt to cover a combination of knowledge and skill development. Five components can be identified:

1 The company – objectives, policies and organisation.

2 Its products.

3 Its competitors and their products.

4 Selling procedure and techniques.

5 Work organisation and report preparation.

The first three components are essentially communicating the required level of knowledge to the salesperson. The first component will probably include a brief history of the company, how it has grown and where it intends to go in the future.

Table 14.6 Skills development

Stage	Description
1 Unconsciously unable	Trainee does not think about skills.
2 Consciously unable	Trainee reads about skills but cannot carry them out in practice.
3 Consciously able	Trainee knows what to do and is reasonably proficient in individual skills but has difficulty putting them all into practice together.
4 Unconsciously able	Trainee can perform the task without thinking about it; skills become automatic.

Policies relevant to the selling function, for example, how salespeople are evaluated and the nature of the compensation system will be explained. The way in which the company is organised will be described and the relationship between sales and the marketing function, including advertising and market research, will be described so that the salesperson has an appreciation of the support s/he is receiving from headquarters.

The second component, product knowledge, will include a description of how the products are made and the implications for product quality and reliability, the features of the product and the benefits they confer on the consumer. Salespeople will be encouraged to carry out their own product analyses so that they will be able to identify key features and benefits of new products as they are launched. Competitors will be identified and competitors' products will also be analysed to spotlight differences between them and the company's products.

Some training programmes, particularly within the industrial selling arena, stop here, neglecting a major component of a training programme – selling procedures and techniques. This component involves an examination of the factors analysed in Chapter 8 and will include practical sessions where trainees develop skills through role-playing exercises.

The final component of the programme – work organisation and report writing – will endeavour to establish good habits among the trainees in areas which may be neglected because of day-to-day pressures. The importance of these activities on a salesperson's performance and, hence, earnings will be stressed.

Methods

The lecture

This method is useful in giving information and providing a frame of reference to aid the learning process. The lecture should be supported by the use of visual aids, for example, professionally produced PowerPoints. Trainees should be encouraged to participate so that the communication is not just one way. Discussion stimulates interest and allows misunderstandings to be identified and dealt with.

Films

These are a useful supplement to the lecture in giving information and showing how a skill should be performed. They add an extra dimension to a lecture by demonstrating how the principles can be applied in a selling situation. In terms of the stages of learning skills, lectures and films take the trainees up to the point of being consciously unable. They will show what they are required to do, but they will lack the experience to put the theory into practice successfully.

Role playing

This learning method moves the trainees into the stage of being consciously able to perform a skill. It allows the trainees to learn by their own successes and failures in a buyer–seller situation. Feedback is provided by other group members, the sales trainer and by audio-visual means.

Seeing oneself perform is an enlightening and rewarding experience and can demonstrate to the trainee the points raised by other members of the group. Without this dimension some trainees may refuse to accept a fault, e.g. losing the buyer's interest, simply because in the heat of the selling discussion they genuinely do not notice it. Playback allows the trainee to see the situation through the eyes of a third person and problems are more easily recognised and accepted.

Role playing has its critics. Some say that trainees do not take it seriously enough and that by its very nature it is not totally realistic. Its main value is in teaching inexperienced salespeople the basic skills of selling in a less threatening environment than real selling. The selling process can be broken up into a series of activities, e.g. opening and need identification, sales presentation and overcoming objections, each of which requires a special set of skills. Role playing can be used to develop each set of skills in a series of exercises which gradually build up to a full sales interview. A role-playing exercise designed to develop skills in need identification is given at the end of this chapter.

The degree of success achieved by role playing is heavily dependent upon the skills of the sales trainer. When the trainees have at least a modicum of sales experience, it is good practice to allow them to devise their own sales situations based upon actual experiences. The briefs so produced are then exchanged between trainees so that each is presented with a situation which is new to them but which, at the same time, is realistic.[28]

Case studies

Case studies are particularly appropriate for developing analytical skills. Trainees are asked to analyse situations, identify problems and opportunities and make recommendations for dealing with them. They can be used, for example, in setting call objectives. A history of a buyer–seller relationship is given and the trainee is asked to develop a set of sensible objectives for his or her next visit.

In-the-field training

It is essential that initial training given to trainees is reinforced by on-the-job training. The experience gained by real-life selling situations plus the evaluation and feedback provided by the sales manager should mean that the salesperson moves solidly into the final stage of the learning skills process – unconsciously able. The salesperson does the right things automatically, just as a driver can co-ordinate the set of skills necessary to drive a car without consciously thinking.

Although unconsciously able is the final stage in the learning process, it does *not* describe a finite position beyond which improvement cannot take place. Field training is designed to improve the performance of the experienced as well as the newer salesperson. In order to achieve this the sales manager needs to do the following:

- analyse each salesperson's performance

- identify strengths and weaknesses

- gain agreement with the salesperson that a weakness exists

- teach the salesperson how to overcome the weaknesses

- monitor progress to check that an improvement has been realised

There may be a strong temptation during a sales interview for a manager to step in when it is obvious that the salesperson is losing an order. Whether he or she succumbs to this temptation will depend upon the importance of the order, but to do so will undoubtedly reduce the effectiveness of the training session. Ideally, the sales manager should use the situation as an opportunity to observe and evaluate how the salesperson deals with the situation. Stepping in may save the order but cause resentment on the part of the salesperson, who loses face with the customer. This may jeopardise future sales and damage the manager's relationship with the salesperson.

Generally, salespeople will respect criticism which they feel is fair and constructive. To achieve a sense of fairness, the sales manager should begin the post-interview assessment session by listing the positive points in the salesperson's performance. S/he should then ask the salesperson to relate any aspects of the sales interview which could be improved upon. If the salesperson realises that s/he has a weakness, then the manager does not have the problem of convincing him or her that a difficulty exists.

It is inevitable that some weaknesses will not be exposed in this way and the manager will have to explain them to the salesperson. However, since the manager has earlier praised other aspects of performance, the salesperson is unlikely to reject the manager's criticisms out of hand. Having gained agreement, the sales manager will then suggest methods to overcome the problem. Perhaps s/he will take the role of the buyer and engage in a role-playing exercise to rehearse the way in which a problem should be dealt with before the next call, or simply instruct the salesperson and suggest that s/he applies what has been said at the next call.

Evaluation of training courses

A widely adopted framework for evaluating the effectiveness of sales training is the four-stage training model proposed by Kirkpatrick.[29] Training evaluations are classified into four categories:

1 **Participants' reactions to the training course.** Reactions are measures of how the sales trainees feel about various aspects of a sales training course. They are, therefore, similar to traditional measures of customer satisfaction. It is assumed that when salespeople dislike a training course, little effort will be put into learning and using the material. Conversely, if sales trainees enjoy the training they will learn more and be more motivated to use the material.[30] Typically, reaction measures focus on value-adding aspects of the training such as satisfaction with the instruction, satisfaction with the course content, and general course satisfaction.[31] Research by Leach and Liu (2003) suggests that there is a positive link between reaction measures and knowledge retention, i.e. the more trainees are satisfied with a sales training course, the more they retain selling knowledge from it.[32]

2 **Acquisition and retention of knowledge and attitude change.** Acquisition and retention of knowledge can be assessed by pen and paper tests when the training objectives are the provision of information (e.g. product and competitor information). When training objectives involve the teaching of selling skills, pen and paper tests will be supplemented with evaluated role

plays. The study by Leach and Liu[33] indicates that trainees whose level of knowledge acquisition was higher were more likely to transfer learned material to the marketplace.

3 **Changes in work behaviour.** Behaviour change evaluations measure the extent to which salespeople modify their job-related behaviour due to sales training. This is often referred to as 'transfer of learning' and is crucial to the success of a sales training course. Learning transfer evaluations often involve direct observations of the sales trainee in the workplace by sales managers. The Leach and Liu[34] study suggests that assessment of the degree of learning transfer to the job is an important aspect of evaluation since it is linked to organisational outcomes, i.e. the more trainees apply what they have learnt from the sales training course, the better their achievement of desired organisational outcomes such as improved selling effectiveness, enhanced customer relations and higher levels of organisational commitment.

4 **Organisational outcomes.** These evaluations measure the extent to which a sales training course has contributed to the achievement of the objectives set out by the company. Six organisational sales training objectives[35] are often used:

- increased sales volume

- improved customer relations

- increased salesperson commitment leading to lower levels of staff turnover

- decreased selling costs

- improved control of the salesforce

- better time management

Although the most relevant, these measures are usually the most difficult to specifically attribute to the sales training course. Hence, it is useful to know that learning transfer (which is easier to measure) is a good predictor of organisational outcomes.

A study by Stamford-Bewley and Jobber sought to identify the methods used to evaluate training courses among a sample of companies in service, consumer and industrial sectors.[36] The results are shown in Figure 14.6. It appears that only 57 per cent attempt to measure changes in sales volume which may occur as a result of the course. More popular were field visits with salespeople (78 per cent) where the sales manager would subjectively gauge whether ability had improved as a result of the training course.

Training sales managers

To succeed as a sales manager requires a formidable set of skills and roles[37] including the following:

- developing close relationships with customers and an in-depth understanding of customers' businesses

- partnering salespeople to achieve sales, profitability and customer satisfaction goals

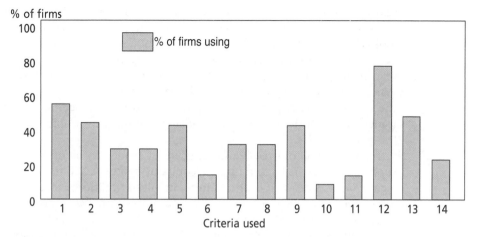

% of firms

Key: Criteria used to evaluate training course
1 Change in sales net volume
2 Change in sales net value
3 Change in sales volume per call
4 Change in sales value per call
5 Number of new accounts gained
6 Number of old accounts lost
7 Order/call rate
8 Order taken/target
9 Coverage of territory
10 Length of time representatives spend with customer
11 Length of time representatives stay with company
12 Ability shown during field visits
13 Questionnaire at end of course
14 Questionnaire at some time in the future

Figure 14.6 Criteria used to evaluate training courses
Source: Stamford-Bewley, C. and Jobber, D. (1989) *A Study of the Training of Salespeople in the UK*, University of Bradford School of Management Working Paper.

- co-ordinating hybrid salesforces of telemarketers and field salespeople

- keeping up to date with the latest technologies impacting the sales function

- learning marketing skills to identify potential business opportunities and recommend strategies

- working with other functional areas to achieve overall corporate goals through customer satisfaction

- continually seeking ways to exceed customer expectations and create added value in buyer–seller relationships

- creating a flexible, learning and adapting environment for the sales team

- developing teaching, analytical, motivational, organisational, communication and planning skills

The sales manager's job is becoming increasingly demanding because of the environmental changes discussed at the beginning of Chapter 4. Yet the training of sales managers appears to be neglected in many companies. Information on the extent of sales manager training is based on US studies which show that not only are most sales managers not being trained adequately, but also that most are not being formally trained at all.

The US survey conducted by Anderson, Mehta and Strong showed that 57 per cent of sales managers reported their company failed to provide them with formal sales management training.[38] They speculate that one reason may be that companies assume a newly promoted 'top salesperson' ought to be able to pass their selling skills on to other salespeople and thus smoothly make the transition from successful salesperson to successful sales manager. However, this argument overlooks the large differences between the job of a salesperson and that of sales manager. While salespeople achieve their goals largely as a result of their own efforts, sales managers accomplish their goals largely through the efforts of the salesforce. Whereas the salesperson requires self-management, selling and negotiation skills, the sales manager requires a much broader range of managerial, administrative and leadership skills. Hence it is not surprising that top salespeople do not always make the best managers.

For those who did receive training, most tended to be on-the-job coaching by supervisors or peers backed up by a company-sponsored course or seminar at a college or university. Most of the training involved traditional methods such as group discussions, role playing, case studies and motivational speakers (see Table 14.7).

The topics most frequently covered were motivation, goal setting for salespeople, leadership skills, training evaluation, territory management and time management (see Table 14.8). Very little attention was given to profitability analyses (by product category, market segment, salesperson, territory or customer type) indicating that sales managers were not being given essential financial skills to support their job.

Research by Dubinsky, Mehta and Anderson[39] examined the link between sales managers' satisfaction with training programmes and training content. Training satisfaction is increased for lower-level sales managers when the course addresses a wide range of issues such as conducting sales meetings, budgeting, company knowledge, customer relations and social responsibility. Such a wide array of topics provides a solid foundation for such managers in their present jobs and in the future as they gain promotion. For higher-level sales managers, training satisfaction is enhanced when the course includes general management issues, management of physical distribution, learning about company policies, planning and control activities and competitor knowledge. Such information has direct relevance for such managers as they affect the design and execution of sales and marketing strategies. Of particular interest is the greater level of training satisfaction for senor sales man-

Table 14.7 Methods used to train sales managers

Method	%
Group discussions	72
Role playing	64
Case studies	50
Motivational speakers	46
Computer simulation games	44
Seminars (up to four weeks long)	44
Videotapes/films	40
College courses	24
Correspondence courses	16
In basket exercises	10
Videoconferencing	8

Source: Anderson, R.E., Mehta, R. and Strong, J. (1997) 'An empirical investigation of sales management training programs for sales managers', *Journal of Personal Selling and Sales Management*, 17(3), pp. 53–66.

Table 14.8 Topics covered in sales training programmes

Topic	%
Motivating salespeople	82
Goal setting for salespeople	76
Leading salespeople	66
Training salespeople	64
Evaluating salespeople	64
Territory management	62
Time management	60
Developing sales strategies	58
Strategic sales planning	56
Recruiting new salespeople	52
Organising salespeople	52
Sales forecasting	50

Source: Anderson, R.E., Mehta, R. and Strong, J. (1997) 'An empirical investigation of sales management training programs for sales managers', *Journal of Personal Selling and Sales Management*, 17(3), pp. 53–66.

agers when control activities are included in the programme. The inclusion of a range of control tasks such as profit analysis by territory/customer type/salespeople/market segment/product category, analysis of selling costs and market share analysis enhances training satisfaction. This is gratifying given the need for sales managers to be more profit-orientated.[40]

14.4 Conclusions

This chapter considered motivational theory and practice as applied to the sales area. A number of theories were examined:

1 Maslow's hierarchy of needs theory

2 Herzberg's motivator/hygiene theory

3 Vroom's expectancy theory

4 Adams's inequity theory

5 Likert's sales management theory

Motivation in practice is focused on the use of the following:

• financial incentives

• sales quotas or targets

• meetings between salesperson and manager

• sales contests

Successful leaders change their style depending on the situation. Sales training involves the development of a programme which enhances selling skills. The components of a training programme and methods used were examined before the skills required for sales management were outlined.

The next chapter explores two other management considerations: sales organisation and compensation.

References

1 Maslow, A.H. (1943) 'A theory of human motivation', *Psychological Review*, July, pp. 121–35.

2 Pullins, E.B. (2001) 'An exploratory investigation of the relationship between sales force compensation and intrinsic motivation', 30, pp. 403-13; Holmes, T.L. and Srivastava, R. (2002) 'Effects of job perceptions on job behaviors: implications for sales performance', *Industrial Marketing Management*, 31, pp. 421–8.

3 Paul, W.J., Robertson, K.G. and Herzberg, F. (1969) 'Job enrichment pays off', *Harvard Business Review*, March–April.

4 Dessler, G. (1979) *Human Behaviour: Improving Performance at Work*, Prentice-Hall, Englewood Cliffs, NJ.

5 Vroom, V.H. (1964) *Work and Motivation*, Wiley, New York.

6 Adams, J.S. (1965) 'Inequity in social exchange', in Berkowitz, L. (ed.), *Advances in Experimental Social Psychology*, 2, Academic Press, New York.

7 Tyagi, P.K. (1990) 'Inequities in organisations, salesperson motivation and job satisfaction', *International Journal of Research in Marketing*, 7, pp. 135–48.

8 Likert, R. (1961) *New Patterns of Sales Management*, McGraw-Hill, New York.

9 Churchill, Jr, G.A., Ford, N.M., Walker, Jr, O.C., Johnston, M.W. and Tanner, Jr, J.F. (2000) *Sales Force Management: Planning, Implementation and Control*, 2nd edn, Irwin, Homewood, IL.

10 PA Consultants (1979) *Sales Force Practice Today: A Basis for Improving Performance*, Institute of Marketing, London.

11 Shipley, D. and Kiely, J. (1988) 'Motivation and dissatisfaction of industrial salespeople – how relevant is Herzberg's theory?' *European Journal of Marketing*, 22, 1.

12 Coulaux, C. and Jobber, D. (1989) *Motivation of Consumer Salespeople*, University of Bradford Management Centre Working Paper.

13 Kotler, P. (2003) *Marketing Management: Analysis, Planning and Control*, 5th edn, Prentice-Hall, Englewood Cliffs, NJ.

14 Jobber, D. and Lee, R. (1994) 'A comparison of the perceptions of sales management and salespeople towards sales force motivation and demotivation', *Journal of Marketing Management*, 10(2).

15 Coulaux, C. and Jobber, D. (1989) *Motivation of Consumer Salespeople*, University of Bradford Management Centre Working Paper.

16 Anderson, R.E., Hair, Jr, J.F. and Bush, A.J. (1992) *Professional Sales Management*, Irwin McGraw-Hill, New York.

17 Churchill, G.A., Ford, N.M., Walker, Jr, O.C., Johnston, M.W. and Tanner, Jr, J.F. (2000) *Salesforce Management*, Irwin McGraw-Hill, New York.

18 Futrell, C.F. (2000) *Sales Management*, Dryden Press, Orlando.

19 Huczynski, A. and Buchanan, D. (2004) *Organizational Behaviour: An Introductory Text*, Financial Times Prentice Hall, London.

20 Goleman, D. (2000) 'Leadership that gets results', *Harvard Business Review*, March–April, pp. 78–90.

21 Goleman, D. (2000) op. cit.

22 Huczynski and Buchanan (2004) op. cit.

23 Huczynski and Buchanan (2004) op. cit.

24 Learning International Organization (1988) 'Selling strategies for the 1990s', *Training and Development Journal*, March.

25 Vroom, V.H. (1964) op. cit.

26 Krishnan, B.C., Netemeyer, R.G. and Boles, J.S. (2002) 'Self-efficacy, competitiveness and effort as antecedents of salesperson performance', *Journal of Personal Selling and Sales Management*, 22 (4), pp. 285–95.

27 Bush, V.D. and Ingram, T. N. (2001) 'Building and assessing cultural diversity skills: implications for sales training', *Industrial Marketing Management*, 30, pp. 65–76.

28 Wilson, M. (1999) *Managing a Sales Force*, Gower, Aldershot.

29 Kirkpatrick, D.L. (1959) 'Techniques for evaluating training programs', *Journal of the American Society for Training and Development*, 13 (11), pp. 3–9; Kirkpatrick, D.L. (1996) 'Great ideas revisited', *Training and Development*, 50, 1 (January), pp. 55–7.

30 Warr, P.B., Allan, C. and Birdi, K. (1999) 'Predicting three levels of training outcome', *Journal of Occupational and Organizational Psychology*, 72 (3), pp. 351–75.

31 Morgan, R.B. and Casper, W.J. (2000) 'Examining the factor structure of participant reactions to training: a multidimensional approach', *Human Resource Development Quarterly*, 11(3), pp. 301–17.

32 Leach, M.P. and Liu, A.H. (2003) 'Investigating interrelationships among sales training evaluation methods, '*Journal of Personal Selling and Sales Management*, 23, (4), pp. 327–39.

33 Leach, M.P. and Liu, A.H. (2003) op. cit.

34 Leach, M.P. and Liu, A.H. (2003) op. cit.; Research by Wilson, P.H., Strutton, D. and Farris, M.T. (2002) 'Investigating the perceptual aspect of sales training', *Journal of Personal Selling and Sales Management*, 22 (2), pp. 77–86, also supports the relationship between the transfer of learning and sales performance.

35 Honeycutt, Jr, E.D., Howe, V. and Ingram, T.N. (1993) 'Shortcomings of sales training programs', *Industrial Marketing Management*, 22, pp. 117–23.

36 Stamford-Bewley, C. and Jobber, D. (1989) *A Study of the Training of Salespeople in the UK*, University of Bradford Management Centre Working Paper.

37 Anderson, R.E. (1996) 'Personal selling and sales management in the new millennium', *Journal of Personal Selling and Sales Management*, 16(4), pp. 17–52.

38 Anderson, R.E., Mehta, R. and Strong, J. (1997) 'An empirical investigation of sales management training programs for sales managers', *Journal of Personal Selling and Sales Management*, 17(3), pp. 53–66.

39 Dubinsky, A.J., Mehta, R. and Anderson, R.E. (2001) 'Satisfaction with sales manager training: design and implementation issues', *European Journal of Marketing*, 35, pp. 27–50.

40 Anderson (1996) op. cit.

Practical Exercise

Selling fountain pens

This exercise can be used to develop the skills required for effective selling outlined in Chapter 8; that is, need identification, presentation and demonstration, answering questions and handling objections, and closing the sale. The salesperson's profile is given below. The salesperson should be given at least 15 minutes to study the range of pens on sale (see Figure 14.7). The role play can be video-recorded and played back in front of the class to provide a focus for discussion.

Salesperson's profile

You are a salesperson in a stationery department of a small store. For a few minutes a customer has been looking at your range of quality pens. The person comes up to you saying, 'I'm looking for a good fountain pen.'

You take the interview from this point. You have a display of six fountain pens (A–F) with the features shown in Figure 14.7.

Source: The authors are grateful to Mr Robert Edwards, sales training manager, UKMP Department, ICI Pharmaceuticals, who devised this exercise, for permission to reprint it.

PEN	Filling method	Price	Spare nibs	Spare cartridge cost	Nib size/ type	Construction material (all with pocket clips)	Shape	Colours	Other features
A	Capillary refillable	£15	£2.50	—	Medium/ gold	All-metal 'gold' finish	Round	'Silver'/ 'gold' tops	Barrel has to be unscrewed to refill with an easy grip feature; guaranteed for two years; screw cap; spare italic nib supplied; made in the UK 
B	Cartridge, 3 spare	£12	£1.50	£1 for 4	Medium/ gold	Metal/ plastic tops	Round	Black/ 'silver'	Very slim enclosed nib; screw cap; guaranteed for one year; made in France 
C	Cartridge, 2 spare	£10	£1.50	£1 for 4	Medium/ steel	Metal/ plastic	Round	Various/ 'silver' tops	Bulky easy-to-hold style; screw cap; guaranteed for one year; made in Italy 
D	Cartridge, 4 spare	£10	£1.30	£1 for 6	Fine/ steel	Plastic with 'silver' top	Round	Various/ 'silver' tops	Superslim variety; enclosed nib; screw cap; guaranteed for two years; made in France 
E	Cartridge, 1 spare	£9	£2.00	£1 for 6	Fine/ steel	Plastic	Triangular	Black/ red/ blue	Push-on cap; one year guarantee; made in Germany 
F	Cartridge, 1 spare	£7	£4.00	£0.60 for 4	Broad/ steel	Metallised plastic	Round	'Silver'	Choice of left-/ right-hand nib; push-on cap; guaranteed for six months; made in the UK 

Figure 14.7 Fountain pen features

Examination Questions

1   It is impossible to motivate, only to demotivate. Discuss.

2   You have recently been appointed sales manager of a company selling abrasives to the motor trade. Sales are declining and you believe that a major factor causing this decline is a lack of motivation amongst your salesforce. At present they are paid a straight salary, the size of which depends on length of service. Outline your thoughts regarding how you would approach this situation.

15 Organisation and Compensation

Objectives

After studying this chapter, you should be able to:

1   Appreciate the advantages and disadvantages of different salesforce organisation structures
2   Compute the numbers of salespeople needed for different selling situations
3   Understand the factors to be considered when developing sales territories
4   Strike a balance between various sales compensation plans
5   Establish priorities in relation to customers, travelling time, and evolving call patterns

Key Concepts

- compensation plans
- key account selling
- key or major account salesforce
- organising a salesforce
- team selling
- workload approach

15.1   Organisational Structure

Perhaps the classic form of **organising a salesforce** is along geographical lines, but the changing needs of customers and technological advances have led many companies to reconsider their salesforce organisation. The strengths and weaknesses of each type of organisational structure, as illustrated in Figure 15.1, will now be examined.

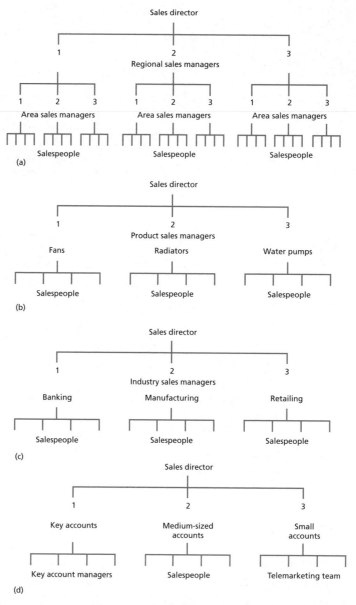

Figure 15.1 Organisation structures: (a) geographical structure – the area sales manager level is optional: where the number of salespeople (span of control) under each regional manager exceeds eight, serious consideration may be given to appointing area managers; (b) product specialisation structure; (c) industry-based structure; (d) account-size structure

Geographical structure

An advantage of this form of organisation is its simplicity. Each salesperson is assigned a territory over which to have sole responsibility for sales achievement. His or her close geographical proximity to customers encourages the development of personal friendships which aids sales effectiveness. Also, compared with other organisational forms, e.g. product or market specialisation, travelling expenses are likely to be lower.

A potential weakness of the geographical structure is that the salesperson is required to sell the full range of the company's products. They may be very different technically and sell into a number of diverse markets. In such a situation it may be unreasonable to expect the salesperson to have the required depth of technical knowledge for each product and be conversant with the full range of potential applications within each market. This expertise can only be developed if the salesperson is given a more specialised role. A further related disadvantage of this method is that, according to Moss, salespeople in discrete geographical territories, covering all types of customer, are relatively weak in interpreting buyer behaviour patterns and reporting changes in the operational circumstances of customers compared with salespeople organised along more specialised lines.[1]

Product specialisation structure

One method of specialisation is along product lines. Conditions which are conducive to this form of organisation are where the company sells a wide range of technically complex and diverse products and key members of the decision-making unit of the buying organisations are different for each product group. However, if the company's products sell essentially to the same customers, problems of route duplication (and hence higher travel costs) and customer annoyance can arise. Inappropriate use of this method can lead to a customer being called upon by different salespeople representing the same company on the same day. When a company contemplates a move from a geographically-based to a product-based structure, some customer overlap is inevitable, but if only of a limited extent the problem should be manageable.

Customer-based structures

The problem of the same customer being served by product divisions of the same supplier, the complexity of buyer behaviour which requires not only input from the sales function but from other functional groups (such as engineering, finance, logistics and marketing), centralisation of purchasing, and the immense value of some customers have led many suppliers to rethink how they organise their salesforce. Companies are increasingly organising around customers and shifting resources from product or regional divisions to customer-focused business units.[2]

Market-centred structure

Another method of specialisation is by the type of market served. Often in industrial selling the market is defined by industry type. Thus, although the range of products sold is essentially the same, it might be sensible for a computer firm to allocate its salespeople on the basis of the industry served, e.g. banking, manufacturing companies and retailers, given that different industry groups have widely varying needs, problems and potential applications. Specialisation by market served allows salespeople to gain greater insights into these factors for their particular industry, as well as to monitor changes and trends within the industry which might affect demand for their products. The cost of increased customer knowledge is increased travel expenses compared with geographically determined territories.

Magrath looked at the way industrial sales specialists levered up sales by virtue of applications expertise.[3] Because they knew so much about the industry, they were welcomed as 'fraternity brothers' by customers.

Account-size structure

Some companies structure their salesforce by account size. The importance of a few large customers in many trade and industrial markets has given rise to the establishment of a **key or major account salesforce**. The team comprises senior salespeople who specialise in dealing with large customers that may have different buying habits and demand more sophisticated sales arguments than smaller companies. The team will be conversant with negotiation skills since they are likely to be given a certain amount of discretion in terms of discounts, credit terms, etc., in order to secure large orders. The range of selling skills required is therefore wider than for the rest of the salesforce, who deal with the smaller accounts. Some organisations adopt a three-tier system, with senior salespeople negotiating with key accounts, ordinary salespeople selling to medium-sized accounts, and a telemarketing team dealing with small accounts. A number of advantages are claimed for a key account salesforce structure:

1 *Close working relationships with the customer.* The salesperson knows who makes what decisions and who influences the various players involved in the decision. Technical specialists from the selling organisation can call on technical people (e.g. engineers) in the buying organisation and salespeople can call upon administrators, buyers and financial people armed with the commercial arguments for buying.

2 *Improved communication and co-ordination.* The customers know that a dedicated salesperson or sales team exists so that they know who to contact when a problem arises.

3 *Better follow-up on sales and service.* The extra resources devoted to the key account mean there is more time to follow up and provide service after a major sale has been made.

4 *More in-depth penetration of the DMU.* There is more time to cultivate relationships within the key account. Salespeople can 'pull' the buying decision through the organisation from the users, deciders and influencers to the buyer, rather than the more difficult task of 'pushing' it through the buyer into the organisation, as done with more traditional sales approaches.

5 *Higher sales.* Most companies who have adopted key account selling claim that sales have risen as a result.

6 *The provision of an opportunity for advancement for career salespeople.* A tiered salesforce system with key (or national) account selling at the top provides promotional opportunities for salespeople who wish to advance within the salesforce rather than enter a traditional sales management position.

The term *national account* is generally considered to refer to large and important customers who may have centralised purchasing departments that buy or co-ordinate buying for decentralised, geographically dispersed branches that transcend sales territory boundaries. Selling to such firms often involves the following:

1 Obtaining acceptance of the company's products at the buyer's headquarters

2 Negotiating long-term supply contracts

3 Maintaining favourable buyer–seller relationships at various levels in the buying organisation

4 Establishing first-class customer service

The customer or small group of customers is given special attention by one key person (often known as a national account manager) or team headed by this person. This allows greater co-ordination than a geographically-based system where each branch would be called upon by a different salesperson as part of the job of covering his or her territory.

This depth of selling activity frequently calls for the expertise of a range of personnel in the supplying company in addition to the salesperson. It is for this reason that many companies serving national accounts employ **team selling**.

Team selling involves the combined efforts of such people as product specialists, engineers, sales managers and even directors if the buyer's decision-making unit includes personnel of equivalent rank. Team selling provides a method of responding to the various commercial, technical and psychological requirements of large buying organisations.

Companies are increasingly structuring both external and internal sales staff on the basis of specific responsibility for accounts. Examples of such companies are those in the electronics industry, where internal desk staff are teamed up with outside staff around 'key' customers. These company salesforces are able, with reasonable accuracy, to forecast future sales levels at these key locations. Further, an in-depth understanding of the buyer's decision-making unit is developed by the salesperson being able to form relationships with a large number of individual decision-makers. In this way, marketing staff can be kept informed of customer requirements, enabling them to improve products and plan effective communications.

New/Existing account structure

A further method of sales organisation is to create two teams of salespeople. The first team services existing accounts, while the second concentrates upon seeking new accounts. This structure recognises the following:

1 Gaining new customers is a specialised activity demanding prospecting skills, patience, ability to accept higher rejection rates than when calling upon existing customers, and the time to cultivate new relationships.

2 Placing this function in the hands of the regular salesforce may result in its neglect since the salespeople may view it as time which could be better spent with existing customers.

3 Salespeople may prefer to call upon long-established customers whom they know rather than prospects where they might face rejection and unpleasantness.

Pioneer salespeople were used successfully by trading stamp companies to prospect new customers. Once an account was obtained it was handed over to a maintenance salesperson who serviced the account. This form of salesforce organisation is used in the CCTV, freight and copier industries.

New account salespeople have been found to spend more time exploring the prospect's needs and provide more information to management regarding buyer behaviour and attitudes than salespeople working under a conventional system.[4] The deployment of new account salesforces is feasible for large companies with many customers and where there is a continual turnover of key accounts which have to be replaced. The new account structure allows better planning of this vital function and eliminates competition between prospecting and servicing.

Functional specialisation

In industrial selling, companies sometimes separate their salesforces into development and maintenance sales teams. The development salespeople are highly trained in handling very technical new products. They will spend considerable time overcoming commercial, technical and installation problems for new customers.

A major reason why companies have moved to a development/maintenance structure is the belief that one of the causes of new product failure is the inadequacy of the salesforce to introduce the product. Perhaps the cause of this failure is the psychological block each salesperson faces in terms of possible future problems with the buyer–seller relationship if the product does not meet expectations. Because of this, the salesperson is likely to doubt the wisdom of giving an unproven product his or her unqualified support. Employment of a development sales team can reduce this problem, although it is often only large companies which can afford such a team. Its use can provide other advantages, including clarity of purpose, effective presentation and reliable feedback from the marketplace. Some pharmaceutical companies use this form of salesforce organisation.

Mixed organisation

This section has discussed the merits and weaknesses of the major sales organisational structures. In practice a combination may be used. For example, in order to minimise travelling expenses, a company using a two-product group structure may divide the country into geographically-based territories with two salespeople operating within each one.

Like many selling decisions, the choice of sales organisation is not a black and white affair, which is why many salesforces are a blend of general territory representatives and specialists. Many companies use all forms of selling simultaneously: for very big accounts they use key account specialists; for the balance of small and medium accounts they use general territory representatives, perhaps supplemented by product application specialists who help generalists across several territories.

The challenge to any sales manager is to know how to assess the options. Financial, customer coverage and organisational flexibility trade-offs need to be made. The company must balance hard numbers with what the customer wants, which often means some form of specialisation, and what the competition are providing. Increasingly, the customer wants to buy total solutions and demands value-added services rather than one-off transactions.

As companies internationalise, consideration of salesforce organisation on a global scale needs to be made. The following case discussion covers a number of relevant issues.

Organisation for international sales

A common method of organising international salesforces is to adopt the same approach as that taken in the domestic market. Many multinational corporations use the simple geographical method within a given country or region. However, international companies that have wide product lines, large sales volumes and/or operate in large developed markets prefer more specialised organisational forms such as customer- or product-based structures. For smaller markets, as found in developing economies, such specialisation may not be economically viable, leading to geographical organisation.

Language also affects international salesforce organisation. For example, territories in Belgium are often divided by language – French to the south and Flemish in the north – or countries are combined as with Austria and Germany because both use the German language. Similarly, Switzerland is often organised into different regions based upon usage of the French, German and Italian languages, while some companies combine Central America into a single sales region.

Some considerations when deciding upon international salesforce organisation are as follows:

- geographical size
- sales potential
- customer expectations
- product line width
- current selling practices
- language spoken

Geographical structures tend to be used in less developed markets, when a single product line is sold and for small sales volumes. Product- or customer-based organisation is more likely in large developed markets, for broad product lines, and where the large sales volume justifies specialisation.

Sources: Based on Hill, J.S. and Still, R.R. (1990) 'Organising the overseas sales force: how multinationals do it', *Journal of Personal Selling and Sales Management*, 10(2), pp. 57–66; Honeycutt, Jr, E.D. and Ford, J.B. (1995) 'Guidelines for managing an international sales force', *Industrial Marketing Management*, 24, pp. 135–44; Samli, A.C., Still, R.R. and Hill, J.S. (1993) *'International Marketing'*, Macmillan: New York.

15.2   Determining the Number of Salespeople

The workload approach

The **workload approach** allows the number of salespeople needed to be calculated, given that the company knows the number of calls per year it wishes its salespeople to make on different classes of customer. Talley showed how the number of salespeople could be calculated by following a series of steps:[5]

1 Customers are grouped into categories according to the value of goods bought and potential for the future.

2 The call frequency (number of calls on an account per year) is assessed for each category of customer.

3 The total required workload per year is calculated by multiplying the call frequency and number of customers in each category and then summing for all categories.

4 The average number of calls per week per salesperson is estimated.

5 The number of working weeks per year is calculated.

6 The average number of calls a salesperson can make per year is calculated by multiplying (4) and (5).

7 The number of salespeople required is determined by dividing the total annual calls required by the average number of calls one salesperson can make per year.

Here is an example of such a calculation. The formula is:

Number of salespeople =

$$\frac{\text{Number of customers} \times \text{Call frequency}}{\text{Average weekly call rate} \times \text{Number of working weeks per year}}$$

Steps (1), (2) and (3) can be summarised as in Table 15.1.

Step (4) gives:
Average number of calls per week per salesperson   = 30

Step (5) gives:

Number of weeks		= 52
Less:		
Holidays	4	
Illness	1	
Conferences/meetings	3	
Training	1	9
Number of working weeks		= 43

Step (6) gives:
Average number of calls per salesperson per year   = 43 × 30
                                                     = 1,290

Step (7) gives:

$$\text{Salesforce size} = \frac{47,000}{1,290} = 37 \text{ salespeople}$$

When prospecting forms an important part of the salesperson's job, potential customers can be included in the customer categories according to potential. Alternatively, separate categories can be formed, with their own call rates, to give an estimation of the workload required to cover prospecting. This is then added to the workload estimate derived from actual customers to produce a total workload figure.

The applicability of this method is largely dependent upon the ability of management to assess confidently the number of calls to be made on each category of customer. Where optimum call rates on customers within a particular category vary considerably, management may be reluctant to generalise. However, in a company quoted by Wilson,[6] although call rates varied between one and ten calls per day, for 80 per cent of the days seven or eight calls were made.

The method is of particular relevance to companies who are expanding into new geographical territories. For example, a company expanding its sphere of operation from England to Scotland could use a blend of past experience and judgement to assess feasible call frequencies in Scotland. Market research could be used to identify potential customers. The workload approach could then be used to estimate the number of salespeople needed.

15.3 Establishing Sales Territories

Territory design is an important organisational issue since it is a major determinant of salespeople's opportunity to perform well and their ability to earn incentive pay where incentives are linked directly to territory-level individual performance. Faulty territory design decisions prevent the best use of expensive selling activities and can harm salespeople's attitudes, behaviour and effectiveness when they believe they have been treated unfairly in territory allocation. Indeed research has shown that the more satisfied sales managers are with territory design, the greater the level of salesperson and sales unit effectiveness.[7] It is therefore important for sales managers to pay much attention to the establishment of effective territories. Their task can be aided by developments in information technology and these are discussed in Chapter 12.

Table 15.1 Workload method

Customer groups	No. of firms	Call frequencies per year	Total
A (Over £1,000,000 per year)	200	× 12	2,400
B (£500,000–£1m per year)	1,000	× 9	9,000
C (£150,000–£499,000 per year)	3,000	× 6	18,000
D (Less than £150,000)	6,000	× 3	18,000
Total annual workload			47,400

There are two basic considerations which are used to allocate salespeople to territories. First, management may wish to balance workload between territories. Workload can be defined as follows:

$$W = n_i t_i + n t_k$$

where W = workload; n_i = number of calls to be made to customers in category i; t_i = average time required at call for each category i; n = total number of calls to be made; t_k = average time required to travel to each call.

This equation is useful because it highlights the important factors which a sales manager must take into account when assessing workload. The number of calls to be made will be weighted by a time factor for each call. Major account calls are likely to be weighted higher than medium and small active accounts since, other things being equal, it makes sense to spend longer with customers who have higher potential. Also, calls on prospects may have a high weighting since salespeople need extra time to develop a new relationship and to sell themselves, their company and its products. In addition, the time required to travel to each customer must be taken into account. Territories vary in their customer density so travel time must be allowed for in the calculation of workload.

The data will be determined partly by executive judgement, e.g. how long to spend with each customer type on average, and, where a salesforce already exists, by observation, e.g. how long it takes to travel between customers in different existing territories. These data can be obtained during field visits with salespeople and estimates of current workloads calculated. For new sales teams the input into the formula will of necessity be more judgemental, but the equation does provide a conceptual framework for assessing territory workload.

The second consideration management may wish to use in working out territories is sales potential. Equalising workload may result in territories of widely differing potential. This may be accepted as a fact of life by some companies and dealt with by assigning their best salespeople to the territories of higher potential. Indeed, moving salespeople from lower to higher potential territories could be used as a form of promotion. If company policy dictates that all salespeople should be treated equally, then a commission scheme based upon the attainment of sales quotas which vary according to territory potential should establish a sense of fairness. However, if, after preliminary determination of territories by workload, sales potentials are widely disparate, it may be necessary to carry out some adjustment. It may be possible to modify adjacent territory boundaries so that a high potential territory surrenders a number of large accounts in return for gaining some smaller accounts from a neighbouring lower potential territory. In this way differences in sales potentials are reduced without altering workload dramatically. If this is not easily done it may be necessary to trade off workload for potential, making territories less similar in terms of workload but more balanced in terms of sales potential.

Designing territories calls for a blend of sound analysis and plain common sense. For example, it would be illogical to design territories purely on the basis of equalising sales potential if the result produced strips of territory which failed to recognise the road system (especially motorways) as it exists in the country today.

Territory revision

A sales territory should not be considered a permanent unit. The following factors may suggest the need for territory revision:

- change in consumer preference

- competitive activity

- diminution in the usefulness of chosen distribution channels

- complete closure of an outlet or group of stores

- increases in the cost of covering territories

- salesforce complacency

Before deciding that changes are necessary, a number of aspects of the sales effort should be investigated. The most common indicators that something might be wrong with the territorial structure is falling sales volume. However, great care must be taken before accepting this as a reason for territory revision. Sales may be falling because the selling and promotion effort within the territory is not as effective as it should be. If this is the case, then it is not the boundaries of the sales area that need revision.

Salespeople may be calling only on the prospects which offer the greatest potential. If there is no systematic plan for the territory, salespeople may make a poor job of planning their calls and this may result in an increase in non-selling time (e.g. travelling time). Furthermore, the supervision may be at fault. If sales personnel are not supervised properly, they may lose their enthusiasm for the job or even for the product.

Before changes are implemented, a reappraisal of market potential should take place. It may be that the original distributors of the products are in need of replacement or motivation because they have become disenchanted with the company, its products, or policies. Consumer acceptance of the product may need to be investigated before territories are revised. This may require a limited market survey. The current activities of competitors should also be investigated.

If territories are to be revised, the salesforce must be fully informed about the extent of the changes and the reasons behind them. The extent to which the boundaries are changed will be governed by the need to increase coverage, reduce costs or increase sales. The sales manager should enlist the aid of supervisors and salespeople when the task of altering territories begins.

While the overall design of territories, size, number of customers, etc., are the responsibility of the sales manager, once allocated, the salesperson too (sometimes in conjunction with the sales manager) can play an important role in managing this territory such as to achieve maximum sales effectiveness. In fact, much of this aspect of territory management comes down to effective self-management on the part of the salesperson. Information technology can aid territory management and revision as discussed in Chapter 12.

15.4 Compensation

Compensation objectives

Sales managers should consider carefully the type of **compensation plan** they wish to use. This is because there are a number of objectives which can be achieved through a compensation scheme. First, compensation can be used to motivate a salesforce by linking achievement to monetary reward. Second, it can be used to attract and hold successful salespeople by providing a good standard of living for them, by rewarding outstanding performance and providing regularity of income. Third, it is possible to design compensation schemes which allow selling costs to fluctuate in line with changes in sales revenue. Thus, in poor years lower sales are offset to some extent by lower commission payments, and in good years increased sales costs are financed by higher sales revenue. Fourth, compensation plans can be formulated to direct the attention of sales personnel to specific company sales objectives. Higher commission can be paid on product lines the company particularly wants to move. Special commission can be paid to salespeople who generate new active accounts if this is believed to be important to the company. Thus, compensation plans can be used to control activities.

Types of compensation plan

When designing compensation plans, sales management need to recognise that not all of the sales team may be motivated by the thought of higher earnings. Darmon identified five types of salespeople:[8]

1 *Creatures of habit.* These salespeople try to maintain their standard of living by earning a predetermined amount of money.

2 *Satisfiers.* These people perform at a level just sufficient to keep their jobs.

3 *Trade-off-ers.* These people allocate their time based upon a personally determined ratio between work and leisure that is not influenced by the prospect of higher earnings.

4 *Goal-orientated.* These salespeople prefer recognition as achievers by their peers and superiors and tend to be sales quota orientated with money mainly serving as recognition of achievement.

5 *Money-orientated.* These people aim to maximise their earnings. Family relationships, leisure and even health may be sacrificed in the pursuit of money.

The implication is that sales management need to understand and categorise their salespeople in terms of their motives. Compensation plans can only be effectively designed with this understanding. For example, developing a new plan based upon greater opportunities to earn commission is unlikely to work if the sales team consists only of the first three categories of salesperson. Conversely, when a sales team is judged to be composed mainly of goal- and money-orientated salespeople, a move from a fixed salary to a salary and commission system is likely to prove effective.

There are, basically, three types of compensation plan:

- fixed salary
- commission only
- salary plus commission

Each type of compensation plan is evaluated below in terms of its benefits and drawbacks to management and salespeople, while Figure 15.2 shows how a sales target can be associated with a fixed salary, commission only, or salary plus commission system. If the target is achieved, sales costs are equal no matter which system is used.

Fixed salary

This method of payment encourages salespeople to consider all aspects of the selling function rather than just those which lead to a quick sales return. Salespeople who are paid on fixed salary are likely to be more willing to provide technical service, complete information feedback reports and carry out prospecting than if they were paid solely by commission. The system provides security to the salesperson who knows how much income s/he will receive each month and is relatively cheap to administer since calculation of commissions and bonuses is not required.

The system also overcomes the problem of deciding how much commission to give to each salesperson when a complex buying decision is made by a number of DMU members who have been influenced by different salespeople, perhaps in different parts of the country. Wilson cites the case of a sale of building materials to a

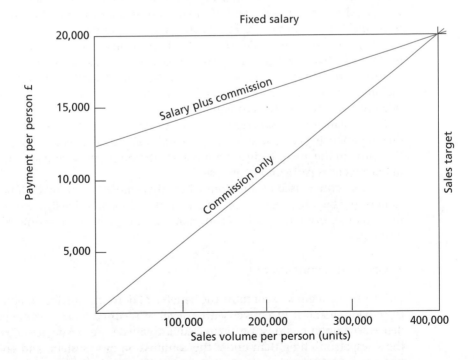

Figure 15.2 Compensation and sales volume

local authority in Lancashire being the result of one salesperson influencing an architect in London, another calling on the contractor in Norwich and a third persuading the local authority itself.[9]

However, the method does have a number of drawbacks. First, no direct financial incentive is provided for increasing sales (or profits). Second, high-performing salespeople may not be attracted, and holding on to them may be difficult using fixed salary since they may perceive the system as being unfair and be tempted to apply for jobs where financial rewards are high for outstanding performers. Third, selling costs remain static in the short term when sales decrease; thus the system does not provide the inbuilt flexibility of the other compensation systems.

Because of its inherent characteristics it is used primarily in industrial selling where technical service is an important element in the selling task and the time necessary to conclude a sale may be long. It is particularly appropriate when the salesperson sells very high value products at very low volumes. Under these conditions a commission-based compensation scheme would lead to widely varying monthly income levels depending on when orders were placed. A Chartered Institute of Marketing study found that roughly one-third of salespeople are paid by this method in the UK.[10]

Commission only

The commission-only system of payment provides an obvious incentive to sell. However, since income is dependent on sales results, salespeople will be reluctant to spend time on tasks which they do not perceive as being directly related to sales. The result is that sales personnel may pursue short-term goals, to the detriment of activities which may have an effect in the longer term. They may be reluctant to write reports providing market information to management and to spend time out of the field to attend sales training courses, for example.

The system provides little security for those whose earnings may suffer through no fault of their own and the pressure to sell may damage customer–salesperson relationships. This is particularly relevant in industrial selling, where the decision-making process may be long and pressure applied by the salesperson to close the sale prematurely may be detrimental.

From management's perspective the system not only has the advantage of directly financing costs automatically, but also allows some control over sales activities through the use of higher commission rates on products and accounts in which management is particularly interested.

It is most often used in situations where there are a large number of potential customers, the buying process is relatively short and technical assistance and service is not required. Insurance selling is an example where commission-only payments are often used.

Salary plus commission

This system attempts to combine the benefits of both the previous methods in order to provide financial incentives with a level of security. Since income is not solely dependent upon commission, management gains a greater degree of control over the salesperson's time than under the commission-only system, and sales costs are to some extent related to revenue generated. The method is attractive to ambitious salespeople who wish to combine security with the capability of earning more by greater effort and ability.

For these reasons it is the most commonly used method of compensating salespeople, although the method of calculating commission may vary. Extra payment may be linked to profits or sales generated, at a constant rate for all sales or only after a certain level of sales has been generated. Payment may be based upon a fixed percentage for all products and customers or at a variable rate. Alternatively, a bonus (a given monetary sum) may be paid on the accomplishment of a particular task (e.g. achieving a sales target, opening a certain number of new accounts). The results of two surveys[11] which have examined the use of salary, salary plus commission/bonus and commission only are shown in Table 15.2.

15.5   Conclusions

Two management functions – organisation and compensation – have been discussed in this chapter. There are three methods of organising a salesforce:

- geographical

- product

- customer

The customer-orientated approach has four variants:

- market centred

- account size

- new/existing accounts

- functional

Determining the number of salespeople needed may be accomplished by the workload approach.

Establishing sales territories will be determined by attempting to balance workload and sales potential.

Table 15.2 The use of compensation methods in the UK

	Manufacturing firms (%)	Industrial distributors (%)
Salary only	34	15
Salary plus commission/bonus	66	81
Commission only	—	4

Sources: Manufacturing firms – Avlonitis, G., Manolis, C. and Boyle, K. (1985) 'Sales management practices in the UK manufacturing industry', *Journal of Sales Management*, 2(2), pp. 6–16. Industrial distributors – Shipley, D. and Jobber, D. (1991) 'Sales force motivation, compensation and evaluation', *The Service Industries Journal*, 11(2), pp. 154–70.

Finally, the three major categories of compensation plan were examined. These are the fixed salary, commission only and salary plus commission.

The next part of the text looks at the final area of sales management – sales control.

References

1 Moss, C.D. (1979) 'Industrial salesmen as a source of marketing intelligence', *European Journal of Marketing*, 13, p. 3.

2 Homburg, C., Workman, Jr., J.P. and Jensen, O. (2000) 'Fundamental changes in marketing organization: the movement towards a customer-focused organizational structure', *Journal of the Academy of Marketing Science*, 28, pp. 459–78.

3 Magrath, A.J. (1989) 'To specialise or not to specialise?' *Sales and Marketing Management*, 141(7), pp. 62–8.

4 Moss, C.D. (1979) 'Industrial salesmen as a source of marketing intelligence', *European Journal of Marketing*, 13, p. 3.

5 Talley, W.J. (1961) 'How to design sales territories', *Journal of Marketing*, 25 January, 3.

6 Wilson, M. (1999) *Managing a Sales Force*, Gower, Aldershot.

7 Piercy, N., Low, G.S. and Cravens, D. (2004) 'Examining the effectiveness of sales management control practices in developing countries', *Journal of World Business*, 39, pp. 255–67.

8 Darmon, R.Y. (1974) 'Salesmen's response to financial initiatives: an empirical study', *Journal of Marketing Research*, November, pp. 418–26.

9 Wilson, M. (1999) *Managing a Sales Force*, Gower, Aldershot.

10 PA Consultants (1979) *Sales Force Practice Today: A Basis for Improving Performance*, Institute of Marketing, London.

11 Avlonitis, G., Manolis, C. and Boyle, K. (1985) 'Sales management practices in the UK manufacturing industry', *Journal of Sales Management*, 2(2), pp. 6–16; Shipley, D. and Jobber, D. (1991) 'Sales force motivation, compensation and evaluation', *The Service Industries Journal*, 11(2), pp. 154–70.

Rovertronics

Going where others might fear to tread . . . but still needing direction

Rovertronics was established in 1965 by Arthur Sullivant, an Oxford-educated cybernetics scientist who invented one of the first artificial intelligence chips, which has subsequently been developed so that now they have the world's first autonomous robot. The robot is known affectionately as 'Fearless Freddie' – Fearless because it can manoeuvre itself into places that would be dangerous for humans to reach. Current applications include bomb disposal and minesweeping for the armed forces, reactor troubleshooting in the nuclear energy industry and maintenance of sewerage networks. At the moment the company is very product myopic and product development ideas are generated through technical inspiration rather than user needs – a typical entrepreneurial company driven by the ideas of its eccentric owner.

The current plant production runs to five per year of a single model. Rovertronics sells each one for £50,000, which covers costs and a small margin of profit plus a small amount for research and development. Sullivant does not have commercial savvy, but has sensibly secured full intellectual property rights and world patents for this unique product. One of the weaknesses of his lack of commercial acumen is that he has paid virtually no attention to the sales function. Currently customers seek out the company and business is developed purely by chance.

The company has attracted the interest of a consortium of City banks that have realised the potential of the product and wish to invest heavily in the organisation in order to make it more commercially driven. Obviously the bankers have no managerial experience and have released a specification for a management consultancy to put together a cohesive sales and marketing plan to exploit the company's potential and the product opportunities. The investors are particularly interested in innovative ideas for the following areas:

- salesforce organisation – structure, territories

- compensation

- number of salespeople required initially

- any other ideas to help the organisation realise its full potential (e.g. sales strategy, new market opportunities)

The class will be split into four groups, two groups representing consultancies competing to advise the company on its business development strategy, a team of bankers, and a fourth group of observers. The consultancies are given 30 minutes to develop a five-minute presentation that meets the bank's requirements. The bankers will award the contract to the consultancy with the most innovative bid, or may decide to put it out to tender again if neither is deemed satisfactory. Each group will give a presentation to the bank's representative summarising their credentials and overall strategic approach to redeveloping the firm. Then the bank's representative will give some feedback on each presentation and announce the winning consultancy (or announce that none of the consultancies have won the task).

The proposals of the consultancies will be evaluated on the basis of their responses to the three key areas outlined above and any exceptional considerations that might crop up.

Source: Written by Andrew Pressey, Lecturer in Marketing, University of East Anglia. Neville Hunt, Lecturer in Marketing, University of Luton.

Practical Exercise

Silverton Confectionery Company

Silverton Confectionery is a growing Berkshire-based company specialising in selling quality chocolates and sweets at higher than average prices through newsagents and confectioners.

At present their span of operation is limited to England and Wales, which is covered by a salesforce organised along geographical lines. Each salesperson is responsible for sales of the entire product line in his or her territory and for seeking out new outlets in which to develop new business. The system works well with Silverton's salespeople, who are well known by their customers and, in most cases, well liked. The salesperson's responsibilities include both the selling and merchandising functions. They are paid on a salary plus commission system.

The success of this company, which has exploited a market niche neglected by the larger confectionery companies, has led Silverton management to expand into Scotland. You, as national sales manager, have been asked to recommend the appropriate number of salespeople required.

The coverage objective is to call upon all outlets with a turnover of over £200,000 three times a year, those between £100,000 and £200,000 twice a year and those below £100,000 once a year. As a first step, you have commissioned a market research report to identify the number of outlets within each size category. The results are given below.

A salesperson can be expected to call upon an average of 60 outlets a week and a working year, after holidays, sales meetings, training, etc., can be assumed to be 43 weeks.

Category	No. of outlets
Under £100,000	2,950
£100,000–200,000	1,700
Over £200,000	380

Discussion Question

How many salespeople are required?

Examination Questions

1 The only sensible way to organise a salesforce is by geographical region. All other methods are not cost efficient. Discuss.

2 How practical is the workload approach to salesforce size determination?

Part Five   Sales Control

This final part consists of two chapters, the first of which considers sales forecasting and budgeting. The sales forecast is important because it is from this forecast that sales, marketing and company plans are based. If the forecast is incorrect then plans for the business will also be incorrect. The place of forecasting in planning is considered in terms of levels of accuracy required in forecasting. An explanation is given of quantitative techniques and qualitative techniques of forecasting as well as the strengths and weaknesses of each. The budgetary process is then examined with particular emphasis on the sales budget. This can be described as the sum total of all of the projected sales of individual members of the salesforce. This is achieved through individual sales targets and quotas.

Salesforce evaluation concludes the book. Chapter 17 examines the salesforce evaluation process and the reasons why this is important for the company. Measures of performance are considered, including quantitative and qualitative measures. A key question to be asked in the context of evaluation relates to winning or losing orders. Questioning skills and the ability to identify weak and strong answers are considered to be useful here. Finally, the role of appraisal interviewing is discussed.

16 Sales Forecasting and Budgeting

16.1 Purpose

It is of utmost importance that the sales manager has some idea of what will happen in the future in order that plans can be made in advance. There would otherwise be no point in planning and all that has been said in the previous chapter would be negated. Many sales managers do not recognise that sales forecasting is their responsibility and leave such matters to accountants, who need the forecast in order that they can prepare budgets (dealt with later). Sales managers do not always see the immediate need for forecasting and feel that selling is a more urgent task. Indeed, the task of forecasting by the sales manager is often delayed until the last minute and a hastily put together estimation with no scientific base, little more than an educated guess, is the end result. The folly of such an attitude is examined during this chapter.

When one is in a producer's market – similar to the situations in the immediate post-war years as described in Chapter 1 – there is less of a need for forecasting as the market takes up all one's production; it is less a matter of selling and more a matter of allowing customers to purchase. However, in a buyer's market the situation is different. The consequence of over-production is unsold stock which is costly to finance from working capital borrowings. The marginal money, i.e. the cost of borrowing the last unit of revenue, comes from the bank overdraft, which is at least base rate of borrowing plus 1 or 2 per cent. It can therefore be seen that over-production and holding stock can be costly. Conversely, under-production can be detrimental as sales opportunities might be missed due to long delivery times and business might pass to a competitor that can offer quicker delivery.

Thus the purpose of the sales forecast is to plan ahead and go about achieving forecasted sales in what management considers to be the most effective manner. It is again emphasised that the sales manager is the person who should be responsible for this task. The accountant is not in a position to know whether the market is about to rise or fall; all that can be done is to extrapolate from previous sales, estimate the general trend and make a forecast based on this. The sales manager is the person who should know which way the market is moving, and it is an abrogation of responsibility if the task of sales forecasting is left to the accountant. In addition, the sales forecasting procedure must be taken seriously because from it stems business planning. If the forecast is flawed then business plans will also be incorrect.

16.2 Planning

It has been established that planning stems from the sales forecast and the purpose of planning is to allocate company resources in such a manner as to achieve these anticipated sales.

A company can forecast sales either by forecasting market sales (called **market forecasting**) and then determining what share of this will accrue to the company or by forecasting the company's sales directly. Techniques for doing this are dealt with later in the chapter. The point is that planners are only interested in forecasts when the forecast comes down to individual products in the company.

We now examine the applicability and usefulness of the short-, medium- and long-term forecasts insofar as company planners are concerned and look at each from individual company departmental viewpoints.

1 *Short-term forecasts*. These are usually for periods up to three months ahead and are really of use for tactical matters such as production planning. The general trend of sales is less important here than short-term fluctuations.

2 *Medium-term forecasts*. These have direct implications for planners. They are of most importance in the area of business budgeting, the starting point for which is the sales forecast. Thus if the sales forecast is incorrect, then the entire budget is incorrect. If the forecast is overoptimistic then the company will have unsold stocks which must be financed out of working capital. If the forecast is pessimistic then the firm may miss out on marketing opportunities because it is not geared up to produce the extra goods required by the market. More to the point is that when forecasting is left to accountants, they will tend to err on the conservative side and produce a forecast that is lower than the trend of sales, the implications of which have just been described. This serves to re-emphasise the point that sales forecasting is the responsibility of the sales manager. Such medium-term forecasts are normally for one year ahead.

3 *Long-term forecasts*. These are usually for periods of three years and upwards depending upon the type of industry being considered. In industries such as computers three years is considered long term, whereas for steel manufacture ten years is a typical long-term horizon. They are worked out from macro-environmental factors such as government policy, economic trends, etc. Such forecasts are needed mainly by financial accountants for long-term resource implications and are generally the concern of boards of directors. The board must decide what its policy is to be in establishing the levels of production needed to meet the forecasted demand; such decisions might involve the construction of a new factory and the training of a workforce.

In addition to the functions already mentioned under each of the three types of forecast, other functions can be directly and indirectly affected in their planning considerations as a result of the sales forecast. Such functions include the following:

1 It has been mentioned that production needs to know about sales forecasts so that they can arrange production planning. There will also need to be close and speedy liaison between production and sales to determine customer priorities in the short term. Production also needs long-term forecasts so that capital plant decisions can be made in order to meet anticipated sales.

2 Purchasing usually receives its cue to purchase from production via purchase requisitions or bills of material. However, in the case of strategic materials or long-delivery items it is useful for purchasing to have some advance warning of likely impending material or component purchases in order that they can better plan their purchases. Such advance warning will also enable purchasing to purchase more effectively from a price and delivery viewpoint.

3 Human resource management is interested in the sales forecast from the staffing planning viewpoint.

4 It has already been mentioned that the financial and, more specifically, costing functions need the medium-term forecast to budget. Later in this chapter we discuss the role of the sales forecast in the sales budgetary procedure and how such a function operates. The long-term forecast is of value to financial accountants in that they can provide for long-range profit plans and income flows. They also need to make provision for capital items such as plant and machinery needed in order to replace old plant and machinery and to meet anticipated sales in the longer term.

5 Research and development (R&D) will need forecasts, although their needs will be more concerned with technological matters and not with actual projected sales figures. They will want to know the expected life of existing products and what likely changes will have to be made to their function and design in order to keep them competitive. Market research reports will be of use to R&D in that they will be able to design and develop products suited to the marketplace. Such a view reflects a marketing orientated approach to customer requirements. Here reports from salespeople in the field concerning both the company's and competitors' products will be useful in building up a general picture; such information will be collated and collected by the marketing research function.

6 Marketing needs the sales forecast so that sales strategies and promotional plans can be formulated in order to achieve the forecasted sales. Such plans and strategies might include the recruitment of additional sales personnel, remuneration plans, promotional expenditures and other matters as detailed in Chapters 3 and 4.

A useful model, proposed by Hogarth, involved three interactive forecasting components: the person performing the task of forecasting, the actions that are a consequence of that person's judgements and the ultimate outcome of that judgement.[1] This model is shown in Figure 16.1.

The individual making the forecast is represented in the scheme in terms of beliefs relating to the forecasting task. This judgement relates to acquiring and pro-

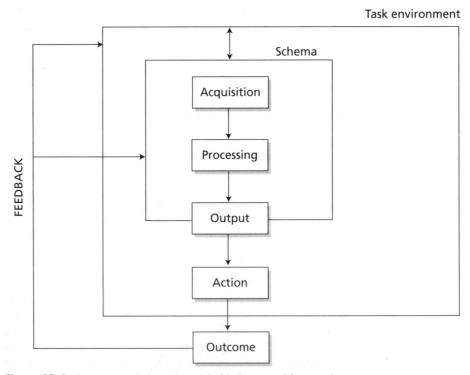

Figure 16.1 A conceptually based model of judgemental forecasting
Source: Hogarth, R. (1975) 'Cognitive processes and the assessment of subjective probability distributions', *Journal of the American Statistical Association*, 70 (350), pp. 271–89.

cessing information and the output from this information. This is then translated into action which is the sales forecast. The outcome refers to action that along with external factors then produces the final forecast. Feedback points are included as corrective measures that might be needed as the forecast becomes reality.

It can thus be seen that an accurate forecast is important because all functions base their plans on such forecasts. The short-, medium- and long-term forecasts all have relevance to some business function and, in the absence of reasonably accurate forecasting where such plans are not based on a solid foundation, they will have to be modified later as sales turn out to be different to those predicted in the sales forecast.

Now that the purpose of sales forecasting has been established, together with its role as a precursor to all planning activity, we can look at the different types of forecasting technique, bearing in mind that such forecasting is the responsibility of the sales function. Such techniques are split into two types: qualitative techniques and quantitative techniques.

16.3 Levels of Forecasting

Forecasts can be produced for different horizons starting at an international level and ranging down to national levels, by industry and then by company levels until we reach individual product-by-product forecasts. The forecast is then broken down seasonally over the time span of the forecasting period and geographically right down to individual salesperson areas. These latter levels are of specific interest to sales management, for it is from here that the sales budgeting and remuneration systems stem, as we discuss later in the chapter.

However, companies do not generally have to produce international or national forecasts as this information is usually available from recognised international and national sources. The company forecaster finds such data useful for it is by using such information that product-by-product forecasts can be adjusted in the light of these macro-level predictions. It is also from these market forecasts that the company can determine what share it will be able to achieve through its selling and marketing efforts. These marketing efforts involve manipulating the marketing mix in order to plan how to achieve these forecasted sales (e.g. a price reduction could well mean more sales will be possible). Once it reaches a detailed level of product-by-product forecasting, geographically split over a time period, it is then termed the 'sales forecast', which is more meaningful to sales management. Indeed, it could be said that this is the means through which sales management exercises control over the field salesforce and, as we describe later, this is the revenue-generating mechanism for the entire sales organisation of a company as seen in the example of Airbus that now follows.

Towards the wild blue yonder

Airbus is producing a super-jumbo, the A380. Boeing is going for speed rather than size with its Sonic Cruiser. Who is on the right path?

At Blagnac airport, near Airbus's headquarters in Toulouse, foundations have been prepared for the largest covered space in Europe. This is where the world's biggest airliner, the A380, was assembled for its maiden flight in April 2005. Metal is now being cut for full-scale production of parts of its giant body in Airbus factories in Germany and France. This is the first manifestation of a $US10.7 billion programme to develop a rival to the Boeing 747, the 416-seater jumbo that has enjoyed a monopoly in big airliners for over 30 years. Airbus, which opened for business in 1970 – the year of the jumbo's first commercial flight – has now caught up with Boeing in market share. The A380 will enable it to tackle its great rival right across the product range.

Airbus's decision in December 2000 to proceed with a 555-seater super jumbo sets it head to head with Boeing's 747 for the first time. Boeing will tweak the jumbo here and there, improving its performance, but its big effort is going into an entirely different aircraft, the 250-seater Sonic Cruiser, which flies at 98 per cent of the speed of sound.

Championing speed rather than size suggests that Boeing thinks most future growth will come from frequent point-to-point flights, rather than those that go through the big hubs. Airbus, by contrast, still sees a healthy market for a relatively low-cost super-jumbo to connect the world's biggest airports. Both companies agree that air travel will triple over the next 20 years, but disagree on how the demand will be met.

Source: Adapted from *The Economist,* 27 April 2002, p. 75.

16.4   Qualitative Techniques

Qualitative forecasting techniques are sometimes referred to as judgemental or subjective techniques because they rely more upon opinion and less upon mathematics in their formulation. They are often used in conjunction with the quantitative techniques described in section 16.5.

Consumer/User survey method

This method involves asking customers about their likely purchases for the forecast period, sometimes referred to as the market research method. For industrial products, where there are fewer customers, such research is often carried out by the sales-force on a face-to-face basis. The only problem is that then you have to ascertain what proportion of their likely purchases will accrue to your company. Another problem is that customers (and salespeople) tend to be optimistic when making predictions for the future. Both of these problems can lead to the possibility of multi-plied inaccuracies.

For consumer products it is not possible to canvass customers through the sales-force. The best method is to interview customers through a market research survey (probably coupled with other questions or through an omnibus survey where ques-tions on a questionnaire are shared with other companies). Clearly, it will only be possible to interview a small sample of the total population and because of this the forecast will be less accurate. There is also a question of the type and number of questions one can ask on such a sample survey. It is better to canvass grades of opin-ion when embarking on such a study and these grades of opinion can reflect pur-chasing likelihoods. One can then go on to ask a question as to the likelihood of purchasing particular makes or brands which will, of course, include your own brand or model.

This method is of most value when there are a small number of users who are pre-pared to state their intentions with a reasonable degree of accuracy. It tends, there-fore, to be limited to organisational buying. It is also a useful vehicle for collecting information of a technological nature which can be fed to one's own research and development function.

Panels of executive opinion

This is sometimes called the jury method, where specialists or experts are consulted who have knowledge of the industry being examined. Such people can come from inside the company and include marketing or financial personnel or indeed people who have a detailed knowledge of the industry. More often, the experts will come from outside the company and can include management consultants who operate within the particular industry. Sometimes external people can include customers who are in a position to advise from a buying company's viewpoint. The panel thus normally comprises a mixture of internal and external personnel.

These experts come with a prepared forecast and must defend their stance in committee among the other experts. Their individual stances may be altered fol-lowing such discussions. In the end, if disagreement results, mathematical aggrega-tion may be necessary to arrive at a compromise.

This type of forecasting method is termed a 'top down' method whereby a fore-cast is produced for the industry. The company then determines what its share will be of the overall forecast. Because the statistics have not been collected from basic market data (from the 'bottom up') there is difficulty in allocating the forecast out amongst individual products and sales territories, and any such allocation will prob-ably be arbitrary. Thus the forecast represents aggregate opinion and is only useful when developing a general, rather than specific product-by-product forecast.

A variation of this method is termed 'prudent manager forecasting' whereby company personnel are asked to assume the position of purchasers in customer companies. They must then look at company sales from a customer's viewpoint and 'prudently' evaluate sales, taking into consideration such factors as external econ-omic conditions, competitive offerings in terms of design, quality, delivery and price and whatever other factors are considered relevant to making an evaluation of the company's sales.

Salesforce composite

This method involves each salesperson making a product-by-product forecast for their particular sales territory. Thus individual forecasts are built up to produce a company forecast; this is sometimes termed a 'grass-roots' approach. Each salesperson's forecast must be agreed with the manager, and divisional manager where appropriate, and eventually the sales manager agrees the final composite forecast.

Such a method is a bottom-up approach. Where remuneration is linked to projected sales (through quotas or targets) there can be less cause for complaint because the forecast upon which remuneration is based has been produced by the salesforce itself.

A variation of the above method is termed 'detecting differences in figures' and here each stage in the hierarchy produces a set of figures before meeting. The salesperson produces figures, broken down by product and customer, and the area manager produces figures for the salesperson's territory. They then meet and must reconcile any differences in figures. The process proceeds with the area manager producing territory-by-territory figures and meeting with the regional manager who will have produced figures for the area, until it eventually reaches the sales manager and the entire forecast is ultimately agreed.

The immediate problem with the salesforce composite method of forecasting is that when the forecast is used for future remuneration (through the establishment of sales quotas or targets) there might be a tendency for salespeople to produce a pessimistic forecast. This can be alleviated by linking selling expenses to the forecast as well as future remuneration.

When remuneration is not linked to the sales forecast there is a temptation to produce an optimistic forecast in view of what was said earlier about customers and salespeople tending to overestimate. The consequence of the above is that a forecast might be produced that is biased either pessimistically or optimistically. As a corollary to the above it can also be argued that salespeople are too concerned with everyday events to enable them to produce objective forecasts and they are perhaps less aware of broader factors affecting sales of their products. Thus their forecasts will tend to be subjective.

Delphi method

This method bears a resemblance to the 'panel of executive opinion' method and the forecasting team is chosen using a similar set of criteria. The main difference is that members do not meet in committee.

A project leader administers a questionnaire to each member of the team which asks questions, usually of a behavioural nature, such as 'Do you envisage new technology products supplanting our product lines in the next five years? If so, by what percentage market share?' The questioning then proceeds to a more detailed or pointed second stage which asks questions about the individual company. The process can go on to further stages where appropriate. The ultimate objective is to translate opinion into some form of forecast. After each round of questionnaires the aggregate response from each is circulated to members of the panel before they complete the questionnaire for the next round, so members are not completing their questionnaires in a void and can moderate their responses in the light of aggregate results.

The fact that members do not meet in committee means that they are not influenced by majority opinion and a more objective forecast might result. However, as a vehicle for producing a territory-by-territory or product-by-product forecast it has limited value. It is of greater value in providing general data about industry trends and as a technological forecasting tool. It is also useful in providing information about new products or processes that the company intends developing for ultimate manufacture and sale.

Bayesian decision theory

This technique has been placed under qualitative techniques, although it is really a mixture of subjective and objective techniques. It is not possible to describe the detailed workings of this method within the confines of this text; indeed it is possible to devote a whole text to the Bayesian technique alone.

The technique is similar to critical path analysis in that it uses a network diagram and probabilities must be estimated for each event over the network. The basis of the technique can best be described by reference to a simple example. As this chapter does not easily lend itself to the provision of a case study that can encompass most or all of the areas covered, a practical exercise, followed by questions covering Bayesian decision theory, has been included at the end of the chapter which should give the reader an insight into its workings.

Product testing and test marketing

This technique is of value for new or modified products for which no previous sales figures exist and where it is difficult to estimate likely demand. It is therefore prudent to estimate likely demand for the product by testing it on a sample of the market beforehand.

Product testing involves placing the pre-production model(s) with a sample of potential users beforehand and noting their reactions to the product over a period of time by asking them to fill in a diary noting product deficiencies, how it worked, general reactions, etc. The type of products that can be tested in this manner can range from household durables, for example, vacuum cleaners, to canned foods such as soups. However, there is a limit to the number of pre-production items that can be supplied (particularly for consumer durables) and the technique is really of value in deciding between a 'go' or 'no go' decision.

Test marketing is perhaps of more value for forecasting purposes. It involves the limited launch of a product in a closely defined geographical test area, for example, a test town such as Bristol or a larger area such as the Tyne-Tees Television area. Thus a national launch is simulated in a small area representative of the country as a whole, obviously at less expense. It is of particular value for branded foodstuffs. Test market results can be grossed up to predict the national launch outcome. However, the estimate can only cover the launch. Over time, the novelty factor of a new product might wear off. In addition, it gives competitors an advantage because they can observe the product being test marketed and any potential surprise advantage will be lost. It has also been known for competitors deliberately to attempt to sabotage a test marketing campaign by increasing their promotional activity in the area over the period of the test market, so introducing additional complications when assessing the final results.

Quantitative forecasting techniques are sometimes termed objective or mathematical techniques as they rely more upon mathematics and less upon judgement in their computation. These techniques are now very popular as a result of sophisticated computer packages, some being tailor-made for the company needing the forecast.

It is not proposed to go into the detailed working of such techniques because they require specialist skills in their own right; indeed a single technique could take up an entire textbook. Some quantitative techniques are simple while others are extremely complex. We now explain such techniques so you will have an appreciation of their usefulness and applicability. If the forecasting problem calls for specialist mathematical techniques then the answer is to consult a specialist and not attempt it on the basis of incomplete information given here. Quantitative techniques can be divided into two types:

1 *Time series analysis.* The only variable that the forecaster considers is time. These techniques are relatively simple to apply, but the danger is that too much emphasis might be placed upon past events to predict the future. The techniques are useful in predicting sales in markets that are relatively stable and not susceptible to sudden irrational changes in demand. In other words, it is not possible to predict downturns or upturns in the market, unless the forecaster deliberately manipulates the forecast to incorporate such a downturn or upturn.

2 *Causal techniques.* It is assumed that there is a relationship between the measurable independent variable and the forecasted dependent variable. The forecast is produced by putting the value of the independent variable into the calculation. One must choose a suitable independent variable and the period of the forecast to be produced must be considered carefully. The techniques are thus concerned with cause and effect. The problem arises when one attempts to establish reasons behind these cause and effect relationships; in many cases there is no logical explanation. Indeed, there is quite often nothing to suppose that the relationship should hold good in the future. Reasoning behind causal relationships may not be too clear at this stage, but once the techniques are examined later in the chapter it should become self-evident. The first set of techniques examined are those concerned with **time series analysis**.

Quantitative techniques (time series)

Moving averages

This method averages out and smooths data in a time series. The longer the time series, the greater will be the smoothing. The principle is that one subtracts the earliest sales figure and adds the latest sales figure. The technique is best explained through the simple example given in Table 16.1. It can be seen that using a longer moving average produces a smoother trend line than using a shorter moving average.

These data are reproduced graphically (see Figure 16.2) and it can be seen that averaging smooths out the annual sales figures. Five-year averaging produces a smoother line than three-year averaging. One can then produce a forecast by extending the trend line, and it is up to the individual forecaster to decide whether three-year or five-year averaging is better. Indeed, it is sometimes unnecessary to smooth the data (in the case of a steady trend) and the technique is then termed trend projection. Generally speaking, the more the data fluctuate, the more expedient it is to have a longer averaging period.

Exponential smoothing

This is a technique that apportions varying weightings to different parts of the data from which the forecast is to be calculated. The problem with moving averages and straightforward trend projection is that it is unable to predict a downturn or upturn

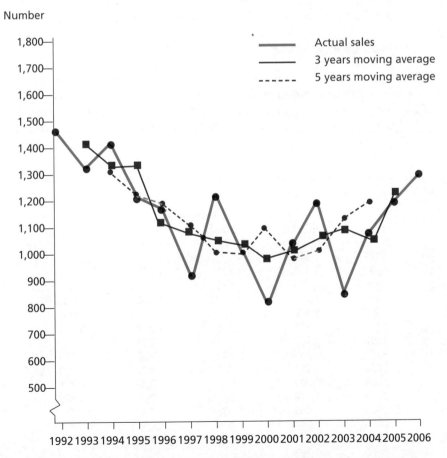

Figure 16.2 Office Goods Supplies Ltd: annual sales of briefcases, moving averages

in the market (unless the forecaster deliberately places a downturn or upturn in the data). In this technique the forecaster apportions appropriate degrees of 'typicality' to different parts of the time series.

It is not proposed to explain the detailed mathematics behind the technique because this is not a sales forecasting textbook. Instead, the statistics used in the previous example have been taken and from these weightings have been applied to earlier parts of the series. These weightings are applied by the forecaster according to his or her own judgement as to how 'typical' earlier parts of the data are in the production of a forecast (although there is a mathematical technique for deciding this if necessary). The result is shown in Figure 16.3.

In the moving averages technique the forecast will take some time to respond to a downturn or upturn, whereas with the exponential smoothing method the response can be immediate. In the example in Figure 16.3 the forecaster has apportioned greater weightings to downturn periods of trade than to upturn periods, and the forecast will thus reflect another downturn period for 2007. Had a moving averages forecast been used, this would have produced a less steep continuum of the 2005–6 upturn trend.

In practice the technique is simple to operate, but it is essentially a computer technique. The forecaster can very simply alter the smoothing constant for different periods to produce a number of alternative forecasts. The skill lies in determining the degree of weightings for earlier and later parts of the time series.

Time series analysis

This technique is useful when seasonality occurs in a data pattern. It is of particular use for fashion products and for products that respond to seasonal changes throughout the year. It can be used for cyclical changes in the longer term (such as patterns of trade) but there are better techniques available for dealing with such longer term

Table 16.1 Office Goods Supplies Ltd: annual sales of briefcases, moving average

Year	Number	Three-year Total	Three-year Average	Five-year Total	Five-year Average
1992	1,446	–	–	–	–
1993	1,324	4,179	1,393	–	–
1994	1,409	3,951	1,317	6,543	1,309
1995	1,218	3,773	1,258	6,032	1,206
1996	1,146	3,299	1,100	5,855	1,171
1997	935	3,228	1,076	5,391	1,078
1998	1,147	3,027	1,009	4,953	991
1999	945	2,872	957	4,810	962
2000	780	2,728	927	5,049	1,008
2001	1,003	2,957	986	4,706	941
2002	1,174	2,981	994	4,805	961
2003	804	3,022	1,007	5,186	1,037
2004	1,044	3,009	1,003	5,470	1,094
2005	1,161	3,492	1,164	–	–
2006	1,287	–	–	–	–

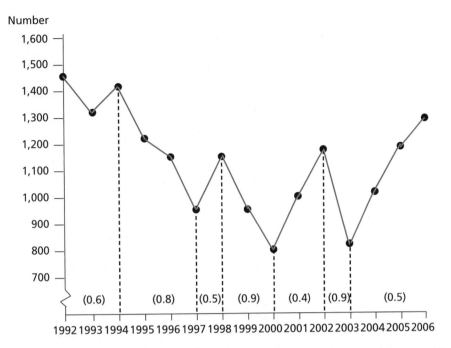

Figure 16.3 Office Goods Supplies Ltd: annual sales of briefcases, exponential smoothing (weighting shown in brackets)

trends. Thus its best application is where the seasonal pattern is repeated on a fairly regular annual basis. These seasonal movements are measured in terms of their deviation from the aggregate trend.

The technique is best explained graphically by using data from the previous example. The quarterly sales of briefcases have been taken for Office Goods Supplies Ltd for the years 2002–2006 (see Table 16.2), and it can be seen that sales exhibit a seasonal pattern, with a peak of sales in the final quarter of each year.

When the sums of quarterly deviations from the trend are added, the resultant sum is +40 in this particular case (see Table 16.3). The total sum must equal zero, otherwise it would mean that a positive bias would be built into the forecast. However, this correction must come from all figures equally, and is calculated as: 40/4 = +10

Therefore +10 must be subtracted from each quarter's figures. The corrected figures are then:

Quarter	1	2	3	4
Corrected deviations	−292	−19	−328	+639 = 0

In this particular example these figures must now be divided by 4 to produce a yearly aggregate (because four years' data have been used in their compilation) and the figures from which the forecast will be derived are as follows:

Quarter	1	2	3	4
Deviations	−73	−5	−82	+160 = 0

Table 16.2 Office Goods Supplies Ltd: quarterly sales of briefcases

Year	Quarter	Unit sales	Quarterly moving total	Sum of pairs	Divided by 8 to find trend	Deviations from trend
2002	1	207				
	2	268	= 1,174	= 2,295	287	−64
	3	223	1,121	2,136	267	+209
	4	476	1,015	= 1,934	242	−88
2003	1	154	919	1,723	215	−53
	2	162	= 804	= 1,643	205	−78
	3	127	839	1,779	222	+139
	4	361	940	= 1,935	242	−53
2004	1	189	995	2,039	255	+8
	2	263	= 1,044	= 2,110	264	−82
	3	182	1,066	2,156	269	+141
	4	410	1,090	= 2,197	275	−64
2005	1	211	1,107	2,268	284	+3
	2	287	= 1,161	= 2,346	293	−94
	3	199	1,185	2,433	304	+160
	4	464	1,248	= 2,497	312	−77
2006	1	235	1,249	2,536	317	+33
	2	350	= 1,287			
	3	200				
	4	502				

The figures in Table 16.4 are an extension of data at the end of Table 6.2 and these have been derived as follows. Unit sales are added to provide a one-year total. This total then summates the one-year moving sales by taking off the old quarter and adding on the new quarter. The quarterly moving totals are then paired in the next column (to provide greater smoothing) and this sum is then divided by 8 to ascertain the quarterly trend. Finally, the deviations from trend are calculated by taking the actual figure (in unit sales) from the trend, and these are represented in the final column as deviations from the trend.

The statistics are then incorporated into a graph and the unit sales and trend are drawn in as in Figure 16.4. The trend line is extended by sight (and it is here that the forecaster's skill and intuition must come in). The deviations from trend are then applied to the trend line, and this provides the sales forecast.

Table 16.3 Office Goods Supplies Ltd: sum of quarterly deviations from trend

Quarter	1	2	3	4
Year				
2002	–	–	−64	+209
2003	−88	−53	−78	+139
2004	−53	+8	−82	+141
2005	−64	+3	−94	+160
2006	−77	+ 33	–	–
Sum	−282	−9	−318	+649 = +40

Table 16.4 Office Goods Supplies Ltd: forecasted trend figures and deviations from trend that have been applied

Year	Period	Trend	Deviation	Forecast
2006	3	326	−82	244
	4	334	+160	494
2007	1	343	−73	270
	2	352	−5	347
	3	360	−82	278
	4	369	+160	529

In the example in Figure 16.4 it can be seen that the trend line has been extended on a slow upwards trend similar to the previous years. The first two figures for periods 3 and 4 of 2006 are provided as a forecast, as this is a function of the calculation. These two periods of course passed, and it can be seen that the forecast is slightly different to what happened in reality. Proof that forecasting is never perfect! The four quarters of 2007 have been forecasted and these are included in the graph.

The technique, like many similar techniques, suffers from the fact that downturns and upturns cannot be predicted, and such data must be subjectively entered by the forecaster through manipulation of the extension to the trend line.

Z (or zee) charts

This technique is merely a furtherance of the moving averages technique. In addition to providing the moving annual total, it also shows the monthly sales and cumulative sales; an illustration of the technique shows why it is termed Z chart.

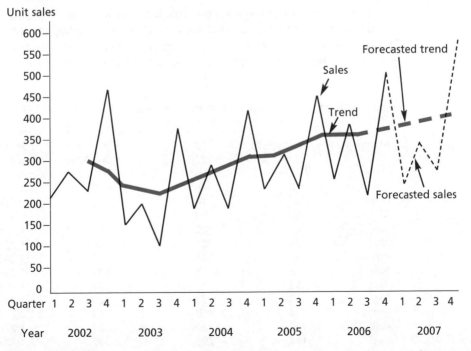

Figure 16.4 Office Goods Supplies Ltd: quarterly sales of briefcases and one-year forecast

Each Z chart represents one year's data and is best applied using monthly sales data. As a vehicle for forecasting it provides a useful medium where sales for one year can be compared with previous years using three criteria (monthly, cumulative and moving annual).

The sales of briefcases for Office Goods Supplies Ltd have been provided for each month of 2005 and 2006 and this is sufficient to provide data for the Z chart as can be seen in Table 16.5. The figures in Table 16.5 are then transposed graphically in Figure 16.5.

Moving annual sales are obtained by adding on the new month's figure and taking off the old month's figure, 12 months previously. The cumulative sales are obtained by adding each month to the next month, and the bottom line of the Z is the monthly sales.

The method is very much a comparison by sight method and in this case would be used for the medium-term (one-year) sales forecast. However, as a serious method for prediction its uses are limited; its main use is for comparison.

Miscellaneous

This final section briefly outlines two computer-based techniques; to describe their workings in detail would take a disproportionate amount of space together with a detailed knowledge of mathematics. They rely in their application upon sophisticated computer packages. If the reader wishes to pursue the techniques further, then a software specialist would advise on their applicability and the degree of accuracy for the desired intention. This is not to say that the forecaster (say the sales manager) should necessarily need to have a detailed knowledge of the technique that is being applied. All s/he needs to know is what the forecast will do and its degree of accuracy.

The first of these techniques is Box-Jenkins, which is a sophistication of the exponential smoothing technique that applies different weightings to different parts of the time series. In the case of this technique, the computer package takes earlier parts of the time series and manipulates and weights parts of this against known

Table 16.5 Office Goods Supplies Ltd: monthly sales of briefcases 2005–6

Month	Unit sales 2005	2006	Cumulative Sales 2006	Moving annual total
Jan	58	66	66	1,169
Feb	67	70	136	1,172
Mar	86	99	235	1,185
Apr	89	102	337	1,198
May	94	121	458	1,225
Jun	104	127	585	1,248
Jul	59	58	643	1,247
Aug	62	69	712	1,254
Sep	78	73	785	1,249
Oct	94	118	903	1,273
Nov	178	184	1,087	1,279
Dec	192	200	1,287	1,287

Unit sales

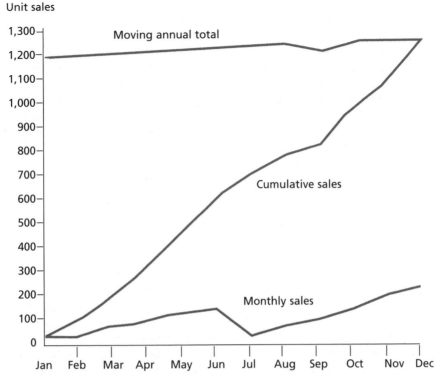

Figure 16.5 Office Goods Supplies Ltd: monthly sales of briefcases, Z chart for 2006

sales from later parts of the time series. The weighting that provides the best fit is finally deduced and can then be used for the forecast. It is reasonably accurate for short- and medium-term forecasting.

The other technique is termed X-11 and was developed by an American named Julius Shiskin. It is a decomposition technique and breaks a time series down into trend cycles, seasonal cycles and irregular elements. It is an effective technique for medium-term forecasting and incorporates a number of analytical methods into its computation.

Quantitative techniques (causal)

Leading indicators

This method seeks to define and establish a linear regression relationship between some measurable phenomenon and whatever is to be forecasted. It is not appropriate to enter into a discussion of the technique of linear regression within the confines of this text; should you wish to pursue the technique further, most reasonably advanced statistical texts will adequately describe the method and its applicability.

The best way to explain the technique is to consider the following simple example. The sale of children's bicycles depends upon the child population, so a sensible leading indicator for a bicycle manufacturer would be birth statistics. The bicycle manufacturer will therefore seek to establish a relationship between the two and, if the manufacturer is considering children's first two-wheeler bicycles (say, at age three years old, on average) then births will precede first bicycles by three years. In other words first bicycles will lag births by three years.

The example is obviously an oversimplification, and there are forecasting packages available that permute a number of leading indicators; i.e. they are indicators which are ahead of actual sales. It is possible to provide the permutation that best fits known sales, where the sales are lagged in time and the indicator is leading. The permutation that best fits the known sales to the indicator (or permutation of indicators) is the one to use in the forecast. Thus the permutation is constantly under review as time goes on. As forecasts pass into actual sales, so the forecasting permutation is modified to take account of most recent sales.

This more sophisticated type of forecasting uses what is known as correlation analysis to establish the relationship. Again the reader is directed to any reasonably advanced statistics text for a fuller explanation of its workings and implications.

Simulation

This forecasting methodology has become possible with the widespread use of computers. Leading indicator forecasting establishes relationships between some measurable phenomenon and whatever is to be forecasted, whilst simulation uses a process of iteration, or trial and error, to arrive at the forecasting relationship. In a reasonably complicated forecasting problem (which most are that utilise this technique) the number of alternative possibilities and outcomes is vast. When probabilities of various outcomes are known, the technique is known as Monte Carlo simulation and depends upon a predetermined chance of a particular event occurring (it is no coincidence that the technique derives from probabilities worked out for gambling games).

We cannot explain the technique further without entering into complex mathematical discussions and explanations. Insofar as this text is concerned, it is sufficient that you are aware of the technique; if further information is required, an expert forecaster should be consulted.

Diffusion models

Most of the techniques discussed so far have depended upon a series of past sales for the company and the industry to be available before a forecast can be calculated. However, when new products are introduced to the market which are not simply extensions or redesigns of old products, then the technique for estimating sales comes from a body of theory called the diffusion of innovations. One of the authors made a study of the subject 20 years ago and produced a forecast for video-recorders that utilised the Bass **diffusion model**.[2]

Again, as with most causal techniques, the mathematics are complicated and the best advice for the sales manager seeking to apply such a technique to a new product would be to seek the advice of a specialist. This is essentially a computer technique and its computation is complicated. Basically, diffusion theory assumes that the new product has four basic units:

- the innovation

- the communication of the innovation among individuals

- the social system

- time

The theory goes on to say that the innovation can be categorised into one of the following groupings:

- continuous

- dynamically continuous

- discontinuous

This is a hierarchical listing, with the innovations being more widely removed from previous technology as one moves further down the list. This means that the further down the hierarchy the innovation is placed, the lower will be the degree of likely acceptance. In the early days of a product innovation, knowledge must be communicated to as many individuals as possible, especially those who are likely to be influential in gaining wider appeal for the innovation. This communication process is broken down into formal and informal communication. These two elements are fed into the forecasting model and as such the model can be applied without large amounts of past sales data. The formal communication is controlled by the company and includes such data as advertising expenditure and sales support for the launch and the informal element relates to such matters as family and reference group influences.

Once the innovation has been launched, a measure of the rate of adoption is needed in order to produce a useful forecast. Products are born, they mature and eventually die, and it is important to the forecaster using this technique that the first few points of the launch sales are known in order to be able to determine the rate of adoption. Thus a forecast can be made using only a small amount of data covering the early launch period. An assumption is therefore made that the product being considered has a life-cycle curve and that new product acceptance is through a process of imitation, i.e. later purchasers will follow the innovators.

Use of computer software in sales forecasting

Software has been written designed specifically for forecasting purposes. The problem with any listing of such software is that it quickly dates, so if it is proposed to use a software package then the best advice is to consult an up-to-date listing. The following is a list of more generalised packages that have withstood the test of time.

EXEC*U*STAT from Mercia Software Ltd. Combines business statistics with high-quality graphics output. It provides for quick analysis of data.

FOCA from Timberlake Clark Ltd. Offers modern quantitative forecasting of time series using exponential smoothing, spectral analysis, Box-Jenkins and adaptive filtering.

MINITAB from CLE.COM Ltd. A general-purpose data analysis system that is easy to use. Its features include descriptive statistics, regression analysis with diagnostics, residual analysis and step-wise procedures, time series analysis including robust smoothers and Box-Jenkins operations.

RATS from Timberlake Clark Ltd. An econometric package that performs time series and cross-sectional regression. It is designed for forecasting of time series, although small cross-sectional and panel data may also be used.

SAS/ETS from SAS Software Ltd. An econometrics and time series library which provides forecasting, planning and financial reporting. It contains procedures for time series analysis, linear and non-linear systems simulation and seasonal adjustments, and its applications include econometric modelling and cash-flow planning as well as sales forecasting.

SORITEC from Timberlake Clark Ltd. Includes non-linear and simultaneous estimation techniques, simultaneous non-linear simulation and solution, a full matrix processing language and transfer function estimation.

SPSS-PC+ from SPSS (UK) Ltd. A fully interactive data analysis package with full screen editing facilities, data entry and validation and a range of analytical and reporting procedures.

STATGRAPHICS from Cocking & Drury Ltd. A statistical and graphics package that includes plotting functions (2D and 3D), descriptive methods, estimation and testing, distribution fitting, exploratory data analysis, analysis and variance, regression analysis, time series analysis including Box-Jenkins ARIMA modelling, multivariate and non-parametric methods and experimental design.

STATPAC GOLD from Molimerx Ltd with batch and interactive processing and good graphics which requires less memory than most other packages.

This listing only documents those packages that are available in the UK; many more are available in the USA.

16.6   Budgeting – Purposes

It was outlined at the beginning of this chapter that an organisation needs to budget to ensure that expenditure does not exceed planned income. It has been shown that the sales forecast is the starting point for business planning activities. The company costing function takes the medium-term sales forecast as its starting point, and from this budgets are allocated to departments (or cost centres). Budgets state limits of spending; they are thus a means of control. The company can plan its profits based upon anticipated sales, minus the cost of achieving those sales (which is represented in the total budget for the organisation).

The consequence of an incorrect medium-term forecast can be seen as the company profit plan will be incorrect. It has already been mentioned, but is re-emphasised here, that if the forecast is pessimistic and the company achieves more sales than those forecast, then potential sales might be lost owing to unpreparedness and insufficient working finance and facilities being available to achieve those sales. Conversely, if the forecast is optimistic and sales revenue does not match anticipated sales, then revenue problems will arise, with the company having to approach a lender – probably a bank – to fund its short-term working capital requirements (which can be expensive if interest rates are high). This latter factor is a prime cause of many business failures, not necessarily because of bad products or a bad salesforce, but through insufficient money being available to meet working capital needs. These problems stem from incorrect medium-term forecasting in the first place. The following budgeting practice used by Kraft gives an illustration of budgeting methods.

Alternative types of budgeting

There are a number of budgeting types to choose from. Kraft uses a mix of the following:

1 Zero based budgeting

In a dynamic business it often makes sense to 'start afresh' when developing a budget rather than basing ideas too much on past performance. This is appropriate to Kraft because the organisation is continually seeking to innovate. Each budget is therefore constructed without much reference to previous budgets. In this way, change is built into budget thinking.

2 *Strategic* budgeting

This involves identifying new, emerging opportunities, and then building plans to take full advantage of them. This is closely related to zero based budgeting and helps Kraft to concentrate on gaining *competitive advantage*.

3 Rolling budgets

Given the speed of change and general uncertainty in the external environment, shareholders seek quick results. US companies typically report to shareholders every three months, compared with six months in the UK. Rolling budgets involve evaluating the previous twelve months' performance on an ongoing basis, and forecasting the next three months' performance.

4 Activity based budgeting

This examines individual activities and assesses the strength of their contribution to company success. They can then be ranked and prioritised, and be assigned appropriate budgets.

Source: *http://www.thetimes100.co.uk/case_study* with permission

16.7   Budget Determination

Departmental budgets are not prepared by cost accountants. Cost accountants, in conjunction with general management, apportion overall budgets for individual departments. It is the departmental manager who determines how the overall departmental budget will be utilised in achieving the planned-for sales (and production). For instance, a marketing manager might decide that more needs to be apportioned to advertising and less to the effort of selling in order to achieve the forecasted sales. The manager therefore apportions the budget accordingly and may concentrate upon image rather than product promotion; it is a matter of deciding beforehand where the priority lies when planning for marketing.

Thus, the overall sales forecast is the basis for company plans, and the sales department budget (other terms include sales and marketing department budget, and marketing department budget) is the basis for marketing plans in achieving those forecasted sales. The sales department budget is consequently a reflection of marketing's forthcoming expenditure in achieving those forecasted sales.

At this juncture it is useful to make a distinction between the *sales department budget* and the *sales budget* (see section 16.8). The sales department budget is merely the budget for running the marketing function for the budget period ahead. Cost accountants split this sales department budget into three cost elements:

1 The *selling expense budget* includes those costs directly attributable to the selling process, e.g. sales personnel salaries and commission, sales expenses and training.

2 The *advertising budget* includes those expenses directly attributable to above-the-line promotion (e.g. television advertising), and below-the-line promotion (e.g. a coupon redemption scheme). Methods of ascertaining the level of such a budget are as follows:

   (a) A percentage of last year's sales.

   (b) Parity with competitors, whereby smaller manufacturers take their cue from a larger manufacturer and adjust their advertising budget in line with the market leader.

   (c) The affordable method, where expenditure is allocated to advertising after other cost centres have received their budgets. In other words, if there is anything left over it goes to advertising.

   (d) The objective and task method calls for ascertainment of the advertising expenditure needed to reach marketing objectives that have been laid down in the marketing plan.

   (e) The return on investment method assumes that advertising is a tangible item which extends beyond the budget period. It looks at advertising expenditures as longer-term investments and attempts to ascertain the return on such expenditures.

   (f) The incremental method is similar to the previous method; it assumes that the last unit of money spent on advertising should bring in an equal unit of revenue.

   (a) assumes that increasing sales will generate increasing promotion and vice versa, whereas the converse might be the remedy, i.e. a cure for falling sales might be to increase the advertising spend. (b) assumes status quo within the marketplace. (c) does not really commend itself because the assumption is that advertising is a necessary evil and should only be entered into when other expenditures have been met. It quite often happens in times of company squeezes that advertising is the first item to be cut because of its intangibility.

The cure for the company ailment might rest in increased promotional awareness. (d) seems to make sense, but accountants contend that marketing personnel will state marketing objectives without due regard to their value, and such objectives may not sometimes be related to profits. (e) and (f) seem to make sense, but the main difficulties are in measuring likely benefits such as increased brand loyalty resulting from such advertising expenditures, and determining when marginal revenue equals marginal expenditure. In practice, firms often use a combination of methods, e.g. methods (d) and (e), when deciding their advertising budget.

3 The *administrative budget* represents the expenditure to be incurred in running the sales office. Such expenses cover the costs of marketing research, sales administration and support staff.

The marketing manager (or person responsible for the marketing and selling functions) must then determine, based upon the marketing plan for the year ahead, what portion of the sales department budget must be allocated to each of the three parts of the budget described above. Such expenditure should of course ensure that the forecasted sales will be met as the forecasting period progresses.

What has been stated so far relates to the sales department budget; the sales budget itself has not been dealt with. The sales budget has far more implications for the company and merits a separate section by way of explanation.

16.8   The Sales Budget

The **sales budget** may be said to be the total revenue expected from all products that are sold, and as such this affects all other aspects of the business. Thus, the sales budget comes directly after the sales forecast.

It can be said that the sales budget is the starting point of the company budgeting procedure because all other company activities are dependent upon sales and total revenue anticipated from the various products that the company sells. This budget affects other functional areas of the business, namely finance and production, because these two functions are directly dependent upon sales. Figure 16.6 best explains the sales budgeting procedure.

Figure 16.6 represents the way that cost accountants view the budgeting procedure. From the sales budget comes the sales department budget (or the total costs in administering the marketing function). The production budget covers all the costs involved in actually producing the products. The administrative budget covers all other costs such as personnel, finance, etc., and costs not directly attributable to production and selling.

The sales budget is thus the revenue earner for the company and other budgets represent expenditures incurred in achieving the sales. Cost accountants also have cash budgets and profit budgets, each with revenue provided from company sales. It is not proposed to go into why they split into cash and profit budgets. If you want to know more about the mechanisms involved here, then any basic text on cost accountancy should provide an explanation.

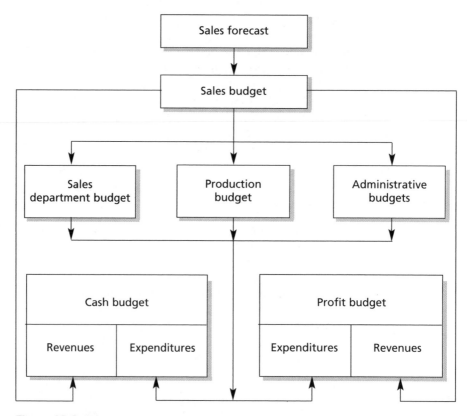

Figure 16.6 The budgetary process

16.9 Budget Allocation

The sales budget is a statement of projected sales by individual salespeople. The figure that reaches the individual salesperson is sometimes called the sales quota or sales target and this is the amount that must be sold in order to achieve the fore-casted sales. Such quotas or targets are therefore performance targets that must be reached, and quite often incentives are linked to salespeople reaching (and surpass-ing) such quotas or targets. Such incentives have already been covered in Chapters 14 and 15.

Each salesperson knows the individual amount they must sell to achieve their quota, and such quotas are effectively performance targets. Quotas need not necess-arily be individually based, but can be group based – say, collectively throughout a region – with everybody from the regional or area manager downwards equally sharing the sales commission. Quotas may also be for much shorter periods than the one year. The entire year's budget may be broken down in the same manner, say, month by month. When administered like this the time horizon is more realistic and immediate than one year. Thus, there is more of an incentive for a salesperson to achieve the quota or target.

For established firms the most common practice of budget allocation is simply to increase (or decrease) last year's individual budgets or quotas by an appropriate percentage, depending on the change in the overall sales budget. However, periodically it is sensible to review individual sales quotas to establish if they are reasonable given current market conditions.

The first step in this procedure is to attempt to determine the sales potential of territories. Usually surrogate measures will be employed to give at least relative measures of potential. For consumer products, disposable incomes and number of people in the target market may be used to assess relative potential. For industrial products, the number and size of potential customers may be used. Another factor to be taken into account is workload. Obviously two territories of equal potential may justify different quotas if one is compact while the other is more widespread. By assessing sales potential for territories and allowing for workload, the overall sales budget can be allocated in as fair a manner as possible between salespeople.

Not only does the sales quota act as an incentive to the salesforce but it also acts as a prime measure of performance. The next chapter looks in detail at the whole area of evaluation of sales personnel.

16.10   Conclusions

The purpose of sales forecasting has been explained and it has been emphasised that this function rests with sales management. Its importance to the planning process has been established; without reasonably accurate forecasting, planning will be in vain. The purpose of forecasting has been considered in the short, medium and long term, and the usefulness of each has been established within the major functions of any manufacturing or service concern.

Forecasting has been considered under the headings of qualitative and quantitative techniques, with the latter being split into time series methods and causal methods. Qualitative techniques and time series methods have been explained in the amount of detail required to give you a working knowledge of their application. However, causal methods depend largely upon the use of the computer, and computation relies to a great extent upon advanced mathematics. As such, the techniques have been described, but not explained in workable detail.

Finally, the importance of the sales budget in motivating and controlling the salesforce was considered. The sales budget, which is determined by the sales forecast, is broken down into sales quotas or targets for individual salespeople and regions. Monetary incentives may be linked to the attainment of quotas and may be used as a yardstick of achievement.

References

1   Hogarth, R. (1975) 'Cognitive processes and the assessment of subjective probability distributions', *Journal of the American Statistical Association*, 70 (350), pp. 271–89.

2 Lancaster, G.A. and Wright, G. (1983) 'Forecasting the future of video using a diffusion model', *European Journal of Marketing*, 17, p. 2.

Practical Exercise

Classical Reproductions Ltd

Background to the application of Bayesian decision theory

It has been mentioned throughout the chapter that since the 1960s we have seen the development of sophisticated statistical techniques for problem-solving where information is incomplete or uncertain. The new area of statistics has a variety of names – statistical decision theory, simple decision theory and Bayesian decision theory (after the Reverend Thomas Bayes, 1702–61). These names can be used interchangeably, but for the purposes of this case we use the term Bayesian decision theory.

Bayesian decision theory is a relatively new and somewhat controversial method for dealing with future uncertainties. Applied to forecasting, the technique incorporates the firm's own guesses as data inputs into the calculation of a sales forecast. There are essentially two ways of conceiving probability:

• as a physical property, inherent to a physical system

• as a measure of belief in the truth of some statement.

Until the late 1950s most statisticians held the first view of probability, with the probability of an event being the relative frequency with which the event might occur. Since this period there has been a rethink on the meaning of probability and it is now regarded more as a measure of belief. This latter approach is termed Bayesian statistics. The Bayesian view is that probability is a measure of our belief and we can always express our degree of belief in terms of probability.

To use the Bayesian approach, the decision-maker must be able to assign a probability to each specified event or state of nature. The sum of these probabilities must add to one. These probabilities represent the strength of the decision-maker's feeling regarding the likelihood of the occurrence of the various elements of the overall problem. It is because of the subjective nature of the process in generating these probabilities that Bayesian decision-making is so useful in solving business problems for which probabilities are often unknown. It is also the reason why many practitioners often reject the Bayesian approach; in fact some of the more conservative statisticians have termed it 'the quantification of error'!

In practical business problems, decisions are often delegated to persons whose levels of expertise should be such as to enable them to assign valid probabilities to the occurrences of various events. These probabilities will be subjective evaluations based on experience, intuition and other factors like available published data, all of which are acquired prior to the time that the decision is made. For this reason such subjective probability estimates are referred to as the prior probability of an event.

In business decision-making we must decide between alternatives by taking into account the monetary repercussions or expected value of our actions. A manager who must select from a number of available investments should consider the profit and loss that might result from each option. Applying Bayesian decision theory involves selecting an option and having a reasonable idea of the economic consequences of choosing that action.

Once the relevant future events have been identified and the respective subjective prior probabilities have been assigned, the decision-maker computes the expected payoff for each act and chooses the one with the most attractive expected payoff. If payoffs represent income or profit, the decision-maker chooses the act with the highest expected payoff.

The Bayesian technique can be used to solve quite complex problems, but in this example we give a relatively simple problem by way of illustration and explanation. However, the principles are similar for simple or difficult problems.

Bayesian decision theory applied to Classical Reproductions Ltd

This UK manufacturer of fine reproduction English furniture is considering venturing into the US market. The company is to appoint an agent who will hold stock and sell the furniture to quality retail stores.

In order for the firm to gain economies in freight charges, consignments need to be fairly large and it is planned that the first consignment will be £2 million worth of furniture.

This type of furniture is particularly fashionable in the USA at present and commands high prices. The management of Classical Reproductions expect the furniture to remain heavily in demand so long as US economic conditions remain buoyant. If economic conditions take a turn for the worse, then demand and prices will fall dramatically, because such products are a deferrable purchase.

To finance the manufacture, shipping, warehousing and other costs associated with the venture, the company is raising capital from a bank. Although the venture looks sound there is uncertainty as to the future direction of the US economy over the next 12 months. The decision facing management is whether to risk going ahead with the venture now, when demand for their products is going to be high but with the possibility of the economy deteriorating, or to postpone the venture until the US economic outlook is more certain, but during which time tastes might change.

Let us assume that the management feel that the direction of the US economy could go in one of three ways in the next twelve months:

- continue to be buoyant
- a moderate downturn
- a serious recession

The direction of the economy is an event (E) or a state of nature that is completely outside the control of the company. Let us also assume that management has decided on three possible courses of action (A):

- export now while demand is high

- delay the venture by one year

- delay the venture by two years

Management has made a forecast of the likely expected profit for each of the possible courses of action for each of the three possible events, and this information is shown in the table below.

Events (E)	Actions (A)	Export now (£)	Delay 1 year (£)	Delay 2 years (£)
Economic conditions remain good		800,000	600,000	500,000
Moderate downturn in economy		450,000	370,000	200,000
Economic recession		−324,000	50,000	80,000

Management wishes to make the decision that will maximise the firm's expected profit. They assign subjective prior probabilities to each of the possible events:

Event	Probability
Economic conditions remain good (A)	0.4
Moderate downturn in economy (B)	0.3
Economic recession (C)	0.3
	1.0

These prior probabilities are now incorporated into a decision tree (see Figure 16.7) which is made up of a series of nodes and branches. The decision points are denoted by a square and chance events by circles. The node on the left (square) denotes the decision the firm has to make. Each branch represents an alternative course of action or decision. Each branch leads to a further node (circle) and from this, further branches denote the chance events.

The expected value (EV) should now be calculated for each forecast and then totalled for each alternative course of action. This is done in the following 'payoff table' by multiplying the expected profit for each event by their assigned probabilities and summing these products.

Action 1 – export now:

Event (E)	Probability	Expected profit (£)	Expected value (£)
A	0.4	800,000	320,000
B	0.3	450,000	135,000
C	0.3	−324,000	−97,200
Total EV for this alternative			£357,800

Action 2 – delay 1 year:

Event (E)	Probability	Expected profit (£)	Expected value (£)
A	0.4	600,000	240,000
B	0.3	370,000	111,000
C	0.3	50,000	15,000
Total EV for this alternative			£366,000

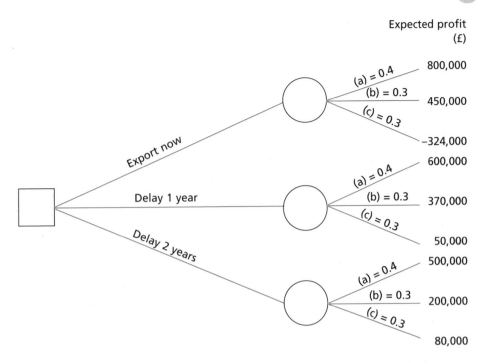

Expected profit
(£)

Figure 16.7 Decision tree for Classical Reproductions Ltd: (a) economy remains buoyant;
(b) moderate downturn; (c) recession

Action 3 – delay 2 years:

Event (E)	Probability	Expected profit (£)	Expected value (£)
A	0.4	500,000	200,000
B	0.3	200,000	60,000
C	0.3	80,000	24,000
Total EV for this alternative			£284,000

The firm decides to delay the venture by one year because the maximum expected payoff is associated with this. Since the act is selected under conditions of uncertainty, the EV of £366,000 is referred to as the EV under uncertainty and the act is referred to as the optimal act.

In this example the probabilities that have been assigned to events have been prior probabilities, so called because they have been arrived at prior to the acquisition of sampling or experimental information. As a rule, these prior probabilities are subjective, representing the decision-maker's belief that various events will happen. The analysis which is carried out using these prior probabilities is called prior analysis. Following prior analysis, the decision-maker must decide whether to go ahead with the optimal act indicated by prior analysis, or to obtain further information in the hope of making a better and more certain decision.

Additional information may be obtained by conducting a survey, by carrying out an experiment or by some other means. If this additional information is acted upon, the decision-maker will have to substitute new probabilities for the prior probabilities. Another analysis will then have to be undertaken using this new information. These new probabilities are called posterior probabilities.

Naturally, generating further information can be costly and the decision-maker must decide if the potential result is worth the cost. To extend this final point, let us find the expected value with perfect information when the prior probabilities are as follows:

(A)   Economic conditions remain buoyant   = 0.4
(B)   Relative economic decline   = 0.3
(C)   Recession   = 0.3

If economic conditions remain buoyant, the optimum choice would be to export now. If there is a moderate downturn in the economy, the optimum choice would still be to export now. If there is a recession, the optimal choice will be to delay for two years. Thus we find the expected value of perfect information (EVPI):

£479,000 − £366,000 = £113,000

This value of £113,000 can be interpreted as the expected opportunity loss for the optimal act under uncertainty and is the cost of uncertainty. The decision-maker can do no better than obtain perfect information, so this figure is the maximum s/he would be willing to pay for additional information that s/he knows will be less than perfect.

Discussion Questions

1   Carry out a full decision analysis for Classical Reproductions Ltd, using the following information.

Calculation of expected profit with perfect information

Event	Profit for optimal act	Probability	Expected value (£)
A	800,000	0.4	320,000
B	450,000	0.3	135,000
C	80,000	0.3	24,000
			£479,000

Prior probablities for the various events for the next twelve months are:

(A) = 0.3

(B) = 0.4

(C) = 0.3

2   Carry out a pre-posterior analysis and find the expected value of perfect information (EVPI).

3   Having applied Bayesian decision theory to this example, what do you consider are its advantages and disadvantages?

Travelodge service with Q-Max Workforce Management

This exercise questions something that is not covered in the text – action needed to be taken by management in the case of a system breakdown. It is felt that this is best tackled in discussion form rather than attempting to prescribe a solution.

With 250 Travelodges all over the UK, travellers are never far from a good night's sleep. With well over 60,000 calls per week being received at the Travelodge Reservation Centre, sleep is the last thing on anyone's mind. The good news is that recent changes to the allocation of shifts and rotas have meant that management can now sleep easy and customers are assured good service.

Travelodge promotes the concept of providing everything that is required for a good night's sleep with luxury Hypnos beds, free car parking in most locations and check out completed on arrival. Visitor's do not pay hotel rates when all they need is a stopover. This approach is working and the Dudley Reservation Centre has experienced an increase in demand along with additional enquiries prompted by the Internet and group bookings.

The Travelodge Reservation Centre has more than 170 advisers spread across two teams covering London and the rest of the country. In addition, there is a team of 20 people dealing with group bookings. The focus has increased to sales at the Centre with the appointment of five sales managers and five sales co-ordinators. This two-tiered management system makes for improved communication and control in terms of coaching and scheduling advisers on a daily basis.

According to Ellen Jones, Workforce and Planning Manager: 'We have introduced a new way of working within our Q-Max Workforce Management system. This means that sales managers and sales co-ordinators have access to Travelodge Live. This enables them to make agent changes without having full access to the system. Previously team managers would ask Planning Department to make changes and that was time consuming and not always accurate. We realised we needed to change the way of working with Q-Max on several levels.'

Exceptional Q-Max Users

Travelodge has been using Q-Max for more than seven years and was able to see how the system could be adapted to fit the new ways of working. Adrian Ward, Consultant at Q-Max Systems said: 'Ellen Jones and her team are exceptional users of Q-Max; they utilise the majority of the functions within the product which means it fits well with the way they operate. This became particularly apparent in terms of the mix of part-time and full-time staff.'

A good example of how Q-Max has helped to improve planning and service is how non-flexible fixed hours staff are now scheduled alongside part-time and more flexible full-time advisors. There are many students and part time mothers working in the Reservation Centre who only work evenings and weekends. Previously these fixed-hour people were added to Q-Max after the more flexible full-time staff had been allocated their shifts. There were rules in the system that insisted that each adviser did two late shifts each week and one and a half weekends in four. By moving everyone available on to large fully flexible rota taking into account the fixed hours of the part-time advisers Q-Max was able to reduce the number of manual changes required and separated the situation where Travelodge could be understaffed during the week and overstaffed at weekends. Full-time advisers were guaranteed every other weekend off so they could plan weekends away and social activities.

The benefits of a flexible rota

The benefits of this rota have been that part-time and full-time flexible staff work fewer evenings and weekends and fixed hours people get the work and hours that they want. In addition, service has improved as there are the right number of advisers available for call volumes that can rise from 4,000 calls on a Sunday to 10,000 on Monday and Tuesday.

Ellen Jones explains: 'The changes to the system were to alleviate pressure so that we had the maximum number of people when we needed them most. This has definitely been the case and advisers are happy with the new arrangement. We have noticed that absenteeism has reduced and suspect this is the effect of new rotas and improved job satisfaction. We are still providing a minimum of four weeks' and a maximum of six weeks' notice in terms of working hours so people can plan around their shifts. The sales managers are also happy with the new arrangement because with advisers covering 7 am to 10 pm and often a mixture of both part-time and full-time people it is easier to schedule specific times for coaching, i.e. when quiet times are predicted.'

With sales managers taking responsibility for updating Q-Max in terms of absence through sickness, coaching, etc., the Resource Planning team are able to concentrate on devising new ways to maximise efficiency. Ellen and her assistant use the Q-Max Optimiser in conjunction with deviation reports to allocate overtime. They also use Q-Max to schedule time for managers to receive calls at peak times. All managers are trained to take calls at busy times and this ability to include them when using the Optimiser has been useful. There are plans to use Q-Max for the group bookings team who are scheduled manually at the moment.

Plans for the future

Travelodge plans to expand the Reservations Centre as the appeal of a good night's sleep without hotel prices increases. Ellen Jones concludes: 'Q-Max has been used within Travelodge for so many years because it is a fantastic system that works really well. The ability to change the way in which it works to suit changes in the way we work has meant it remains fresh and appropriate at all times. The service we receive from Adrian and the rest of Q-Max means we are kept up to date with how to use the system to its best ability. Our recent experiences have proved it is a flexible and powerful product that enables us to deliver levels of service our customers demand.'

About Q-Max Systems Limited

Q-Max Workforce Management is a day-to-day management system to calculate the number of agents required to respond to customer demand. The Q-Max Optimiser evaluates within seconds schedule changes required to meet service levels. Q-Max also has a Long Range Forecaster, Shift Scheduler and Agent Adherence and self-service Agent Desktop features.

Q-Max (www.q-max.co.uk) is the most widely installed workforce management system in the UK and is also installed in 43 countries worldwide.

Source: *www.prartistry.co.uk* with permission

Discussion Questions

1 What might be the implications associated with a possible breakdown of the Q-Max computing system?

2 Suggest how management might cope with such an eventuality.

Practical Exercise

Pizza Ristorante

Thawing the frozen pizza market

Dr. Oetker has recently entered the UK market with the launch of its flagship 'Pizza Ristorante' frozen pizza brand, but until now little in the UK has been known of the company that is one of Europe's leading food manufacturers. So, who is Dr. Oetker?

A pharmacist from Bielefeld, Germany, Dr. August Oetker founded the Oetker Group in 1891. Today the group has grown to become one of Germany's largest family-owned companies with an annual turnover of more than £3.5 billion.

And the key to this success? A simple philosophy – that 'Quality is the Best Recipe', both in business and its products.

Quality is the best recipe

Pizza Ristorante has the responsibility of launching Dr. Oetker in the UK, and the company is more than confident it will succeed. Pizza Ristorante promises an authentic pizzeria taste, and that's exactly what you get. Research indicates that 76 per cent of consumers prefer Pizza Ristorante to its competitors,[1] obviously enjoying the balance of a genuinely thin and crispy base with generous, quality toppings that result in a pizza which raises the standard for the entire frozen pizza market. Initially the brand, which is a European bestseller, will be available in four core varieties: Mozzerella, Speciale, Funghi and Hawaii, with an extended range consisting of Salame, Tonno, Quattro Stagione and Vegetale.

Peter Franks, Sales Director for Dr. Oetker (UK) Ltd, comments: 'Consumers have become disenchanted with frozen pizzas, often considering them to be of poorer quality than their cousins in the chilled cabinet. Pizza Ristorante will turn this perception on its head, offering the quality and taste you expect from your local pizzeria with the versatility and convenience you expect from your freezer.'

Formula for success

Dr. Oetker has plenty of experience when it comes to launching into new markets, and is already market leader in many of the 23 European countries in which its pizza brands are available. The company forecasts similar success in the UK, as Peter Franks explains: 'Pizza Ristorante is prepared from the finest ingredients to satisfy consumer demand for a quality frozen product. In addition, looking at the market, the Thin & Crispy sector is dominated by own label, and the introduction of a branded product offering true quality at a competitive price can only add value. Our aim is to stimulate a static market by encouraging consumers to revisit the frozen pizza category by sampling the uniquely authentic pizzeria taste Pizza Ristorante delivers.'

Investing in the future

The launch is being supported with a fully integrated marketing campaign including a £5 million TV advertising campaign, focusing on the quality and convenience of the thin and crispy range, PR, in-store POS, sampling and promotional support.

The product is excellent, the research positive and the financial investment second to none, but will Dr. Oetker succeed in the UK? Well, if quality is indeed the best recipe, and consumers seem to agree it is, it would take a brave man to bet against it.

Recent developments

It was reported in *The Grocer* on 13 July 2002 that sales of the new range, launched in March, hit the £3 million mark in multiple grocers and Co-ops in May. This impressive figure, likely to have been generated by a heavyweight TV campaign, equated to an 11 per cent share of the total frozen pizza market during that month. However, figures for June suggest that only one out of two consumers have repeated their purchase, with latest figures for the four weeks to 16 June dropping to under £1.5 million. Own label still dominates the market with average monthly sales of around £8 million. Vice President, Axel Andree, told *The Grocer* that he believed Dr. Oetker would become the number one pizza brand in the UK within three years, sparking speculation that the company may enter other sectors of the UK food market.

Note

1 Independent Market Research, September 2001

Source: Adapted from article originally in *The Grocer*, 18/5/02, p. 30; 13 July 2002, p. 48. Reproduced with permission.

Discussion Questions

1 Franks wants a system of forecasting that will provide as accurate a picture as possible of first year sales in order to satisfy demands from head office who are sponsoring the launch of Pizza Ristorante. Advise Franks as to the best system he might adopt.

2 Franks also wants the new salesforce to be incentivised to ensure a good product launch. He recognises the importance of the sales budget in motivating and controlling the salesforce. Given the background of the case, advise Franks on the best way of setting sales quotas or targets for salespeople and how these might be used as a yardstick when measuring achievement.

Examination Questions

1 What is the place of sales forecasting in the company planning process?

2 Distinguish between qualitative and quantitative forecasting techniques. What are the advantages and disadvantages associated with each approach?

3 Define the differences between a sales forecast and a market forecast.

4 How might a government forecast or a forecast from a trade association be of specific use to a medium-sized company?

5 How does the sales department budget differ from the sales budget?

6 Discuss the importance of the sales budget in the corporate budgetary process.

Salesforce Evaluation

After studying the chapter, you should be able to:

1 Understand the meaning of salesforce evaluation

2 Understand the salesforce evaluation process

3 Know how standards of performance are set in order that sales can be achieved

4 Understand how information plays a key role in the evaluation process

5 Set qualitative and quantitative measures of performance

Key Concepts

- appraisal interviewing
- qualitative performance measures
- quantitative performance measures
- salesforce evaluation
- salesforce evaluation process

17.1 The Salesforce Evaluation Process

Salesforce evaluation is the comparison of salesforce objectives with results. A model of the evaluation process is shown in Figure 17.1. It begins with the setting of salesforce objectives which may be financial, such as sales revenues, profits and expenses; market-orientated, such as market share; or customer-based such as customer satisfaction and service levels. Then, the sales strategy must be decided to show how the objectives are to be achieved. Next, performance standards should be set for the overall company, regions, products, salespeople and accounts. Results are then measured and compared with performance standards. Reasons for differences are assessed and action taken to improve performance.

17.2   The Purpose of Evaluation

The prime reason for evaluation is to attempt to attain company objectives. By measuring actual performance against objectives, shortfalls can be identified and appropriate action taken to improve performance. However, evaluation has other

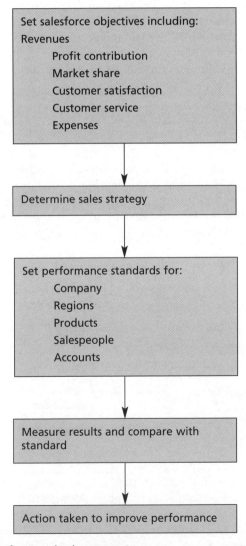

Figure 17.1 The salesforce evaluation process

benefits. Evaluation can help improve an individual's motivation and skills. Motivation is affected since an evaluation programme will identify what is expected and what is considered good performance. Second, it provides the opportunity for the recognition of above-average standards of work performance, which improves confidence and motivation. Skills are affected since carefully constructed evaluation allows areas of weakness to be identified and effort to be directed to the improvement of skills in those areas.

Thus, evaluation is an important ingredient in an effective training programme. Further, evaluation may show weaknesses, perhaps in not devoting enough attention to selling certain product lines, which span most or all of the sales team. This information may lead to the development of a compensation plan designed to encourage salespeople to sell those products by means of higher commission rates.

Evaluation provides information which affects key decision areas within the sales management function. Training, compensation, motivation and objective setting are dependent on the information derived from evaluation, as illustrated in Figure 17.2. It is important, then, that sales management develops a system of information collection which allows fair and accurate evaluation to occur.

The level and type of control exercised over international salesforces will depend upon the culture of the company and its host nations. The boxed case discussion highlights some important points.

Controlling international salesforces

The degree to which sales teams are controlled may depend upon the culture of the employing company. Many European and US companies are profit focused and so emphasise quantitative (e.g. sales and profit) control mechanisms. Many Japanese and Asian companies use less formal and less quantitative evaluation systems.

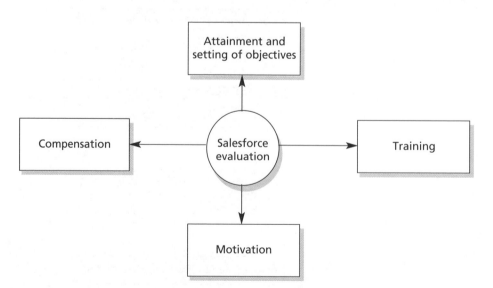

Figure 17.2 The central role of evaluation in sales management

Control systems must take into account the local conditions in each overseas market. Furthermore, they should account for the type of salesforce employed (expatriates or foreign nationals). Systems that are used at home may be appropriate for expatriates, but for foreign nationals they may be alien to their culture and way of doing business.

Source: Based on Honeycutt, Jr., E.D. and Ford, J.B. (1995) 'Guidelines for managing an international sales force', *Industrial Marketing Management*, 24, pp. 135–44.

17.3 Setting Standards of Performance

Evaluation implies the setting of standards of performance along certain lines which are believed to be important for sales success. The control process is based upon the collection of information on performance so that actual results can be compared against those standards. For the sales team as a whole the sales budget will be the standard against which actual performance will be evaluated. This measure will be used to evaluate sales management as well as individual salespeople. For each salesperson, his or her sales quota will be a prime standard of sales success.

Standards provide a method of fairly assessing and comparing individual salespeople. Simply comparing levels of sales achieved by individual salespeople is unlikely to be fair since territories often have differing levels of sales potential and varying degrees of workload.

17.4 Gathering Information

The individual salesperson will provide much of the information upon which evaluation will take place. S/he will provide head office with data relating to sales achieved by product/brand and customer, a daily or weekly report of the names of customers called on and problems and opportunities revealed, together with expense claims.

Such information will be supplemented by sales management during field visits. These are important in providing more qualitative information on how the salesperson performs in front of customers as well as giving indications of general attitudes, work habits and degree of organisational ability, all of which supplement the more quantitative information provided by the salesperson.

Market research projects can also provide information on the sales team from customers themselves. A specific project, or a more general one which focuses on the full range of customer–seller relationships, e.g. delivery, product reliability, etc., can provide information on salespeople's performance. A market research study commissioned by Perkins Engines found that salespeople with technical backgrounds were basing their sales presentation on features which were not properly understood by their audience.[1] This led Perkins Engines to retrain their salesforce so that their sales presentation focused upon a simple presentation of features and the customer benefits which arose from those features.

Finally, company records provide a rich source of information for evaluation. Records of past sales levels, calls achieved, expense levels, etc. can provide bases for comparison and indications of trends which can be used both for evaluation and objective setting.

17.5 Measures of Performance

Quantitative measures of performance

Assessment using **qualitative performance measures** falls into two groups. For both groups, management may wish to set targets for their sales team. One group is a set of input measures which are essentially diagnostic in nature – they help to provide indications of why performance is below standard. Key output measures relate to sales and profit performance. Most companies use a combination of input (behavioural) and output measures to evaluate their salesforces.[2] Specific output measures for individual salespeople include the following:

- sales revenue achieved

- profits generated

- percentage gross profit margin achieved

- sales per potential account

- sales per active account

- sales revenue as a percentage of sales potential

- number of orders

- sales to new customers

- number of new customers

All of these measures relate to output.

The second group of measures relates to input and includes:

- number of calls made

- calls per potential account

- calls per active account

- number of quotations (in part, an output measure also)

- number of calls on prospects

By combining output and input measures a number of hybrid ratios can be determined. For example:

1 Strike rate = $\dfrac{\text{Number of orders}}{\text{Number of quotations}}$

2 Sales revenue per call ratio

3 Profit per call ratio (call effectiveness)

4 Order per call ratio

5 Average order value = $\dfrac{\text{Sales revenue}}{\text{Number of orders}}$

6 Prospecting success ratio = $\dfrac{\text{Number of new customers}}{\text{Number of prospects visited}}$

7 Average profit contribution per order = $\dfrac{\text{Profits generated}}{\text{Number of orders}}$

All of these ratios can be applied to individual product and customer types and help to answer the following questions:

(a) Is the salesperson achieving a satisfactory level of sales?

(b) Is sales success reflected in profit achievement?

(c) Is the salesperson 'buying' sales by giving excessive discounts?

(d) Is the salesperson devoting sufficient time to prospecting?

(e) Is time spent prospecting being rewarded by orders?

(f) Does the salesperson appear to be making a satisfactory number of calls per week?

(g) Is s/he making enough repeat calls on different customer categories?

(h) Is s/he making too many calls on low-potential customers?

(i) Are calls being reflected in sales success?

(j) Are the number of quotations being made reflected in orders taken?

(k) How are sales being achieved – a large number of small orders or a few large orders?

(l) Are the profits generated per order sufficient to justify calling upon the account?

Many of these measures are clearly diagnostic. They provide pointers to possible reasons why a salesperson may not be reaching his or her sales quota. Perhaps s/he is lazy – not making enough calls. Perhaps call rate is satisfactory but call effectiveness, e.g. sales per call, is low, indicating a lack of sales skill. Maybe the salesperson is calling on too many established accounts and not enough new prospects.

Ratios also provide clues to problem areas which require further investigation. A low strike rate (order to quotations) suggests the need for an analysis of why orders are not following quotations. Poor call effectiveness suggests a close examination of sales technique to identify specific areas of weakness so that training can be applied more effectively.

A further group of quantitative measures will explore the remuneration which each salesperson receives. The focus will be on expenses and compensation. With respect to expenses, comparisons will be made between salespeople and between current year and last year. Ratios which may be used include the following:

- expenses/sales revenue generated
- expenses/profit generated
- expenses per call
- expenses per square mile of territory

Table 17.1 A comparison of the usage of salesforce evaluation output criteria between small and large organisations

Evaluative criteria	Small firms %	Large firms %	Statistically significant difference
Sales			
Sales volume	87.2	93.1	
Sales volume by product or product line	61.2	80.3	*
Sales volume by customer or customer type	48.2	59.5	
Sales volume per order	22.4	26.7	
Sales volume by outlet or outlet type	22.4	38.9	*
Sales volume per call	12.9	24.4	*
Market share	32.9	57.3	*
Accounts			
Number of new accounts gained	58.8	55.7	
Number of accounts lost	44.7	42.7	
Amount of new account sales	57.6	54.2	
Number of accounts on which payment overdue	41.2	38.2	
Proportion/number of accounts buying full product line	14.1	16.0	
Profit			
Gross profit generated	58.8	48.9	
Net profit generated	38.8	42.7	
Gross profit as a percentage of sales volume	47.1	45.0	
Net profit as a percentage of sales volume	38.8	34.4	
Return on investment	28.2	26.7	
Profit per call ratio	12.9	12.2	
Orders			
Number of orders taken	48.2	38.2	
Number of orders cancelled	14.1	13.7	
Order per call ratio	25.9	29.0	
Strike rate $\frac{\text{Number of orders}}{\text{Number of quotations}}$	37.9	40.5	
Average order value	28.2	26.0	
Average profit contribution per order	21.2	16.8	
Value or orders to value of quotations ratio	29.4	21.4	
Other output criteria			
Number of customer complaints	23.5	22.3	

Note: *indicates significant at $p < 0.05$.

Such measures should give an indication of when the level of expenses is becoming excessive. Compensation analysis is particularly valuable when:

- a large part of salary is fixed

- salespeople are on different levels of fixed salary

The latter situation will be found in companies which pay according to the number of years at the firm or according to age. Unfairness, in terms of sales results, can be exposed by calculating for each salesperson the following two ratios:

- total salary (including commission)/sales revenue

- total salary (including commission)/profits

These ratios will reveal when a compensation plan has gone out of control and allow changes to be made before lower paid higher achievers leave for jobs which more closely relate pay to sales success.

A study by Jobber, Hooley and Shipley surveyed a sample of 450 industrial products organisations (i.e. firms manufacturing and selling repeat industrial goods such as components and capital goods such as machinery).[3] The objective was to discover the extent of usage of sales evaluation criteria among small (less than £3 million sales turnover) and large (greater than £3 million sales turnover) firms. Table 17.1 shows that there is a wide variation in the usage of output criteria among the sample of firms and that large firms tend to use more output criteria than small organisations.

Table 17.2 shows that the use of input criteria is also quite variable, with statistics relating to calls the most frequently used by both large and small firms. Again,

Table 17.2 A comparison of the usage of salesforce evaluation input criteria between small and large organisations

Evaluative criteria	Small firms %	Large firms %	Statistically significant difference
Calls			
Number of calls per period	49.4	69.7	*
Number of calls per customer or customer type	15.3	37.4	*
Calls on potential new accounts	56.5	53.8	
Calls on existing accounts	55.3	61.8	
Prospecting success ratio: (Number of new customers) (Number of potential new customers visited)	28.2	32.8	
Expenses			
Ratio of sales expense to sales volume	38.8	45.4	
Average cost per call	21.2	30.8	
Other input criteria			
Number of required reports sent in	42.0	42.0	
Number of demonstrations conducted	23.5	22.3	
Number of service calls made	21.2	23.1	
Number of letters/telephone calls to prospects	14.1	7.7	

Note: *indicates significant at $p < 0.05$.

there is a tendency for large firms to use more input criteria when evaluating their salesforces.

The growth in the penetration of personal computers is mirrored by the development of software packages that provide the facilities for the simple compilation and analysis of salesforce evaluation measures. The creation of a databank of quantitative measures over time allows a rich source of information about how the salesforce is performing.

These quantitative measures cannot solely produce a complete evaluation of salespeople. In order to provide a wider perspective, qualitative measures will also be employed.

Qualitative measures of performance

Assessment along qualitative lines will necessarily be more subjective and take place in the main during field visits. The usual dimensions which are applied are given in the following list:

1 *Sales skills*. These may be rated using a number of sub-factors:

- Handling the opening and developing rapport.
- Identification of customer needs, questioning ability.
- Quality of sales presentation.
- Use of visual aids.
- Ability to overcome objections.
- Ability to close the sale.

2 *Customer relationships*.

- How well received is the salesperson?
- Are customers well satisfied with the service, advice, reliability of the salesperson, or are there frequent grumbles and complaints?

3 *Self-organisation*. How well does the salesperson carry out the following?

- Prepare calls.
- Organise routeing to minimise unproductive travelling.
- Keep customer records up to date.
- Provide market information to headquarters.
- Conduct self-analysis of performance in order to improve weaknesses.

4 *Product knowledge*. How well informed is the salesperson regarding the following?

- His or her own products and their customer benefits and applications.
- Competitive products and their benefits and applications.

- Relative strengths and weaknesses between his or her own and competitive offerings.

5 *Co-operation and attitudes*. To what extent will the salesperson do the following?

- Respond to the objectives determined by management in order to improve performance, e.g. increase prospecting rate.

- Co-operate with suggestions made during field training for improved sales technique.

- Use his or her own initiative.

What are his or her attitudes towards the following?

- The company and its products.

- Hard work.

An increasing number of companies are measuring their salespeople on the basis of the achievement of customer satisfaction. As Richard Harrison, a senior sales manager at IBM, states: 'Our sales team is compensated based on how quickly and how efficiently they achieve customer satisfaction'.[4]

The study by Jobber, Hooley and Shipley also investigated the use of qualitative evaluative measures by industrial goods companies.[5] Table 17.3 shows the results, with most criteria being used by the majority of sales managers in the sample. Although differences between small and large firms were not so distinct as for quantitative measures, more detailed analysis of the results showed that managers of small firms tended to hold qualitative opinions 'in the head', whereas managers of large firms tended to produce more formal assessments, e.g. in an evaluation report.

As mentioned earlier, the use of quantitative and qualitative measures is interrelated. A poor sales per call ratio will inevitably result in close scrutiny of sales skills, customer relationships and degree of product knowledge in order to discover why performance is poor.

Sales management response to the results of carrying out salesforce evaluation is shown in Figure 17.3. Lynch[6] suggests four scenarios with varying implications:

1 *Good quantitative/good qualitative evaluation*. The appropriate response would be praise and monetary reward. For suitable candidates promotion would follow.

2 *Good quantitative/poor qualitative evaluation*. The good quantitative results suggest that performance in front of customers is good, but certain aspects of qualitative evaluation, e.g. attitudes, report writing and market feedback, may warrant advice and education regarding company standards and requirements.

3 *Poor quantitative/good qualitative evaluation*. Good qualitative input is failing to be reflected in quantitative success. The specific causes need to be identified and training and guidance provided. Lack of persistence, poor closing technique or too many/too few calls might be possible causes of poor sales results.

4 *Poor quantitative/poor qualitative evaluation*. Critical discussion is required to agree problem areas. Training is required to improve standards. In other situations, punishment may be required or even dismissal.

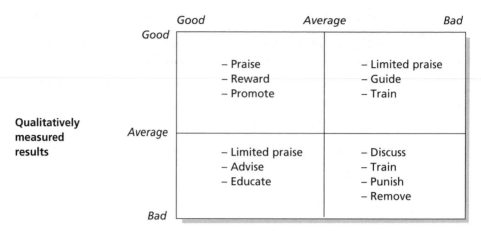

Figure 17.3 Salesperson evaluation matrix

For an evaluation and control system to work efficiently, it is important for the sales team to understand its purpose. For them to view it simply as a means for management to catch them out and criticise performance is likely to breed resentment. It should be used, and be perceived, as a means of assisting salespeople in improving performance. Indeed, the quantitative output measures can be used as a basis for

Table 17.3 A comparison of the usage of qualitative salesforce evaluation criteria between small and large organisations

Evaluative criteria	Small firms %	Large firms %	Statistically significant difference
Skills			
Selling skills	81.9	86.9	
Communication skills	77.1	85.4	
Knowledge			
Product knowledge	94.0	90.8	
Knowledge of competition	80.7	83.1	
Knowledge of company policies	56.6	68.5	
Self-management			
Planning ability	77.1	76.2	
Time management	54.2	61.5	
Judgement/decision-making ability	74.7	68.5	
Report preparation and submission	63.9	77.7	*
Personal characteristics			
Attitudes	91.6	88.5	
Initiative	92.8	83.1	
Appearance and manner	90.4	86.9	
Aggressiveness	45.8	50.8	
Creativity	49.4	56.9	

Note: *indicates significant at $p < 0.05$.

rewarding performance when targets are met. In essence, controls should be viewed in a positive manner, not a negative one.

Winning or losing major orders

A key qualitative evaluation question that sales managers have to ask is: 'Does it appear that we are going to win or lose this order?' This is particularly important for major sales. For example, a sales manager may be asked by the managing director: 'Will you find out whether the Saudis are really going to place that new big aero engine order? I have to tell the board next week so that we can decide whether we will have to expand our plant.'

The obvious response would be to ask the salesperson in charge of the sale directly. The problem is that many salespeople delude themselves into believing they are going to be successful. How do you come to terms with the fact that you are going to lose an order worth £5 million? Asking the direct question 'Bill, are we going to win this one?' is likely to get the answer 'Yes, the customer loves us!' What the salesperson really means is that the customer likes the salesperson, not necessarily the product.

Consequently the sales manager needs to probe much more deeply in order to assess the situation more accurately. This involves asking a series of who, when, where, why and how questions. It also means that the sales manager needs to work out what would be considered acceptable (winning) answers, and what would be thought of as unacceptable (losing) responses. Table 17.4 gives an example of the use of this procedure in connection with a £10 million computer sale. The losing answers are thin and unconvincing (e.g. the director of MIS would not have the power to authorise an order of this size).

The salesperson is deluding him- or herself and misleading the sales manager. The winning answer is much more assured and provides clear, credible answers to all of the questions (e.g. an executive director is likely to have the power to authorise a purchase of this magnitude).

If the outcome is a losing answer, the sales manager has to decide how important the sale is and how important the salesperson is. If they both have high potential, the sales manager, sales trainer or top salesperson should work with him or her. S/he should be counselled so that they understand why they are being helped and what the sales manager hopes they will learn. In the process, they will also realise that management cares about their development and the success it can bring to both parties.

If the salesperson is viewed as having high potential but the situation has low potential, only a counselling session is needed. Usually it is best done at the end of the day, driving back from a call, using an 'oh, by the way' introduction, and avoiding serious eye contact. By these means the salesperson's ego is not offended.

When the salesperson does not have high potential but the sale does, the alternatives are a little nastier. Perhaps the salesperson would be a candidate for redeployment to a more suitable post. When neither the salesperson nor the sale has much potential, the basic question is whether the salesperson is redeployed before or after the sale is lost.

Table 17.4 Winning and losing orders

Question	Poor (losing answer)	Good (winning answer)
Who will authorise the purchase?	The director of MIS.	The director of MIS but it requires an executive director's authorisation, and we've talked it over with him or her.
When will they buy?	Right away. They love the new model.	Before the peak processing load at the year end.
Where will s/he be when the decision is made – in the office alone, in his or her boss's office, in a meeting?	What difference does that make? I think s/he has already decided.	At a board meeting. But don't worry, the in-supplier has no one on their board and we have two good customers on it.
Why will they buy from us? Why not their usual supplier?	S/he and I go way back. They love our new model.	The next upgrade from the in-supplier is a big price increase, and ours fits right between their models. They are quite unhappy with the in-supplier about that.
How will the purchase be funded?	They've lots of money, haven't they?	The payback period on reduced costs will be about 14 months and we've a leasing company willing to take part of the deal.

17.6 Appraisal Interviewing

Appraisal interviewing can provide the opportunity to identify a salesperson's weaknesses and to give praise when it is deserved. One method is to ask the sales-person to write down 5–10 expectations that they hope to achieve during the next year, e.g. to go on a presentation skills course, to go on a time management course, to have monthly sales visits from their sales manager, to meet targets, to move into marketing, etc. The sales manager then sits down with the salesperson and goes through this list, breaking it down into quarterly (three-month) sections. At the end of each quarter they have another meeting to see if expectations have been met or shifted in any way. These meetings also provide an opportunity to give or withdraw recognition and acceptance.

17.7   Conclusions

This chapter has explored the sales evaluation process. A model of the evaluation process is described. It begins with setting objectives, moves to the determination of sales strategy, the setting of performance standards, measurement of results against standards and finishes with action taken to improve performance.

A more detailed look at the kinds of measures used to evaluate salespeople was then taken. Two broad measures are used – quantitative and qualitative indicators. Such measures can be used to evaluate, control and motivate salespeople towards better performance.

References

1   Reed, J. (1983) 'How Perkins changed gear', *Marketing*, 27 October.

2   Oliver, R.L. and Anderson, E. (1994) 'An empirical test of the consequences of behavior-based and outcome-based sales control systems', *Journal of Marketing*, 58 (4), pp. 53–67; Oliver, R.L. and Anderson, E. (1995) 'Behaviour and outcome-based sales control systems: evidence and consequences and hybrid governance', *Journal of Personal Selling and Sales Management*, 4 (4), pp. 1–15.

3   Jobber, D., Hooley, G. and Shipley, D. (1993) 'Organisational size and salesforce evaluation practices', *Journal of Personal Selling and Sales Management*, 13 (2), pp. 37–48.

4   The quotation appears in Jap, S.D. (2001) 'The strategic role of the salesforce in developing customer satisfaction across the relationship lifecycle', *Journal of Personal Selling and Sales Management*, 21 (2), pp. 95–108.

5   Jobber, D., Hooley, G. and Shipley, D. (1993) 'Organisational size and salesforce evaluation practices', *Journal of Personal Selling and Sales Management*, 13 (2), pp. 37–48.

6   Lynch, J. (1992) 'A new approach to salesperson evaluation', *Proceedings of the European Marketing Academy Conference*, Aårhus, July.

Practical Exercise

Dynasty Ltd

Dynasty Ltd is a radio paging service that has operated since the mid-1970s when radio pagers took Hong Kong by storm. Hong Kong still has the world's highest concentration of population carrying radio pagers, currently estimated at around 2 million. When the Hong Kong government decided to introduce a new telecommunications technology called CT2 (cordless telephone generation two), Dynasty jumped on the bandwagon of contenders in pursuit of a licence. After some negotiation it was awarded one of the four licences to operate a CT2 network in Hong Kong. The company is about to launch this service.

Raymond Chan is Dynasty's sales manager with the task of setting up a salesforce. Whilst CT2 is a sophisticated technology, Chan feels that a deep understanding of the technology is not a prerequisite for his salespeople. Instead, how to deal with customers, who tend to be very time conscious and results orientated, is more important. He believes that CT2 is a personal product. The new recruits should have experience in selling products to end-users and must have broad social contacts.

When reviewing his recruitment plan with his superior, John Lee, it became apparent that Lee had different ideas. Lee is a strong advocate that new recruits must be familiar with the product and its technology since that is what they are selling. An inside knowledge of these new products would also impress would-be customers and give the salespeople an edge over the competition. Lee favours recruiting from within the telecommunications industry, since such people are familiar with the developments of the technology. Apart from that, they are likely to talk the same language as people working in engineering, technical support and service.

Discussion Questions

1 Justify what general factors you consider should be taken into account when recruiting salespeople for the positions described in the exercise. In particular, suggest how the performance of such salespersons could be evaluated.

2 State whether you agree with Chan or Lee, or neither.

3 Suggest and justify the kind of commission structure that you would put into place.

Practical Exercise

MacLaren Tyres Ltd

MacLaren Tyres is a company involved in the import and marketing of car tyres manufactured in Asia. David MacLaren established the business in 1990 when a friend living in Singapore told him of the supply of tyres from that area which substantially undercut European prices. Although Asian tyres were not as long lasting as European (average 18,000 miles compared with 25,000), they were produced to a high standard which meant that problems like weak spots, cracks and leaks were no more serious than with European tyres.

MacLaren believed that a viable target market existed for the sale of these tyres in the UK. He was of the opinion that a substantial number of people were interested primarily in the purchase price of tyres. This price-sensitive target market could roughly be described as the mid–lower income family that owned a second-hand car which was over three years old.

He decided to buy a consignment of tyres and visited tyre centres to sell them. Initially business was slow but gradually, as distributors began to believe in the quality of the tyres, sales grew.

MacLaren was general manager and had recruited five salespeople to handle the sales function. A brief personal profile produced by MacLaren of each of his salespeople is given below.

Profiles of MacLaren salespeople

Peter Killick

Joined the company five years ago. Has an HND (business studies) and previously worked as an insurance salesperson for two years. Aged 27. Handles the Tyneside area. Gregarious and extrovert.

Gary Olford

Joined the company three years ago. No formal qualifications but sound track record as a car salesperson and, later, as a toy sales representative. Aged 35. Handles the Manchester/Liverpool area. Appears to be hard working but lacks initiative.

Barrie Wilson

Joined the company at the same time as Olford. Has an HNC (mechanical engineering). Was a technical representative for an engineering firm. Aged 28. Handles the London area. Appears to enjoy his work but lacks the necessary 'push' to be really successful in selling.

Ron Haynes

Joined the company three years ago. Has a degree in industrial technology. Previous experience includes selling bathroom suites and textile fabrics. Aged 29. Covers the Birmingham area. Appears to lack enthusiasm but sales record is about average.

Kevin Harris

Joined MacLaren Ltd two years ago. Has a degree in business studies. Only previous experience was as a marketing assistant during the industrial training period of his degree. Aged 25. Handles the Bristol area. Keen but still very raw.

Salesforce data

MacLaren decided that the time had come to look in detail at the sales records of his sales representatives. His plan was to complete a series of statistics which would be useful in evaluating their performance. Basic data for the last year relevant to each salesperson are given below.

	Sales (£000s)	Gross margin (£000s)	Live accounts	Calls made	Number of different customers called upon
Killick	298	101	222	1,472	441
Olford	589	191	333	1,463	432
Wilson	391	121	235	1,321	402
Haynes	440	132	181	1,152	211
Harris	240	65	296	1,396	421

Market data

From trade sources and from knowledge of the working boundaries each salesperson operated in, MacLaren was able to produce estimates of the number of potential accounts and territory potential for each area.

	No. of potential accounts	Territory potential (£000s)
Killick (Tyneside)	503	34,620
Olford (Lancashire)	524	36,360
Wilson (London)	711	62,100
Haynes (Birmingham)	483	43,800
Harris (Bristol)	462	38,620

Discussion Questions

1 Evaluate the performance of each of MacLaren's salespeople.

2 What further information is needed to produce a more complete appraisal?

3 What action would you take?

Examination Questions

1 Quantitative measures of the performance of sales representatives are more likely to mislead than guide evaluation. Do you agree?

2 Produce a balanced argument that looks at the differences between qualitative and quantitative measures of sales performance.

3 If a company loses a potential major order what should sales management do to alleviate the risk of this happening again?

Examination Technique

Introduction

Many able and talented students fail to do justice to themselves in examinations. This section is designed to help remedy the problem of under-achievement by providing guidelines on effective ways of preparing for examinations. Before dealing with points of detail, the importance of positive thinking needs to be emphasised; intending examinees must have confidence in their potential. Confidence can be developed by giving yourself adequate time to prepare for examinations and by paying attention to the following points on examination technique.

Planning and Setting Objectives

Only very talented or very lucky candidates can sit down and do their revision the night before the examination. The majority of individuals need to plan their work and set themselves objectives. By doing this, substantial improvements in examination performance can be achieved.

The need to plan and organise work prior to an examination is self-evident, but in practice substantial numbers of examinees pay insufficient attention to this aspect of preparation. A first stage in planning is to obtain a good idea of what is expected by examining a copy of the relevant syllabus. This will state the general objectives of the programme and detail topics to be covered. If you are studying for an examination which is set and marked by the college you are attending, obtaining a syllabus should be a simple matter of requesting it from your tutor, assuming that you have not been given one at the outset of the course. Candidates for examinations set by an external body can obtain a syllabus from the examining authority. Usually this will be quite detailed and give a precise indication of the relative importance of topics. Once you have obtained a syllabus, check it carefully against your course notes to ensure that they provide a complete coverage of topics.

The next stage in planning involves finding out about requirements for the examinations by obtaining copies of past papers and checking that there have not been any changes in examination regulations since the previous paper. Amongst the most important pieces of information you will derive from examination papers is the amount of time available to answer each question. As part of your revision programme you should practice completing answers to questions within the time limit. This point cannot be stressed too strongly. To use a sporting analogy, it is clear that many students prepare for an exam as if for a marathon, by practising writing long essays, and during the examination find for the first time that they have to take part in an 800 metres event. The specimen examination answers which are frequently available for professional examinations provide a useful aid when trying to establish the type and length of answers required.

Finding out the date and time of the examination is obviously important and allows you to draw up a revision timetable. For most people 'little and often' is a more effective and less painful way of revising than intensive and lengthy periods over a short period of time. However, it must be admitted that circumstances and individual preferences do not always permit or require this general rule to be followed. A revision timetable will therefore reflect your own particular needs, but should attempt to be as specific as possible about time allocations and topics to be covered.

Once you have drawn up a timetable, check the topics covered against those indicated on the syllabus to ensure a match between the two. If possible, set objectives for each topic on the timetable and check progress against these. Few people will be able to work precisely to every aspect of their timetable because of unforeseen circumstances, but do attempt to catch up on the schedule as soon as possible, even if it requires extra work. However, do not study late at night, particularly immediately prior to the examination; this might actually impair your performance and, even worse, your health.

Revision

It is impossible to give hard and fast rules about when to start revising, but about eight weeks before the examination is a reasonable guideline. It is possible to start earlier, but most students will not have finished their course of study before this time. Many students leave much less than eight weeks for revision, but this may result in limited or superficial coverage of the syllabus and over-heavy reliance on 'question spotting'.

The importance of active learning cannot be overemphasised when revising. Innumerable candidates for examinations have spent hours and hours reading as part of their revision programme without actually remembering or understanding anything but a fraction of their work. One effective way of promoting active learning is to take brief notes on the topic being revised. These brief notes should incorporate all the sources of information relevant to the topic such as lecture notes, textbooks, examples, your own ideas and so on. When making notes try to write down key points and space notes out so you can find topics quickly at a later date. Diagrams and illustrations can be used, as these serve as useful aids to one's memory.

Some students find it useful to condense their notes at each successive revision session. What starts out as reasonably detailed notes on a particular topic is eventually reduced to a few basic statements and key words that provide leads into the main aspects of the problem.

Another useful way to promote active learning is to set tests every few days on the areas you have revised. Many students do not find it easy to set such tests. It may be possible to obtain the co-operation of a tutor to set the tests, but in any event past examination questions and discussion questions from textbooks should provide help when setting these self-evaluation tests. Of course it is important that the time allocated to the test is closely related to the time available during the examination. When the test has been completed, evaluation of performance is important and, although self-evaluation is fundamental, the views of fellow students, tutors or other hopefully knowledgeable third parties can be invaluable.

A revision aid that is much under-utilised is studying with groups of other students who are revising for the same examination. This form of group work provides a forum for pooling information, questioning ideas and evaluating performance. The organisation of such groups can take many forms including brainstorming sessions, individual presentations on selected topics, informal discussions of questions and so on. One of the main benefits of this approach to revision is that it encourages brevity and a full understanding of subjects which have to be discussed with fellow students. It is, of course, vital that discussions concentrate on the work for the examination and are not sidetracked on to other perhaps more pleasant topics.

Reading and Remembering

It has been pointed out that long hours spent reading do not necessarily result in the effective acquisition of knowledge and note-taking is one way of improving learning while reading. However, the process of reading about a subject also involves skills that can be improved. The most obvious point about different individuals' reading skills is the speed at which they read. Some people read much more quickly than others, and if this can be combined with good understanding, it is obviously an advantage when revising. At the same time fast reading speeds for their own sake are not necessarily advantageous; understanding and remembering are the ultimate objectives.

Quick and efficient reading can be developed by paying attention to a number of points. First, it is helpful to adopt a comfortable, but not soporific position in good light and approach the reading in a positive manner rather than viewing it as an unpleasant task. Then it is wise to develop the habit of reading in sections, i.e. looking at the meaning of sentences as a whole rather than concentrating on each word in isolation. This practice of reading in sections is not easy to describe, but the more you read with this principle in mind, the more your reading skills are likely to improve. A further point to bear in mind when developing an approach to quick and efficient reading is not to read for too long. Although there are individual differences in this respect, approximately 30 to 40 minutes at a time is usually the maximum span before a break of several minutes should be taken.

It is important to re-emphasise the importance of making brief notes on material being read. These should include details of points not fully understood so you can pursue them with your tutor or study group.

A valuable spin-off of reading widely is that it can help improve your vocabulary. A good vocabulary is undoubtedly an invaluable asset when it comes to interpreting and answering examination questions. Unless you are quite clear about what particular words in an examination question mean, you are going to waste time thinking about them and ultimately may completely misinterpret the question. To avoid this pitfall it is good practice to make a list of words encountered in your reading which cause difficulty, along with their dictionary definition. This list should be committed to memory and the words should be used where appropriate in self-evaluation tests.

The role of good note-taking and self-evaluation tests in promoting effective learning have already been stressed. Another way to remember information is by using word association. Perhaps the most common way of using this technique is to take the first letter of each of the words to be remembered and to make them into another word. For example, AIDA can be used to remember the key factors in selling and for advertising, namely, attention, interest, desire and action. Other word association techniques might involve making up simple stories or rhymes. The objective of all of these aids to remembering is to increase your familiarity with, and ease of recall of, the subject matter being revised.

Remembering and Applying Knowledge

The main objective when revising is to collect together all relevant information and attempt to remember it in context. However, this is not an end in itself since it is necessary to be able to use this information to answer the examination questions. Practice in applying knowledge to questions before the examination is as important as remembering it. Probably the most common cause of students under-achieving in examinations is that they do not answer the question. Instead they just write down an expanded version of their notes on the topic, which are unlikely to address themselves to the particular issues raised in the question.

The problem of applying knowledge is relatively simple if the examination questions are predominantly descriptive. This type of question merely requires you to demonstrate your knowledge about a particular topic without having to demonstrate higher level skills of analysis. Such questions will typically start with words such as *describe*, *state*, *outline*, *explain* and *define*. When answering descriptive questions, include relevant definitions and explanations of all the points required by the question. Good answers will probably also include examples and/or empirical evidence to illustrate the points covered.

Analytical questions pose much greater difficulties in terms of using knowledge to answer a question. The hierarchy of skills illustrated in Figure A1.1 indicates the broad difference between descriptive and analytical questions.

Questions that are analytical in nature will start with words such as *discuss*, *evaluate*, *assess*, *criticise* and *analyse*. This type of question requires the examinee to show

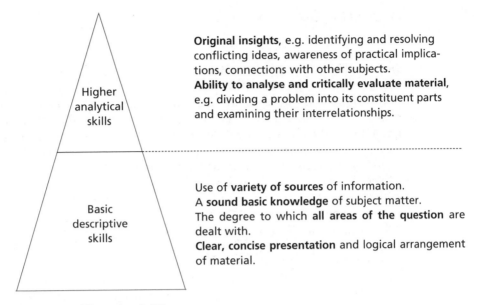

Higher
analytical
skills

Original insights, e.g. identifying and resolving conflicting ideas, awareness of practical implications, connections with other subjects.
Ability to analyse and critically evaluate material, e.g. dividing a problem into its constituent parts and examining their interrelationships.

Basic
descriptive
skills

Use of **variety of sources** of information.
A **sound basic knowledge** of subject matter.
The degree to which **all areas of the question** are dealt with.
Clear, concise presentation and logical arrangement of material.

Figure A1.1 Hierarchy of skills

early in the answer that the question is understood and to set up a framework for the remainder of the answer. It is then important to present the relevant points of view, support them with examples and show awareness of the criticisms that can be levelled at particular points of view. An answer to an analytical question should end with a conclusion that briefly summarises the key issues and presents the student's own considered judgement on the topic.

Some questions will have a clear descriptive component and an analytical component as in the following example: 'Identify the main elements of the marketing mix and assess their relative importance for marketing consumer durables.' In such cases it is reasonable to assume that the descriptive part will be allocated a lower proportion of the total marks than the analytical component. This should be reflected in the amount of time spent in answering the two parts of the question.

Examination Nerves

Careful revision and preparation should help to minimise the problem of examination nerves. Last-minute panic could mean not obtaining the mark one's preparation warrants. It is important to keep calm and believe in yourself. Those individuals who are particularly prone to stress should talk about it with friends, family or welfare counsellors, as the very act of discussing the problem may help to reduce anxiety. Everyone finds examinations stressful to some extent, but if the exams are approached in a positive manner and by a candidate in good physical health, this stress should not be harmful. Of course if there are health or other medical problems a doctor should be approached well before the examination and the relevant details brought to the attention of the examining authority.

Answering Examination Questions

Once under examination conditions, and when the examination questions have been distributed, it is vital that time is taken to read all the instructions and questions carefully. If questions are then rated in terms of whether they can be adequately answered, it should finally be possible to list the required number of questions in the order they will be attempted. As a general rule it is wise to begin with a question where the subject matter is well known. This helps to build up confidence and means the more difficult ones can be left until later.

The next step is to make an essay plan after thinking about the question for a few minutes. This plan will consist of brief notes made on the answer paper in which the main points and structure of the essay will be outlined. Writing an essay plan helps to give direction to an answer and enables the scope of the answer to be gauged. Gauging the scope of an answer is an important prerequisite to deciding how much time can be devoted to its component parts. It is good practice to start your actual answer on a new page and when it is finished to lightly cross out the essay plan. The plan should, however, be included as part of the examination.

When writing an essay under examination conditions, students should attempt to make their writing as legible as possible as this will avoid trying the patience of the examiner who ultimately marks the paper. Other simple but important points to remember include numbering the answers correctly and making sure that any additional papers have your name on and are attached to the answer book in the correct order.

One of the keys to success during an examination is correct pacing, so that an equal amount of time is spent on each answer. This skill should have been developed during revision and cause few difficulties during the examination. If a question has not been finished during its allocated time it should be brought to a swift conclusion and the next one commenced. The value of completing all of the required number of questions cannot be overemphasised. It is difficult to get a good overall mark if the final question is not attempted or only just started when time expires. Allow time for planning before each question.

Answers should be written in a clear and logical manner with as good a style as the conditions permit. As time is at a premium, avoid waffle; do not keep repeating certain words. It is not usually necessary to rewrite the question before starting – this wastes valuable time. Refer to the question on the examination paper and circle key words as appropriate. The length of an answer is obviously dependent on size of handwriting, time available and knowledge of the subject, but as a general rule at least two or three sides of A4 paper are needed to write an adequate answer.

The style in which an examination answer is written depends on the nature of the examination and the particular question asked; some papers require an answer in essay form, others require reports, and in some instances the examinee must present an analysis of a case study. It is important to research the issue of the required style of answers and to practise preparing them before the examination.

Essay-type answers can take many forms but will usually have the following components:

(a) an opening paragraph which goes to the heart of the question and gives an indication of how the problem will be approached

(b) the main body of the answer in which the examinee puts forward a reasoned case supported by appropriate facts and empirical evidence

(c) a conclusion which draws together the strands of the argument and relates them back to the question

There is no doubt that some students find writing essays under examination conditions difficult. In such cases it may be possible to introduce some greater degree of structure by using numbered headings and sub-headings within answers. However, these should not denigrate into notes; on the whole this style is more appropriate to descriptive rather than analytical answers.

Case studies are an increasingly common feature of many examinations and may require answers to be presented in report form. Any question that specifically asks for a report will almost certainly involve a proportion of total marks being awarded for layout and presentation of the answer. In these circumstances, examinees must take care over the form of their answer by paying attention to correct report format, although allowances will be made by the examiner for the fact that it has been prepared under examination conditions.

Conclusion

Passing examinations is not an end in itself. A course of study should be seen as a vehicle for personal development and improved understanding. It may also help individuals to obtain a new or better job. Those students who select their course of study carefully, apply themselves diligently and revise in a systematic manner should be able to cope with the final hurdle of an examination without too much difficulty. Obviously, things do go wrong on occasions and most people do fail a few examinations during their education, but this should not be seen as the end of the world. Opportunities for retaking the examination or other courses of study are usually available if mishaps do occur.

Further Reading

Sales functions/techniques

Barber, M. (1997) *How Champions Sell*, McGraw-Hill, Maidenhead.

Bird, D. (1998) *How to Write Sales Letters that Sell*, Kogan Page, London.

Chaffey, D., Mayer, R., Johnston, K. and Ellis-Chadwick, F. (2000) *Internet Marketing*, Pearson Education, Harlow.

Claybaugh, M.G. and Forbes, J.L. (1992) *Professional Selling – A Relationship Approach*, West Publishing, New York.

Denny, R. (1996) *Selling to Win*, Kogan Page, London.

Fisher, R. and Ury, W. (1989) *Getting to Yes: Negotiating Agreement Without Giving In*, Business Books, London.

Foss, B. and Stone, M. (2001) *Successful Customer Relationship Marketing*, Kogan Page, London.

Gabay, J. (1996) *Teach Yourself Copywriting*, Hodder and Stoughton, London.

Hafer, J.C. (1993) *The Professional Selling Process*, West Publishing, St Pauls, MN.

McDonald, M. (1996) *The Pocket Guide to Selling Services and Products*, Butterworth-Heinemann, Oxford.

Manchester Open Learning (1998) *Making Effective Presentations*, Kogan Page, London.

Murdock, A. and Scutt, C.N. (2003) *Personal Effectiveness*, Butterworth-Heinemann, Oxford.

Oberhaus, M.A., Ratcliffe, S. and Stauble, V. (1993) *Professional Selling: A Relationship Process*, Dryden Press, Fort Worth, TX.

O'Connor, J. and Galvin, E. (2000) *Marketing in the Digital Age*, FT Prentice Hall, Harlow.

Schiffman, S. (1997) *25 Top Sales Techniques*, Kogan Page, London.

Schiffman, S. (1997) *High Efficiency Selling*, Wiley, New York.

Sales management

Allen, P. (1993) *Selling: Management and Practice*, 4th edn, Pitman, London.

Anderson, R.E., Hair, J.E. and Bush, A.J. (1992) *Professional Sales Management*, McGraw-Hill, New York.

Churchill Jr, G.A., Ford, N.M. and Walker Jr, O.C. (2000) *Sales Force Management: Planning, Implementation and Control*, 2nd edn, Irwin, Homewood, IL.

Donaldson, B. (1997) *Sales Management, Theory and Practice*, Macmillan, Basingstoke.

Futrell, C.M. (2000) *Sales Management*, Dryden Press, Fort Worth, TX.

Jobber, D. (ed.) (1997) *CIM Handbook of Selling and Sales Strategy*, Butterworth-Heinemann, Oxford.

McDonald, M. and Rogers, B. (1998) *Key Account Management*, Butterworth-Heinemann, Oxford.

McDonald, M., Rogers, B. and Woodburn, D. (2000) *Key Customers: How to Manage Them Profitably*, Butterworth-Heinemann, Oxford.

Noonan, C. (1997) *Sales Management*, Butterworth-Heinemann, Oxford.

Wilson, M. (1999) *Managing a Salesforce*, Gower, Aldershot.

Index